OPEN QUESTIONS IN ANALYTICAL PSYCHOLOGY

D1706401

Open Questions
in Analytical Psychology

Proceedings of
The Thirteenth International Congress
For Analytical Psychology
Zurich, 1995

Mary Ann Mattoon
Editor

DAIMON
VERLAG

Copyright © 1997 by Daimon Verlag,
Am Klosterplatz, CH-8840 Einsiedeln, Switzerland.

Zurich 1995: Open Questions in Analytical Psychology
edited by Mary Ann Mattoon.
The translators of individual papers are given on the final page of each
translation.
Cover design by Veronika Vizner van der Linden.

ISBN 3-85630-555-6 (hard-cover)
ISBN 3-85630-556-4 (paperback)

All rights reserved. This book, or parts thereof, may not be reproduced
in any form without written permission from the publisher.

Contents

Couples, Families and Groups

Analyst-Training

Past and Future

Alphabetical List of Authors

Editor's Preface

The Thirteenth (triennial) Congress of the International Association for Analytical Psychology was held August 20-25, 1995 at the Kongresshaus in Zurich, the birthplace of analytical psychology. This was the first Congress to be held in Zurich since 1968. The theme, "Open Questions in Analytical Psychology," drew a record number of proposals (at least 220) and led to a record number of presentations: 60 sessions comprising 83 papers.

This meeting was the largest gathering of Jungians ever. Participants registered for the entire Congress numbered a total of 700: 391 analysts, 223 candidates, and 86 "auditors." In addition, 177 day cards were issued. Of the 32 Societies that were member groups before the Congress, at least 28 were represented, as were 30 countries. Three additional Societies were admitted to IAAP at the business meeting. The total number of analysts who are IAAP members stands at 2080.

The program represented by the papers in this book was embedded in a variety of rich "extracurricular" offerings, many of them taking advantage of the Zurich setting. From the opening reception in the courtyard of the Swiss National Museum to the concluding excursion on the Lake of Zurich, participants had opportunities to experience the city (with its surroundings) that was home to C.G. Jung for virtually all of his adult life. There was a guided tour to the Marc Chagall Windows in the Fraumünster Church; a stroll through the Zurich Altstadt (old city); a concert of 16th, 17th and 20th century music; gatherings in homes of Swiss colleagues; daily open house at the C.G. Jung Institute (now in the suburb of Küsnacht); a social evening hosted by the Institute Students' Association; and historical lectures at the Zurich Psychological Club. These lectures, dating from 1916 (James Kirsch), 1930 (Emma Jung), 1936 (Alexandra David-Neel) and 1949 (C.G. Jung), were read by Congress participants in their original languages. Following the Congress, participants had the opportunity for a four-day tour of places that were of particular significance in Jung's life.

Special meetings were organized around topics: activities in Eastern Europe, research and the IAAP newsletter. Other meetings brought together sub-groups: child therapists, sandplay therapists, training candidates, graduates of the Zurich Institute, directors of training, editors, and French-speaking analysts and candidates.

***

The Congress theme opened the way for presentations on a wide variety of topics. Indeed, as Adolf Guggenbühl-Craig mentioned in his opening presentation, even questions that have been considered to be answered remain open to new theorizing and new experience. And certainly there are many questions that have not been answered extensively, some not previously addressed.

The first ten papers (following the remarks of the First Vice-President and the Mayor of Zurich) were those presented to the morning plenary sessions, offered here in their order of presentation. Each morning paper was followed by a general discussion led by the chairperson for that meeting.

Following these ten are the papers that were presented in eight sets of afternoon sessions, usually six simultaneously, and a set of early morning sessions. As a help to the reader in finding areas of interest, the editor introduced the categories (from among several possible schemes) indicated in the table of contents. Many of these categories have appeared in Proceedings from earlier Congresses. Others may indicate some shifts in the foci of the thinking of Jungian clinicians, scholars and researchers.

A few papers are joint productions of two or more persons; such authors' names appear sequentially at the beginning of the paper and, in the table of contents, are connected by "with." Names of authors of individual papers in one program are separated by commas. If only a summary appears, it is so indicated. With two exceptions (who are identified by name and city only), presenters are analysts. Each analyst is identified by place of practice and group of voting membership in IAAP. (An analyst who is a member of more than one group has an IAAP vote in only one.)

Of the papers presented at the Congress, only two do not appear here, by their authors' decisions that the material did not lend itself to printed form: those of Peter Ammann and Jean Shinoda Bolen.

***

The official languages of the Congress were English, French, German and Italian. If a paper was delivered in a language other than English, it has been translated and the original language indicated. The translator's name follows, if it is available.

Because of space limitations, many of the papers had to be reduced in length for publication here. A few presenters requested that this fact be footnoted specifically in relation to their papers.

Editing was designed for clarity, enhancing each author's contribution while retaining individuality of writing styles, and for consistency in notation and usage: references, spelling of words, italicizing dreams and visions.

References to Jung's *Collected Works* are indicated in the text by volume number and paragraph number. CW-B refers to Supplementary Volume B, a re-issue of the original *Psychology of the Unconscious* (revised as CW5). Other Jung references include:

AP = 1925 *Seminars on Analytical Psychology*
CD = *Children's Dreams*
DS = *Seminars on Dream Analysis*
Let-1 and Let-2 = Jung's *Letters*, Vols. 1 & 2
MDR = *Memories, Dreams, Reflections*
VS = *Visions Seminars*
ZA = *Zarathustra Seminars*
FJ = *Freud-Jung Letters.*

Freud's works are indicated, insofar as possible, as SE (*Standard Edition*) and their volume numbers.

Other textual citations follow the format of the *Publication Manual* of the American Psychological Association. They indicate author and date, keyed to the reference at the end of the paper or group of papers. Each reference is in the language cited by the presenter. Non-English titles are accompanied by their English equivalents when the reference cited is known to have appeared in English.

American-style punctuation and spelling are used, according to the University of Chicago *Manual of Style*. Non-English words in the texts have been translated into English, unless they are terms – such as those from alchemy – that are well-known to readers of Jungian works or are available in a standard English dictionary. Words that are used in a special sense by Jungians are spelled as in the Collected Works, except for "Self" (self in the CW), which has a meaning in Jungian psychology that is not shared by other schools, and for words with which a particular author chooses to depart from Jung's practice.

The terms "patient," "client" and "analysand" are used as the individual author sees fit. The identity of each individual to whom an author refers is disguised.

Graphics are placed as much in keeping with the author's request as possible, taking into account optimal use of space. The complete set of *Rosarium* plates is presented between the two papers that use it.

Manuscripts were typed on computer disk by Beverly Cicchese. Jennette Cook Jones assisted the editor with refining some translations from Italian. Copy editing was done by Bonnie L. Marsh.

Mary Ann Mattoon
Minneapolis, Minnesota, U.S.A.
June 1996

Opening Remarks

Verena Kast
St. Gallen, Switzerland
First Vice-President, IAAP

It is my pleasure to welcome you to the scientific part of our thirteenth international congress here in Zurich, 40 years after the International Association for Analytical Psychology (IAAP) was founded here.

Jungian psychology has emanated from Zurich, has been disseminated, and has found recognition and criticism worldwide. It has been received and further developed in each one of you in an individual expression and with different emphases, according to your interests. As you "return" to Zurich now, this conference takes place against a background of deep meaning, reflected in numerical totality. Thirteen is the number of moon-months in a year. Forty is four times ten: a symbol of entirety. The experience of totality lets us pause for a moment; afterward, a new departure must follow. You bring your view of Jungian psychology back here to its source and, in conversation, we reflect together on what is important to us about analytical psychology as it stands today, and what should be changed or added.

Psychologists of the same school, mostly practitioners, take completely different views on therapies and theories that become strung together or exist side by side. If we could agree that every theory is provisional, that it should be questioned continuously, that results should be shared and verifiable as much as possible, then the relation between theory and practice can be a lively one. Indeed, conferences can be vital to a theoretical direction.

However, things do not work this loosely. Theories serve not only the establishment of truth or the finding of the best possible strategies of action; they also serve the definition of one's identity. The person who changes parts of a theory may be seen as a renegade, even a denigrator who will not be seen, not be read, will be overlooked. In the formation of theories, it is not just a matter of modifying and presenting a theory for discussion in order to allow for its best possible handling in practice or for it to be considered. Rather, the sum of the theories also builds an ideology and guarantees the identity of a psychological direction. Changes, therefore, may be overlooked.

We who have gathered here have different theoretical positions. In my estimation, these positions have to do not only with different educational sites and their specific beliefs but also with Jungian psychology as such. It is very important to some colleagues to introduce Jungian psychology into the general psychotherapeutic discussion in an increasingly differentiated manner. Political events further this position and these efforts. Almost all of us must prove, for instance, that our form of therapy conforms to scientific criteria of effectiveness. The majority of us may complain about this requirement, but when we adhere to it, it can improve the communication between us Jungians, as we have experienced at various meetings. Thus, our actions will become more outwardly transparent.

Almost as a counter-reaction, there are colleagues who turn more toward the "esoteric" aspects of Jungian psychology. It is important to remember that Jungian psychology has never simply followed the mainstream of scientific psychological discourse, that it has always occupied itself with "hidden things" which were accepted less easily but have exerted a lively effect on the psychoanalytic schools. These two directions of research and thinking should not exclude each other; they complement each other well if one does not feel threatened each time by the "other side" and if one is not under the impression of having a corner on the truth. When it comes to psychological theory, it is not actually a matter of truth but rather of a possible view of reality. After all, we Jungians also wish to have our place and our say in the world of therapy. It is of the utmost importance as well that we lift up our voices – that we speak about that which can be spoken about – and that we also remain silent in those areas where in our therapies we encounter the unspeakable. The conversation about these mainstreams will be important at this Congress.

Our theme, "Open Questions in Analytical Psychology," becomes us very well. The human being is unfathomable; we are in for a surprise over and over again. A psychology without open questions would not do justice to the essence of humanity. At this moment, however, depth psychology stands somewhat in a headwind after having been idealized for a long time. The psychoanalytic schools stand under suspicion of ideology, and Jungian psychology is no exception. Quite the contrary; it is held against us that belonging to a school places its members under obligation of a consensus that inhibits thinking and research, thus possibly hindering therapeutic progress.

Open questions mean exactly that consensus is not claimed. The individual presenters – and you who will be conversing with the presenters – will formulate that which has remained open for you in Jungian psychology. Questions will be asked. Whether we will actually risk addressing the more explosive open questions and stepping into a constructive dialogue with each other regarding them remains to be seen.

Many of you have entered suggestions for presentations and workshops in a wide area of topics. In an overview of these suggestions, specific fields of interest stand out. As was to be expected, we have many interesting contributions to the clinical picture and therapeutic techniques with adults, children, families, and couples; including themes of incest, violence and early dreams. The criteria for selection of topics to be developed, as well as questions regarding training and supervision, are very interesting. The themes range from the area of efficacy of Jungian psychotherapy all the way to psychological research on symbolism in art, imagination, and alchemy. The analysis of the destruction of the environment on one hand and a bio-psycho-social phenomenon such as AIDS on the other hand creates a connection to current social themes. The question of the psychology of women in the Jungian context, especially the connection between the social role of women and its effect on the analytic relationship, seems to remain open. More so than in other years, the theme of the connection between body and analytical psychology has been offered, as well as the connection between music and analytical psychology. Could this latter theme have to do with the fact that music reaches feelings in a great breadth and depth and that we are turning toward feelings – which after all make up the core of our identity – in a new manner?

In order for such a Congress as this to become possible, a great deal of work is done by a few colleagues. The program committee under the direction of Murray Stein had to choose from a large selection of exciting offers. Then there was the Swiss organizing committee under the direction of Hans Jürg Brunner and Ruth Amman. They have organized this Congress with judiciousness, imagination, and flexibility. We give warm thanks to them and to their assistants as well as to other colleagues of the Swiss Society who are members of the organizing committee. Tom Kirsch has kept his watchful eye on the whole.

We have agreed once more to have each morning presentation given by a colleague who has not previously made a plenary presentation at an international Congress; this will allow us to come to know the thinking of as many colleagues as possible in the course of the decades. We have succeeded again in holding six parallel programs each afternoon. That means, of course, that each of us cannot hear all the presentations, but it presents the possibility of conversing with each other in smaller groups and to place our own experiences into a widened context.

Zurich is a very special place and will elicit special emotions. We hope that the stimulation and the connections that have emanated from Zurich in the past will influence our Congress as well. I hope for us to spend a stimulating and exciting week together, fostering old friendships and forging new ones, and that you will carry your experiences from here out into the world.

Translated from German by Yvonne Cherne

Address by the Mayor of Zurich

Joseph Estermann

Many of you have come here from distant places in order to take part in the Thirteenth International Congress for Analytical Psychology. It is a great pleasure for me to welcome you to the city in which analytical psychology originated with Carl Gustav Jung.

I was wondering whether the Congress organizers might have had a special reason for holding tonight's opening reception in this very place – the inner courtyard of the Swiss National Museum. As mayor I might content myself with the explanation that this spot was selected because it is both picturesque and centrally located, a slightly exotic setting which invariably impresses visitors from abroad. I would be very pleased if you could feel comfortable here and were able to establish some first contacts with colleagues from all over the world. However, since psychologists have a professional propensity to see deeper meanings and hidden motivations behind what are simply matters-of-course to us lay people, allow me to come up with a few speculations of my own as well.

You may have asked yourselves how old might be the venerable walls surrounding us: those windows and hatches, towers and battlements, bays and balustrades. They might even bring to mind images of those warlike Swiss foot soldiers who, during the Middle Ages, put the fear of God into whole armies of mounted knights commanded by European kings and emperors. I hope you will not be too disappointed if I tell you that the buildings which house the Swiss National Museum are by no means a former medieval fortress or anything of the sort, but were constructed between 1893 and 1989, in the age of historicism, whose outstanding attribute is, according to one author, the "representation of being architecturally at a loss." The modern republic of Switzerland was just about 50 years old at the time and eager to erect, on the threshold of the twentieth century, a monument that could serve as a symbol of national unity by memorializing the power Switzerland once had been. Unfortunately, the architectural quality of the building was not quite up to these lofty claims. Indeed, the great exhibition room had to be closed down six months ago for safety reasons.

But perhaps the architectural design of this museum reminds you of another edifice more familiar to you. I mean Jung's tower in Bollingen on Upper Lake Zurich, which he built with his own hands. But while Jung's tower is a witness to his life history – to the process of his own individuation – and makes no claim to eternal life, the National Museum is an example of a construction of national identity that is fragile in more senses than one. For societies are no less subject to fractures in their development than individuals.

When the International Congress for Analytical Psychology congregated in Zurich in 1968, its participants were able to observe such a fracture practically right before their eyes. At that time great numbers of young people filled the streets with their public protest, smashing the post-war myth of never-ending progress. And today you are again in a place which bears witness to such a historic cleavage. This time I am not referring to the museum walls, but to the pleasant-looking green space you see in front of you: You will hardly believe me if I tell you that this is the notorious needle park where countless young people succumbed to hard drugs. Today, Zurich no longer has an open drug scene, and the park was recently refurbished and re-opened for public use. Whether the Zurichers will profit from the opportunity remains to be seen. Perhaps the memories of the recent past are still too raw, too undigested for them to venture into this area light-heartedly.

You may have seen also photographs of James Joyce standing at Zurich's "Platzspitz," peering down into the river. The Platzspitz is the place, just a few steps from here, where the waters of two rivers flow into one another: those of the Sihl, which hails from the mountains and brings down mud, uprooted trees and the like during thunderstorms; and those of the River Limmat, a pure, calm waterway emanating from the Lake of Zurich. You couldn't have picked a better spot for tonight's get-together to illustrate Jung's discovery that good and evil combined constitute the equivocal nature of life itself.

Like good and evil, questions and answers are interconnected in a dialectic relationship. Questions are no less a prerequisite of the human existence than answers; they may be even more important. True, answers and assured facts are essential if we want to put things into practice. But they can also lead to rigidity and even petrifaction, which must be loosened up again in a long and sometimes painful process. Asking the right questions may show the way back to sanity; it may help in giving up spurious convictions and facing truth. In this sense, the locality in which we are now is a reminder exhorting us not to withdraw into the tower of illusory beliefs, but to tackle the problems with which our society is confronted with open eyes. Asking the right questions is not easy, as we have known ever since Perceval, who was unable to penetrate the secret of the Holy Grail until he asked the proper question. Nor may the right to ask questions be denied, as in Wagner's "Lohengrin," for there is nothing that exists solely, unquestionably of itself. As far as answers are concerned, I believe that no answers are better than wrong ones. Take for instance Kafka's short story "Die Prüfung" (The Examination), in which you may read the following: "Wer die Fragen nicht beantwortet, hat die Prüfung bestanden." That is, "Candidates who do not answer the questions will pass the examination." If you still insist on answers, let me refer you finally to a anti-war song by Bob Dylan, whose famous refrain goes, as you will surely recall, "The answer, my friend, is blowing in the wind."

Ladies and gentlemen, I do wish you a fruitful exchange of questions and answers, of knowledge and experience, as well as a pleasant stay in Zurich.

Plenary Sessions

No Answer is Still an Answer

Why Many Psychological Questions Must Stay Open

Adolf Guggenbühl-Craig
Zurich, Switzerland
Swiss Society for Analytical Psychology

The title of this Congress, "Open Questions in Analytical Psychology," implies that there are different kinds of questions in Jungian psychology. First, there are questions that have been answered by now. Second, there are open questions, questions that have not been answered but may be answered in the future – or may never be answered.

The questions that have been answered should be easy to find. Typology seems to be one. Extraversion/introversion and the four functions – thinking, feeling, intuition and sensation – have now become part of everyday language. There is a dominant function, an auxiliary function and an inferior function. You all know this psychological and intellectual masterpiece: this refined, stimulating, sophisticated and dynamic Jungian typology. Everything in this typology seems clear; few if any questions remain open.

Is that actually the case? Are the four functions valid? Could there not be nine functions, or sixteen, or any other number? Could there not be completely different kinds of functions? Are these functions not outdated nineteenth century psychology? Is it true that feeling is the opposite of thinking and intuition the opposite of sensation? Is it true that the thinking of a feeling type is inferior? I observe, for example, that feeling types often think accurately.

Do these types really exist? Or are they just a grid, a pattern that we put on the different personalities, the same way we put a grid on a map of a particular landscape? There are many different grids possible. Is the Jungian typology the most accurate? Or do not all typologies distort the psychological reality? Is Jungian typology, like many other typologies, just an expression of our need to create order, to have some orientation in the bewildering variety of human characteristics?

Let us take something more central to psychology than typology, namely the unconscious. Every Jungian seems to know what the unconscious is and how it has to be understood. Some questions may be unanswered still, but basically we know what we are talking about.

Is this really the case? Because the unconscious is unconscious, we know only indirectly what it is and what is supposed to be in the unconscious. And what is the collective unconscious? Beneath the individual unconscious lie the different layers of the collective unconscious; of the family, of the city or village, of the nation, of humanity and eventually even of the whole creation. But what is this collective unconscious really and what are these different layers? Are we just talking about common denominators? Or are we talking about independent psychic structures or centers of energy? Is there an anima familiae, an anima populi, an anima mundi, and so on?

A colleague of mine said he would flunk any candidate in an examination of basic Jungian principles who would say that the collective unconscious is an entity like the individual human soul. But would that be fair? Some of us are more like the French rationalists of the eighteenth century, and some share the ideas of the German romantics who talked of the "Seele des Volkes" (soul of the people). It seems to me that the notion of the unconscious, especially the notion of the collective unconscious, raises more questions than it can answer. Is the idea of the unconscious not just a way out of the fact that the psyche is mysterious and inexplicable?

Let us come to the archetypes, a centerpiece of Jungian psychology. Where these are concerned clarity should reign. Here we seem to have more questions answered than open. But what are archetypes really? Are they – so to speak – eternal? Have they been in this world since "the big bang"? Have they always been here, or did they slowly develop in the course of history of animals and humans? Are they typical reactions within typical recurring situations, which then become archetypes? And anyway, how many archetypes are there? Five, eight, ten, a hundred, or even more? Or do the archetypes not exist at all? Is it not as if we illuminate a part of the psyche with a torchlight and then give a special name to that part?

We say that the gods personify archetypes, but there are many different gods all over the world who seem to have little to do with each other, even if we try to connect them with the archetypes we think we know. Thus, one could conclude that there are innumerable archetypes or that archetypes are just the result of our concentration on a particular spot in our psyche, as when we look at the cloudy sky. We can see all kinds of figures in the clouds and yet they are only clouds.

Wherever we look, we see only open questions.

Let us turn to the dreams which are so important for us and which we seek to understand. But when we talk about dreams, we get into trouble again. Are the researchers right who claim that dreams are only an attempt to get rid of the garbage of our souls? But even supposing the dream really does express something very significant to our souls, can't every dream be interpreted in many different ways, perhaps all of them fairly convincingly? People who think they can use dreams as oracles must remember that the oracle of Delphi was usually misunderstood completely.

Not everything can be an open question; there must be some questions answered in analytical psychology. Let us take the so-called final aspect of our psychological life. We observe that most psychological happenings, including psychological disturbances, seem to be aiming at something, to include a finality. Every neurosis seems to point somewhere, give a direction for the future, have a meaning. But we cannot be sure. Again: Is it only Jungians who see this finality? The final aspect of a particular psychological symptom might seem to be fairly obvious in the individual case – but obvious only to a Jungian observer and not to a behaviorist, for instance. The idea of finality certainly fulfills our need for meaning, our need to understand the aim of psychological life. But that need is a psychological phenomenon too.

I think the concept of individuation and the understanding of the Self is one of the greatest contributions of Jung to psychology. We all know what individuation is meant to be. It doesn't just mean to become strong, efficient and healthy. It means to become connected with all the layers of our soul, the conscious and the unconscious. It means to become an individual personality that is, however, in close contact with the collective unconscious. Individuation is much more than just a healthy development; it means being on a spiritual path and being connected with the community.

Is individuation really what it is supposed to be? And is it really achieved by having more and more analysis? Most practicing analysts have hundred of hours of training analysis behind them. And yet can we say that analysts are more conscious, wiser and more guided by eros than the average citizen? If analysis is really the way of individuation, then why are we analysts not better human beings, more conscious and even more kind?

I am questioning the way to individuation, not individuation itself. But closely connected with individuation is the concept of the self, the Jungian Self, which is not quite the same as the self of Kohut, or any other concept of self. The Self according to Jung is not mainly an organizing center of our soul, the nucleus of our soul, or one pole of the ego-Self axis. The Self is the "divine spark" in us. But once, in a lecture at the Zurich Institute I used the word "divine spark" to characterize the Self, I found that none of the students present had heard the expression "the divine spark in us." And yet: the divine spark in us may be the origin of eros and thanatos of love and of our destructive drives, of evil. So there are many open questions concerning individuation and the Self.

What about animus and anima? Again questions. Are anima and animus archetypes like other archetypes? The classical definition was that women have an animus, their male part, and men have an anima – their female part. But many modern Jungians, including me, say that men and women both have an animus and an anima. Archetypes belong to everyone and if animus and anima are archetypes, they belong both to men and women.

And what about the question: What are men and what are women psychologically? What is masculine and what is feminine? Is there a feminine psyche and a masculine psyche, or are the two psyches the same? For a while it was "in" to say there is no real psychological difference between men and women and even between the feminine and the masculine. It is all cultural, therefore artificial. Now again we hear that even the brain structures of men and women are different, and therefore we might conclude that men and women really are different, that there exists a masculine and feminine soul. So perhaps the difference between masculine and feminine is not only cultural. More open questions.

As soon as we consider theory all kinds of questions arise, which are difficult to answer. But when we go into the practical side of psychology and of our work, then things become clearer and many questions are answered. In therapy we know more or less what has to be done and we have not so many questions left unanswered.

Is this really so? We Jungians ourselves cannot even agree if one hour a week is usually best for most of the patients, or two hours, or maybe even five hours a week, and we can't even agree if one should have sixty or seventy hours all together, or maybe five hundred or six hundred hours. Is it really the more the better, or would less be better?

The behavior of the analyst during the hour is open to dispute also. Should we keep the so-called frame as strictly as possible, or should we relax our attitude? Should we sometimes make a few personal remarks, or even general remarks about the weather, about cultural or political events? Should we, when somebody brings us a bunch of flowers immediately try to interpret why these flowers were brought, or should we just smile and accept the flowers with thanks? Staying with the technique raises the question how to deal with dreams. Here again we have many questions. Should we interpret dreams or just take them phenomenologically, as the existentialists do? Is it really valid that there are initial dreams, which point out what course the therapy will take, or is the idea of the significant initial dream just an attempt to smooth over our insecurity at the beginning of an analysis?

We are surrounded by unanswered questions, which bring all kinds of difficulties. Nowadays society and insurance companies require of us proof that we have successful results in psychotherapy and analysis and that these results have been obtained with minimal costs. Jungians all over the world try hard to prove that their work is successful, but then the question arises: What does "successful" mean? Does it mean that you eliminate symptoms? Or does it mean that you help the client to individuate? Does it mean that the client gets in touch with another dimension of soul – for instance religion and philosophy, or does it just mean becoming healthy but a bore? Or does it mean becoming politically more aware?

Let us look at a different topic: selection and training of psychotherapists. Nobody can explain precisely what one must look for in selecting future psychotherapists. There are some hints here and there that the future analyst should have a certain interest in people. But even these criteria are just speculations; maybe someone who is more interested in psychology in general than in individual people is an excellent analyst, too. We just do not know in advance who has the ability to constellate the healer in the client and who has not, or if there really is a healing ability.

The situation becomes even more confused when we look at training. The tendency up to now has been: the more the better. Six hundred hours of personal analysis is better than 400 hours, and 900 better than 600 hours. But is this really so? Is it not possible that there is a limit? Perhaps we ask too many hours of personal analysis in the training and just make people infantile and dependent, deterring them from ever being on their own. By having too many hours of training analysis, we, without realizing it, may select people who really enjoy being led, being eternal immature students. But will these be good analysts and psychotherapists? Maybe the good analysts are the ones who say: "Enough is enough. Now I want to work on my own and I do not want to be a student and a child forever."

Nothing but unanswerable questions are found, even if we go into the larger field of the general development of humanity. Do human beings really become more loving, or at least more conscious? If humanity still exists in a million years, will it have changed for the better or the worse? Or if in two years another star crashes into our planet, would the end of humanity hit us at the height of our psychological development? There is certainly movement in the psychological development of humanity, and there is movement in depth psychology. But I strongly suspect that people who expect that depth psychology makes a better world will be disappointed over and over, perhaps always.

My time is too short to examine all Jungian psychological ideas and Jungian psychotherapeutic procedures. But when I looked around, intensely as I did, I found only open questions.

All this sounds very pessimistic; what can we do? After all, we work, and we have certain ideas about what we are doing and about the psyche. Some analysts become cynical, or they defend themselves against the basic insecurity by becoming Jungian fundamentalists. Other analysts, when they see that they do not get answers about the basic questions in Jungian psychology may try, even at an advanced age, to find answers in other schools of psychology. But if they live long enough they probably will find again that they have to choose again between "no answers" or naiveté.

We must accept that the soul, which is our main interest, can never be understood precisely. All we know is that there exists something like soul – because that is us – and that all we can do is to dance around this soul, approach it from different angles, but we never really catch it. The very essence of the science of soul, of psychology, is that no answers are ever given, that everything is always open. All we can do is to create different images, stories and symbols about the life and nature of the psyche. These mythologies are more or less adequate to the soul. And, by logical thinking, we can create psychological theories or hypotheses. For instance Jung, after he experienced anima, figured out that in women there must be something corresponding to anima, and so got the idea of the animus in women. But fantasizing and imagining we can always find new images, and by rigorous thinking new hypotheses and theories. We can approach the human psyche with our anima, with images and stories, or with the animus – with rigorous logic. Men and women both may have animus and anima – but neither animus nor anima can ever fathom the depth of the psyche.

What is more: Our images and theories about soul have to change again and again, because the psyche changes. Some images and thoughts may be adequate today and inadequate tomorrow. And all that we are doing, saying, imaging, thinking about soul depends again on our individual soul, not only on the "objective psyche."

All we know is that human beings have something, are something, that we call soul or psyche and that this very mysterious phenomenon can be approached only by speculations, hypotheses, mythologies, images, and so on. But because there is no other way to approach the phenomenon of soul does not mean that it does not exist and it does not mean that we have to give up. The soul is far too important for us to behave the way the nineteenth century psychologists did: pretend that soul should be abandoned altogether, because it complicates psychology.

We are a bit stuck. We could say: Well, if that is the case, it doesn't really matter what kind of psychology you choose or want to work with; just let us pick up anything. Let us pick up the ideas and techniques of a depth psychological school that is "in," is fashionable. Let us just be with the hoi poloi, with the psychological crowd. This at least gives us a secure economic basis.

The choosing of the "right" depth psychology, however, is very important. We have to choose the one which suits us best, not the one that is the most fashionable. We have to choose the one with which we feel most comfortable, which appeals most to us.

Whether a psychology really pleases us depends not on the structure of the psychological images, but mainly on their philosophical or religious roots. All the theories of any depth psychology school are rooted in a "Weltanschauung," (world-view) and a "Menschenbild" (image of human nature).

We often choose unconsciously. We automatically prefer the psychology that corresponds most to our own philosophical or religious roots. A religious psychotherapist probably cannot become sincerely a Freudian analyst because the philosophical roots of

Freudianism lie in materialist causality. But the philosophically materialistic psychotherapist should choose Freudian psychology and certainly cannot choose Jungian psychology, because Jung stressed the religious dimension of the soul or – to put it more generally – insisted that there is a dimension to existence other than the purely material or the purely causal one. For a Promethian – a person convinced that we eventually can rule the world – it may be quite appropriate to become a behaviorist, because behaviorism fulfills the idea that the psyche in some way can be ruled. Thus, our philosophical and religious roots usually determine the choice of our psychological mythology and our psychological theories.

Depth psychological hypotheses, theories and mythologies never can be taken at face value; they are only playful images and thoughts in our attempt to come a little closer to the phenomenon of soul. But these images and hypotheses and mythologies with which we try to catch and represent soul are an expression of their philosophical or religious roots.

Eclecticism, by the way, is not the answer either. Any psychological theory, hypothesis or mythology must express the underlying philosophy and religion. It does not help to pick up something here and something there, to be a bit Jungian, and then follow a little some other school. The belief that one can pick up the best of everything is in some way rather touching and very optimistic, but the different philosophical, weltanschaulich and religious roots contradict each other, and so then do the psychological mythologies and images. Eclecticism then becomes bizarre, incoherent.

The title of this Congress, "Open Questions in Jungian Psychology," is an excellent one. It describes what Jungian psychology, indeed all depth psychology is: one big open question. Perhaps the word "question" is actually wrong. Questions always imply that there might be an answer now or in the future. But the aim of depth psychology is not to give answers; it does not describe and state facts the way physics may do. Psychology is a refined song and a beautiful dance, addressed to the soul; this song and dance is strongly influenced by the basic attitude of the singer and dancer.

I have simplified matters a great deal. A particular philosophy or religion usually rules collectively, while the philosophical and religious roots of each human being are mixed and even full of contradictions. The question arises: "What are we really doing? What does our work consist of, if depth psychology has only open questions? If it works only with mythologies, images and theories about the soul, which are connected with various philosophical and religious roots?"

I see more and more that most psychotherapy has a strong ritual character: based on, accompanied and explained by a particular mythology. With the psychotherapeutic ritual and its mythology we try to constellate healing or – to put it mythologically – we try to constellate the archetype of the healer in the client, who then does the healing.

What we call the frame and psychotherapeutic technique are really rituals. Our explanations for them are the mythology that goes with the ritual. Although many analysts don't realize that they work with rituals and mythologies, different schools of psychotherapy have different mythologies, expressed in different rituals, all trying hard to constellate healing. Consequently, most serious schools of psychotherapy have about the same healing effect.

What about thoughts, hypotheses, products of animus? Can they be ritualized too? I am not sure. They may constellate the healer without ritual. In a healing atmosphere, psychological animus thinking can be curative. That is perhaps why so-called cognitive therapy has a curative effect, for instance, in depressions.

About Jung's philosophical and the religious roots much has been written, and there is little agreement. Are they generally Christian of the Zwinglian variety? Many theologians deny that and see even an enemy in Jung. Were his roots gnostic? Were they even pagan, platonic, or neoplatonic? Was Jung a child of the romantic thinkers? Of his many roots, I don't know which appeal to you. I may be able to see my philosophical, ideological, or religious roots but it is very difficult to see them for 2000 people. Each has a particular combination of philosophical and religious roots; it would be preposterous to declare mine as those of all Jungian analysts. Perhaps one could say the following: Jungian psychology – mythology, images, thoughts and theories – is based on some kind of transcendental view of the psyche. What we think, what we see and experience with ourselves and the world, is not the final reality. There is something else behind everything. Everything is greater and deeper than we think at first; therefore we talk of depth psychology. A Jungian psychology without any transcendence – in the experience that something shines through the actual existence – is very difficult to imagine.

As Goethe writes in Faust, "Alles Vergängliche ist nur ein Gleichnis" (everything mortal is only a symbol). Even we humans are only symbols: not in the Jungian sense, but in the platonic sense.

I have come to the conclusion that Jungian psychology – all depth psychology – knows only open questions. Depth psychology is "bodenlos" (bottomless), never can hit the ground, has no secure base. Its object – the soul – can never be caught, can never be explained, remains a mystery. We search for it, and we try over and over again to represent it. We do this with stories, with mythologies, with images, with models, with thoughts and hypotheses. That is why psychology is so full of possibilities to be creative – to use this overstretched word. We can continually create new stories, new mythologies, new images, new thoughts, new ideas. These are not created out of thin air; they are expressions of the soul. They reflect it partially, but they can never be precise. Once in a while a gifted individual creates a whole new mythology or a whole new chain of thoughts – Freud, Jung, Heinz Kohut, Otto Kernberg, Melanie Klein, and others. We less gifted ones use their creations, always changing them according to our own needs, according to our roots and of course according to the needs of clients. Love of the soul is a passion that never can possess the object of its love.

My view may seem despairing, but it is quite the opposite. Millions of people fall in love and sing thousands of songs about love, yet nobody can explain passionate love and why somebody falls in love with a particular person. But this does not remove the enthusiasm for love. The same applies to psychology; we never can find answers, only questions, yet our passion for soul and psyche remains as strong as ever. We are all, as psychologists and psychotherapists, not soul technicians or soul manipulators. We cannot explain soul, but we care for the soul; we are passionate caretakers of the soul.

Sexual Acting Out and the Female Analyst

Coline Covington
London, England
Society of Analytical Psychology

Starting with Freud's and Jung's first experiences of working with female patients, some attention has been given to the subject of male analysts who are tempted to act out or who do act out sexually with their female patients. Much less attention has been given to sexual acting out by female analysts.

Despite the title of my paper, I am not discussing actual instances of sexual acting out between female analysts and their patients. Neither do I want to take the position that all instances of acting out, sexual or otherwise, are a "bad thing." The question I am addressing has less to do with morality than with the reasons for sexual acting out and whether it is analysis.

Case

John was 44 when he started analysis with me. He had had a previous, three-year analysis with a man when John was in his 20s, and he had seen a psychiatrist intermittently since that time. John was a very successful businessman and was at a crucial point in his career: being considered for a substantial promotion. The last time he had received a promotion, he had had a breakdown; it was the anxiety of another breakdown that had brought him to me. He handled his first session as a seasoned patient, giving me a full historical synopsis of his life, making links between himself and his father, who had also been a powerful businessman but always a remote figure within the family. The only time that John revealed any feeling was when he told me that his mother had been American – as he assumed I was – and that she had been beautiful. She too was portrayed as a powerful and distant figure.

John then returned abruptly to the subject of his career and his anxiety about losing his promotion. For a brief moment, when he had been describing his mother, John had shown some warmth toward me, smiling at me in a slightly seductive way. Then I felt as if he had poured cold water on me. I thought he was telling me about his anxieties about being potent, and specifically that, if he was promoted to his father's powerful position, he would be punished. He wanted to discover that he was attractive as a man but he equated being attractive with being punished. It became clear that John had constructed a competent false self behind which his real self was trapped in a nightmare world of seduction followed by the threat of castration.

In the second session, John recounted a recurring dream in which *he had committed a murder and could not find anywhere to hide the body. The body was that of a woman.* John linked this dream with his sexuality and said in a tantalizing way that he had a secret that he was always trying to hide: He secretly saw himself as a woman. We could see then that it was his passive, homosexual identity that he was failing to conceal and to bury in the dream. He confessed to having a compulsive fantasy of watching a little girl sticking the handle of a spoon up her bottom and then being hosed with cold water by a punitive mother. The fantasy took different forms, but always consisted of anal penetration accompanied by a punitive, phallic mother. John was afraid that his mother would punish him for wanting to be a woman, yet he felt that he could be attractive only if he was a woman.

Since his twenties, John regularly had sought out prostitutes who would enact this fantasy for him. He did not want sexual intercourse with them; what excited him was having them put their fingers up his anus. His search to find a phallic mother in these prostitutes had become an addiction which had enabled him to carry on with his version of reality: to continue being his mother's homosexual lover and, thus, to avoid competing with his powerful father. John's fear of feeling desire for his mother was so great that it could be circumvented, in his mind, only by his becoming a girl. This defense was beginning to break down, however, as he became increasingly anxious about being caught. At the same time, he admitted that he wanted to be caught and, finally, to be allowed to be a man.

John made it clear to me that he expected me to make sense of these matters and to provide him with a manual, as he so aptly put it, which he could follow. I felt that John was asking me, like the prostitutes, to penetrate him. He wanted to find in me that phallic mother who would make him feel safe under her control. His technique of seduction was to try to make me feel powerful, so that he could continue to hide his masculinity and thereby keep us both as the bisexual couple in his inner world. Thus, he transformed the failure of oral and phallic eroticism into anal eroticism and he remained fixated to that position.

John's erotic transference to me, hinted at in the first session, began to unfold. He appeared at my door promptly, usually panting from his exertions to arrive on time, and from excitement. He would then lie on the couch and stretch out, his hands nearly touching me, sitting at his side. I remained where I was, being careful not to move away from him; he would certainly have taken such movement as a sign of rejection. John needed to know that I would not try to escape, as he felt his mother had, from his desire to touch me and to be touched by me. He soon began saying that his sessions were the only times in his week that felt constructive, how much he looked forward to them and how his wife was convinced that he had fallen in love with me. I became his idealized, beautiful and cruel mother from whom he expected the "cold water treatment." His intense fascination with, and hatred of, his beautiful mother was tangible. He would turn and stare at me with icy, penetrating eyes, behind which I could sense his anxiety about feeling different in me. Whenever he was able to accept warmth from me, he would immediately put me to the test and become insistent on knowing my thoughts and feelings about him. He became obsessive about controlling me. When he felt particularly frustrated by my failure to respond in the way he wanted, he would refuse to speak or would tell me there was no point to anything and the only real solution was suicide. The moment John felt unwanted by me in his mind, he would threaten to bugger me and destroy the analysis; then we would be "in the shit together." Feeling blackmailed whenever he did not get his way with me, I imagined that he had been subjected to this kind of treatment from his mother. Rather than interpreting John's behavior as an attack against me, which would have served to reinforce his expectation of being seen as bad, I spoke about his fear of allowing himself to receive warmth from me and his fear of what this might lead to, since this was a new experience for him.

As John was able to feel increasingly dependent on me, what emerged was his need to find a responsive mother who could accept his desire for her and recognize him as desirable. It also became apparent that he identified with the sadistic, controlling mother who had severely punished John when he went against her wishes or showed signs of independence. John's continual pressure on me to allow him to touch me threatened to elicit a re-enactment of his mother's rejection, thereby confirming his belief that he was essentially unlovable, which he attributed to his having a bad penis (i.e., his failed masculinity). This also meant that John could remain, in secret, his mother's emasculated love object and sustain his fantasy that mother preferred him over father. No parental intercourse was allowed to take place in his mind, so that John could maintain an illusion of being in control over me and over the primal scene. Thus, he did not know that he could arouse someone's desire or love; he only knew how to control, seduce, manipulate and ultimately to be unlovable. John wanted to convince me of his nastiness so that he could stay with me forever as my "hopeless case," while harboring the fantasy that by sacrificing himself – his sexual identity – he would win me over. The pressure to allow him to touch me came not only from his need to control me but also from his intense need to internalize me, to internalize a living and different mother who could then continue to exist inside him; that is, to achieve object constancy.

The degree of control to which John had been subjected and to which he subjected others had left him in a lifeless and empty world, around which he had to construct a narcissistic shell for survival. While he could present a good show, it also belied his constant need to impress himself on others and to use others as a mirror to reassure himself of his existence. Like a magician, he would pull glittering tricks out of his hat; out of an empty, mindless space; out of his anus.

Here John appeared as the trickster in his most frightening, unrelated aspect. In the transference, John felt he needed to perform for me. Because he was not powerful, he had tried to present a pretty show for his mother; he had wanted to give her a glittering penis in order to make her feel that she had a vagina and to enhance her power. Off stage, John lived alone, in a place he described as his ice tower, surrounded by glittering mirrors where he had grown to despise the sight of himself. His principal technique for denying this inner reality was to keep as many balls in the air as possible, taking on more and more projects at work and creating an endless stream of sexual fantasies in which he was the onlooker, identifying with a woman who was being tantalized or tortured sexually by another woman, or the naughty little girl who must be punished for her misbehavior. Thus he could remain, in his mind, a man and a woman at the same time.

This compulsive fantasying enabled John to maintain his illusion of bisexuality and to deny his psychic reality. These fantasies could never evolve or lead anywhere; he used them within the analysis to entertain me, in a masturbatory way, as a defense against revealing his real feelings and desires. When such fantasying happens in analysis, a kind of anti-narrative is established which is both boring and static. If the patient's desire for relationship is not recognized, the situation can lead also to an intensification of symptoms. In John's case, his need to excite me and seduce me derived from his need to create some sense of life, to make me come alive in his mind and to ensure that I would stay with him. Inevitably, this situation felt demanding and devoid of feeling. Consequently, at the end of one of his discourses, no matter how brilliantly delivered, we would both be in the ice tower, frozen in time.

This repetitive and inauthentic narrative had been constructed in John's previous analysis. He and his analyst had evolved an account of John's life, close enough to his persona that he could add it to his repertoire of mental devices. In his need to be brilliant for his mother, he remembered and reproduced his analyst's interpretations, seemingly verbatim. While they may have been correct theoretically, they had had no transmutative effect. He had remained in his ice tower, untouched. I imagined that the previous analyst had been unable to assume a passive, feminine role; hence he had continued to act as John's powerful father with whom John was frightened to compete and whom he could only imitate. In retrospect, perhaps the most promising feature of John's first session with me was the flicker of passion he showed when he referred to his beautiful mother, associating me with her. Here was the possibility of something igniting between us that might lead to melting his icy encasement. My difficulty was in finding a way to touch him with words; he had no mind yet with which he could receive and assimilate them. Words were like narcissistic objects for John, used defensively to simulate relating. Initially, I found that I could touch John and give him warmth concretely through the tone of my voice and the expression in my eyes.

John emphasized that the only way the analysis could be fruitful was for us to be on equal terms. He told me all of his thoughts and secrets; it followed that I should tell him mine. He would argue that it was only by means of this reciprocity that he would ever believe he could be cared for. John wanted me to play the role of his beautiful mother with whom he had felt on equal terms, who had been there exclusively for him. His desire for there to be no difference between him and his mother meant that no parents could exist in his inner world. Similarly, he wanted to eradicate the distinction between us and to destroy the analysis. He wanted not only to be close to me, but to control and possess me, in as concrete a way as possible, so that he would have access to my body and my mind at all times. The intensity of John's demands on me revealed the strength of his hatred and destructiveness, but also the extent to which his oral needs had been frustrated. John seemed to have had hardly any experience of a loving breast; instead, he had felt his mother's desire for him as coming from her need to feel excited, in order to feel alive.

In the countertransference I felt no desire for John at this point; I felt numb. John seemed to want me to be his prostitute, whose body he could control or, alternatively, to be my prostitute. Either I had to be without feelings and a mind or John had to be the mindless one. We could not both have feelings at the same time. When I said this to John, he recalled having been held once by his previous analyst when he had broken down in tears and how he had only felt uncomfortable and frightened. He linked this experience to a memory of caressing his mother affectionately when she had been in tears, and of his sudden fear that she would require him to become her lover and allow him to take his father's place. Thus, his attempts to give or receive affection had either been frustrated or had become eroticized. He could not transfer his need to give and receive affection onto someone else; all his libidinal desires remained cathected onto this seductive and rejecting internal mother. His way of defending himself had been to dissociate himself, going numb. As a result, there was no link in John's mind between true affection and sexual desire with a differentiated object.

After several months, John was having five sessions a week and would have seen me on weekends if I had agreed. He described me as the center of his world, his every act being directed toward gaining my recognition. He wanted to regress more and more, not in order to progress, but to fuse with me in a symbiotic state. When he was not with me, especially over weekends, he would torture himself with the idea that, because I did not tell him about my life, he was unwanted. Thus, he turned me into his rejecting mother in a masochistic attempt to control me.

At this time, his sexual fantasies had largely stopped; they reappeared only occasionally, on weekends and breaks. In their place, John was beginning to fantasize about being touched by me and touching me, which he would describe in great detail, looking at me longingly. His desire seemed to be a bottomless pit; nothing would suffice except total possession of me. John also made me feel like the beautiful mother in the narcissistic transference who had seduced her child so that he would not grow, colluding with his wish to take revenge against his father. John wanted to make me have loving feelings toward him so that he could control and frustrate me as he had felt controlled and frustrated by his mother. But more importantly, he needed to elicit from me a loving mother whom he could establish as a good and enduring internal object and who made him feel like a desirable man. He was in search of a mother who could relate to him, enjoy him and help him to grow.

As John was able to differentiate increasingly between a controlling mother and a receptive one, he could experience feeling wanted as a man for the first time. With the discovery that I was different from his mother, he could begin to desire me as a separate object, not a narcissistic one, and to ask for love. He had only known what it was like to be wanted as a selfobject for his mother, as a narcissistic extension of her. In her reflection he could see only emptiness. There was no mother to receive his desire, no breast wanting to be desired; he had never experienced this primary potency. He had to develop a pseudo-potency, and a pseudo-thinking, as was evident in his always identifying with the woman in his sexual fantasies. He could never allow himself to be the man and to develop his own mind. I think this was also indicative of his early identification with his mother, an adhesive identification which had formed in place of ordinary projective and introjective processes.

His call for a reciprocal relationship was correct in that he had failed to receive this at a basic level. Initially, in his need to feel that he could get inside me, John became a detective and spied on me and on my house. He also pieced together a biography of me. In a similar way he had had to be a detective in relation to his mother who remained largely inaccessible to him. He also wanted to know about my private life so that he could take the position of my partner, thereby breaking the boundary and eliminating father, with the ultimate aim of reducing us to a single entity.

The pressure I felt to respond to John's needs, and specifically to his depression, was also his way of communicating to me the pressure he had felt as a child to alleviate his mother's depression, as well as the futility that whatever he tried to do would never be enough. Try as he might, he could never fill in for his absent father whom he saw as the source of his mother's depression. If I had been depressed, as his mother had been, it might have led to a destructive re-enactment of their relationship. As it was, in my neurotic countertransference, John represented that depressive father whom I had wanted to rescue, the depressive parent we all know and have within us. Had I not been aware of this, my countertransference feelings might also have led me to act out with John and to have become the phallic mother he wanted me to be for him, who could not bear for him to be separate and to grow.

As John fell more intensely in love with me, he put increasing pressure on me to demonstrate my feelings toward him, to gratify him, and to break the boundary of analysis. He continued to beg me to allow him to touch me and especially to kiss me. I was increasingly drawn to him, toward the image of my own depressed father that I saw in him and my desire to make him feel potent. I also understood John's desire to touch and to be touched as not simply relating to a primitive level of need, but as indicative of his need to find a responsive and spontaneous mother, who could demonstrate to him that she was not afraid of his feelings. Rather than responding in a concrete way to John's requests I found that, when I could respond spontaneously in words, John was able to feel touched by me and less frightened of his loving feelings. Part of the aim of the erotic transference is to elicit the spontaneous response from the analyst in order to feel that it is possible to express loving feelings safely. Without this, there can be no freedom to think or to symbolize because fantasy had to be continually blocked and controlled.

There was a delicate balance in the level of frustration that John could bear. If I remained silent for too long John would feel pushed away and, in his mind, I would revert back to his icy mother. He would become again the rejected little boy who felt sadistic contempt for women and who expected to be controlled by them. Then he would attack me, as his defense against feeling totally annihilated. Only by my interpreting John's attacks as his defense against his need to express loving feelings toward me, was he able to come out of hiding again. It became increasingly difficult to resist John's demands to touch me and to be touched. He made me feel that I was cruelly depriving him; a part of me longed both to mitigate his suffering and to expel this cruel mother from the transference. I knew that I had to contain for us both the feelings of frustration, longing and hatred that were so unbearable for John. I imagined that his mother had felt deeply frustrated and angry at his often aloof father and could not bear to feel close to John, especially as he grew older. John experienced a sadistic frustration which denied his needs. By gradually being able to identify this controlling part of himself, which would push people away and leave him more isolated and rejected than ever, John was able to gain increasing control over his destructive and omnipotent impulses and to bear frustrations while being able to hold onto his loving feelings at the same time.

It was important to recognize that the sexual tension within the transference and countertransference came about when John tried to resolve his need for affection through sexuality. In this respect the erotic transference manifested John's need to be close to a mother and a father, as well as his wish to repair the primal scene that was lacking and to find his own sexuality. His aggression resulted from his need to be held and accepted by a mother who could recognize him as different from herself.

When John could see his need for affection, he was able to change. He had a series of dreams which seemed to indicate a significant shift in his inner world, toward the establishment of a good internal object with which he could relate. The dreams depicted John's becoming closer and closer to me sexually, until we were on the brink of making love. These dreams were so highly charged that John said he was left with the sense that they had not been dreams at all, but had actually happened. Because he felt he could elicit this response from me, albeit in his dreams, he was able not only to bear the frustration he felt when he could not actually seduce me but also to allow himself to be more potent outside the analytic relationship. He then had the following dream:

I was walking down the street at night and a man in drag was following me. I kept telling him to go away and he wouldn't until I got frightened and hailed a taxi and left. I was then at a party and talking to an actress. She was very self-conscious and was looking at everyone else in the room to see if they noticed her. I told her she should be careful not to do the same part all the time and to get type-cast; she should try doing different parts, that this would be better for her career. Then I was in another taxi seated in-between an older woman on my right and my father on my left. I was stroking the woman's thighs and felt very affectionate towards her. We then went into a restaurant; my father left the room. I embraced the woman, said good-bye to her and went into a large room where I was soon

*joined by a younger woman. I don't remember what she looked like.
I knew she was going to become my wife.*

This dream seemed to chart the stages of John's analysis and of
his anima development, from his original identification with a
phallic mother (the man in drag) to a more narcissistic persona who
was reminiscent of the magician, to finding himself in-between his
parents, able to express his sexual and loving feelings toward his
mother without being rebuked and without triumphing over father,
and finally about to embark on a marriage.

This dream marked the final stage in John's romance, during
which he had to relinquish the fantasy of being always in intimate
contact with me. This was the period of weaning which John had
never experienced. His behavior toward me changed markedly. As
he felt increasingly active and potent, he could imagine making love
to me differently, this time as himself, as a man.

Discussion

When patients, such as John, want to act out sexually with the
analyst, they are demonstrating their need to find, first, a loving
breast and, second, an empathic father. For John, there was a failure
at both the pre-oedipal and oedipal stages. Failure to meet these
needs results in a narcissistic defense which prevents the child from
being able to think, to have a mind – to know what he is missing. For
John to have known about his unresponsive mother – who could not
help him to develop and grow – and his absent father, who could not
help him to separate from mother and become a man, would have
been unbearable. These lacks could be known only when he was
able to find and internalize a different relationship within which he
could be himself and have a mind.

Initially, John's coldness and his attempts to control me were his
way of maintaining his gender confusion and his narcissistic
defense. In the case of female patients, my experience is very
similar. These women also want to convince me of their unlovability
and to turn me into a phallic mother or a cold, rejecting father. In
such cases it is important for the female analyst to recognize the
paternal transference and the negative oedipal transference. Failure
to do so may reinforce in the patient the sense of being rejected for
having sexual desires and push the patient into homosexual retreat.
For John the only way of remaining close to his father was through

homosexual identification. Similarly, failure to recognize the negative oedipal transference may promote a malignant narcissistic attachment in which the female patient is never able to become a woman in her mind because she cannot separate from mother and allow the parents to be together in the primal scene.

While the erotic transference stems from a failure to resolve oedipal conflicts, the failure often goes back to the early relationship with the mother in which her feelings, particularly her infantile needs for a responsive mother, make her frightened or overwhelmed by her baby's needs. Thus, she is unable to receive the baby's projections and to differentiate these from her own. If this process goes wrong, there is never a strong enough attachment to support separation. In effect, weaning becomes impossible and there is no safe container for imagination and thought to unfold. The negative messages the child receives at this early stage of development lead to feelings of worthlessness and to confusion of sexual identity, which in turn lead to the perpetual attempt to deny desire and loss, just as the parents have done. To protect himself from this unbearable frustration, the male child turns himself into a girl in his mind and feels castrated, becoming in adulthood the lesbian lover of a phallic woman. In a similar way the female child turns herself into a boy in her mind because she cannot accept being castrated, and becomes in adulthood the homosexual lover of a passive man. Both deny they are men and women as part of a system of denial of psychic reality, as a defence against unbearable frustration. This homosexual identification later serves as a defense against the recognition that the child cannot marry mother or father. Oedipal frustration cannot be breached when the child's earlier experience of desire has been frustrated and denied. Such a defense inevitably blocks the possibility of thought and symbolic process because there can be no inner space; the need and desire for the other is denied when it has been unmet. The task of the analyst is to meet this desire with words – and to frustrate it.

For both male and female analysts there are two danger areas in treating patients who manifest erotic transferences. The first is the failure to meet the patient's desire with understanding. The second is, if there is no such understanding, the failure to frustrate this desire. In the first danger area, the analyst can only contain the patient when the ego is not ready to understand; the second is what the analyst must do when the patient's ego is ready to understand. If the analyst fails to be receptive to the patient's desire and, like the patient's parent, denies these needs in herself, the patient – if healthy enough – may terminate the treatment. But it is also likely that the treatment will continue and the analysis will become interminable, with analyst and patient locked in a sado-masochistic relationship. Then the patient is likely to develop a stronger false self as a protection against the realization that primitive needs are still not being met, and are experienced as being overwhelming.

From the analyst's viewpoint, the patient's not actually changing, and continuing to suffer, serves as a constant reminder of the analyst's uselessness and thereby assuages his or her guilt about failing to provide the recognition and empathy which the analyst may never have received, either from parents or analysis. As with John, this problem is often apparent with patients who have had many years of previous analysis during which very little has changed, due to the analyst's resistance to recognizing the erotic transference. If the analyst's response is defensive and frightened, it will send the patient into an anal or oral sadistic state. Then the patient will stop the erotic transference through guilt and not through understanding. The ego can understand what is happening only by working through in the transference. In John's case, for example, he wanted to touch me in order to discover the difference between anal intrusion and sexual penetration. When this could be talked about, it could be discovered and worked through.

One feature these patients have in common, is their failure to have felt or expressed any closeness or attachment to their previous analysts. As one patient said, "I always thought it was against the rules for analysts to have any feelings for their patients." What also commonly occurs is that the failure to recognize and analyze the early dependency needs drives the patient into a homosexual solution (or reinforces this solution) as a narcissistic defense. The patient's history is then re-enacted within the analytic relationship and the analyst takes on the role of the parent whom the patient can only hate, because loving feelings are too frightening. Thus, the patient cannot separate to form new loving attachments.

In the case of the analyst who is able to respond to the patient's desire but is unable to frustrate the patient and is actually seduced, the analyst is caught in a parental countertransference to the patient. The analyst who has an abusive image of a primal scene, or who has not resolved the depressive position, and remains within a two-person (pre-oedipal) state of mind, will find it more difficult to resist acting out sexually. In this case the repressed desire to remain

exclusively with mother or father is fulfilled along with the destruction (in fantasy) of the parents who have been experienced as only
cruelly frustrating or rejecting.

If we imagine Oedipus in analysis, he would certainly have
developed an erotic transference; it would also be clear that his
search for a loving mother was due to his early abandonment. If
Jocasta had been Oedipus' analyst, she might have been tempted to
rescue him and to respond to his desire for her. Oedipus might prove
irresistible if Jocasta's own pre-oedipal needs had not been met. Her
own longing to feel wanted might make it too difficult for her to
frustrate Oedipus in his desires. In this way, analyst and patient may
re-enact the patient's history of having been sexually abused by a
parent. It is understandable that Freud would have come to this
conclusion in his treatment of hysterical women.

The strength and virulence of the erotic transference stems from
this primitive need of the infant to feel wanted. This is the cry of the
patient who says, "For analysis to work, I have to fall in love with
you and you have to fall in love with me." My version of this
statement would be slightly different. For such an analysis to work,
the patient does have to fall in love with the analyst. In turn, the
analyst has to allow herself to be the object of her patient's love and
to respond with warmth and analytic understanding. By these means
she can provide an experience of empathic frustration within which
the patient can emerge and grow.

Female Perversion

Scenes and Strategies In Analysis and Culture[*]

Anne Springer
Berlin, Germany
German Society for Analytical Psychology

In the chapter of his memoirs devoted to Freud, Jung wrote:

Incest and perversions were no remarkable novelties to me, and did not call for any special explanation. Along with criminality, they formed part of the black lees that spoiled the taste of life by showing me only too plainly the ugliness and meaninglessness of human existence. That cabbages thrive in dung was something I had always taken for granted. (MDR, p. 166)

As a further introduction, another quotation from Jung:

An artistically gifted patient produced a typical tetradic mandala and stuck it on a sheet of thick paper. On the back there was a circle to match, filled with drawings of sexual perversions. This shadow aspect of the mandala represented the disorderly, disruptive tendencies, the "chaos" that hides behind the self and bursts out in a dangerous way as soon as the individuation process comes to a standstill, or when the self is not realized and so remains unconscious. (CW9-I, par. 689)

Jung did not report what exactly the patient offered as an image, nor did he specify the relationship between the good front side and the shadowy and chaotic reverse side. The patient probably wishes to be seen by the analyst with the tension and the links between the parts that she has presented. There are difficulties in grasping the relationship between the image and the chaotic reversal in the analytical process. Cabbage may grow well on a dungheap, but how does that work?

The words perversion, perversity, perverse give rise to unsettling thoughts and feelings in many people in our culture; it has to do with

---

[*] Abbreviated version

the forbidden, hidden, embarrassing, frightening, and in a strange way both attractive and repulsive. Moral value judgments crop up that are supposed to work in opposition to this dark fascination but are unable to do so.

Female perversion until recently appeared in the psychoanalytic literature (apart from the school of Melanie Klein) only as the exception, usually in the description of special pathologies such as kleptomania, or as a controversial classification of homosexuality. With the exception of Freud's "Three Essays" (SE7), the widely expressed opinion was that some men are perverse; women are neurotic, psychotic or borderline. Only recently have we seen systematic consideration of female perversion in the psychoanalytic field; we are more likely to find such accounts in the libraries of pornography or in treatises on sexual science.

After his break with Freud, Jung no longer studied perversion systematically. He referred to it in some cases as pathological but was not interested specifically in its genesis or its inner structure. We frequently find negative connotations when Jung speaks about the perverse in the context of his break with Freud. In his efforts to distance himself, "perverse" was an anti-psychoanalytic battle cry to the well-known outbursts of 1934. There he speaks of "infantil-perversen Jargon gewisser Neurosenfälle, welche sich durch die Besonderheit der Freudschen Psychologie auszeichnen. Es ist geradezu grotesk, daß der Arzt selber in jene Denkweise verfällt, die er am andern mit Recht als infantil beanstandet und darum heilen möchte" (CW10, par. 356). On the other hand, Jung encourages the analyst to view the bizarre and strange in their extremities as possible elements and expressions of individuation. (See also Guggenbühl-Craig, 1976.)

Almost as an aside, Jung makes comments that contribute to the comprehension of the perverse. More recent work (e.g., Fordham, 1988, Wyly, 1989) is also important for an understanding of the perverted person and relationship from a Jungian point of view.

My interest here is in examining the perverse structural elements of women as I have encountered these in the analysis. I came to see these structural elements as perverse only as a result of learning these special patients' lack of progress in analysis, and countertransference reactions which were highly confusing for me.

Definitions of Terms

1. Perversion: Making hate (not love) with sexual performance that is obligatory, compulsive, fixated, and rigid. (Kaplan, 1991, p. 40).

2. Difference between male and female perversion: Males relate to external partial objects; for women the site of perversion is their own whole body or another whole body which they unconsciously fantasize as part of their own body.

Perversion and perverse structural elements, like almost everything pathological represent a complex mental performance. According to Morgenthaler (1987), their inner psychic function protects against disintegration by overwhelming excitation, which can lead to psychosis or, if coupled with impulses to act, can result in suicide.

The perverse is always to be seen as defense of the self. With women it simulates in a defensive way a wholeness and completeness that is intended to eliminate the reality of the other sex (not-self). As Fordham (1988) suggested, the perverse is a pseudo-androgyny, the hermaphrodite at the beginning of the opus.

Case Study

Frau L. was one of four patients who all posed similar problems for me. At the start of the analysis, she is 32 years old, a successful lawyer suffering from depression, back-pains and difficulties at work. She copes well with large tasks, but often manages smaller tasks only after overcoming considerable anxiety, accompanied by an element of pleasure that I came to recognize only later. She is very thin (looking almost anorexic), attractive and well-mannered, wearing expensive and fashionably styled clothes. Despite being attractive, she seems strangely unerotic. She is carefully made up; in her narrow face her eyes seem remarkably large, hungry and childlike. She has come to analysis because of severe depression and because all relationships break down. She had lived in a series of longer, heterosexual relationships, and had been left shortly before analysis began. She speaks in staccato; her body emanates something of a marionette. In the preconsultation she says dryly, "The analysis is the final attempt to make a go of my life." Her facial expression switches confusingly between momentary petrification, which suggests profound desperation, and the beaming charm of an omnipotent maiden.

We agree on analysis three times a week, lying down. She had saved a considerable sum of money which would cover costs her health insurance would not meet. The initial dream: *The patient is given flowers by a female colleague* [in waking life married with two children, to whom the patient has an apparently negative attitude.] In the dream *the patient accepts the flowers*. The accceptance seems condescending; the patient says that in the dream, but when retelling it she has been moved by the friendly act. She is also condescending in the way she tells the dream to me. She seems to be saying, "I am being good; I will tell my dreams. I hope you can make something of it all." The aggressive aspect is alien to her consciousness. The start of the analysis is determined by the patient's clinging to the hope that her lover will come back. The analysis circles for some 150 to 160 hours around this relationship and two others, showing the following pattern: She meets a man who treats her sadistically and aggressively. She is fascinated, plays with the idea of falling in love with him, and now fantasizes total closeness and fusion, while at the same time eliciting from him hurtful words and deeds. She recognizes her role rationally but is unable to resolve it. In this phase of sadomasochistic entanglement she rejects genital sex, eagerly registers every small sign of tenderness from her partner, only to denounce it immediately as being insufficient. She masturbates alone at home for hours on end.

The tormenting process intensifies, accompanied by growing diffuse excitation. At the same time, her massive fear of people grows. She knows that she must break with the man for her own self-esteem, but she is unable to do so. In the sessions, she eventually becomes unreachable, enclosed in herself. She also seems unreachable when dealing with family entanglements: Her parents are controlling but not caring; her brother marries and she feels deserted by him. However, she cannot separate from the family because of financial ties, though these are clearly maintained by the patient. The partner relationships end with her being left, after long tormenting scenes. A briefly emerging anger with the partner is withdrawn immediately. At this point she says, "Better this way than me becoming a shrew; then I could stand myself even less and would have to kill myself."

The patient has no female friends. She is ashamed, can't display her misery to women, they – I – did everything better than she anyway. The fear of her jealousy becomes clear at this point, and gradually becomes partially accessible to the patient.

She keeps her sexuality and her sexual fantasies – including the masturbation fantasies – out of the sessions. It is noticeable that she never really loses her charm. She talks a great deal in the short periods of silence, as if she had disappeared. When she is silent, she kills almost every idea and almost every feeling in me. Her body – if she refers to it at all – is a thing, an assembled machine. Her body must be thin, otherwise it is objectionable. Her uterus is a burden. Children would make her swell up. She says, "I would not be good for children; I can't play." Frequently she enters the consulting room with arms slightly apart and a spring in her step, like a little girl who has just been told, "Don't go and get your nice clothes dirty." When it comes to my holidays she briefly becomes an angry little princess. In turn, I feel like a servant maid who shouldn't be making any fuss; I am getting paid. In the sessions I become irritated and tired at the same time. But she is obviously trying hard to be a good and productive patient. On the other hand, I feel a growing need to inquire aggressively, inquisitively – invasively – and in a strangely excited way, searching for a way of discharging tension and reviving myself. Outside the sessions, she occupies my thoughts to a considerable degree, but unproductively. In the sessions I increasingly feel that I don't understand her anyway.

From the text, the dreams and the fragments of memories, I gradually form a fragmentary and confusing inner image of the mother: a large, thick-skinned woman, mostly silent but aggressive in bursts, who degraded the father in front of the patient but felt extremely dependent on him; a mother who told her daughter with every new boyfriend, "He isn't good enough." As a small child, and through adolescence, the patient remembers herself as being very aggressive. She almost always played alone, climbing daringly in the garden and house. In addition to concern, I feel an aggressive indifference; "Let her fall down out of the tree; I can't change it" – an aggressively tinted separation fantasy. After the patient has explained much of her childhood pastimes over a number of sessions, she comes to the next (181st) session and says, "But in the evening I crept into bed with my mother, both of us in front of the television." I feel some anxiety, then brief but intense sexual excitation, without fantasy or emotion. Strangely there occurs to me the patient's new man-friend, about whom she has spoken in glowing tones. She is in love with him, but he doesn't sleep with her. He is a homosexual, practicing masochist: for the patient a tender friend, acting his sexuality in a sadomasochistic hell.

For the first time in this analysis I have the impression, at the moment of physical excitation, that I am able to reach a missing part of the patient. I ask, "Who seduces whom?" The patient starts, then says: "The door to Mother's bedroom had a translucent pane of glass, and through it you could see something of her, large, always pink nightdresses. In bed I always slid up to the top where she lay. Then she scolded me and pulled me back down again. She always wanted me to sleep there. She had said: "Naughty girl, but better than your brother, he's roaming around outside. You won't be like daddy, we don't need him here." She caressed me, but at night she stuck her finger into me down there, and I pretended to be asleep. I always thought "I'm bad" because it had excited me so; she shouldn't notice anything. One time I crept away; she said I was bad. She always had chocolates in bed. The patient's voice has become that of a six-year-old child. For the first time she cries: a confused, miserable, deserted child.

Later discussions between the patient and her brother – and diffuse memories which gradually come together – indicate that as a small child she was probably masturbated regularly by her mother if she did not go to sleep and was crying, just as she calmed herself with endless masturbation in the loneliness and torment of her relationship with men. In the subsequent sessions she cries a lot, from anger alternating with sorrow. Then, in the 200th session, the patient again reports the sexual scenarios of her homosexual boy-friend and his fear of AIDS. She still likes him, but is annoyed that he keeps a part of his life inaccessible to her just as she has kept a part of her life inaccessible to me. She says, "I should stick with my fantasies; that way you can't get AIDS." I say, "When you mastur-bate, you enjoy without danger." The patient: "Since I was 15, I have had a fantasy which always does the trick. I imagine I am a great queen in a room with glass all the way round, and a ceiling and floor of glass too. Outside are people: men, women and children. The people can see me; otherwise they can't be there, if they can't see me. But they can only be there if they hurt themselves, have sex. Each one is there for me. I fetch into the room one that I want, but he can't do anything to me in the room, just look together with me at what they are doing outside."

Shortly before developing this central masturbation fantasy in adolescence, the patient had experienced a double loss and was suicidal. Her dog, which she had loved but also tormented and sexually stimulated, had died; she also lost the therapist her parents had engaged in view of her aggressiveness and non-conformity, and with whom she had fallen in love. She was alone and lonely, as she had been as a baby and small child. From this period of time the personality developed as I came to know it: a princess-like femininity as masquerade for a child, constantly threatened by disintegration under the pressure of sorrow, anger and longing. The princess masquerade included the sexualized seduction, coupled with the desire for revenge. The fear of disintegration demonstrated itself as a fear of being overwhelmed by a diffuse sexualized excitation. For the helpless baby there was nobody really and constantly there.

In the analysis she naturally defended the seductive entanglement which had served her so long as necessary defense and as a possibility for living. She was aggressive, her sadism became cheaper and she expressed a powerful wish for revenge, in the analysis and at work.

The newly found and injured baby began only slowly to feel, let me feel and to play in a non-masturbatory way; for example, with ideas about how she would redesign my room, safe in the knowledge that I would survive the resulting destruction. As a way of understanding this, I suggested that she go looking round in my body: "What is where?" And, she asks, could it really be that she did not have a very small penis inside herself? Ashamedly and triumphantly she discloses that she had always assumed its actual existence. There are repeated setbacks due to severe feelings of guilt with which she responds to good experiences. The feelings of guilt lead to self damage: a short anorexic phase, a disfiguring hairstyle, extreme self-doubt in her work, emptiness and inconsolable desperation after professional success. In the meantime, for the time-being, the treatment has reached a conclusion (after 380 sessions). The patient lives, free from symptoms, in a relationship with a man who is probably somewhat soft; they have separate apartments. She finds it reassuring that she can return to the analysis when children become a topic in the relationship.

Transference/countertransference

Once the patient had been able to reach me by projective identification to my body, the transference and countertransference could be identified much more clearly. Her childhood fate was re-enacted in the here and now and back to the pre-oedipal time, the world of her inner object and thus also of her real object relationships. The inner world of the patient was dominated and determined by the experience of a dangerous and sexualizing mother, who regarded the child as an extension of herself and who arranged a perverse scenario with the child. Krämer (1980) said: "I speculate that [incestuous mothers] could not enjoy their own genitals for sexual pleasure, but masturbated the genitals of their incompletely separated and individuated children as dehumanized extensions of the maternal body" (p. 330). This could be said about abusing female analysts, too.

The child introjected the experience of this perverse mother. The reversal of the mother – turning aggression into apparent love – sat tightly in her. At the same time, the perverse fantasies and relationships, as well as the perverted treatment of her body, served as defense against the diffuse anxiety, anger and sadness of a deserted child. In the central masturbation fantasy, the mother later turns the smallness and vulnerability of the baby daughter into apparent greatness and autonomy, perhaps following a fantasy of the mother that she is her devalued phallus. Now the patient seduces instead of being seduced, and can revenge herself. She can see and be seen, which wasn't possible in childhood and in her relationships in adult life, because good objects and good experiences would have rocked the stabilizing defenses too much. She experienced coitus in adulthood – as well as analysis – as psychically empty, merely as a discharge of tension (frigidly) or as using a man to please herself (as masturbation). In the transference she enacted the mother-child pair who do not understand each other, in changing constellations with the over-reaching and stimulating mother, but also with her identification with the perverse mother. By means of projective identification, mother and daughter confront each other in the transference.

From this moment on, the patient was able to draw on rudimentarily good experiences with a woman – the paternal grandmother – in order to allow an approach to a good object, the analyst. The central masturbation fantasy of the patient, however, characterizes the long period of abuse, the perversion of the analytic situation. The queen in the glass room wants to be seen, and left alone, wants to be understood but kills the thinking/feeling process. She denies her solitude and lack of happiness, and attacks the analytic process with unconscious pleasure.

The "Analysis" as a Danger of Masturbation for Two

How are we to understand what we do when, as Jung (CW16) so vividly describes it, we share as the analytic pair in the bath that also contains the mud? Let me answer with the striking words of a non-Jungian, but which Jungians can second. Joseph (1985) writes:

> *[Transference] must include everything that the patient brings into the relationship. ... Much of our understanding of the transference comes through our understanding of how our patients act on us to feel things for many varied reasons; how they try to draw us into their defensive systems; how they unconsciously act out with us ... trying to get us to act out with them; how they convey aspects of their inner world built up from infancy – elaborated in childhood and adulthood – experiences often beyond the use of words, which we can often only capture through the feelings aroused in us, through our countertransference, used in the broad sense of the word.* (p. 157)

In my interventions I had to be careful, including in my choice of words, so as not to get involved in the relationship entanglements but to take these apart – to analyze. Anything else would have meant getting involved in the archetypal level of the primitive androgyny, the primitive hermaphrodite. My task, therefore, was to make myself available as a sufficiently good object, to offer again the archetypal images of a good mother and a mother-child relationship which makes separation possible, and then to help to fulfill these.

I was helped by the few publications available on the problem of perverted transference. Steiner (1993) describes the perverse, fragmented confusion of inner objects as a result of incomplete inner separation into good and evil parts. The fragments group to form an inner-psychic path that infiltrates the good parts, attacks them from within and dominates them – a sort of inner-psychic masked mafia. In opposition to this negative process, it was important in the analytic regression to initiate a new and beneficial separation and differentiation process.

Constructions of Femininity

The questions the patient asked explicitly and implicitly in the transference, were: "Am I a woman? What sort of woman am I? How did I become a woman?" These questions, which the patient wanted answered but whose answers she feared, concerned her femininity. In the history of this woman before and during the analysis, what do I find?

The mother could not provide adequate support for the daughter's efforts to achieve separation, but used her as a selfobject in the function of a transitional object. The daughter – stuck in her development – developed images of women in her own inner-world, in her inner relationships, which largely fit the negative mother complex: possessive, devouring, providing poorly. On the other hand, there were positive elements from the paternal grandmother. They probably allowed the mental (and possibly physical) survival of the patient, as well as a rudimentary ability to recognize in me a good object. Further, the daughter identified with the projected image of the mother: the well-behaved daughter who did not rob and injure the mother by her own separation, but who remained dependent, the princess daughter who lets herself be worshipped. As an object for the daughter's immense anger, which was really aimed at the mother, the mother offered the men she had devalued, for two contradictory reasons: "Don't become dependent on men as I am on your father. Everything you need you get from me. You are everything (both sexes) for me." And a second message: "Without a man you are nothing, I am dependent on a man – your father – and don't believe that you can have more autonomy than I."

The image of the inner parental pair is sadomasochistic in structure. Good heterosexual and same-sex pair images are underdeveloped and, with much less experience, are fragile and threatened. In this inner chaos, the patient "chose" a specific construction of femininity: A primitive androgyny – primitive because it remains concrete (I have a penis) – guarantees staying with the mother and apparent independence in the world. The father remains pale, impotent, a possession of the mother, offering an opportunity for identification only in terms of achievements.

As a woman the patient sought in men the other and better mother, but repeatedly internalized the sadomasochistic pattern. Every attempt to achieve a good pair-image was successfully attacked by the inner sadomasochistic parental pair, which was masked as a good pair, both intrapsychically and in reality. A primitive androgyny had to be maintained against this in a holistic fantasy and autonomy fantasy, supposed to offer salvation, in the shut-up, perverse inner and outer relationship world, and in the transference. Such staging of a holistic fantasy, preventing separation, is described by Jung (CD). There he speaks of people's bisexuality (what I call "primitive androgyny"), refers to it as an archetypal fact, and says:

*Under certain conditions, the active presence of such archetypes ...
in the child's unconscious can give rise to "perversions." Then the
children do strange, disgusting things which nevertheless have
symbolic meaning. That is, they show behavior that at one moment
is too clean and at another too dirty. For example, a nine-year-old
boy eats toads because he has a horror of them; a four-year-old city
child picks up excrement in the fields. A country child would never
do that. ... It is the unconscious search for original unity which gives
rise to such behaviors. They should really not be called perversions
but rather faults in upbringing which are later mostly compensated
for. That original, primitive image therefore leads not only to the
strangest painful, disgusting satisfactions, but also acts as a defense,
for example, in people who pick their noses or have oral "coitus"
with a fountain-pen. Such activities are needed as a protection; in
effect people form a circle with themselves. In fertilizing themselves
they demonstrate that they are completely self-sufficient, the completely circular original being. ... In that state nothing more can
touch them.* (pp. 47-48)

Here we find important components of modern psychoanalytic
thought on perversion and perversity, and of modern Jungian
thought (e.g., from Fordham), valid for both sexes but which take on
a particular complexity for women.

On the one hand, the female persona of these patients shows the
partially unconscious primitive androgyny fantasy through clothes,
hairstyles and ideology formations. On the other hand, it consists of
a facade, a secondary, constructed femininity. Frau L. seemed to me
like a puppet on a string. Very late in their analyses, these patients
(who had all been sexually attacked by their mother or nanny)
reported extensively, in a shy but triumphant manner, how they had
quite consciously decorated themselves as women with elements of
fashion and items from the arsenal of socially recognized female
gestures and movements. This "Womanliness as a Masquerade,"
described by Rivière (1929), serves in turn self-deception, self-
protection, but also brings about the expression of the unconscious
anger of these women by its triumphant deceptive character. The
apparent craziness of the masquerade is in its message: I am only
feminine, but in fact I am everything.

It is craziness, in the sense of an inherent fragmentation and
contradiction that cannot be resolved in this crazy cosmos, which
inspires the search for an image capable of encompassing the whole
of this tension, both as a way of bringing matters to a head and as a
means of defense against anxiety. It was in the course of this search

that I thought of Lilith. Lilith is also threefold – the terrible, child-devouring, disappointed mother, the vulnerable baby, and the glittering and exciting seductress – accompanied in the myths by unimportant, castrated, smaller male demons, which can be thought of as triumphal compensation after the lost struggle with Adam, and as justification for the anxiety about challenging Adam at all: Why should Lilith want to fight with a man who is already devalued? (See Hurwitz, 1980).

Commenting on this type of construction of femininity – a woman creates herself anew – Rivière (1929) writes: "The reader may now ask how I would define femininity and where to draw the line between genuine femininity and the 'masquerade.' I do not pretend that there is a difference; may it be natural or secondary, in fact it is the same" [my translation]. If this is true, it is unsettling.

Frau L. and the other patients are therefore perhaps doing something against a specific background of conflict and with specific psychic functions which women do in our culture when they use the typical features of "normal femininity." It is not a coincidence that the masquerade is such an important topic in Anglo-American feminist theory. It is deceptively easy for women to see the figure portrayed by Glenn Close in "Fatal Attraction" merely as the image of male fantasy. It is also a caricatured but very concrete presentation of elements of "normal femininity": She wants her lover for herself, and she wants to have his baby, whatever the cost. All her actions say: Better to kill desperately and pleasurably for this purpose than to be alone. Are all women perhaps also Lilith? Why is the androgyne modern in such an extent? Are we part of a world becoming more perverse? Perhaps the disorientation of patients like Frau L. will cause us to question our assumptions about the dichotomy of the sexes which we maintain with anxiety. There are innumerable constructions of more male or more female identity. Our constructions are still used much too often, but not as shorthand for a basic polarity; the dichotomy tends to protect us against fear of variety. The formulation of the anima/animus pair is an important step in this context. Wieseltier (1994) said:

> *To be fascinated by identity means being fascinated by the idea of wholeness. Identity offers to bring together the split-off parts of a life and to form a unity out of them, a whole life that makes sense. This may produce a psychic and an aesthetic satisfaction as well. But – is there really nothing worse than a life that does not present itself as something that makes sense as a whole?* [My translation]

These are not the words of an analyst but a journalist, writing about the defensive search for identity and the false search for entirety.

Just as we can sit as men or women in a defensively determined identity which imprisons the opposite and keeps everything disquieting at a distance, the defensive need for a false harmony and wholeness, which has always contained and already knows everything, can also come to dominate analysts and their schools. This, perhaps, could then be perverse.

Translated from German by Richard Holmes

References

Fordham, M. (1988). The androgyne: Some inconclusive reflections. *Journal of Analytical Psychology, 33,* 217-228.
Guggenbühl-Craig, A. (1976). Psychopathologia sexualis und Jungsche Psychologie. *Zeitschrift für Analytische Psychologie, 7-2,* 110-112
Hurwitz, S. (1980). *Lilith, die erste Eva.* Einsiedeln, Switzerland: Daimon.
Joseph, B. (1985). A clinical contribution to the analysis of a perversion. In B. Joseph, *Selected Papers.* New York: Routledge.
Joseph, B. (1989). Transference: The total situation. In M. Feldman & E.B. Spillius (Eds.). *Psychic Equilibrium and Psychic Change: Selected Papers.* New York: Routledge.
Kaplan, L.J. (1991). *Female Perversions: The Temptations of Emma Bovary.* New York: Doubleday.
Krämer, S. (1980). Object-coercive doubting: A pathological defensive response to maternal incest. *Journal of American Psychoanalytic Association, 31,* 325-351.
Malcolm, R.R. (1988). The mirror: A perverse sexual phantasy in a woman seen as a defence against a psychotic breakdown. In E.B. Spillius (Ed.), *Melanie Klein Today.* London/New York: Routledge, in association with the Institute of Psycho-Analysis.
Morgenthaler, F. (1981). *Homosexuality – Heterosexuality – Perversion.* Hillsdale, NJ: Analytic Press.
Rivière, J. (1929). Womanliness as a masquerade. *International Journal of Psycho-Analysis, 10,* 303-313.
Steiner, J. (1993). Perverse relationships in pathological organizations. In J. Steiner, *Psychic Retreats.* London/New York: Routledge.
Welldon, E.V. (1988). *Mother, Madonna, Whore: The Idealization and Denigration of Motherhood.* New York: Columbia University Press.
Wieseltier, L. (1994). Against identity. *The New Republic,* Nov. 28.
Wisdom, J.O. (1988). The perversions: A philosopher reflects. *Journal of Analytical Psychology, 33,* 229-248.
Wyly, J. (1989). The perversions in analysis. *Journal of Analytical Psychology, 34,* 319-337.

Bridging Analytical Psychology and Research

A Sandplay View

Harriet S. Friedman
Los Angeles, California, U.S.A.
Society of Jungian Analysts of Southern California

Over the past ten years there has been a dramatic information explosion in both the psychological and physiological fields. This explosion is a result of the powerful convergence of many different sources of information, including accessing information and conducting research in new ways. A concern of mine has been: Has our own field of analytical psychology been able to integrate these data and also benefit from new understandings? The scientific world and its findings have much to offer us, and our archetypal symbolic approach has much to offer the scientific world.

A "marriage" of these two perspectives could only benefit both fields of human endeavor. This marriage would require the Jungian archetypal tradition of bringing together the opposites. I can affirm personally that my study of sandplay research has greatly enhanced my understanding of the sandplay experience.

I hope to stimulate your imagination, to consider how the integration of the scientific world view with the practice of analytical psychology might add both to your ability to conceptualize and to the art and craft of your analytic practice. I am using sandplay slides of both children and adults to illustrate how research methods can be joined with a symbolic and archetypal perspective in order to deepen our understanding of the work.

Sandplay is a particularly good vehicle to illustrate the marriage between research and practice; its roots run deep in both these worlds – something I discovered when a colleague, and I began writing a book (Mitchell & Friedman, 1993) on the history of sandplay. To our surprise we learned that there have been almost 70 years of active research concerning sandtray work. Quickly we became convinced that this research must be made available to enhance sandplay therapists' understanding of the images that unfold in the sand. In a world which is becoming more demanding of proof as to the efficacy of psychotherapy and analysis, sandplay offers one of the few in-depth documented validations of our work. Indeed, it is here in Zurich that the sandplay archives reside, containing hundreds of cases from all over the world. These cases, accompanied by supporting research, detail the process and validate some of the major contributions of Jungian psychotherapy to the field of mental health.

There are pioneers of sandplay, people who have described the tools we use today for research and practice and who have given us a wealth of information. They include: Margaret Lowenfeld, Charlotte Buhler, Erik Erikson, Ruth Bowyer, Hedda Bolgar, Liselotte Fischer, L.N.J. Kamp, Kay Bradway, Estelle Weinrib, Ruth Amman, Joel Ryce-Menuhin, Kaspar Kiepenheuer, Hayao Kawai, Yushiro Yamanaka, and finally our own Jungian pioneer, Dora Kalff. Several researchers have created their own developmental norms for the sandtray. Their academic research is valuable to me as a frame of reference, just as Kalff's symbolic approach is valuable.

Now, to show how scientific understanding can deepen knowledge of the sandplay creations of children and adults, let us turn to some photos. My photos follow the categories developed by Bowyer, researcher and colleague of Lowenfeld's. Bowyer, who is still living in Scotland, made major contributions to the literature on sandtray. She served on the academic staff of the University of Bristol, and later in the Psychology Department at the University of Glasgow. I find her work to be unusually clear and straightforward. She studied the sandtrays of 50 children and 26 adults, ages two to fifty, and established developmental norms. Sandtrays mainly from my own practice illustrate her categories.

As you observe the photos, following the various stages of development that weave in and out of the sandtrays, please remember that we are witnessing archetypal development: either age-appropriate development or development disrupted by wounding at a crucial stage. As with all major symbolic images that erupt from the psyche, some of them shine through with a multitude of meanings. As you look at these photos, I suggest that you turn one eye inward and pay close attention to which scenes, which motifs in the sandplays resonate with you personally, as you may do when listening to a dream. For me, observing the places that touch me personally in a sandplay can become a particularly rich source of information from which to grow and can provide insight that the intellect cannot. As Jung wrote in 1927, "Often the hands know how to solve a riddle with which the intellect has wrestled in vain" (CW8, par. 180).

Bowyer's First Category: The Use of Space

The first category Bowyer created was the area of the tray used. Bowyer found that, with increasing age, a greater and greater area of the tray is used. Older children use more of the tray and show a firmer sense of boundaries.

These first three trays in the photos were created by very young children. They illustrate what is typical of two-, three-, and four-year-old children as they work in a sandtray environment. Then we can contrast these young children's trays with those of older children and adults, to see the progression as well as the similarity in development, and see the child in the adult. Bowyer's research shows that very young children typically use only a small section of the tray; the rest of the tray is ignored and sand may be spilled over the sides. The research also tells us that issues of boundaries and outer reality are disregarded; often heaps of toys are flung into the tray. First, let us look at how two very young children use space in the tray.

The first tray (Fig. 1) was done by a two-and-a-half year old who was brought unannounced into a session with her mother, who was in treatment with me. The child went immediately over to the tray, picked up a watering can close to the tray, and watered only a small portion of it. An older child with more eye-hand coordination would probably have moistened more of the tray and would have done so with more focus. This particular child then tipped over the watering can and left it there, half in and half out of the tray, indicating a lack of boundaries. What we see here is typical and normal for this very young age group.

A tray (not shown) – done by a four-year old – contained cars, trucks, and people heaped together in the center. There was noticeably more chaos and complexity, and numerous objects used in a freely disorganized fashion. Yet all the objects remained inside the tray, boundaries recognized, and more of the tray used than in the previous one, done by a younger child. This tray had a chaotic quality to it, often seen in trays of four-year-olds.

Bowyer's research tells us that, after the age of five, normal children begin to use the space out to all four sides of the tray. A tray

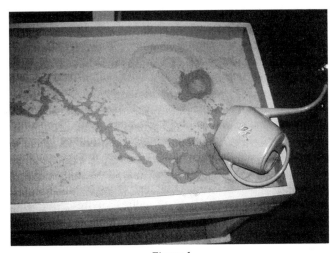

Figure 1

Figure 2

(Fig. 2), done by a healthy nine-year-old boy, illustrates how an older child uses the space. Notice how the wedding scene uses much more of the tray than the two previous trays.

A big developmental jump was evident in the sandtray (not shown) of a 40-year-old man in an enraged and regressed state. This man had been accused at work of acting inappropriately toward a customer. He felt misunderstood and wrongly accused. This situation evoked childhood feelings and memories of having been misunderstood and wounded, growing up in a chaotic, cult-like religious environment. His family moved when he was around the age of five. He used space similarly to the expressions of a young child's chaotic tray. His sandtray illustrated the rage and chaos he was feeling. To me, this man's tray suggested that of a young child and was a powerful communication of the overwhelming feelings he had experienced as a child under age five. These feelings evidently were alive for him again.

Another tray (not shown), in which only a small portion of the tray was used, was that of a 42-year-old woman. The woman, the oldest of seven children and married to a musician, expressed the despair and lack of identity she was feeling in her life; she conveyed her feelings in a very youthful manner. As the oldest child in her family of origin she had learned to devote herself to helping and serving others. Her tray, depicting only a piano, her husband's instrument, communicated to me the barren state in which living for and serving others had ultimately left her.

A tray (not shown) of a 37-year-old woman illustrates how the entire space is used when there has been a significant healing experience. The feeling of centeredness, liveliness, connection to her own spirituality, and the strong statement of increased consciousness was symbolized by lit candles and feathers, clearly communicating her strong sense of self.

Bowyer's Second Category: The Expression of Aggression

Bowyer's second category deals with the question of how the expression of aggression changes as normal development unfolds. She found that two-to three-year-olds often poke, fling, and bury miniatures. She found that four- to six-year-olds use dramatic activity in moving the toys around in the tray, and often make noises or speak for the miniatures they are using.

A creation (not shown), depicting two monsters, eating up a mother and father, was done by a five-year-old boy while he made growling noises and moved the figures about. Without being aware of these developmental norms, one might conclude that this is a very disturbed child, instead of realizing his behavior is quite typical and appropriate for his age.

A seven-year-old boy, whose parents had divorced when he was two, used the miniatures and the sand (Fig. 3) to create two clearly delineated camps that conveyed his anger as well as his parent's

Figure 3

Figure 4

divisiveness. There are two armies shooting at each other while, in the middle of the tray, he goes back and forth in a canoe between the two camps. As he was creating this tray and moving the canoe back and forth while making shooting sounds, he said, "This is how it feels to come home to my mom's house after I've been with my dad all weekend long. The fighting just never stops."

A tray (not shown), demonstrating an immature level of development was done by a 40-year-old unmarried woman who had come to treatment in great distress after impulsively having had an abortion. She had thrown away what she now believed was her last chance to have her own baby. She told me that her mother had talked her into the abortion. She was now overwrought, full of remorse, suffering feelings of loss and that she had been tricked by her mother once again. As she made the tray, she repeatedly thrust a snake forward, as if it were biting at a mask, and spoke about how she had always been forced to act in ways her mother dictated. I wondered if the snake depicted her mother's aggression or her own anger. She felt consumed with rage at her mother. The tray depicts quite a young stage of aggression and supports my view that earlier wounding can be seen in a tray.

From 12 years of age through adulthood, the moving of objects around in the tray appears to subside as clients become more aware of their aggressive feelings. They appear content to depict these feelings in the tray without needing to move figures around, interact with them, and make sounds for them.

A tray (Fig. 4), reflecting a more mature level of development, was made by a 27-year-old woman. Aware of what she was depicting, she commented that one side of her tray showed an idyllic scene; the other, a plane crash. She used verbal comments rather than moving the objects around. She did not understand the meaning of the tray, but she said it was a satisfying experience to her. These two mounds also looked like breasts to me. Some time after this tray was made, she was diagnosed with cancer in the right breast.

Bowyer's Third Category: Control Issues

As we have seen in trays from earlier developmental periods, little or no control was shown by two- to three-year-olds; their trays were typically chaotic, undifferentiated, and disorganized. Control appears to expand from five to ten years of age, as evidenced by an increased use of fencing. Ten years old is the peak age for using fences and other literal structures of control. After the age of 11 there is less use of literal controls, such as fences and signs, and more use of symbolic controls. After 11, control of the scene in the tray is depicted more often by topological features such as mountains and streams.

An 11-year-old girl's tray (Fig. 5) demonstrated how fences are often used around age 10, the peak age for fences. A high level of sexual energies, as symbolized by horses, is safely differentiated

Figure 5

Figure 6

from the domestic, more feminine energies, all appropriate at this prepubescent age.

The tray (Fig. 6) of a 29-year-old man reflected his feeling of being betrayed in a love affair. The woman with whom he had planned a life had left him for another man. When he was 11 his mother had died suddenly. The upper area of devastation, portraying his wounding, is literally fenced off, much as a ten-year-old would do, to protect the new growth. I was pleased to see that growth was possible even in his current depressed state, and hopeful that future analytic work would help him to manifest these potentials for a new life.

Adults use more themes of symbolic control and fewer literal controls. A 47-year-old woman was feeling abandoned because her last child had just left for college. The woman's tray (Fig. 7) poignantly displays a theme of symbolic control. As a child her father had fought in World War II. He had left home when her mother was pregnant with her and had not returned until she was five. The parents divorced two years after he returned. This woman had never recovered from her early and prolonged yearning to be part of an intact family. Now, decades later, with her last child departing, these feelings – depicted by the hand attempting to hold together her diminishing family – were becoming overwhelming.

Bowyer's Fourth Category: The Use of Sand

For me the information regarding the use of sand has been especially helpful. For years I have been fascinated and intrigued by the many different ways that both children and adults use the sand. Bowyer noted that young children use sand for pouring, pushing, and burying. After age seven, the constructive use of sand for creating roads, waterways, buildings, and paths appears to depend on individual personality traits more than on age differences. Bow-

Figure 7

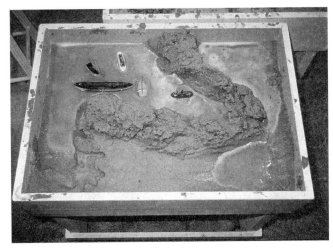

Figure 8

Figure 9

yer found that the constructive use of sand indicates an ability to use inner resources creatively, in an attempt to enlarge or restructure the tray and, symbolically, one's own world. She also found that the constructive use of sand suggests average or above-average intelligence.

A tray (Fig. 8) done by a nine-year-old boy whose mother had died when he was three, was accompanied by a story about boats that were trying again and again to get to the safe harbor. His use of sand to construct a safe harbor showed a high level of creativity and healing potential.

An 11-year-old's structure (Fig. 9) is adorned with shells, rocks, and the American flag. He had been accepted into a Little League baseball team, at long last. What an effort this tray was for him and what pleasure he took in viewing it when it was finished! In this achievement the Self has certainly been constellated.

A tray (Fig. 10) done by a 39-year-old woman, a university administrator who had just had a professional paper accepted into a prestigious journal. To her, it felt like a culmination of her inner and outer work. The similarity of these trays is striking, with both trays suggesting that the Self has been touched in a profound and deep way.

The use of sand in the next tray (not shown) was particularly touching to me. This 30-year-old woman had been told by her gynecologist that she might never become pregnant due to a physical deformity. Her creative use of the sand, as well as her depiction of her grief, suggests that she is attempting to take in this fate.

Six months later she did a tray (Fig. 11) with several egg-shaped stones placed in a uterus-like enclosure. When I saw it, I was silently hopeful that she had conceived. Indeed, two weeks later she joyfully shared with me that she was pregnant. These next two trays were made during her pregnancy. Another one (not shown) was done three months into the pregnancy: a primitive goddess figure on a swollen pregnant belly. A third tray (not shown) was made six weeks before the birth. The goddess figure now stands upright, overlooking the scene while the human infant stands between the two breast-like mounds.

Bowyer's Fifth Category: The Contents of the Tray

Bowyer's last category is about the content of the tray. She found that with increasing age, realism increases, miniatures are more integrated, and a time perspective is often included. Trays of children of the same age show great similarities under eight years of age; after that individual differences begin to emerge.

The content and story told in a sandtray (not shown) done by a six-year-old, shows both realism and fantasy, although not as clearly as those done by older children. Her older sister had died when this girl was 18 months old. She placed a nest on top of a tree and then took one of the eggs and dropped it on the sand, saying, "The

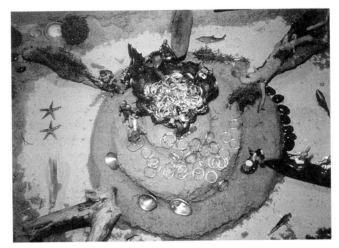

Figure 10

Figure 11

mommy bird is looking for her egg. She can't take care of her other eggs because she just keeps looking for her lost egg."

A realistic tray (not shown) by a 12-year-old boy depicts a baseball team playing on a baseball diamond – a mandala – with cavemen looking on. The boy said, "The cavemen stand on the side as the game is coming to a close. They remember how these guys never even used to be able to throw a ball." This tray was done just as his therapy was terminating. It was true that he had been

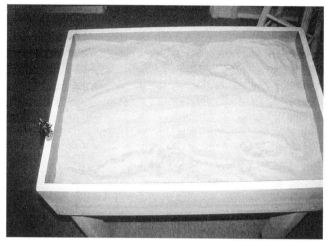

Figure 12

Figure 13

physically immature and frightened of entering into the world as well as the game of life. Here he is a true participant in life, all played out on a diamond, a unifying symbol of the highest level of the Self.

A 45-year-old business man was highly skilled and hard-driving. At age two, he had lost his father. His tray (Fig. 12) was like that of a two-year-old who is reluctant to use space. In making it he manipulated the sand for a long time and then got up and chose one miniature – a death figure (Fig. 13). As I watched him do this, I remembered that he had told me that he had a lifelong fear of dying suddenly of a heart attack, like his father.

The same man, six months later, made a tray (Fig. 14) that is still quite sparse, much like that of a younger child, but he chose some fairly robust figures. They enliven the scene, although one of them is a wounded man who has lost an arm. When I saw a milkmaid bringing milk (Fig. 15), I felt hopeful that this might be the therapeutic milk to heal his wounds.

We all realize that words do not allow the fullest and deepest expression of meaning. Words are the language of consciousness; the unconscious speaks primarily in images. As a non-verbal technique, sandplay can provide cross-cultural communications of the soul. Like dreams, the images that emerge in the sand are snapshots of the unconscious for us to behold and thus to reach a deeper understanding.

Figure 14

Figure 14

Today, research continues to play an important role in the evolution of sandplay as a therapeutic medium. Jungian therapists' enthusiasm for the use of sandplay in clinical practice is shared by the larger therapeutic collective. It has become evident to many of us worldwide that, because sandplay is visual and experiential rather than verbal, it offers us an opportunity to witness the universality of personal experience through images only – no ideas, no concepts, no cognitions.

As I was surveying sandplay research for my book, I began to wonder what had happened to the emphasis on research that was well established by Jung in his discoveries early in this century. He was infinitely curious about other sciences and sought to cross-fertilize his own theories and speculations with knowledge from them. He prided himself on being an empirical scientist, as evidenced by his research and development of the Word Association Test. The appropriation of Jung's theory of typology into the Myers-Briggs Type Indicator has made an enormous impact, especially in the area of career counseling.

Unfortunately, the tradition of scientific empiricism has not been broadly sustained in analytical psychology. While there has been some movement toward the scientific communities, I am urging that we build on what some of our community has already begun. Jung was willing to use statistical and experimental methods to investigate his intuitive hunches. It is my belief that, were Jung alive today, he would be open to findings regarding psychotherapy and other scientific research and be willing to use such methods in studying, improving, and deepening his understanding of the manifestations of the unconscious.

It is crucial for us who practice analytical psychology to be receptive to scientific knowledge that can inform and enrich our work. A wealth of research is currently going on in our field: on dreams and dream activity, brain functioning, the effect of ultradian and circadian rhythms, short- versus long-term therapy, the effects of imagery and visualization on the auto-immune system – to mention a few. Recent discoveries in brain research confirm that anatomical and biochemical changes occur in the brain when psychological development takes place. These are exciting findings that indicate a broad scientific basis for the work we do.

Most of us have taken, historically, an intuitive, archetypal, symbolic way of looking at sandtrays because this way has been familiar to us. We are finding, however, that this view is complemented by a cognitive, linear, and structured approach to understanding how age and trauma influence the making of sand worlds. Might not our goal as Jungians be an integration of the two? Facilitating this right- and left-brain integration is as enriching as putting words to music – or music to words.

Becoming familiar with developmental research has helped me better to understand emerging aspects of the Self in the sandtrays of children and adults. It has helped me identify adults who experienced a cataclysmic event at an early age, sometimes even alerting me to the approximate age at which this event occurred. These trays of adults who have experienced early trauma are often surprisingly similar to young children's trays. I hope you see evidence in the trays depicted.

My intuitive view that sandplay can identify traumatic events is supported by a 1937 study by Erik Erikson. Erikson was interested in examining character development. He asked Harvard students to create dramatic scenes using miniatures. One of the most striking findings to come out of that study was that, even though the students were all English majors, they did not build scenes representing themes from literature or theater. Instead, very personal and intimate scenes emerged that could only be connected to traumatic events these students had experienced in childhood. Current research continues to expand our knowledge base in this as well as other areas.

One important open question to consider is whether we continue to observe the psyche in the same way we always have, or is it appropriate now to integrate the thoughtful application of scientific research to inform our work? Von Franz (1992) states that for psychology to reach over to other fields of science should not present any fundamental contradictions and that indeed psychology should keep pace with the findings of the other sciences.

Edinger (1984) addresses the issue of these two poles when he writes: "It is already widely recognized that the pursuit of scientific knowledge as the highest goal of human endeavor is inadequate to the needs of the whole man; a return to the intellectually naive standpoint of concrete religious faith is equally inappropriate to the modern mind. A genuinely new goal and purpose for human existence is required" (p. 258). Echoing Jung, Edinger proposes how this conflict could be moved forward: "Out of a conflict of mutually exclusive duties can emerge the third, transcendent condition, which is a new quantum of consciousness" (p. 21). Perhaps all of us today can begin to sow the seeds of reconciliation between these opposites, to bring about the possibility of this new consciousness.

I am surprised to find myself in this position, to be seized by scientific ideas. I have had a very classical Jungian training and, for many years, have felt comfortable in a symbolically-oriented framework. Indeed, I was drawn into sandplay work by being intrigued by the symbolic and archetypal dimension of the trays. Then, as my understanding of the trays evolved, I began to integrate other ways of knowing that included a more logos-oriented approach.

Earlier in this paper I mentioned the challenge of the integration of the rational-scientific and the symbolic-intuitive approaches. When I came upon the figure of the milkmaid, it seemed to symbolize this goal beautifully. It is not always an easy task to carry the two sides, especially for those of us who have been entranced for so long in the symbolic way. It has been a challenge for me to explore the coming together of the left- and right-brain approaches to sandplay. As we Jungians move into the twenty-first century we must meet the challenge of continuing to follow our intuitive beliefs as well as explore the application of an empirical model. In meeting this challenge, as we move into the Aquarian age so beautifully symbolized by this water carrier, we help both sandplay and analytical psychology to move into a new millennium. In so doing, may our attitude be as balanced as is the milkmaid's.

References

Edinger, E. (1984). *The Creation of Consciousness: Jung's Myth for Modern Man.* Toronto: Inner City Books.

Mitchell, R. & Friedman, H. (1993). *Sandplay, Past, Present, and Future.* London: Routledge.

von Franz, M-L. (1992). *Meaning and Order: Psyche and Matter.* Boston/London: Shambhala.

Demons in the City

Kaj Noschis
Lausanne, Switzerland
Swiss Society for Analytical Psychology

In discussing our psychological relationship with cities, I shall suggest a frame for understanding what cities can do for our souls: seeing value in our urban life in contrast to the current trend of return to nature, such as hiking. A paradox of our Zeitgeist can be phrased in the following terms: We have come to believe that human beings have created inhuman cities without soul. We must go into nature to make contact with soul. While there may be good reasons for understanding this opposition of city and nature, I maintain that where people are living together and where there is urban activity, there is soul. Western Christian heritage makes us doubt about this, but dismissing urban life may make us ignore important soul-making opportunities. (See Hillman, 1975.)

The Western Heritage

Cities in the Western cultural tradition are influenced by Greek, Roman and Christian thought and behavior. Since ancient Greece there has been in Europe a tradition of urban planning. We can describe planning as a rational effort at ordering buildings and the spaces between buildings, both having hoped-for influence on behavior. When we plan cities we are already moving away from spontaneity and irrationality. Planning and building cities is a conscious exercise.

However, since cities are places where human beings live, unconscious aspects also will demand recognition and expression. This has happened in cities through the centuries. How? We as urban dwellers are confronted with demons in the city – demons in the Greek meaning of the word: good and bad spiritual beings. But before doing that we need to look at representations of cities historically.

The Earthly and Heavenly City

In fifth century (BC) Greece, Hyppodamus – recognized as the first urban planner in Europe – had a grid-plan for the town of Miletus. For Aristotle, who called Hyppodamus the inventor of the *ariste politeia* (perfect city), the plan of Miletus was the spatial translation of harmony into city life. Indeed, the relation of the spatial and social characteristics of urban life has fascinated humankind throughout history. A spatial model is intended to create conditions for a good life in a city. City models have not always meant urban planning but they all have intended to improve conditions of urban living.

Within the Christian heritage the most influential model – although it is not spatial – is The City of God, described by St. Augustine between 412 and 426 A.D. Augustine wrote just after the barbarian invasion of Rome by Alaric in 410. His explicit aim was to defend the recently established Christian religion against criticism expressed in Rome. Influential Romans thought that the sacking of their city was due, perhaps, to the abandonment of their previously revered pagan gods. St. Augustine (1952) built his work on the opposition between the City on Earth and the City of God. "Because some live according to the flesh and others according to the spirit, there have arisen two diverse and conflicting cities, [and] we might equally well [say] because some live according to man, others according to God" (p. 379).

By opposing the Earthly City to the Heavenly City, St. Augustine contributed to a major split in the Christian attitude toward cities. The representation of the City of God increasingly affirmed itself as an ever more perfect city and moved further and further away from human reality. Human beings lost touch with the City of God as a vital principle and found themselves confined to "living according to the flesh."

Augustine said that faith and piety are the hope for a City on Earth which would be a religious and social project of renewal among people. There have been periods when faith and piety have had an eminent place; in cities they have been the motors for some of the most impressive and lasting achievements in Christian architecture and planning. I refer here mainly to cathedrals and monasteries. These constructions testify to the attempts at creating Cities of God on Earth. From the sixteenth to the eighteenth centuries, with the Christianization of the New World, we again have testimonies on how Jesuits in Latin America, for instance, constructed entirely new settlements with urban plans that explicitly aimed at creating Cities of God on earth. (Ironically, they were all destroyed, eventually, in wars against other Jesuits' imposing slavery in these same regions).

However, the reality of most urban life through the centuries is in increasing contrast with this model. Events as experienced by urban dwellers correspond to the City on Earth described by Augustine and are even closer to the pagan Rome so despised by him. New forms of relationship were possible, but life in growing human settlements became increasingly promiscuous. Thus cities generated a sense of freedom, of more choice than peasant life. However, the risk is that one feels "lost in the flesh."

Yet this risk is a possible reason for the impact of clear and rigorous views such as those of St. Augustine. For instance, he vigorously attacked the polytheism practiced in Rome, affirming that, with many gods behaving themselves in the most licentious manner, it was almost necessary that Romans would fall into the same behavior. His is a strong argument for a change in favor of the Christian God and adopting the City of God as a model.

The adoption of the Christian God did not help in changing behavior and feelings, even if people established the two Cities in their imagination. Consequently, the two started growing apart from each other. The centuries that followed St. Augustine have not shown much change in citizens' behavior.

In the later Middle Ages there was a particularly strong emphasis on humans as sinners. The human condition is miserable because of the original sin; the City of God becomes then unattainable. We can find testimony to this in many northern European paintings from the fourteenth and fifteenth centuries. Here the holy figures – mainly the announcement to Mary or the holy family – were painted outside the city walls; God is not in contact with life inside those walls. Or, when heavenly Jerusalem is painted, it is without people.

A counter-example is the Italian Renaissance, seemingly a period when the City of God was closer and perhaps attainable. Apart from the splendid buildings erected during this period, there were paintings with the holy family inside urban environments. Yet, in general I find that, in the Christian urban world, the distance between the City of God and the City on Earth has increased through the centuries.

The Tower of Babel

St. Augustine referred to many sources from the Bible, but the following centuries mainly reverted to two such sources. One is the reference to John's gospel with its violent images of the earthly Babylon – also named the Great Prostitute – as opposed to heavenly Jerusalem glittering in material and spiritual splendor with a few angelic creatures as sole inhabitants. The motive of human arrogance and defiance of God remained a constant theme for centuries, often using images from the Tower of Babel:

> *And the Lord came down to see the city and the tower, which the sons of men had built. And the Lord said: "Behold, they are one people, and they have all one language; and this is only the beginning of what they will do, and nothing that they propose to do will now be impossible for them."* (Genesis, 11:5-6, Revised Standard Version)

Having thought in this manner, God punishes people by dispersing them and having them speak different languages. Exegesis has seen the construction of the Tower of Babel as mostly an image of human arrogance and as a defiance of God. In forgetting God, humans are living "according to the flesh." The Tower has become an image of the earthly city of Babylon as a bad place. Thus, the opposition is reinforced, between the City on Earth and the City of God.

If we keep strictly to the biblical text, God becomes afraid of humans building cities. The building of Babel shows that nothing is impossible for humans. God intervenes, introducing the opposition between human construction and construction by God. The opposition is not formulated as a human view.

One of the most remarkable paintings on the subject is the painting of the Tower of Babel in 1563 by Breughel, now in the Kunsthistorische Museum in Vienna. It is a most impressive painting, with hundreds of humans working like ants, systematically, with energy and continuity. It is an astounding document on human energy and dedication to a grandiose collective project. It is easy to understand – if I may say so – that God would be impressed by such an effort. It is most certainly a monument to the glory of humanity, but is it not perhaps also an attempt to realize the City of God on earth? I believe that Breughel's answer is yes. His main view – and a reason for his popularity – is to look at life as an effort to work and live together. If there is a place for God, it must be in the everyday life of people in cities; the City of God is too far away. What we care about is Babel. We do care about what we construct. Babel may mean that we don't care anymore about God, but it may mean that God is in everyday life. Thus, we can say that the Tower of Babel is a monument to God.

Let us remember, also, other paintings by Breughel involving the holy family or Jesus. The holy figures are seen as ordinary people, in the middle of a crowd that doesn't care. There is constantly this double perspective: No one cares about God, and the divine presence is just ordinary people. My view is that Breughel responds to the tremendous distance that had become apparent between the City on Earth and the City of God. It is in ordinary life that spirituality must be sought – not somewhere far away. Breughel's Tower of Babel painting reminds us of the construction of cathedrals some centuries earlier when at least the people involved in that activity were building the City of God on earth.

Breughel's painting shows the Tower of Babel before God intervenes. God's intervention is incomprehensible for humans and suggests an egotistical God cut off from human life. That is perhaps what Breughel points at: What people do in cities is an expression of the City of God, while what God does is incomprehensible. In the sixteenth century the opposition between the City on Earth and the City of God had become so strong that the only way out, perhaps, was to reintroduce God in the city. Otherwise human life would have been completely reduced to suffering because it is in opposition to God. In Breughel's time, such views may be related, more generally, to the emergence of Protestantism.

The City and Nature

Despite the advent of Protestantism and Breughel's popularity even during his own time, the centuries to follow did not "mix" or "fuse" these two cities. Breughel was forgotten and rediscovered only in the nineteenth century. The Christian church, in all its varieties, kept the image of the City of God far away from human reach. The Enlightenment tried to solve the difficulty by liberating humanity from faith. But the image of Babylon as the City on Earth remained. If planning pursued the City of God, life has handed the city over to Babylon. During the industrialization of the nineteenth century, Babylon again became very fashionable as an image and as a model. In this same period Romanticism discovered nature as a remedy. Humans can escape Babylon and find the soul by finding nature. We have inherited this view and live with it today. An empty city could qualify for the City of God, but not an inhabited city. Even today, in architectural magazines, it is rare that people are represented. The model is one of pure spirit, without flesh – the model of St. Augustine. A recent example of this model is the rationalist movement with its square lines and boxes as buildings. These forms are expressions of reason only, similar to the plans of the Jesuits in South America. They ignore the complexity of human beings and their feelings – as if it would be possible to live only rationally; to do away with feelings, fantasies and shadows. Thus, rationalism can be seen as the most recent – perhaps unwitting – attempt to impose the Augustinian City of God.

Yet we live in inhabited cities and are confronted with life according to the flesh every day. The Earthly City has its attractions for us. But as inheritors of the Christian tradition we are not very comfortable with this attraction. To look for soul we continue to look for "purity" and, as we cannot do this in the city, we do it in the back-to-nature mode, following Romanticism.

The Garden of Eden is the image for an original state of purity in humankind, closely associated with nature: Adam and Eve live with animals and abundant fruit trees surround them. The Garden was on earth and bodies did not know sin. After being chased from the Garden, humans multiplied and started building settlements, moving from a state of nature to a state of culture. Babylon appeared. Cities became places where humans grow away from God. Paradise – the Garden of Eden – becomes the image of a lost natural state that might be attained after life, in spirit, and yet might be in contact with nature – a good reason for going "back to nature." In contrast to Babylon is the image of Heavenly Jerusalem, unattainable by humanity on earth and hardly attainable in heaven. In any case, Heavenly Jerusalem is cut off from Earthly Babylon.

Thus, psychologically, Western culture perpetuates a difficult relationship between humans and the city. Breughel might have turned it around: God's relation to the humanity that builds cities is incomprehensible. With this dichotomy in mind we can now take a closer look at city life.

Emotions and City Life

The emotional content of urban life is made up primarily of encounters and events in our daily life. Many such events can touch us deeply: an eye contact with someone we don't know, a dramatic scene, unexpectedly meeting someone we do know. We also seek intense emotional experiences in the city: adventure, wished encounters, the excitement of being in some particular place, of buying something, of doing something. We feel excitement, joy, sympathy, enthusiasm, but also fear, hate, disgust. (See Noschis, 1984.) Throughout history cities have exercised a fascination on the imagination of human beings and continue to do so. Novels, poetry, paintings and movies depict our relation to cities. And they do it with soul. Urban emotions are associated mainly with people and places, with feeling communion or the need to create distance. Feeling part of something and feeling isolated. Babylon fascinates and scares us with its daily diet of trouble, desire, altruism, day-dreaming; but also brutal sex, crime, drugs of all sorts. But could this not be the context where we can look also for soul? I find it an excellent place to meet figures such as shadow, anima, animus – directly or indirectly.

St. Augustine saw urban life as a perpetual opposition between two representations: The City of God – mystic home of the predes-tined souls – and the City on Earth, whose citizens are consciously or unconsciously allied against God. This opposition is expected to continue to the end of time. So far Augustine seems to have been right in his prediction. Throughout Christian history we have been caught in this fight, and mostly we feel that we have lost it to Babylon on Earth.

A different perspective is possible. In a way it is a pre-Augustin-ian perspective, polytheism. In another way it is a post-Augustinian perspective, the purely spiritual nature of the divine. The description of "depraved" which Augustine applied to the Romans does not need to be related to polytheism versus monotheism, but to how we relate to Gods or God in the city.

We have fallen into a trap by wanting to measure the distance that separates city life as it is from an ideal model of life. In that sense we can only remain depraved. What we need is a frame for understanding and giving meaning to activities that are part of city-life – shopping, going to restaurants, encounters or as life conditions such as being candy-vendors, nightclub dancers or doorkeepers. My point here is to recognize the possible spiritual dimension of such activities; in doing them we relate to transcendent figures; this cannot be thought or done as long as we are caught in the opposition between Heavenly Jerusalem and Babylon on Earth.

Demons in Greece and Rome

In ancient Greece and Rome the relationship with the main Gods (capitalized here to indicate their importance) was based on practical requests: rain, bread, health, advice and peace. Gods needed offerings; they were done ritually by the community. Gods were pleased or were not pleased with the offerings and the community would be awarded its request or continue to suffer. These material offerings and rituals were also spiritual: talking to transcendent figures. Although in Greece and Rome Gods had specific domains, concerns and powers, these were not so absolutely defined at the time. Depending on the place and circumstances where cults were practiced, one Olympian God could be invoked for everything, having a monotheistic status. Thus, distance between humans and God could be a reality both in Greece and Rome. In addition there were other divine beings, closer to humanity and closer to places. They probably even precede historically the Gods shared by Greece and Rome. Demons were such intermediary figures in Greece. Daimon etymologically is part division (daiomai), destiny: something separated from us, but having to do with us. The term suffered a complete transformation of meaning into something negative for Christianity while, in Greece, Demons were generally positive but sometimes negative beings.

Demons were beings of a higher order than humankind; they were never humans and did not have human bodily nature. They would manifest themselves through events that happened to a person, but also in that person's inner life – as we remember from Socrates. Thus the difference between Demons and Gods is more a question of degree than of essence. Demons were more personal and accessible to humans. We might see them also as having a connection with fetishism – as spirits embodied in or attached to or conveying influence through certain material objects. Historically they probably originated in the country – attached to natural objects and animals – before moving to the city.

Also in Rome there was, even before Greek influence, a recognized presence of Genius for men and Juno for women. Genius and Juno were invisible personalities, separable from – yet closely attached to – the life of visible human beings. An independent power with whom to relate, for instance, "*indulgere genio*" (to do one's Genius a pleasure) or "*defraudare genium*" (to cheat the Genius of an enjoyment). It was believed that Genius came into existence with the birth of the person it pertained to; it could even be considered to exercise control over the individual. Things and places would have their own Genius, for instance *genius loci*. Close to genius as spiritual beings were the Lares, the household spirits. There was first the *Lar familiaris*, then *Lares compitum* (of the neighborhood) and other Lares connected with localities. Thus, we understand that places and objects also would connect to spirit and activities. All workers, for instance, would have a Genius or Demon above them. Activities, sacrifices and offerings were done for Demons. But material offerings had a spiritual dimension: They were a way to make contact with these transcendent figures and, let us venture, to develop an interior dialogue.

St. Augustine (1952) offers a vivid description of demons according to Apuleius of Madaurus (125-180 AD), follower of Plato and author of "Socrates' God" (and of "The Golden Ass").

Apuleius when speaking concerning the manner of demons, said that they are agitated with the same perturbations of mind as men, that they are provoked by injuries, propitiated by services and by gifts, rejoice in honours, are delighted with a variety of sacred rites, and are annoyed if any of them be neglected. ... Demons are of an animal nature, passionate [I suggest here "passionate" instead of "passive in soul"], rational in mind, aerial in body, eternal in time. (p. 275)

If we today would view much of our urban behavior as commerce with demons, we would qualify most of our activities as spiritual – as soul-making. Working – selling and serving – for money but also for our demons or the place's demons; shopping for ourselves but also for our demons; experiencing emotionally because of places and people, but also because of our demons. In adopting such a view we could recognize that in these daily events there is much more at stake than just doing what we have to do or want to do. With a recourse to demons we could bring life to our relation to cities, and we would have at our disposal a psychologically relevant description of human inner life and struggle. Instead of being caught in moral views that despise city life and activities, we would be taking care of ourselves and could find soul.

Augustine is very critical of these pre-Christian beings and explicitly states that demons are the messengers of the devil. They have nothing to do with spiritual life and must be avoided. Yet St. Augustine (1952) talks also about spiritual creatures, intermediaries between God and human beings: angels. They are very important because they are the inhabitants of the City of God and they show us the way to reach it. The City of God

> *is celebrated by the holy angels, who invite us to their society, and desire us to become fellow-citizens with them in this city; for they do not wish us to worship them as our gods, but to join them in worshipping their God and ours; nor to sacrifice to them, but, together with them, to become a sacrifice to God.* (p. 314)

Compared to demons, angels are entirely good and pure; they don't want offerings but prayers. Thus, the difference is not the absence of demons – in the original Greek sense – but that there should be no sacrifice directly to demons. Later, this would become a dogma for the Church: People sacrificing to demons would be condemned, whereas the only accepted form of relation to demons would be the one proposed by St. Augustine where we ourselves are the sacrifice.

Demons in the City

Yet in daily life we do not feel that we are a sacrifice to God. Perhaps in some heroic postures and moments, but not in daily life, and particularly not when we are in a city and go to a restaurant or go shopping. On the other side of the desk, we are a sacrifice – as vendors, or servers in a restaurant – but even in these activities we will rarely say that we are in contact with superior beings. Yet in such activities and, when considering buying something or going to a restaurant we may reach far beyond material acts. If we view such activities as relating to demons, then we accord a spiritual dimension to these events. By re-introducing the notion of offering more than just prayers we reinstate a pre-Christian attitude and gain the possibility of viewing spirituality as it occurs in our daily urban commerce.

But one major change, consequent to Judeo-Christianity, is particularly relevant to our argument. It is precisely the transition in worship from material offerings and sacrifices to prayers. Limiting worship to praying creates the conditions for a less concrete and more imaginary relationship with God. Yet something in human beings seems simultaneously to resist the idea of a god to whom we relate only in imagination. We also want something concrete. Let us call this the pagan part; it wants to continue with offerings and sacrifices.

However, as we in the Christian heritage are not supposed to do it to God, we act because "we have to" or "for others" or "to earn our living" or "for pleasure," without recognizing anything spiritual in our actions. My contention is that, in our urban life, we pay tribute regularly to our demons. People working in the advertising business say that we buy images, not objects or services. Such images have to do with our demons or – to say it differently – with the City of God or, in yet another perspective, with the Self. With a particular activity – in buying something important, in going to a restaurant, in accepting an unexpected encounter – we relate to an image, we make a sacrifice to our demon, we attempt to transcend the material event.

If we view urban life in this manner we may be able to pursue an inner dialogue beyond the material considerations that are necessarily involved. This is what demons helped do in Greece and Rome and what I believe they can still do today, notably with the help of analysis. Make sense of our daily lives; make daily events more consciously into the quest for the Self that our life anyway attempts to be. This attitude would give added respect to many workers in the city: the candy-vendor, the nightclub dancer, the doorkeeper. They all have a genius they relate to.

Conclusion

Today we may be able to consider polytheism again with respect, because we have been able to move God inside us. Romans paid tribute to their genius "out there"; we might accept that we honor our genius "in here." After centuries of being scared about our condition and about the punishment of God, we may become able to consider the divine as a dialogue that is possible everywhere. We are pagan polytheists in our daily life. Let us value it. In analysis we meet different aspects of ourselves. We first meet these in our daily activities, generally urban, and we find them in our dreams and take them into the analyst's office. There we eventually realize how far-reaching these encounters are.

Our choice is either to remain Augustinian, and ignore most of urban life, or to re-become Roman. Today we give assistance, if not to a revival of polytheism, at least to a growing sympathy for Greek gods. It may not be necessary to be so literal, to know exactly with which God we are in contact, as they, too, may have undergone some changes during these centuries. Demons then might offer a better image. They don't need any mythological naming; they are more personal, or tied to a place's history.

More important, although Demons have moved into ourselves, we still need to make them offerings to gain their favor, to keep them calm, to understand better. In doing this we may be reaching for soul.

Adopting a polytheistic perspective to urban life will not stop us from going out to look for spirituality in Nature, but it may offer us a frame for looking at everyday urban life as an important place where we can contact the Self.

References

Augustine, St. (1952). *The City of God* (M. Dods, trans.). Chicago/London: William Benton.

Hillman, J. (1975). *Re-Visioning Psychology*. New York: Harper & Row.

Noschis, K. (1984). *Signification Affective du Quartier*. Paris: Meridiens-Klincksieck.

The Bipolar Split in Analytical Psychology

Donald F. Sandner
San Francisco, California, U.S.A.
Society of Jungian Analysts of Northern California

My concern in this paper is the present situation, causes, and possible fate of the split in analytical psychology between the (so-called) symbolic and clinical groups. Although not rigidly defined, the symbolic group centers on the use and amplification of unconscious symbolism, the clinical group on the use of regression and interpretation. They are not mutually exclusive; they may even be complementary, but – human nature being what it is – they have become oppositional. Samuels (1985) has reviewed the history of this split, describing it in terms of an archetypal orientation on one end, a developmental one at the other, and a classical one in between. My discussion is not from the viewpoint of an objective observer, but from the personal experience of one who has been in the middle of the controversy.

My part of the story begins with my brief time, in 1959, as a student at the C.G. Jung Institute in Zurich. I was in the last year of psychiatric residency at Stanford, and this visit was my elective study. I was on a very slim stipend which I stretched as far as it would go – in this case, to Zurich. The golden years of the Analytical Psychological Club – when Jung, Emma Jung and Toni Wolff were teaching – were over. Jung was ill and came only rarely to the Institute. Emma and Toni were dead, but the most brilliant students and collaborators with Jung were still in their heyday, and students from all over the world came to hear them.

Jolande Jacobi was the most extraverted of the group, and she actually spoke personally with most of the new students. It was generally assumed that since you had come to the Jung Institute, you would want a classical Jungian analysis, but if you wanted the "other" you could get that "down the road." Dr. Jacobi, however, announced at one of our initial meetings that she would do either Jungian or Freudian analysis. Being somewhat flamboyant, she stood out like a sore thumb from the others. But she was a natural teacher; not too deep but very passionate. If it had not been for her enthusiastic reaching out, we as green newcomers would have felt entirely unnoticed.

Barbara Hannah was there, too, in full bloom; she was giving a thorough course on the Brontes. She spoke about them effortlessly, without notes, as if she knew them personally. She spoke about the greatness of their works, but also about the many details of their private lives. (She was partial to Branwell.) It was one of those situations in which you might find out more about the Brontes than you wanted to know. Miss Hannah was the school marm, one of the best. She was aware of the depths behind the facades, and she was unstintingly honest and straightforward. In her biography of Jung, she was one of the few early ones who wrote about his relationship with Toni Wolff.

During my stay in Zurich, in spite of our coffeehouse gossip about everybody and everything, the relationship between Toni Wolff and Jung was not mentioned. I found out about it only much later. In the case of a great man – unfortunately perhaps – in the end not much remains hidden. Posterity is patient, but relentless.

The undisputed star of the group of lecturers was Marie-Louise von Franz. Her instantly available erudition and profound insight into Jung's concepts were amazing. Someone remarked that von Franz was more Jungian than Jung himself. Perhaps that meant that she was more organized, coherent and intellectually clear.

She and the other speakers presented a humanism that was free and all-embracing, but still rooted in psychology. Their humanism was Kantian in the largest meaning of that philosophy. Mythology, theology, literature, history, and language were presented not only for the wonders of their own discipline, but also as products of the psyche in its larger function. Their motto might have been: The study of psychology is the study of everything (even the Brontes) as products of the mind. You can imagine what effect this had on an already susceptible young man raised in mid-Illinois. It was a revelation, nothing less. I, in fact, read all of Jung that was then available in English in "one long sitting."

That fact brings us squarely back to the theme of this paper. Such a wonderful outpouring of creativity always has a hidden but considerable shadow, and I was not the only one to fall into it. That shadow could be characterized under two headings: inflation, and neglect of the transference. But they are closely connected. Many of us were caught up in the grandeur of Jung's psychology – the road to inflation. One could first analyze the shadow, which shouldn't take too long, perhaps a few months. Then with the help of deep dreams one could come to terms with the anima or the animus. And then one could tackle the Self.

I think that even in those days I had the common sense (perhaps from that midwestern boyhood) to realize that one could not buy self-realization so cheaply. It took Jung a lifetime; it would take us no less. I wonder if Jung knew how truly he spoke when he said that he would rather be Jung than a Jungian. We are left with the fruits of his genius and a powerful model on which to build, but we are also left with his shadow as well as our own. And so we are full of doubts $\longleftarrow$ and contradictions. We must find our own ways, shoulder our own burdens, not Jung's. And that, in the nature of things, is how it should be.

Then there is the second element of the shadow of those early times: the neglect of the transference. Even though Jung admitted to Freud that transference was the alpha and omega of analytic therapy, neither of them took their own shrewd insight to heart. It was the custom when I was in Zurich, as it has been reported to have been 20 years earlier, to go easily from one analyst to another. In earlier days, for example, one could see Toni Wolff for six months, and then see Jung who, after a period of time with him, would send one to see Emma. If you were seeing a woman, perhaps you needed to see a man, or you needed to see someone who specialized in some branch of symbolism, and so on. They simply did not see the transference as we see it now. For Freud as well as Jung in the early days, the transference was an obstacle that had to be dealt with, perhaps by interpretation or dream analysis. I think now most of us, however great our other differences might be, see the transference not as an obstacle, but as the centerpiece of analytic therapy, the mainspring dynamism by which the therapeutic process unfolds. Jung understood this theoretically but not so well in actual practice.

Behind this confusion about the transference there was a more hidden disparity. We were dealing with two very different kinds of $\swarrow$ analyses: that which included spiritual growth as part of individuation and spanned a lifetime; and that which was directed toward emotional injuries of childhood and infancy that extended into the present as complexes. The latter kind of analysis involved heavy use of regression and was expected to do its work within a limited number of years. We never got these two straightened out, and we were often trying to do them both at once even though the methods, guidelines and goals were quite different. It is still so.

The first kind of analytic therapy, the kind that was practiced by Jung himself and by his early students in Zurich, can be called dream-centered, or vision-centered. Dreams and visions are analyzed and elucidated through association, amplification, active imagination and serial integration (analyzing a series of dreams as one continuum). Much work in writing, studying, visualizing and drawing dreams can be done by the patient outside the analytic hour; thus, meetings can be less frequent. The patient and analyst usually sit vis-à-vis, and the work of dealing with regression and the transference, often an archetypal transference, is done mostly in the dream work. The dream itself is the temenos for this kind of therapy and its great value is that it reaches the deepest layers of the patient's psyche. Using intuition as its major function, it orients itself to the patient's entire process of individuation over a lifetime. For that reason it can accommodate itself to frequent changes of analyst, shorter periods of work spread out over a longer time, with the expectation that the patient will do much of the work outside the analytic session. This kind of analytic work is particularly useful in mid-life, illness, or old age and the time before death; it is essential for a person with strong spiritual leanings (though it need not be the only analytic work for such a person). According to Jung's idea of individuation, this kind of work tends to create a symbolic system of life values rooted in sacredness, and offering access to a spiritual path. The religions of the Plains Indians have much in common with this view, relying on the vision quest and big dreams to guide the seeker.

There are weaknesses in this kind of work. I have already mentioned some. Not everyone can remember dreams, or connect them to everyday life. Very strong repressed feelings may be indicated in dreams, but not experienced. Also this work is easier for intuitives who, unfortunately for us, do not represent the entire population.

In the Zurich of the 1960s, we were thoroughly imbued with this dream-centered analytic work, and we went home to the United States and other countries expecting to put it into full practice. I returned to complete my training at the C.G. Jung Institute of San Francisco. The group of analysts there was minuscule compared with the overwhelming presence of the Freudians. When I told my supervisor in residency of my intention to take up Jungian analysis, he looked at me as though I were one of the walking dead.

I went into analysis then with Jo Wheelwright. It was certainly not a classical Jungian analysis. It did not center on dreams although dreams were a part of it, but it was relationship-centered, relying on the feeling function. We sat face-to-face, there was some regression, and a good deal of dream work, but the relationship was central and authentic. He did not imitate Jung or anyone else. He was completely himself, for better or worse, and for that I am grateful. It was a close, instinctual father-son relationship, but it was also sacred. The two poles were united in a contained relationship.

Such relationship-centered therapy also has its shortcomings. There may be too much looseness of the container. Really intense feelings of rage, hatred, envy or greed may not be contained well. There is the possibility of avoidance of deeply unconscious material, or arousing sudden transference reactions, and not resolving them. Such cases are not rare. But when the connection is good, and the repressed material not too primal, this therapeutic work can be very real, powerful, and effective.

But this was the 1960s in San Francisco, and the great wave of the hippie era was soon upon us. Some saw it as enlightened humanism; others saw it as irresponsible hooliganism. At any rate in such works as Bob Dylan's songs "Tambourine Man" and "All Along the Watch Tower," the Rolling Stone's "Sympathy for the Devil" and the Doors' "Break On Through To The Other Side," it did seem that popular culture touched the deep psyche. Some called it the Crack in the Cosmic Egg. I remember heading home one evening, and waiting at the point where Haight Street meets Golden Gate Park as a parade of Krishna devotees made their way with a full sized Juggernaut in their midst.

Jung, with his archetypal symbolism, his interest in myth and fairy tales, and his concept of individuation was part of the hippie scene. My office was visited by many people talking about psychedelic experiences, communal styles of living, sexual freedom, and return to the land. Interest in Jungian psychology grew enormously; we frequently had sell-out weekend conferences. Those were the days; I thought they'd never end, but they did. They came to their highest point at the birthday celebration for Jung's hundredth birthday hosted by the University of California at the Miyako Hotel in 1975. It was packed to the rafters with people enthusiastic about Jung's ideas. There was even a big birthday cake. It was a celebration of archetypal dimensions, and it was – to my memory – the last of those great conferences.

After 1975, slowly at first, a great change came over the Jungian world. Where before everything had been reasonably cohesive, now there was a discernible split. I first became sharply aware of this at the IAAP congress in Jerusalem in 1983. I heard one young woman, possibly a candidate, say to another that she never wanted to hear the word "symbol" again. I thought at first she must be in the wrong place, but then I began to see that she was not alone in this sentiment. The split between the "symbolic" side of Jungian psychology, what I have referred to as dream-centered, and the "clinical" side, here represented by the relationship and regression-centered models, had begun in earnest. The flaws in Jung's psychology were brought vividly to the fore: failure to recognize the power and destructive potential of the transference, failure to give due recognition to the need for developmental regression, and serious boundary problems leading to ethical violations, including analysts' sexual relations with patients.

There was a growing realization that, despite the enthusiastic claims, Jungian therapy in its classical form could not cover all the needs of a psychotherapeutic practice, even a highly specialized analytic one. Classical Jungian analysis produced some great successes; especially in people who were hungry for an inner spiritual life, who could find it nowhere else, and who were mature enough to contain and reduce the inflation that invariably accompanies it. But at times this kind of analytic work could not meet the demands of regressive complexes, awakened by the transference and flooding into the psyche from earlier, sometimes infantile states. Such cases may need a different model of therapy to which I have already referred as regression-centered. This model is based on Freudian psychoanalysis, but has been modified greatly by such investigators as Melanie Klein, Heinz Kohut, R.D. Laing, D.W. Winnicott, Ronald Fairbairn, Harry Guntrip, and most notably by Michael Fordham, whose efforts to bridge Freudian and Jungian concepts has been greatly undervalued by both sides.

The original idea in regression-centered work, which has been greatly modified since, was that the analyst was expected to remain objective, relying on the patient to produce free associations. No personal reactions or even polite amenities were permitted. The container was to be very tight. In order to further facilitate regression, the patient was to come several times a week, perhaps four or five, and lie on the couch, which put him/her into a vulnerable, child-like position in relation to the analyst.

The analyst's traditional response to this regression is interpretation, largely – but not entirely – based on thinking. Thinking along rational and lucid lines yields a useful picture of one's childhood and its subversion. It even makes sense of the confusing welter of feelings going on in the transference at any moment. It can be validating and liberating, especially in regard to the personal unconscious as it is affected by infancy and childhood. This form of therapy can contain intense feeling, and can be reparative in a most satisfying way. Someone has compared it to knitting up a torn garment, or in this case a torn life. Its shortcomings are that it is expensive and time-consuming, the relatively objective nature of the analyst may be felt as cold or even hostile, it does not usually touch the archetypal layers of the deep psyche – although that may happen – and it sometimes evokes the most intense regressive feelings of need and dependency, which can be very difficult to resolve.

By 1989, at the time of the Paris Congress, there were growing insights into the limitations of Jung's psychology, and also growing awareness that, as a person, Jung was not the ideal we had allowed ourselves to imagine. Hans Dieckmann gave us a particularly good metaphor: It is never so dark as at the base of a lighthouse. Jung, we realized, had a considerable shadow. The accusations about his anti-Semitism had always been around, but now, as direct quotations were assembled and investigations made, there seemed to be a good deal of truth in them. I will not rehearse all of that – you have heard it before – but there is one part of it that is difficult to accept. At the Paris Congress there was a report by Aryeh Maidenbaum and Stephen Martin that, even after the Hitler era, there was a quota system for Jews in the Analytical Psychology Club in Zurich, a system that lasted until 1950.

There was also severe criticism of Jung's relationship with some of his women patients which indicated a disregard for the transference and the boundaries it imposes. Michael Fordham (1993) stated that he was angry with Jung for talking one way about the transference and acting another. There were also critics who felt that Jung liked power much more than he admitted. There were many instances in which his influence over his followers, admirers and patients seemed to go too far. As we see it now, there were a great many dual relationships in Zurich. Almost every one who knew him admits that Jung had a poor feeling function, and one woman analyst who saw him in the 1930s described him as monstrously insensitive.

Having said all this, I find myself still filled with gratitude for the great mentor who gave so generously of his gift to all of us. Perhaps it is a mark of maturity in our group to learn to live with that ambivalence. If one can learn to live with the loss of one's ideals, perhaps one can even learn to live with one's own shadow. Then the shadow of a great man does not obscure his greatness.

We stand here in the middle of the 1990s in some disarray. We have found many inadequacies in our psychology; we have discovered many imperfections in our founder. There are quarrels in our Societies, some having split into two or more groups. Our goals and our future are cloudy and divisive. Where do we go from here?

By way of pointing to a deeper level of our problems, I offer a Native American trickster story called, appropriately enough, "Why Raven Isn't Perfect" (Goodchild, 1991). Raven is a cultural trickster figure from the Northwest Coast. He is also a creator and hero. He, along with Coyote, has much to teach us, and here is part of it.

There were two Ravens, both snow white, and they were busy creating all the creatures of the world. (Perhaps they were like Freud and Jung creating new kinds of therapy.) But whenever one of them, the good Raven, would create a beautiful creature, the other would – in a nasty, critical way – destroy it. For instance, when the good Raven made a beautiful fish with perfect balance and symmetry, and rainbow-hued scales, and was standing back to admire it, the other Raven rushed out of the nearby woods, raised his huge foot and stomped on the fish. Then the good Raven's heart tensed with hate; for there, instead of the beautiful fish, a flat flounder flopped about his feet.

"If you keep doing that," said the good Raven (who wasn't so good anymore), "I'll kill you." But the bad Raven persisted and with some subtle trickery and a not-so-subtle sharp axe, the good Raven (which was which now?) killed the bad one. As the good Raven stared down at his dead twin he moaned: "What have I done?" He tried to wipe the blood from the feathers, but it could not be removed; it spread over him and grew darker until his once-white feathers were as black as the winter's night. "It is happening in my heart, too," he moaned. "It is darkening as if my brother's spirit had moved in beside my own. What will happen now? Will I ever make a perfect creature?" (Will we ever make the perfect therapy?) He began to make creatures again, but they all had serious flaws. The deer was fleet and graceful, but he was a coward. The bear was large and strong, but he was greedy. Finally he made humans, but there was always something wrong with them, too. He noticed that those who were sensitive and kind were also weak and ineffective, and those who were strong and confident were neither kind nor tolerant.

The black Raven almost despaired, but finally he said: "In all these creatures I have made something perfect, as I aspire to be, but in these same creatures, there are great flaws and evil intentions, as my brother would have wished. Just once more I will try to make a perfect being, but inside me I will have to hold my brother's bad spirit away from my own."

Carefully Raven made soft long hair, the color of autumn light. Next he fashioned the body, shaping it to fit perfectly in its world, not too large and not too small. Then slowly he breathed upon it. Then he stood back watching life fill its lungs.

When the other creatures, especially the devious fox, saw this perfect creature they were mad with hate and envy. Raven saw that as soon as he put the creature down they would destroy it. "Stand back," he said, and he rolled the still wet creature over the sharp pine needles on the ground. Then he let it go, and when fox rushed up to strike it, his paws were pierced with the needles and they stuck in him as he ran away howling. Raven saw this and from deep within him – somewhere near where the spirit of his bad brother sat beside his own good spirit – a new sensation came rushing into his throat. Then Raven laughed the first laugh in all the world.

The moral here is not only that a sense of humor might save us from quarreling to our own destruction; this story is about warring opposites and integrating the shadow. As I have given it some thought, it seems to me that the porcupine is not such a bad symbol for individuation; he is humble, unassuming, he goes about his vegetarian way with no heroic attributes, and he is well protected. One might do worse, since for the moment we cannot solve all the important questions that beset us. On both sides of our current polarity, as always, we fear that in compromising we will lose our treasure. So we must gather what skills and integrity we possess, practice the therapy that seems right for each of us, recognizing that people really are different in their perceptions, in their functioning, in their thinking and feeling and every other way. What one can do another can't, and what one cherishes as the best is of indifference or scorn to the other. To keep to our way we must be open, aware and yet protected with a hide full of sharp needles. Our way of integrating will become clear, but for now it is a slow process, reminding me of the old joke question: "How do porcupines make love?" and the answer which fits for us also: "Very carefully!"

Many people are now becoming aware that we could destroy the unique core of Jungian psychology in our zeal for the perfect kind of analysis. Is it possible to do full justice to regressive and symbolic-centered therapy in one analysis, or by one analyst? Is it possible to offer a full-range analytic practice under the name of Jung alone? Probably not,

In spite of our differences, we have something very powerful in common – the strength and transformational ability of the transference. The training and ability to use that power consciously puts us, as long-term therapists, apart from all other kinds of psychotherapy. It is a treasure that Freud and Jung have bequeathed us and, like the porcupine, it needs protection. The transference-countertransference interaction is the nuclear energy of Analytical Psychology, and we must learn to handle it carefully. I have come to believe that every practicing analyst should have at least one hour of supervision a month with anyone of his/her choice. I also think this should be continued from the beginning to the end of one's professional career.

Long-term therapy, consciously using the transference-countertransference, is a discipline of its own, and it should be responsible to itself. It isn't standard medical care, and will not be in the foreseeable future. Since events – especially in the United States – have forced our hand, we will see if long-term analytic therapy can exist without the help of insurance companies, government subsidies, or outside financial support. In other words, is it worth it to the analysand? My guess is yes. My analysis, surely one of the turning points in my life, was paid for without insurance, and many of my colleagues can say the same.

The overall experience of analysis continues to be of crucial importance to many people, and they will continue to make whatever sacrifice must be made to obtain it. No other experience offers such a deep insight into the nature of one's humanity: not only its wonderful accomplishments, but also its cruelty and destructiveness. As Jung said: "One does not become enlightened by imaging figures of light, but by making the darkness conscious" (CW18, par. 335). That is the core work of analysis and it can be done only within the mighty dynamism of the transference-countertransference.

Making conscious the terrible shadow of human life has been one of the greatest works of the twentieth century, and it has barely begun. Freud revealed the shadow of sexuality in sadism. Winnicott, Fairbairn, Guntrip and others have emphasized the importance of hatred and destructiveness in the human psyche. And finally Jung, as far as he was able, brought into consciousness the shadow of God. These discoveries form our main guide into the twenty-first century. Socrates' ancient dictum "Know thyself" is still the main hope for our survival, and we have just begun – considering World Wars I and II, the Holocaust, the possibility of nuclear war, exploding overpopulation and environmental destruction – to know what that means. Can we bear to know?

F. Scott Fitzgerald once said that the mark of a first-rate mind is the ability to hold two opposing ideas at the same time and still function. If we can do that consciously, then we can recognize bipolarity as a fundamental function of the psyche which is a pre-condition (or goad) to creativity, and not the work of an enemy. It is the spirit of the dark brother who sits always beside one's heart. If we as individuals – and as a group – can do that, we should be able to hang together. But if we can't, we most assuredly will hang separately. No one of us, or one part of us, can know the whole way of the psyche. The work needs us all.

References

Fordham, M. (1993). *The Making of an Analyst: "A Memoir."* London: Free Association Books.
Goodchild, P. (1991). *Raven Tales*. Chicago: Chicago Review Press.
Samuels, A.(1985). *Jung and the Post-Jungians*. London: Routledge & Kegan Paul.

Modern Infant Research and Reductive Analysis

Mario Jacoby
Zollikon, Switzerland
Swiss Society For Analytical Psychology

Infant research, in the last decades, has become an extensive field with broad implications. In this paper I hope to give an overview of the field looking to the question: What might Jungian analysts embrace from the findings of infant research? More particularly, in light of these findings, does it still make sense to speak of "reductive" analysis? (For the distinction between "Infant Research," done mostly in the United States, and "Infant Observation," pioneered by Esther Bick, see Covington, 1991, and Zinkin, 1991).

Why am I so interested in the findings of modern infant research, particularly as described and elaborated by psychoanalysts such as Lichtenberg (1983, 1989, 1992) and Daniel Stern (1985)? I find the issues currently under investigation by infant researchers to be of fundamental human significance: issues concerning the basic, universal nature of the human being. Seen from a Jungian perspective, one could say that infant research studies describe with great precision and in minute detail the process by which the Self – the central archetype of order – incarnates itself in the individual person.

In the manner of a Platonist, I like to imagine that there is a pre-existing Idea concerning human nature, even if its formation took millions of years in an evolutionary process. This universal Idea incarnates itself in the individual infant and organizes its maturation and development. It is as if Nature (or a creator of the universe, if you prefer) has a pre-existing conception of the human species. This thought is expressed mythologically in our Jewish/Christian tradition, according to which humans are created in God's image. Indeed, there is a mysterious knowledge operating in every individual, beginning in the prenatal state, of how to be and how to mature into a human being, as distinguished from growing into an ape or a dog, for example. And since we humans are social beings by nature, society influences this process of maturation from the beginning of the individual's existence and at every step of the way thereafter by means of interactions with significant others.

I do not have the illusion that, thanks to infant research, we now can find final answers concerning the mystery of human soul. Nor can we arrive at a definite knowledge of the infant's subjective experience. But it may be that we can approach a more definite grasp of the inherited dispositions that organize our psychic experience.

Researchers use modern instruments such as time-loops, videos, body diagnostics and highly differentiated experiments to study the infant's behavior during periods of 24 hours, especially in interactions with the caregiver. Going beyond their data concerning this behavior, they also attempt to draw conclusions about the actual experiences of babies. But it is to their credit that they are careful to bracket those areas of their theories that are tentative and hypothetical. What especially appeals to me is that, even though many of these researchers are originally Freudians by persuasion, they want to look at infants and mother/infant interactions in a fresh way, daring to call into question some widely-held theoretical assumptions. And many of their findings, granted that they are tentative, make sense to me and to my work as an analyst.

My interest in these findings does not mean that I am drawn to "reductive" procedures, in the sense of explaining complex psychological phenomena by reducing them to a single infantile cause. Jung usually spoke about reductive analysis with a slightly derogatory tone, although he did find such analysis necessary in order to treat certain neurotic states. It is understandable that Jung had become allergic to the proud certainty of Freud and the early psychoanalysts whenever they found a "nothing but" cause for neurotic, cultural and religious phenomena. To Jung, this attitude seemed terribly one-dimensional.

On the question of "reductive" analysis I recommend an excellent paper that was published just at the time when I was in the midst of my struggle with this issue. Siegelman (1994) supplies many convincing reasons for replacing the rather devalued term "reductive" with the term "developmental" analysis. Since she has provided a convincing criticism of the term "reductive," I find myself free to focus mainly on some findings of infant research and their potential usefulness for analysts.

On Intersubjectivity

The similarity between modes of infant experience and those of some basic adult experiences is striking. For example: I see connections between the findings of infant research and Jungian analysis. In enthusiastically sharing these with you, I inevitably hope for some understanding and resonance which would strengthen my confidence to continue with this endeavor. Your response would mirror to me that I am not completely off the mark. Likewise a comparable, basic hope for understanding and resonance has been observed among infants from seven months onward. According to Stern (1985), this hope marks the beginning of the infant's "intersubjective sense of self," with its basic need to share experiences with the mother, and its expectation of a good-enough affect-attunement.

This statement in itself is not big news following the publications of Michael Balint, D.W. Winnicott and Heinz Kohut. But of particular relevance to an analyst are the detailed observations concerning the extent to which this very need brings about a corresponding sense of self and stimulates particular aspects of the infant's socialization. The infant finds that some behaviors meet with a welcoming response from the environment and some do not. In such interactions with significant persons, "recognizing validation" and "social referencing" take place, for better or worse. Mothers can react to the infant's activities and affective states with a number of different signals, consciously or unconsciously.

A short example from Stern (1985, p. 222): One mother reacted with a depressive signal every time her one year-old son did something uncoordinated, such as knocking over an object or damaging a toy. This consisted of long expirations, falling intonations, and "Oh, Johnny," that he could interpret as "Look what you've done to Mummy again." Gradually, Johnny's exuberant freedom became more circumspect. His mother had brought an alien affective experience into an otherwise neutral or positive activity, which in time turned into a quite different kind of lived experience for the boy.

What sort of lived experience would I have if I shared some enthusiasm with you in connection with ideas that I am playing with, and if these ideas offended some Jungian, Kleinian – or whatever – belief, such that you felt alienated and rejecting? On an emotional level, could this experience not be described as a variation of the infant/mother interaction in the here and now? If my entire being and self-worth were invested in this interaction, the rejection could be a shattering experience. Such are the experiences of infants.

I usually have an array of defense strategies at my disposal, none of which the infant has yet developed. If infants have to build up primitive defenses at too early an age, they tend to develop pathology. As an adult, I may defend myself by devaluing adverse opinions others have of me. Indeed, I may be able to accept rejecting criticism, even when it hurts, not only as an attack but also as a challenge to inquire further into the matter and to look within myself. Thus negative criticism may turn into social referencing that operates in a productive way.

But the basic intersubjective needs, with their effect of recognizing validation and social referencing, are similar in the baby and in the adult, especially the needs to be seen, heard and understood. They seem archetypally given and become a central issue at the approximate age of nine months.

These findings, about intersubjectivity and the importance of affect-attunement, play an enormous role in the analytic relationship. Sooner or later patients usually repeat in the transference whatever early intersubjective experiences they have had. The analyst may try to find the roots of these experiences by watching the patient's dreams, memories, associations and – last but not least – countertransference reactions. The analyst may try to reconstruct the patient's early intersubjective experiences, thus doing the sort of therapeutic work that classical Jungians may call reductive.

But far from becoming fixated to the past, an analyst and analysand are engaging in an intersubjective process that takes place in the here and now. The experience of the present may be distorted by the prejudices and expectations stemming from the past, but by seeking to understand and empathize, the analyst may implant a new affective experience into the patient's emotional system. If the fit between the partners in analysis is good enough, a new social referencing may take place. The influence of the analyst's personality and value system may result in a change of attitude in the patient. Such a change may open new possibilities for experiencing life in the present and opening doors for the future. Thus, even if we focus on childhood issues – something that few of us do consistently – we are rarely working only reductively.

The Sense of Self and Motivational Systems

Findings that are particularly interesting for Jungian analysts include infant researchers' preoccupation with the infant's sense of self. It has been observed that the infant has such a sense that long predates any image or representation of the self. That is, the infant senses its own self instinctively long before it can know consciously: "This is me." Observation shows that the infant can distinguish between itself and other persons (beginning with the caregiver) immediately after birth. Thus is confirmed a point Fordham (1969) made many years ago when he postulated his concept of the primary self. Although infant researchers understand by "self" our sense of self, they are convinced that the sense of self and its maturation are central concerns of the infant's life, much more so than the vicissitudes of the instinctual drives. Lichtenberg (1991) even speaks of a groundplan for the infant-environment system which wants to be followed and realized.

Lichtenberg wants to replace the concept of instinctual drives with the idea of basic inborn motivations that are accompanied and enhanced by respective basic affects. According to Lichtenberg, the infant is motivated by needs for regulating its physiological requirements, and by needs for attachment which later develop into a need for affiliation. Then there is the motivation to explore the environment and to assert oneself there. Very important for survival are the motivations for reacting aversively, either through contradiction or retreat. Sensual needs are felt from the beginning which, after a certain time, will be intensified also by sexual needs. These inborn motivations are operative throughout the life-span. (See Lichtenberg, 1989.)

The Sense of a Core Self

Integrative processes also have been discerned which, in the first month of life, form the sense of a "core self." After the age of one to two months the core self allows the infant to experience intentions and motivations as its own – the self as its own agent. The infant's sense of its body, its boundaries, of coherence and continuity have also come alive. No longer are the oral drives of psychoanalytic doctrine so central; the sense of the core self is central. Of course, orality plays its part, especially in the interactions with mother, but so do such needs as eye-contact, holding, snuggling, vocalizing and interest-arousal through play.

Infant researchers emphasize that these experiences with the caregiver are not experiences of symbiotic fusion. In spite of the fact that the infant's sense of self changes in relation to the activities of the caretaker – through feeding, changing diapers and playing – the boundary between self and other remains intact. According to Stern (1985), this phenomenon can be described more accurately as relatedness to a "self-regulating other" than as merging. Again, it was Fordham who, years ago, spoke of the infant's boundaries between self and others.

The function of the self-regulating other may be operative also in the analytic situation. Some clients may feel reassured, relieved or emotionally contained for the moment simply by hearing the analyst's voice on the phone, by entering the atmosphere of the consulting room, or by experiencing the analyst's listening presence. This is not to overlook the experience of other analysands, who cannot stand such longing for intimacy, who are afraid and ashamed of such dependency, and who deny all these feelings.

The Sense of a Verbal Self

Stern (1985) observed that the "verbal sense of self" begins at the age of 15 to 18 months, equivalent to Margaret Mahler's "rapprochement phase." At this time, with the acquisition of language, a burst of growth takes place, which could be likened to a revolution. The time coincides with the beginning of the infant's capacity to take itself as the object of its own reflection. Thus, an "objective self" comes into being beside the "subjective self" of earlier phases. The desire of children at this age to look with fascination at their own reflection in the mirror is a clear indication of this phase, as is the development of the capacity for symbolic play. Through language, many skills can be practiced at a level not previously possible.

But language is a double-edged sword; it both enriches and limits the field of common experience. Only parts of the original global experience can be expressed in words; the rest remains inaccurately named and poorly understood. Language thus drives a wedge between two modes of experience: one that can be lived only directly, another that can be verbally expressed. To the extent that experience becomes linked to words, the growing child becomes distanced from the spontaneous flow of experience that had characterized the preverbal state. Thus the child gains entry into its culture at the cost of losing the strength of wholeness of its original experience.

> *The self becomes a mystery. The infant is aware that there are levels and layers of self-experience that are to some extent estranged from the official experiences ratified by language. The previous harmony is broken. For the first time the infant experiences the self as divided and rightly senses that no one can heal this split.* (Stern, 1985, p. 272)

Isn't this familiar ground for Jungian analysts also? Are not the main activities within the analytic field designed to build bridges between those two modes of experience, helping to cope with this split? Are we not dealing with the relation or non-relation between the ego and the unconscious? As analysts we try to find a bridge to those realms that have been left to lead a nameless but nonetheless very real existence, including creative and/or destructive resources in the psyche. In adults they may express themselves in dreams, fantasies, symptoms, affects and behavior.

Here may lie an explanation of how analysis can be a "talking cure." By means of interpretations we give language to unnamed realms of experience and thus invite them to become a part of our conscious world. By means of language we attempt to ratify experiences that had been fended off by shame- or fear-barriers, because of their incompatibility with ego-values. It is true that Jung was skeptical about words; he was aware of how often they serve defensive, rationalistic purposes. Yet he developed the word-association experiment, showing how certain words are triggers of feeling-toned complexes. The choice of words in the analyst's comments, reactions and interpretations is essential, in addition to body language and voice inflection. The use of a particular word may determine how and whether we can cross the bridge to the preverbal realm of experience, a realm that is not yet verbalized or cannot be verbalized, but may be symbolically depicted. Sometimes the analyst has to be the first one to give a name to something that had remained unspeakable.

In describing the development of the different aspects of the sense of self I must not fail to mention a point that Stern (1985) made: that higher stages of the sense of self do not simply replace the previous ones. Each "stage" is more than passing; it represents an abiding way of being in the world. Over a lifetime each can develop, differentiate, become renewed or enriched; but a stage can also remain undifferentiated, become atrophied or split off.

The Question of Infantile Fantasy

According to Lichtenberg (1983), infant researchers have been unable to ascertain a world of images – including fantasy activity – during the first year of life. Recognizing the mother when she is present does not mean that the infant is capable of producing an image or idea of her when she is absent. Researchers have found, however, that the infant retains memories of many interactions with the mother: episodes that take place in the course of feeding, changing and communicating with each other. That is, the infant retains various episodes that occur in the presence of the self-regulating other, especially those episodes that keep repeating themselves with small variations. Thus, rather than speaking in terms of inner images of mother or father *per se*, we can speak of memories of interactions and the expectation of the repetition of such interactions. In the episodic memory of the first year of life, the significant other is not maintained in the form of a discrete person, but rather as an influence on the regulation of the emotional and physical state. I have been watching myself in this respect and have found that my own memory is at its best when recollecting how interactions with people have made me feel. These feelings are the last memories I lose over the years, and may represent the deepest roots of memory-contents. However, this experience may be related to psychological type.

I find it interesting that the ever-recurring individual episodes are recorded in memory in a general form or even a pattern. Stern (1985) speaks of "representations of interactions that have been generalized" (RIGs). RIGs form a kind of inner knowledge for the infant, garnered from experience about how the interactions with others affect the infant's state. Such representations take on a more or less generalized form, and are not limited to concrete interactions with the personal mother. From a Jungian standpoint, the ability to form a general representation out of countless independent experiences is something that we attribute to a creative, structuring power, which we call the archetype. This raises another question: To what extent can one consider these first representations of interaction, with their expectations, as the root of what Jungians call complexes? I tend to answer this question affirmatively. (See Jacoby, 1993.) Kast (1994) came to the same conclusion.

If the findings of infant research are correct, we must do more than differentiate between pre-verbal and verbal states; we must also hypothesize a state in which images and fantasy are not yet available. One might call this a "pre-pictorial state." This puts the Jungian idea of the primordial image into question, because it is not the image that is primordial in the individual psyche. But what about the archetype?

Archetype and Affect

For me, the theory of archetypes is not invalidated by those findings. The archetype is, in Jung's words, an "inherited mode of psychic functioning, corresponding to the inborn way in which the chick emerges from the egg, the bird builds its nest" (CW18, par. 518). Seen from inside, from within the realm of the subjective psyche, it may clothe itself in suitable symbols. Yet, according to Jung, the archetype may not always take the form of an image. Thus, archetypes are at work in the psychic functioning and experiencing of the infant, even if not in the form of symbolic imagery.

According to the findings I have been describing, a case can be made that the earliest archetypal experiences manifest themselves in relation to rhythmically repeated patterns that regulate the physical and emotional state of the infant. The infant experiences a range of bodily sensations plus different kinds of rhythm, having to do with its mother's and its own heartbeat and with the cycle of states the newborn goes through during a 24-hour period. If the mother functions as a good-enough self-regulating other, she mediates, through the regularity of her dealings with the child, a kind of primary "world order." Thus an archetypal pattern unfolds that does not possess the quality of image and symbol but is active in the category of time, the temporal ordering processes, and their associated affective states. These processes regulate tension and relaxation; they direct movements, perceptual stimuli and bodily sensations. All the basic inborn affects such as joy, surprise, interest, distress, rage, disgust, fear and shame manifest themselves also in the dimension of amplitude or intensity. One thinks of a sudden joy, or of a sadness that builds slowly over time. It may come on all at once, subside again quickly, rise to a sudden peak, or slowly ebb away. In musical language these are expressed with the terms *accelerando, sforzando, ritardando*, and of course also *forte* and *piano*. More so than visual imagery, music and dancing speak to our most primary and archaic emotional states.

Stern (1985) speaks here of "vitality affects" which express the basic emotional disposition, the "temperament" of a person. If the infant's inborn emotional disposition is too much at variance with the basic temperament of the mother, there may be great difficulty for them to attune themselves to each other. It goes without saying that those vitality affects have a great influence on the atmosphere of the analytic field. They go a long way in determining whether a therapeutic alliance has a facilitating potential or is a mismatch.

To a certain extent, the issue of matching temperaments has long been self-evident to sensitive analysts, as well as the attempt at affect attunement. For instance, when I listened to audio-tapes of analytic sessions that some able trainees brought me for supervision, I could hear the trainee's modulations of affect-expression, be it in tone, loudness or softness, speeding up, or slowing down, which empathically responded to the way the patient expressed his or her emotional issues.

Conclusion

To be receptive to findings from infant research does not mean a necessity for any radical change of methods – at least not for Jungians. On the contrary, a pioneer of infant research such as Lichtenberg (1992), has made many proposals for a new psychoanalytic technique that increasingly resembles the Jungian approach. Just a brief example: Due to the great importance of mutual eye-contact in infancy, Lichtenberg (1991) now finds it therapeutically essential to move out of the traditional position behind the couch, where the analyst is unseen by the client and cannot see the expression of the client's eyes.

Still, the question remains: What might Jungian analysts embrace from the findings of infant research? As a matter of instinct we may be doing already much that I have been talking about. At least I have many "Aha-experiences" when encountering this material. Even so, these findings are important in directing our attention to qualities of interaction that have been too much in the background or simply taken for granted. For a very long time, the focus of most Jungians was more or less restricted to the contents of the unconscious; we devoted far too little attention to the subtle pathways by which the unconscious motivates interactions between analyst and client. Thus, the findings of infant research have increased considerably my sensitivity to the feeling issues emerging in the interactive field. These findings have made me more aware of the great emotional significance of the language we choose, of the function of the self-regulating other, the possibility or impossibility of affect-attunement, the emotional nuances behind and between the lines of discourse concerning manifest contents. I may be responsive also to the motivational system that is dominant, moment-for-moment, in the analysand's emotional state. When is he or she motivated to engage in the shared work of exploration? When are attachment needs in the foreground that divert attention away from exploration? Are sexual fantasies dominant – which the patient is trying to fend off – that result in a form of aversion against analyzing, against my presence, operating as a form of resistance?

I find it less and less meaningful to juxtapose reductive versus symbolic, clinical versus archetypal. I feel that I accompany my clients best when I succeed in being there in an empathic and introspective mode, in order to do justice to their conscious and unconscious issues, while simultaneously giving sensitivity and free space to the emotional nuances of the interactions in the here and now of the therapeutic field. If Lichtenberg (1991) speaks of a "groundplan of the infant-environment system, which wants to be followed and realized," I want to add that this groundplan is archetypal and thus it is also operative in the analytic situation – on a much more complex level. Thus, the findings of infant research may contribute to a more sensitive grasp of what is taking place on an emotional level and what is therapeutically necessary within the interactive field. And finally, these findings may begin also to provide some new hypotheses concerning the most fundamental features of our emotional life, and the factors that contribute to or inhibit its maturation and differentiation. To my mind, it all circles around the inexhaustible question: What is the nature of humans?"

References

Fordham, M. (1969). *Children as Individuals*. London: Hodder & Stoughton.
Jacoby, M. (1993). *Shame and the Origins of Self-Esteem*. London/New York: Routledge.
Kast, V. (1994). *Vater-Tochter, Mutter-Sohne*. Stuttgart: Kreuz.

Lichtenberg, J. (1983). *Psychoanalysis and Infant Research*. Hillsdale, NJ/ London: The Analytic Press.

Lichtenberg, J. (1989). *Psychoanalysis and Motivation*. Hillsdale, NJ/London: The Analytic Press.

Lichtenberg, J. (1991). Oral communication.

Lichtenberg, J. et al. (1992). *Self and Motivational Systems*. Hillsdale, NJ/ London: The Analytic Press.

Siegelman, E. (1994). Reframing 'reductive' analysis. *Journal of Analytical Psychology*, *39*-4, 479-496.

Stern, D. (1985). *The Interpersonal World of the Infant*. New York: Basic Books.

Mercurius Duplex

Archetypal Defense Against Early Trauma

Donald E. Kalsched
New York, NY, U.S.A.
New York Association for Analytical Psychology

A diabolic trickster figure often appears in the dreams of patients who have suffered early trauma. "Diabolic" comes from the Greek *dia-ballein* meaning "to throw across or apart." This seems to be the "intention" of our figure – to tear apart the inner world in order to allow living to go on in compartments. Jung's word for this "throwing apart" was *dissociation;* our diabolic figure appears to personify the psyche's dissociative defenses where early trauma has made psychic integration impossible. In a clinical vignette we shall see how this diabolic image murders a suffering, innocent child in the dream of a patient who had just begun to risk infantile dependency feelings in the transference. This gives us a clue as to the intrapsychic function of our dark trickster, who seems to operate as an archaic defense against emerging dependency feelings toward real objects in the world. In a second vignette, a very different side of our trickster reveals itself at an advanced stage of healing in an early-trauma patient. Here, in the midst of ongoing grief work, our mercurial imago appears to protect and help re-integrate a vulnerable child-aspect of the patient, instead of attacking it. This benevolent activity describes the "other face" of our duplex image and helps us understand why the antonym for the word diabolic is "symbolic" from the Greek *sym-ballein*, meaning to "throw together" or integrate.

Early Trauma

I use the word "trauma" to mean any experience that causes unbearable psychic pain or anxiety, ranging from the shattering, devastating experiences of child abuse so prominent in the literature today to the more "cumulative traumas" of many emotionally impoverished childhoods. These experiences include the more acute deprivations of infancy described by D.W. Winnicott as "primitive agonies," the experience of which is "unthinkable." The distinguishing feature of such trauma is what Heinz Kohut called "disintegration anxiety," an unnameable dread associated with the threatened dissolution of a coherent self.

To experience such anxiety threatens the annihilation of the human personality, the destruction of the personal spirit, which must be avoided at all costs. Because such trauma may occur in early infancy before a coherent ego is formed, archaic defensive operations come into play to prevent the "unthinkable" from being experienced.

Now what does it mean to say that archaic defenses prevent something from being experienced? In the early days of psychoanalysis we would have said that the incompatible drive or idea was repressed, made "unconscious." It was kept unconscious by defenses of the ego, creating "horizontal splits" in the psyche. That was before we knew much about pre-verbal levels of anxiety or pre-ego levels of defense. Since the work of Melanie Klein, Ronald Fairbairn, Winnicott, and W. R. Bion, we realize that early childhood trauma creates "disintegration" or "annihilation" anxiety or, following Erich Neumann, "mythological levels" of anxiety. Such anxiety, flooding the fragmentary, infantile ego, requires what Leopold Stein originally called "defenses of the Self" to distinguish them from ego-defenses. The idea of defenses organized by the primal Self, prior to ego-consolidation, was applied further by Fordham (1974) and by Proner (1986). My object here is to elaborate this promising idea, as it applies to trauma.

Defenses of the Self are archaic and typical: archetypal defenses. They constitute the psyche's effort to protect the immature ego from disintegrative levels of anxiety that might destroy the essential personal spirit of the individual. This spirit is the mysterious essence of animation in the personality: what Winnicott called the secret "true self" and what Jung, wishing to underscore its transpersonal origins, called the Self (both light and dark), the indestructible center and totality of human personality. The incarnation of this essence of individuality must never be violated even if destroying the host personality (suicide) is necessary or, in less severe cases, driving the spirit out of the mind/body unity.

People who have suffered early trauma have had their hearts broken by unbearable psychic pain. They may go on living outwardly "normal" lives, but something in them has been broken; their spirit has left them. Often they tell us this. They have resigned themselves to a kind of un-alive, un-dead existence. They remember that "everything changed" after a certain childhood event – a major move, a parental divorce, or a serious illness. These courageous patients have taken over their own self-care – or, more precisely, the archetypal world has taken over this care – because a facilitating human environment has broken down.

Archetypal defenses accomplish this self-care by the dismembering of experience, which allows living to go on, but "dis-spirited living" – in compartments, separated by what we now call "vertical splits." The normally integrated components of experience include both somatic and mental elements: affects and sensations in the body; thoughts, images and cognitive mechanisms in the mind. Meaningful experience requires that bodily excitations, including archaic affects, be given mental representation so that eventually they can reach verbal expression. With splitting, unbearable infantile affects and sensations from the body are not permitted to acquire symbolic mental representation but are retained in the somatic unconscious in the disintegrated form that Bion (1967) called "beta" elements. The result is psychosomatic illness or what McDougal (1985) referred to as alexithymia – patients who have no words for feelings and who, as a result, are "dis-affected" or, in the language of the current discussion, "dis-spirited."

The Diabolic Figure and His/Her Activities

As analysis with early trauma patients proceeds, a remarkable process unfolds in which the archetypal defense personifies itself in dreams. This process seems to occur only after a containing field of safety has been established. Dreams in which the archetypal defense appears usually follow moments in the transference where elements in the early vulnerability and its accompanying anxiety are repeated. In the dreams of trauma patients I have seen, the diabolic side of the trickster-figure has performed the following acts: cut the dreamer's head off with an axe, brutally raped the dreamer, petrified the dreamer's pet animals, buried a child alive, seduced the patient into performing sado-masochistic sexual favors, trapped the dream ego in a concentration camp, tortured a patient by breaking his knees in three places, shot a beautiful woman in the face with a shotgun, and a variety of other destructive acts, the purpose of which seems to be to drive the patient's terrified dream-ego into a state of horror, anxiety and despair.

How do we understand this phenomenon? It is bad enough that our hapless patient suffered unbearable real trauma in early childhood. Now the psyche seems to perpetuate this trauma in unconscious fantasy, flooding the patient with continued anxiety, tension and dread – even in sleep. When I first began to encounter this persecutory figure, I thought I was witnessing the attacks of what Jung would have called the negative animus. But the figure was not always male, not always contrasexual to the dreamer and could appear in animal form. If anything, our diabolic figure appeared to fit best with Jung's description of the archetypal shadow. But this also was problematic, because on rare occasions in analysis, after an extended healing process, the previously malevolent figure would change its countenance in dreams and present a more benevolent protective side. It then appeared that in some primitive fashion this very same figure was "trying" with great forethought, to protect some traumatized remainder of the patient's true self from further violation – sometimes to soothe, and if necessary anesthetize, this enfeebled childhood spirit with alcohol or drugs, in order to protect it against unbearable pain.

These reflections and clinical experiences with our diabolic introject forced me to recognize that I was dealing here with a kind of emissary of the original Godhead or Self which appeared to have taken over the care of the traumatized patient's inner world in the absence of adequate ego mediation. This figure seemed to have at its disposal all the primitive aggression that should have been available for adaptation but which, because of early trauma, was directed back into the inner world. Paradoxically, the figure seemed also to embody a primitive, protective form of "love" and was thus a "duplex" imago – mercurial in nature – representing both libido and aggression, Eros and Ares, fusion and splitting, linking and what Bion called "attacks against linking."

Jung pointed to the Old Testament Yahweh as precisely such a figure, saying that Yahweh is "both a persecutor and a helper" (CW11, par. 567) and describing how the antinomies in God are gradually integrated through Job's lonely suffering. But Job was not in analysis, and even Jung's inspired interpretation of the poem leaves us with very little understanding of the processes through which the ambiguous Yahweh-Self becomes integrated in the life of the individual. Another favorite "*complexio oppositorum*" of Jung's was Mercurius Duplex; here we have a figure whose dynamic energies are "closer" to the processes of transformation that go on in depth psychotherapy.

Mercurius Duplex as Archetypal Defense

For Jung, Mercurius was a favorite example of the Spirit archetype, hence his designation "Spirit Mercurius." He was the essential animating spirit of alchemy's transformative procedures: the winged, soaring one of the alchemical opus. If the bird of Hermes escaped the retort, the whole alchemical process had to be started all over again. As Jung pointed out, every experienced alchemist took great precautions to avoid this tragic result, "sealing his bottle with magic signs and setting it for a very long time over the lowest fire, so that he who is within may not fly out" (CW13, par. 250). The dreaded escape of Mercurius from the alchemical retort is analogous to what happens when early trauma interrupts the normal process of individuation: The animating personal spirit escapes the mind/body container. It cannot remain embodied – or "gradually incarnate" in the mysterious process that Winnicott called "personalization" or "indwelling." Here we confront a paradox: The archetypal force responsible for driving the mercurial personal spirit out of the body following trauma is the diabolic aspect of the spirit archetype itself, Mercurius Duplex.

Once he has occupied the patient's mind, our black magician functions as an archetypal defense, an inner system of self-care. Usually the mediating spirit of transformation, Mercurius now becomes a non-mediating force, interrupting the normal flow of libido between self and world outwardly and between affect and image inwardly, mistaking every new opportunity for growth as a possible threat and dissociating the mind accordingly. Once the archaic defense is established, there is a further erosion of affect-tolerance and an attack on any perceptions that risk arousing emotion or introducing disintegration anxiety. The spirit cannot re-enter the body/mind unity. This is true "auto-immune disease" of the psyche.

We don't usually think of the Spirit Mercurius as diabolic, preferring to see him as the winged spirit, the messenger of the gods. But Jung has no such rosy picture of him. On his dark side he represents the chthonic spirit. He is associated with the female serpent-daemon Lilith and with the dissolving spirit of Saturn which

destroys everything. As the transitional god presiding at all boundaries, borders and threshold crossings, he is the great mediator, the
link, gluing the opposites together, but in his "retrograde" function
he can break the connections he creates. Then he becomes the
splitter, an attacker of linking, the "cutter." As Jung said, "if
Mercurius is not exactly the Evil One himself, he at least contains
him" (CW13, par. 276).

"Big Nurse and the Baby"

Some years ago, a young female therapist I was supervising
called me for a special consultation. A young female patient,
familiar to us both from prior supervisory sessions because of her
amazing resistance to the psychotherapy process, was having a kind
of "breakthrough," my supervisee said. But accompanying this
breakthrough there was a dream that disturbed both her and the
patient.

The patient in question, who was then a 23-year-old, exception-
ally beautiful, highly narcissistic woman, showed all the aspects of
early childhood trauma that leads to an inner world menaced by
dissociative defenses. Early incest with her own alcoholic father was
paired with both emotional and physical neglect from her depressed
mother. The patient had held herself together through this traumatic
childhood by identifying with a tough counter-dependent persona or
false self. A serious drug problem began at the age of 14 and almost
led to her death.

Several years later she began psychotherapy. The incident I am
reporting occurred two years into her process. For the first two years
there was great resistance – many missed appointments, late appearances and other manipulations testing the reliability of the therapeutic container. Slowly she had begun to trust her therapist and to feel
some modicum of safety. Then came the breakthrough session my
supervisee was concerned about. In recent weeks, the patient had
begun to report with great awkwardness and shame that she had
"feelings" about her therapist. She was unable to talk about this any
further and these feelings of emerging dependency and "love" were
followed by the usual counter-dependent anger, cynicism and
impenetrability. During the session in question, the patient had been
unusually vulnerable in her presentation of these new "feelings" and
even cried a bit. The next session she canceled. When contact was

Donald E. Kalsched

re-established the patient reported a traumatic dream from the night before her canceled session.

> *I am in a hospital room with a baby. I am about 14. The baby is screaming and crying and close to dying. I don't know what to do. I don't feel I can "look" at the baby because I'll disintegrate. A big nurse who has been standing in the doorway watching all this comes in (she's really huge!) She starts to give the baby injections in the stomach. I realize she is trying to kill the baby but no-one will believe me. The nurse says that the baby will be OK if it pees, but I know that she is lying and means to kill the baby. I'm helpless to do anything. I wake up crying.*

In associating to this dream, the patient thought that she herself was the baby. But then the question became, who was the big nurse? Was this a transference image of the therapist? My supervisee had been reading Langs (1976) about "therapeutic misalliances" and had to ask herself if perhaps she harbored phallic sadistic feelings toward her patient. But she was aware only of mild irritation over the canceled appointments and seemed fully conscious of this. Also, none of the patient's associations supported this equation of the big nurse with the therapist. In fact, the problem seemed to be that the patient was beginning for the first time to trust the therapist as a "good" outer object and this was the scary part. She was beginning to feel dependent feelings (the baby) but was "afraid to look" at them, lest she be flooded with disintegration anxiety.

From a Jungian standpoint, the big nurse is a threshold figure of "huge" proportions, suggesting something titanic, larger than life or archetypal. We also note that she is duplicitous – a trickster. She is lying about her true intentions in order to make herself seem benign. Or is it possible that her very "killing" of the baby has a benign rationale that we do not understand. She gives injections in the stomach. Vaccine injections for rabies (madness) are given there. Is it possible then that she is "trying" to quell the madness of this screaming infant by "killing" it as a representative of infantile dependency. Killing in the psyche would be equivalent to total dissociation. As if to support this hypothesis, we note that the patient is 14 in her dream – the age at which she began to abuse drugs, that is, anesthetize herself against feeling.

The big nurse seems to personify an archetypal self-care system: a superordinate duplex survival-Self-figure whose intended healing, integrating functions have been pressed into the service of the psyche's dissociation and hence survival-in-pieces. This survival-

Self has the patient's unmet infantile needs as its "client." The screaming infant represents the re-emergence of dependent longings within the transference which are starting to embody as genuine affect – longings of this woman's dissociated spirit that are beginning to be experienced as grief. This dangerous new development threatens the survival-Self with a possible integration of previously dissociated experience, a "re-membering" and embodiment of early infantile longing which (we must imagine) was traumatically injured, ushering in disintegration anxiety. Thus each new opportunity for the ego's healing with a real object represents the danger of re-traumatization to the survival-Self, the big nurse. "She" will not share her care-giving functions with the therapist and insists that the dependency feelings emerging in the patient stay dissociated (killed).

If we take the foregoing analysis seriously, we must admit that trauma itself does not split the psyche. Rather, an archetypal inner figure occasioned by the trauma does the splitting. And this figure is much more than just an "introjection of the outer perpetrator," as writers on trauma commonly allege. A "traumatogenic" imago haunts the psyches of traumatized people: an imago that makes it very difficult to decide whether child abuse is an historic event or something going on continually in the inner world and often leading to "retraumatization" in the outer world. It is not enough, for us as analysts, to condemn trauma and its terrible effects on the psyches of innocent victims. No doubt actual child abuse, ritual abuse, and incest are much more common crimes against children than we ever thought possible. But we should keep in mind there is also a sadistic, abusing agency in the psyche, and one that commits incest. As Jung himself noted in 1912, "Fantasies can be just as traumatic in their effects as real traumata" (CW4, par. 217).

When the Spirit Returns to the Body

A final case illustration of the positive side of our diabolic Mercurius as he seems to supervise a process of the spirit's return to the body shows the trickster in his positive, integrative role. My patient was a middle-aged woman who had lived in poverty most of her younger years. The family was evicted from each trailer park or motel; the mother was drunk most of the time. Her father was off at war until she was two and, when he returned, brought warfare into the house in the form of alcoholic rages and beatings of the mother.

My patient was in constant fear but she tried as best she could to hold things together – to care for the other children – to give them the childhood she was losing as the years went by. She became the little mother of the family: cooking the meals, making the beds, dragging the mother out of bars. At some point in this process, around the age of four or five, this valiant little girl who was later my patient, simply gave up. Her spirit just left. All the color went out of her life. The rest of her childhood, she said, was experienced in black and white.

Prior to her therapy with me, this patient had gone to a workshop where she did a kind of active imagination; the image she had was part of her motivation for therapy. In her vision,

> a male guide came and took her into a temple. Deep inside this stone sanctuary, in a darkened room, was a female child lying on a kind of altar. But the child was stone. Slowly, as my patient stayed with her, the child came to life. She opened her hand; inside was a star. The star sparkled, beautiful and golden, but then slowly it took the shape of a sheriff's badge and the vision ended.

My patient's association to the sheriff's badge was an important link to the dream that I will cite. During this time she worked at an adoption agency and was often involved in placement proceedings. At her agency, whenever a birth-mother gave up her child for adoption, the local sheriff would serve papers, making it official that the mother was giving up all rights to the child. My patient always hated this procedure and felt it was adding insult to injury for the birth mother.

This all came out later. At the time she had the vision, this woman knew that the girl child in the temple was also herself. It made sense to her that the child was stone, because the woman felt frozen in her body, split off from her emotions and her sexuality, deeply depressed.

In her subsequent therapy with me, after many sessions spent exploring her early life and trauma history, there emerged an experience of trauma in the transference. This had to do with her rage and grief that the "love" she felt for her analyst could not be lived out in the "real" world and that some of the mutuality she had imagined in our relationship was illusory. This led to a back and forth, withdrawal and re-connection cycle in the sessions which, in retrospect, I see as the gradual transformation of her mercurial defense. Her demon would whisper "See, I told you so – he doesn't care; you're just another case – and he would pull her out of relationship to me. Then, after her angry withdrawal, we would somehow restore the feeling connection and the work could proceed.

During this difficult process of "grief work," something began to happen that I can only describe as her spirit returning to her body. The dream I have mentioned gave us both an image of when, in childhood, her spirit had left. Ironically, her spirit's departure was only "possible to be dreamed" when conditions were safe for it to return. Her dream was set in the context of her adoption agency work:

I am in a house where a little girl apparently lives and all kinds of lawyers are present. A case is being developed to get this little girl out of a traumatic environment with her parents by terminating parental rights. The head lawyer is drawing a chart on the wall showing how the child gets anxious whenever the father or mother is present. Nearby is the child's grandmother; she loves the child intensely and is there for her protection from the mother and father. I am the case-worker in this situation. I see that the grandmother will give the child up, but is not letting on how terrible she feels. She has to be tough and unfeeling to create the appearance that there is no feeling for this child in this family, because she wants the head lawyer to get this child out. I take the grandmother outside and hold her very tightly in a full body hug, in order to draw out her feelings. We both start to cry. I know she must feel all of her grief. She's willing to lose this little girl because she knows it's the only way to save the child.

Then I look up and I see the little girl looking down from an upper window and at this point I realize the child is also me. I/she am about four or five years old. I motion for her to come down and as she does this I realize she's not a real child, but a kind of ghost-child. She's all ethereal and sort of floats down to us. I put her in her grandmother's arms so she can feel all the love we have for her as she is released into safety.

As my patient reported this dream she felt an enormous sadness but didn't know why. Following a long silence, I said to her simply that I thought this dream was about what happened to her when she was four or five: that she could no longer live as a whole person then and that a part of her had to be "released" into safety. I said that this had been a terrible loss – one she had been unable to grieve until now, and that she could have this dream now because, paradoxically, after our work together, this child was returning to her body.

She was now strong enough to feel her loss and let it mean something.

This interpretation made sense to her and brought up still more affect which continued for the rest of the hour. This experience is an example of how, when the psyche is ready, a dream can bring together affect and image to create meaning which in turn makes further suffering possible – this time meaningful suffering – that can be incorporated in the deep narrative history of an individual's life.

My understanding of this dream and the prior vision of the stone child is that at the age of four or five, when the little girl had her hopes for life broken and gave up her spirit, something in the psyche I have described as the archetypal mercurial defense was there to catch it. This figure, I propose, turned this child into stone and put a star in her hand – a star that symbolized both its imperishable, irreplaceable essence and, as sheriff's badge, the "sign" that this child's spirit had been given up "officially."

The dream pictures the moment of her spirit's release. The head lawyer and the grandmother I interpret as differing aspects of her mercurial-guardian self-care system. Together, they are "tricking" the family. The head lawyer and grandmother are collaborating to make sure the spirit-child will be released into safety and the patient, now having descended into her body, makes sure this child feels loved as she is "released." The "full-body hug" bespeaks the patient's new-found embodiment.

We can think of this moment also as the release of the Spirit Mercurius from his defensive functions, for his real work as a psychopomp and mediator of what alchemy calls the "greater *coniunctio.*" At least this is one way to envision what my patient and I experienced as a remarkable deepening of the work at this time. Over the following weeks, her dreams started to cohere around a particular telos or direction, the sessions felt more mutual and collaborative, everything slowed down and there was a sense of gratitude for the meaning of the work.

These grace-like experiences, I propose, are those in congress with the same shimmering God whose diabolic shadow we have been wrestling with all along. Now God turns an other face and blesses the patient and our efforts with a light that comes from all this darkness, like Lucifer's light, the *lumen naturae*, the light of nature itself. Here is the transcendent function, the capacity for imagination restored, the renewed possibility of a symbolic life.

We encounter here a supreme irony in our work with the psyche. The self-same powers that seemed so set on undermining our therapeutic efforts – ostensibly devoted to death, dismemberment and annihilation of consciousness – are the very reservoir from which new life, fuller integration and true enlightenment derive, if they are humanized through the transformative process of "good enough" analysis. We come closer here to understanding the devil's self-description in *Faust*. When asked "Who are you then?" the devil responds:

> *Part of that Power which would*
> *the Evil ever do, and ever does the Good.*

References

Fordham, M. (1974). Defenses to the self. *Journal of Analytical Psychology*, *19*-2, 192-199.

Proner, B. (1986). Defenses of the self and envy of oneself. *Journal of Analytical Psychology*, *31*-3, 275-279.

Where Man's Shadow Falls

Reflections on Jung and Women

Giovanna Carlo
Rome, Italy
Italian Center for Analytical Psychology

It is a foregone conclusion among the initiated that men understand nothing of women's psychology as it actually is, but it is astonishing to find that women do not know themselves.

C.G. Jung

In this epigraph, Jung deplored the scant consciousness that women have of themselves. It was a recurring theme, both in his letters and in his seminars during the 1930s. Why have women, to whom Jung attributed a special talent for introspection, used it to fathom the psychology of the men in their lives, more than to untangle the knotty problems of their inner world? The most immediate and traditional answer is that women are guided by the eros principle and pay close attention to whatever fosters their relationships. But as we well know, human beings cannot overcome their conflicts with others if they have not first found some peace within themselves.

Projecting the Self onto a person of the opposite sex, in the view of analytical psychology, reveals a still-primitive phase of one's individuation process. Even so, the worst sort of romantic love still torments the bodies and souls of many women, without their being able to work symbolically for spiritual awakening. I refer to the passion that kills the joyous and fertile aspects of a relationship and transforms it into the cult of a pitiless divinity who demands martyrdom as the eventual outcome. That "ghostly lover" (Harding, 1933/1969) still claims his victims 60 years later from apparently adjusted and serene wives, successful professional women and even adolescent girls who seem much less conventional in regard to traditional women's roles.

When Jung was a child he had already perceived his "ties to the infinite" through those natural elements outside himself: water, fire and the stone he sat on in the garden of his home. At the age of nine, however, he was not even aware of the changes in his mother's body as she expected another child. It is probable that if Jung's sister had left us written evidence of her own precocious intuition of Being, she would have included her mother's body, with which she – like any girl – would have identified. The correspondence of Body-House-Cosmos constitutes a kind of religious experience that, according to religious historian Mircea Eliade, has belonged to all of humanity in not so remote times.

In the first half of a woman's life nature has already reminded her frequently that the biological destiny of the species follows its own ways, transcending her ego's choices. Yet this first experience of the Self, in which the ego's consciousness feels itself to be an object, rather than the subject, is experienced in the body. (This also happens to men, although in a much less pointed fashion.) The experience finds no designation or symbolization in patriarchal western culture. Rather, it is neglected, denied, forgotten, technicalized by medical science and covered up by the silence and the shame of the current moral codes.

The Christian mythology of the West does not deny either room or importance to women's roles. On the contrary, compared to the social position that women held in Greek and Roman culture, Christian myths have conspicuously revalued women. Yet ignoring the role of the body, as the germ of future spiritual experiences, has asked a woman to deny her primordial identity and to be transformed into a genderless human being. She has been lacerated in the conflict between her physical experience, symbolically considered to be a worthless burden, and a spiritual tension that, in order to be expressed, demands negating the palpable unfolding of life itself.

It is significant that, when he was directly studying a feminine individuation process (VS), Jung felt the need to turn to oriental philosophy and the transfiguration of the body as it has been described in the Tantric tradition of Kundalini yoga.

These seminars (1930 to 1934) are important for their numerous reflections on women's psychology. Jung states that, on a symbolic level, the image of the divine form produced by a woman's psyche can be nothing but a feminine figure – as in a man's case, the personification is always masculine. The paradoxical nature of the Self and its bipolarity renders it viable as a type of impersonal condition on the one hand and, on the other, as a full consciousness of its own specific nature. Consequently, gender identity – even on this level – is a fact that cannot be discarded. Jung (VS) writes,

> *It is quite indifferent to the spirit of nature whether you are a man or a woman; what you do does not matter. Yet, of course, in a certain sense it matters very much, since it is all done on the command of that figure that says in the same breath: "Go into the world, do not go into the world."* (p. 456)

If the images of light, as well as those of darkness, are expressed in female figures during a woman's individuation process, it must be said also that our traditional books of mythology, theology and psychology are meager on this point. The problem is of no small concern. It is precisely because the Self is a category that is not grasped immediately on the conceptual plane that its symbolic representation has such a marked influence on our chances of living it and remembering it as a significant experience. I do not mean that no woman has experienced and recorded her own individuation process. Yet it is for just this structural insufficiency of our symbolic code that women's testimony is hardly able to become an integral part of our therapeutic, psychological, and academic contemporary culture.

Researching cultures other than our own is important here. In some of those mythic tales the heroine does not wait to be saved by a hero, and does not suffer for love alone. Fathers and brothers are fought and loved, but the heroine does not wait for their response in order to be situated existentially either in regard to herself or to other women. An example of this is the Sumerian myth of Inanna, which Perera (1981) has brought to the attention of psychologists.

Not only fathers, but also mothers have passed on the only symbolic code they have known: the patriarchal one in which it appears natural that women are defined by a masculine vision of reality. With love, but also with a kind of deaf rancor, we women have attempted to adapt ourselves to the images of femininity that have been produced essentially by men. It is perhaps for this reason that, as Polly Young-Eisendrath (1986) wrote, "I have yet to encounter an adult woman who did not evaluate herself in some highly convincing way as uniquely deficient or inadequate" (cited in Wehr, 1987).

All the most serious and psychologically significant research in the feminist field agrees on the necessity of finding new linguistic categories. Until now the symbolic void has forced women to define themselves negatively, in respect to what they are not, and what they do not feel, rather than defining themselves around what they are and want to become. On the European scene, Irigaray (1986), in her essential essay on the medieval myth of the serpent-woman Melusina, has declared courageously that women's spiritual evolution has been arrested by the absence of a divine female model of inspiration. This, Irigaray affirms, has burdened the spiritual growth of all humankind. I am thinking of such American women theologians as Ruether (1985); the new "witches," in the eyes of the ecclesiastical hierarchy, are attempting a feminine hermeneutics of sacred texts. I am thinking as well about writers such as Heilbrun (1988) who, in the struggle to define new expressive styles, draw disapproval, or dismissal, from newspapers and universities.

I am thinking also of von Franz (1983), of the wholehearted simplicity that she has in her work as an analyst and teacher. She wrote:

The incarnation of God in Christ was felt to be a momentous, collective religious experience. In the case of the ancient mother-goddess, however, the desire to incarnate in a human daughter was never fulfilled. In practice this means that since woman's form was not recognized, neither was the woman. (pp. 30-31)

The freedom and originality of Jung's thought are extraordinary, when we consider the spirit of the times in which he lived as a man and as a scholar of psychiatry. We must not forget that, when Jung was a medical student, the university texts were compiled mostly by positivists who described women's minds and bodies, without ever having closely observed even their wives. When empirical data failed to confirm their theoretical descriptions, they did not hesitate to borrow poetical expressions from romantic literature testifying to the "unfathomable mystery of the eternal feminine."

In this respect women are probably a little more advanced than their male companions. They are more used to listening to and reading, with all due attention, what the most brilliant male minds have produced over the centuries, if only in school. The reverse cannot be said for the majority of our male colleagues. They often avoid women's studies with the same aplomb and feelings of respectful discretion that nineteenth century gentlemen felt in avoiding a lady's private chambers. Thus, feminist psychological studies meet the same fate of marginality that has always characterized Jung's works. Even now many psychoanalysts and psychotherapists completely ignore Jung's writings without feeling that there is a lacuna in their educational background or that their therapeutic skills are less than valid.

In Jungian works, one frequently finds a methodologically illegitimate superimposition of the anima archetype, as experienced in a man's mind and body, and the feminine dimension as it empirically corresponds to a woman's body and consciousness. Jung himself has repeatedly cautioned against sliding from one dimension to another. Even though, as human beings, we well understand his tripping over his own shadow; as scholars we cannot pardon it.

Jung's shadow can be found in the reprimands voiced by eminent theologians against his psychology of the divine. Buber (1952), for example, considered it to be a religion of "purely psychic immanence." In Buber's words, by exclusively defining the image of God as an archetype of the collective unconscious, Jung risked undervaluing transcendence, which has always been an important symbol of humanity's religious heritage.

Maffei (1987) noted that a strong need to ascribe significance to every psychological experience reverberates throughout the Jung's works. It is a sort of *horror vacui* (terror of the void) that does not allow one to confront completely the dark night of the soul. Jung had faced it, nonetheless, with utmost psychological courage, during the dark years following his break from Freud.

Perhaps it is for this reason that Jung tended to project onto feminine figures a natural antidote to that dramatic sense of psychological solitude. At times these were archetypes, at other times flesh and blood women. He described those women who were not contaminated with a negative animus as being gifted with a wise and simple love of life. This gift is a species of a priori eros that is more credible as the destination of an arduous journey toward psychological maturity than as innate in a feminine ego. From the diary Esther Harding kept of her encounters with Jung we know that, "To go in search of his anima a man must adopt a *feminine* attitude, while for a woman to struggle against the animus is sufficient; that is whatever is *male* in herself," (McGuire & Hull, 1977, pp. 322-23). If Jung meant by this that a woman, in order to mature, must free herself of that self-hating internal saboteur – that misogynous personage who uncritically adopts the paradigms of the patriarchal culture introjected since infancy – I share his opinion. I cannot maintain, however, that the psychological characteristics of a woman's masculine dimension can be reduced to these historical elements. If it were so, we should have to imagine a parthenogenesis of feminine consciousness.

It is surprising that Jung, notwithstanding the extraordinary experience gained during more than 50 years of contact with human suffering, could still have written, in a letter addressed to Mary Bancroft,

A man's helplessness can be real; a woman's is one of her best stunts. As she is by birth and sex on better terms with nature, she is never quite helpless as long as there is no man in the vicinity. (Let-2, p. 270)

After having witnessed the pain and existential angst of many women patients, could we assent to this statement? Can we therefore believe that the *felix culpa* of Eve resulted only in Adam's being exiled?

Perhaps the moment has been reached for women to perform that sacrifice which can contribute so much to humanity's spiritual growth: renouncing the pretense of being goddesses. To conquer men's admiration and approval, we let them believe that the numinous capacity to give biological life brings with it the possibility of participating in its highest and most spiritual meaning.

Recalling the well-known sense of humor of the head of our school, I conclude with a jest. A young woman psychologist once asked me if Jung's writings were still relevant for a woman. I laughingly answered, "Of course, above all when not speaking about women." For Jung, as for the poet T.S. Eliot, the truth,

> *... is the only the unattended*
> *Moment, the moment in and out of time,*
> *The distraction fit, lost in a shaft of sunlight ...*

Translated by Peter Gardner

Laura Cervellati Telmon
Rome, Italy
Italian Association for the
Study of Analytical Psychology

A wide range of literature has been published on women, but the relationship of the feminine psyche and its shadow needs further exploration. This exploration cannot be done in isolation, since the individual develops in a complex intermingling of personal factors with other conditions, both internal and external. Talking about woman and her shadow once again is meaningful only if we relate it to those individual and collective themes in which she is participating at this particular time.

Men and women have had to face huge, transforming events this century. The extraordinary development of science – and its technical by-products – has forced us all to deal with social and political situations that have subverted traditional values, habits and structures. From different angles, according to their gender and individuality, men and women have found themselves disoriented and helpless before the external world and in understanding interior processes.

It is revealing that one of the first nosographical expositions of the psychoanalytic movement was Freud's publication, between 1882 and 1885, of five cases of hysteria in female patients. After that, Freud would adopt as his the dogmatic words, "Anatomy is destiny." He concluded in 1937, during the last period of his speculation regarding female sexuality:

> *The war between sexes is not the only factor responsible for neurotic conflicts. ... Through penis desire and virile protest, after having crossed all the stratifications, we reached the basic cornerstone, the end of our activity. ... In the end, the refusal of femininity cannot be anything but a biological factor: the great enigma of sexuality.* (SE23, p. 212, Italian edition)

In addition, as Hillman (1972) writes, the early Jung "who was particularly open to a new vision of the conscience," also describes "a high degree of conscience ... (which) is characterised by an increased awareness, by a predominance of direct volitive character and by an almost complete lack of instinctive determinants" (p. 259). Indeed, Jung wrote:

These images go back to the sun god Apollo. ... It is probably no accident that the two most important discoveries which distinguish man from all other living beings, namely speech and the use of fire, should have a common psychic element. Both are products of psychic energy. ... In Sanskrit ... the word "tejas" [means ... cutting edge, fire ... beauty ... strength ... passion dignity, semen.] (CW5, par. 237)

Male superiority, in which the fixity of rules and sexuality of Apollo's character were coordinated, could not but correspond to the splitting, removal and projection on the other polarity.

Despite the fact that dampness was attributed to the feminine as an important value with its own creative potential, it remained an inferior, shadow quality. It was only later with Jung and the contribution of the Jungian school, that many aspects of the feminine psyche have found recognition and placement.

Although many Jungian authors have written about women, I mention only Jung's 1927 work, "Woman in Europe" in which he writes, "Woman begins where man's shadow falls" (CW10, par. 236). This sentence recognizes the presence and interpretive possibilities of the feminine archetype, to whose images a great part of Jung's work would be devoted.

The emergence of an archetype is never fortuitous. It is nurtured over many years of incubation and entails – in both the collective life and its meeting with the individual – structured resistances and conflicts, before becoming personal and historical conscience. With its biological, instinctive and psychic energy and its push of original necessity, it represents a decisive risk to constituted order as well as to those individuals who find themselves contacting it in order to "create a soul."

Woman has suffered from man's projection on her, shaped by a masochistic acceptance of power and the predominant strength of male dominion. She has identified herself in that historical and social conscience and in logos, which were not the elaboration of her own experience but of opinion and a shadow as much as a collective conscience. Thus, she was allowed to share the supremacy of reason, and of a power that, if not directly expressed in social extraversion, showed its introverted intensity in the world of the family, compensating fears and frustrations.

In accepting the undisputed priority of the role of the mother, which is fixed in canon and attitudes, woman was invested with unlimited and numinous power. This power compensated for the diminutions that obliged her – in a masochistic means of escape – to neglect whatever potential the male dominion did not recognize, both in the image of inferiority – idealistically imposed and "scientifically proven" – but in violent experimentation on her body and sexuality. In this way, Eve, the mobile and curious maid "puella," was led by her devil toward the tree of knowledge in order to cross – together with Adam – the threshold of a world without time toward the world of history, conflict, life and death. In the resulting shadow she became a symbol of guilt and, thus, an epitomization of the body and evil.

The symbol of this transformation had to be redeemed by Mary and alchemically sublimated in Sofia, even though Augustine identified this "happy" guilt as an element of limitation, of discrimination and contact between the world of being and the condition of the ego.

In the fairy tales told to her children, the young woman becomes a shadow, a source of fear and nightmares. She often escapes into the woods from the court of castles of a hostile world. This mythical figure of the witch is restless, bent over herbs, filters and nocturnal, shadowy mysteries of nature.

In the crisis of the contemporary world, men and women are both displaced. They feel inadequate before the emptiness of conscience, of ideological uncertainty. Yet they have different incapacities regarding the finding of new vectors for transformation, since the models on which patriarchal civilization built its order are inadequate and dangerous.

Behind the solar hero, carrier of the conscience, the contemporary man now finds himself thinking about the instincts upon which he acted, removing aspects of the shadow and attributing to the name of conscience sublimations of violent impulses. The woman also feels this, but somehow knows that her guilt is deeper and more archaic. The female knows that she lacks a specific elaboration of her essence and, in respect of the supremacy of logos, she moves – uncertainly – in conflict and dramatic confrontation with herself. This is the inevitable labor toward the birth of her consciousness.

In this crisis of passage the woman, gripped by anguish and fear and caught between external forces and internal requests, has found the first expressions of her rebellion in protest and anger. She has opened new spaces with this combative animus, re-balanced old injustices and opened new possibilities for the feminine.

However, the animus – with its libidinal push – is not yet conscious. Acted out by the unconscious and not in a dialectical position with it, the animus does not always take the shadow into account. Instead it makes use of a secondary paternal identification and runs the risk of using a structured – but not structuring – aggression. Thus, it compensates for a deeper and denied insecurity and masochism.

Now, in the disintegration of the endured – or exploited – identification of the patriarchal world and in the search for a specific existential reality, the phases of transformation are more dramatic and painful for the woman. Hers is not the equivalent of the male process in which the detachment from the mother, fraught with difficulty and characterized by grief, has taken place; it gives a man recognition of his diversity and puts him ahead in the position of the Other, a preliminary and necessary condition for the process of selection and development; that is to say, of conscience. In the same transition, the woman does not have the equivalent support to help her overcome the anguish of a greater betrayal, and to feel naturally different from the maternal figure.

For the daughter, detachment from the mother means struggling not only against the mother but – in preparing herself for separation – struggling against herself, denying her natural identity, disowning affinities and fearing identities. According to Jung (CW9-I), the leitmotif of this complex is, "Anything, so long as it is not like Mother!" (par. 170): refusing the primary love, living with fear and repulsion of the body, of contact "with that human being who was our mother" (par. 172). The new in us only seems to be able to build itself through guilt and betrayal, projecting on her the most obscure, lacerating and terrible forms of the eternal image of archetypes.

In the face of the cruel, cynical, clinical definition of the schizophrenic mother, we listen to the sufferings not only of daughters during hours of analysis, but also of mothers, rent by the most opposite feelings, knowing how much anguish and cost is entailed in the relationship between such close feminine realities.

In the fixity of the roles which she has accepted for millennia, woman also tried to remove conflicts that were adjusted or minimized by such roles. She accepted as natural a certain passivity and "laziness" that Jung interprets as an incestuous and deathlike regression. We find this passivity in the most serious depressions without an object and, in psychosis, the bearer of a silent death wish. At the same time, the woman naturally knows the rhythms of her physiology. Menstruation, the central fact of her biological sexuality, is the only thing, according to Claude Levi-Strauss that can still link us to nature.

Women are closer to the alternation of life and death. It is sufficient to think about how high the death rate has been, even in recent times, from giving birth – both for mother and child – and how it is sometimes necessary to opt for saving the life of one or the other. Consequently, shadows are present in pregnancies and post-partum depression. Each woman is assumed to be the trustee and bearer of an energy and ambivalent power. A woman's fear of instincts becomes overwhelming: developing into fantasies of omnipotence; envy toward children, men and novelty; fixed in the more archaic rites of the Great Mother.

It is the misogyny of a woman toward women that makes her look at her sister with diffidence and hostility. It is the negation of herself that so many times in the past – although now less frequently, especially in adolescents – made her confess with bitterness that: "I did not want to be a woman, I do not like being a woman."

Eluding the struggle with the shadow – allowing it to occupy our psychic space – means avoiding the risk of being able to discern, separate the forms, surrender to the seducing and absorbing charm of the shadow that is found in serious depression. It also means risking that possibility of transformation for which, after the with-drawal of projections, the shadow can gather its primary and irreducible contents.

The necessary renunciation of an alienating identification puts the woman in direct contact with her shadow and at the same time with her potentiality. She is concentrated on listening to the deeper and archaic voices of her own nature, in order to elaborate them in a conscience which cannot be a hostile and aggressive opposition; that is to say, independent from the male logos. The conscience has a different and peculiar form, still indeterminate, mobile and perhaps as anxious as the vital tension can be in the necessary break of transformative processes.

Perhaps now the woman, recognizing only partial aspects, cannot yet say at which stage her conscience is. She probably knows clearly what she does not want and cannot accept; she knows she can accept only that in which instinct, feeling and thought can coexist harmoni-ously.

This is the moment of research, of recognition of something new that she feels to be possible but not yet integrateable with the Self. It is the beginning of a dialectic situation of unconsciousness, a self-world of images and basic experiences, in which the process of "creating a soul" takes place.

Abandoning fixed roles, no longer using a protective manner, exacts the price of regression and depression that many women are paying. They are driven by an obscure and unidentifiable force, which finds its expression in confused discomfort and sterile rebellions because it is too violent and immediate. In refusing many aspects of past security, the woman is trying to give shape to an "Eros" that is vital, reaching out toward the world and authentic relationships.

The witch has been seen as the forerunner of the French Revolution. Another revolution, now taking place before our eyes, is probably even bigger, as vast as the geographical and cultural areas involved. The contemporary world is collapsing, possibly in a definitive way. But there is a development of different awarenesses, apparently disconnected; some ephemeral, others perhaps carrying a movement that may be.either reversible or it may be inexorable. Woman knows that she is one of the essential parts of this movement and revolution; being so is a dynamic and dialectic component of a choice. The mysterious and religious world of matter, which renews itself in the infinite number of life forms, is the millenarian, phylogenetic and ontogenetic of feminine knowledge, which reconnects the self to a remote past and coagulates in the deeper vital sentiment of feminine awareness and dignity.

Woman is also going through the Faustian descent to the land of the Mothers, which contains potential experience and memory of a knowledge greater and never completely comprehensible to the ego and daily ego habits.

Translated from Italian by Nissau

References

Buber, M. (1952). Eclipse of God; Studies in the Relation between Religion and Philosophy. New York: Harper.

Harding, E. (1933/1970). *La Strada della Donna* (The Way of All Women). Roma: Astrolabio.

Heilbrun, C. (1988). *Scrivere la Vita di Una Donna* (Writing a Woman's Life). Milano: La Tartaruga.

Hillman, J. (1972). *Il Mito dell' Analisi* (The Myth of Analysis). Milano: Adelfi.

Irigaray, L. (1986). Donne Divine. In AA VV (Various Authors) *Melusina, Mito e Leggenda di una Donna Serpente*. Roma: Utopia.

Maffei, G. (1987). Brevi riflessioni su alcuni commenti di Jung relativi alla sofferenza, *Rivista di Psicologia Analitica*, n° 36.

McGuire, W. & Hull, R. F. C. (1977). *Jung Parla, Interviste e Incontri* (C.G. Jung Speaking; A. Bottini, trans.). Milano: Adelfi.

Perera, S. B. (1981). Italian *La Grande Dea* (Descent to the Goddess: A Way of Initiation for Women). Milano: Red.

Ruether, R (1985). *Womanguides: Reading Toward a Feminist Theology*. Boston: Beacon Press.

von Franz, M.-L. (1983). *Il Femminile nella Fiaba* (The Feminine in Fairy Tales). Torino: Boringhieri.

Wehr, D. (1978). *Jung and Feminism: Liberating Archetypes*. Boston: Beacon Press.

Young-Eisendrath, P. (1986). New contexts and conversations for female authority. Unpublished Manuscript. Colloquium for Social Philosophy, Pennsylvania State University.

The Soul of Underdevelopment

The Case of Brazil

Roberto Gambini
São Paulo, Brazil
Associate of Graduate Analytical Psychologists
(Zurich Institute)

A major question still open in analytical psychology is the relationship between individual and society, between psychology and history. Jung laid the foundations for a new understanding of this complex relationship when he stated that both individual and collective life are ruled by archetypes and by basically the same laws – since macrocosm and microcosm are the same. Society for him has never been an abstraction, but a real and concrete entity composed of real individuals connected to each other and to the whole. Jung had two vantage points: He perceived a certain historical configuration correlated with individual complexes; for example, his analysis off the Nazi period ("After the Catastrophe," CW10) and each person's shadow, and he could see in a single individual a particular expression of a larger whole. Jung never dissociated a person from genealogical and historical roots, nor from socio-cultural context.

There is still a good deal of work to be done, however, both in theory and in methodology, before we reach a greater cooperation between Jungian psychology and the human sciences. Also, our research tools need sharpening.

I come from a country that is part of that gigantic entity known as the Third World, encompassing perhaps 80 percent of humankind. I cannot ignore this fact, and I think Jungian psychology in a country such as mine should not have the same priorities and characteristics as in First World countries. Whenever I address this topic, I like to play with the idea of what Jung would be studying if he lived in a country such as mine. Certainly native Indian mythology, ethnology, history and geography, culture, religious symbolism, symbols of the soul, the collective unconscious of the masses, and above all: What does it mean to belong to the third team? This is not exactly what official psychology courses or analysts' training programs teach.

In addition to being a Brazilian with Italian grandparents, I have the good or bad luck of coming from the social sciences. For these reasons, it was inevitable that I chose as my subject, "The Soul of Underdevelopment."

It was exciting to study social sciences during the 1960s. We all believed that we would make some significant contribution to an impending revolution which would redeem our country. In those days intellectual Marxism was a religion, although no one recognized it as such. We believed in the science we made and in its beneficial effects if only it were applied correctly to change our society. We students read a lot, we had many intellectual and ideological debates. Most of the books had to be read in their original languages. Our recently elected president of Brazil, whose student I was, belonged to that group. Other scholars of that time have also reached power positions.

One of the key concepts proposed by the social sciences in the 1960s was that of underdevelopment. Through this concept, young students became aware of the country's actual condition and, at the same time, had a kind of diagnosis and an action plan. The great goal of all was to overcome underdevelopment, whether through violent or peaceful means. For this purpose we had to deal with two great tasks: (1) finding a "correct" way to think and analyze the problem, in order to create an adequate collective consciousness and (2) selecting the best kind of political action to change that negative reality.

It was stimulating to participate in this process, but there was much exaggeration, much ideology. People soon became too radical, thinking that they would make a revolution with books or with words. Some chose the path of clandestine political militancy and suffered the bloody consequences of the crushing repression unleashed by the military dictatorship that soon put an end to democracy. Others preferred to avoid acting out, but we all carried this sign of the 1960s: eagerness to diagnose the country's sickness.

In those years psychology in Brazil was even more silent than it is today. Very few people had heard about Jung; Jungian analysis was introduced only at the end of that decade. The study of underdevelopment was not done through a psychological approach, and may not be today. Each of the social sciences – sociology, political science, history, economics, anthropology – chose one angle of this revolutionary concept of underdevelopment to analyze the problem. Why "revolutionary"? Because it is one thing to say that the world is divided between rich and poor, developed and non-developed countries – since this pair of opposites is archetypal, the strong and the weak – but another to avoid this pair using the prefix "under."

Well, what is underdevelopment? It is a perverted development. It is a development done in a sick way. It is something that could become, does not quite succeed, but remains below its full potential. What comes to reality is a perversion of what could have been. A non-developed country, in the twentieth century, is archaic and retrograde, with high illiteracy and child mortality rates. It lacks a national government and an export production; it lives basically on a local, staple economy.

This was not our case, nor was it the case in many countries in the so-called Third World. In Brazil there has always been a split between advanced and backward regions and, since World War II, São Paulo was already the largest industrial center in Latin America. Our Gross National Product has been growing and certain privileged sectors of society could very well belong to the First World. Nevertheless, the country is not developed, nor is it archaic. The concept of underdevelopment does not mean that the country is half-way, in a middle position. As in a chronic disease, the prognosis it that, because of structural factors, it will take a very long time before the country will outgrow its negative condition. The politically active sectors of society waved this flag and the question of under-development was taken up with passion by popular songs, drama, film and literature. When one said "underdevelopment," one instantly had a fighting standpoint and was full of indignation.

This very concept has been instrumental for some of the best analyses of our society and for some highly creative moments in our culture. These analyses were able to unveil our tragic condition, our identity and our unlived possibilities, thus contributing to a rise in our social awareness. To my knowledge, academic psychology, engulfed as it was by positivism and Skinnerian research, never used this concept.

As we know, sadly, underdevelopment has not been overcome in Brazil, despite improved statistical rates, propaganda and the good life of an elite that holds more than 90 percent of the national wealth. Social indicators demonstrate that the historical pattern survives. Brazil has grown, but poverty has grown too. São Paulo's financial center develops, but unskilled workers and their families live close to misery – some 30 million people. This pathological structure has never been altered. Indeed, our growth generates pathology. Our population is getting poorer, more underfed and shorter in average height. Expansion and degradation both come together as a curse. We are the eighth largest economy worldwide, but hundreds of children die every day of malnutrition. Our sociologist-president puts it briefly: "Brazil is no longer an underdeveloped country, but an unfair country." It seems that injustice is our original, essential sin.

Underdevelopment has not been overcome, but this word is no longer in use. It was banished, along with the banners of the left wing, and has not been replaced. Today people talk about modernization, opening markets and industrialization, but an image has been lost. That is my concern.

The president's statement that I quoted is very recent. It will soon be five centuries since we came as a people under the spell of another sentence, this time by the Pope: "There is no sin below the Equator." What kind of a people is this, comprised between these two sentences? The Pope's statement declares that, in the society just about to be created in the newly discovered lands, the shadow would rule. In sixteenth century Catholic Europe, the shadow was kept under relative control by ethical institutions and civil law; extreme abuses such as human exploitation, slavery, manslaughter – in one word, explicit evil – were condemned and punished. The shadow stayed in a corner, pressed for a way out to be lived and projected. Thus, when a vast geographical area was opened under the rubic, "Here it is allowed," the shadow disembarks on the shore and runs free, proclaiming gladly: "I made it! This is home!" The first European inhabitants, who were left in Brazil after the conquerors sailed back to Lisbon, were common criminals who were given the choice of colonizing as an alternative to prison. They are our true founding forebears.

If we analyze this shadow and this notion that there is no sin below the Equator, step by step we acquire a psychological (not just a socio-economic) understanding of slavery, first of Indians and later of Africans; upon these two races Christianity's shadow was to fall. Indians and Africans were seen as naturally inferior and ruled by the Devil, in a time – indeed up to now – in which "civilized" humans had not reached enough psychology maturity to admit the barbarism and destructiveness of their own shadow. Beyond that, our analysis has to take into account the greedy, rapacious attitude of white people behaving toward America as if it were a tree full of fruit just waiting to be plucked, the cornucopia of abundance. You can see these images in many allegorical paintings and tapestries of the Baroque period in Europe. "Take all you can" was the motto that drove the conquerors; who just took away, expropriated, kidnapped and violated as if the land belonged to no one until they arrived. Our first anti-ecological act – in 1500 – was cutting down brazilwood, much in use then as a red dye for fabrics. I consider this the starting point of rain forest devastation, but our children don't learn it at school. Civilization begins as destruction of nature and of the land's ancestral soul, especially by means of an enforced conversion of the Indians to Catholicism.

Can we conceive a relationship between the loss of a country's ancestral soul and its underdevelopment? Why is it that the vast majority of underdeveloped countries have the richest ancestral cultures of all humanity? Think of India, China, Tibet, Nepal, Pakistan, Sri Lanka, Egypt, Sudan, the African Continent, the Middle East, Turkey, Greece, Mexico, Guatemala, Peru, Bolivia, Equador and Brazil. These countries carry the residues of humanity's oldest cultural traditions. What is Egypt today, this very country that thousands of years ago created a mythology that still fascinates us by its capacity for expressing the mysteries of the soul and of life after death? There is a sharp, brutal cut. What is the relationship between today's Greece and that of the gods, modern Guatemala and that of an amazing Mayan astronomy? And Brazil which, unlike its Inca neighbors, never had a high material culture, but whose native people were already settled in the Amazon forest 10000 years ago, or – as has been discovered only a few years ago – 30000 in the Northeast?

What does it mean if we think that a country like Brazil – some 10000 years ago – had its territory already allotted to highly organized tribes, each with its own mythology, religion, social organization, material culture and language? In a word, these natives – who would be so degraded and annihilated in the course of time – had already worked out the basic human tasks: surviving, interacting, procreating and finding meaning in life. There we have a very rich psychic layer, as Jung used to say, in which archetypes and images lay imprinted like cave paintings. Jung has said that psyche and earth intercommunicate, as if certain regions of the planet had a characteristic soul, as if psyche and matter coexisted at a psychoid level. In India, for instance, one is exposed to something very ancient. The land is impregnated by an ancestral soul, not visible at once and only perceptible to those interested in finding it.

How does our history begin? As they set their feet on newly discovered land, did the Portuguese say: "This land is inhabited by a noble and ancient soul, let us bow before it, let us learn from it, respecting it as a supreme value"? No; a thousand times no. Had it been so, our history – the history of conquered lands – would be different. These words never have been uttered. What was said, in the learned centers of a sixteenth century Catholic theology, was that the Indians had no soul and were closer to beasts than to human beings. The settlers would say: "Let us give them a soul through baptism; when they die they can go to Heaven and finally be released from the Devil their father." Jesuits, as soldiers of Christ, had to fight the Devil and his soulless offspring, the Indians. In this way was our ancestral soul first attacked.

Here I have to make short a very long and cruel story, but the main point is: What has this loss of soul to do with our modern problem? How has our society been shaped and, therefore, how has our collective contemporary soul been formed? Our unique Indian heritage was integrated only in the peripheral outer aspects of our culture, not at its heart. Our society was built upon the actions of Portuguese adventurers; men walking after their shadow, greedy men who want only gold, emeralds, brazilwood, slaves, land. What kind of a nation can spring from such men? And I mean males, because no white woman took part in the conquest. Women, like the anima, were absent. The first cell of our society was formed by white men mating with Indian women, giving birth to hybrids who spread along the immense Atlantic coast.

Indian women were the first house servants in Jesuit settlements and the Great Mother of the Brazilian people. Our children don't learn this at school either; our collective consciousness does not register this genealogy. Even Jungians don't care to study this mother mythology, paying more attention to that of Babylonia. The Indian mother is not a figure of our collective consciousness; she was erased like a mistaken word in a text. She was a silenced mother, since she could not educate her children according to her tradition. She gives birth and she feeds, but she cannot transmit an identity. Losing her original place in the tribe, to which she could no longer return after mating with a stranger, she was bound to join the new settlements. Having lost her roots, how could she transmit to her children something she no longer possessed? She lost her existential basis and not even her language would her children speak; "mother tongue" is actually father's tongue. And what about the father? He was not interested in this kind of son, a bastard who would never fit in his paternal society. In Portugal, this first Brazilian is but an outcast, a pariah.

Who is this first Brazilian, our ancestor, with no place for himself? He doesn't know who he is. He finds no possible identification either with father or mother. As one of our leading anthropologists (Darcy Ribeiro) says, a nation had to be created so that these people could at least belong to something. Our land was nobody's land, it was below the Equator, and its people had no name, no face, no identity of their own. What then would their soul be like? It was a wandering soul. Unaware of its own place, whether Paradise or Hell. I see the Brazilian soul as a wonderful thing – as many foreign travelers have depicted it – precisely because of its mixture, but at the same time an outcast in its own land. A penitent soul, it ignores its own essence and origin. That is how we began as a nation.

It is high time that we look at these facts. We no longer need to research the history of the ruling class, but that of the little people, because in those inferior layers of society we can find a genuine and not a transplanted soul. In matters of soul there can be no imitation, but only the real thing. Settled far away from patristic houses and urban centers, the descendants of intermixed Indians, Africans and whites created their unique ways of living and believing, of enjoying life, of eating, singing, working, building and telling stories. Our folklore, our popular traditions are genuine, much more so than the ruling class culture that we have absorbed. As the colonization of Brazil was based upon the absorption of a foreign culture, the ancestral soul treated to the unconscious and gradually stopped manifesting itself in upperclass culture. A genuine expression of the soul is found only in the humble, underprivileged sectors of society.

Academic history – and psychology, too – never had exactly this approach. Pre-Jungian psychology does not know how to work with a paradox, and cannot say, as Jung did, having learned it with the alchemists: Gold is to be found in the gutter. Persons' higher value lies in their inferiority. Patients' progress is right there where they suffer most. This paradoxical psychology can say: Truth is not in appearances, but in what lies hidden. I am interested in what is not obvious. The essence of a human being is not in the persona, but in the still unconscious Self. These words imply a distinctive psychological, theoretical and methodological standpoint. When a patient comes to us, we are not so interested in a curriculum of victories; we will not work with that, but with the part that suffers, the part that is not adapted, inferior, stupid, unconscious, perverse. With that we will work.

We do not have an integrated science that looks at our underdeveloped reality from this paradoxical viewpoint, that would enable us to perceive things which still do not exist. To overcome underdevelopment both intellectually and in practice, we must see that which a given society could become. Much in the same way as we analysts train our senses to capture germs of the future personality in our patients, looking at what is invisible to them and to everyone else. If we cannot see objective indications in the unconscious material, we have to be able to spin therapeutic fantasies around our patients. Otherwise, we are bound to work with normative models of how a person can change or how a person should be.

In the same way as an analyst looks at a patient and imagines that person in a better condition, we should be able to look with critical and loving eyes at our country, at our soul and ask the same therapeutic questions: Where is the wound? Where does it come from? Where are germs of development to be seen? All of us who lag behind in the race for progress must not imitate the winners, but be able to formulate an image of what we want to become. This imagining is not achieved by an individual, nor by the president or the constitution – but only by an activated collective psyche.

When, at a certain historical time, the archetype of future is constellated in the collective unconscious of a nation, its people have a dream and make a projection of what they want to become. The problem is that most underdeveloped countries no longer dream about their future. In the 1960s Brazil had a passionate dream of development. But as this dream was followed by a military dictatorship and its heavy repression, all dreams shrank and imagination lost its wings. What would then be the general psychological state of the Brazilian people? First: it is a state of under; we are not what we could be. Second: it is a regressive state; we give up projecting change. Third: it is a depressive state; we have lost our enthusiasm and have accepted chronic failure. Corruption cannot be stopped. Inflation has reached unimaginable heights. No authority succeeds in curbing criminality, hunger, poverty, juvenile delinquency and violence against children. It takes a long time to say yes, there is sin below the Equator; yes, there is a moral rule to keep the shadow in its place.

The soul of such a nation is in a deplorable state; it is reduced to silence. It is so full of shame, so humiliated, that it hid in a corner. There it suffers in silence, creating all sorts of disharmonies and maladies by its very absence. Where can the soul speak? In dreams, in all forms of art, in religion, in collective emotions, feelings and facts that mobilize the whole population. It is speaking very, very quietly now in our part of the world. In the last decades our culture has not been especially creative; one does not hear strong voices expressing the feelings and the real psychological condition of the nation in defense of justice, morality, truth and social change. One does not hear a woman's voice embodying the archetype of the Compassionate Mother in defense of street children killed by the police and other brutalities. And mind you, Brazil is the largest Catholic country in the world, dedicating thousands of churches to the Mother of Christ. But She doesn't come down from Heaven to interfere in our dramatic affairs through the hearts of real women and men. The soul is also silenced for lack of voices and we all fall into resignation, cynicism or apathy.

We must have all these hard facts in mind when we do our work in a Third World country. Because big and small, nation and individual are alike, as Jung showed us, using the wisdom of alchemy. I think of my country – and of many others – as a patient with an inferiority complex, our national sickness. Or then with inferior feeling. Since we do not evaluate ourselves properly, we magnify our defects and lose sight of our qualities. Our self-image is distorted because we look at the wrong mirror; either a foreign one, which leads us to imitation and fake values, or a broken mirror. We feel completely down, as a lost case. We need the right mirror, one that shows the real image and promotes feelings of pride for what is genuinely ours: from geography to culture, from genealogy to myth.

Television is a mirror. Every night, our most popular TV network shows a caricature of the country, pasteurizing regional and social differences. Even the language spoken in soap operas is artificial. Characters behave in a sociologically unreal way, as if life took place only in a living room where people never worked but just talked and gossiped. You look at it so much that you begin to see yourself with that haircut, those clothes, that way of talking. Over 70 percent of our people are of mixed racial origin, but our TV shows very few blacks or the real Brazilian stock – hybrids – except for stereotypes. The Indian mother has never been shown once in 45 years of broadcasting. All the same, television is a mirror, newspapers are mirrors, the movie screen, the printed page, the school book, the elementary teacher. They are all mirrors, all distorting mirrors. And the analyst, too, is a mirror.

A psychotherapist working in a country such as ours must be trained to make a cultural diagnosis. The context in which both therapist and patient interact cannot be ignored. Is there a deep root that sustains both of them? What is the existential basis on which these two people stand in this city, in this country? It is alienating to practice psychotherapy in São Paulo as if we were in Zurich or New York; there are sociological differences that imply psychological differences. Not that Jungian tradition and theory should be undervalued and put aside in a sort of psychotherapeutic carnival. Rather, we must develop a standpoint of our own, searching for our specific traits. For us Jungians, the question is: What does our collective unconscious look like? Which are our myths? How are we affected by decades of political misdemeanor? How are we influenced by our specific habitat? Perhaps just psychological concepts are not enough. We must animate our psychology with a living and individuated soul before we can hope to heal the soul of underdevelopment.

Theoretical Issues

Lack of New Metaphors in Analytical Psychology

Giuseppe Maffei
Lucca, Italy
Italian Association for the
Study of Analytical Psychology

Analogy is that which compares two different domains where a pair of elements is clarified, assessed and evaluated, thanks to a second pair of elements; for example, old age is to youth as evening is to morning. Metaphor is a kind of condensed analogy, which consists in taking one element from each of the two pairs; for example, "old age" of the day or the "evening" of life. If we maintain that the unconscious is a layer of psychic life, we are condensing an analogy between geological structures and psychic ones. There is a clear tendency in science to turn analogies into metaphors, a trend toward eliminating the intermediate terms and tightly linking the other two. In its extended form, analogy keeps separate the domains it compares. Metaphor, on the other hand, creates a sort of new psychic object and potentially a new subject for study; metaphors are at the center of a semantically more complex and, therefore, a more constructive domain than that created by analogies. As proof that a metaphor has a specific level, we can consider the fact that in poetry, at least, metaphors cannot be paraphrased. If they are paraphrased they lose their value and effectiveness. "Metaphors can be metaphorically defined as a lie which tells the truth, confusion which clarifies, a detour which leads directly onto the main road, blindness which enables one to see" (Murray, 1975, p. 287).

It is important to consider also that, in literature, metaphors have a meaning in a specific text, whereas in science they have a more general meaning. If, for example, we accept Bohr's analogy between atoms and the solar system, the analogy is valid for all atoms. If, on the other hand we take a poetic analogy, it is valid only in a specific text. Metaphors often originate spontaneously and point to a new way of looking at the world. For example, in the statement "John is a lion," the metaphor describes experience differently from that resulting from the mere perception of John. It shows us the world in a new light. For this reason, the term "metaphor" can be used to refer to all scientific concepts; for the very fact of being formulated in language, they can never coincide with the real. Therefore, they constitute a unique "metaphoric" domain.

Scientific concepts as metaphors

If one considers scientific concepts to be metaphorical, the problem of scientific truth can be seen from a different standpoint from that in positivistic science. And it is generally accepted now that "truth" is not attainable because the observer's viewpoint is a major consideration. Two issues are obvious. One is the greater or lesser value of metaphors; the other concerns the very possibility of scientific development.

With regard to the first problem, is it possible to have criteria that could enable us to choose among different metaphors and to avoid an extreme relativism? This problem has not been solved satisfactorily.

As to the development of science: If there were an attainable truth, scientific development could be seen as getting closer and closer to it. The hypothesis that scientific concepts are a way of getting closer to reality is now the subject of a great debate. Tagliagambe (1992) maintains that, when it comes to considering the object of reality and the object of knowledge, we are faced with two different domains, but they represent "aspects of reciprocal inter-penetration which cannot be neglected" (p. 33).

According to this theory the reality with which science deals does not coincide with the actual object. This object remains outside scientific analysis, and does not coincide with the object of knowledge. The reality in which science is interested lies on the border between these two realms.

The state of metaphors

The development of psychoanalysis and of analytical psychology becomes a particularly interesting subject for study. If there existed a truth and a direct route to it, the possible considerations relative to the development of knowledge would be secondary. But if knowledge develops in a non-linear way, and is linked to a complex plurality of factors, the analysis of the way knowledge develops becomes a good subject for investigation. Let us consider the state of metaphors first in the field of psychoanalysis and then in that of analytical psychology.

In psychoanalysis the presence of four levels of metaphors is demonstrable:

First, those forming the basis of the field (e.g., the unconscious psyche and psychic conflict); Second, those where there is reference to other fields of knowledge (e.g., geological stratification, the laws of hydraulics, and organ functions). Perron (1991) and others have spoken of such metaphors as representations of partial aspects of a more general theory.

At this level we can place also those metaphors important in the history of psychoanalysis, in certain geographical and historical circumstances. They have not claimed to be metaphors representative of mental functioning in its totality but have brought about important advances in theory. Also, metaphors have often originated outside psychoanalysis: for example, René Spitz's theory of organizers, Imre Hermann's "power of grasping," Didier Anzieu's "lopelle" (ego-skin), and Freud's use of the amoeba image. The importance of these metaphors is reflected in the concept of symbiosis, which originated as a biological concept and was taken over by analysts. It made possible the theorizing of a genetic point of view and an exploration of the subjectivity of the patient and of the analyst – in transference and countertransference – as well as an unprecedented exploration of ambiguity.

These metaphors do not call into question the more general, scientific metaphors. Rather, they expose them to the tension of continuous rethinking, which prevents them from being turned into dogma. The second level is particularly important, since the relationship established at this level between psychoanalysis and other sciences avoids the closing of psychoanalysis. Rather, it maintains a tension opening toward the exterior, a tension that favors development.

The third and fourth levels are made up of those metaphors that do not have a precise metapsychological status: theoretical models which are often personal, with even less claim to be general. They have the function of representing conceptualizations lying between the clinical and the metapsychological. These are metaphors that do not aspire to become important; they are among the implicit theories present in the minds of all analysts.

From observation of the psychoanalytic field, my basic thesis is that there is coexistence of these different levels of metaphors along with continuous movement and replacement between the metaphors and between the levels. All the complex work that has taken place within the field of psychoanalysis is made possible not only by one of these levels, but by the complexity of their relationships and the maintenance of an unbridgeable gap between various levels. Some authors believe that we have virtually exhausted the possibility of creating new metaphors; metaphors in psychoanalysis are all linked to analogies with the body and these associations have been exhausted. I believe that reality is unknowable and therefore inexhaustible and that exhausting the production of new metaphors cannot possibly result from exhausting reality. The history of psychoanalysis seems to show that wherever one of these metaphorical levels or a metaphor within one of these levels has taken on a hegemonic position by wanting to swallow up the other levels and other metaphors, the evolution of theory has been blocked. Examples are Wilhelm Reich and rigid Freudian, Kleinian and Lacanian orthodoxies.

We do not have open clinical and theoretical activity unless we accept the existence of a wide gap between theoretical and clinical, within which different levels of metaphor are, in their turn, separated by gaps. I do not deny the importance of a strong theory in the name of an empiricism that is characterized by the hiding of its own implicit theories; I maintain merely that a strong theory cannot be hegemonic. The ability to cure and the ability to think exist only if the analytic mind has a firm grasp of the presence of these gaps, and if there is no desire to close them. It is their presence which gives a theory its strength. In the psychic activity of analysts it is necessary to work and think within strong parameters that are linked to one's own analytic experience. Otherwise, a confusing situation arises. But for analysts to survive we must consider the unconscious within a theory that does not dismiss it.

If we examine the literature of analytical psychology, we do not find metaphorical work intermediate between clinical and theoretical, as is the case in psychoanalysis. The Jungian world, with some exceptions, seems condemned to a repetition of its metaphors. To identify some reasons for this difficulty in theoretical progress, I am devoting particular attention both to the "subjectivistic" epistemology of Jung and to the consequences of the emphasis on archetypes, by Jung and by many analytical psychologists.

We could think that there is no need for work intermediate between clinical and theoretical; analytical psychology is close to clinical experience. The lack of intermediate work can be considered a positive quality, providing opportunities for development. If illnesses are gods and psychopathology can have its basis in mythology, then analytical psychology possesses an appropriate and functional system of metaphors. Our task would be "to rethink ... or re-imagine psychopathology by examining behaviour with an eye to myth" (Hillman 1972, p. 202) and this re-examination would make the modern intermediate structures superfluous. Rooting ourselves in myths we could see most of the conceptual work in the field of analytical psychology as a little foam at the top of a powerful wave. But why have we not been able to create new metaphors and new myths?

I find that an effort to produce new metaphors is fundamental. Even if, in hard sciences such as physics, the aim of science is not so much to know the truth as to formulate the rules of the structure of the real by means of thought and instruments, this awareness should not make us lose sight of the need for a continuous restructuring of our knowledge. In our field there remains open, for example, the problem and the scandal of psychic illnesses. If it were not so, we would run the same risk as an ecology that does not take into account the characteristic human wish to improve the environment. The love of old metaphors should not excuse us from attempting to change them into other metaphors.

These characteristics of the field of analytical psychology are linked both to the ways in which Jung approached the issue of knowledge and to the characteristics of his personality. Nagy (1991) has traced Jung's scientific attitude back to Kant's conviction that it is through the experience of inborn moral awareness that humans can get near to the knowledge of the real. Jung's epistemological thesis seems to be, however, that the only certainty we have is our knowledge of the interior world.

The knowledge of God is expressly considered impossible. But also the real knowledge of the physical world is considered impossible. Thus we have come back to the world of the mind; or, as Jung preferred to say, to the world of the psyche or of the anima. This formulation enabled him to accept psychic contents as valid at the same time as he was denying the rationalized or dogmatic expressions of these same contents. (Nagy, 1991, p. 30)

This is an essential point: Why rid this fundamental revaluation of the human psyche of the fact that *esse in anima* (being in soul) can also signify the creation of new metaphors? Why should the importance of "esse in anima" involve a hyper-estimation of what was imagined by our forebears – as if modern humans could not create new myths and symbols?

Jung spoke about a dream in which the figure of a child appeared. In the middle ages, Jung says:

> *The child would have been called the Christ Child and the people of that period would neither have dreamt nor known about Tammuz or Dionysus. Modern humans understand [the little naked child] in a much more psychological way than ever before ... as a psychological fact. In a thousand years he may have a completely new name, but this will only be a new expression for the same old fact.* (DS, p. 183).

A participant in Jung's seminar asked, "In terms of modern symbolism, what would you call the child?" Jung: "I always use metaphors to indicate these things. If I were to give this child a name, I would be catching him and killing him. We could get attached to the word; but if I say Puer Aeternus, using a metaphor, we all understand what it means." Participant: "Does a modern symbolism exist?" Jung: "No. There is no such thing. I definitely prefer not to invent a cage in which ... I had captured the Puer Aeternus" (DS, p. 184).

To understand what had been meant by divine child as a psychological fact is no minor matter; we can well find a modern name. Jung suggests "puer aeternus" because it is a metaphor. But would not any other appropriate word have been the same? Puer aeternus, a Latin name with its associations, perhaps implies less risk of creating a cage, but a different word might have been used. Why then endow the ancients with the power to find new metaphors and deprive the moderns of this same possibility? Let us listen to Jung again:

> *Now, concerning my concept of the anima, I have been reproached occasionally by scholars for using an almost mythological term to express a scientific fact. They expect me to translate her into scientific terminology, which would deprive the figure of its – or her – specific life. If you say, for instance, that the anima is a function of connection or relationship between conscious and unconscious, that*

is a very pale thing. It is as if you should show a picture of a great philosopher and call it simply Homo sapiens; ... *a picture of a criminal or an idiot would be* Homo sapiens *just as well. The scientific term conveys nothing, and the merely abstract notion of the anima conveys nothing, but when you say the anima is almost personal, a complex that behaves exactly as if she were a little person, or at times as if she were a very important person, then you get it about right.* (DS, pp. 485-96)

Considering these observations, the lack of an analytical psychological field made up of different levels of metaphor assumes importance and can be reflected on. While most of the theory has been developed at a metapsychological level by re-proposing terms of the past, the statements relative to a prospective attitude – and therefore open to the possibility of the new – have not been developed adequately, precisely because the ability to produce new words has been expunged from "esse in anima." The strange thing is that Jung knows very well that it is a question, today as in the past, of different names given to something unknowable. But then he generally lets the most obsolete term prevail as the nearest to this unknowable thing. He is implicitly aware of the constructive value of language. Otherwise, how could he be so attentive to its history and how could it be possible to conceive the statements present in *Psychological Types* (CW6), from which it is clear that there is no knowledge of the world that is not related to the attitude of the subject?

Jung says: "The language I speak must be ambiguous, must have two meanings, in order to do justice to the dual aspect of our psychic nature. I strive quite consciously and deliberately for ambiguity of expression, because it is superior to unequivocalness and reflects the nature of life" (Let-2, p. 70). He is affirming the poetic and metaphoric value of language while avoiding a paternal attitude that would on the one had affirm metaphors that are exact and recognizable as such, and on the other regard as inadequate to express reality. The problem, complex but unavoidable, lies in the fact that everything is partly made up of its name. We cannot help thinking of Jung's father and about the hypothesis that Jung may have needed to base his descent not on the plain words of his own father, but on archetypes, the ancient mythical ancestors. He was a very lonely man; one could now think that this loneliness may have been the origin of his way of thinking.

The word "narcissism" has lost the negative meaning it had in the past and it points, at least for some people, to the personality structure of those people who have been unable to develop a good relationship with the early objects of love and have thus been compelled to grow in a more or less complete loneliness. These people often experience a remarkable interior growth but they hardly ever succeed in having an open relationship with others.

All we know about Jung's childhood points to solitude. When I maintain that Jung never managed to have a full relationship with other people, I mean that his relationship with them needed a mediation through archetypes. The conceptions relative to the *unus mundus* are already involved in the relationship Jung had with the well known stone of childhood; they deny the difference between the outside world and the inside one.

Also important are his theological conceptualizations in which God was never conceived as wholly other: "It is therefore psychologically quite unthinkable for God to be simply the 'wholly other,' for a 'wholly other' could never be one of the soul's deepest and closest intimacies – precisely what God is. The only statements that have psychological validity concerning the God-image are either paradoxes or antinomies" (CW12, par. 11, n6).

Returning to the consequences of this problem in the development of analytical psychology we could refer briefly to psychoses, which Jung knew very well. But why has his ability for "esse in anima" with psychotics not produced new metaphors? He used the term "participation mystique" and meant by this a phenomenon similar to what now is called "projective identification." Why has the latter term been invented outside analytical psychology? And why (apart from the essential work by Michael Fordham) has the concept of Self had to wait for the theorists of self psychology in order to bear metapsychological fruits? It is true that the others do not read Jung very much. But would it not be apt, in order to get out of this repetitive conceptualization, to analyze these questions deeply, to apply ourselves to our metapsychology?

Why, even if we have freed ourselves of the idea of linear scientific progress, is it not possible to create new metaphors useful for the development of our field? Have we not dwelt too long on work that has been done already? Can we conceive a future which is not just a repetition of what has been bequeathed to us? We seem to believe Jung when he says that "Analytical psychology is a reaction against the exaggerated rationalisation of consciousness which, seeking to control nature, isolates itself from her and so robs man of his own natural history" (DS, p. 380). Now that this rationalism seems to be mostly outdated in modern science, could we not consider that the historical and cognitive function of analytical psychology could change?

This paper may seem excessively critical, but it has sprung from an authentic desire for growth and development in analytical psychology.

Translated by Francesca Phalen

References

Hillman, J. (1972). *The Myth of Analysis*. Dallas: Spring Publications.

Murray, E. (1975). The phenomenon of the metaphor. In A. Giorgi et al. (Eds.), *Dusquesne Studies in Phenomenological Psychology* (Vol. 11, pp. 281-300). Pittsburgh: Dusquesne University Press.

Nagy, M. (1991). *Philosophical Issues in the Psychology of C.G. Jung*. New York: State University of New York Press.

Perron, R. (1991). Des divers sens du term 'modèle' et des leurs usages possibles en psychoanalyse. *Revue Francaise de Psychanalyse, 55*, 221-232.

Tagliagambe, S. (1992). Filosofia, scienza, realtà e verità. *Metaxú, 13*, 18-40.

Why it is Difficult to be a Jungian Analyst in Today's World

Andrew Samuels
London, England
Society of Analytical Psychology

Among the open questions in analytical psychology, three are my concern here: (1) mourning for Jung; (2) making our theory and practice "good-enough"; (3) psychoanalysis. As I am attempting a broad survey of our field, I must generalize. I hope, however, that my remarks are tempered by respect for difference, diversity and individuality; and that making general statements can be the first step to making more differentiated contributions.

My comments arise from my personal experience of travel and friendship with academics (in various disciplines), psychoanalysts and, of course, co-workers in the Jungian world. I have been fortunate in that some of my work has found acceptance in psychoanalytic and academic circles. My hope is that readers of these words will not spend too much time wondering if I am right or wrong, but will ask themselves if they see what I am getting at and whether or not it is relevant to them in their situation. My impression is that the frankness I seek is usually found in the bars and restaurants that surround a Congress and not on the floor of the Congress itself.

These days, in addition to being a post-Jungian, I consider myself a critical analytical psychologist. When I visit universities to teach I ask students to do a simple association exercise to the word "Jung." So far, I have had about 300 responses. By far the most numerous are replies such as "Freud" or "psychoanalysis" and words like "Nazis" or "anti-Semitism." Working through these difficult responses is part of the general experience of being a Jungian analyst in today's world. But I am glad to be Jungian. And my title is not "Why it is impossible to be a Jungian analyst in today's world."

Mourning Jung could prove rather central for us, precisely because our Congress is in Zurich. My feeling tells me that it is a time for honoring Jung the man and focusing on what he brought to our field. But I perceive also a problem of unresolved mourning that needs attention. We are not alone in having a problem with mourning. Robert Wallerstein, then President of the International Psychoanalytical Association, reflected in his 1988 presidential address that "For so many of us [psychoanalysts] Sigmund Freud remains our lost object, our unreachable genius, whose passing we have perhaps never properly mourned, at least not in an emotional fullness" (p. 9).

I think we have a problem with our identity as a group, post-Jung. Are we even a group? Are we a profession, a community, a movement, even – as some critics claim – a cult? Whatever we are, we do not even have a settled and consensual account of our history – as the work of "revisionist" historians of analytical psychology such as Sonu Shamdasani, Eugene Taylor, Jay Sherry, John Kerr – as well as my own – shows. Like the psychoanalysts, we have to live with the undermining of our cherished Ur-cases, such as Miss Miller, the Solar Phallus Man and the Tantric Yoga Woman. Personally, I do not feel that Jungian analysis should undergo a product recall because its intellectual and scientific foundations now seem so shaky. That would miss the point about analysis as a healing art. But I am worried that too many of us want to brush this kind of thing – such as the difficulties in relation to the politicization of the original text of *Memories, Dreams, Reflections* – under a carpet. (See Shamdasani, 1995.)

Until we mourn Jung fully, we cannot achieve an optimal distance from the contributions of other psychotherapists. Too close an adherence to Jung the man means that the notion of participating in a generic or eclectic psychotherapy training, by following a Jungian "track," is not possible in most places that I have visited. I see this limitation as intimately connected to the problems of mourning, identity and historical insecurity that I have been outlining.

Among the relatively few places where it is possible to follow a Jungian track within a broader psychotherapy formation or training, many are located in what I call the "frontier" areas of the Jungian world, such as Russia and the former communist countries. There it is possible to hear a young therapist explain how she studies Jung along with neuro-linguistic programming, for instance. There is a freshness and a willingness to mix and match to be found in the frontier areas that is not inhibited by a concern whether this is acceptable or not because, in a sense, the renaissance of psychotherapy in those countries is bound to be unorthodox and eclectic.

In Britain and Australia (and a very few places in the U.S.), it is becoming easier to follow a Jungian track in a university context as part of the wider, emerging discipline known as psychoanalytic studies. But to be part of this exciting development, one must adopt at least the persona and probably also the substance of the inquiring and skeptical academic.

My concern can find expression in concrete organizational and constitutional reform of the IAAP. We urgently need to work out a model of affiliate membership for groups in the frontier areas and for academic membership of our Association. Perhaps there could be also a category of "Jungian analytical psychotherapist" in anticipation of qualified practitioners who have followed a Jungian track but are excluded from IAAP at present.

In these remarks on mourning Jung, my intent has been to get beyond an idealization-denigration split. In the SAP (Society of Analytical Psychology, London), where I trained, and in some Jungian circles in other countries, there has been a vogue to focus in a negative vein on Jung's personal problems, for example, his supposed infantile psychosis: the idea sanctioned by Winnicott (1964) as vitiating the utility of his ideas. Such personalization of the issues is something I have tried to avoid; psychobiography should not be decisive in theoretical dispute. The denigration of Jung by Jungian analysts is as much a sign of incomplete mourning as is any idealization of him. Holding this balance is very difficult. When I published my work (1993) on Jung and anti-Semitism, I received several reviews that accused me of being "soft" on Jung and even of "whitewashing" him. I was accused of being stuck in an idealization. Yet many colleagues in the Jungian analytic world felt that my father complex was showing and that I was indulging in a split-off denigration of (Father) Jung. Apparently, all we can do is to work at avoiding the split.

My second question is whether our theory and practice are good-enough. I want to ask if we think that, as a group, we have dealt well-enough with such problems as elitism, sexism, racism and anti-Semitism – not as difficulties of Jung but our difficulties as Jungian analysts today. It is just too slippery to say that all these are due to Jung's personal complexes or reflect the values and attitudes of his time. I have tried (1993) to show how, if you seek to make a knee-jerk defense of Jung by arguing that his reprehensible qualities are all congruent with his epoch, you end up discovering that they were not.

My own reply to this question is, broadly speaking, positive and optimistic. I think that a very substantial attempt has been made to address some of the problems regarding Jung's ideas and that this can be seen now as providing a base for a post-Jungian or critical analytical psychological intervention in key debates in depth psychology and psychoanalysis. For we will know whether our theory and practice are good-enough only by testing them in a wider arena than that provided by the consulting room. Some examples of the form our interventions might take reflect my own personal interests. Other Jungian analysts will be stirred by other issues.

In psychoanalysis, there is much discussion about the relation between past and present and, in particular, over the status of "infancy" and "childhood" in relation to the emotional, existential and social situation of the adult client. When interpreting in terms of the infantile psychological life of the client, what is a psychoanalyst really doing? Is it a question of a transferential repetition? And is this factual (what Freud called a "construction" and now is called "reconstruction")? Or is it a question of meaning and hermeneutics?

New light can be shed on these and the many other possibilities by introducing Jung's technique of amplification in relation to the interpretation of clinical material in infantile terms. With this in mind, we would consider the analyst's amplifying the client's material as connecting it up in word and emotion with something or someone from the client's far-off past. The analyst would be doing this for all the usual reasons that analysts amplify clients' material: to make thin and personalistic material more "ample," to turn up the volume so as to "hear" the material better, to provide a dimension of meaning that takes personal distress onto social and collective levels.

Thus, instead of amplifying by means of myth and fairy tale, or the stuff of contemporary culture, we amplify by means of adducing an infantile dimension to the interactions and phenomena of the analytic session. When the client is distressed at the upcoming holiday break references to separation anxiety, fantasies of starvation and abandonment may be understood as amplifications.

I have found a ready response to this idea when presenting it to audiences of psychoanalysts and psychoanalytic psychotherapists. For them, it has the virtue of being more detailed and somehow "empirical" than justifying past-oriented interpretations in terms solely of the *meanings* of past events.

A second example of the utility of our good-enough theory and practice concerns the giving of here-and-now transference interpretations. Strachey (1934) argued that the only change-inducing interpretations were of the transference situation at any moment of the analytic session. This view was expanded subsequently to include the entire transference-countertransference dynamic. Here the psychic action was felt to be hottest. It was also the realm where Michael Fordham and the other early members of the developmental school thought the classical Jungians weak. Thus, transference interpretations are a hot professional issue for Jungians as well as Freudians.

Matters developed in psychoanalysis to such an extent that some (or even many) psychoanalysts, especially in Britain and Latin America but lately elsewhere as well, began to over-indulge in what one critic, Nina Coltart, called "you-mean-me interpretations." The analyst hears a story about an inefficient garage mechanic and says, "You mean me." Or there is a wise person in a dream: "You mean me." I realize that no one is going to say, "Yes, that's what I do; I totally exaggerate my importance to the client and, resting on Strachey, am going to save my interpretive libido for here-and-now interpretations only. I truly believe in the primacy of process over content." No one will say that and maybe there are no Jungians of whom it is true. But, if psychoanalysts such as Coltart are to be believed, such a belief has become an undesirable or at least disputed possibility in Kleinian and post-Kleinian psychoanalysis. I argue that Jungian psychology's habitual employment of broad cultural perspectives may be useful in relation to this problem – which by now is a problem for us, not just for the psychoanalysts.

One way of understanding the obsession with the dogma of the mutative here-and-now transference interpretation is to see it as a manifestation of an out-of-control monotheism: "Thou shalt have no other analyst before me." Only a monotheistic culture could have desired, never mind achieved, the boiling down of the wealth of psychic matter in any analysis into a one-strand, monotonous litany of "you mean me." Once this cultural point is grasped – and similar observations could be made about many aspects of so-called clinical technique which are by no means natural things – then the analyst is freer to use here-and-now interpretation in a selective and responsible way. This is everyone's goal of course. But what I have wanted to show is how a Jungian angle helps to intervene in an important psychoanalytic debate.

A further example of the utility of good-enough theory concerns the thorny question of national psychology. European fascism taught us to be careful about constructing any scheme, let alone a hierarchy, of the nations of the world. It is argued that globalization of the world's economy has rendered the nation-state a thing of the past. But the positive role of nationalism as a liberating trend in history is quite overlooked as a result of the negative effects of ethnic nationalism, for example, in the Balkans.

Jung's work in the 1930s on questions of national psychology should be continued. Obviously, the hope is to get beyond crude definitions (e.g., the English are reserved, Germans rigid, Americans materialistic, Jews pushy). We need a method, and I feel that an international association is well-placed to continue with the research into national psychology that Jung initiated. Does it exist? Can we verbalize it? Who says what it is? This research could be an important contribution to conflict resolution psychology.

My final example of how our theory and practice may be of use in today's world is work done on tempering Jung's theory of complementarity and the opposites (see Samuels, 1985, pp. 92-94 and 112-116 for a summary). Let's reconsider our way of dealing with homosexuality and the hidden homophobic elements in a developmental theory that rests so much on the "contrasexual" (i.e., heterosexual) components of the psyche. If we image growth as involving an internal marriage of opposites or even merely an interplay of opposites, and if we image such opposites as heterosexual, where does that leave a homosexual person? Critics of psychoanalytic theorizing about the combined internal parental couple – supposed to symbolize the summit of psychic fecundity and maturity – have made similar observations regarding psychoanalysis to these of mine on Jungian theory.

It is not satisfactory to state that the contrasexual opposites are meant to be taken metaphorically. We know that the raw material of a metaphor pulses with considerable emotional power. Nor is it enough to say that everyone comes from a heterosexual union. There is no reason why that should have become such a central image of psychological growth and maturity save for the cultural valorization of heterosexuality. The debate we can have about the opposites and getting beyond contrasexuality/heterosexuality should be linked with the debate going on in psychoanalysis about getting beyond the image of the combined internal parental couple.

The last of my questions here is the question of psychoanalysis. I feel that we have a closeness-distance problem. Some of us, and some of our organizations, have come too close to psychoanalysis; others have remained too distant from it. Again, no analyst and no organization is going to admit to either problem. Thus, the issue seemingly can be discussed only informally – in the bars and restaurants. We still have work to do to clarify what we feel about Jung's break with Freud and about our present-day relations with psychoanalysis. I have been suggesting for some time that we devote one of our Congresses to those themes.

One question I would dearly love to see discussed more openly is the question of whether or not we feel a clinical deference toward the psychoanalysts. At many Jungian Congresses and conferences, I have felt keenly that such a deference exists. Sometimes, it rests on Jung's tendency to sexual acting-out, which is understandably worrying for Jungian analysts. But Freud's own technique was amazingly loose by today's standards. Thus, there is something illogical here. I am sure that, if we were to discuss our clinical inferiority complex, we would identify certain traditional Jungian clinical techniques that could be developed further, for example, amplification and active imagination. What concerns me is that we are importing psychoanalysis wholesale rather than using it critically. I see this as a worldwide trend and not something restricted to one or two societies, mainly in Britain.

We can walk tall, clinically speaking. If we do, then something will shift in the tendency for us to acknowledge the achievements and contributions of Freudian psychoanalysts while they do not acknowledge us. I get frustrated reading about all the rapprochement between Jungians and Freudians that is supposed to have taken place. It is a one-sided rapprochement. A more assertive attitude on our part, tempered by the kinds of critiques I have been discussing, could lead to a more responsive attitude on their part.

I cannot end on such an upbeat note. Having begun by wondering if we had worked through our mourning for Jung, I came to the thought that some of us have tended to import psychoanalysis wholesale. If my readers could accept for a moment that some of us have been insufficiently critical of psychoanalysis and many of us have not really mourned Jung, then a new way – new, in that it differs from my earlier (Samuels, 1985) classification of the practitioners of analytical psychology – would be to see four main groupings in Jungian analysis today:

(1) the *fundamentalists* who have not mourned Jung and are stuck to him.
(2) the *classical school* who are moving onward within the Jungian traditions.
(3) the *developmental school*, using psychoanalysis in a critical spirit but remaining proudly and recognizably Jungian.
(4) the *psychoanalytic school* who have really ceased to be Jungian in most important respects but are left with their historical institutional affiliation to analytical psychology.

Polly Young-Eisendrath
Burlington, Vermont, U.S.A.
New York Association for Analytical Psychology

In every setting in which I've worked (except independent practice) – from being a professor at Bryn Mawr College to being a research psychologist and teacher at a psychiatric hospital to being an author – I have been translating Jung's ideas. That is, I have been communicating with people who have little or no interest in Jung, but who are committed to understanding and practicing psycho-dynamic psychotherapy. From graduate students to residents, my typical everyday audience has come to Jung with skepticism. Even in my private practice, I have often had patients who know nothing about Jung, who can barely pronounce the term "Jungian," and who come to see me simply because I have been recommended as an effective psychotherapist.

What I have to say, then, needs to be understood as the product of a particular person who has been influenced a great deal by the larger world of psychoanalysis and developmental psychology, one who has been speaking with, and writing for, mostly people who do not worship at Jung's altar.

A major way in which I have developed as a Jungian analyst and as a person, over the past ten years or so, has been through the challenges to my Jungian stance, provided especially by feminism and post-modernism, critiques of the human sciences raised from epistemological and ethical grounds. My "difficulty" has been in attempting to speak about these issues and concerns, with my

Jungian colleagues. I have often felt isolated and lonely in attempting to revise analytical psychology in the face of important questions raised by some forms of post-modernism. I consider my remarks here to be an invitation to my colleagues to reflect on the useful methods and ideas of this important cultural development.

Post-Modernism

Post-modernism is a broad critique of the grounds for truth claims. It is not limited to the human sciences, but it has played a major role in the revision of psychoanalytic concepts, such as the drive and structural models and the oedipus complex. Post-modernism has been unfolding in all major disciplines from science to literature, from linguistics to psychology, from art and architecture to religion over the past 25 years. Many of my Jungian colleagues have reacted to this critique as if it were a mosquito; they have ignored it or brushed it away or swatted at it. Some have confused post-modernism with its most skeptical branch – the French philosophy called "deconstruction."

Deconstruction is a skeptical philosophy that analyzes claims to truth ultimately as social, political or power constructs. This philosophy has been extended into psychoanalysis by several theorists, especially some prominent followers of the French psychoanalyst Jacques Lacan. Although deconstruction has something to offer, I do not find its approach highly compatible with Jung.

There are several affirmative branches of post-modernism that continue, revise and expand some claims made by Jung about the psychic basis of reality. Hermeneutics and constructivism, as well as theories of narrativity, are all useful epistemological tools that can help us better understand our work and ourselves in analytical psychology. Freudian psychoanalysts were close to losing their way, especially in reducing their concepts to a weak version of mythologized biology when they began to take note of post-modern methods. Post-modern and feminist critiques have resulted in a vast and healthy renewal and development of many fields within contemporary psychoanalysis, from object relations to attachment studies.

Before we Jungians can begin to engage more fully within a post-modern dialogue, we would have to do what many Freudians have already done: review, revise and understand the claims we make to universal status for our fundamental ideas. Archetype, complex, the collective unconscious and the Self are examples of ideas that need to be examined and revised.

Affirmative post-modernism, rooted in the philosophy of Kant, is developed further in Hegel, Heidegger and Wittgenstein, finally reaching its contemporary refinements in Quine, Rorty, Taylor, Kuhn, Putnam and many other philosophers whose commentaries can be clarifying to our work. These philosophers have raised important questions about what constitutes "truth" in the natural and the human sciences. Their analyses are often illuminating for depth psychological work.

When Jung and Freud were originating psychoanalysis, there had not yet been a fullblown critique of realism (as in the biological realism of instincts, hormones and drives) or idealism (as in the idealist premise of mental forms, such as archetypes, that precede human interpretation). The world has changed since then, and no account of biology or mental forms can be taken as self-evident. A sample of the kinds of questions raised and their relevance to analytical psychology is presented in the following brief review of a few of my favorite quotations from some prominent philosophers of post-modernism.

The first quotation is from philosopher of science T. S. Kuhn, who is best known for his work on the structure of scientific revolutions. He teaches at the Massachusetts Institute of Technology (MIT) and has spent his career studying the epistemology of natural sciences. He argues in this passage that the natural sciences – like the human sciences – have a hermeneutic base; the natural sciences are not dealing with "brute data" or anything that resides somewhere outside human interpretation and conceptual schemes. Kuhn (1991) says:

> *The natural sciences of any period are grounded in a set of concepts that the current generation of practitioners inherit from their imme-diate predecessors. The set of concepts is a historical product, embedded in the culture to which current practitioners are initiated by training.* (p. 22)

That is, the claims of natural sciences are themselves hermeneutical, the result of interpretive systems. These claims are not "more objective" or "more true" than claims made by human sciences, except as they are used within their own systems of investigation. The interpretive bases of the natural sciences establish the condi-tions for investigating, exploring and demonstrating truth within their own frame of reference. At this time, the claims to truth made by the natural sciences are often accepted by society-at-large because we have come to assume that scientific methods will reveal truth or reality more reliably than other methods. Nevertheless, the methods of the natural sciences are rooted in human interpretations and contexts.

Kuhn goes on to say, however, that practitioners of the natural sciences behave differently in their practice from those in the human sciences. What practitioners of the natural sciences mostly do, once they have established their methods and questions,

> ... *is not ordinarily hermeneutic. Rather they put to use the paradigm received from their teachers in an endeavor I've spoken of as normal science, an enterprise that attempts to solve puzzles like those of improving and extending the match between theory and experiment at the advancing forefront of the field.* (p. 22)

The human sciences, by contrast, follow a practice that is interpretive or hermeneutic through and through. Although the natural sciences are interpretive at base, they operate as though they were working from an objective context. Little of what characterizes the human sciences resembles the normal puzzle-solving research of the natural sciences. The practice of natural sciences does occasionally and unexpectedly produce a paradigm-shift, or a new way of understanding truth and method, as Kuhn is famous for showing. But paradigm shifts are rare and not part of the design of normal science. Those who discover these paradigm-shifts are not seeking them and may even fail to recognize what the discoverers' findings signal. In the human sciences, on the other hand, we take as our goal the production of new and "deeper" interpretations. This very different interpretive stance constitutes a major epistemological difference between the natural and human sciences, Kuhn believes.

Another philosopher of science, Hilary Putnam – also of MIT – argues from a different angle that there is no such thing as a "fact." Although he spent much of his career defending a certain kind of biological realism, Putnam (1989) ultimately says: "To talk of 'facts' without specifying a language to be used is to talk of nothing; the word 'fact' no more has its use fixed by the world itself than does the word 'exist' or the word 'object'" (p. 114). When we Jungians, or our Freudian colleagues, attempt to ground our truths in biology or morphological structures or mathematical formulas, we are not escaping the hermeneutical circle, and we may be obscuring our own enterprise.

If we attempt to explain our interpretive methods by resorting to natural sciences – for instance, in claiming that archetypes relate to genetics, biochemistry or evolutionary biology – we have made a major epistemological error. We have not made our own thinking more objective or coherent; we have simply turned to a wholly different world to explain what we need to understand from our own backyard, our own methods and theories. Not only are the truths of the natural sciences (like those of human sciences) grounded in interpretation, but their methods are so different from ours as to make comparisons suspect.

On the other hand, any claim that archetypes are timeless, elemental or transcendent forms that exist somehow beyond us will be dismissed as "foundationalist" or "essentialist" among post-modern thinkers. Essentialism is the belief that essences or meanings arise in themselves, outside the context of human interpretation. If we give essentialist status to archetypes, then we tend to sound like naive idealists or realists who believe that our concepts arise from some source other than consensual agreement among a community of thinkers.

It is possible and, in my view, critical to our on-going existence as a human science, to interpret analytical psychology in a hermeneutical context. This context is entirely consistent with Jung's later paradigm of the psychological complex with an archetypal core, uniting what had been the collective and the personal unconscious. As a theory about predisposition, archetype is on a par with many other theories of perceptual-motivational organization. Beginning with Kant's concept of a *synthetic a priori*, the idea of an innate releasing or responding system in the embodied mind, has been refined and developed. Archetype, as a predisposition to form an emotionally charged image, provides a link between the emotional intelligence of the individual and its cultural expression in art, literature and religion. Similarly, readily construed and clarified as hermeneutical and constructivist theories are the idea of the dialectical tension of opposites (transcendent function), some aspects of Jung's theory of psychic reality, and his later theory of the Self as a function or process.

The tremendous philosophical contributions of Kant, Heidegger and Wittgenstein have shown us clearly that we are always agents or authors of our own perceptions and experiences. Experiences do not come to us from "out there" or "in here," but are shaped by us in interaction with a changing environment. We are always limited by our own embodiment and emotions. As MacIntyre (1977) puts it:

> *We are never in a position to claim that now we possess the truth. ... The most that we can claim is that this is the best account which anyone has been able to give so far, and that our beliefs about what the mark of "a best account so far" are will themselves change in what are at present unpredictable ways.* (p. 455)

This argument, when fleshed out, effectively undermines all forms of essentialism and fundamentalism. There is no way to escape our own interpretations. This does not mean, however, that we are all solipsists or subjectivists. Because we are all embodied in more or less the same bodies, there are some elements of our world construction that we share. In terms of epistemologies, when we have clarified our premises within any discipline or method, then we can talk of "facts" and "truth" according to our own parameters.

I think that Jung would not disagree with MacIntyre, and yet I have heard some of my colleagues speak as though they were certain they had privileged knowledge of ancient, universal Truth – coming from Self, dream, or archetype. If we lose track of the fact that we have formed a particular interpretive community with certain assumptions and roots, then it is likely that we will lose our way altogether in this post-modern world.

Racism, Sexism and Anti-Semitism

Over the past ten years, I have tried – along with Andrew Samuels and others – to examine the premises and assumptions of analytical psychology for an understanding of how and what we practice. Because we have had only one African-American colleague in the United States, I had to ask myself how our assumptions might be racist. I found some answers in our accounts of cases – including dreams – which often are rooted in Eurocentric biases: seeing the world only from an elite, white, European perspective. Nothing is wrong with this perspective in itself. Our founders were elite, white Europeans and they could not have had any other perspective. All theories begin somewhere.

We are in a different world now, however, and we recognize more self-reflectively how our theory shapes our thinking, as much as vice versa. Jung did not live late enough into the twentieth century for post-structuralism to affect him deeply. But we have lived into this post-modern period and are challenged now to examine our inherited assumptions and how they may shape us.

Within the frame of post-modernism, we find that our assumptions are not inviolate, but can be questioned: What does it mean to claim that an archetype is universal? Why would we say that the shadow is dark or black? What does it mean to say that the anima connects a man to life whereas the animus connects a woman to objectivity? What does it mean to take the hero myth as the basis for individuation? And so on.

As a feminist, I have been shocked often at the way we women in Jungian groups have been labeled and stereotyped. Sometimes there is a belittlement of female authority, labeled as "animus possession." Other times there is a stereotyping of female abilities and powers by various goddess labels. Let us try to understand why we might want to maintain the biased language of archetypal masculine and feminine. Knowing now that these are not universal, biological phenomena, but simply ways of thinking, how do we want to express sex and gender differences in our psychology?

I have often needed the help of historians and anthropologists to figure out why we have inherited certain concepts. I want to feel that my colleagues are open to understanding what happened between Jung and Freud in the complicated history of Jewish and anti-Jewish influences on the development of analytical psychology. I have welcomed the clarification that Andrew Samuels and others have brought to seeing how and why Jung may have manifested some anti-Semitic tendencies during the 1930s, and how this has affected our concepts and community since.

This issue of anti-Semitism bears directly on healing the split in the larger psychoanalytic circle – the split that has continued until today. Suspicions about Jung's anti-Semitism are, in my view, one of the greatest unspoken barriers between us and the rest of the psychoanalytic community. When others ask me why our psychoanalytic colleagues do not study Jung, the answer I most often give is that we have not healed the split regarding Jung's conduct in the 1930s in relation to National Socialism in Germany.

Conclusion

In presenting these comments my hope is to open more dialogue with colleagues on the issues that have been troubling me as a Jungian. The larger enterprise of psychoanalysis is alive and well at the end of the twentieth century, at least in part because it has taken seriously the critiques emerging from feminism and post-modernism. I have been in many fruitful debates and dialogues around these issues in Freudian groups. I hope that analytical psychology can travel the same path.

References

Kuhn, T. (1991). The natural and the human sciences. In D. Hiley, J. Bohman and R. Shusterman (Eds.), *The Interpretive Turn: Philosophy, Science, Culture*. Ithaca, NY: Cornell University Press.

MacIntyre, A. (1977). Epistemological crises, dramatic narrative, and the philosophy of science. *The Monist, 60,* 453-472.

Putnam, H. (1989). *Representation and Reality*. Cambridge, MA: MIT Press.

Samuels, A. (1985). *Jung and the Post-Jungians*. London/Boston: Routledge & Kegan Paul.

Samuels, A. (1993). Jung, anti-Semitism and the Nazis. In *The Political Psyche*. London/New York: Routledge.

Shamdasani, S. (1995). Memories, dreams, omissions. *Spring, 57,* 115-137.

Strachey, J. (1934). The nature of the therapeutic action of psychoanalysis. *International Journal of Psycho-Analysis, 15,* 127-159.

Wallerstein, R. (1988). One psychoanalysis or many? *International Journal of Psycho-Analysis 69-*1, 3-29.

Winnicott, D.W. (1964). Review of *Memories, Dreams, Reflections*, by C.G. Jung. *International Journal of Psychoanalysis, 45,* 450-455.

Neurobiological Theory and Jungian Metapsychology

Auspicious Correspondences

David I. Tresan
San Francisco, California, U.S.A.
Society of Jungian Analysts of Northern California

This paper has two purposes. The first is to review the relationship of depth psychology to modern brain research, the second to elucidate the status of Jungian psychology in relation to the neurosciences. In recent years, psychoanalysis and, by association, all of depth psychology is under serious attack due to a dearth of scientific corroboration. The subject of an ongoing debate is whether the clinical practice of depth psychology will or should continue to exist. The reality of this challenge is seen in decreased insurance funding for long-term psychotherapy and the demand for research proofs of efficacy. A body of clinical theory that is in frank variance with how the brain works probably will not survive as a mainstream treatment modality. My explorations have impressed me with the irony that, although Freud intended to ground his psychology in the biological sciences, it is Jung's psychology that fits much more readily with modern neuroscientific findings.

The present conditions regarding depth psychology and the neurosciences stem from two considerations. The first is that psychology has broadened the range of data it considers appropriate for scientific research and now accepts as legitimate for investigation of the phenomena of consciousness, intentionality, meaningfulness, the quality of experiences and other subjective events. This is a radical change and flows from the relatively recent demise of behaviorism as the reigning paradigm in psychology and from the similar demise of orthodox Freudian drive theory as the main arbiter of depth analytic work. Second: The neurosciences, like psychology, have accepted as data the field of subjective experience. Moreover, the neurosciences have developed non-invasive means of investigating the functioning human brain *in vivo* such that private experience can be measured and even visualized while in progress. The 1990s have been designated the Decade of the Brain by the U.S. Congress; in Japan a similar focus is called the Japanese Human Frontier Programme. In England the Brain Research Association was formed in the 1960s and is "committed to the view that the brain was bigger than any of its constituent disciplines" (Rose, 1993, p. 45). Indeed, the constituent disciplines are numerous, ranging from the traditional sciences and philosophy to the newer sciences such as molecular biology and computer sciences. Generative work is afoot in all these fields but, with few and largely inconsequential exceptions, depth psychology is not part of this effort, nor, of course, is analytical psychology.

The history of depth psychology's relation to neuroscience is unfortunate. Freud's metapsychology is seriously flawed and, contrary to the title of this paper, there is no Jungian metapsychology. We must extrapolate the Jungian brain from Jungian psychology; that is what I intend to do in order to critique this psychology. The word metapsychology is a term from the Freudian lexicon; it refers to the presumption that psychology is rooted in and derived from its biological substrate. I have heard many people refer to "metapsychology" or, more likely for Jung, "metaphysics" when they mean "metatheory." Etymologically Freud's use of the expression has always seemed to me a subversion of the term since he refers more to a stratum "below" psychology (its foundations) than to one "beyond" psychology. (In Aristotle's use of the prefix *meta,* his *Metaphysics* was so named because it was the fifth volume in a series and the one that lay on the shelf beyond the fourth, which was entitled *Physics.*

In truth, Freud's metapsychology has had inauspicious consequences for Freudians and, consequently, for depth psychology in general; the clinical principles derived from it cannot be verified consistently in practice and are often heuristically inept explanations of human behavior and cognition. So little was understood of the anatomy and physiology of the brain in the latter nineteenth century that Freud swiftly foundered in his early attempt at creating a neurology for psychologists – an attempt entitled "Project for a Scientific Psychology" (SE1), which he recorded in two notebooks written in 1895 and sent to Wilhelm Fliess. According to Strachey (SE1), Freud gave up this effort because he could not derive consciousness from biological processes. However, Sulloway

(1992) claims that Freud never abandoned the Project but was unable to formulate a biological basis for pathological repression. This subject which was to have been presented to Fliess in a third notebook but was never written.

It is a testimony to his integrity that Freud put aside the Project or, at least, did not insist on its scientific veracity. Unfortunately for the same virtue, he retained a number of psychological principles which he worked out in these 1895 writings and continued to defend but did not openly attribute to his biological theorizing. Among the ideas that derived from the Project are "the concepts of primary and secondary processes, the principles of pleasure-unpleasure, [energy] constancy, and reality testing; the concept of cathexis; the theories of psychical regression and hallucinations; the systems of perception, memory, unconscious and preconscious psychic activity; and even ... wish-fulfillment theory of dreams" (Sulloway, 1992, p. 19). According to Strachey (SE1), Freud referred to his biologically based ideas as underlying much of his thought even through his metapsychological modifications from 1914 to 1923 and until his death in 1939. By apotheosizing these theories without owning up to the source of their conception, Freud foreclosed a much-needed debate and, in effect, retarded the progressive alignment of neurology and depth psychology.

The most unyielding aspect of Freud's quasi-biological psychology is its dependence on reductionism, a principle that has been part and parcel of all science of this and the last century and before, and a more comprehensive term than that of "reductive analysis." Reductionism is a philosophical concept that addresses the way we, and especially scientists, tend to explain events that occur in a physical world taken to be real. Speaking of such scientific realism, philosopher of science Ian Hacking (1983) states that it "has, historically, been mixed up with materialism, which, in one version, says everything that exists is built up out of tiny material building blocks" (p. 24). It is the breaking down of phenomena to these tiny building blocks (or to intermediate-size ones) that constitutes the practice of reduction, which assumes that the greater is explained by the smaller and, in effect, that the greater – if all be known – is precisely the sum of the smaller. Moreover, reduction presumes that later events are explained by earlier ones and that a lower (or earlier) explanatory level, when fully known, replaces an upper level that has been explained. Thus, we presume causation: that a present event is caused by the action of its antecedent elements. Depth psychologists may fear – rightly – that science aims to reduce all mind (and spirit and soul) to an inanimate and mechanistic brain and to eliminate completely the reality of psyche *sui generis.* I think that this is a fear well justified by our experience with the hegemony of nineteenth and twentieth century scientism, behaviorism, and ortho-dox drive theory.

How then are we to think about the relationship of mind and brain without reducing the former to the latter? Pervasive though it is, reductionism has an alternative that is not dualism. It is an alterna-tive that has been with us since the beginning of this century and even well before, but has begun only recently to flower into verifiable theories and concepts regarded seriously by the world of science. Jung belongs in this current of events. Although he never shook off the demands of the scientific materialism of his age Jung – in temper and in practice – espoused a way alternative to reductive materialism which he nonetheless did not conceptualize and articu-late in systematic and operationally communicable theories accept-able to the science of his time. Only now is that kind of formulation taking place, and it is tantamount to a paradigm shift. Of this shift, psychologist and Nobel Laureate Roger Sperry (1993) has this to say:

> *What is involved is the age-old reductionist-holist issue. ... A new way of reasoning, a new logic, or different reference frame for causation was needed. In other words what reversed the scientific ban on consciousness was not new evidence, but a new logic. ... The key concept here, that of downward causation, though simple, has seemed to give more trouble than any other. According to traditional atomistic or microdeterminist science, everything is determined from below upward following the course of evolution. Brain states determine mental states, but not vice-versa. In the new view, how-ever, things are doubly determined, not only from lower levels upward, but also from above downward.*
>
> *... Scientific materialism, with its exclusive atomistic, reductive physicalist approach, has been in error all along, excluding, not only the mental but also, in principle, all autonomous macro, emergent, or holistic explanations.*
>
> *The recognition of the major causal role thus played by the higher, more evolved forces of both human and nonhuman nature gives science a vastly changed view of the entire natural order. The mental, subjective, vital, and social forces are given their due, as well as physics and chemistry. No longer is science incompatible with the humanities, values, or ethics. Perhaps of most importance,*

for present purposes, the great divide between science and religion is removed – at least for liberal, nondualistic theology. (pp. 10-12)

In short, the nondualistic alternative to reductionism is a concept closely related to downward causation, namely, the concept of emergence in which successively higher levels emerge from lower ones but with the understanding that, although dependent on them in some degree, the higher levels are neither caused by the lower nor are reducible to them. What is postulated is 1) that reality as we know it is constituted of many simultaneously existing levels, each of which is real and ontologically substantive; 2) that each level has its own laws and phenomenological characteristics; 3) that the laws governing relationships between levels are different for each interval and 4) are neither causal nor linear and are, in fact, neither fully known nor understood nor even necessarily understandable. Philosophers have led the way here (e.g., Hare, 1952; Davidson, 1970; Kim, 1993). Higher levels are said to supervene on lower or subvenient ones whence they emerge. Used most recently in modern context to speak of how moral ethics relates to natural law, the word supervenence has had specific usage also in the conceptualization of the mind/brain problem. Mind, it is said, supervenes on brain. Thus lies the way to ponder the relationship of mind to brain, giving each its reality, affirming relatedness between the two, acknowledging degrees of dependency, but not reducing one to the other.

Sperry sounds very much like Jung, and emergence sounds very much like Jung's synthetic method of analysis. Indeed, they are the same in spirit and in practice with regard to the acceptance of top-down in addition to bottom-up causation (as well as sideways causation seen as an intrinsically limited ordering principle). In Jung's time reductionism alone reigned as the acceptable scientific method and emergence as a scientific principle was disallowed.

Emergence as a theory for psychology warrants a short discussion in order to locate Jung in this tradition and especially to bring the concept up to its most recent formulation. For this purpose, emergence may be viewed as having three historical aspects. The first, known from time immemorial, manifests as religion, holistic philosophy, and art; it has been perennially disavowed as science. Jung exemplified this conflict within himself in the form of the anima voice which accused him of being an artist and not a psychologist – that is, not a scientist. The second current within emergence is the vitalistic tradition, which postulates that life is

patterned by a force or forces over and beyond the blind evolutionary happenstances that eventuate in survival of the fittest. This line
of thought leads ineluctably to the notion of a supraordinate intelligence, a God-concept, and as such it is also excluded from serious
consideration by traditional science. Jung's psychological theory
seemed to gravitate to this position in mid-career with his postula-
tion of a Self concept but at the same time it subtly and persistently
retained an epistemologically noncommittal stance appropriate for
psychology but incompatible with revealed religion. (See Nagy,
1991.) According to Henderson (1995), this remained Jung's theoretical position until his death. The third way of thinking about
emergence has not been available to the human mind until the last
two decades or so of the twentieth century. Like the second current,
the third also presupposes a supraordinate ordering principle. This
principle, however, does not flow directly from a supraordinate
intelligence but from the way matter automatically sorts itself out
under certain circumstances. These newly discerned self-organizing
principles are data-driven, definable in mathematical terms, objectively verifiable and, as such, constitute the scientifically respectable core of the paradigm shift that the modern-day concept of
emergence represents. (See Beckermann et al., 1992.)

The conditions that predispose toward emergence are 1) a large
number of elements 2) having multiple relationships with each other
3) all put in motion according to simple rules of involvement 4)
which then proceed to self-organize in non-linear ways 5) into
patterns that continue to change over successive generations with or
without further input 6) into ever more complex organizations. For
my specific purposes here, there are two kinds of activity that satisfy
these conditions. One is neurobiological activity in the brain. The
second is the mental activity that goes on between analyst and
analysand.

With regard to the working of the conditions for emergence in the
consulting room, consider that the mental productions of both
analyst and analysand in an analytic hour may be seen as creating
three interlinked psychological fields, one emanating from the
analyst, one from the analysand, the third a common field emanating
from the participants together. All three fields are in constant
change, and the common field is continuously being shaped in
reciprocal communication with each individual one. That is, each
person changes the common field and, in turn, is changed by it.
Irwin Hoffman has labeled this view of the transference/counter-

transference situation "social constructivism." It is not far from Jung's ideas about transference and countertransference in which all possible vectors exist at all times in the analytic situation among the participants, the ego consciousness, and the unconscious of each. It is also consonant with Jung's metaphor in which the analytic relationship is conceptualized as a chemical reaction and the two parties as chemical ingredients. Regardless of which theoretical tradition is invoked, the common field, or the "analytic third" as T.H. Ogden calls it, serves as a continuous *pot pourri* or subvenient base for emergent activity.

The salient question for clinical psychology is the nature of how emergent or spontaneously creative activity within the analytic situation engenders higher mental states. Clinically, the paths diverge between what happens according to the Jungian schema in contrast to what happens in emergence theory. Jung maintains that an encounter between ego consciousness and the unconscious creates a "third way" (this is not Ogden's "analytic third"). Otherwise said, the encounter between ego and the unconscious creates a spiritual or symbolic state of mind, into which the ego or the solely empirical attitude is absorbed and transformed. In the schema of emergence, the symbolic emerges from the concrete under appropriate conditions but does not have an encounter with it, and the two levels never blend to form a third. Instead, the symbolic supervenes on the concrete, and both levels, the symbolic and the concrete, remain preserved as integral realms, each with its own ongoing characteristic manifestations and laws. That is, in emergence theory the level of non-symbolic and physicalistic existence is not recast through encountering an archetypal or other symbolic level nor, as a result, does there appear any sort of human-spirit amalgam. Unlike in emergence doctrine, Jungian theory seems willing to collapse reality levels into one another, a phenomenon we know clinically as ego-inflation.

Irrespective of the possible conflation of levels and its clinical implications, Jung's theoretical world is an ordered emergent one consisting of four realms that supervene on one another. In the diamond diagrams of *Aion* (CW9-II), Jung posits a mineral world, plant world, animal world (with humans at the apex) and ultimately a spiritual world. The collective unconscious may be seen as yet a further and more comprehensive emergent level in the form of a circle composed of the four basic realms bent back on themselves. In 1921 Jung (CW6) coined two synonyms for the process of emergence: "synthetic" method and "constructive" method. Near the end of his life, still conceptualizing outside the letter but within the tradition of emergence, Jung postulated two new phenomena, the most implausible of all his constructions: synchronicity (CW8) and UFOs (CW10). The formulation of synchronicity was an attempt to describe a psychophysical law that defined a special kind of relationship between the realms of mind and matter. UFOs, according to Jung, were actual manifestations of a realm of reality different from our usual reality. These two theoretical statements are the most suggestive evidence that Jung, in consonance with emergentist doctrine, envisioned an ontologically multilayered universe. They also represent the furthest limits of Jung's emergentist ideas.

Up to this point, illustrations of supervenience and emergence have relied on discussions of mental events and mental life. As we move to the juncture between mental life and brain, we approach that cleft in reality that has never been conquered: not by Descartes' pineal gland nor by John Eccles' "psychons," which are but quantum-sized pineal glands that are putatively found among dendritic spines. What does it mean to say that mental life supervenes on brain? We do not know how inanimate matter produces mind, but what we seek are the psychophysical laws that mediate the two realms of mind and brain, with the hope that the specifics of the relationship will instruct us further about how psyche works and about the clinical effects.

Unfortunately, the psychophysical laws we seek are still unknown; thoughts and feelings are far from being reducible to mathematical descriptions. We are still at a stage of brute correlations as compared to readily discernible relationships. Some think that such reductions never will be possible and that psychophysical laws never can be known because of the vast number of variables involved. Others think that the problem is not a methodological one but is intrinsically unsolvable. Nonetheless supervenience, emergence, and the mind are being addressed forthwith in the metaphysical literature of philosophy – albeit rather theoretically – and speculation, especially by depth psychologists whose knowledge of psyche is far from theoretical, is very much in order.

Of the three areas of mind/brain confluence that have clinical relevance – learning, memory and the capacity to symbolize – space constraints allow me to discuss only the third. Controversy is inevitable since there is no one reigning paradigm at this time for understanding mind and brain, and, contrary to the title of my paper, there is not one neurobiological theory but many.

With regard to symbolization, the key concepts are generativity and health. In the Jungian tradition, psychic health depends on the continuing ability to generate ever more comprehensive symbolic realities: in effect, ever more inclusive higher-order categorizations. The healthy psyche may be pictured as a set of continuously propagating nesting boxes, each box representing a virtual reality that is comprehended by the next larger one. Spiritual life may be regarded as the upper and outermost box symbolizing a succession of comprehensive paradigms each of which include the notion of infinity as one structural feature and also an appropriate affective dimension. Emerging progressively to such extensive paradigms takes a lifetime. Even if one is propelled there at once, it takes a lifetime to decipher the experience. For these reasons, Jungian psychology has tended to be a psychology of the latter half of life. As Jungians, we tacitly postulate that health in aging correlates with the continuation of emergent activity, plus the development in time of broad paradigmatic views, sometimes called "spiritual" or "wise."

Unfortunately, what constitutes health and superhealth in aging has never been clarified, for the amount of research in this area is relatively minuscule. Recently, a community of nuns have donated their brains posthumously to such research. The working hypothesis is that the unusual amount of ongoing intellectual activity in these nuns' lives preserves the functional and physical integrity of their brains. These are spiritual people as well as intelligent ones and the hope is that the spiritual dimension is being considered alongside the intellectual.

If, indeed, health correlates not only with a continuing intellectual atmosphere but with an ongoing capacity for emergence, Jungian psychology as a treatment modality is uniquely constituted in the field of psychology; Jungian theory and practice has always been especially attuned to a vertical consideration of life. Its particular expertise has to do with interlevel relationships, including the processes through which one symbolic level emerges from another, the way that levels "invade" one another (e.g., invasion by the collective unconscious), and the laws governing the healthy and destructive effects of such events. This is in contrast to such schools as that of object relations, which have a more horizontal organization. These concern themselves more with the intralevel relationships and perspectives specifically of the empirical and physicalistic world and retain the rational, linear, and causal presumptions germane to that realm.

The ability to name objects is related to an area of the left temporal cortex. The ability to name actions depends on the intactness of a prefrontal area. The ability to form global concepts such as soul, spirit or infinity is not localized in any one part of the brain, but is thought to be generally distributed and to rely on the frontal lobes. That is all we know at present regarding the neurology of the highest order mental processes. How, we may ask, does the brain embody such higher order information? What neurobiological states correspond to subjective experiences of wholeness, spirituality or health in general? What neurobiological events and stages are involved in the learning process? Why can one person effectively attain to these levels of comprehension and another not? What conditions promote and enhance such learning? All these questions are still unanswered and largely uninvestigated.

In all of this, there is a part that depth psychologists, Jungians in particular, may be able to play. We know about emergence in the area of psychology, especially in the form of the capacity to symbolize. More than anyone else we are in a position to recognize such events and to define the phenomenological and psychological processes that go into moving from the concrete to the symbolic, from the symbolic to the more comprehensively symbolic (e.g., the archetypal). Any research in neurobiology on higher order symbolic functioning will have to collate with accurate phenomenological and subjective descriptions. It behooves us to find or help develop a psychological testing instrument that discerns the capacity to symbolize or, at least, to identify and register the need for such an instrument. A discriminating study regarding the capacity to symbolize and the ability to discern the differences between levels of symbolization would be a unique contribution to research in the neurosciences.

Since Jung's death in 1961, the world of science has ceased to be unarguably reductive and causal. It is accepted now that biological and other processes do not occur in straight-line functions and never have, and that the Second Law of Thermodynamics, the tendency toward entropy which Freud as a reductionist accepted forthwith and with which Jung grappled so tortuously, is not a fully satisfying explanation of reality as we know it. Jung did not define the "present era" nor was he precise or thorough in discerning and articulating its rules, but he did live its tenets, calling them science before their time. In resisting reductionism and espousing the spirit of emergence, his legacy is a body of psychological theory not fully complete but not in significant variance with the new paradigm nor with the workings of the brain as we are coming to know them.

It is not the purpose of this paper to grant any kind of special prize to Jung nor to claim that, like a Leif Erikson, he should belatedly be granted primacy of discovery regarding a psychology that largely concurs with brain functioning. In fact, it is my hope that by rethinking the brain, all psyches will recognize a totem ancestor which at the outset of life is neither Jungian nor Freudian nor of British middle school (combining Freudian and Jungian) extraction but simply an amazingly plastic, uniquely organizable, three pounds of wondrous biological material that we each carry in our skulls. It is to be hoped that the common possession of this organ by all of us and the increasing ability to arrive at common agreements about how it works will help diminish the nasty partisanship in the name of truth that has characterized the field of depth psychology from the time of its inception in the early 1900s to the present – but I doubt it.

References

Beckermann, A.; Flohr, H.; Kim, J., Eds. (1992). *Emergence or Reduction? Essays on the Prospects of Nonreductive Physicalism.* Berlin/New York: Walter de Gruyter.

Davidson, D. (1970). *Actions and Events.* Oxford: Clarendon Press.

Hacking, I. (1983). *Representing and Intervening: Introductory Topics in the Philosophy of Natural Science.* Cambridge, England: Cambridge University Press.

Hare, R. (1952). *The Language of Morals.* Oxford: Clarendon Press.

Henderson, J. (1995). Personal communication.

Kim, J. (1993). *Supervenience and Mind: Selected Philosophical Essays.* Cambridge, England: Cambridge University Press.

Nagy, M. (1991). *Philosophical Issues in the Psychology of C.G. Jung.* Albany, NY: State University of New York Press.

Rose, S. (1993). *The Making of Memory: From Molecules to Mind.* New York: Anchor/Doubleday.

Sperry, R. (1993). A powerful paradigm made stronger. *Psychological Science Agenda,* Sept-Oct., 10-13.

Sulloway, F. (1992). *Freud: Biologist of the Mind.* Cambridge, MA/London: Harvard University Press.

Archetypal Foundations in the Unification of Psychology, Physics and Biology

Alchemical *Informatio* and Jung's Synthetic Method

Ernest Lawrence Rossi
Malibu, California, U.S.A.
Society of Jungian Analysts of Southern California

Recent explorations of Jung's synthetic method have important implications for current developments in the theory and technique of analytical psychology. The theoretical aspect is focused on Jung's understanding of the alchemical *informatio* and its current incarnation as the concept of information that is playing a leading role in the unification of all the sciences. The technique aspect has to do with our daily work as analysts: facilitating the evolution of consciousness and healing via the transcendent function and new approaches to Jung's synthetic or constructive method.

The Alchemical Informatio *and Archetypal Psychology*

In international science meetings and publications, there is a new movement toward unification by using the concept of information as a common language. Many areas of scientific specialization are seeking common concepts that can spur new discoveries in mathematics, physics, biology, psychology, the social sciences and even the humanities. The new movement is an expression of an important transition in the concept of the objective psyche: a spontaneous evolution and an archetypal expression of the transcendent function. The alchemical concept of the informatio is being rediscovered as information in computer science, physics, and psychology and biology and as a unifying principle that can bridge all areas of science. This is particularly true in the new field of mindbody science where information in the form of messenger molecules and their receptors appears to be a way of bridging the Cartesian gap between psyche and soma that has plagued the healing arts for the past 200 years.

Stonier's (1990) mathematical conception of the evolution of information in the universe from the Big Bang about 15 billion years ago to the development of life on earth and finally to Jung's conception of the Self is a development with significance for psychology. Physicists currently hypothesize that the Big Bang itself originally evolved out of a quantum flux (variation in the electromagnetic field). Recent advances in "string theory" suggest that the fundamental building blocks of nature – such as electrons, quarks, gravitons – are all expressions of the way vibrating strings squirm and twist in space. The unification of nature in this current "theory of everything" may seem remote from our daily work as analysts until we recall one of Jung's favorite quotations from alchemy, the axiom from Hermes Trismegistus' *Tabula smaragdina*: "What is below is like what is above, that the miracle of the one thing may be accomplished." Niels Bohr, the father of quantum theory, used this same archetypal idea when he announced the "correspondence principle" whereby the laws of quantum physics governing the very small, like the vibrating strings, must be chosen mathematically to correspond with the classical laws of Newtonian physics that we experience in our everyday life. Recent research illustrates how these minute vibrations or oscillations at the innermost essence of nature may correspond with Jung's transcendent function as it is expressed in the entirely natural daily and hourly rhythms of our mindbody communication and healing – what I call the "wave nature of consciousness and being."

For the ancient Greeks the entire universe was made up of matter. It took almost 2000 years to realize that another principle that we now call "energy" was equivalent to matter. This was immortalized in Einstein's famous equation: $E=MC^2$ (Energy equals Matter multiplied by the square of the speed of Light). It is only within our generation that some scientists are speculating that energy and information are also equivalent. Stonier (1990) calculates that one energy unit (entropy) equals approximately 10^{23} bits of information. One of the most challenging frontiers of science integrates Stonier's equation of information and energy with Einstein's equation, to obtain an experimentally verifiable formula for the equivalence of the three basic concepts – matter, energy and information – in the evolution of life and the psyche.

From this perspective we can understand how the ancient alchemical dream of facilitating healing of the body as well as psychological and spiritual transformation by studying informatio –

literally "in form" – may be on the verge of becoming a reality. Since matter has structure and organization in form, we can no longer doubt that life itself, the organization and form of our physical body, is actually a form of information. The questions that now assail us are: Is the information that makes up the organization of the matter that makes up our body of the same nature as the information we express as words, ideas, images, thoughts, feelings, intuitions and sensations? Is verbal information really equivalent and transformable into the structural information of body and visa versa? Could we thus use the information of words that we exchange in psychotherapy to transform and heal the body? Is information the common denominator, the bridge between mind and matter?

Jung used the concept of the *psychoid* as the bridge between mind and matter. Can Jung's psychoid be amplified appropriately by the currently evolving conception of the equivalence of information, matter and energy? A few quotes from Jung suggest that what he called "psychoid" does gain a new scientific foundation with our modern concept of information. We could easily substitute the word "information" for "psychoid form," for example, when Jung writes, "The psychoid form underlying any archetypal image retains its character at all stages of development, though empirically it is capable of endless variations" (CW13, par. 350). The equivalence of information, energy and matter in current science was intuited by Jung when he wrote, "the physicist does not believe that the transcendental reality represented by his psychic model is also psychic. He calls it *matter*, and in the same way the psychologist in no wise attributes a psychic nature to his images or archetypes. He calls them "psychoids" (CW18, par. 1538). Jung's use of the term "archetype" in these contexts strongly suggests that the archetype is itself a form; form of information. Indeed, it would appear that Jung's archetypal psychology potentially finds its clearest field for modern evolution in studies of the equivalence of information, matter and energy as they are expressed in mindbody healing and individuation. (See Rossi, 1996.)

Stress, Messenger Molecules and the Transcendent Function

Let us now explore the extent to which information can be understood as the common denominator in the flow of communication between mind and body, conscious and unconscious, in the transcendent function as well as more specific areas such as psychoimmunology and healing. Previously I have illustrated four critical stages of the circular loop of communication between mind and gene. Stage One is the process of data collection by which all sensations and perceptions from the outer world are transduced by the central nervous system in the limbic-hypothalamic-pituitary system into the hormones that regulate all the adaptive processes of the body: temperature and appetite regulation, adaptation to stress, sexuality, growth and healing. Most of us who went to school a generation ago were taught that the nervous system was the connecting link between mind and body. We now know that hormones, now called "messenger molecules," are the older, original form of communication in life at the single cell level before huge multicellular organisms, such as humans, with about six trillion cells evolved.

The central nervous system evolved about four billion years ago only in response to the need for a faster form of communication (neurons with neurotransmitters carrying the signal between one nerve and the next) from one end to the other of large multicellular organisms. Even now, the older messenger molecule receptor system regulates the functioning of our nervous system with what are called "neuromodulators." We now know that most of the messenger molecules from the pituitary, the master gland of the mindbody, are released in pulses or rhythms every hour and a half or so. These molecules flow through the blood stream to all cells of the body where they are picked up by receptors on and within the cell. I propose that this messenger-module-receptor system that regulates all cells of mind and body as well as the entire nervous system is the basic communication pathway between the conscious and unconscious that Jung called the "transcendent function."

This messenger-molecule-receptor system of mindbody carries signals from the outside world to the center of life within our cells to turn genes on and off so that the body can respond adaptively to shock, trauma and stress. This is Stage Two of mindbody communication wherein information of the genes is transcribed into mRNA (messenger Ribonucleic Acid) that will serve as a blueprint for the cell to make new proteins to facilitate adaptation, growth and healing as well as the structural foundation for new consciousness. Glaser and others (1990) published the first experimental evidence that psychological stress such as medical students experienced during medical exam week actually could turn off a gene (the interleukin-2 receptor gene) so that the normal process of transcription did not take place. We may take this as direct experimental evidence of mindbody communication. The famous Cartesian gap between mind and body has been bridged by a form of communication called the "messenger-molecule-receptor system."

Glaser's research gains even more profound significance for a general theory of mindbody healing when we realize that other independent medical researchers (Rosenberg & Barry, 1992) have found that interleuken-2 is a messenger molecule of the immune system which tells certain white blood cells to attack pathogens that cause diseases, including cancer cells. Thus, the purely medical research of Rosenberg and the holistic medicine of Glaser, in the developing field of psychoimmunology, have found the same bottom line in mindgene communication at the level of gene expression. I hypothesize that mindgene communication will become the new criterion for evaluating all forms of holistic mindbody healing. Whatever the holistic method, we can test whether it facilitated mindbody communication and healing by taking a blood sample to determine whether gene transcription took place. An easy and reliable test of whether mRNA is made so that new proteins can be synthesized for growth, healing and new consciousness.

Yes, even God would have to pass our mRNA-gene test if she came down from the clouds to heal a lame child's withered limb. When we do our mRNA test on the miraculously healed limb we will expect to find the evidence that all the normal mRNA-gene transcriptions are operating as they do in a normal limb. Or do you believe that God would heal the limb by placing some sort of special spiritual substance in there to make the withered limb work?

Stage Three in the general cycle of mindbody communication is represented as the process of gene translation by which the mRNA from the genes is used as a blueprint for the cell to make new proteins that can make enzymes to: 1) facilitate the energy dynamics of the cell (yes, this would be the source of psychic energy as well); 2) drive the metabolism of the cell for growth and healing of the matter or structure of life; and 3) form new messenger-molecules and receptors to modulate the ever-changing informational systems of mindbody communication and consciousness.

Stage Four of the mindbody communication loop is the flow of messenger molecules released by cells into the blood stream where they can flow to the brain within about a minute, to turn on and off the neural networks that encode memory, learning, behavior, emotions, imagery – virtually everything we call "psyche" or "mind." This regulation of mental experience by messenger molecules of the body is a two-way street that is now well documented by two decades of experimental research on state-dependent memory, learning and behavior. (See Rossi, 1993, 1996.) It can account for our shifting moods and fantasies every hour and a half or so throughout the day in what is called the "Basic Rest Activity Cycle" (BRAC) as well as our nighttime periods of dreaming (REM sleep). Moods, fantasies and dreams are the basic stuff of Jungian psychology.

Healing and The Wave Nature of Consciousness and Being

It takes about an hour and a half to two hours for a complete loop of communication (cybernetics) from mind to gene and back again. We are all familiar with the term "circadian," the 24-hour rhythm of the daily cycle. The term "ultradian" has been coined recently to refer to any cycle less than 20 hours. Our heart rate, pulse, breathing and the BRAC are all examples of ultradian rhythms. A massive amount of experimental data now suggests that the hour and a half BRAC that we all experience as rhythms of optimal performance and healing in everyday life has its source in the mindgene communication loop at the cellular-genetic level. (See Lloyd & Rossi, 1992, 1993.)

The peaks of these rhythms when we are asleep is the approximately 20 minute REM dream state. When we are awake we experience ultradian performance peaks for about 20 minutes that alternate with ultradian healing responses for about 20 minutes at the low end of the cycle when most people feel a temporary fatigue. I hypothesize that these ultradian healing response periods correspond to the 20 minutes it usually takes for signals at the cellular-genetic level to carry out the critical Stage Two of gene transcription. When we ignore our natural mindbody signals of fatigue and the need to take a break we may be setting up the conditions for what I call the "ultradian stress response" wherein excessive "stress proteins" are produced at the cellular-genetic level in a desperate effort to cope with the excessive demands we are making on ourselves. When this condition continues over time it can lead to a chronic elevation of stress hormones with attendant consequences such as a suppression of our immune system, high blood pressure, anxiety, and depression. This natural 20-minute rest-healing period that normally takes place every hour and a half or two throughout the day can lead us to experience the ultradian healing response or the ultradian stress response. (See Rossi & Nimmons, 1992). I hypothesize further that this is the psychobiological basis of what has been called the "hypnoid" and the *"abaissement du niveau mental"* (a lowering of mental level). Let us trace the history of these concepts and their relationships to the wave nature of consciousness and being.

Jean-Martin Charcot believed that there exists a special state of consciousness which occurs periodically, somewhere between sleeping and waking. He called it "hypnoid" and identified it as a source of hysteria and many psychological problems. He believed that this state is something like hypnosis, but could appear spontaneously. He did not know why it appeared, but hypothesized that it is much like the experience of being caught up in a dream. At such times, he believed, any strong emotional stimulus could become imprinted on the mind in a neurotic fashion. When we cannot rest, we become prone to highly-charged emotional states, anxiety, irritability, and depression. Charcot sought in vain a biological basis for such a hypnoid state. Another century of research was required before laboratory scientists coined the term "ultradian" and recognized that our nighttime dreams take place every 90 to 120 minutes, while our waking daydreams follow the same rhythm.

Pierre Janet noticed that, at various times through the day, we experience periodic fluctuations in our mental status (abaissement du niveau mental). During these periods of abaissement, Janet found that the psyche loses some of its capacity to synthesize reality into a meaningful whole, especially if we encounter a powerful emotional event. During the abaissement we tend to be emotionally vulnerable; we can register life experiences but cannot properly "digest" them. The emotional experience floats in our unconscious mind unassimilated, in effect jamming the gears of the mind. Janet hypothesized that such unassimilated experiences could become the seed of psychological or psychosomatic illness, obsessive thought patterns, phobias – all sorts of behavioral problems. Many chronic problems, he believed, were the result of the mindbody's continuing, frustrated effort to make sense of the original disturbing experience. Janet believed that there was an underlying physiological source of these abaissements during the day that were somehow associated with stress and exhaustion.

It was Freud's genius to recognize the essential connections between the sources of psychopathology and creativity in everyday life. In their early classic volume, *Studies on Hysteria*, Breuer and

Freud recognized that the hypnoid state was somehow related to "abnormal states of consciousness" as well as the ordinary everyday "absence of mind" but they were puzzled about it. It would taken another 50 years before researchers found that there is an entirely natural "absence of mind" that takes place for 10 to 20 minutes every 90 to 120 minutes or so throughout the day. I hypothesize that this is the natural psychobiological basis of what Milton H. Erickson called the "common everyday trance," a natural form of self-hypnosis.

Jung's Synthetic or Constructive Method

The relationship between Janet's abaissement and the symptoms of ultradian stress, healing, creativity, and the transformation of character were described by Jung as follows:

> The abaissement du niveau mental, *the energy lost to consciousness, is a phenomenon which shows itself most drastically in the "loss of soul" among primitive peoples, who also have interesting psychotherapeutic methods for recapturing the soul that has gone astray. ... Similar phenomena can be observed in civilized man. ... Carelessness of all kinds, neglected duties, tasks postponed, willful outbursts of defiance, and so on, all these can dam up his vitality to such an extent that certain quanta of energy, no longer finding a conscious outlet, stream off into the unconscious, when they activate other, compensating contents, which in turn begin to exert a compulsive influence on the conscious mind.* (CW16, par. 372)
> The archetypes are formal factors responsible for the organization of unconscious psychic processes: they are "patterns of behavior." At the same time they have a "specific charge" and develop numinous effects which express themselves as affects. The affect produces a partial abaissement du niveau mental, *for although it raises a particular content to a supernormal degree of luminosity, it does so by withdrawing so much energy from other possible contents of consciousness that they become eventually darkened and unconscious.* (CW8, par. 841)

Jung also wrote the clearest description of the rhythmic or wavelike character of emotional complexes and imagery before the term "ultradian" came on the scene:

> The complex can usually be suppressed with an effort of will, but not argued out of existence, and at the first suitable opportunity, it

reappears in all its original strength. Certain experimental investigations seem to indicate that its intensity or activity curve has a wavelike character, with a "wave-length" of hours, days or weeks. This very complicated question remains as yet unclarified. *(CW8, par. 201, emphasis added)*

I submit that Jung's "very complicated question" is answered, at least in part, by our developing understanding of the ultradian wave nature of consciousness in stress and healing. We have come full circle, from the classrooms of nineteenth-century Paris and Vienna to our current exploration of the wave nature of consciousness. From the "hypnoid state" of Charcot and the "abaissement" of Janet as the source of psychopathology to Freud and Jung's recognition of its role in healing, creativity, and the evolution of consciousness; each of these pioneers seemed to describe much the same phenomenon: There are special time periods of potential stress or healing that come on us naturally. Each described mindbody state occurs when our balance of consciousness and capacities shift, rise and fall, leaving us not fully awake, nor quite asleep. All these pioneers had glimpsed a "royal road" to our inner mindbody with a potential for pathology as well as personal growth.

I have illustrated previously how a typical psychotherapy session uses the psychobiological dynamics of an ultradian Basic Rest Activity in deeply experiential psychotherapy by whatever name: the original emotional catharsis method of Freud as well as the highly numinous encounters with the Self that Jung called "active imagination." I propose that this is the psychobiological essence of Jung's synthetic or constructive method leading to the "transcendent function." I have found a parallel between the four stages of the classically described creative process – 1) data collection, 2) incubation or emotional arousal, 3) illumination or insight and 4) verification – and the natural arousal, crisis or peak performance and the natural relaxation phases of the BRAC. Further, in Stage One, when the patient is searching for the problem, Jung's "sensation function" is most appropriately engaged. As the patient moves on to the second stage, Jung's "feeling function" obviously becomes more prominent. In the third stage we would expect that Jung's "intuitive function" would come into play as new consciousness is experienced. The essence of creative experience often occurs during a period of creative inner work – active imagination – wherein patients are so involved within the numinosity of their transformation that they are often silent and apparently unresponsive to outside cues. I hypothesize that these creative moments of original psychological experience correspond to the synthesis of new proteins in the brain. (See Rossi, 1996.)

Finally, only in the fourth stage, verification, does Jung's "thinking function" have its best role. It may be surprising for most therapists to recognize that conscious cognition, meaning and understanding usually come last, at the end of the creative experience. The body as sensations, perceptions and feeling usually comes first as has been documented previously (Rossi & Cheek, 1988). All too often, however, when the patient begins to experience emotional arousal in Stage Two the therapist becomes insecure and hastily jumps in with premature interpretations and cognitive structuring that cuts off the nascent private period of creative experience. This is the most common error by therapists who have no appreciation of the periodic nature of the transcendent function. The basic facts of the wave nature of consciousness and being imply that we all experience a complete unit of mindbody communication and healing every hour and a half or two with a potential for new consciousness and Self creation. The novel mapping of Jung's psychological functions on the four stages of the creative process is artificial and only approximate. It can be taken only as a heuristic guide for the therapist rather than another procrustean bed into which to fit the patient.

There is something fundamentally new in this mapping of the four stages of the creative cycle onto our natural psychobiological ultradian rhythms of performance and healing. Analysis is something more than a "talking cure," more than an "I-Thou dialogue," and certainly more than the "art of interpretation." Numinous experiences in analysis engage us at the deepest levels of mindgene communication when the transcendent function is involved in utilizing our natural ultradian rhythms. According to this view, Jung's synthetic or constructive method is deeper than the mind level; it engages us at archetypal levels of transformation in the matter-energy-informational dynamics of the collective unconscious, expressed at all levels from the cellular-genetic to our numinous experiences of the Self. I have described elsewhere (Rossi, 1996) this new vision of Jung's synthetic or constructive method. It has stimulated the development of a host of new approaches to facilitating active imagination and the transcendent function.

References

Lloyd, D. & Rossi, E. (1992). Ultradian Rhythms in Life Processes: A Fundamental Inquiry into Chronobiology and Psychobiology. New York: Springer-Verlag.

Lloyd, D. & Rossi, E. (1993). Biological rhythms as organization and information. *Biological Reviews, 68*, 563-577.

Rosenberg, S. & Barry, J. (1992). *The Transformed Cell: Unlocking the Mysteries of Cancer.* New York: Putnam/Chapmans.

Rossi, E. (1972/1985). *Dreams and the Growth of Personality.* Pacific Palisades, CA: Palisades Gateway Publishing.

Rossi, E. (1993). *The Psychobiology of Mind-Body Healing* (rev. ed.). New York: Norton.

Rossi, E. (1996). *The Symptom Path to Enlightenment: The New Dynamics of Self-Organization in Hypnotherapeutic Work.* Pacific Palisades, CA: Palisades Gateway Publishing.

Rossi, E., & Cheek, D. (1988). *Mind-Body Therapy: Ideodynamic Healing in Hypnosis.* New York: Norton.

Rossi, E. & Nummons, D. (1991). *The 20 Minute Break: Using the New Science of Ultradian Rhythms.* Pacific Palisades, CA: Palisades Gateway Publishing.

Stonier, T. (1990). *Information and the Internal Structure of the Universe.* New York: Springer-Verlag.

Psychological Type in Relation to Archetype

Wayne K. Detloff
El Cerrito, California, U.S.A.
Society of Jungian Analysts of Northern California

In my early years of working with Jung's contributions, his theory of psychological types seemed almost totally separate from his theory of archetypes and the collective unconscious. Over the years I have come to realize how much the two areas have in common. There is an innate propensity toward patterning, relatively independent of outer experience. In addition, psychic energy and emotion are active in relation both to the archetypes and to the psychological type.

My thoughts here are influenced by two factors: (1) a long practice of depth analysis and extensive experience in a wide range of clinical settings and (2) quantitative data collected over three decades from a great variety of people, including newly convicted felons, the full range of patients in and out of hospitals, staff in various institutions, middle-class couples and students.

Often when we review in our minds patients who seem to have something in common, we may not think of ourselves as doing research. We note that certain patients have some experience or problem in common and we wonder whether they have something else in common, a quality shared by many of them. Almost automatically we wonder whether it is different with gender or age. When done with some thoroughness, we now increasingly call this process qualitative or phenomenological research. I suspect that most of us are doing a great deal of this kind of research, in an informal way.

It may be that not all the cases are explained best by the same formulation and that we need to look for better ways to make meaningful subgroups beyond gender or age. Psychological type often is an appropriate moderating variable. Quantitative methods enable us to establish subgroups, especially with a large number of cases.

Although I cite research using quantitative methods, the real creativity is not in the statistical methods, nor in the computers that facilitate those methods. These methods and computers are tremendously helpful in managing the tedious and complex tasks inherent in a wide range of problems: in testing hypotheses as well as in storing, retrieving, and showing subtle, complex inter-relationships of a huge number of variables. One can find subtle relationships among variables that can elude even the most finely honed intuition. But the creativity begins with deciding what to ask of the computer and picks up again with what the computer has produced. One asks – rightly – "but what does that mean?"

To answer the question of meaning requires just the right researcher. A researcher, who knows the data well and is also an experienced clinician, finds in this question a special place for creativity. Working back and forth between the quantitative data with large numbers of subjects and the qualitative data of smaller numbers of cases found in clinical experience may result in the convergence of the quantitative and the qualitative approaches. When the two approaches fail to converge, it is important to understand that failure; then a convergence may become possible. Studying the interaction between the two approaches allows one to enrich and, in a sense, validate the other.

Many of Jung's ideas were formalized many years after his word association experiments, where the roots of his ideas lie. Over time he recognized deep patterns manifest at various levels. In his word association experiments he used the most sophisticated statistics of that time. He continued to use statistics later in his life, even in relation to the difficult problems inherent in synchronicity. I find it easy to imagine that, if Jung were still with us, he would find creative uses of the mathematical developments that are facilitated by computer.

Psychological type seems to be the archetype for the development of ego consciousness. The Self has the potential for the development of each of the types and, thus, for the development of the ego. The development of the psychological type tends to proceed in an orderly manner unless there are disruptive influences in the experiences of the patient. This process is clearer in adults but seems to be similar in children.

Jung never stated, to my knowledge, that the psychological type could be viewed as the archetype for the development of the ego, but this formulation seems to me consistent with his giving the English translation of his book on psychological types (CW6) the subtitle, "The Psychology of Individuation." Initially, there may need to be further development of the primary function and then of the auxiliary function. This development may occur more or less simultaneously with analysis of the shadow. For individuation in the classical sense, the third function and finally the fourth, the inferior function, are deeply involved. The sequence is rarely this clear and neat, but a general trend or pattern underlies the process. Once the type begins to be established, there is a probable sequence of further development, unless it is impeded in some way. There may be a crisis for a person whose original and natural predisposition is strong but thwarted.

In a recent survey (Bradway & Detloff, in press) nearly 200 California analysts and candidates were asked their opinion about the relative importance of five possible determinants of psychological type. By far, an inborn tendency due to genetics (chromosomes) was rated highest; 69 percent ranked genetics number one, for an average of 52 percent of the influence. Intra-family dynamics was a clear second determinant. There were three other possible choices: (1) inborn tendencies due to fate/karma/previous lives/synchronicity; (2) interpersonal experiences outside of family (teachers, peers, admired persons) and (3) birth order. Two early published research studies on introversion/extraversion (Eysenck, 1956; Gottesman, 1963) point to a genetic predisposition. Other, more recent studies tend to affirm the heritability of introversion/extraversion. Unfortunately, the extent to which the concepts used by those researchers fit Jung's description is not clear, but a big overlap is likely. These studies used the model of identical versus fraternal twin. My own unpublished research also uses the twin model and includes the attitudes and the four functions. This research uses my unpublished research edition of a types questionnaire as the criterion and shows a genetic predisposition for attitude and functions.

Family hassles often are based on a child's strong disposition that is in conflict with the parental expectations. Recognition of this situation can lead to helpful interventions. For some people, it is a huge step for them to acknowledge that there is another legitimate way of being that is different from their own. The therapist's explanation of this conflict usually reduces the destructive tension and leads to more tolerance and relatedness, with sincere interest in the differences. Then, even a little understanding of the nature of the differences and how they are manifest on an interpersonal level or in terms of learning styles, is tremendously valuable. I have been impressed with how well children often make use of direct help in this area, even when the adults have discouraging limitations.

We need words and concepts that are as clear and precise as possible, without simplifying or limiting in a way that closes out some of the essence. I am fond of a statement that has been attributed to Einstein: that he liked simple explanations but no simpler than the real world. When working clinically, the context of a word or concept often saves us. The problem becomes more severe when we do formal research, or, perhaps to a lesser extent, when we talk to colleagues about important aspects of case material. Perhaps we are concerned with areas that are not yet sufficiently conscious to have an adequate vocabulary and a clear enough concept. I am often troubled by the ease with which we use words and concepts with an underlying assumption that everyone understands what we say exactly as we intended.

A related problem has to do with "Barnum" effect: statements that can be true without discriminating one person from another. This phenomenon was named after P. T. Barnum, the circus pioneer of the last century. After Meehl (1956) suggested serious consideration of the term, others reported research on the use of vague statements (e.g., "You enjoy a certain amount of change and variety in life"); double-headed statements ("You are generally cheerful and optimistic but get depressed at times"); model characteristics of the subject's group, such as students ("You find that study is not always easy"); and favorable statements ("You are well liked by others"). These statements can be largely true without discriminating one person from another.

I first learned to exploit this phenomenon as a kind of parlor trick before I had any clinical training and before it became known as the Barnum effect. One can convince people that more is known about them than there is any rational way of knowing. To a large extent, this is based on the person's being unconscious and gullible. My present interest in the phenomenon is to enable us to be as conscious and clear as possible in the vocabulary and concepts we use. At the same time, I believe that important areas are by their nature not yet sufficiently conscious for us to have an adequate vocabulary. It may be that introverted feeling or introverted sensation types are likely to be less verbally fluent, especially around deeply important personal concerns.

A related reason for interest in the Barnum effect is, for the most part, beyond the scope of this paper. My conviction is that this effect is often important to transference/countertransference. My concern is that the transference be "earned" and not merely the result of the Barnum effect. Often we have little control over matters of transference but at least we can be careful not to make unwarranted assumptions.

In general, paper-and-pencil inventories have not been considered to contribute much at the deepest level. I have become convinced that the archetypal level of our being can be manifest at all levels and that we can come to recognize these patterns including via paper-and-pencil inventories.

We are familiar with the parental archetypes, the contrasexual archetypes, the shadow, and the archetypes behind major life events: birth, death, marriage, and transitions between stages of life. Where else might we look for deep patterns? Should other patterns be viewed as facets or variants of these basic patterns?

Several areas are possible in response to the first question, but the response to the second is by no means clear. Henderson (1962) first introduced one of the most carefully worked-out contributions, which deserves careful attention. He described the four cultural attitudes: social, religious, aesthetic, and philosophic. More recently he updated his work and added a psychological attitude. (See Henderson, 1984, 1991.) He discussed these patterns in the context of layers of the unconscious; the cultural attitude lies between the primordial unconscious and the personal unconscious. His thesis clarifies issues that I consider basic.

The patterns associated with birth order seem to have an archetypal basis. Stewart (1992) has studied well-known historical people in relation to their birth order. My pilot study using people's birth order and their response to a list of descriptors has produced a long list of correlations that are being ordered so as to be more comprehensible.

Ideas that have lived through time are prime candidates for archetypal themes, especially if the ideas seem to apply cross-culturally. Phylogenetically, gender has been around much longer than parenting and thus may be the basis for the oldest archetypes. Gender as the physiological substratum for the feminine and masculine principles is central to one of the oldest recorded documents, the *I Ching*. The terms feminine/masculine principles, logos/eros principles, and the contrasexual archetypes seem to be used without adequate delineation. We need to be clear about each of the terms and their relation to the functions of feeling and thinking.

Astrology is one of the most potent areas to look for archetypal patterns. Whether or not you believe in the synchronistic aspect of astrology, it has developed into one of the most elaborate systems for viewing the universe. When I first spoke to my friends and colleagues of these patterns in astrology as archetypes, the responses often involved varying degrees of reservation, skepticism, and dismissal. Since then, at least four authors (Burt, 1988; Greene, 1978, 1983, 1984; Hamaker-Zondag, 1980, 1984, 1985, 1988, 1990; Howell, 1987, 1990) in astrology have used the concept of archetype. In addition, some of the astrological concepts are related to psychological types.

As has happened so often when I have had the impression that I had an original thought, I found not only the basis of the thought in Jung's writing but quite a clear expression of the idea. So it was with my relating astrological patterns to archetypes. Then, I must consider that I might have read what Jung said. I fear that there are many instances in which, try as I may, I cannot always credit people in my outer life who have contributed to what I think of as my own. It is a sobering concern.

In astrology each element, sun sign, or planet represents a node that, like other symbols, can be grasped or understood. Each node has the potential for being energized. The constellation of these nodes constitutes the background forces in a person or situation. It may be that some of the astrological configurations are more appropriate for some clinical situations than are more commonly used concepts, especially if we can sharpen our understanding and use.

The recent interest in the Enneagram is another impressive example. The Enneagram is said to have been part of a secret oral Sufi tradition for hundreds of years and rarely given in its entirety to any one individual. Each of the nine points describes certain characteristics or propensities which interact according to patterns described in the Enneagram itself. It is uncertain whether that which is now readily available truly corresponds to the original tradition. However, the enthusiastic response of those introduced to the Enneagram in its present form suggests an archetypal quality.

The deep patterning with which we are concerned here may be reflected whenever one finds a connection between the body and the psyche. Thus, one might look to somatotypes (Ernst Kretschmer,

William H. Sheldon, or Stanley Keleman), chirology, and dermatoglyphics.

Jung has mentioned Kretschmer, whose book (1921) was published in the same year as Jung's *Psychological Types* (CW6). Jung pointed out a basic difference in the two approaches: Kretschmer starting with the body, Jung with the psyche. In 1929, Jung wrote "I personally have the impression that some of Kretschmer's main types are not so far removed from certain of the psychological types I have enumerated." (CW8, par. 222) To my knowledge, Jung never elaborated on this comparison. As late as 1957, Jung stated (Let-II, pp. 346-348) that he considered the comparison of somatic and psychological types as completely unsolved, pointing out that somatic characteristics are permanent and virtually unalterable facts whereas psychological type is mutable in personality development and especially in neurotic disturbances. I find, also, strong influences from experience.

Spier's (1955) study of hands (for which Jung wrote an introduction) would have had limited use for me without the help of the late Kate Marcus, a Jungian analyst who had studied with Spier. I have not yet undertaken a quantitative study, but, on the basis of clinical experience, I have a strong conviction about the importance of the study of hands. When certain features are constellated in the hand I can predict, with considerable confidence, some aspects of psychological types as described by Jung. I am indebted to the late Charlotte Wolff, who helped me to see that the hand can be viewed as a visible interface between early embryonic development and experience.

Cummins and Midlo (1961), two anatomists at Tulane Medical School, coined the term dermatoglyphics and established the specialty with that name. Dermatoglyphics focuses on the fine lines (papillary ridges) of the palms of the hand and the soles of the feet, which have been used for identification since the turn of the century. In the first trimester after conception, the fine lines of the hand of the embryo are laid down and are relatively unchanging throughout life. There is extensive, careful, and detailed research on dermatoglyphics, mainly by anatomists, geneticists, and anthropologists. There are about thirty medical syndromes which have been shown to have associated dermatoglyphic findings. Some of these syndromes, especially those involving the X and Y chromosomes, have psychological features. There is also recent research suggesting a connection with sexual orientation in men.

Later, the secondary lines of the hand appear and continue to change throughout life. These secondary lines seem to relate to experience of deep archetypal impact: the relationship of the body to the psyche. Marcus and I had noted independently the change in Jung's hand print from before his near fatal heart attack and after. These findings were later published by Debrunner (1974).

My research has been both phenomenological and quantitative. The interaction of the phenomenological approach with the clinical experience and the use of quantitative approaches as adjuncts is central to my research. This research has stimulated my thought about the patterning in the psyche, especially its manifestation at the level of paper-and-pencil responses. Any one observation may be understood best in relation to psychological type and at other times by one of the archetypes. At still other times, the archetype and the psychological type seemed to be interacting and it is difficult to know how much to attribute to the type and how much to the archetype.

When Marie-Louise von Franz first visited California in the early 1950s, she lectured on the puer aeternus. I was already familiar with the amplification material by Jung and Kerényi (1949). The lecture by von Franz helped me to see more clearly how this archetype looked in everyday life. Her description struck me as being much like an extraverted intuitive and I began to wonder if there were a special affinity of an archetype and a psychological type. It took time for me to recognize the archetype in sensation types. This was the beginning of a realization that there is a subtle and clinically very important relationship of archetype and type on the ego and behavioral level. The way an archetype is experienced by the person in whom it is active and the way it can be observed in the person's behavior are very different, according to the person's typology. Recognizing this archetype changed my whole perspective on the then current psychiatric nomenclature, where we had often diagnosed people identified with the puer archetype as sociopathic or psychopathic. The failure to include such nuances in our clinical discussions is a loss.

Jung's writings often start with an image from the unconscious which is then amplified to enable us to infer the archetype and its meaning. Osterman (1968) showed the propensity to patterning throughout the universe. A profound propensity for deep patterns becomes central in my investigations, whether we speak of an archetype, introversion/extraversion as an attitude, the four functions, or logos/eros principles.

The extensive list of descriptors that I have amassed facilitate people's rating how well the descriptor applies to themselves or to someone they know well. The descriptors – mostly adjectives and traits, with a few phrases – were limited to about the eighth grade reading level so that wide usage would be possible. Friends, graduate students in clinical psychology, and colleagues were "judges," to minimize the influence of my own temperament. An initial selection of about 3000 items – including some orienting variables derived from previous research – was reduced to about 1500. Responses to the 1500 by a large number of people is the basis for further reduction to a more manageable number. My approach is to use widely different samples of people, gathered over decades of time. Items which hold up under these conditions should have the widest possible applicability. I am still in process of eliminating the least valuable descriptors.

Working with these descriptors has already been helpful to me in clarifying, extending, and confirming some basic concepts. The goal is to develop clinical and research tools that will make Jung's contributions more available beyond the Jungian community. The first priority has been a thorough study of problems related to Jung's typology. A clinical and research tool to evaluate type with unprecedented thoroughness is forthcoming, perhaps first in an experimental edition. The second priority is to select the very best descriptors for discriminating within a wide range of problems such as I have described here. There is an underlying working hypothesis which is not formulated concisely but is explained partially in the remainder of this paper. Basically, it assumes that the more or less conscious ego and behavioral patterns are an inseparable manifestation of patterns found at all levels, including the deepest archetypal patterns, though the ego and behavioral patterns have the added elements of the more personal level.

There are serious and complicated methodological problems. In the course of many years, I ran a huge number of factor analyses. I would never give up factor analysis but there are serious problems in its use that have not been recognized sufficiently in the literature. One simply cannot rely solely on a mathematical solution. Fortunately, there are some ways of reducing the magnitude of these problems, but space limitations prevent my discussing them here. Comparison of traditional methods with some of the principles more recently derived from artificial intelligence and Rasch's (Linacre, 1994; Wright & Masters, 1982) work is part of developing these tools. To my knowledge, this is unprecedented anywhere in psychology.

To start with, each descriptor I have used has a certain face meaning. Some of the descriptors are similar on the literal level. (E.g., if the responses to "shy" and "bashful" are highly correlated, there is little surprise.) More interesting is words' relating to a concept such as introversion. The same words may relate also to a neurotic quality not explained by introversion.

Most important is a constellation of responses to words from a more or less conscious ego point of view, which then point to a deep pattern that we call an archetype, such as: introversion/extraversion as attitudes, one of the four functions, or logos/eros principles. It is not quite the same as arriving at a score by adding the number of correct responses to a series of carefully chosen arithmetic problems. To a large extent, such a score measures learned skills involving mostly conscious ego functioning. In the case of Jung's concepts, we are often concerned with a conscious ego point of view and an associated constellation in the unconscious as in typology, or we are concerned with a conscious ego functioning which has its roots in the unconscious.

Here it seems useful to make my point by recalling a Buddhist saying, "The finger that points to the moon is not the moon," or Alfred Korzbyski's saying "The map is not the territory." My intent is to use a constellation of responses to descriptors for pointing to a deep patterning that has its roots beyond the ego. At this point, it is the inferred deep patterning that is of interest, not the individual descriptor. A pattern or concept is reflected that the respondent would otherwise have no way of formulating. Likewise, an observer can respond to the descriptors in relation to the observed person and thereby allow for describing the person according to concepts that are unfamiliar. This approach is based on personal and clinical experience that when a pattern is important, active, and becomes energized for the individual, the pattern of responses to the descriptors will be more clearly differentiated. That is, the response to individual items will have more clarity or conviction, and the patterns of responses will be more consistent and coherent.

From a research point of view, such an "objective" instrument enables research results to be replicable and more comparable with other studies using the same criteria. Research possibilities are almost endless. For example, one may want to study the effect of the typological match of therapist and patient under various conditions: short term versus long term, initial response versus long-term developments, experienced therapists versus less experienced therapists.

Clinically, such an instrument can be used in a way somewhat analogous to a "second opinion." There are times when one might want to check one's judgment against an independent view. This can be true, especially, for a clinician still developing skills in the area in question. Or, there are times when the material presented by the patient is not clear and being more clear would be helpful to the process. In a "classical analysis," one might choose to wait until material clarifying the issues comes forth, but not all situations allow such waiting. Indeed, we might question whether waiting is necessarily better.

In summary, my focus has been on the propensity for patterning as seen in both psychological type and archetype, along with possible additional areas. The way the archetype manifests on the ego and behavior level may seem different according to psychological type. My approach to research uses both phenomenological and quantitative methods which complement each other. The two methods tend to validate each other, or raise new questions. Descriptors can be used to develop clinical and research tools.

References

Bradway, K. & Detloff, W. (in press). Psychological type: 32-year follow-up. *Journal of Analytical Psychology.*

Burt, K. (1988). *Archetypes of the Zodiac.* St. Paul: Llewellyn.

Cummins, H. & Midlo, C. (1961). *Finger Prints, Palms and Soles: An Introduction to Dermatoglyphics.* New York: Dover (corrected republication of work first published by Blakiston, 1943).

Debrunner, H. (1974). Changes in the hand lines of C.G. Jung. *Spring,* 193-199.

Eysenck, H. (1956). The inheritance of extraversion-introversion. In H.J. Eysenck (Ed.), *Readings in extraversion-introversion, theoretical and methodological issues* (Vol. 1). New York: Wiley (1970).

Gottesman, I. (1963). Heritability of personality: A demonstration. *Psychological Monographs, 9* (Whole No. 572).

Greene, L. (1978). *Relating, an Astrological Guide to Living with Others on a Small Planet.* York Beach, ME: Weiser.

Greene, L. (1983). *The Outer Planets and Their Cycles: the Astrology of the Collective.* Reno: CRCS.

Greene, L. (1984). *The Astrology of Fate.* York Beach, ME: Weiser.

208 Wayne K. Detloff

Hamaker-Zondag, K. (1980). *Astro-psychology.* New York: Weiser.

Hamaker-Zondag, K. (1984). *Elements and Crosses as the Basis of the Horoscope: Jungian Symbolism and Astrology* (Vol. 1). York Beach, ME: Weiser.

Hamaker-Zondag, K. (1985). *Planetary Symbolism: Jungian Symbolism and Astrology,* (Vol. 2). York Beach, ME: Weiser.

Hamaker-Zondag, K. (1988). *The Houses and Personality Development: Jungian Symbolism and Astrology* (Vol. 3). York Beach, ME: Weiser.

Hamaker-Zondag, K. (1990). *Aspects and Personality.* York Beach, ME: Weiser.

Henderson, J. (1964). The archetype of culture. In A. Guggenbühl-Craig (Ed.), *The Archetype.* Basel/New York: S. Karger.

Henderson, J. (1984). *Cultural Attitudes in Psychological Perspective.* Toronto: Inner City Books.

Henderson, J. (1991). The psychological attitude. In *Symposium on cultural attitudes in honor of Joseph L. Henderson, April 7, 1991.* San Francisco: Friends of ARAS, Jung Institute.

Howell, A. (1987). *Jungian Symbolism in Astrology.* Wheaton: Theosophical.

Howell, A. (1990). *Jungian Symbolism in Astrological Signs and Ages.* Wheaton: Theosophical.

Jung, C. & Kerényi, C. (1949). *Essays on a Science of Mythology: The Myth of the Divine Child and the Mysteries of Eleusis* (R.F.C. Hull trans.). Bollingen Series XXII. New York: Pantheon.

Kretschmer, E. (1921/1951). *Physique and Character, an Investigation of the Nature of Constitution and of the Theory of Temperament* (2nd ed.). New York: Humanities Press.

Linacre, J. (1994). *Many-facet Rasch Measurement.* Chicago: Mesa.

Meehl, P. (1968). Wanted – a good cookbook. *American Psychologist. 11,* 263-272.

Osterman, E. (1968). The tendency toward patterning and order in matter and in the psyche. In J.B. Wheelwright (Ed.), *The Reality of the Psyche.* New York: Putnam's for the C.G. Jung Foundation.

Spier, J. (1955). *The Hands of Children: An Introduction to Psycho-chirology* (2nd Ed.). London: Routledge.

Stewart, L. (1992). *Changemakers: A Jungian Perspective on Sibling Position and the Family Atmosphere.* London/New York: Routledge.

Wright, B. & Masters, G. (1982). *Rating Scale Analysis: Rasch Measurement.* Chicago: Mesa.

Stages of Life

The Torch Bearers

Puers as the Chosen Ones

Avi Baumann
Jerusalem, Israel
Israel Association of Analytical Psychology

Clinical work with ten cases of second-generation Holocaust survivors – and other second generation Jewish refugee-immigrants to Israel – showed that many of the subjects had difficulty entering adult life, assuming roles, finding suitable professions, marrying and settling down. After working for some years more with such cases, I now realize that there are other problems and difficulties: *puer* states with all their accompanying phenomena, or the *senex* side of the archetype, which becomes significant in patients who are traumatized too early. The "senex" immigrants have adapted well to collective norms and their puer side sits well in the shadow. But they have difficulty, as adults, in finding meaning to their lives. My comments reflect, in addition, my own experience as an Israeli, born to a generation of immigrants who, as youths, escaped from Germany and Austria during the Second World War.

I realize also, as part of the process of maturing into adulthood, the importance of attachment to our broader roots. Bringing about an encounter with these roots is part of the parents' role in helping the child to bridge the gap from childhood to adulthood. The parents undertake this role best if they are attached meaningfully to their own pasts.

But what happens when the parents themselves are torn away from their past and unable to transmit it? What if they can depend only on the future? What kind of conscious and unconscious messages does the child receive? What does it mean to grow up? Does the child want to? Perhaps he or she has something worthwhile to say as a child or – for the male – as a puer. Before forcing him to grow up, we should try to hear the call of the puer, remaining first in the archetypal realm and moving from there to the personal level through the etiologic and clinical pictures by which the condition reveals itself.

At the archetypal level, two different points can be emphasized for better understanding of the puer's nature. Von Franz (1970) emphasizes the attachment of the puer to the mother archetype; he appears as the son/lover and not as the youth. Von Franz does not perceive him as a principal counter to the senex; in this way she misses the socio-cultural collective influence and its possible fertilization by the inspirational nature of the puer.

Hillman's (1979) emphasis is well-placed. He developed the idea of the puer-senex continuum and interaction as a possibility of growth or as a danger of being possessed. Only in a personal situation can a puer sometimes become united too closely with the mother complex or with other complexes; at the archetypal level, the puer complex must be examined separately. Like Jung, Hillman describes the puer archetype as the principle of growth and renewal – a creative movement. Youth and freshness are not committed to heavy tradition, and by nature, incorporate a great deal of naivete. In contrast, but not to be considered separately, is the senex – old man – personification of the archetypal principle of time, order, decisive principles, crystallization of law and rules of this world's culture and history. In understanding the puer as part of the senex-puer continuum, we must examine the socio-cultural background we are dealing with, in order to give place to the senex pole and, thus to give some ground to the puer.

To study the puer-senex in the Holocaust generation and the succeeding one seems too extreme, but I broaden it to include the issue of the new generation after the stress of migration. My hypothesis is that, in a forced migration of uprooted people, there are enhancing factors in both generations that cause the puer to be active. There is an abrupt early "weaning" of the child, pseudo-maturity and, later in life, a clinging to adolescence and its attendant phenomena. An important factor is the difficulty encountered by the previous generation: uprooted from its well-known surroundings and supportive social-cultural environment, and having to adapt to a new situation and, to a certain extent, being dependent on the offspring. To comprehend better the puer-senex as part of generation interaction and its impact on the individual, it is necessary to understand the issue in the specific context of the new Israeli collective that has been established over the last five or six decades.

The New-Old Collective

Israel, "Alt-Neuland" (old-new land) – as the visionary, Theodore Herzl, called it – is a state that was established mainly out of a mixed population of Jewish immigrants from all over the world, especially Europe and the Arab countries. Many of them came, not of their own free will, but as refugees fleeing their countries of origin. Although they arrived while Israel was still fighting for its existence and independence, for them Israel was not merely a symbolic, but a real haven of refuge. Landing in the new homeland stirred in most of these immigrants a series of new/old feelings, even a sense of redemption. These new feelings of affiliation, reinforced by the deep, painful disappointments in their past, aroused in them enormous expectations and hopes. They tended to idealize the new nation and its "Israeliness," and to degrade the past of the Diaspora – the Jewishness. Zionism tried to be more like the distant biblical past than the recent Jewish past of the Diaspora. The new, idealistic Israelis felt that they must be proud and strong, with heads held high and shoulders back, actively contrasting with the picture of the weak, bent Diaspora Jews. A painful split, albeit an artificial one, began between the Israelis and the Diaspora Jews, which would take many years to heal. People were encouraged to forget their pasts, the places they came from and even their cultures. Some even felt ashamed of their origins with their victimization, and tried to hide it. Differences in people's pasts and cultures, and the uniqueness of each group, were regarded as threats to national unity. Thus, people became ambivalent toward their own identities.

Denial of their origins caused considerable damage to the creative life of these people. The collective, although not yet consolidated or based on its true foundations, assumed a large measure of power over the individual. The new, inexperienced collective was quite dogmatic and nationalistic, unsure whether to be ideological, religious or tribal. There were strong influences of parent archetypes projected onto the land; heroes and myths of old came alive once more. The archetype of resurrection and rebirth, the one most relevant to our study, was felt everywhere. Behind all that, in the shadows, lurked the picture of the wandering "Shtetl Jew" of the Diaspora, who survived persecution and the wounds of the Holocaust with its deep traumas, rages and anxieties.

The father of one of my patients wrote to him on the day of his bar mitzvah:

To my son: Never have I had a day of joy; never real happiness;
always the Ghetto, the great war, Auschwitz. No ... No! you must not
cry; you should not take a pill; you are not ill and you are not crazy.
It is reality come back through the memories. You don't cure it; you
don't anesthetize it. This is your life, and tonight you can celebrate,
because from that death, those ashes and the blood, new life
emerged. There is a boy, a Jewish boy, and a victory! This is our
celebration! You are our victory!

My patient's father commented, "That was one of the few nights
that I slept without a pill."

Let us turn to the smaller unit in which the actual generation
interchange is taking place. There the child is socialized, and
receives most of his or her ability to become an adult in a given
society. When we analyze the various factors in that system in a
condition of immigration, and try to determine which of them is
crucial for us to understand the etiology of the unconscious complexity of the puer archetype, we see that there are parents' factors
and children's factors.

The parents' factors are the wounds sustained on tearing away
from their families and their previous culture: failure to adapt to the
new environment; detachment from the inner child; depression at
having given up on the meaning of their own personal selves; the
impossible expectations, both conscious and unconscious, of the
child; and last, but not least, the parents' ability or inability to pass
the child through to the outside world of society and culture.

The child's factors are sensitivity and intuition: ability to read the
parents' messages; the need to help the parent emotionally. It is the
creative, spiritual child, one who is more open to the archetypal
world and to that of the parents, who will be tuned in to them and
will be more susceptible. The child with greater cultural, social and
spiritual needs which have not been met will feel the split in the
parents' identity and will suffer.

The Families of Holocaust Survivors

Those who survived the Holocaust were, in most cases, the only
ones remaining in their families and are still in fear of annihilation.
To have a part in building the new country, creating a new family
and having children was most important and healing. The new
country symbolized life and continuity. Their children, in their new
home, became the sunshine, source of warmth and light for the

parents. Also, Israel was proof of victory over the Nazi intention to destroy the nation. The children became the *raison d'être* of their parents' lives. There is a great deal of research describing the parents' expectations from their children, claiming them as compensation for their loss and using them as substitutes for those destroyed. (See Trossman, 1968; Sigal & Rakoff, 1973) Rather than being individuals in their own right, the children became symbols of their parents' loss. It appears, then, that the expectations projected onto the child's role of memorial to the parents' loss were the reasons for the severe separation difficulties that most of these children suffer. It seems that both generations suffered unavoidable pain. The parents built their identities around the new generation; their own lives were restricted to surviving, after being cut off from their inner life and their past. The children gave up their identities, becoming the hopes, promises and extensions of their parents.

One might ask why in such a situation – being such a support and being rewarded for maturity – the child chooses, instead, to become a puer, refusing to assume an adult state? In such a stressful situation, it would appear easier to understand children who successfully pass through adolescence without crises, but pay the price of getting caught in the senex state. They continue to be the serious ones, meeting the norms of the collective through the expectations of their parents and they build up, even earlier, a falsely mature self as a way of existence. But what about the puers? What are they aiming at?

Onto the puer types the characterization of puerile adolescent personality has been thrust. All of them were youthful and creative, wore sunny smiles and were full of enthusiasm. They were sensitive to the analyst, carrying a sense of hidden omnipotence and ambitious to do something important and meaningful. Inwardly, however, they felt very old, tired and detached, saying that they knew exactly what it meant to be a grown-up. To them, it meant being unattractive, empty and depressed, with no creative soul. In all the cases, one can feel the pressure on the child, of his or her importance to the parents, and an enormous need to satisfy the parents, even to the extent of the children's sacrificing themselves.

Wardi (1990) writes about two main messages transmitted from the parents to their children and sealed in their souls. The first is to remind the world of what happened in the Holocaust; the second is to fill the void created by the loss of their dear ones. It seemed that they had to continue to play the role of those that had been lost but, for them, there was no real attachment to the past. Anything before the Second World War just wasn't there. So the message was, "You are the generation that must continue, but behind us there is only destruction, death and emotional vacuum. You have to build the family and the nation, and sometimes even to give your life for them." Underneath, of course, were the shadowy emotions of deprivation and sometimes a hidden envy. Of course there was also a message of the proof of victory.

Case No. 1: Yuval

We encounter a hero, brave and strong. We have already read his father's letter to him on his bar mitzvah.

For Yuval to come to analysis was another new injury. He had always thought of himself as strong, brave, young and talented, with no need of anyone's help. He was the apple of his anxious, depressed but ambitious father's eye, and also of his poor mother, a Holocaust survivor. His parents found each other on their way to Israel. They did not acclimatize well to their new country, and Yuval was always ashamed of their old-world behavior. He sought treatment because of the symptoms he was presenting: jumpiness, attacks of panic, wild gestures. Otherwise he would not have come. He jumped from job to job, unable to find real interest in any of them. He began every new enterprise with a burst of excitement that faded very quickly. He took a wife, knowing he would leave her soon after. One foot was already on the way out. He was quick, intuitive and full of ideas that he never could apply. Here he was writing a book, and there composing a new song. He has just found a wonderful, new puella, but tomorrow he will meet the true one.

From childhood, Yuval had to face his broken father, trying hard to read his needs, frustrations and inability to be happy. His fantasies fluctuated between becoming a millionaire – saving his father from his feeling of being poor – and being an artist, because he was creative, talented and musical. One of the first dreams Yuval brought to the treatment was:

> *I am making a very vigorous climb on a steep hill; a fiery torch is in my hand and my parents and my sisters are following me. It is a gloomy, dark night; my father and mother look like two refugees, wearing ragged clothes. I am glad I have the torch, which is beautiful and gives light, but I feel my legs hurting me more and more. I look down at them and see that I am barefoot and bleeding. It becomes harder and harder and more and more painful to walk.*

The situation created in the dream was clear: Yuval began to realize the role he plays in his family and in his life anywhere. He talked of what he did in the army: the risks he took, the sacrifices he made, his readiness to do anything in order to save others and be the officer of whom his father was so proud.

For Yuval, coming to analysis was like retirement after a long period of labor. He confessed how afraid he was, how childish he was underneath and how much he wanted someone to discover his disguise. Yuval was preoccupied with the mood of the therapist. Sometimes, he was more sensitive to me, my moods, health and expectations than I was myself. He knew how to satisfy and be the star patient. There was much twinship transference and a feeling of brotherhood that was healing, probably, for both participants. After taking up his role as a savior, Yuval calmed down and gradually revealed and confronted his puer face – which was his true one. Analysis made him aware of his omnipotent powers and his wish to do something great and important for his family and for the nation. But underneath was the need to save his father in order to have one.

Yuval also revealed a great deal of spiritual interest; in the analysis, this interest shifted to a greater interest in his father's family, past and culture. Yuval discovered that he had grown up without a father, without anyone to guide him, with no cultural heritage or past, or any real tradition. He came to realize how different he felt from the typical Israeli man. His discovery of how Jewish and how much more European he was gave his identity a new dimension. Yuval had to give up his torch and his inflated feelings and begin to heal his own wounded feet. It was difficult and painful to mourn his inability to be a proper child, stealing bits of it, like a thief, whenever he could. Yuval gave up his torch only when he could have another kind of light, another consciousness, for his own true self.

Case No. 2: Gili

Gili, in his late twenties, came for treatment because of inability to continue his vocation of social worker, inability to establish steady relationships, all coupled with terrible anxiety regarding marriage and settling down. Like Yuval, Gili was charming, creative, full of enthusiasm, had a beautiful smile and was always optimistic and cheerful. He was addicted to movies and books, reading everything new and living much of the time in a world of fantasy. Both his parents were Holocaust survivors. His father, a very nervous man, would even beat Gili in a frenzy of rage when he brought his food back from school uneaten and hidden in his drawings. Gili was the favorite son, the bright one, the one who was supposed to raise the family's achievements.

He recounted, "I was the family project, the scholar that my father had never been, and the cultured one that both of my parents were not. My father decided that I was to be a doctor while he worked as a clerk in the office of a medical center, always trying to pass himself off as a real M.D." In treatment he confessed, "Even from childhood I knew that I was playing and acting as if I really was a genius, and in fact, there were times when I actually believed it."

For Gili, it was a lightening of his burden to have a vessel, where he could at last begin to be himself and stop being a project of a new father (the therapist). He always found himself being put into that niche, but he always backed away. "Don't you fall into that trap," was his hidden message to me. He enumerated the many people who had been disappointed in him when he failed to fulfill his promises. Gradually Gili became aware of the puer side of himself, which held him high and distant from his confusion, depression and identity issue. He was afraid of life, of growing up, taking responsibility and being an empty, melancholic senex like his father. Confronting his depression was important, yet frightening. Gili had numerous night-mares and anxieties that emerged during the analysis: "No one prepared me for this life: no one told me about the real world. I feel like an orphan, wandering around; a real, lost project." That was the beginning of the emergence of Gili's true self. From the cheerful, promising puer came the orphan and the true self, and Gili now knew why he clung for about ten years more than he should have to the role of Peter Pan from never-never land.

Gili saw in me a father figure who could accept him, but who also was able to see through his posturing, and not let him play his unnecessary games. At the beginning of treatment, Gili greatly feared that my disappointment with him would cause me to abandon him. He tried very hard to be a perfect patient, wanting to bring success to me, my reputation and especially my new ideas in the field. For Gili, too, as for the others, it was very difficult to emerge from the puer state and transform it into something more meaning-ful. He suffered greatly while coming to terms with his limitations, his inability to work properly, his inadequacy in entering adult life.

Part of Gili's motivation in giving up the puer state was the new meaning that he found in getting married, having a family and assuming the responsibilities of fatherhood, which later became the most important part of his life. He even told me that he sent his wife to develop a career while he took over "the big project" of raising their children. He found it rewarding and perhaps even healing when recalling and coping with his own orphan state. Recently, he has changed jobs, having been accepted as a worker in a new project for gifted children, combining arts and sciences. For Gili, it appears to be compensation for his own culturally-deprived childhood.

In these cases, one was the project of the family; the other was the hero who, with his new, fresh spirit, would be the father's savior and the pride of the whole family. It was Miller (1979) who introduced the term "the gifted child": the child who is especially sensitive to the parents' needs and probably does self-damage by being too devoted to the parents' wounds. This mutually sensitive parent-child system has a strong impact on the child's psyche, influencing the strength of the ego and the rapidity of the child's growth, especially when the parents had undergone a trauma.

In earlier years, the second generation used to be called "the generation of the desert." They had been born on the way to the new Israel, between two cultures, midway between two stages of the Jewish nation. They were quicker to adapt to the new situation than were their parents. Their sensitivity and instant maturity resulted in an inability to assume adult roles when the time came. They claim, "I know the story of being grown up and adult. What's the big deal?" Spoken like a cynical, melancholic old senex.

Discussion

There are two levels of interaction between puer and senex: the collective level and the personal one, the macro and the micro. With the trauma of the Holocaust and subsequent uprooting, one can see the causes and effects that brought about the painful occurrence of the puer complex.

We have seen how the new-old collective was created, in the course of the building of the new country. We saw the detachment of the immigrants from their roots, culture and social systems, their clinging to the new piece of land as an anchor, countering the trauma of their abandonment. They saw it as their investment in hope and dependence on new ideals and a future generation. We have seen the split that occurred between the new and the old. Living in this intense atmosphere of redemption and rebirth revived many old themes from the distant past, like the old-time heroes from archetypal layers. This constituted a favorable atmosphere for emergence of the puer.

Returning to the perspective of the personal-familial level, children were mostly overprotected and had enormous importance for their parents. They were exposed very early in life, whether consciously or unconsciously, to a great deal of their parents' misery and helplessness, and were given all kinds of impossible messages about being the "victory" and the reason for their parents' life. This is a heavy burden to lay on a child who cannot protest and has no legitimate way to bear the suffering. Being unable to display one's own weaknesses and flaws is a crucial factor in the development and maintenance of the puer's inflated wishes to save, heal and redeem. Busy with the redemption of others, he forgets about his own. Hillman (1979) emphasizes the splitting of the puer-senex continuum as a crucial factor in the creation of the negative senex: cynical, depressive, discouraging; and the hypermanic puer – hovering, detached or fading.

The split could be caused either by the parents' overly difficult life, by their spiritual damage or their lack of attachment to their own broader roots. In the case of a lack of roots, they will transmit to the child a lack of meaning, inducing a cynical way of dragging the burden of life, teaching the child that life is all a struggle, with no pleasure.

By understanding the reasons on one hand and the prospect toward which the puer is aiming on the other, we can go beyond the one-dimensional prism through which von Franz (1970) views the puer syndrome. We can also broaden the solution she suggests. Because she emphasizes work and an ability to be committed as the main problems and not as symptoms of a deeper wound, her approach appears to be somewhat didactic and preaching, lacking in healing qualities. Looking at her words according to Hillman's concepts, her voice is coming from the negative side of the senex, which the puer can arouse easily.

Beneath the surface of this colorful but sometimes irritating picture presented by the puer, lies a child who, though wounded, does not cease looking for a lost childhood and does not give up trying to understand better how to become a true adult with a true self. Like Icarus or Peter Pan, the puer will fly higher and higher, whirling, until he gets into a crisis and falls down. His main motivation is not narcissistic – although it can be seen in that way – but to get into the true secrets of life. Whether tradition, art, or nature, he will approach each in a fresh, naive way. Like the child in "The Emperor's New Clothes," he can become obsessed with truths. He can become a wandering, drifting, lonely person, looking for all kinds of experiences, as if there had been no one to initiate him into the world and its secrets.

In analysis it seems that the real meaning and true secrets of life can come only after he gets in touch with his own wounds: the deprivation, the orphaned state, loneliness and detachment. Only then, as a grown-up, mourning his childhood and "crying his cry," as Hillman called it, will he get out of his inflation and a new meaning will emerge. The puer does not need a mother in the sense of milk or mirroring his narcissistic needs. He needs a place and another adult who believes him, accepting his puer side and giving him space to cry his own tears by coming to terms with his incapability and his failure to save his parents. He needs someone who will help him cease needing to be a chosen child, to cease searching for a healing elixir for the mother or being the parents' project, and to give up the torch, making room for a new light that will illuminate his true child self.

Perhaps, after a working through the personal healing, there will come a need to be in touch with the parents' past, and following that, with his broader Jewish roots, or others that are so important for his identity, attachment and stability. As a result of his reintegration, this new connection to his Jewish origins now becomes part of the restoration of the Self.

References

Hillman, J. (1979). Senex and puer. In J. Hillman (Ed.), *Puer Papers*. Dallas, TX: Spring Publications.

Miller, A. (1979). *The Drama of the Gifted Child and the Search for the Self*. London/Boston: Faber & Faber.

Sigal, J.; Rakoff, D. (1973). Some second-generation effects of survival of Nazi persecution. *American Journal of Psychiatry, 43,* 320-27.

Trossman, E. (1968). Adolescent children of concentration camp survivors, *Journal of the Canadian Psychiatric Association, 12,* 121-23.

von Franz, M.-L. (1970). *Puer Aeternus: A Psychiatric Study of the Adult Struggle With the Paradise of Childhood*. Boston: Sigo Press.

Wardi, D. (1990). *Memorial Candles* (in Hebrew). Jerusalem: Keter Publishing.

The Art of Unlearning in the Third Age

Marianne Jacoby
London, England
British Association of Psychotherapists

Some of the art of unlearning lies in distinguishing between what can be unlearned, and what cannot. The idealizations of, and prejudices about, old age can be unlearned, whereas the inborn tendencies – which we can summarize, in the Jungian way, as being when introverted tendencies outweigh the extraverted, or vice versa – seem to be constitutional and remain largely unchanged. But even here the distinction between what can and cannot be unlearned is not simple. Individuals differ and, after a long life, differences among them increase.

I am in my eighty-eighth year, and ascribe to myself the position of senior apprentice to the art of unlearning. But the words "the art of unlearning," are not mine alone. I took them from R.D. Laing. He mumbled them in his intuitive way, barely conscious of what he said. We were at a committee meeting held to decide the title of a congress, where Laing was to be the central figure. Yet nobody else had heard his words. He never repeated them; I never forgot them.

Laing – he wanted to be called "Ronnie" as an assurance that we loved him – may have been thinking of the art of meditation. But I am not good at meditating. Closer to me is Jung's "active imagination," which is a second cousin to meditation.

Much later, I added to this title "in the third age." The words were unknown to us in the 1960s, and are not widely familiar now. It is even less well known that the term has its origin in classical history.

Although I have never heard of a first or second age, the third age has a formidable history. Its origin is in the *Iliad* (Book I, line 253). Homer introduced us to the eminent King Nestor of Pylos, the king of the third age. History will have it that the king waged war not only with the first and second generations, but continued with the third generation of his own old age. Homer comments on the heroic king with pride: "He gave no grounds for sorrowful old age" (Book 10, line 79). I suggest that, if we need a patron of our old age, we claim

King Nestor, thus dating our historical roots back more than 2500 years. In those ancient days old age, whether it was sorrowful or not, was expected to begin at 60.

The number 60 exerts an extraordinary spell even in our own day. Sixty is an archetypal number: It denotes totality. We have inherited this magic quality of 60 from the Sumerians who lived in Mesopotamia some 4000 years ago. The Sumerians invented a sexagesimal counting system in which all measurements were based on 60 – and the spell is not lost on us. We count 60 seconds for our minute, 60 minutes for our hour, and six times 60 for our year of roughly 360 days. Therefore it will seem that our retirement age at 60 or 65 is not as arbitrary as many of today's 60-year-olds think.

In those ancient times, the majority of women did not live beyond 60 years of age. They had either died in childbirth or did not recover from it. Since then the situation has changed to the exact opposite. By the year 2030, according to forecasts, 75 percent of people over 60 will be women. This imbalance is new even for the majority of the women and men who are now in what we call our third age.

The many women and the few men who make up the population of the third age, carry – unconsciously – those of yesterday's assumptions and prejudices which should become conscious so that they can be unlearned and shed. The help of therapists or counselors ought to be available for both individual and group therapy. We need to take into account that today's third-agers grew up in the era of strict obedience and adherence to the youth cult: to look old was to look ugly. They have also learned to keep faith with the hallowed, Herculean spirit of the Protestant work ethic. It makes up the indelible part of a third ager's frozen superego.

A 91-year-old friend of mine told me that she had no time to phone me because she was too busy. She had been a workaholic all her life. A 70-year-old patient remembered her father's dictum, "A full day's work is a reward in itself." Whenever yesterday's work ethic collides with the new unhurried sense of time in old age, it causes confusion in the disenchanted third-ager, who does not understand the world any more.

I use my theme as a magnet which, left undisturbed, draws to itself its own relevant material, memories and images from mythological sources. Following the basic themes is my suggestion of a role model for the post-patriarchal third-age woman. I shall illustrate the unlearning, or the lack of it, with the cases of two aged patients and Jung's model of animus and anima. Following this comes an elaboration of Jung's notion that life is a transitus.

I can experience the art of unlearning by having recourse to Jung's active imagination. At first the two seem odd bedfellows. But they reinforce one another; each requires unlearning as an art. The imaginer, like the artist, is the protagonist of fantasies. These can become a real experience only if the imaginer unlearns conscious interference and allows spontaneous images to emerge; you let yourself dream while you are awake. With a passive attitude, you follow your active dreaming.

The professional artist works in much the same way. Active imagination is a private art; it is only for me. Yet not quite. For it forges a link between me, the me-ness and the otherness in me. I can be a tree or a mountain or a vintage Ferrari. Or it is my body, being part of nature, that invokes the otherness. This is especially noticeable if the body is ill. For the similarity between an ailing body and a gnarled oak tree or a cedar tree, more than 200 years old, is debatable. I do not deny trees a measure of natural consciousness.

A patient in his early sixties used active imagination in his therapy with me. He was a talented stage designer; golden opportunities beckoned to him. But he spoiled them by letting his rigid ego interfere, with its defensive method of manic stubbornness. I had to listen to his torrent of complaints; he felt interfered with by the managements of the theaters. They wanted him to make changes when designs were too elaborate and expensive. But Bert, my patient, would not give in. In one session, he did a longish bit of active imagining.

During his imaginary wanderings, he came to stand in front of a door with gold door-handle and door-plate. He desperately wanted to open this door but an old man, who had the key to the door, stubbornly and grumpily refused to hand the key over to Bert. This was the end of the session, and we did not come back to the grumpy old man; during the next sessions, other problems seemed more important. But, a fortnight later, Bert was upset; he had gone out and, without being aware of it, had left the key stuck in the front door on the outside. Luck had been with him; nobody had noticed the key. When he found the key, he didn't make the connection with the golden key of his imagination, but I did, and told him that the key problem had come back with a vengeance. We understood that the stubborn old man by the door was a personification of Bert's old attitude of stubbornness and grumpy defiance. He could confront it now. He unlearned his stubbornness, accepting the necessary compromises. Sure enough, the golden key was now in his hand and opened the door to golden opportunities. He became a well-known stage designer; his obituaries were in leading newspapers in Sydney, London and New York.

Turning now from the private world to the collective aspects of the third age, I shall sort out my fantasies about the preponderance of third-age women. Never have there been so many women confronting so few men. Thus, women mirror themselves in other women. The complementary opposites of female and male can be expected to disappear. As there is no longer an equal proportion of yin and yang, the third age is going to carry an overload of yin. Yet it seems possible that the most awakened women will take the opportunity of developing their own psychic male potential. This is not altogether new to younger generations of women. Some feminine identities, those that fit most smoothly into the dependence on the vanishing patriarchal males, can be unlearned. Whenever the feeling function is alert, it assesses the values and worthiness of attitudes and, in this case, sets in motion a process of devaluation. Accordingly, outmoded attitudes can be left behind. Instead of the old routine responses, a new flexibility can take over that lessens the burden of old age, allowing it to travel light. Also the body loses weight and height in very old age.

The awakened grandmothers, great-grandmothers and third-age unattached women have the opportunity to act as social mothers, thereby creating social families such as clubs and "togethernesses" of all kinds and enabling the passive and depressive loners to make new bondings, late in their lives. One hopes that there will be enough psychotherapists who will help them to keep the new bonds meaningfully. If thousands of women make their own contributions, however small, to the third age, they will create a new culture, which could unburden the sense of responsibility of the younger generations toward their elders.

Yet the huge problem remains as the support rate of the younger generations to the third-age pensioners is expected to halve between now and the year 2030. We should neither forget nor try to solve the not-yet problem of the year 2030.

I find it interesting to look back for a moment to Jung's essay, "Woman in Europe" (CW10), which he wrote in the 1920s – when Jung was only in his fifties. Much of what he wrote then is now out of date. We are 70 years further in the development of female and male psychology. Yet Jung's model of the contrasexual elements in our psyches is still valid for us today – even though what I call "today" must remain an assumption.

The contrasexual potential in women is the animus. It indicates a mature creative spirit. In fact, the Jungian literature is teeming with inspiring female authors. And there are as many, if not more, such Freudian authors.

Jung called the feminine psychic potential in men the anima, denoting a besouled empathic imagination. Both animus and anima have negative aspects, too, which do not add to their popularity. The negative animus in women makes them argumentative, wanting to lay down the law. The negative anima in men makes them sentimental and moody.

I have waited – without conscious interference – for the emergence of a role model that would fit the new masculine woman. It appeared in the wake of my browsing through Greek mythology; Athena, beloved daughter of Zeus, fits the model. After Zeus had fallen out with one of his several wives, he took on the birthing himself. What a reversal of parental roles! Thus Athena was born from her father's head, fully grown and fully armored.

Athena is no one's wife, mistress or mother; yet she is a woman. Her epithet is authority and care for others: for women, children, impetuous warriors and listless, indecisive, failing heroes or "patients." I find the Athena figure a fitting model for us as female therapists, as well as for the male therapists who are attracted by Athena as an adorable anima figure. Her image of authority and care determines the behavior pattern of female and male therapists; image and behavior are a unit that will be a safeguard whenever the therapy is in crisis.

There is no Athena without the Zeus model. His model can be aligned to the heads of our profession; Freud, Jung and many more are all available for individual choice. The Athena-Zeus model also relates to patients if a woman's relationship to her mother is overshadowed or outshone by her relationship to a prominent father.

However, one warning is required: not to go too far in identifying with an Olympian goddess. Our egos cannot tolerate the weight of such inflation. A drop into a depressive unworthiness, or into the Jungian shadow, would be inevitable.

Now I am submerging in my memories of 60 years ago. In 1935, I had an interview with Anna Freud in Vienna. She sat at the other side of her writing-desk, facing me. When she told me: "We do this" or "We think that," the "we" meant herself and her father. At the time of the interview I was young and awe-struck. Now, six decades later, I can relate the concrete reality of Miss Anna and Professor

Sigmund Freud to the archetypal pattern of the couple: Athena and Zeus. It belongs to the art of unlearning in the third age to let go of the fascination with external objects and perceive their archetypal background.

It is wonderful to sit back and let feelings, intuitions and associations attach themselves to memories and make sense of them, and thus come to understand them as "total objects," as Melanie Klein would call them. It is a blessing of the third age to have enough leisure time for revising memories and fantasies.

But the third age has negative aspects: loners' clinging to the past and maintaining that they are too old to learn the unlearning. And there are the melancholics who have no sense of the passing of time, who love the dead and the yesterdays more than the living of today. But a measure of melancholia is indispensable during the third age. So much loss is mourned, of the once-familiar relationships, home, environment, and youthful body image. And for many third-agers there is the loss of their former independence. The third-age ego has to unlearn and to devalue many of the precious habits of self-control that were taken for granted before frailty and fatigue set in.

The third age has its own shadow that makes it unpopular with younger generations. Untrained third-agers have the habit of talking too much. They seem to sense, often unconsciously, that there will be a limit after which they will be silent forever. Hence, while they are here, they get in as much talk as they possibly can. But they remain unaware of the fact that they omit to listen. And what the audience hears is the annoying, interminable, repetitive, unaddressed talk of a self-appointed orator. He or she will impart the same news to everybody. Any pair of anonymous ears is good enough.

Next in line of unpopular third-agers are those who forget. Many third-agers dislike themselves and get so discouraged and angry when they notice that they forget, that they won't try to train their capacity to memorize. In addition, there is the fear of Alzheimer's disease. It is not as frequent as it is dreaded. Another task for third-age therapists is to give help in memory training.

A male patient is a stand-in for the 25 percent, the third-age males of whom I know too little as patients. When he started therapy, just before he entered his sixties, his self-image was that of a loser and loner. The one and only reaction to his bad world was his grim anger: residual, paranoid-schizoid anger. When it exploded in the sessions, I let it blow over my head and disappeared in my chair. But because I could understand why he was so angry, it never occurred to me to terminate the therapy, nor would he stop attending. The unlearning of his hatred took the first ten years of therapy. But he needed not only the psychotherapy in my consulting-room. He also needed a physiotherapy of his own brand, which took place outside in the world. He, a Ph.D. mathematician, by then in his late sixties, became a runner – of races. I was sure that, with each drop of sweat he lost on his cross-country races, a drop of anger was lost as well.

One day he reached a watershed – a breakthrough. As I opened the door, my patient stood there poker-faced. A broad red ribbon hung from his neck. Fastened to the ribbon was a first prize in the shape of a big circular medal. Perhaps it was of pure bronze, but symbolically it stood for the pure gold of the Olympic winner. He had pulled my leg and I had a good laugh. During the next ten years of his mind and body therapy, his anima developed. It prompted him to practice active imagination in classical music. He bought a viola and joined a string quartet. Instead of his old poor-man's outfit, he now dressed with good taste. I allowed myself enough flirtation to comment on his good looks.

Yet in many of his daily habits he remained the introverted loner he had always been, notwithstanding the fact that he had become a happy grandfather. His introversion may have been constitutional, as Jung would have it, or acquired in childhood conditions, as W.R.D. Fairbairn would have it.

Generally speaking, to be alone and to introvert is better suited to old age than is extraversion. An extremely extraverted woman patient of mine – in her seventies – relied on a continuous supply of stimuli from external objects. When these failed her, she could only fall asleep.

As for myself, I veered either to Jung's or to Fairbairn's points of view. But I always felt that much of my introvertedness was forced upon me. The family behind me had more than one skeleton in the cupboard which made it imperative for me to become a psychotherapist, a Jungian, by preference. My aim was to lay the ghosts to rest: those of my own family and those of my patients. I also remember from early childhood my burning desire to get out into the world, which looked to me brimming over with promise, as it still does.

Jung called the afternoon of life the "sundown of the grand parabola's downward curve" (CW8, par. 798). According to the third-age time-scale, Jung was still a "minor," not yet 60, when he published this essay. He believed in the completeness of life. He stated, when he was almost 80: "Doubt and insecurity are indispensable components ..." I certainly go along with him here. But then he added, "of a complete life." And then he repeated: "If one lives properly and completely" (Let-II, p. 171). I ask myself who can assess whether one lives completely. Yet I am sure that for many third-agers the vision of a complete life will be a great comfort. But I find such completeness of life a tall order, too tall for myself. I am only an apprentice, albeit a senior one.

At this point in my essay, when I found it difficult to continue, I turned to D. W. Winnicott's imagery. I could tune into it. He said, about five months before he died: "Sooner or later the process of growing smaller starts, and it is painful at first until you get used to it." And again: "A great deal of growing is growing downwards. If I live long enough, I hope I may dwindle and become small enough to get through the little hole called dying." I feel that Winnicott's vision is akin to my basic theme of unlearning and of shedding, as a process that goes on indefinitely.

I got stuck here once more until I browsed in Jung's *Letters*. Unconsciously I was looking for a passage which I had forgotten, consciously, but years ago I had annotated it in the margin. "We should recognise," Jung reminded us, "that life is a transitus [transition]." He continued: "There is an old covered bridge near a village in Canton St. Gallen [near Jung's tower at Bollingen]. It carries the inscription: 'All is transition'" (Let-II, p. 169).

The most treasured memory of my childhood is a bridge over the Rhine. This bridge was so huge that when, as a child, I walked on my own I could never get to the other side. But now the bridge is for me – symbolically – the passage in time, a transition from one world to another. And I am once again incapable – or not yet capable – of getting to that faraway other side. I have an image of the third-agers moving, each on an individual transit, across this bridge of time.

With my persistent objection to completeness, I do not claim any degree of completeness for this talk. I take it for granted that you will have found points and aspects missing that I never thought of, not even in my dreams. I am only too aware that in about a year's time I would make up a different talk on the very same theme, of putting the art of unlearning apposite active imagination.

Would that we had the Swiss villager's motto, "All is transition," posted on our Channel Tunnel. But that is unthinkable!

An Individuated Life

An Interview with Elizabeth Osterman

Susan Bostrom-Wong
San Francisco, California, U.S.A.
Society of Jungian Analysts of Northern California

Elizabeth Osterman of San Francisco reflects on her life – 40 years as a Jungian analyst – and her connection to the Self. She tells her story of individuation, the founding years of the San Francisco Institute, and her meeting with Jung. She also speaks about her love for another woman and the sad but meaningful death of this life partner. Lastly, at age 80, she reflects on facing her own death.

For copies of the tape (80 minutes). Inquire: Susan Bostrom-Wong, 423-38th Ave., San Francisco, California 94121 USA.

Body and Psyche

The Relationship Between Psyche and Body

Eastern Perspectives

Shirley See Yan Ma
Toronto, Ontario, Canada
Ontario Association of Jungian Analysts

Jung's work on the sixteenth century alchemist Gerhard Dorn and subsequent recognition of the *mysterium coniunctionis* as: "the Western equivalent of the fundamental principle of classical Chinese philosophy, namely the union of *yang* and *yin* in *tao*" (CW14, par. 662) has built a bridge for psychological understanding between the East and the West. Within the forum of analytical psychology, what can the East and the West learn from each other despite their differences? Our focus is on the psyche-body aspect of this question; we hope it will generate more questions and reflections.

In most Western societies, the body is a discrete entity, separate from thought and emotion. Modern Western medicine views the body as made up of nuts and bolts; the doctor is a mechanic who fixes the body like a machine. In China and other Asian societies, the body is an open system linking social relations to the self; emotion and cognition are integrated into bodily processes. The traditional Chinese view treats the body as a garden; the doctor is a gardener who cultivates the garden according to the cosmic forces in the universe.

In Chinese alchemy the opus is achieved and experienced through the body. This tradition reflects a spirituality that is grounded in the organic unity of psyche and body. Once this unity is experienced, it becomes a way of life that can be cultivated consciously and lived.

A brief overview of the Chinese alchemical opus as it is understood through analytical psychology is in order. As Eastern healing techniques such as acupuncture, Shiatsu, and Reiki are being incor-

porated increasingly into the therapeutic community; this exploration may provide deeper insights for analysts into the nature of
psyche-body integration.

Chinese symbolic thinking has maintained a quality of *participation mystique*; the psychic and material aspects of a person are not
differentiated. To the traditional Chinese doctor, a change effected
on the physical plane automatically has a corresponding effect on
the psychic plane, and vice versa. Thus, in this paper, the word
"psyche" implies "body," and "body" implies "psyche."

Basic Chinese Cosmological Views

The Eastern approach to the whole person reflects the basic
cosmological view that respects the organic unity of the human
being and the correspondence between humans and nature. That is,
the body is regarded as a microcosm in symbolic resonance with the
social and planetary macrocosm. The ancient Chinese divided the
psycho-physical cosmos into a periodic two-fold rhythm, a reciprocal enantiodromial yin-yang motion: alternating rhythms in which
spatial and temporal elements are not separable. They regulate (*tiao*)
and harmonize (*ho*).

Through the five basic elements of Wood, Fire, Earth, Metal and
Water, the movements of the inner and outer worlds are correlated
intimately in an intricate system of interdependence and mutual
regulation. Outwardly, humans move with the forces of the seasons,
directions and time. Inwardly, the internal organs relate through the
movement of Ch'i (energy) and Blood via the energy channels in the
body. The unity of psyche and body is further reflected in the fact
that the Ch'i – the basis for all physiological processes – is also the
basis for emotional and mental processes. The loss of balance and
harmony between the yin and yang organs will give rise to disease,
which obstructs the natural movement of Ch'i. Healing is the
restoration of this balance.

The Body as Instrument in the Chinese Alchemical Opus

In Chinese alchemy the *tao* can be experienced through the body,
which is the instrument through which one can cultivate and develop
self-realization. The notion of *tao* coincides with the *unus mundus* –
the unity of existence which underlies the duality of psyche and
matter. Jung said, "If mandala symbolism is the psychological

equivalent of the unus mundus, then synchronicity is its parapsychological equivalent" (CW14, par. 662).

The experience of tao is the Chinese expression of the experience of the Self – one's wholeness – symbolized by the center, the light, or the golden flower. According to the inner elixir tradition which began in the first century, tao in itself is beyond human conceptualization. But tao can be experienced consciously during meditative breathing when the introversion of psychic energy reaches its climax. This experience of tao is symbolized by the hexagram *fu*, to denote returning to the original oneness – the root of life – to begin to live a new, transformed life. (See Miyuki, 1967.)

The mysterious point of contact between the timeless and temporal gives birth to consciousness, which must be cultivated further in one's lifetime by constructing a subtle body around oneself through breath meditation (*Ch'i kung*). More specifically, the alchemical opus, or elixir, is produced by transforming the three fundamental physical and psychic substances in the body. They are: *Ching-Essence*, *Ch'i-Energy* and *Shen-Spirit*. Each of these substances has a material and a psychic aspect and is associated with an internal organ located in the lower, middle and upper elixir fields in the body.

The process of transforming these substances is expressed through the Taoist motto: "through compounding Ching-Essence, Chi-Energy is transformed; through compounding Chi-Energy, Shen-Spirit is transformed; through compounding Shen-Spirit, one returns to Non-being (Tao)" (Chang, 1963, p. 136).

The kidney contains ching-essence – or *Ch'i-before-heaven* – which is the foundation of all *yin* and *yang* energies in the body, thus the source of vitality and stamina. Symbolized by water, the trigram *kan*, the kidney signifies a timeless equilibrium with its inner dynamism.

The spleen contains *Ch'i-after-heaven* which determines the source of Ch'i and Blood in the body. Symbolized by Earth, the center of totality, the Spleen signifies the spiritual principle of the expanding feminine, which brings the spirit into material and spatial manifestation.

The interplay between ching-essence and Ch'i-energy – the Ch'i-before-heaven and Ch'i-after-heaven – signifies a *hieros gamos* of heaven and earth in which the two principles exchange their attributes. The unification of the two fields signifies the coming together of an eternal order and the just-so-ness of reality. The realization of both is manifested in the heart, which houses the Shen-Spirit in the upper elixir field.

The Heart houses the Shen-Spirit which is the most subtle, non-material form of Ch'i. Symbolized by fire and the trigram *li*, Shen-Spirit draws its basis and nourishment from the mental, emotional and spiritual faculties of all the Yin organs. It is the root of life and consciousness. Shen-spirit gathers and unites *Po*, the Yin-soul and *hun*, the Yang-soul.

The Lung houses Po, Yin-soul, which is the spirit of the body. During life it is attached to the body; at death it returns to the earth. Po brings Ching-Essence into the spheres of sensation and feeling and gives the body the capacity of movement, balance and co-ordination. Without po, the potentially vital substance of Ching-Essence would be inert. Thus po regulates somatic consciousness.

The Liver houses hun, the Yang-soul, which complements Shen-Spirit and Ch'i-Energy. During life, hun is contained and integrated by shen-spirit. At death, hun returns to heaven. Hun regulates and harmonizes the emotions, supports intuition, and provides a link to the unconscious and to the world of imagery, dreams and symbols. Hun represents the totality of the transcended spirits of Ching-Essence, Ch'i-Energy and Shen-Spirit, which after death join the land of the ancestors. As an ancestor in heaven, one provides benevolence for one's descendants. While on earth, one would cultivate the elixir in order to connect to the ancestors in heaven.

The Role of Feeling in the Alchemical Opus

As far back as the second century B.C. when the *Yellow Emperor's Classic on Internal Medicine* was compiled, emotions were seen as causes of disease; emotions can disturb the internal organs and consequently the harmony and movement of Ch'i and Blood. Each organ was thought to produce a certain energy which resonates with specific emotions. Anger resonates with the Liver, joy with the Heart and Liver, worry with the Lung and Spleen, pensiveness with the Spleen, sadness and grief with the Lung and Heart, fear with the Kidneys, and shock with the Kidneys and Heart. Only when emotions are excessive and prolonged can they cause injury to the organs. Thus, what we today identify as stress was seen as causing diseases.

External factors can give rise to excessive emotions which affect particular organs. Conversely, the state of the internal organs can affect or bring about corresponding emotional states. For example, if Liver-Yin is deficient due to dietary factors, it causes Liver-Yang to rise and cause irritability. Or, if one is habitually angry at a particular person, this also can cause Liver-Yang to rise.

Chinese medicine as it has been practiced through the centuries takes emotions into account when treating illness. Psychological symptoms are explained in terms of disturbance of Ch'i associated with the various organs. For example, excessive internal heat (*huo-chi-ta*) suggests irritability, anger and anxiety. A wet and sticky heart (*tsim tsap-tsap*) suggests discomfort in the chest, palpitations of the heart, anxious and depressed feelings. This approach has given Chinese medicine the advantage of psychosomatic integration.

The search for the tao from both Confucian and Taoist perspectives has encouraged the development of psyche-body training via meditative breathing exercises as a form of psychological intervention. However, this approach has delayed acceptance in the East of the contributions modern psychology and psychiatry have made to the diagnosis and treatment of mental and emotional disorders.

Epidemiological studies of illness patterns in the Orient in the past two decades show that somaticization is the chief idiom through which patients experience, perceive and articulate psychological and psychiatric problems. For example, depression is not considered a psychological condition, but is labeled as Kidney Deficiency (*shen-kuei*) and treated accordingly.

Chinese doctors were found to make frequent use of the nineteenth century term *shen-ching-shuai-jo* (neurasthenia) as a general diagnosis for neurotic and emotional disorders. As the pressures of modern life increase, this diagnosis may not be specific enough, and Chinese doctors and patients may begin to turn to some of the psychological concepts of the West. The time may be coming when Eastern and Western traditions will correct their imbalances: the West becoming more tuned into body-mind integration, the East moving away from a strictly somatic viewpoint.

It was Jung who first recognized the psychological significance of the wisdom of the *I Ching* and Chinese alchemy, introduced to him by Richard Wilhem in 1929. Jung's insight has initiated a genuine dialogue between the East and the West on a depth level. As the forces of globalization accelerate toward the twenty-first century, it is our task as analysts to see that this dialogue continues and to ensure that "the fire does not go out" (von Franz, 1984).

Summary

In the Chinese alchemical tradition, the search for the tao and the experience of it are a way of life, to be practiced in and through daily life. Miyuki (1967) has suggested that consciousness of a high level "must be circulated through the entire body to make the body a house of the Mind of Heaven, where Light is the master" (p. 77). The achievement of harmony is symbolized by hexagram 63, which expresses the secret of the *I Ching*. In this state one returns to the Source, the Void that is not empty, and the language is silence.

Chinese spirituality, as expressed through the alchemical opus, is rooted in life and in nature, and grounded in the organic unity of psyche and body. Once this unity is experienced, it becomes a way of life that can be cultivated consciously and lived. Embodied in this way of life is the experience of the continuing unfolding of the mystery of a cosmic Eros which corresponds to an individual's urge to individuation and which, paradoxically, leads men and women to a state of universal relatedness with existence.

Western Perspectives

Lucinda Sykes, M.D.
Toronto, Ontario, Canada

The subtle energy body is a concept identifying the interface between psyche and material body at a level where psyche and body form a functional unit. It deserves recognition because it answers a limitation in our Western scientific model of the body. Jungian psychology has much to contribute to its development.

The past 30 years have seen an accelerating study of mind-body by scientists from several disciplines and perspectives. Evidence increases for a complex interplay that is imaged most effectively as a unity, but no such image has been developed in our scientific conceptual framework. Rather, science identifies a material, mechanical body composed of parts causally related and generating psyche through the mechanism of brain biochemistry. This one-sided model is strained to accommodate the evidence of a reciprocal influence of psyche on body.

The subtle body concept provides a Western response to the East's assumption of psyche-soma in unbroken totality. It also bridges the schism between biological psychiatry and the analytical psychologies, which are seen to have opposite but complementary perspectives on this one fact of psyche-body interplay.

Jung referred to the subtle body repeatedly, usually concluding that it remained "speculation" because so little was known. In his most detailed discussion (ZA) he said:

> *The part of the unconscious which is designated as the subtle body becomes more and more identical with the functioning of the body, and therefore it grows darker and darker and ends in the utter darkness of matter. ... Somewhere our unconscious becomes material. ... One must include not only the shadow – the psychological unconscious – but also the physiological unconscious, the so-called somatic unconscious which is the subtle body.* (p. 441)

Using Jung's description, what can a Western observer say about the subtle body now? One quality of the subtle energies that is already apparent is the value of meditation. Regular meditation has been shown (Benson, 1975) to confer long term health benefits, and the term "relaxation response" has won some acceptance in the medical literature. Here begins an assimilation of Eastern understandings into a Western context.

Body influences psyche and psyche influences body; through the subtle body, there is a functional unity. Material body, especially as brain, can be seen as producing psyche. This is the basis for the psychopharmacology that has revolutionized psychiatry. However, we also observe psyche "producing" body: such mental practices as meditation, hypnosis, biofeedback and visualization all can bring immediate change to body chemistry and functioning. The level of the subtle energies is open to influence from either "direction" of the West's duality of mind and body.

Implications of Modern Physics

The material and mechanistic body of the mainstream biomedical model can be seen as a microcosm of the classical Newtonian-Cartesian universe. For physicists, this universe underwent a radical change in this past century, especially with the theories of relativity and the quantum mechanical model. At various points in his writing, Jung responded to the psychological implications of modern physics. For example:

> *The psyche, inasmuch as it produces phenomena of a non-spatial or a non-temporal character, seems to belong to the microphysical world.* (Let-I, p. 395)
> *Physics has demonstrated ... that in the realm of atomic magnitudes an observer is postulated in objective reality. ... This means that a subjective element attaches to the physicist's world picture, and ... that a connection necessarily exists between the psyche to be explained and the objective space-time continuum.* (CW8, par. 440)

His interchange with physicist Wolfgang Pauli led to elaboration of Jung's principle of synchronicity and of "acausal orderedness" in general. He described a quaternio developed with Pauli: "This schema satisfies on the one hand the postulates of modern physics, and on the other hand those of psychology" (CW8, par. 964). These considerations relate to a central question: How do our Western understandings of matter and of psyche correlate? In the junction of these models will be the subtle energy body.

Archetype in the Subtle Energy Body

That Jungian psychology can provide a useful modeling of the subtle energy body is not surprising, in that the subtle energies are psychic energies – at the level of matter – of collective significance. As Jung commented:

> *Archetypes ... are inherited with the brain structure – indeed they are its psychic aspect. ... They are the chthonic portion of the psyche ... that portion through which the psyche is attached to nature.* (CW10, par. 53)
> *The archetypes are formal factors responsible for the organization of unconscious psychic processes.* (CW8, par. 841)
> *The archetypes are not found exclusively in the psychic sphere, but can occur just as much in circumstances that are not psychic.* (CW8, par. 964)
> *Psychology investigates the basis of consciousness until ... nothing more can be seen but effects which have an "organizing" influence on the contents of consciousness. ... The qualitatively rather than quantitatively definable units with which the unconscious works, namely the archetypes, therefore have a nature that cannot with certainty be designated as psychic.* (CW8, par. 439)

The two major Eastern body energy systems – oriental ch'i/ meridian and Indian prana/chakra – indicate an organized dynamism of energy in the body which is, at least in part, subject to conscious experience and intervention. This quality of organized psychic energy can be seen as an extension of archetypal patterning into the physiological or "infra-red pole" of the spectrum metaphor as elaborated by Jung: "The dynamism of instinct is lodged as it were in the infra-red part of the spectrum whereas the instinctual image lies in the ultra violet part" (CW8, par. 414).

This continuum of archetypal-instinctual influence suggests the interplay of image with the subtle energy flows at the opposite "pole" of the spectrum – and, hence, into the material body. This interrelation is evident in the use of image in the Eastern body traditions. It also underlies the interplay of image and body observed in analysis and Western "bodywork." Image can affect body and body can respond with image. The medium of exchange is through the subtle energy body, as organized by archetype.

Subtle Energy Body as Field

Von Franz (1980) has offered a general definition of the idea of field in the natural sciences: "It is a network of relations in every situation. ... Now I propose to use the hypothesis that the collective unconscious is a field of psychic energy, the excited points of which are the archetypes" (p. 61). This idea of a field of psychic energy can be applied fully to the dynamic patterning of the energies in the Eastern body traditions. The model of field also applies to the microphysical world of modern physics.

Here is a Western imaging of the psyche/body interface: that of a field of psychic energy which animates both psyche and the material body – a field that tends to organize into archetypal patterns. These are patterns at the infra-red end of instinctual dynamism, in a continuum with the image and idea of the "ultra-violet" pole. This patterning is of the "psychoid" level of psychic energy.

Subtle Energy Body as "Irrepresentable"

The diversity of body energy systems can be understood with Jung's observation that "the archetypal representations mediated to us by the unconscious should not be confused with the archetype as such. They are very varied structures which all point back to one essentially 'irrepresentable' basic form" (CW8, par. 417).

Therefore, systems representing archetypal patterning at the subtle energy level should not be confused with the subtle body as such. They are conscious representations of "irrepresentable" forms. In the case of Eastern systems, there can be historical and cultural influences not necessarily relevant to Western needs, even though the subtle energy level they represent is a collective phenomenon.

It is likely that there can be several systems (as conscious representations of the "irrepresentable"), perhaps even with some contradictory aspects. Western physics can be comfortable with ambiguity (e.g., electrons can be both particle or wave) but Western medicine is slow to accept nature as indeterminate.

Conclusion

This ultimate "irrepresentability" of archetype resonates with Jung's repeated warnings against a blind imitation of Eastern traditions. He suggested that "It is likely that the yoga natural to the European proceeds from historical patterns unknown to the East." (CW11, par. 873) Historically, our Western standpoint will have to include Western science and Western medicine.

The subtle energy body is a Western concept of psyche and body in functional union. The development of this concept would allow us to integrate into our current model evidence for a level of psyche-soma in unbroken totality – whether this is the evidence gleaned from Eastern body energy systems or the evidence from our own scientific investigation. "We should then be in a position to build on our own ground with our own methods" (CW11, par. 773).

References

Benson, H. (1975). *The Relaxation Response*. New York: Avon.

Chang, Chung-Yuan (1963). *Creativity and Taoism*. New York: Julian Press.

Miyuki, M. (1967). *The Secret of the Golden Flower: Studies and Translation*. Diploma Thesis, C.G. Jung Institute, Zurich.

von Franz, M.-L. (1980). *On Divination and Synchronicity*. Toronto: Inner City Books.

von Franz, M.-L. (1984). Personal communication.

The Uses of Adversity

Intentional Pain, the Body, and Individuation

Arthur D. Colman
Sausalito, California, U.S.A.
Society of Jungian Analysts of Northern California

The centrality of pain in human development has intrigued psychological, religious, and spiritual disciplines as long as consciousness has been embodied in humans. As Jung says in many ways throughout his writings, "Every step forward along the path of individuation is achieved only at the cost of suffering" (CW11, par. 411). My concern here is to explore situations in which body pain is induced intentionally, either by self or society. The context of this exploration is my personal and clinical experience with body pain. I am concerned with the relationship of pain to individuation theory, particularly the stages of the *coniunctio*, and in learning more about how this relationship might aid patients in pain.

A strategy of studying intentional pain in order to learn more of pain's role in individuation may seem gratuitous. There is certainly enough unsolicited pain in our lives without needing to focus on torture, sadomasochism (s/m), and various forms of religious asceticism. My intent, however, is to study the extremities of pain in order to learn more about the more usual ranges of pain – much like studying aphasia in order to learn more about language. Extreme and taboo forms of pain can be viewed – depending on context and intent – as sacred or profane, ecstatic or disgusting, spiritual or perverse, righteous or immoral. Like the real and symbolic role of incest in human love, it is just these extreme and liminal taboo behaviors that are so often connected, however ambivalently, to developmental transitions and life change.

Some recent personal experiences connect pain with themes of individuation. More than a year ago I attended a small conference on shamanism and psychology. After a long day many of us repaired to a hot pool to talk, under a starry Rocky Mountain sky. In the bath were several Jungian analysts and candidates along with other students of shamanism and psychology. The group included a 30-year-old Lakota-Sioux, "Jim." That evening I had presented my researches on the use of pain in shamanic initiation and its relation to s/m. The slide presentation included juxtapositions of historic crucifixions, other mortifications and tortures of saints, the traditional Lakota-Sioux Sun Dance and a variant of it along with other "s/m rites" – performed by a spiritual sect in the United States to commemorate AIDS victims – and piercing and tattooing in Mentawaii shamanic initiation in Indonesia. The presentation was considered extremely provocative. Many thought it broke new ground in bringing pain into our work; Jungian analyst Don Sandner called it the "shadow of the Jungian shadow." But some objected to what they conceived of as disrespect in mixing the sacred and the profane. One member of the audience had vomited and a few left during the presentation.

These reactions were understandable for many reasons, including the timing of the talk. Several hours before my presentation we all had participated in a physically difficult sweat lodge of great heat and body constriction for the purposes of purification and vision. Just hours before that we had listened to two Jungian therapists describe their own participation in the Lakota Sun Dance in which – after days of fasting, chanting and dancing – their chests and shoulders were pierced with large hooks fastened to trees which they pulled until the hooks ripped from their flesh.

The Sun Dance they described had its origins as a dance of thanksgiving and praise to the sun, which appeared in the midst of a storm just in time to save the Lakota tribe from starvation and exposure after a long period of being snowbound high in the mountains. The Sun Dance had been outlawed in the early 1900s. However, the national laws against this sacred dance had been repealed recently and the Sun Dance is now danced regularly as part of the modern Lakota initiation ceremony, as well as for special kinds of healing. The participation of these two non-Indian men in the ceremony was rare, and their descriptions were profoundly ecstatic and spiritual. They felt imbued with strong healing powers after the ceremony and the desire to share that power with those in pain. It was politically and emotionally problematic to link their experiences with some of the slides I had shown.

As we bathed in the waters, pondering the power of spiritual fashion, I could not help noticing that Jim's naked body was covered with many scars and tattoos on his chest, back and shoulders. I asked him about these marks and he said some of them came from his participation in the Sun Dance since age six, when his father had put the two hooks in his chest skin and guided him through the long dance, including the agonizing ripping of flesh that ended it. He had participated in more than 20 such ceremonies. The tattoos had come after a stint in the Army. His body looked quite like the pictures I had seen of men and women who pierced their bodies in a variety of s/m rituals and also of the bodies of tortured Holocaust and South American kidnap victims.

Months later, I attended a clinical discussion at a Jung society where an analyst discussed a patient whose behavior included sadomasochistic rituals which he described as the spiritual center of his life. Our clinical discussion revolved around how to get rid of his symptom – behavior modification was mentioned – as well as the childhood origins of this symptom and its effects on his object relations in the present. There was no discussion of any possible spiritual function of his symptom or the role of pain in this man's individuation. It was as if a taboo had been joined; to break it was to risk group censure.

Jung's alchemical prescription for individuation includes: "the torture of initiation, the indispensable means of leading him (the initiate) toward his destiny" (CW11, par. 410). Yet we all usually assume the "torture" to be psychic. If the case had dealt only with psychic pain and suffering, or even physical pain without a pseudo-sexual context, the discussion would have reached deeper, more meaningful realms. Sandner's comment about intentional pain being the "the shadow of the Jungian shadow" seemed most pertinent. He was referring to the difficulty we Jungians often have in dealing with certain kinds of darkness. We all agree that pain is at the center of individuation but it is also clear that some kinds of pain and some contexts of pain are more acceptable to us on this road than others.

The notion of the intentional inflicting of pain for the purpose of pleasure and/or spiritual knowledge is, I think, problematic for Jungians who thus accurately reflect the judgments of Western culture in general. For example, we do not accept or consciously condone physical torture in our prisons or painful childbirth in our hospitals; we see this attitude as progress toward more "humane" values, part of our attempt to create a more enlightened culture. Yet the same cultures that have promulgated these advances are almost completely addicted to violence. This addiction is evident in the toys we give to our children, the movies we watch, the wars we make –

and watch. We are, after all, the perpetrators of the most savage and far-flung violence in human history. I speak of the holocausts of genocide, war without limit, and massive willful death-dealing impoverishment of a consciously contrived, two-tiered socio-economic structure. These dark institutions are as much a hallmark of us, of the Western cultures of enlightenment, as are salutary advances in health, law, and human rights. Is it possible that our enlightened taboos and repressiveness toward certain forms of pain and suffering are connected to the violence of our immediate past and present generations?

The intentional inflicting of pain for the purpose of pleasure or self and societal knowledge is a main concern of Foucault (1975), a remarkable and controversial French philosopher. He contrasted the apparently "barbaric" treatment of the condemned criminal in the eighteenth century with the "humanized" life-long totalitarian incarceration of condemned criminals in the nineteenth and twentieth centuries. Foucault questions which punishing condition was more horrible and more useful. It is not that he would advocate a return to hot wax and chopped-off limbs. Rather, he pointed out that public execution – or the public shame of having homeless people in our midst – forces society to feel responsible for its use of sadism, its policy of torture and the pain it creates. Foucault believes that our penal and other isolating institutions hide our collective shadows from ourselves thereby preventing collective growth, very much the way narcotizing in an individual life may prevent the individual from developing.

At the end of this life, Foucault (1982) moved closer to our field by focusing on the "institution" of sexuality. He argued that even intimate, subjective bodily experiences, including sexual experiences, are profoundly affected by the same subtle coercion of "enlightenment." His understanding of any human faculty lived fully was that it must include pain and the nearness of death. In sexuality too, the "limiting experience" must be measured in the presence of the truthsayer, the body in pain, including the taboo world of sadomasochism. Foucault had turned directly to the most vulnerable core of the individual as the target of this coercion. For him the control of sex is tampering with the *prima materia*, "the relation to the self in the experience of the flesh" (p. 211). Foucault's later writings do not deal with the specifics of his own sadomasochistic practices but he saw them as philosophical adventures, a work in progress. A year before his death, he talked of the body's sexuality as an "ethical substance" which, if confronted without societal intervention, produced sexual moralities tied to individual exploration rather than societal coercion. "The kind of relationship you ought to have with yourself, is what I call ethics – that which determines how the individual is supposed to constitute himself as a moral subject of his own actions" (1983, p. 352). This last work produced a view of adult development very close to the Jungian ethic of individuation.

Foucault's last work also borrowed from the larger s/m movement in which self-discovery is linked to a variety of body practices and to self-discovery. Musafar (1992b), a leader of this movement and editor of one of its journals, *Body Play,* states his credo: "I personally feel that the pursuit of Change-of-Bodystates can be a powerful way to explore one's own spirituality – can be a way to prepare one to live life more fully and consciously, even prepare one for the ultimate Change-of-Bodystate called 'death'" (p. 3).

What Foucault and Musafar are suggesting is hardly foreign to the alchemical texts Jung used. Thus, Jung excerpts from the Ostanes text Zosimo's vision of the torments that the "prince" desires for his initiates:

> *I am Ion, the priest of the innermost hidden sanctuary, and I submit myself to an unendurable torment. For there came one in haste at early morning, who over-powered me and pierced me through with the sword, and dismembered me in accordance with the rule of harmony. And he drew off the skin of my head with the sword, which he wielded with strength, and mingled the bones with the pieces of flesh, and caused them to be burned upon the fire of the art, till I perceived that I was transformed and had become spirit. And that is my unendurable torment.* (CW13, par. 86)

In a footnote, Jung places this vision "in the wider context of rebirth symbolism. Consequently it plays an important part in the initiation experiences of shamans and medicine men, who are dismembered and then put together again" (CW11, par. 346, n9). This description of initiation must not be taken literally but the tendency to "symbolize" this sadomasochistic vision misses part of the point. The splitting of mind and body is a function of our language, our prejudices, and our taboos. As we know, shamanic dismemberments are hardly symbolic. They are very real bodily experiences; actual pain is of their essence. The initiations of Siberian shamanism, for example, fuse mind and body in any number of painful realities including: extreme cold, frostbite, fasting, starvation, isolation, body constrictions, fear of animal attack, animal attack. The visions of Zosimo are both part of a well-known literature of sexual excitations and also painfully close to the very real tortures of the Inquisition visited on Jews, infidels, and the alchemists themselves.

Consider for example the Balinese tooth-filing ceremony which involves unanesthetized filing of the eye teeth of pubescent girls and boys in order to get rid of their "animal nature." Here we have a rite of puberty associated with great pain. To the outsider it looks like cruel and inhuman torture, but it takes place in a context of cooperation by the participants, their families and their community. From watching these ceremonies, I can attest to the terrible pain inflicted on these youth. The file was very coarse and the initiator was very strong. The smell of burning flesh filled the air and yet the children, despite their own tears and cries, demanded more and more filing. They wanted more because they required an ordeal in order to become men and women of standing in their community. This ceremony/ordeal is, like so many puberty rites, a form of intentional pain sanctioned by the community. It is also what Musafar (1992a) defines as "body play, the deliberate, ritualized modification of the human body which is either made a part of a culture or if it is seen as a threat to established social order and institutions, then forbidden" (p. 5). To Musafar "body play" is an avenue for exploring many facets of human nature: aesthetic experience (tattoos, piercing, corseting), spiritual expression (fasting, isolation, extreme heat and cold, immobilizing in extreme meditation postures); and community bonding (the Ball Dance, Sun Dance and other ceremonies where a variety of these rites of pain are used in a group context).

Currently within the United States and Western Europe there is a surfeit of s/m activities, some sacred and some profane. We have intentional pain and body change techniques in innumerable contexts and unprecedented scale from surgical cosmetics, tattooing, piercing, flogging, to vision quests, fasts, long silence, day- and week-long meditation. Each of these behaviors must be understood in a context of intent. Consider the northern California-based Black Sun Dance in which 30 to 50 men and women meet for week long ceremonial rites including the Ball Dance, the Sun Dance, and a variety of sexual negations, ritual flagellations and other practices, all dedicated to the deaths of friends who suffered and died with AIDS. This ceremony begins with a talking circle in which each participant states the intent of his or her practice. In a ceremony I attended, most of them were enacting and symbolizing their own suffering and loss in ceremonies of pain powerful enough to embrace the death/rebirth archetype. The body in these ceremonies was the sacrificial altar for personal and community growth.

It is difficult for most of us to be open to these explorations without a range of strong negative feelings. When I became interested in this area, I had been in more or less continuous severe back and leg pain for almost seven years, followed by equally painful (though blessedly healing) back surgery. Before these experiences with acute and chronic pain, and despite an affected tolerance and lip service to the sanctity of all behavior, I shared the common attitudes toward s/m. But in the midst of my own experiences with pain, I lost much of the judgmental part of my reactions. With each month and year of chronic pain that I experienced I felt less horror at hearing about and watching piercing, flagellations, body constrictions, and the variety of "humiliations" involved in these practices and ceremonies. Rather I felt open, compassionate and even identified with the intent of their practices and love for the people involved. I was drawn to enter into these rituals for myself; the possibility of experiencing pain and being able to stop it, an experience that had not been possible for me for seven years, was terribly seductive. So was the possibility of sharing pain with others instead of being so alone with it. Eventually, however, I decided that I could not join their ceremonies as an active participant, though I did participate as a drummer during some of the ceremonies. Thus, I was able to gain an immediate appreciation of the powerful personal quest that s/m can represent for some people.

My explorations in this field began from within my own pain. As I pursued my researches of intentional sadomasochistic activities, I heard about and saw abuse and debasement without any apparent redeeming features. But I also saw many activities of great spiritual power, activities that have been present as part of serious religious practice since time immemorial – and I understand why. My researches led me finally to a suffering community of men and women who had seen too many friends die and had learned how to invoke "intentional" pain as a doorway to mourning. Pain delivered them into sacred space during their ceremony and, for some, into the crucible of their own individuation.

I return now to the question of how pain works in the individuation process and why it is such an important constant in human development. In individuation theory, pain is both the handmaiden and antagonist of individuation; this paradox is at the heart of pain's role in the individuation process. On the one hand, our hope for what Jung calls "the supreme realization of the innate idiosyncrasy of a living being always hostage to the painful consequences of ignoring society's strictures" (CW17, par. 289). In extreme situations an individual may be punished, tortured, and made scapegoat if he or she challenges the collective ethic at a level deemed crucial to its survival. (See Colman, 1995.)

On the other hand, being tethered by rules and roles made by others is in itself extremely painful, especially when we have lived in the collective world long enough to be ripe for more consciousness as an individual. The same "torture" society inflicts to exact obedience can also force the individual toward freedom. Recognizing this, we can understand better the sentiments of those who voluntarily don the hairshirt, seek flagellation, gratefully ascend the cross, dance under the high desert sun straining against the chest hook and say that we must all long for pain, must seek it out, call it our friend if we are to find ourselves, live our lives as sacred. What we refer to as the perversions of s/m, then, are also inevitable elements of every religious, spiritual and mystical tradition which asks its adherents to eschew society's whip and push past the pain-enforced collective norms to confront one's own needs and desires directly.

This transformative and separating power of pain in individuation resides in its relation to the body. Such pain forces a consciousness that has the potential to move us beyond a body-mind relation based on projections and idealizations. The human psyche disconnected from the body can twist and turn almost every psychic phenomenon to give it pseudo-meaning. The body in pain makes a mockery of such rationalizing abstractions. Unlike almost every other interior state of consciousness, physical pain "has no referential content. It is not of or for anything" (Scarry, 1985, p. 4). Pain can illuminate but it can bring permanent disintegration also. It does not promise surcease or psychological growth, although that may emerge from the work engendered by it. There is no inherent value in the stabbing onslaught of the myocardial infarction, the agony of perforation of a stomach, the torture of severe back spasm. Pain forces us to stark reality here and now without psychic justification. It is this awesome meaninglessness that strips us of our collective opiates and connects us to a powerful confrontation with our own individual truth.

The separation of the individual from the collective body, furthered by pain, corresponds in alchemical terms to the first stage of the coniunctio, the formation of the *unio mentalis*. In Jung's description thereof – a union between soul and spirit in the context of separation from the body – a central image is of decapitation; the head is split from the body. "The aim of this separation was to free the mind from the influence of the 'bodily appetites and the heart's affections' and to establish a spiritual position which is supraordinate to the turbulent sphere of the body" (CW14, par. 681). We need only to appreciate the "out of body" experiences of the patient beaten as a child, the child "seeing" it (but not feeling it) from the upper corner of the room, completely divorced from his or her body, and the "adult child" still able to disassociate mind and body at times of stress, to understand this alchemical mechanism at its most concrete and pathological. Jung's visions at the time of his heart attack, and shamanic healing visions during fasting, isolation and self-inflicted pain, are more developed examples of the same process.

In the second stage of the conjunction, spirit and soul are conjoined once again with the body. The cycle of adult development – especially in later life – requires this return, on different terms it is true, but still a rejoining of psyche to the physical body and the collective body, in order for the first stage of the individuation cycle, the journey of separation, to have meaning. In psychological terms, healing through the power of projection must give way to reconnection. Even in the most compartmentalized and hardened projection system – multiple personalities – there is a powerful pressure for reintegration of the personalities, driven by the pain of loss of the whole.

Thus, even as pain separates us from our body, it activates the tether that calls us back to our bodies and our collective body. The developmental separation that the first stage of the coniunctio affords is increasingly balanced by the suffering that isolation brings: loneliness, disconnection, and meaninglessness. As the *separatio* does its individuation work, we develop new levels of pain: the pain of unfulfillment, of unrequited love, of undone service that forces an enlightened return, the return that Buddha, the Bal Shem Tov, the present Dalai Lama and other spiritually gifted individuals model.

In the second stage of the conjunction the alchemical recipe for reunion is the production of caelum, "the heavenly substance in the human body, the 'truth'" (CW14, par. 697). In order for the conjunction to go forward caelum must be mixed with a series of ingredients: honey, celandine, rosemary, the Mercurialis plant, red lily and human blood. Blood is considered the most important of these nutrients for, as Edinger (1995) says "What has cost us blood, we never forget" (p. 294).

Surely pain's elixir too must be included in this recipe: perhaps the venom from the serpent Skadi used to punish Loki or the agonizing pecking of the liver of Prometheus bound to that rock, for pain, like blood, unites in a way we never forget. Pain, the separator, transforms the vessel itself, breaking it or strengthening it. If the vessel holds, pain grounds us in the body by despoiling of all illusion that body, soul, and spirit are not one. Anyone who has experienced profound pain for a goodly length of time will know this amalgamating potential; the mind-body separation that pain initially fostered cannot endure pain's abiding presence. If the vessel holds, separation between physical pain and psychological pain slowly gives way and resolves into a more inclusive state, first at the level of the unconscious and later in ego consciousness as well. The individual or subgroups working at the second stage of the coniunctio are therefore in a place to lead rather than follow the culture.

We may understand the mind/body split of Western medicine as an absence of adequate societal vessels to contain the pain, allowing this tension of opposites to be transcended and transformed. But even if our collective healing culture maintains an exaggerated separation between mind and body, this polarity is transcended by many people in pain and most importantly by some of the well initiated, "wounded" healers who serve them. Thus, all profound initiations in the healing arts from shamans to surgeons are anchored in an ordeal with an obligatory requirement for pain and sacrifice. We want to know that the surgeons to whom we entrust the blocked arteries of our hearts and brain can endure a 14-hour operation. We want analysts to be rigorously analyzed and in that or other initiatory process to have faced their own pain in the world of flesh and blood.

In the individuation process, then, pain serves as truthsayer and trickster: at times representing individual consciousness, at times collective consciousness; at times their separation, at times their joining. Pain is mercurial, paradoxical and uncontrollable. Above all uncontrollable. Pain is not a medicine that can be dispensed in appropriate dose and temporal span and then inactivated and excreted having done its work. Coming with or without warning, with or without intent, pain changes our life in unpredictable directions. To some who know too much pain, there may be a feeling of moral repugnance in equating the pain of loss of a loved one, of illness, of bodily damage, with pain that is willfully induced. But pain, like psyche, is not a moral force. When nature is unobliging or, paradoxically, when the pain in our lives is too profound and out of control, some may need to challenge themselves and the gods and introduce the potential of pain to create sacred time and space for change. Challenges like these, when not imposed on others, cannot be understood or judged through the lens of personal or societal taste. Rather, they should be honored as the expression of the individual's and society's insistent need for sacrifice and meaning, no matter how instigated and achieved.

When Jesus was nailed on the cross at Golgotha – an agony of hunger, thirst, burning skin, body constriction, piercing and humiliating exposure – he cried out *"Adoni, adoni, lamah sabachtoni"* (Father, father, why hast thou forsaken me?). Pushed by extreme pain and the nearness of death, he spoke directly to feelings of betrayal and loss of faith. Theologians have argued for centuries about the meaning of these final words. To me, pain – for Jesus as for so many men and women – was truthsayer. His suffering cut deep into his denial, inflation and the messianic mission of a man who, firmly in the shadow of the Jewish tradition, believed he was the ultimate chosen person, the son of God. In accepting his human body and its feelings, his profound teachings gain even greater stature, for we are able to identify directly with his suffering and his message. In that moment of extreme pain and profound truth, Jesus – like Buddha before him – left the realms of the Gods, spirit and soul without body, and returned to his body, his community, his humanness and his death. In doing so a suffering, bleeding man on a societal cross became an embodied symbol of the individuation process, a symbol which has remained powerfully sustaining through two millennia of human pain.

The suffering and sacrifice of Jesus and others like him remain alive for us because they reassure us that the path of individuation requires pain and a mortal wounding, that the pain we experience we may need. Individuation is limited by the willingness to submit to pain and its consequences. Pain is truthsayer and trustmaker. Those who come to know pain are either traumatized and damaged by the experience or healed and stronger for it. But those who do not know

pain cannot know a critical part of themselves and therefore ultimately cannot trust themselves.

Many who encounter the extremities of pain do not survive it with
integrity. The vessel cracks and breaks and development is attenuated, perhaps for a lifetime. Then pain has become the fixed center
of meaning rather than an inevitable part of development. Living
with pain without fixing development in its thrall requires living in
the tension of opposites between hope and acceptance. Finding a
viable balance does not lead to a cessation of pain but a transcending
relation to body and mind, an altar of experience leading to a new
relation to Self which is hinted at in the last stages of the coniunctio.
During my own long sieges of pain, I glimpsed something of what it
means to live with body and mind truly together, a state in which that
"indestructible thing" was an ever-present connection with a larger
entity of experience. I have been with patients in severe pain for long
periods of time who have made this state their own. Those who use
the extreme technique of inducing pain to test their own limits are in
search of such transcendence and sometimes find it. Ultimately pain,
intentional or otherwise, will have its way with us. Only love can
match its power to hold us in the tension between hope and
acceptance until both are transcended. It is then that Shakespeare's
entire quote, the title of this paper speaks most clearly:

> Sweet are the uses of adversity;
> Which, like the toad, ugly and venomous,
> Wears yet a precious jewel in his head.
> And this our life exempt from public haunt
> Finds tongues in trees, books in the running brook,
> Sermons in stones and good in everything.
> I would not change it.
>
> *As You Like It*, Act II, Scene 1

References

Colman, A. (1995). Up from Scapegoating: Awakening Consciousness in
    Groups. Evanston, IL: Chiron.
Edinger, E. (1995). *The Mysterium Lectures*. Toronto: Inner City Books.
Foucault, M. (1975). *Discipline and Punish* (A. Sheridan, trans.). New York:
    Vintage/Random House.

Foucault, M. (1982). The Subject and the power. In Hubert L. Dreyfus and Paul Raibinow, (Ed.). *Beyond Structuralism and Hermeneutics.* Chicago, IL: University of Chicago Press.

Musafar, F. (1992a). *Body Play, 1*-1, Menlo Park, CA: Insight Books, p. 5.

Musafar, F. (1992b). *Body Play; 1*-3. Menlo Park, CA: Insight Books, p. 3.

Scarry, E. (1985). *The Body in Pain: The Making and Unmaking of the World.* New York: Oxford University Press.

The Psyche's Response to the Trauma of AIDS

Part I

Gilda Frantz
Santa Monica, California, U.S.A.
Society of Jungian Analysts of Southern California

Anyone who wants to know the human psyche would be better advised to bid farewell to his study and wander with human heart through the world. ... He would reap richer stores of knowledge than text books a foot thick could give him, and will know how to doctor the sick with real knowledge of the human soul.

C.G. Jung

He who learns must suffer. And even in our sleep, pain that cannot forget falls drop by drop upon the heart, and in our own despair against our will, comes wisdom by the awful grace of God.

Aeschylus

This epidemic will ultimately inspire works of great beauty and power. It is an irony of life. Some of the greatest creative works of Man have been born out of pain and suffering. So what is evil, in that case? We think of the epidemic as a bad thing and I, for one, am not exactly jumping for joy at the thought of my oh-so-likely to be foreshortened life ... and yet, when I think of what the gift to the future will be from this ... the art, the dance, the theater, literature and music that will derive not so much from the global kind of response to the disaster that is AIDS, but from the personal loss, I have to wonder.

Maybe what is evil is not necessarily what causes suffering, but suffering without some kind of gain, either in insight, depth of being, or creative expression. The idea is hard to express precisely. Maybe there is an evil response that is the key to suffering.

Carl Frantz, 1952-1992

The trauma experienced by the psyche in AIDS is beyond the ability to articulate, of anyone who does not have the disease. We who try are like foreign correspondents, deeply touched by our subject but remaining witnesses. In the American branch of the Jungian community we have lost three, possibly four analysts and one candidate to AIDS. We have lost also children, lovers, sisters, brothers, friends. Many of us around the world who treat individuals with AIDS or HIV know that the work is meaningful and life-enhancing. We witness the courage and beauty of conscious living and dying; the acceleration of the individuation process is extraordinary.

At the onset of the plague in the United States, gay men were the hardest hit, but the virus has not remained selective. Now there is no discrimination based on gender, color, or age. HIV has infected 17000000 individuals in the world; one million of these are in the United States, where one in every 100 adult males is HIV-infected, one in every 800 females. As of January 1995, the World Health Organization (WHO) documented 1000000 cases of AIDS worldwide. Approximately half of these people have died. WHO predicts that, if the disease continues to spread at the same rate, by the year 2000 the cumulative total of HIV positive cases will be between 30000000 and 40000000 worldwide. Every ten minutes a woman dies of AIDS; every seven minutes a man dies of AIDS.

Jung warned us not to get caught in a collective way of thinking or reacting. Yet I ask myself, are we Jungians avoiding a collective trap by avoiding responding to AIDS – or are we in denial? I find denial in our silence. Denial and homophobia. Why do we, who understand the psyche and know its beauty and its depth, fail to raise our collective voice and proclaim our allegiance to those afflicted, our gay brothers or sisters? Of course there are individuals – including John Beebe, Robert Bosnak, Robert Hopcke, Barry Miller, Harry Wilmer and Scott Wirth – who have written about AIDS from their individual perspectives. That is what we analysts do, isn't it? We articulate our own experiences and then share them with the collective. But AIDS has been ravaging men, women and children for 15 years; it is past time for us to take responsibility and to speak. Because AIDS has touched my own life, it is time for me to speak up. As John Beebe said reference to AIDS in the Jungian analytic community, "It is no longer them, it is now us" (1995).

Earlier in this century Jung's concern about collective engulfment was spawned by two world wars that ravaged the planet. The image of psychic infection sweeping individuals away into an unconscious collective tide was not Jung's concern at the end of his life, however. Shortly before he died, Jung (Let-II, p. 592) wrote that becoming whole does not take place on a desert island;.we need to be related to the few and to the many in order to see ourselves.

Imagine that you are 35 or 40 years old and you have just been told that this horror, this dreaded malignant thing, this wasting disease, is inside you. You have already buried your lover as well as many friends and acquaintances. With your friends and lovers gone, who will take care of you when you become ill? You are horrified by the news, but not surprised. You knew you were at risk when last year you learned of the death of someone with whom you had been intimate. You know that, unlike cancer, AIDS has no period of remission, no known cure. The stigma of the AIDS sentence makes you feel that you have been cursed by God, and you know you are going to make the ultimate sacrifice.

Imagine that you are gay, have always felt different, have always lived outside society, stigmatized. This is a typical American gay experience. You are the Other. Like other minorities, you are the carrier of the shadow projection. Because of this projection, some of your friends have been beaten up, "gay-bashed," and you have heard of many killings incited by such hate.

Imagine you are a woman in the prime of life, married with children and a career, yet haunted by the long-ago affair you had with an IV-drug abuser in college. You are feeling ill and have gynecological symptoms that don't sound anything like HIV, but you seek help. Eventually you learn that, not only do you have HIV, but so do your young children. You try to take this in, and as you begin to accept this reality, you become a person you have never been before. You become more courageous, your life is now utterly transformed, and you are the most frightened person on the planet. How can you live with this? One woman who is dealing with this trauma says:

> *I allow my work and my children to fill my time, so I don't have to think about those things on a daily or hourly basis. I couldn't get through the days if I did. The best thing I can do for my children is be with them, look them straight in the eye, answer their questions as best I can, and remain involved in their lives. ... They know I have a disease. I don't know if they're relating it to what their dad had – and I don't know if I want them to relate to it, because I am not sick, yet. [The media] try to make me an exception. I am not unusual. There are a lot of women with small children who are [HIV] positive, women who are devastated, women who are scared to talk about it. I know, because they come to me.* (Fisher, 1994)

Speaking is a 45-year-old mother, artist, activist, philanthropist, who learned in 1991 that she was HIV-positive. She raises an issue women with HIV often must face: children and family.

When I read the daily paper, I look first at the obituaries, particularly of people whose death was AIDS-related. I saw one for a ten-year-old boy, who was related to a senator from Texas. The boy had died of AIDS, his death following the AIDS deaths of his father and mother. I read all the AIDS obituaries and say my own good-bye to each individual. I have not yet seen such an obituary for a woman.

The following quotations are taken from the journal of my son Carl Frantz, who was a gifted man, a gay man. By sharing some of his thoughts and feelings, written after he had learned that he was in imminent danger of developing the full AIDS syndrome, I hope that you will be able to hear the voices of thousands of men, women, and children who have been afflicted by a tragic plague that is now in its fifteenth year. Reading his words, perhaps you will feel the psyche's response to the trauma of AIDS. You might have written the words that he wrote when at 37, he first learned he was HIV-positive.

I want my life back. I want to wake up tomorrow and find out they mixed up my files, and that my test results are better than they thought. I have been thinking about what happens when I die. Part of me would like to think that, wherever the soul goes, I will be able to see Dad and Grandma and ... others who have gone before me. There is a part of me that also believes at least a little in reincarnation. That prospect frankly horrifies me. I don't know if I want to go through all this again. Growing up is hard. Living life is hard. Facing mortality when barely halfway through one's life is really hard. I mean really facing it. I have been aware of it in an abstract way for years. I think that's what adulthood is really about: realizing that you aren't immortal after all, that Death will also happen to you. [This realization] has made me more cautious about life, risks, etc. [But] it is not the same as facing the sudden high potential that I am unlikely to live out my full life span.
That's ridiculous, of course. However long we live is our full life span. What I mean is that fantasy of living to a ripe healthy old age, and dying in my sleep with a smile on my face, when I am fully ready to let go of life.

Then, a few months later, after a visit to his physician:

This is a day when my almost-worst fears come to pass. Today I find out that, healthy as I have been, my T-cells are far lower than I would hope. In fact, I am dangerously close to a level ... to start worrying about coming down with real AIDS. ... I may have to accept the fact that I am never likely to really achieve anything in my life. How much time do I have left? Do I suddenly begin working like a fiend and imagine that I will make some posthumous impact on the world? Do I have some great vision of "what it is all about" to write or paint for the world? I have the strongest feeling that such aspirations are nothing more than Puer fantasies. Vainglorious imaginings to temper the blow that my ego was struck today. Ultimately the only thing that I can achieve is my life. ... I must cultivate a source of inner strength. I must become centered. I wonder how far I can or should or will set my sights now? I face the prospect of a painful and lingering, degenerative death. That is terrifying. If this is the death I will face, I hope I will be able to do as Rick did, and know the right moment to say, "Enough ... stop the medication. Just keep me comfortable." I pray I will not surrender hope prematurely, either.

Later that same day:

I will not waste my days sitting around, whining and moaning "Why me?" Why ANYONE? ... There is no mourning for anything I MIGHT have wanted to do with my life. Now I have the certainty of the ultimate uncertainty. There are lots of hopeful unknowns facing me and a great sword, suspended by a slender thread, hanging over me. I don't know how many days I have, months, years that remain for me to use at the peak of my health. With luck, a few years, and by then there may be new hopes; without luck, less. Many before me have gone to their deaths hanging onto those hopes. However, now it is still time to live my life. ... I will live my death when the time comes. Whatever else there is time for, there is time for inner work. This must go on.

I facilitate a support group at a local hospital for "significant others" of people with AIDS. I volunteered about six months after my son died, feeling that leading it would be helpful to the group and my own healing. This group, unschooled in Jung's work, responds very enthusiastically to many of his ideas. I initially became a member of this support group when my son was hospitalized with cryptococcal meningitis and pneumonia. Participation in a group was a unique experience for me because, like many classically trained Jungians, I had avoided groups. When Carl was first diagnosed with HIV, he swore me to secrecy. Thus, I had no one I could talk to. Now being with individuals who were in the same boat was life-saving. Carl was experiencing such severe pain that morphine didn't bring relief, and I was in utter distress. I was able to talk to the group about my own pain. Secrecy, I later learned, is a common reaction to the trauma of assimilating the reality of AIDS. Secrecy is born out of a valid fear of loss of job, insurance, and friends, but I think that in the beginning a person with AIDS feels shame.

Carl wrote the following while he was processing his own feelings of shame:

> *I am overtaken by unheralded moments of deep sadness. I find an old friend popping up in my thoughts. … I remember it from when I was struggling with acknowledging my own homosexuality; I was so terribly mindful of the pain the news would bring, the shame, and how that impacted on my own sense of personal failure. Now the same feeling rears its ugly head. I need to tell my sister what the situation is, and it is so hard for me to do. (It is already enough to have done this to Mom.) … At the same time, I know how bad I felt when I realized how long my friend Bill had known about his condition and not told me. I was hurt. I felt excluded as a friend. And I used to call him a "sister." M. really is my sister. I can't protect her from this pain. I am not so great a vessel as to contain it all within myself. Deep down, I know this. "So great a vessel" indeed. I can't even hold my own feelings together, let alone contain all this pain! [He then fantasizes] … Um … waiter? Excuse me, but my life didn't come out quite the way I ordered it. Would you please send it back to the kitchen and have them do it again for me. I hate to be a bother, but this life is much too salty for me. I'm on a special diet. Could I have something else instead? I guess not. I guess I better call her and get it over with.*

Survivors who are HIV-negative often experience guilt and rage in a way not dissimilar to survivors of any catastrophe. This year alone, based on the above statistics, a minimum of 8 000 000 individuals will be left bereft and grieving. This experience of multiple loss and the pain of continuous grieving is the constellation of the Job archetype in the persons with AIDS and their loved ones. Gay men and lesbian women find that a kinship circle of choice can understand them in a way that "straight" society – even supportive families – does not. I know of men and women who experienced utter rejection when they "came out" to their families. They were told not to speak to their parents about "this" again and certainly never to bring their friends home. Where would such individuals go, if not to their gay brothers and sisters? In the gay community family values are alive and well, at a time when the conventional nuclear family in the United States is threatened with continuing fragmentation. Gay men and lesbian women reconstitute a solid family after they leave their homes of birth. They do this in two ways: through creating a family unit of their own and having a child, either by a donor or by adoption, and by creating a kinship family circle complete with "sisters" or "brothers" and even a friend they may refer to as "mother." In the gay community the loss of someone to AIDS is a loss from one's "kinship family," one's social life, and one's identification with a subculture. When friends die in multiples we can see the resemblance of the AIDS crisis to wars, when whole villages were annihilated.

In my work as volunteer facilitator of the support group, I see lovers (many of whom are HIV-negative), parents, sisters, in-laws, wives, ex-lovers, roommates, and husbands. One young man who developed AIDS lived with his parents, who had no idea of his sexual orientation.

The attendance at this drop-in group varies from eight to 16. We talk about everything: dying, living, sexual problems (especially the sexual frustration of the partner), suicidal feelings, God, health, anger, fear, loathing, love. A woman with multiple personality disorder attended one evening, on a pass from the local psychiatric hospital because her woman lover had AIDS and was in jail under a suicide watch. One member had suffered the deaths of his father and mother, within four months of each other, and the loss of his job while caring for his ex-lover. The group consists of family members of origin and family members of choice. No one in this group has ever asked how the person with AIDS was infected.

Just as each person with AIDS feels fear about what will happen in the future, so do significant others suffer similar concerns. In the AIDS community this is called anticipatory grief and is a terrifying experience of constantly expecting the next illness, or worse. The feelings of those who have HIV or AIDS rise and fall, depending on their T-cell count and their subjective state of health. To call it an emotional roller coaster is an understatement. There is a saying: "When someone you love has AIDS, you have AIDS."

Claude Levy-Bruhl's observation of *participation mystique* applies here. My personal experience and clinical observation are that this total participation is necessary and life-giving in the case of AIDS. But this sense of oneness can complicate things. Partners or caregivers find themselves identified with the mother archetype. While I was with my son in his time of dire illness, I felt a power surge through me unlike anything I had ever felt. I was able to use this power and to recognize that I was being infused with archetypal strength. I had the readiness of a wild animal able to spring into action in a split second to protect her young. Without this help, I doubt that I could have survived. Mine was not simply a maternal reaction; it happens to fathers and to male lovers.

How we look at the mother archetype needs to be rethought, especially in relation to AIDS, where issues of living and dying are constellated from day one. As in birth, the presence of the mother archetype is needed in the death experience. Today many a woman is present with her child in the death process, just as they were in the birthing process. As are fathers and lovers.

Part II

Scott Wirth

San Francisco, California
Society of Jungian Analysts of Northern California

Although my focus is on the impact of HIV on gay men in the United States, I am well aware of the many other populations also affected heavily by the epidemic, as well as its universal impact. I also speak as an HIV-negative individual, with the limits of this perspective.

The Latin root of "immune" is *munis*, in English "duty" or "service." When the Latin prefex *com-* is added to *munis* we get *communis*: "common" or "universal" or "public." Another variation is "sharing burdens." The Latin evolved into the Old French *comun* or *commune*, meaning "belonging to all." From there evolved such words and phrases as communicate, communion, communism, community, communicable, commoner, commonplace, common sense, common law, common denominator, common cold and commonwealth. Words like municipal, munificent and remunerate also developed from *munis*. We find many rich etymological amplifications to bear in mind as we consider some social and psychological meanings of HIV disease in our time.

I am a psychologist whose clinical practice specializes in work with gay male patients in San Francisco. Twenty years ago I began seeing an openly gay analyst-candidate who became a certified analyst while I was under his care. At the same time, I began to practice psychotherapy myself, with an idealistic vision of growing into a gay wounded healer, passing on to other gay souls the kernels of transformative processes that were being offered to me by my gay wounded healer analyst. I was also in the first group of gay and lesbian doctoral-level psychology interns to train in the first psychiatry department outpatient program whose specific mission was to serve the gay and lesbian community of San Francisco. This clinic was like a commune: a group of gay citizens who banded together for the common good of the gay community, to do our service, our duty, to share the burden of overcoming societal homophobia.

I know that I am not alone. Indeed, I believe that nearly all gay or lesbian individuals experience, as I do, their sexual and affectional orientation as fateful: an inner mystery, a secret, a sacred dimension of their being. That inner fate was lived alone and largely unmirrored in a 1950s childhood and a 1960s adolescence. It finally met, in young adult life, 1970s outer cultural and therapeutic supports. The experience was and is unspeakably beautiful, bringing an expansion of consciousness, a personal flowering. In the 1970s, millions of gay and lesbian individuals migrated to major urban centers such as San Francisco to secure for themselves and each other a time and place for freedom and affirmation of identity. These urban sanctuaries conferred certain forms of immunity on the individuals living in them. For me the containers of Jungian analysis and meaningful community work were my main sanctuaries.

Other gay men entered other sanctuaries and opened themselves to each other, lowering defenses on many levels. To compensate for childhood and adolescent years spent in psychological hiding, young adult gay men hungrily sought and found mirroring affirmation from each other. Many gay men freely communed sexually with each other, having no idea that a deadly virus was breaking into the Dionysian aspect of their sanctuary. Except for the extremely rare case of a hepatitis-B death, the greatest consequence of gay free love then was the hassle of a trip to the VD clinic, a case of the crabs, or a course of antibiotics.

Among the cruelest aspects of the HIV epidemic is the fact that a large portion of those carrying the virus were young men and women infected in the expansive, sexually exploratory 1970s. This was before a viral agent was discovered and its patterns of transmissibility were medically and epidemiologically analyzed. Working primarily with gay men, each of whom is psychologically assimilating the AIDS epidemic, I repeatedly see my patients feeling betrayed or undermined by the same homosexual eros that healed them. AIDS dropped like a bomb on their psychological cathedral, their temple. Dionysus had magnanimously sanctioned, even enthusiastically encouraged, experiences of fluidity, spontaneity, disinhibition and risk-taking. Apollo suddenly ascended in 1981, demanding radical alterations of consciousness and behavior, requiring large measures of rationality, caution and separation. The imagery of walls brought up to protect one's immune system, to guard one's separate, individual existence, rapidly became ubiquitous: latex condoms and dental dams; abstinence, sobriety and monogamy; sexual guidelines and negotiations; phone and computer sex; dry sex and sex at a distance, non-penetrative sex, masturbatory sex and less sex. Skin barriers not crossed, orifices closed.

As gay men blossomed into their various gay identities in the 1970s they had experienced an enantiodromia from the not-being of childhood and adolescence to being. One might think that the advent of HIV in the 1980s might bring a regression to not-being, a depressive throw-back to the underground False Self adaptations gay men made to survive the "abnormal environmental conditions" of childhood and adolescence. I see some of these regressive tendencies in my clinical practice.

But more of what I see are expressions of individuation. More often than not, the exploring work that my patients did on themselves in the Dionysian 1970s serves them now. For most gay men, that decade included a profound experience of adolescence: rebellion, peer group associations, limit-pushing, immortality illusions – all of it, and in generous portions. Almost universally during their actual teenage years, these men's sexual development had remained frozen. By the time it developmentally thawed and their adolescent life experience had cooked, they often found themselves about 30 chronological years old.

With eight or ten erotically-unlived adolescent years taken away on the front end of life, gay men already knew about time warps. With HIV making off with anywhere from 30 to 60 years of normal life span on the back end, this knowledge of compressed time seems to create a more intense heat in the vessel of the psyche, in the analytic container.

Sustaining multiple losses over a 14-year period is a traumatic experience. I think we will be studying the long-lasting effects of the traumatic impact of HIV disease on the individual psyche for decades, just as study goes on today of the psychological impact of the Hiroshima bomb or of Holocaust survivors, their children and grandchildren. It is too soon to know the full range of psychical scarring, the closing down of sensitivities and imaginative space in the human psyche. Here we are 14 years into the AIDS epidemic and this is the first Jungian Congress to address AIDS at all. We are just beginning.

Over the 14 years of the AIDS epidemic I have worked with about 55 gay men diagnosed with HIV disease and with another 70 who have tested HIV-negative or do not know their HIV status. I have found, of course, wide variations in individuals' manner of working psychologically with HIV. Trauma can be worked with and sometimes transformed. I find four varieties of psychological process, each undergone by at least ten of my gay clients. All these patterns were helped along significantly by the exigencies of AIDS, including its traumatic aspects. A few characteristic patterns of response:

(1) Men who let their grief carry them to deeper reaches of themselves, leading to a less inhibited, more passionate pursuit of personal goals, a clarification of priorities, a letting go of superfluous activity and hollow interpersonal relating. To different extents, awareness of AIDS has helped these men to give birth in themselves to greater experiences of pleasure, relatedness and health.

(2) Men who were facing a loved one's death or their own, but with whom it was often clear from the start that we would not be doing regressive analysis. These men may be younger or more naive; they may have come for therapy without much time to live; or perhaps they did not have the inclination to do long, slow analytic work. Yet the work we did could be moving, often with moments of I-Thou relating. In this work, we honor the powerful mystery of death and their capacity for facing it. Especially the younger men – in their twenties or early thirties – remind me of these words from Stephen Crane's *The Red Badge of Courage*: "He had been to touch the great death, and found that, after all, it was but the great death. He was a man."

(3) Men who were so shaken by the AIDS epidemic that they embarked on a process of letting go of compulsions and/or addictions, including chemical dependencies. Many of them re-examined their pattern of sexual relating and defined for themselves changes they wished to make, often including abstaining from addictively acting on sexual impulses with anonymous partners. Working

through the psychodynamics underlying their addictions allowed some of these men to explore seriously intimacy with a partner, often for the first time.

(4) Men whose AIDS suffering led them to a heart-stirring experience of what French philosopher Auguste Comte termed *"vivre pour autrui"* (to live for the sake of others). Very often the physical wasting of their own or a loved one's body brought these men into profound compassionate connection with the sufferings of persons unknown to them, perhaps children with HIV disease, Africans suffering from AIDS and starvation, or people with terminal cancer. In more than a few instances, this social or global empathy led to contemplative spiritual practice; in other cases it led to volunteer service work, political activism, artistic expression or combinations of these. This spirit of giving back to *communitas* something of what one has received therefrom finds expression in Tony Kushner's closing words to *Angels In America*: "This disease will be the end of many of us, but not nearly all, and the dead will be commemorated and will struggle on with the living, and we are not going away. We won't die secret deaths anymore. The world only spins forward. We will be citizens. The time has come."

These are a few of the positive outcomes in my psychotherapeutic and analytic work with gay men dealing with HIV disease. I will save for another time going into the failures, the stalled courses of treatment, the bitter and cynical deaths, the cases where psychic and physical trauma were too intense to work with, the instances where hardwon consciousness was precipitously eroded by physical debilitation and dementia, where there was no return from the underworld, where the work was cut short by sudden death.

In our work, we undergo the experience of termination more times than we can count. Our patients finish their work with us and, when the treatment has gone well enough, patients go on to live fuller lives, enriched by their encounters with the unconscious in the analytic temenos. Sometimes we hear later about how some aspect of the analytic experience of a given patient endured but mostly, of course, we never hear from our patients again. To one degree or another we content ourselves with conscious or unconscious fantasies of our patients' futures, with images of the continuing evolution of their consciousness rippling or sprouting or regenerating: this way or that, out into life, helped, fertilized or inspired by the work once done in our consulting rooms.

Analytic work with the dying quickly and coldly undercuts this level of concern. For the dying there will be no usual future, no coming back years later, no work afterward with another analyst. No more therapeutic silence, only complete silence. There will be no patient remembering an analyst, no yellowish dream journals looked through years later. When analysis terminates with the patient's death, where do the living analyst's fantasies go of the patient's future? Which evolution of consciousness, which rippling or sprouting or regenerating: this way or that, out into death. This, then, is the sacred work of termination for the analyst: to allow oneself to be penetrated by the transcendent as decisively as the AIDS virus infects the human body.

Part III

Kim Storch
Analyst-candidate
San Francisco, California, USA

We've seen the horrors when the world remains silent.
What if no one said a word, to see, to bear witness, to speak
from the heart.

Amnesty International

The psyche's response to any loss or perceived threat is profound. When it is multiple loss that continues over a long period of time, such as occurs with the AIDS/HIV virus, we are dealing with a previously unknown phenomenon.

Many cultures describe a three-to 12-month grieving period for loss of a loved one. It is not difficult, therefore, to understand how many in the gay community suffer from almost constant depression, feelings of hopelessness, reckless living, and apathy. It is not an exaggeration to state that many have lost more than fifty friends, lovers, and chosen family, with little or no time between these losses. Within this community massive energy is spent on caring for the sick and dying. I recall how the gay liberation movement was born out of the depths of grief. On June 28, 1969 we were mourning the very recent death of Judy Garland, at a New York City gay bar, the Stonewall. We were accustomed to enduring regular police harassment as the price for being different. The strength of our emotions that night, however – the magnitude of the grief – demanded that we no longer accept the status quo. For the first time in modern history, gay men stood up for themselves.

We had lived in a state of taboo: a shroud of silence concealed the word "homosexual" and gay was not a word spoken openly. Growing up in Detroit, Los Angeles, and San Francisco, I still never heard about another gay man, or even the word "gay," until 1968. I was not alone in thinking that there was no other person in the world who felt as I did about my sexuality. Literally, all was kept quiet. The faces of gay men were hidden, the voices of gay men were kept quiet and the place gay men were asked to take at the table of life was in the shadows. June 28, 1969 was the day we stood up and said "NO MORE."

It was grief that led to the turnabout in our feelings and behavior. We fought back. First, we threw money at the police, showing them we despised the regular kickbacks they received from the Mafia who owned the bar. When that was not enough, when the police could not understand that money was inconsequential, in our grief we threw bottles and rocks in our first step toward breaking the damning silence. We began the process of gaining our voices, claiming our faces, and taking a place at the table. This was a liminal moment. We could no longer tolerate the old; the new was not yet in focus. But the thought that there could be a path in life, to walk in the light with others, was exhilarating.

It is 25 years later and the thrill is gone. For 14 years a plague has decimated our gay community nationwide.

My own response has been varied: from taking up knitting to providing consultation and training. I have felt overwhelmed with grief, mourning and sadness. Anger and rage alternate with apathy and hopelessness. When I consider the duration of this loss, I have no outer reference point that speaks to a comparable situation. Blatant attempts to shame the gay community with slogans such as "Don't Ask Don't Tell," with the accompanying deception that it is not harmful to the gay community, indicate that there is an enormous collusion of silence. As psychologists we cannot collude in this silence. Few efforts are made to cover up the devaluation and contempt our society holds for homosexuals. I realize that the need for silence speaks to the blank screen of projection gays carry for the patriarchy. Too much light and the projection screen is useless to the larger society.

Imagine, for just a moment, the bind we live in daily. Take off your wedding rings, take down the picture of your spouse, remove the Mrs. from your stationery. Realize now that if you meet someone you came to love, you may be breaking the law. You risk your family and friends, and possibly your life, if you announce your marriage. Small wonder that frustration and rage wash over gay men as we bear witness to the massive numbers of deaths in our community.

In 1981 I was coordinating a crisis unit for San Francisco Community Mental Health. My unit began receiving AIDS patients before the name for AIDS had been created. Fantasy life, shadow projection, and fact all merged as we tried to stay calm in the face of shock, panic, and near hysteria. At the same time I was asked to do some training for crisis unit staffs throughout San Francisco. I saw decisions being made that appeared sound but were actually political, yielding to social and political pressures at the expense of effective action. I saw how easily groups would make decisions in accordance with the politically conservative or religious ethics, ignoring the needs of gay men.

This moment in our history calls for cooperative effective action. We as Jungians can use our knowledge and humanity to provide the "view from the other side." We need to review our perceptions of who is included in humankind and who is pushed into the shadows. We need to become conscious of our stances, to discover which are valid in today's world and which have been passed from one generation to another without consideration and evaluation. Rather than attribute rigid views of behavioral traits to men and to women, survival calls for a review and a redistribution.

I am reminded of a Navajo myth. First there was Changing Woman, who gave birth, through a kind of immaculate conception, to two sons: the warrior chief and the shaman. These are archetypal models of masculinity and are still alive in us today. The warrior chief archetype conquers, the shaman heals and integrates both masculine and feminine components in his identity. The warrior chief's seeming domain over the earth and nature today is clearly not intended in the original myth. The native Americans know that no tribe, no animal has domain over the earth. Yet some people still think this way and would do away with the shaman, in effect trying to kill the second son for the avarice of the warrior chief. If we allow this to occur we deny the implied balance of the myth.

During the conquest of the Americas, Native Americans made a conscious decision not to discuss the role of the shaman, nor the Berdache (the third sex) with Europeans who, it was assumed, could not understand the mystical and spiritual experiences which helped the individual and the tribe determine the relationship to these individuals, many of whom had acquired their position in the tribe through a significant dream directing them on this path.

There was a ten-day period in 1983 when I lost my lover and two of my closest friends. My response was a long period of shock. I fell into a depression. Finally a visit to Alaska forced me to re-enter life. I think it was the combination of nature at its finest and the desire I had for coffee each morning! I had to learn to make a fire in the rain or do without. Risky tasks for me to take on at that time. When I returned home I took up knitting – which is useful in mourning – began doing grief groups in the community and volunteering my consultation skills. I began drumming and participating more in community rituals, especially memorials. Many other gay men have had experiences similar to mine.

> *The ever present possibility of early death leads to a sense of fatalism, with a lack of enthusiasm for long term goal planning. There is simply no equivalent to this experience in the non-gay community. While a pandemic might be compared to natural disasters in which a large proportion of a particular community is wiped out, there are important differences. Ordinarily, when a disaster occurs, broad emotional and financial support (e.g., validation) for the survivors becomes available. For the survivors of AIDS, discrimination and homophobia conspire to keep them socially isolated and stigmatized.* (Crystler, 1995, p. 22)

Repeatedly I have pondered the question "Why are gays the targets of such brutal scapegoating and how can our colleagues, friends and even families, tolerate watching and silently participating in such events? Fourteen years of this plague, relentlessly unfolding but blanketed by enormous silence, points to a collusion in which the sub-group of gay men serves a scapegoating function by carrying a poisonous projection unconsciously perceived as life threatening to the majority culture.

I agree with Hopcke (1989) when he states: "Misogyny and repression of homosexuality as an aberrant phenomenon go hand in hand in Western culture" (p. 6). I have encountered this fear of the feminine in many forms: internalized homophobia within myself and others. When homophobia resides in gay men, it proves to be an insidious roadblock to healthy relationships and demands attention in the clinical setting. If unattended, it leads to ambivalence toward intimacy and, worse, reinforces the negative sexual attitude encountered in the collective. We have an opportunity to speak from the heart rather than continue this collective silence. Whether this takes the form of working with these issues clinically or bearing witness and speaking publicly or in some other creative way, colluding with the silence would be a regrettable path.

References

Fisher, M. (1994). Los Angeles *Times*, February 17.

Hopcke, R. (1989). *Jung, Jungians and Homosexuality*. Boston: Shambhala.

Crystler, J. (1995). Treating multiple loss syndrome. *San Francisco Sentinel*, June 14, p. 22.

The Treatment of Organic Diseases

An Analytic Model

Denise Gimenez Ramos

São Paulo, Brazil
Brazilian Society for Analytical Psychology

A theoretical psychological model is needed, to be applied in the understanding and treatment of "organic" illnesses. My hypothesis is that the organic symptom may correspond to a split in the representation of a complex/archetype, in which the abstract/psychic part was repressed. On being disconnected from the ego, such a symptom recurs compulsively, as if seeking to be integrated into consciousness so that individuation may proceed. (See Ramos, 1994.)

Can it be that becoming conscious of the complex's abstract pole – transducing the symbol from its pathological organic to its psychic/abstract pole – can diminish its pathological organic expression? That is, would such transduction of the symbol improve the patient's health? According to Rossi (1986), it would. Some clinical cases shed light on this question.

The Human Grenade: When the Heart Infarcts (Cardiac disease)

A 57-year-old engineer and senior executive, was referred by his cardiologist after having suffered a myocardial infarct. About three months earlier, he had begun to feel "some sharp pains in the chest," but went to the doctor only when the pectoral pain increased. Then he was hospitalized with an infarct. He discovered that he suffered from arterial hypertension, the probable cause of the infarct. He was referred to analysis for resisting the doctor's recommendation of cutting back on his work pace and changing his lifestyle. The patient took the suggestion that he make time for more leisure to mean that he should increase his sports activities. He took part in a sports tournament that aggravated the clinical picture of hypertension.

The therapy focused initially on his work, to which he devoted about 14 hours a day, not including weekend work. Highly competitive, he walked and spoke rapidly, using aggressive and hostile words about his employees and colleagues. He demanded of them the maximum, as if he and they were in a championship competition. He said he had no friends because he had no time for "idle talk." He set up relationships unilaterally, issuing orders without hearing the replies. Even his sexual life with his spouse was rule-bound and disciplined, "to not upset the mind." To the fifth session, Arthur brought the following dream:

> *I go to a business meeting, but it is taking place in a kind of amusement park. In a shooting gallery I get a nasty shock when I see my youngest daughter held fast as the target in an arrow-shooting contest. The arrows just miss her, and I wake up screaming.*

Associations: the youngest daughter, age 11, was his favorite. She was the only person he was able to kiss; she was not afraid of him and approached him more spontaneously than the others. When he was 11 his maternal grandmother, who was quite affectionate, died. From then on, he became more obedient and rigid, because she was the only person who protected him from his strict and demanding father.

Background: He was greatly afraid of his father, who was "most correct and honest," although distant and given to explosions. His mother passed her time completing domestic tasks with "incomparable precision." She spoke little and never expressed her emotions. He learned from her how "vulgar" it is to express emotion. Both parents expected their son to be brilliant and accepted no evidence of inferiority.

Interpretation: This dream led the patient to speak, for the first time, of his childhood and his parents. Through the dream, we can see the origin of his hyperactivity and of his inflexible attitudes (which, he says, do not bother him). He continued to think that "that's the right way." He was upset only by the threat to his daughter, which I understand as the threatened loss of his emotionality. His anima, still in the infantile stage, found itself threatened by arrows in a work environment (business meeting). The arrows were the hostile and aggressive attitudes normal in his daily life; they would kill what was most dear to him. Arrows in the heart represent an acute (sharp) amorous suffering of which the patient was completely unconscious. They corresponded to the cardiac symptom he was feeling a few days before the infarct. Needing to be "Mr. Tough," he paid no attention to the symptoms until they intensified, forcing him to lie down, something he did not like to do – as shown by his insomnia and state of being constantly alert.

The psyche, by forcing him to the clinic, made him face a conflict, the fruit of an infantile complex. Insofar as he was unconscious of that conflict, it had moved into his body as an infarct, visible in the symbol of "arrows piercing the heart." Other dreams of similar cast followed. We began to perceive that the repressed desire for love had imprisoned him in a cold and objective world. The more he tried to control love, the more threatened he became.

During the eleventh session the patient mentioned that, despite the medicine he was taking to control it, his blood pressure was dangerously high. We worked with his symptom, using the technique of active imagination. I requested that he try, with eyes closed, to "see" what was happening inside his body and where this high pressure had started. After about 30 seconds Arthur related the following image:

> *There is a man running down narrow streets. They seem to be channels, everything is very red. I think they're my veins. This man is running a lot and has a grenade in his hand. He can't stop; he always has to flee. Were he to stop, the grenade would explode.*

This image explains why he had to be on the run constantly. If the outside pressure (pressing business) were to abate, the internal pressure would be unbearable. Now he could see that he always needed to be fleeing, running. He had not known exactly what he feared, but was afraid to stop. We concluded that he feared the emotionality associated with the feminine: of becoming less a man, of weakening and becoming less efficient. Consequently he ran, out of fear. The man with the grenade in his fist was associated with the strict and explosive father who punished him (he now remembered) for the slightest imperfections. The analysis, by touching on this complex loaded with energy and emotionality, worsened the cardiac symptom, in a way. That is, by making him more conscious of the conflict, the analysis made his fear more conscious, increasing his blood pressure: a fight-or-flight reaction that is normal when one is confronted by danger.

Medication or lifestyle changes would have brought only temporary relief to this patient. Actually, he would not have been able to change his lifestyle in any definitive way, because a complex much stronger and more dangerous than heart disease threatened him. Had he not undertaken analysis, any other treatment would have been in vain.

We can understand the grenade-holding man as an aspect of his shadow that emerged as hostility and uncontrollable competitive impulses. With such a shadow, the patient had to be constantly vigilant and ready to flee or fight, as his organic symptom revealed. In the following sessions, we used active imagination with the images that emerged spontaneously: the father in the door to his heart, the injured heart, physical fights with the father, the free and empty heart, the daughter embracing the patient's heart and finally the warm heart, beating slowly.

Last dream of the analysis (29th session):

I was cruising in an enormous gilded boat down a long canal. The boat was moving harmoniously, following the water's movements. At the same time, the banks of the canal grew wider and narrower, helping the boat to pass.

Associations: Gilded boat: boat of the twilight of middle age, which brings a sensation of pleasure and peace such as he had never felt before. Canal that moved: the rhythmic movements of the vaginal canal during birth. It was thus that he felt himself being born.

Interpretation: This dream reveals the birth of a new consciousness and a new rhythm in the dreamer's psychic life. The canals (veins and arteries) were now free to offer passage to a renewed ego (boat).

This was a brief analytic process, focused on an organic symptom, and leading the patient into his process of individuation. When approaching middle age, the individuation process was blocked by a neurosis that the patient with resistance refused to acknowledge. A symbol emerged at the corporeal pole, forcing him to confront his complexes and correct his one-sided development. What might have been lived on the abstract plane had to be experienced synchronistically and unconsciously on the concrete plane, in order to be integrated into his consciousness.

The Stoic: When Joints Flare Up (Rheumatoid arthritis)

A 49-year-old housewife had been suffering from rheumatoid arthritis for ten years. She began to feel pain in her hands and knees around ten years ago, but did not get upset about it until her freedom of movement diminished. Her hand joints already suffered visibly from deformities. The joints of her wrists, elbows, knees, ankles, and toes were affected also, but to a lesser extent. The symptoms worsened when she was tense and irritated. She had been treating the condition with medicine for six years with no improvement.

Obsessed with cleanliness, she worked about 18 hours a day at home. The relationship with her husband was cold and distant. She associated the onset of "pins-and-needles" and of burning in her knee and hands with her youngest daughter's leaving home.

During analysis, she began to associate her excessive work with a defense against the fear of being abandoned; she increased her workload to shut out feelings of loss and solitude. However, in order to avoid annoying anyone, she never complained or argued. Her basic attitude was subservience and modesty. Her desires, always considered "lesser things," were so repressed that they were inaccessible to the patient herself. Revealing her sentiments was at times accompanied by worsening pain. It was as if each repressed emotion corresponded to a contracted muscle, and the possibility of expressing it might be followed by punishment (as her mother used to punish her).

We began to realize that her masochistic and depressive structure had led her to sacrifice herself continually for others. The patient began to recall enjoying music and dancing as a child, and denying herself these pleasures because she felt awkward and stiff. It was as if all that was life and flexibility had been tied up so that the patient was restricted to rigid and limited movements. Her self-sacrifice had been halted only by the illness, which had worsened in the last few years.

Before the illness, she had blindly obeyed all outside requests. Her altruism turned obsessive; when she could not complete a given task she was possessed by a feeling of unbearable anxiety. Eventually she realized that her body was defending her from further abuse.

I proposed to work directly with the illness, once its regressive aspects became more conscious. I asked her to sit comfortably and concentrate, eyes closed, on the most painful joint, which at that moment was her knee. I asked her to concentrate on it, observing what was happening there. The patient described it as a "distress" and "weird soreness which gets better when I put my knees together." As she touched her knees together and then spread them, she realized that this was a defensive movement against an invasion – sexual invasion by her husband. Intense hatred for her husband surfaced, mixed with nausea and repulsion, sentiments she had never realized before.

We began to understand the hardening of this joint as a defensive mechanism against movements imposed against her will. At the same time, the hardening was the best way to express her Self, given the conflict between the wish for power (keep her husband) and eros (hate her husband). Restriction of movement protected the patient from a greater evil: continuing a hateful relationship.

In another session, when the patient concentrated her attention on her right wrist, she reported a heightening of the pain, as if a handcuff were tightly securing her wrist. I asked her to imagine this handcuff tightening even more and then to try to "see" who was on the other side of it. The patient felt the heat rising, as if the handcuff were scorching her skin and "saw" her husband laughing, sadistically holding a key. The image of the husband was mixed with that of her father, and the patient wept with anger and powerlessness. Faced with the power of the two men, she could do nothing. She said, "I am a marionette tied at the wrists and ankles, which dances to the tune they play. I have no will of my own. I walk and jump incessantly at their will. No one protects me. I have to do as they command."

During another active imagination, I proposed to the patient that she concentrate on her body and the joint that called out the most. The patient directed her attention to her atrophied fingers. She was hardly able to open them, so painful was any movement. There returned the sensation of handcuffs on her wrists; she realized that she would have to use her fingers to get free from them. With great effort, she started to move the fingers of her right hand, as if she were opening a padlock on her left wrist. She repeated the motion with her left hand. Her motions were slow and evidently painful. She ended the effort smiling. She knew that she was not free yet, but would have to repeat this movement again and again. Spontaneously she began to do this at home, several times each day. In the following sessions, the patient spoke of a considerable improvement in the inflammation and the pain, principally in her knees, wrists, and fingers.

Although the arthritis has not gone away completely, she no longer feels pain and the inflammation emerges in her hands only when she is tired or stressed. She understands that the illness may return if she detours from the "path of her Self," if she stops "obeying herself" and begins to "obey the others." The arthritis has changed from being a symbol to being a sign: a sign that advises her when she is exceeding a limit and losing her balance.

The arthritis, by stopping her movements, also stopped her defensive, obsessive, and servile hyperactivity. If repression of desire created a feeling of superiority, it also produced intense sorrow and resentments that were accumulating in the joints. By stopping, the organism rebelled against detouring away from normal development. Nodules of sorrow accumulated in the body, signaling the need for transformation. Paradoxically, this illness saved her from a worse evil: continuing to live without desires, unconnected with her Self. The inflamed joints revealed the "inflamed psyche," her silent revolt against the constant violation of her essence.

The Depressive: When Cells Revolt (Cancer)

A 32-year-old teacher sought analysis after surgery to remove a melanoma. After she started analysis, a mammary cyst was found.

The patient was single and lived with her mother. Her father left the family when she was eight years old. Two months before she started analysis, a birthmark on the left side of her right leg thickened, began to itch and bleed. She went to a doctor who diagnosed melanoma, which was then removed. She was very depressed for months before the cancer appeared, because she and her fiancé had broken up about seven months prior. She attributed the illness to her emotional suffering and death wish.

She always had several birthmarks distributed around her body. She associated them with her father, who had similar marks. Upon removing the melanoma, she thought she was cutting a link to her father. She felt both relief and a great fear of losing him.

The patient recounted numerous dreams which have a common pattern: accident, illness, and death. We could understand these dreams as a portrait of the trauma that the patient underwent when her engagement ruptured. Through analysis, however, she began to recall past situations when she probably had already felt the same suffering; they left her lacking energy and depressed. For example, remembering the day when her father left home occasioned pain in the area of the surgery.

We worked intensively on these aspects, and anger began to emerge. She used active imagination to return to the moment of her father's departure and was able then to express her emotions and resentments. In these moments she complained of pain – in the region of the surgical scar – for which there was no medical reason.

Out of her negative mother complex, the patient had difficulty in making female friends; she viewed all women as inferior to men and was alienated from her own body. She took care of it as a duty, rather than with pleasure. She kept it "clean, hygienic, and healthy" as an obligation.

In active imagination, I asked her to concentrate on the operated region and observe what was happening. The patient soon related a scene in which her leg was being stung by mosquitoes, causing great itching. She associated the insects with burns and her father's going away. Memories of the fantasies that occurred when the cancer was diagnosed began to emerge; we now realize more clearly the relationship between the burn, the paternal rejection, and the melanoma. The patient had fantasized as a child that her father would return to cure her from a burn. Thus, as an adult, feeling rejected by her fiancé (father), the same symbol (melanoma/burn) emerged to express this suffering and the attempt to recover paternal love.

She also had dreams, fantasies and thoughts where the main content was her destruction, as well as scenes in which she had been rejected and used by her mother. The patient felt that her vitality was gone. She imagined her death by various modes. At the same time, the emergence in therapy of maternal contents became pronounced and associated with the mammary cyst. The patient felt that her body was against her. She felt that she would die because her body didn't like her. I asked her to use active imagination to talk with her body and ask why it wanted to destroy her.

The image of a gigantic woman appeared. This woman was terrible and hated her. The patient tried to escape. Wherever she ran, the earth opened up into craters. As she tried to hide behind some boulders, rain and lightning bolts fell on her. She left the session deeply afraid and without any resolution. No dialogue was possible.

After drawing the witch-woman (Fig. 1), the patient saw that she was powerless against this terrible woman who, simply because the witch was evil, desired the patient's death. There was no escape; the patient would die in any event. The mother complex, in its negative aspect, elicited the mother archetype, including in its negative aspect as the witch-mother figure. The destructive mother, present in the body of her daughter, wanted the daughter's destruction. The three figures in the drawing are the patient trying to talk with the giant and then, finding her effort in vain, the patient giving up and preparing to die. How could she fight against the witch-mother invading the daughter's own body? It was as if the cells of her body had revolted against her. How can you identify the enemy when it is part of yourself? Some cells tried to destroy the patient. How could she identify them?

The patient sketched herself (Fig. 2) lying down, defeated, with an enormous bleeding wound threatening to crush her. At first

Figure 1

Figure 2

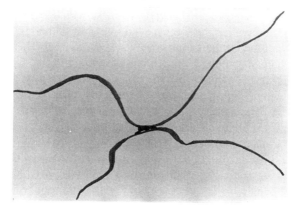

Figure 3

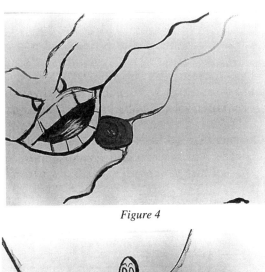

Figure 4

Figure 5

glimpse, she imagined it to be an open breast, with dark spots inside. But then she saw that the spots looked like birds gathering, ready to fly. She reinforced the forms with black ink and took heart at the newly emerged symbol. Even without understanding it, she felt it to be positive.

A drawing (Fig. 3), done in a subsequent session, arose from the suggestion of imagining the cyst in her right breast. The drawing represents the same crushed and defeated woman, imprisoned among the lactiferous ducts. The patient said, "Nothing can flow from my breasts. They are clogged up. There's no milk, just blood. I have no energy to rise. The woman is crushed. I need help." But who can help her?

The next drawing (Fig. 4) is a reply to the question of who could help. There appears here a "devouring monster." The patient's comment was, "He will eat the tumor. Only he can combat the witch. Only another equal to her could defeat her." The crushed woman continues in the lower right corner of the drawing, now praying and asking for aid. According to the patient, the monster is not benevolent; it will help her because it merely wants to thwart the witch. The patient said, "He eats the tumor."

I asked the patient to imagine, several times per day, the monster devouring her cyst. The patient repeated the image five to six times per day and said she felt heat in the region of the cyst.

Within the breast (Fig. 5) we have an oval form between the ducts, in the region of the cyst. The body is that of the monster, but the head is a caricature. The patient said:

I like him. He's funny. He has a sense of humor and controls the monster. The monster ate the tumor already – it's just that he could feel himself powerful and got out of control, attacked me as did the witch. But here he can do nothing, because the guy on top is laughing and putting him in the proper perspective. He says the monster gives no orders. It is transformed into Tipsy Fool [an inflatable weighted toy], who gets pushed from one side to the other, but doesn't give any orders.

Here we verify the existence of two complexes taking part in the formation of her organic symptoms: the negative mother and father complexes. Both expressed themselves – symbolically at the bodily pole – as symptoms, given that unconscious mechanisms impeded their integration into consciousness.

If we take the disease, melanoma, as a symbol, we can see its significance in this process. Wrapped in painful mourning, the patient relives abandonment by her father through the abandonment by her fiancé and reopens a wound stemming from her paternal identification. The birth marks take on the sense of a link to her father; their malignancy may signify the malignancy of the paternal relationship.

The shadow expresses itself in the symbols of the injured, sick, and dead girls – unconscious to the patient – who appeared independent, always ready to help and never needing anything. Here the shadow is active within the body as organic symptoms, showing how serious the injury had been.

In the mammary cyst, we were able to see how the negative mother complex activated the archetype of the great mother in its negative aspect, threatening the body's existence. The mammary cyst was the cyst of the maternal relationship, which had "clogged up" her relation with the feminine/maternal and, at the same time, was an expression of that dysfunction.

The struggle against the negative great mother took place on various levels, but the turning point came with the aid of the archetype of the father. The emergence of a masculine archetypal symbol, the figure of the devouring monster, may signify a struggle between the paternal archetypes, a necessary struggle if the patient was not to stay totally under the thrall of the evil mother.

The process seemed to come under conscious control when the patient realized that she can also control the unconscious monster. Consequently, there emerged figures of the positive animus and logos.

Conclusion

In the cases studied, the organic symptom corresponded to a split in the representation of a complex, where the abstract, psychic part was repressed. The symptom/symbol developed automatically and out of control, revealing its complicated and unconscious character. The use of the analytic model in the patients cited led to the discovery and integration of the abstract pole of the complexes involved. That is, through the analytic model and its psychotherapeutic techniques, it proved possible to transduce the symptoms from their organic pole to the abstract, leading their pathological expressions to diminish gradually and bring about improvement in the patients' general health.

The introduction of the concept of organic disease as symbol resolves the secular dichotomy psyche/body. At the same time, the concept stimulates reflection in defining the limits of the psychological and the biological, of psychology and medicine, a reflection/redefinition already happening in clinical practice.

Translated from Portuguese by Lincoln Berkley

References

Ramos, D. (1994). *A Psique do Corpo*. São Paulo: Cultrix.
Rossi, E. (1986). *The Psychobiology of Mind-Body Healing*. New York: Norton.

Alchemy, Homeopathy, and the Treatment of Borderline Cases

Edward Christopher Whitmont
Sherman, Connecticut, U.S.A.
New York Association for Analytical Psychology

Homeopathy is a highly effective modality for the therapy of certain borderline patients: those for whose fragmented egos impaired cognitional and integrative capacities depth psychological work is ineffective or seriously limited. Homeopathy is like a modern technique of alchemy and of the spagyric arts. Unlike psychotropic medication, homeopathy seemingly does not operate on the level of material chemistry. It works through the "subtle" or "vital energy" body which Paracelsus called the Archaeus. Consequently, it does not interfere with neurotransmitter or hormonal activity, but affects the psychosomatic totality in a direct, normalization of psychoid dynamics. The indications for homeopathic medicines are based on this totality. Even in the treatment of organic disorders, primary emphasis is placed on personality type and psychological makeup. Classical homeopathy supports the individuation process by overcoming the blocking effects of psychoid engrams and, thus, is syntonic with analytic work.

Psychotherapy and the Borderline Problem

Psychotherapy operates on the premise that psychopathology and – frequently – organic suffering, are alleviated through self-awareness and maturational development. Such a development requires self-observation based upon an adequately functioning ego capable of confronting one's shadow. As Jung (CW14, par. 674) sees it, such ego development rests upon a separation between one's "natural" – biologically, instinctually and emotionally determined – motivations and affects, and one's capacities for consciousness: a sense of personal identity and an ability to think rationally and exert willed control over one's actions.

The first separation makes possible the second step: a conscious differentiation and reconciliation of hitherto primitive and potentially pathological affect dynamic into an ethically self-fulfilling personality that can perceive spiritual, ethical and transcendental meaning.

In borderline pathology the embodiment through deintegration of the transpersonal Self, into a complex of identity able to tolerate the stress of polar opposites, is inadequate. In consequence of severe early environmental or a priori traumatization or retardation of psychobiological development, an initially adequate center of conscious identity failed to solidify out of the psychoid, semi-animalic – affect-determined – state of unconsciousness. Since affectivity operates in terms of autonomous-nervous and hormonal activity it possesses a certain fixity and "imprints" itself in reflex, hormonal, neurotransmitter, organ and peripheral muscular structuring and spasticity. The initial ego nucleus is of the nature of a body-ego. Thus, this organic fixation may interfere with further ego-affect separation and shadow confrontation, which can feel like mortification and figurative death.

The attempt to bring about such a self-witnessing and mortifying separation carries the threat of a personality fragmentation and feels intolerable. The extreme form of this non-incarnation we encounter in "hospitalism." Infants raised under biologically adequate conditions, proper nutrition, and hygiene but without hugging, cuddling and loving physical touch, fail to develop and frequently even die. Lacking bodily experience of loving acceptance, the Self withdraws from the intended full incarnation. In less extreme cases, an inadequate ego development fails full cortical control over the limbic and reptilian brain functions. An insufficient scope of the magical-mythological psychoid stratum becomes psychologized. Emotionality remains "characterized by marked physical innervation" ... and a "peculiar disturbance of the ideational process." Emotion is not sufficiently transformed into feeling, nor obsession into thought, drive into willing, and paranoic fears into perception, attention and reflection. Instead of developing into "voluntarily disposable functions," affects and drives remain largely bound up in "the body psychoid" (CW6, par. 681). The elementary motivational force-fields continue to be experienced as extraneous, quasi-macrocosmic rather than microcosmic, psychological factors. The weak ego remains merged with and threatened by the "demons" of obsessive complexes. When the rigid defense system is threatened or tampered with, the ego lives in fear of being carried away or swamped by these "demons."

In this state of affairs adult psychotherapy is limited to supplying a regression experience: an encounter with the unmetabolized and largely unconscious affects in an environment of safety and "holding" support. The ego/non-ego confrontation which Jung considered the first step necessary for individuation, ethical choice and responsibility cannot be attained at this stage. Moreover, the adult or adolescent no longer has the child's plasticity. The distortions and deficiencies have become conditioned reflex activities, encoded in the substance and functioning of musculature, posture and the innervation of organs and neurotransmitter systems. The activities of organs and of the hormonal and autonomic nervous system are altered, first, on the level of the "subtle body." Later, a persistence of these engrams may change what at first was only functional into gross organic pathology.

This dynamic is little accessible to cognitional approaches. In order to modify the pathology of the psychoid, psychotherapy is in need of complementary modalities of precognitional nature. To varying extents, bioenergetics, art therapy, hypnosis, therapeutic regression and (for the treatment of addictions) acupuncture have endeavored to fill this gap. Psychotropic medication addresses itself to the organic level also, but by means of material, chemical interference, with risks of side effects and functional or even organic damage.

The centuries-old spiritual tradition of the spagyric arts considered our problem of soul-body evolution of primal concern, and claimed to have discovered effective ways of dealing with it. Part of what they shrouded in esoteric language, accessible only to intuition or personal initiation, has been developed into an experimentally and clinically verifiable modality that is highly effective. Paradoxically, however, homeopathy has not been given attention by Jungian psychology, even though homeopathy was anticipated and, in principle, spelled out by alchemy.

The Medicamentum Spagyricum

In alchemy, the creation of the *lapis* – equivalent to the individuation process – required first the separation from the *unio naturalis* and second the reintegration of soul-substance into a *unio mentalis*. The alchemists considered that the first part of this process, the separation, could be aided by a medicine, a *medicamentum spagyri-cum*. They considered the *prima materia* of the human state to be the unio naturalis, called chaos, *nigredo, massa confusa,* and "hard to dissolve convolution of body and soul." From this "original semi-animalic state of unconsciousness," the mind was to be extracted and separated by dividing this unio naturalis into a pair of opposites consisting of "instinctuality and rational mind" (CW14, par. 695). That division would bring into existence a soul capable of resisting the influence and compulsions of the body and its instincts.

The medicine was to work by dint of similarity, not oppositeness. Since this medicine was considered the physical equivalent of the lapis and the heavens it was called *"caelum"* and *pharmakon athanasias*. As *caelum* it was held to represent the non-corrupt archetypal substance of the world which could make ill as well as heal all fragmentations of body and soul.

This "heavenly" *medicamentum spagyricum* was produced by extracting a *quintessence* from various substances, but the specific nature or contents of the *arcanum* were not indicated. However, it was affirmed to be of physical nature, a "substance that is not a substance." The arcanum is of physical nature, it is alive, possesses an anima and a spiritus, and even a human-like nature.

The necessity for similarity is stressed repeatedly since, given the spiritual nature of this substance, its helpfulness must depend upon the analogy of its dynamic with the functioning of the person whom it was to heal. Thus, Paracelsus avers that "Never has a hot disease been cured by coldness, nor a cold one by heat. But it has happened that likes have healed likes" (Aschner, 1928, Vol. 2, p. 494). "Man is heaven and earth, and the lower spheres, the four elements and whatever is within them, wherefore he is properly called by name of microcosmos for he is the whole world. ... Thus scorpio cures its scorpio, realgar its realgar, mercurius its mercurius" (Aschner, 1928, Vol. 1, p. 362).

Hence, "Since all of this exists also in the external world the physician must learn upon the illnesses of the visible things their similarity of their coming into being and being dispersed. By virtue of the spagyric art he ought to reduce the bodies to their stuff of origin. Thus he finds out from what substance a particular illness comes. Once he has established all stuffs of origin he knows about all illnesses" (Aschner, 1928, Vol. 1, p. 73).

We can see in these quotations that Paracelsus and the alchemists envisioned the existence of a psycho-physical and spiritual analog to human dynamics inherent in the various substances of the outer world. Their "spiritual" *quintessentia* could be extracted and, by virtue of their similarity to the human situation, they were expected to reconnect the human psychosomatic entity with its corresponding unconditioned archetypal source and, thereby, to heal that which is ill or arrested in its development.

Trained as he was in terms of nineteenth century positivist medical viewpoints and not familiar with homeopathy, Jung was puzzled by such statements. He could not conceive of the possibility of such transmaterial principles as a priori constitutents of matter. Thus, he explained the alchemist's descriptions in terms of projections upon matter which needed to be "taken back" and be recognized exclusively as aspects of the human psyche. Even though he noted that the alchemists repeatedly affirmed that the processes in question involve physical transformation as well as physical substance dynamics, Jung remarked that "if the adept really concocted such potions in his retort he must have surely chosen them on account of their magical significance. He worked accordingly with ideas, with psychological processes, but referred to them under the name of the corresponding substances" (CW14, par. 704). "It never occurred to the alchemist to cast any doubt whatsoever on this *intellectual monstrosity* [sic]" (CW14, par. 695).

For traditional medicine, homeopathy represents as much of an "intellectual monstrosity" as does alchemy, and for the same reason: It works with "substance which is not substance" and considers psychological, psychophysical and somatic dynamics to be equivalent to, hence "similar" to the outer world substances.

Homeopathy

Homeopathy is based on the fact – experimentally and clinically verified – that any medicine will cure that particular disease the symptoms of which are most similar to those symptoms it produces upon healthy persons who consistently ingest the medicine. Such systematic testing of drugs on large numbers of average healthy humans (not on animals), for the sake of eliciting their typical bodily, mental and emotional symptoms is fundamental for the practice of homeopathy. (It is called "proving," from the German word "prüfen," verify). However, such similarity must include the specific gestalt-totality of the disorder rather than fortuitous details.

For instance, the disorder brought about by inhaling onion (allium cepa) duplicates the initial phase of a head cold. A similar state is brought about by the initial, toxic effects of arsenic. Hence, onion and arsenic, in appropriate dosage, abolish a cold when taken during the early phase. However, these substances are not interchangeable; the fit between remedy and patient must be specific.

Suppose a patient evidences the symptoms of a head cold and wants to avoid cold air so as not to feel worse. Onion would be ineffective because the nasal irritation it produces is aggravated by warmth, and indeed is usually relieved by cold. An arsenic irritation, which also duplicates the initial phases of a cold, behaves in the opposite fashion from onion; arsenic is assuaged by warmth. Since we have a patient who seeks heat, arsenic would be the appropriate remedy, the best "fit." (These substances are not the only ones that would apply; for the later phases still others are to be considered.)

The dynamics of the right remedy must include not only the temperature preferences but all the physical, emotional, and psychological characteristics that constitute the patient's given condition and states, even the seemingly irrelevant. An actual case, of course, involves many more variables than the two we have chosen above. The correspondence between remedy and patient has to be personal, constitutionally specific and exactly matched to the descriptive phenomena in the field.

For example – again simplified – given a somatic state such as an intestinal disorder, an attenuated preparation of windflower (*Pulsatilla*) is more likely to be effective with people of mild, timid and yielding disposition than with those of an aggressively irascible temper. The latter type would be more likely to respond to a particular form of strychnine (*Nux vomica*), while another strychnine compound, the St. Ignatius bean, corresponds to psychological states of grief, bereavement and abandonment. Gold, as another example, influences heart and circulatory functioning and affects personalities of serious, over-responsible and depressive, even suicidal tendencies.

Hence, every substance field represents a Gestalt pattern of circumscribed personality traits, temperament, and emotional propensities in unison with biological response patterns and disorders. Every existing substance, when subject to the proving experiment, exhibits a similarity, hence a healing capacity for some human (or animal) disturbed state. In view of the immense number of still unproven substances (the homeopathic materia medica at present contains approximately 1000 or 1500 proven medicines), we assume that for every human affliction there exists a healing substance. Psychobiological response patterns that are aspects of the human life-drama are duplicated in the structural and life activity of the earth's substances. The psychosomatic totalities of ill persons and medicines appear as similar field patterns, mutually inclusive of human and nonhuman, "external" and supposedly "inanimate" substances.

The further "intellectual monstrosity" that makes homeopathy so unbelievable to the minds of the orthodox scientist is its use of dosages that have been attenuated to the point where no molecule of the original drug could still be present. This practice began as follows: When the toxic effects of medicines were added to the similar disease state, the drugs selected on the basis of similarity frequently caused initial aggravations of the condition they were supposed to cure. Samuel Hahnemann, the originator of homeopathy, was guided by some intuition or perhaps familiarity with spagyric tradition. In order – as he thought then – to reduce dosage, he proceeded to dilute his medicines, but in an unusual way. Instead of ordinary dilution he proceeded stepwise in repeated one to ten or one to 100 attenuations, while at each step succussing the resulting solution a hundred times. Eventually, on the basis of trial and error, he came to repeat this process 30 times, insisting upon thorough (100 times) successive shaking for each step. Each of these "dilution steps" is called a "potency."

Hahnemann and his followers found that, on the average, a thirtieth potency produced the smoothest curative effect, without undue previous aggravation of symptoms. This runs in the face of the fact, fortunately as yet unknown to Hahnemann, that, according to Avogadro's number, the probability of any molecule of the original medicine still to be present in such a dilution of 1:100 to the thirtieth power, is about nil. No material or chemical effect can be expected from such a dilution. Nevertheless, these preparations are extremely effective, provided they are prepared in the step-by-step fashion described and administered according to the simile principle. When the simile principle is disregarded or the attenuations have not been carried out by stepwise succession, they are ineffective. On the other hand, when diluted and thoroughly succussed in stepwise 1:10 or 1:100 succession, the continuing presence of "something" in dilutions that exceed Avogadro's limit has been demonstrated by biological, biochemical, and nuclear magnetic resonance methods. (Coulter, 1981, pp. 52-63).

The strangest aspect of this phenomenology is the fact that, while the toxic effect of the substance gradually diminishes in dilutions from the concentrated strength to the thirtieth step, the energetic effect increases as the attenuation is carried further into the ultramolecular realm beyond the thirtieth, to the two hundredth, thousandth, ten thousandth up to hundred thousandth and millionth step. Such high potencies can cause an uproar in delicate conditions, and be even dangerous when administered injudiciously.

Apparently, what we deal with here is not a dilution in the ordinary sense, but another, as yet unknown dispersion of the substance which, while "dematerializing" on the molecular level, preserves and even intensifies its specific characteristics in terms of dynamics. Such highly attenuated, dematerialized "substances" may be likened to spirit, information, or meaning in matter; pointing to a border area where material and nonmaterial dynamic, mind and matter, psyche and soma seem to overlap and appear like varying expressions of basic, encompassing archetypal themes. The operative reality of such encompassing ground-themes, which symbolically depict a "personality," "spirit" or "anima" of substance, has emerged from extended clinical experience.

Evidently the formal patterns underlying or expressing themselves in human dynamics, emotions, conflicts, thought forms and organic functioning correspond to formal and functional elements that also underlie the building stones of our planet as well as of its inhabitants. These patterns are creative, archetypal principles of order and meaning that, in differing "code" forms, embody corresponding functional complex systems on the level of mineral, plant, animal and human body-and-awareness systems. For every human life-theme played out as a complex, somatic pattern there is, apparently, a mirroring energy field that biopsychologically encodes that complex in the substance-body of the earth. The nature of these patterns can be considered psychoid, not psychological. Hence, also on the human level, they operate through the psychoid system and involve somatic as well a psychic effects. These field patterns can be evoked psychically, as we know from work in our consulting rooms. But they can also be evoked via the "essences" distilled out of substance, via "substance that is not substance," homeopathic high potency.

Just as mental and psychological patterns can, by synchronicity, constellate analogous material events, so also can dense "material" substance be "thinned out" and dematerialized into directive principles of order and form, by the process of potentization. The functional connection or essential unity between "inner" and "outer" rests on the principle of analogy, metaphor or similarity. Clinically, this similarity of the substance "personality" to that of the patient serves as therapeutic indication for its use.

For reasons of space I can give only cursory illustrations of the unique way homeopathy depicts these functional "spirit-personalities" of its spagyric medicines and how these viewpoints have been applied in clinical situations. First, however, we must consider the effect on the transference of the therapist's suggesting or offering medication.

Transference Implications

Because of legal restrictions or of their insufficient familiarity with the homeopathic materia medica, many therapists wishing to use homeopathy may have to refer to a qualified homeopathic practitioner rather than dispense remedies themselves. For them the transference implications probably will be not very different from those when they refer a client for diagnostic consultation or for psychotropic medication. The client may fear that the therapist may want to get rid of him or her, as too heavy a burden for the therapist, too difficult a case or a "bad" patient. Conversely, there may result a split transference when the patient plays the medicine against the analytic process and feels that, instead of his or her own work, the medicine is to do the whole job now.

For the analyst who dispenses the medicine, the transference problems arise from the partial shift of archetypal role from that of the relatively neutral observer and partner in the search to the medical model of the director of treatment or all-knowing guru. Needless to say, all the above contingencies, particularly the abandonment, authority, and guru complexes – including those of the therapist – as well as the therapist's countertransferential anxiety, impatience, and authority needs will have to be evaluated and worked through. They will have to be weighted as to appropriate timing and whether the hoped-for benefit of the intervention of giving a medicine balances the problems it may raise.

At times a remedy may have to be withheld temporarily or permanently for the sake of more psychological work. On the other hand, a stalled phase of the treatment may be moved into positive activity by the medicine, with transference issues – hitherto repressed or denied – brought into the open. The unblocking effect on the psychoid level may be more effective analytic work, as was the case in the instances described below. (The first case was my own analysand. For the second Sylvia Perera was the analyst and I was homeopathic consultant.)

Cases

Our first patient was a 25-year-old woman with a severe depression and disorientation of the reality function. She was passive, yet full of fury about imaginary enemies, with obsessive flights of ideas and illusory notions: that her hands or other parts of her body wanted to talk to her or disturb her. She was not interested in school or job activities, because she wanted to "save" her energies. She complained about constant tiredness and a weakness that supposedly prevented any activity, about feelings of emptiness and a sense of being unreal. She felt that she could not control what "happened" to her, that parts of her body were separate. Hence she was afraid that, inadvertently, she might commit acts of violence. For that reason she avoided human contact. Her dress and hair were neglected and looked dirty despite a washing compulsion.

In school she had been diagnosed as "learning disabled" and put into special classes. She sensed contempt from everybody and concluded that there was no point in trying to assert herself and to relate to people except by withdrawing.

After three years of mainly reductive analysis and some therapeutic regression she was relatively well able to understand her problems. She discovered that she was convinced that there was nobody in the world who would understand her, that there was no point in making any effort, since "it all would come to nothing anyway." These feelings centered around her sense of having been neglected and held in contempt by her father who, while "helping" her, made it always quite clear that he preferred her extroverted, cheerful and socially successful older brother. According to her memories, father also had the need to show off and to prove to his children, especially to her, how powerful and smart he was and how wrong and stupid she was.

As she assimilated these insights the obsessive aspects of her condition began to improve. However, her depressions, hopelessness and lethargy remained unchanged.

Eventually she brought dreams. In one *she was trying to drive her own damaged car, but feared that it might be injured further in the effort.* In another *she tried to connect with a woman whom she described as a well-adapted, social person, but felt that her body or her mother did not allow it.* Those dreams I took as speaking not only of her identity with the ineffectual mother but also as referring to a resistance from the *Hyle* (mother, car, body). This resistance I considered a possible call for substance support. The similar medicine would have to reflect the self-image of an angry, even wrathful and embittered, but also discouraged, humiliated and insulted "down and out" person who could not come to herself because of feeling a "nerd," peddler or beggar, worthless, put down and ridiculed, having lost the game before it even started, hence having no chance in life. These features are reflected in the picture of *Psorinum*, a medicine derived from potentizing the content of a scabies vesicle, the "beggar's filth." The substance picture may be likened to a spirit or "demon" of self-contempt, humiliation and neglectful disregard of self and body and of one's human dignity, reflected and materialized in the scabies eruption – a neglect of one's way of meeting the world (skin as the surface where inner meets outer).

One dose of the thousandth centesimal potency brought about a dramatic change. The patient now brought a dream in which *she enjoyed walking and watching a beautiful spring morning's sunrise.* Her posture straightened. She began to pay attention to the way she dressed and, quite spontaneously, got an attractive haircut. Her mood level improved and a first sense of humor began to appear. Most importantly, a shift occurred in the accessibility of the negative transference. Up to that time, she had remained relatively lethargic and withdrawn, at best merely acknowledging interpretations but isolating herself from interaction with the therapist behind a wall of passive aggression – the habitual style she had developed in dealing with her father complex. She began to come out of this lethargic cocoon and to challenge interpretations and even to express resistance. Eventually she allowed her bottled-up anger to show in verbal fights with the therapist. She had a chance to discover that her furious and at times obsessive anger and invectives did not kill the relationship as she had feared it would have done with her father.

Aggressive libido thus found a channel that moved from depression to assertion and self-assurance, expressed in her being able to pull herself together and to apply herself to systematic work. Upon eventual repetition of the dose, she developed an active interest in and a cooperative attitude toward psychological self-understanding and some months after the first dose she decided to go back to college. Analysis continued for several more years, now mostly focused on the working-out of relationship problems.

The next example is that of a middle-aged divorced man. He was the son of an alcoholic father and a paranoid, psychotic mother. As a child he felt he had to take care of his mother yet was often abused, beaten, and almost tortured by her, while having the reality of the situation white-washed. On entering therapy he was suicidal, given to extreme mood swings and at times prone to hallucinatory states and psychotic transference projections of both the sociopathic neglectful father and the abusive mother. He tended alternately to feel himself as a hateful evil and then as a victimized "good boy" and was either excessively clinging or closed off and unable to communicate. He wanted to be a "good father" and take care of his own children and then hated to be bothered by them.

In therapy he was unable to remember a session from one week to the next, although he kept obsessive and copious reports. These reports functioned as if to evacuate and/or accumulate them away into a safer, non-human object and to attempt to destroy the therapist's intentions as his mother's wild envy had nearly destroyed him. Because of splitting and a fragmentary pre-ego he could not hear interpretations or begin to observe the part-aspects of his psyche. The same ground had to be gone over again and again without resulting in any capacity to assimilate insights. Over several years the therapist came to feel that the patient's discriminatory and metabolizing capacities were submerged beyond reach in an insufficiently psychologized affect and drive level. Hence the help of a medicamentum spagyricum seemed called for.

In view of the man's tendency to extremes of dissociated splitting, the first medicine chosen was Anacardium orientale in the two hundredth potency. Anacardium is a nut from the mountains of Eastern India. It has an external coating of an oil which is black, caustic and "bad," but the heart of the nut is sweet. The personality may be called malicious, but with a sweet heart. Dissociation, splitness and separation up to the extreme of schizophrenia are part of its characteristic proving picture. A symptom, mentioned in its proving and clinically typical, is a sense of two wills; one bad, one good. For instance, the description reads: "a deeply religious person feeling impelled to hate and curse god, or feeling impelled to do what one hates and does not want to do" – in this case our patient's alternating and mutually opposed urges.

The effect of this medicine was dramatic. An allergy improved dramatically within the hour, and he was able for the first time in the therapy to express gratitude. In addition to easing his allergy temporarily, the dissociative splitting and obsessive defenses eased considerably. However, the pathology dramatically shifted to the somatic level. He began to suffer attacks of bronchial asthma, severe rheumatic pains and swelling of joints. Affect came to the fore via his body. He could allow himself to feel pain and fear that were projected upon his physical condition; he felt threatened damage from the negative mother as nature: external factors such as the weather. He felt quite dependent on the therapist whom he called almost daily, sometimes several times a day, to report on his physical condition or his fears. Nonetheless he was also still fixed in his habitual patterns and avoided trying new initiatives and ways of relating. But this behavior now seemed to harbor the beginnings of a coalescing core of selfhood.

At this stage a further medicine, carbonate of calcium, was chosen on the basis of its similarity, this time to the man's basic psychosomatic constitutional personality "picture." The criteria for the choice were given by his physical typology – short, obese, flabby body build, sensitivity to external climate factors, particularly wet and cold – and by his basic temperamental habitus: slow, systematic and stubborn, clinging, defensive and one-track minded in the track of his current mood.

The carbonate of calcium is prepared from the middle layers of the inner, snow-white part of the oyster shell. Rather than being used as a chemically "pure" product the oyster calcium is "live" inasmuch as limestone rocks are sedimentary, derived from ancient sedimentation of oyster-like animal life. The essence of calcium, hence, is "oyster-like." The form principle of the oyster is underwater life of a soft gelatinous inner core, capable of producing a pearl in its center around an injuring foreign element. This soft core is surrounded and protected by the hard limestone armor of the closed shell. The oyster "determinedly" clings to any available fixed support. In this sense, then, carbonate of calcium presents itself in the organism like a builder of solid ground amidst the flow of waters. The human parallel theme is protection of the individual physical and mental structure against external and internal influences that might dissolve and overwhelm it.

Calcium people are generally slow, practical, economical, conscientious, responsible, even over-responsible as workers, who steadily plod along. They are reliable partners but hate to be dependent; they are satisfied to build patiently and drag stone upon stone in their work. Work is very important to them but is not competitive or ambitious. They are loyal and duty-bound, often dominated by a perfectionistic super ego, full of "shoulds" and "don'ts." When the activity of this field pattern is disturbed or traumatized, its polar opposite is constellated. Then, like our patient, these people may lack initiative, be too easily frightened – looking for support – too open to influences from their surroundings, too easily affected, hypersensitive or too armored and isolated; in order to compensate for their lack of ability to meet a challenge. They become stubborn and, thus, dependent, passive, withdrawn from social relationships.

This medicine, given in two-hundredth and, later, thousandth potencies, not only completely healed the man's physical symptoms and discomforts but also enabled him to become accessible to analytic exploration and interpretation. As the analysis proceeded, he was able to develop empathy for his genuine suffering and some differentiation from his obsessions. While accepting that he had a "psychotic pocket," he even began to develop a sense of humor. Analysis continued for many years and resulted in an increasingly satisfactory work and relationship life.

Conclusion

The alchemist's spagyric process labored toward the creation of the lapis by aiming at a reduction or approximation of substance to the prima materia, namely the informational field that underlies and "condenses" itself into what we experience as substance. The homeopathic method is a modern form of this process. As the aboriginal, unconditioned, archetypal "purity" of the prima materia is approached, its ordering effect normalizes the corresponding areas of human encoding. In terms of psychological work we speak of the effects of the constellated Self. When, as in psychotic and borderline cases, the way to psychic cognition is barred, it may be opened through the "substance that is not a substance," the spirit or quintessentia of substance.

In the cases I have described, as in most instances, the spagyric medicine helped remove psychoid fixations which hindered the progress of analytic therapy. When the consequences of serious childhood damage, emotional and physical abuse, rape incest, war, concentration and prison camp experiences, drug addiction, or other conditioning have become imprinted somatically, they create stubbornly resistant dissociations and repetition compulsions. In these instances the therapeutic approach benefits from addressing itself also, perhaps even primarily, to the biologic-psychoid substratum: the "subtle" body fields.

Nevertheless, analysis remains essential in these cases and the importance of the psychotherapist is not diminished. The homeopathic substance is helpful in removing an energy block and aids the development of an adequate ego capable of witnessing and confronting the instinctual unconscious. Nevertheless, the substance is not, of itself, capable of removing the underlying personality problems. Moreover, to the extent that adequate cognitional and integrative capacities happen to be available, the reliance on a medicine can be counterproductive. The notion that the medicine could solve one's difficulties of relationship to oneself and others may interfere with the maturational process. On the other hand, when insufficient ego strength and cognitional capacities are major problems, a homeopathic medicine can make the psychological work easier and more effective. But even then, with borderlines and others, psychotherapy has to be continued. Basic life decisions, ethical and interpersonal relationship problems and difficulties as well as one's relationship to one's complexes, to one's creativity and to the transpersonal dimension require the psychological differentiation and the agonizing work of the ego in confronting the unconscious, as the second step towards the achievement of the unio mentalis.

References

Aschner, B., trans. (1928). *Paracelsus, Sämtliche Werke*. (Vols. 1 & 2). Jena: Gustav Fischer.

Coulter, H. (1981). *Homeopathic Science and Modern Medicine*. Berkeley: North Atlantic Books.

AIDS Fantasies in Analysis

Pasqualino Ancona
Catania, Italy
Italian Center of Analytical Psychology

While reflecting on Hermann Hesse's metaphor in his novel *Narcissus and Goldmund*, I noticed an analogy between the Plague and Acquired Immune Deficiency Syndrome (AIDS). What becomes of the Goldmund of the year 2000? And what of the tormented soul that – in roaming aimlessly, in the abuse of sex and lovers – looks for artistic sublimation, symbolizes the eternal and archetypal mother figure? According to Hesse's metaphor, we must dare and risk, in order to fight death – to win or die. The greatest challenge is incest, returning to rebirth.

At the height of this excessive introversion Goldmund finds his double, Narcissus. Narcissus represents the ego, developed and reinforced by contemplation; in this way Goldmund develops the thinking function. He can defeat the dragon and become the prior of the monastery, Mariabronn. The process of transformation, in Hesse's metaphor, is brought about by the Plague and the fear of death. Plague and death are the opportunity to understand the complexity of the libido. In this way the partiality of consciousness is compensated.

Sex may be the way to experiment with the sacred. The transcendent function is activated; every time there is external interference, a limit, it impels the individual to look for other possibilities. This sequence can apply to the image of irrepressible longing and endless desire that never finds its object, and to the search for the absent mother. Thus, Hesse's Goldmund is similar to the roaming heroes: Gilgamesh, Dionysus, Heracles, Mithras.

From Disorder to Order

The basis of research is roaming. It is not possible to deal with the symbolic process without taking instincts into account. The symbol would lose its meaning if not counterbalanced by instinct. In the same way, disorder in the instinctive world would lead only to destruction if the symbol did not give the instincts a guideline. Thus, we realize that the fear of AIDS is an opportunity to move the individual to find again the symbolic referents of the sacrificed instincts.

Not long ago the instinctive world could be expressed without being controlled. Analysts are discovering that the fear of AIDS necessitates finding a guideline for the instincts and provides a collective opportunity to find a symbolic guideline. Jung's theory on the transformation of the libido is illustrated in the Heracles myth.

Heracles' Sacrifice

Only by sacrifice is it possible to achieve success in the process of transformation. Sacrifice does not result in regression or, at least, regression may be positive. Sacrifice is a successful transposition of the libido to the symbolic equivalent of the mother. Therefore, it is a spiritualization of the incestuous libido.

When Heracles dies, he goes up to Olympus and Hera mimes his rebirth from her womb. To achieve this, however, all the defenses of the heroic ego must be eliminated; it is essential that there be a desire to welcome death. In this metaphor we may find an interpretive key to AIDS. The gradual annihilation of the defenses to the point of the wish for death calls to mind AIDS in its pathogenesis – the destruction of immune defenses – as a metaphor of transformation.

The understanding of metaphor enables us to understand AIDS fantasies and dreams. More and more frequently, a sense of disease – showed through dreams and fantasies to be seropositive – opens up the process to restructure the personality. Metaphorically, the annihilation of defenses of the ego is an opportunity to be open to the Self and to transformation.

Heracles' efforts are tests of the heroic ego, elicited by the incest taboo. Mystic thinkers have found in Heracles' labors the emancipation of the soul, gradually freeing itself from the slavery of the body until it reaches deification.

The hostility of the Great Mother, Hera, impedes Heracles from birth in acting out incest, thus denying him the phallic power bestowed upon him by his father Zeus. Such denial enables him to find different ways of increasing his strength in order to face up to sacrifice and rebirth.

Hera – persecutor, dominating anima – imposes the most serious labors on the hero and threatens him with ruin, should he not take action toward performing his heroic deed. Hera represents the tyrannical need to transform the mother complex through the sacrifice of the ego, overcoming barriers and resistance.

Heracles' myth enables us to understand the heroic effort of the ego, thus giving us clues to the problem of AIDS. His final transformation begins with a transgressive incident where his wife Deianira mates with Centaur Nessus, who attempts to rape her. Consequently, Heracles' garment is contaminated with Nessus' blood and sperm. (These are the two elements that are the vehicles of transmission of the AIDS virus.) If we follow Heracles' final experiences that precede transformation, we reach a better understanding of the AIDS phenomenon.

During his journey into Hades, while he is struggling with his twelfth labor, Heracles finds the preconditions for his earthly death. His heroic arrogance compels him to defy the mother complex, the trials and tribulations of the Great Mother Hera. Through Heuristeus, she forces Heracles to capture Cerberus from Hades, as a final labor to achieve male recognition.

Heuristeus, combining the Greek words eurisko and teos, means "discovery of God." He gives Heracles the opportunity to become a god This gift is the beginning of defeat. When Heracles arrives in Hades he is arrogant and menacing but, for the first time, his heroic ego is moved to pity by a plaintive soul.

It is Meleagris' soul. He has died recently, leaving his unmarried sister Deianira alone in their father's house. After disarming Heracles, reminding him that a soul cannot be annihilated, and moving him to pity with his desperate tale, Meleagris asks Heracles to marry his abandoned and threatened sister.

It is only in the depths of the unconscious that the heroic ego may find the opportunity to change a homoerotic feeling. This may happen in the kingdom of an infertile god, Hades, who does not permit anyone to return to the kingdom of the living. The heroic ego that does not accept defeat may compromise and agree to go halfway, when a homo-erotic feeling is present. The feeling may be present in the spirit and not in the flesh. Thus Heracles, on his victorious return from Hades, succeeds in saving Theseus, one of two friends who had been condemned to eternal immobility. When Heracles attempted to set free the other friend, Pirithous, the earth quaked and Heracles was forced to leave him to his terrible fate.

The consequence of this partial rescue is the marriage to Deianira who is both a virgin and a warrior. She is to aid Heracles in fighting against the Driops. From this image we can deduce that homosexual instinctive forces may find an object without one's being aware of it, through relationship with a masculine woman.

The adolescent may feel drawn to homosexuality as an opportunity to identify with his mother, since he is unable to possess her. His inability to be unfaithful to her inhibits his heterosexual development. The tendency to regression may be compensated partially by having as an object of love a female with male attitudes.

Thus, when Heracles returns from Hades, he has the opportunity to experience the homosexual side of his personality. When an undifferentiated instinctive energy structures a confused sexual impulse that we may define as bisexual, this impulse finds many outlets for expression at various stages of existence, corresponding to the various components of heroic myths: radical good, radical evil and all the in-between possibilities of sexual expression.

We are coming to the end of the myth. The deep feeling of rebellion of Heracles' heroic ego to the easy flow of libidinal unconscious energy moves Heracles to murder Nessus on impulse. Nessus was a centaur to whom the gods had given the task to take people from one side of the river to the other. Metaphorically, we can say that Heracles refuses to act out directly his partially unconscious impulse, which is incomprehensible and negative. (Nessus is also a son of Ocean, who well represents the immensity of the libido.) He also refuses the likely link between direct and indirect homosexual desire, between Meleagris' desire and his sister's desire, between a man's desire and his female partner's desire. Is Nessus more excited at the sight of Deianira or at the sight of Deianira at Heracles' side?

Heracles has a strong reaction against this image, just as the heroic ego becomes a tyrant who impedes the unconscious images from coming to the surface. But unconscious forces do not surrender.

Nessus did not die immediately. He still had time to deceive Heracles' wife: pretending that he wanted to do her a kindness, he told her that the blood discharging from his poisoned wound had magic powers, and he advised her to take it and put it into her flask. Then Centaur told her that Heracles would never love another woman if he wore his blood-soaked garment. Deianira took the lethal advice. When Nessus was about to arrive at the river bank and very near death, Deianira took his blood, and hid it in a bronze urn in the house. (Kerényi, 1985, p. 212)

According to some versions, the mixture contained Nessus' blood, to which Deianira added the sperm splattered from his genitals during his attempt to rape her. A variation of the myth – recorded by an Alexandrian poet, Diotimo – defines Heracles as the lover of Euristeus. According to this variation, Heracles fulfilled all the latter's whims because he was in love with him.

The Great Mother Hera, through the choice of homosexuality, directly or indirectly puts Heracles through many trials and tribulations before accepting him as an adult. Whether or not the hero's bisexuality is lived fully or partially, directly or indirectly depends on mythical variants – opportunities.

The final transformation for the heroic ego is the sacrifice of nature, of unrestrained sexuality. The final deification is the guideline of the heroic development of consciousness. But it is Nessus, the transporter – the link – who arranges the final transformation. To find the link again, and the union of opposites in the oedipal triangle, requires great effort on the part of consciousness. When there is no awareness, unconscious energies come to the fore unexpectedly.

Nessus arranges Heracles' atrocious end and deification with the mixture of his blood and sperm. A happy death frees Heracles from the painful knowledge that his body is tormented by his unrestrained sexuality (experienced as a burning sensation in his body).

If there is no dialogue between consciousness and the unconscious and if the link between them is interrupted at the beginning, this may result in harmful behavioral patterns that become fertile ground for the AIDS virus. Nessus, as Ocean's son, is a part of the libido that prevents it from stagnating on only one side of the river. Through Nessus, the ego may take small steps to explore the universal flowing of the libido.

When the dialogue between consciousness and the unconscious is interrupted, the repressed behavioral patterns are acted out in violent form. It is known that the first victims of AIDS were in prejudiced environments, in which homosexuality was split from the rest of the personality. Acting out took the individual by surprise and did not give him time to reckon with the reliability of the partner or the use of condoms, nor with sexuality without any future, lived compulsively at the moment of meeting. The risk and fear of AIDS puts sexuality to the test and denies its true meaning.

Sexual contact becomes but a fleeting moment. Similarly, we can say that other harmful behavioral patterns connected with AIDS, especially drug addiction, appear mainly when a fragile ego wishes to experiment with initiation rites by assuming pseudo-heroic behaviors that permit neither a relationship nor a constructive dialogue with the unconscious. All is resolved in an instant, without previous thought or imagination, therefore without a future. Without a future it is impossible to see the way of the transcendent function.

Transformative Strength of Evil

The verb "to transcend" is derived from the Latin – trans (crossing) scandere (to go beyond) – and used by the sodomite Brunetto Latini who, in Dante's *Divine Comedy*, says: "I advise you to take good care of my Treasure with which I still live; I will say no more." Is the evil of hell – the shadow – a treasure that must be taken care of? We know that the Shadow is the source of the energy for transformation. Setting in motion the imagination opens the way to wider horizons for consciousness. The emotional charge that characterizes contact with the shadow may be dealt with differently in relation to superior psychic functioning.

When thinking is the superior function, the individual's effort is directed toward research and empathic recognition of the split in the dark side of the personality. In contrast, when the superior function is feeling, the individual may be overwhelmed by the discovery of the dark side. Once or several times in life, the shadow may become dominant in the ego and the remainder of the personality may become unconscious. The dark side could represent a "treasure" to be guarded jealously; it could activate the transcendent function each time that the predominance of the ego over the unconscious interrupts the natural process of transformation and individuation.

This interruption is likely to take place if we bear in mind the bipolarity and complementarity of the psyche. During analysis the lessening of the projection enables the individual gradually to recognize the shadow. The next step is to link the shadow to the collective dimension again, thus opening the path to a symbolic quest.

Before this process can take place, the shadow must be recognized as personal potential – until it becomes conscious. In this way the shadow becomes more important and stronger than the ego. Then the strict and unambiguous ego may be shattered by the transgressive potential of the shadow. Thus, the latter encourages the libido in new directions, opening different horizons of consciousness.

Before the advent of AIDS, transgressive behaviors – homosexual contact and drug addiction – were tolerated both by personal and collective images. Now such behaviors tend to be suppressed and inhibited – because they bring to mind AIDS in the personal and collective world of images.

In the days before AIDS, we were conscious that eros represented a way to live our potential for transgression. This consciousness enabled us to become aware of the psyche's attempt to individuate. Today the fear of AIDS could put the brakes on eros. This fear may encourage introjection of erotic tension, to link it to a symbolizing process. On the other hand, the fear of AIDS could induce the individual to risk denying the shadow, because it is closely related to risky behavior. Eros is a vital instinct, but today it carries with it the risk of death. Today, more than in the past, the deep roots of the libido are suppressed by the fear of AIDS when they are represented merely by sexual instincts. This suppression could result in incestuous regression, which would be hazardous for psychic balance.

The long path that leads from erotic fantasy to death has been annihilated in its intermediate stages; erotic fantasy coincides with death. By excluding all probabilities between pleasure and death, the individual automatically imagines a likely death. Between these two extremes the analyst, now more than in the past, experiences a new resistance on the part of the patient and, to a lesser degree, on the part of the analyst.

In the past, work in a setting where imagination and erotic fantasies are developed did not afflict the analyst much if, in the quest for individuation, the patient acted out transgressive sexual acts. Indeed, these acts could represent an element that moves the individual toward the path of transformation by working on the sense of guilt. Today the analyst must bear a sense of guilt and is compelled to work in a limited space, that of not repressing and not acting out. In this space the possibility to act out activates the fantasy of death and divine punishment. We analysts ought to ask ourselves if the present negative publicity against analysis is supported by collective knowledge or collective fantasy. Analysis, more than other psychotherapies, may activate transgressive acting out and risky behavior.

Analysis also gives access to examination of the need for interiorization, a need that is activated by external obstacles to living life freely by following one's instincts. Thus, the moralistic statements deriving from a Catholic environment take on a wider and more complex meaning. According to these statements, AIDS reveals and punishes the prevailing laxity and indecency in today's society. From a metaphorical point of view, we can see that the thought of death, activated by AIDS, could give life a more profound meaning. At the same time, the split in the two aspects of the libido, spiritual and sexual, is the basis for proliferation of repetitive and compulsive sexual behavior.

All efforts to understand this behavior symbolically are lost when there is a split in the libido. The advent of AIDS has given rise to the possibility of being reunited to the spiritual aspect of the libido. If we fail to understand the literal meaning of Catholic warnings and if we try to understand their metaphorical meaning, we can accept even the most bigoted moralistic dogma: that AIDS is the scourge of God expressing rage against a society that has dared to break the rules.

Licentious sexual inclination was "in" during the 1970s. It was boosted by progress in "almighty" science, which was able to overcome once-fatal diseases contracted through sexual intercourse. Thus, homosexual eros was deprived of its symbolic meaning.

At that time many homosexual males considered themselves only as a capitalistic system, producing and distributing sex which happened quickly, often and efficiently. There was no time for reflection or quest for the symbolic. The treasure that Brunetto Latini recommended, with its transformative impulse, had been suppressed for many years.

The fear of AIDS compels many individuals, not only homosexual males, to control sexual behavior more than in the years before the advent of AIDS. This fear impels us to reconsider our life style. The message was once to consume, grow, enjoy yourself, do whatever you feel like doing, going beyond the limits. Now such a life style has changed completely.

But it is true also that eros motivates transgressive behavior that attempts to awaken the libido toward new paths, opening different horizons for the consciousness. Today, the restless, rebellious and undisciplined nature of a human being may take him or her to the threshold of death through the risk of the AIDS infection.

But the more one is able to endure the fear of life, the more one will be able to interiorize the libido, thus linking it with the creative basis of the personality. The question is: How does one descend into the depths of the psyche if the entrance is barred by fear?

A thirty-year-old patient dreams of *being in a field with two schoolmates in the elementary class. They are miners and they are inside two deep pits which exhume a lot of steam.* The schoolmates in the dream are those who made fun of him when he was ten, asking him if he would like to be a miner. (They were alluding to a Sicilian dialect word meaning "to masturbate.")

The dream encouraged him to interiorize his libido and to bear in mind all that he was to see in Hades, by following the miner's metaphor; the miner is one who looks for hidden treasures underground. In the Sicilian dialect the term "minare" (to mine) lends itself to the metaphor in the quest for the psyche underground by means of masturbation, bringing to mind Hillman's (1972) metaphor.

Conclusion

AIDS can be used to advantage. In Jung's theory this statement is comprehensible because of the opportunity to change one's life style, availing oneself of compensatory introversion – compensating the excessive extraversion typical in Western society.

We analysts can sympathize with the Catholic religion whose dogma asserts that AIDS is a divine scourge sent to punish the licentiousness of today's society – if we see this dogma from a metaphorical point of view. In this way we can recognize the psychological meaning of the human need to find the spiritual side of the libido. Thus we may be able to give to society and to the individual advice and suggestions concerning their fears and suffering relating to AIDS.

References

Hillman, J. (1972). An essay on Pan. In J. Hillman & W. Roscher (Eds.), *Pan and the Nightmare.* New York: Spring Publications.

Kerényi, C. (1985). Gli dei e gli eroi della Grecia, Vol. II (V. Tedeschi, trans.) Milano: Garzanti.

Sexual Identity

Gay Identity

Analysis and the Symbolism of Desire

Barry Miller
West Hollywood, California, U.S.A.
Society of Jungian Analysts of Southern California

In the summer of 1994, the *New Yorker* magazine presented two seemingly unrelated statements on the theme of erotic, affective relations between men. The first came in June, a month when hundreds of thousands of people gathered in New York City to celebrate Gay Pride and to participate in an event called the Gay Games, an athletic contest which included more participants than the International Olympics. This first statement appeared as a cover illustration, without commentary, entitled "June Grooms." The background was lavender, the bottom center was a wedding cake with two groom figurines on top. Behind the cake stood two men, one wearing a black tuxedo; the other, in a white tuxedo, held a bouquet of roses. Responses to this cover ranged from congratulatory to outrage.

The second statement came late that summer, in an article by Susan Faludi, "The Naked Citadel," concerning the last publicly-supported military academy in the United States to exclude women as cadets. In the article the male cadets convey their valuing of the intimate, cruel and loving life they share. One cadet summarized it: "Maybe it's a Freudian thing, but males feel more affection with each other when women are not around. Maybe we're all homosexuals." His mentor articulated, "With no women, we can hug each other. There's nothing so nurturing as an infantry platoon. It's like a true marriage. With this security cadets can, without being defensive, project tenderness to each other."

These feelings for this "true marriage" are part of the implicit and explicit homoerotic experiences in a group of men who seem to strive toward the idealization of American masculinity. They do not think of themselves as homosexuals; if one were discovered to be a true queer, he would be disgraced and exiled from the academy.

In this militaristic institution the men are clear that they want their homosexuality in their own form, excluding other forms of it. They know that this depends upon keeping women out. One cadet stated that this male enclave is "the last bastion of male, Christian, heterosexuality." The ultimate defeat to this expression of male eroticism and initiation comes from the state, which does not recognize the need for gender-specific opportunities or protections.

The relentless enemy of the same-gender union on the wedding cake is based in the religions and, in America, the political action groups that bind together on this issue. In September 1994 the *New York Times* published a summary by David Boaz on the numbers of articles about homosexuality and the "gay lifestyle" that have appeared in conservative political publications in the United States. Homosexuality is by far the most frequent subject of political concern, many times more frequently written about and politicized than issues such as crime or violence or poverty. There is an obsession with homosexuality and the images the subject generates. In the way that Communism once was feared in America, the June Grooms – for millions of people – symbolize absolute evil.

These examples are only two in a landscape of multiplying images attached to this complex subject. They represent the range of same-gender sexual involvements and the possibilities of meaning generated by these erotic images and experiences. It may be that what we have come to call "homosexuality" encompasses such apparent contradictions that the difference between the gay grooms and the straight men of the military may not even be sexual.

Same-gender sexual experiences belong to no single group, but are an expression of the very nature of male sexuality. Men differ in terms of the psychological meanings derived from these erotic experiences and in how these meanings are assimilated in the construction of identity. One example of this can be seen in a group of young men and women in Los Angeles who completely identify themselves as gay, but in a ritualistic way maintain cross-gender sexual relations with one another. This in no way interferes with the solidity of their gay identity. "Homosexuality" – with its emerging vocabulary of identity – and its counterpart, "heterosexuality," are certainly not identical with sexuality. However, in the psyche of modern people these words have come to carry such symbolic value that we can barely fathom their effects on our lives and our sense of self.

Around the time of Oscar Wilde the Western mind started to perceive itself as either heterosexual or homosexual. The change was not behavioral, in the sexual experiences of men, but was the way these experiences became contextualized and grew into polarizations. The consequences of this polarization have been pervasive, and destructive in the lives of those of us identified with this schism and therefore tyrannized by it. Foucault (1990), one of the great minds lost in the AIDS epidemic, emphasized the more fluid nature of sexuality, as opposed to the usual fixed categorizations. He concluded, "We must not forget that the psychological, psychiatric, medical category of homosexuality was constituted from the moment it was characterized – Westpah's 1870 article on "contrary sexual sensations" can stand as its date of birth – less by a type of sexual relations than by a certain quality of sexual sensibility. ... The sodomite had been a temporary aberration; the homosexual was now a species" (p. 43).

Halperin (1990), has summarized elements of relationship embedded in historical texts of classical literary relationships between men. Most notably, he amplified the relationship between Gilgamesh and Enkidu of the Sumerian myth. He concluded that the affection between these two figures draws from kinship dynamics and sexual desire or conjugal relations; they are to each other simultaneously brother and wife. The purpose of his study is not to suggest that this couple can be revealed to be latently homosexual, nor a precursor of the contemporary gay man, nor as an image of bisexuality. Rather, Halperin's point is that, in our past, the dynamics of male friendship combined elements and diversities no longer contained in friendship experiences. These elements have been distilled out of male friendships and redefined as appropriate only to conjugal ties, which today would also include the gay marriage. The impact is enormous on male friendship and on expectations that burden sexuality and the institution of marriage.

What these factors mean in the ongoing development of men and the movement of culture is unknown. However, speculations about the history and future of homoerotic experience cannot be separated from the evolution of masculinity, the meanings attached to sexuality and marriage, and to the changing nature of the state.

My observations and thoughts here are meant to highlight only a few of the complexities of same-gender sexuality in men, putting this form of sexual activity into the context of psychological development as amplified in Jung's work. By neutralizing the effects of categorizing male sexuality, we open ourselves to what Jung spoke of as the natural man, where sexuality is mercurial and not categorical. Such a less safe, less comprehended view of male sexuality, may be closer to the range of men's actual experience with erotic libido.

The movement toward splitting male sexual identity has been advanced by the popular forms of psychology. Historically, psychology took up the issue in its function of pathologizing many forms of sexual variance. More recently, in response to the demands from those victimized by this marginalization, psychology has emerged as a source of benevolence and acceptance, but has yet to divest itself from the parent role implied in both these reactions. As carrier of the parental imago, psychology unintentionally recreates a moralistic attitude and abandons its capacity as an observer of psychological phenomena.

The need for relief from the alienation resulting from this splitting and the scapegoating it encourages, brings patients to the psychotherapist greatly in need of acceptance. The struggle between and within the psychotherapist and the patient in seeking the source of this relief determines whether the work will develop into an analysis or supportive psychotherapy. Will the healing be derived out of an immersion in the seemingly more enlightened, humanistic values of the therapist, or from a confrontation and acceptance from the patient's Self? The direction is affected not only by the patient's needs, but by the ability and willingness of the therapist to engage, divested of the power to know what is best for another. The therapist is challenged to define the work as separated from both the admiration and the restrictions that emanate from the conscious reactions of the patient.

To embark upon an analysis opens the possibility that all identity elements may be subject to a dissolution. If the analyst takes a position not committed to the unknown possibilities for the person, the analysis will ultimately demean and subvert the individuality of that patient. The patient is not a "gay man"; he is a man who says he is gay. This would be the same for any socially-induced identity, such as being a Jungian or a heterosexual. These identities are held by conscious and unconscious attachments to symbols that have powerful effects on the individual. Relating to these concepts symbolically, not literally, allows for the evolution of a person's relationship to those symbols. If this psychological attitude is not maintained, the patient – with the analyst's support – may put himself beyond the reach of analysis.

A man in analysis woke out of a nightmare, terrified to realize that his use of sexual categorization had been an attempt to mask his own destructive rage. Identifying himself as gay allowed him to act out destructiveness that his immediate culture would organize and convert into heroism. It is my position that an analysis of any man, whether he thinks of himself as gay or not, begins where Jung described analysis to be: where everything is yet to be discovered. Only then can one reflect upon how a particular identity construction both advances and limits the development of personality.

The majority of men who are building their lives around their desire for other men are contained, like the majority of men in general, in sexual identities that have emerged out of a state of polarization. The result is often a vigorous sense of direction, feelings of belonging and community. For these men, analysis – with its value toward individualization and emphases on separation – might seem to be in a direction opposite to the immediate needs for healing deeply-felt alienation or the urgent demand for establishing a way of life. However, within a phenomenologically-based analysis the mysterious nature of the libido is encountered through sexual desire. There it reveals its implications for the construction and reconstruction of the personality. Thus, the work has a great deal to teach about male sexuality.

In the neutral space of analysis a man can begin to see his sexuality as something other than what has been transmitted by culture. Any patient needs validation, not in homosexuality or heterosexuality, but in the autonomous urge toward action: to integrate his awareness of his own libido, thereby forming a basis for behaving as a separate human being. It is essential that analysis create a space where the libido can be re-experienced, held in awareness between analyst and analysand, protected from the world's thoughts. Without a conscious awareness of impulses and their emergence in the body, the libido flows into the recreation of familiar fantasy and often results in autoeroticism.

A courageous young man working on making conscious the dynamics of his orgasms initially thought of his seemingly chaotic sexual experiences as something he would grow out of and that analysis was his ally for this evolution. In view of the erotic constellation embedded in his experiences, he anticipated an annihilation. Resistance here was a fear of the deconstruction of sexual identity, his most immediate experience of the Self. The intention of analysis is not a dissolution, but conscious observation. Dissolution is, however, a possibility; the fear is understandable.

This patient dreamed that *he was with a man with whom he was "romantically" involved. The two men were joined by a third, a "lover" who was dying of AIDS; the death was being awaited.* Eros was symbolized in the dying man, a lover who links the dreamer to the underworld and also to his aspiration to be someone's lover. The experience the dreamer had been having was to become psychologically "dead" as he fell into the role of "lover" and simultaneously to see the other as "dead" when the other would become the "lover" to him.

The patient is driven not by the desire for death, but by the yearning to be joined with his life. The encompassing vision expressed by Jung is that "The conjunction is a culminating point of life and at the same time a death. ... The anima is the connecting link with the ... eternal images, while ... emotionality involves man in the chthonic world and its transitoriness" (CW13, par. 457). The lover in the dream carries the connection not only to death, but simultaneously to the essential values in life, values that are realized only with the approach of death.

The patient's difficulties in establishing a sense of self, strong enough to endure in his attempt at relationship, could be interpreted as a consequence of prejudices against same-gender union or, more generally, as the problem of the soul connection's finding an expression in a cultural context where masculine autonomy is idealized. These issues need our understanding and attention, although working on them does not bring a resolution. A separation must occur from impinging ideas of attraction and sexuality. Localizing himself in his own bodily experiences helps to establish the man's awareness of the psychological situation with which he is confronted: the encounter with the opposite tendencies which form the archetype of union. Psychological integration necessitates that the analytic relationship highlight the tension, and not seek suppression of the conflict. The transformative work is not in the patient's sexuality but in the emancipation of his spirit.

Where the image of union splits apart, analysis must be applied to these contradictory tendencies of the archetype, with simultaneous awareness of attraction and repulsion, life and death, attachment and separation. In the paradox of experience consciousness is expanded, usually with the sacrifice of a more comforting perspective. If a tragic quality emerges, the work of the analyst is to help contain the tension, not reduce it prematurely or encourage what may be a manic solution.

In following the non-linear movement of libido, changes can occur at the speed of light. What had been an object of desire turns into its opposite, the object of repulsion. Continuity of time is needed to remain conscious of these shifts and to analyze their meanings. Otherwise the patient is left on his own in the critical moments of encountering the unconscious and the material is left outside the analysis. What is analyzed is not reflections on sexuality, but experience itself. The center created between analyst and analysand must become a dynamic force in the ongoing experiences of the patient – perhaps bringing up rage over losing the immediate gratification found in unconsciousness. Here the individual needs the analytic alliance.

Another man dreamed that *the woman previously known to be mother was now revealed to be not the real mother. The real mother was imprisoned in a system of compulsive and primitive fertility.* It is this imprisoned mother who also serves as the foundation for his own psychology of the lover, compulsively giving birth to another's fantasies, as well as using others to carry his fantasies. The mother cannot then rear her children. She returns to the insatiable need for new life over and over again, creating and abandoning the life she has brought forth.

It may be useful to think of these times of fantasy-driven, compulsive states not as a manifestation of the out-of-control baby the patient sees himself to be, but as a mother who lacks control of her functions. It helps to focus the ongoing work not as a maturation but as a restoration of the internal connection to human instinct – localizing the analysis as an experience within the body, present for the hour, with all the potential of the man's full nature.

The evolution of the internal mother is taken up in the dyadic relationship of analyst and analysand. This re-establishment of the maternal psychology is within the analysis itself and specifically not in the maternal attributes of the analyst. Such work, which develops more conscious self-regulatory functioning, is not the goal of the analysis but without it nothing more is possible.

Men often feel that the analytic relationship is a threat to whatever separation has been achieved from the imprisoning psyche. It is the responsibility of the analyst to differentiate from a regressive entanglement, while upholding the legitimate claims for intimacy within the analysis. The establishment of the analytic "couple" is not accomplished through good intentions nor the desire to be helpful, but from differentiating and struggling for what belongs to the analysis. This process requires a clarifying discrimination of what parts of the work belong to the individual – making choices – what belongs to the analytic couple, and what may include others. Analysis involves two people; other seemingly therapeutic or relational activities can be attempts to reduce the analysis to impotence.

A man described how he and his partner were experimenting with anal penetration. They were experiencing tension about the spontaneity; to me it seemed more like willfulness than a sexual yearning. The possibility that penetration might be a psychological experience within our relationship, and not the sexual experience he sought, was difficult for him to contemplate. This possibility stimulated fantasies of contamination to his sexual and emotional expression, threatening his illusion of freedom.

This particular man had made many attempts to develop our relationship along same-sexed psychodynamics, such as father-son or mentor-initiate. While these constellations have enormous values, an analysis must be open to a full range of psychological engagement, including intercourse. This openness encourages the uniqueness and power of analysis, as contrasted with other human encounters. Since the goal of the analysis is spiritual unity and not biological reproduction, gender of the participants is not critical in establishing the contrasexual attributes essential to the process.

When a psychological need, such as penetration, comes to consciousness as an erotic desire, enormous burdens are placed on sexual experience. Gratification is projected not into the encounter with the other, but into an experience of totality where the other person is a vehicle or a conduit for the experience. The body of the other serves as a symbol of transcendence and the situation approaches Jung's description: The sexual projection contains not only the anima, but the Self as well. The resulting range of experience can extend from a powerful sense of ecstasy to severe dissociation. Jung points to the danger here when "the self struggles to make itself manifest and threatens to overpower consciousness. ... It is indeed a self sacrifice when a man gives way to the urgency of the demands of the self and perishes, for then the self has lost the game as well, having destroyed the human being who should have been its vessel" (CW13, par. 433).

Bringing awareness to the experiencing of erotic pleasure may necessitate a complete re-establishment of the individual's sense of what is truly gratifying and what is destructive, overwhelming, or compulsive. Often coming to consciousness through this work is the bleak, previously denied recognition of non-gratification. This awareness, avoided because of the fear and possibility of depression, is fundamental for a man to develop a sense of reality that is based on his actual feelings and his own judgment.

During this time of upheaval in re-perceiving human nature, it is essential to maintain a commitment to pursuing psychological meaning that develops out of the experience of the men we work with and not out of ideas of how we or they would like it to be. We are all under tremendous pressure to conceptualize a bearable, perhaps comforting, path toward wholeness for the patients in our care. Ultimately, however, it is the deeper nature of the psyche and not our own personal persuasions that will determine what is true for any individual.

My intention here has been to emphasize the necessity of seeing the object of erotic desire as a concretization of something which, in its erotic state, is not available for consciousness. Therefore, the characteristics of the object of desire are meaningful only in terms of the subjective, inner reaction of the man. In erotic longing the symbol falls into matter, the body of the man himself, and analysis must follow.

Needing to be made conscious is the individual's own reaction and response to the state of desire, coming to terms with his own libido as an internal phenomenon. The analysis is not so much about what goes on in his head, the familiar fantasies used to manipulate stimulation, but what is happening in his body as he experiences the complexities and power of sexuality. This attitude promotes the differentiation of sexuality from other needs, opening new possibilities, while also supporting a confrontation with loss and limitation. To do this we must submit ourselves, as well as our patients, to the process of analysis where each man's story is heard as a singular event and ideas about his life emerge out of the consciousness of that man himself.

References

Foucault, M. (1990). *The History of Sexuality* (Vol. 1). New York: Vintage Press.

Halperin, D. (1990). *One Hundred Years of Homosexuality and Other Essays on Greek Love.* New York: Routledge.

Homosexuality

Hazel Davis
London, England
Society of Analytical Psychology

A denied – unconscious – prejudice exists, I believe, among analysts in general against homosexuality. A pseudo-acceptance is present but not always discernible in clinical, work where the prejudice can be masked by the "pathology factor." Prejudice is more manifest in the personal attitudes of those in positions of economic power and in political life.

Those of us who have grappled with our own prejudices know that their conquest involves a great deal of psychic pain: a dipping into our own well of self-hatred that is so close to the Self as to be almost indivisible. With that degree of threat, who can blame us for splitting off our personal attitudes, and adopting a "professional" acceptance?

What might be a more solid theoretical model than we have at present for our understanding of homosexuality? We analysts are at different points regarding the understanding of the subject since Jung's time: via research findings, the political and cultural climate, the gay culture, AIDS. All these have affected our psychological approach. I am aware that I am tackling an area of high social anxiety and one in which there is considerable disagreement in analytic thinking.

Prejudice

There is not yet agreement on whether a homosexual orientation is part of the primary Self – unalterable – or determined by variable factors. Despite this open question, Freud's view of homosexual development – in men at least – has remained our starting point. Notions about mother-fixation and arrested oedipal development, albeit with pre-genital modifications, still underlie our analytic approach to homosexuality. Such theories are important but, if we

allow them to become dogma, we severely restrict our understanding of patients. Friedman (1988) crosses the borders of psychoanalysis and biology, genetics and anthropology. He shows convincingly that the collated findings do not fit the Freudian stereotype:
that male homosexuals are more tied to their mothers and have
weaker fathers than heterosexuals. Further, the extensive research
Friedman cites does not reveal more psychological disturbance in
homosexuals than in heterosexuals. Yet the belief is still deeply held
that homosexuality is a manifestation of an immature personality,
narcissism or psychosis.

While not wishing to be prejudiced, we are reluctant to depart
from an established line of thinking, and we lack the necessary steps.
Indeed, many psychotherapy training programs do not accept homosexual candidates. That homosexuality still carries a stigma in the
profession is illustrated by one psychotherapist's writing under a
pseudonym when challenging entrenched attitudes. Again, there still
tends to be an overt or covert sense of therapeutic failure in the
regret that a particular patient's conversion from a homosexual
orientation to heterosexual is not happening. An analyst's frustrated
outburst, "He is not motivated to change," is not uncommon.

The question of what is normal sexuality and what is sexual
perversion is largely a matter of value, according to Stoller (1985).
A perversion, according to this psychoanalyst, may be erotic excitement that is fused with hostility. But, he observes, what makes
excitement out of boredom is, quite commonly, the introduction of
hostility into erotic fantasy.

Stoller's simple observation poses the question of whether there
is an essential rather than a relative difference between the person
who performs a sexually perverse act, the person who keeps from
doing it but fantasizes it, and the person who neither fantasizes nor
enacts, but who gets excited when chancing on it. To the question of
what perversion is, Stoller invites an opposite thought, one tantaliz-
ingly difficult to answer. What specific piece of any individual's
sexual behavior might not be considered a perversion? Is pornography a perversion? All erotic daydreams? Masturbation? Is perversion more clearly so when it is accompanied by "perverse" fantasies? Altogether, Stoller presents a convincing argument that our
line between normal and abnormal sexuality is arbitrary, that there
is no clear "us" and "them."

Nevertheless, we analysts still make judgments and harbor stereotypes such as that homosexual men have effeminate personali-

ties; that they are either active or passive types; that actively homosexual men are potential pedophiliacs and that a close non-erotic relationship, between friends of the same gender, can be labeled as homosexual. Yet the studies that Friedman quotes are well documented, and open-minded inquiry leaves little doubt that such ideas are at best vague and controversial.

The prejudice is striking because a stereotype persists alongside psychotherapy practice where we differentiate levels of psychic disturbance. Thus, in clinical practice we see neurotic and severely damaged homosexuals (as we do heterosexual patients), and we see homosexual symptoms sometimes emerging defensively in heterosexuals or the reverse. The picture is confused because once the Self has been organized along homosexual lines, other developmental psychosexual processes are likely to be negotiated differently, especially at the oedipal stage and in adolescence. A further complexity may result, as with a bisexual patient of mine who had worked out some of his later developmental steps along heterosexual lines. This process left him with persistent heterosexual, as well as homosexual inclinations.

Freud, Klein, Jung

Just how critical is the oedipal conflict and its earlier manifestations in the formation of homosexuality? As we know, Freud centered the development of gender identity on the oedipal stage and supposed previous polymorphous sexuality. According to the Freudian legacy, excited sensations in infancy are not differentiated; in male and female alike they are constellated around the body orifices: mouth, anus and genitals. It seems that Freud's notion of an initial polymorphous sexuality allows for a not unnatural potential of the psyche to organize itself in a homosexual direction. The issue was simpler for Freud than the variety of early male and female identifications that are apparent today. Then, the small boy's awareness of his penis and a fear of castration alone accounted for his letting go of his identification with his mother, to see himself like father instead. The girl's corresponding psychological task was to come to terms with her penis envy.

Since 1905 Melanie Klein and others have formed many theories of infant fantasies, in particular pre-oedipal fantasies about the infant's own and the mother's body. These findings lean toward an interpretation of gender orientation different from Freud's. The

Kleinian notion is that the earliest infant fantasies are archetypal and already contain potentiality toward a heterosexual fit. For Kleinians, the boy or girl discovers rather than learns his or her sexual orientation. Adults who have not discovered the heterosexual orientation are defending against their true nature; homosexuality is judged to be pathological. The implication here is that heterosexuality would be recoverable if the analyst were skillful enough, had time enough, and the patients were sufficiently motivated.

Such Kleinian notions of unconscious infant fantasies, being similar in nature to the archetypes Jung described, have been integrated into many Jungian training programs, just as Jung's conclusions about homosexuality – developmentally speaking – are not dissimilar from Freud's. However, Jung's notion of the anima/animus is different from Klein and different from Freud's polymorphous notion, especially if we allow the masculine or feminine imagery that is spontaneously activated to be independent of the gender of the individual. By understanding a dual unconscious gender potential in this way, we can appreciate more fully the range of masculine/feminine psychic malleability.

A woman patient was protesting about ending her analytic sessions, especially in what she saw as having to submit to me. For this and other reasons her attitude of willfulness came to dominate the sessions. My analytic task was to hold the process steady during her outbursts rather than to give way or overreact to them, thus helping her to discover a reliable internal figure. During this process, she marked a turning point by bringing to a session a poem of George Herbert's, "The Collar." It touched a deep level, akin to anima activity. After the poet's rebellious opening, he wrote:

> *I struck the board, and cry'd, No more.*
> *I will abroad.*
> *What? Shall I ever sigh and pine?*
> *My lines and life are free;*

Herbert ends with a quite a changed experience:

> *But as I rav'd and grew more fierce and wild*
> *At every word,*
> *Methoughts I heard one calling, child!*
> *And I reply'd My Lord.*

For the poet the encounter with his anima as God, through whom he recovered his soul, was an imaginary male-to-male experience. My patient was recognizing the poet's experience as her own. She too was recovering an unconscious part of her anima but her experience was through the female-to-female relationship of the analysis.

To embrace wider understanding of the animus or anima frees analyst and patient from making gender assumptions. This facilitates the countertransference – the analyst's holding of the primal undifferentiated and still unconscious part of the patient's personality – so that it can become a personal part of the relationship. In my experience the transference is most intensely sexual at just such a time as the anima/animus is achieving a different balance.

Clinical Vignettes

Two episodes depict how analytic judgments about a homosexual orientation can affect the therapeutic process. Morgenthaler (1988) shows that the patient's excessive preoccupation with sex is not to be blamed on his homosexuality as such. This view enables Morgenthaler to connect his patient's troublesome impulses with a capacity to love, which had previously eluded him.

The patient has confessed that the only thing that really interests him is the sexual, that at every opportunity he thinks about the cock while other people act as though it were otherwise with them. He works round to proposing that perhaps he and the analyst might get together, suggesting "Maybe we could meet in a sauna sometime."

After a short pause the analyst said, "I don't believe that you'd want that. You prefer doing it with your friends. After all you have come to me for other reasons."

> Patient: *At the beginning certainly, but now it is different. With the men I do it with I cannot talk the way I do to you. Homosexuals among themselves have very little to say to one another.*
> Analyst: *That's not true. Homosexuals can express themselves with great differentiation and enter into genuine love relationships. You can see that in our relationship, even though we don't sleep together.*
> Patient: *Once it gets that way with friends everything afterward is different: non committal, and superficial. Then each seeks another partner for the next night.*
> Analyst: *That is your experience. That explains why you are afraid that we might do it together.*

The patient withdrew a little and said, disappointed, "Actually you are not interested in me. After all you are married and, as an analyst, you keep your distance from everything" (p. 125).

Morgenthaler then works with the analysand's disappointment, interpreting his wanting to withdraw: He is anxious about his growing attachment to the analyst. By accepting the transference and interpreting the immediate anxiety, the analyst enables the patient to reach a different level of intimacy with him. Thus, supporting a patient's sexual orientation can help bring the sexuality into a personal relationship with the analyst, where the fears associated with it can be worked out.

A contrasting episode is from Meltzer (1973), a Kleinian analyst whose writing is much studied in analytical psychology also. Meltzer argues that active bisexuality in an adult is always psychopathological. He treats the homosexual desire of his patient rather than the heterosexual as the problem; he does not make clear why, or invite a consideration of the opposite possibility.

The man is married and in his forties. It had appeared to Meltzer that his patient was making progress in the direction of heterosexuality, indicated in dreams such as of a new organ being installed in an old church, or the roof of an old cattle shed being repaired so that it could be used for calves once more. (The images may have different symbolic meanings for the patient from those for the analyst.) At the same time, he had become depressed about his poor progress in life, in analysis and in work. His sexual relations with his wife had fallen away completely, and were replaced by an interest in the young man with whom he had a sexual relationship before his marriage. He reluctantly reported this dream:

> *Two friends came unexpectedly into his studio: current friend, Ralph, to tell him of his recent appointment to a university post; the other, Mario, bringing him a flask of Italian wine. He was surprised to see them together for he had not even realized that they knew one another. Mario was dressed in the garb of the priesthood. ... The patient felt hard pressed to appear pleased with his one friend's success, due to envy, and with the other's gift, as it was not to his taste. He comforted himself with the thought that Ralph was a bachelor. ... [and] he put Mario's gift on the shelf.* (Meltzer, 1973, p. 117)

Two sides of this analysand may be configured in the dream as Ralph and Mario. Either of these figures could be projected onto the analyst: Mario in his priestly garb (which could represent sexual ambiguity or some kind of moral high ground, and whose offer of wine is not to the patient's taste and goes onto the shelf); or Ralph, a more attractive figure of whom the dreamer is envious, but with whom he would like a relationship. The analyst could understand himself to be either figure and thereby get a feel through the countertransference of the conflicting ways that the patient is experiencing him. This is the kind of approach that Morgenthaler might take.

Meltzer chooses a part-object level of interpretation which does not alter the issue under discussion but, believing only the heterosexual expression of the patient to be the "true self," he treats the homosexual area as defensive. He argues that the polymorphous nature of sexuality is secondary and warns analysts against compromising their stand with any fashionable social acceptance of bisexuality.

He takes a negative, even scornful view of his patient's homosexual desire: "I mean to stress the subtle ways in which ill will, denigration, reduction to part-object status and ingratitude operate [in the dream] so as not to interfere with the patient's [idealized] self-image" (p. 118). Further, "The patient's defensive and eventually defiant attitude about his homosexual activities reveals a heavy defensive commitment." Meltzer rightly expects the "pseudopotency" of the heterosexual adjustment to give way but so that "the addictive aspect of the homosexual one is yielded to analytic enquiry." (It does not yield, apparently, for Meltzer then strains to justify his stance.)

> *Naturally, it will appear descriptively that the analysis has damaged the patient's potency. The [patient's] guilt about representing the analysis to the world, as it were, negatively, does form the core of a depressive attitude toward the impotence which greatly helps to power a thrust for further development toward genuine [heterosexual] potency.* (p. 119)

Meltzer's position is in clear contrast to Morgenthaler's example, where he is not judging the orientation itself as a bar to meaningful and intimate relationships.

Healthy Individuated Homosexuality

The challenge today is to be able to trace etiological sequences without fear of being reductive or pathologizing and to maintain an even-handed valuation of heterosexual and homosexual lifestyles, while also maintaining Jung's teleological perspective. The psychodynamic theories of Freud, Klein and Jung can be helpful, but only if we are genuinely comfortable with psychologically healthy sexuality, whatever the orientation. The goals of individuation – the value of wholeness, internal harmony, a steady and reliable self image, the possession of a non-defensive attitude and the capacity to develop intimate relationships – are the key issues. Jungian principles find an echo in psychoanalytic schools too, such as in Morgenthaler's view that we analysts need to see sexuality primarily as human sexuality that is seeking to find a personal form of expression.

References

Friedman, R. (1988). *Male Homosexuality: A Contemporary Psychoanalytic Perspective*. Newhaven/London: Yale University Press.

Meltzer, D. (1973/1979). *Sexual States of Mind*. Perthshire: Clunie Press.

Morgenthaler, F. (1988). *Homosexuality Heterosexuality Perversion*. Hove/London: The Analytic Press.

Stoller, R. (1985). *Observing the Erotic Imagination*. New Haven/London: Yale University Press.

Identity, Sexuality and the Self in Late Adolescence

Brian Feldman
Palo Alto, California, U.S.A.
Society of Jungian Analysts of Northern California

The most significant developmental task of late adolescence is the establishment of a sense of a coherent identity. In Jungian terms the synthetic aspects of the Self emerge and function to integrate the complexes and introjections, which have both personal and archetypal components. As the adolescent begins to feel more secure about sexuality, goals, and desired life-style, the Self, as a guardian of meaningful experience, becomes an important integrating and synthesizing force. Inner confidence emerges, making possible the establishment of interpersonal intimacy and a capacity to plan and actualize meaningful goals.

Jung used the term "identity" to denote the primitive mental state of *participation mystique,* which implies a non-differentiation of subject and object. He believed that this state of mind is characteristic of early infancy, when a state of identity or fusion exists between the infant and the care-giving figures. Jung believed that the individuation process evolves out of this original state of fusion. I think that the concept of identity formation in analytical psychology now needs to be developed and expanded.

From infant observation research I have not found the infant to be in an on-going state of fusion and identity with the mother during the first months of life. Rather, there is an oscillation between self and other, a rhythm of contact involving states of connectedness and states of separateness. The infant's experience of self emerges out of these fluid states, which have a coherent rhythm and tempo. Both infant and mother experience states of togetherness and separateness from the very beginning of post-natal life. Each infant/mother pair develops a specific rhythm of contact, of separateness and togetherness. Fordham's (1995) model of integration and deintegration in infancy begins to address this type of interactional sequence, but it does not capture fully the sense of fluidity and ongoing dynamic oscillation that is conveyed by close observation of the mother/ infant relationship. While I agree with Fordham that the infant experiences a sense of separateness from the mother at birth, I have observed also that there are states of fusion and identity during the first year of life that are important for the infant's developing self and help to facilitate individuation in infancy and early childhood.

Gender and sexual identity also have their origins within the infant/parent and child/parent relationships. The infant identifies with and introjects the mother's innate, psychic bisexuality. Mother's influence on the baby's sense of gender and sexual identity can be observed via the manner in which she handles her baby, and inferred in the way she talks about and describes both her relationship with the baby and her inferences about the baby's internal life. As development proceeds, differentiations in regard to gender and sexual identity occur. In adolescence, when there is a push to live out sexual impulses, the strengths of the early psychosexual complexes, identifications and introjections are tested. Adolescents are forced to confront both the historical/personal and archetypal/transpersonal components of their sexual and gender identity.

Jung elaborated on the theme of adolescence and identity in commenting extensively on the problem of incestuous desire between mother and son. He stated that "the basis of the 'incestuous desire' is not cohabitation, but the strange idea of becoming a child again, of returning to the parental shelter, and of entering into the mother in order to be reborn through her" (CW5, par. 332). Jung's approach to the problem of incest implies that the adolescent needs to understand symbolically the tension between the desire to regress and remain a child and the desire to assert individuality and autonomy. The separation from the parental figures is fraught with conflict, but becomes resolvable as the adolescent engages in a "heroic" conflict to assert autonomy and independence by using creative and symbolic capacities. Jung focused on the parallels between the myth of the hero and the development of adolescent identity. He saw the evolution of identity as taking place through the struggle for self-definition and meaning, arising out of a confrontation with the creative matrix of the unconscious. In this regard the soul of the adolescent finds its shape, dimensionality and limits through a tunneling into the unconscious until the foundations of the Self are reached.

Jung's description of individuation in adolescence applies aptly to the male, but does not take into account a comparable need for a stable attachment and intimacy between mother and daughter. Gilligan (1982) has commented cogently on the themes of attachment and intimacy which are so significant in the lives of female adolescents. Such themes poignantly and painfully fill the analytic sessions of female adolescents. The female adolescent's need for interpersonal embeddedness provides the foundation from which she can think about herself. Her struggles for self-definition and identity are mediated through the metaphors of connection and attachment; the often detailed analysis of these metaphors within the context of the transference/countertransference relationship is a prominent task of the analytic work. Thus, the hero's quest for separation and self-definition through the battle for deliverance from the mother is more a description of male than of female adolescent development.

Jung's Adolescent Development

The major source of Jung's theory of adolescent identity is, I think, his own adolescent development. In this respect Jung's psychology is a kind of involuntary and unconscious memoir. Jung's life constitutes the seed from which the Jungian tree has grown and flourished. His creative genius emerged in adolescence alongside an expanding consciousness and capacity to reflect upon experience. His identity was rooted, for the most part, in an experiential apprehension of self. He distrusted conceptual and purely intellectual formulations, desiring to experience and know, rather than merely to believe and think. The Cartesian formulation "I think, therefore I am," could be changed to in Jung's case "I experience, therefore I am."

Jung's desire for an experiential understanding of self had as its foundation the experiences of his earlier childhood. These experiences had a profound effect on his emerging self-awareness, especially his dream of the underground phallus, and his reverie of God defecating on Basel cathedral. These formative experiences awakened in Jung a desire to experience the mysteries and depths of his inner life and then to formulate theories based on these experiences. The profound emotional and spiritual impact of these early experiences had a major influence on the development of his psychology during his long and productive life.

The interpersonal backdrop of Jung's adolescent development, emotionally and intellectually, is the conflicted relationship with his parson father and the psychologically and emotionally close relationship with his mother. Jung's father failed to offer the adolescent Jung an adequate model for masculine identification. Jung experienced his father as filled with self doubts, insecurities and anxieties. During Jung's adolescence his father was immersed in a profound spiritual crisis that resulted in his being self-absorbed and largely unavailable emotionally. Perhaps this led Jung in adolescence to forge a closer relationship with his mother who, earlier in his childhood, was separated from Jung for several months while hospitalized for severe depression. This separation was traumatic for Jung and resulted in his feeling insecurely attached to his mother. During his adolescence, his mother was emotionally more present and involved, but not without some resulting emotional strain for Jung.

Jung was deeply identified with his mother during his adolescent years, especially with her uncanniness. She held all of the conventional beliefs, but then Jung witnessed what appeared to be the emergence of a distinct personality described as "a somber, imposing figure possessed of unassailable authority" (MDR, p. 48). The adolescent Jung was sure that his mother consisted of two personalities, one innocuous and human, the other uncanny. When her uncanny personality emerged it was unexpected, mysterious, and frightening.

> *By day she was a loving mother, but at night she seemed uncanny. Then she was like one of those seers who is at the same time a strange animal, like a priestess in a bear's cave. Archaic and ruthless; ruthless as truth and nature. At such times she was the embodiment of what I have called the "natural mind."* (MDR, p. 50)

With great sensitivity, Jung observed that the violence of the separation from the mother is proportionate to the strength of the bond uniting son with the mother; the stronger the bond, the more dangerously does the mother approach the son in the guise of the unconscious. This is the savage mother of desire who threatens to devour the son/hero. This description of the mother/son relationship is evocative of the profound struggle Jung experienced as his need for separation and individuation emerged in the adolescent years. These were themes that Jung expanded cogently.

As an adolescent, Jung had a conflicted view of himself. He described this discrepancy as his "number one" and "number two" personalities, which evolved both through his identification with his mother and his experience of being temperamentally similar to her. At first he experienced his number one personality as a schoolboy who could not grasp algebra and was unsure of himself. His number two personality was an important person, a high authority, a man not to be trifled with; but also skeptical, mistrustful, and remote from the interpersonal realm. As Jung matured, number two became less grandiose and began to feel closer to the earth and the natural elements, the weather, all living creatures and above all close to the night and dreams. In this form number two represented Jung's real or true self. Number two had a close relationship to God and the cosmos, to the realm of the unconscious, and was close to his mother's "natural mind." In this regard his mother's number two offered him the strongest support in the conflict then beginning between paternal tradition and the strange, compensatory products which his unconscious had been stimulated to create. Jung seemed to be searching for a sense of his true self. According to Winnicott (1960), only the true self can be creative and only the true self can feel real. This was the case for Jung. His ongoing sense of authenticity in adolescence involved a contact with both the unconscious and with nature, expressed through his number two personality.

Jung's relationship with his father in adolescence was filled with profound doubt and disillusionment. He was skeptical of all his father said to him, finding it stale and hollow, "like a tale told by someone who knew it only by hearsay and cannot quite believe it himself" (MDR, p. 43). Jung's failed experience of initiation when he was confirmed at age 15 further drove a wedge between father and son. Jung became convinced at this point that his father was consumed with inward doubts. Father's religious belief was based on blind faith and not true experience as was Jung's, for example, in his reverie of the deity defecating on the cathedral.

Jung's failed relationship with his father in adolescence left him with a need to find masculine figures whom he could idealize and find worthy of his admiration. This was to prove a difficult and largely unsuccessful quest. The adolescent homosexual experience that Jung described to Freud in his letters was probably related to his unfulfilled need for closeness and intimacy with a man, yet it left him emotionally devastated. With Freud, Jung was trying to repair the adolescent wound related to his sexual seduction as well as the vast feeling of disconnection which he experienced with his father. Jung found in Freud a man he could idealize, look up to and identify with. Unfortunately for Jung the unresolved conflicts related to his relationship with his father and the adolescent homosexual experience could not be worked through with Freud and perhaps led, in part, to the rupture in their relationship. The profound nature of Jung's conflict becomes clear as he bares his soul to Freud:

> *I have a boundless admiration for you both as a man and a researcher. ... My veneration for you has something of the character of a "religious crush." ... I feel that it is disgusting and ridiculous because of its undeniable erotic undertone. This abominable feeling comes from the fact that as a boy I was the victim of a sexual assault by a man I once worshipped.* (Let-I, p. 95)

There is little mention in Jung's memoirs (MDR) of sexuality or sexual experiences in adolescence. Overt sexuality in adolescence seemed to be suppressed and displaced, largely onto philosophical and religious preoccupations. One significant erotic experience during Jung's adolescence is described as occurring during a vacation in the Alps, visiting the relics and home of Brother Klaus. Jung described the following incident:

> *I was strolling up the hill, lost in thoughts, and was turning to descend when a slender figure of a young girl appeared. She wore the local costume, had a pretty face, and greeted me with friendly blue eyes. As though it were the most natural thing in the world we descended into the valley together. She was about my own age. Since I knew no other girls except my cousins (his only sister was quite young at this point) I felt embarrassed and shy about talking to her.*

While he was walking with her he thought,

> *She has appeared just at this moment and she walks along with me as naturally as if we belonged together. I glanced sideways at her and saw an expression of mingled shyness and admiration in her face, which embarrassed me and somehow pierced me. Can it be possible, I wondered, that this is fate?"* Jung had a brief conversation with the girl. He felt that he could not talk to her about his preoccupations. While outwardly the encounter felt meaningless to Jung, from within it *"not only occupied my thoughts for days but has remained forever in my memory, like a shrine by the wayside."* (MDR, p. 80)

For Jung, being attracted to the girl's innocence seems to have stirred his erotic desire, but it was difficult to come to grips with this at the time; his desire and infatuation with the innocent girl remained largely internal and spiritualized. She represented a component of his anima – an inner figure of feminine innocence – which could not be integrated at that time. Perhaps Jung's attraction to the girl's innocence covered his suppressed erotic and sexual longings.

Jung's adolescence was a time of profound symbolic awakenings as well as deep emotional disappointments. He was able to tunnel into the realm of the unconscious and find within himself a meaningful source of experience for the creation of a sense of identity. His profound inner conflicts, however, were not resolved in adolescence and he entered into young adulthood still needing to define his own sense of self. This task was completed more fully through his own self-analysis in his confrontation with the unconscious after his break with Freud. The interpersonal disappointments of adolescence engendered in Jung a feeling of isolation and emotional vulnerability, but also consolidated his conviction that the most profound healing emerges from within the psyche. Jung's adolescence was thus a fertile period of self-exploration which provided a part of the foundation out of which analytical psychology could grow and develop.

Clinical Jung: A Case of Late Adolescence

Jung described his clinical approach to late adolescence in a case published twice (CW7; CW17); the material must have had a special significance for him. The young man was 20 years old when he saw Jung for the first time. He is described as having considerable intellectual and aesthetic interests. A fascinating dream series from this case helps us to understand how Jung was beginning to conceptualize adolescent identity and sexuality, and how his analytic technique evolved and developed.

On the night preceding the first analytic session the analysand had the following dream: *I am in a lofty cathedral filled with mysterious twilight. They tell me that it is the cathedral at Lourdes. In the center there is a deep dark well into which I have to descend* (CW7, par. 167). The associations are related to Lourdes as the mystic fount of healing. Jung links this to the analysand's search for a cure for his homosexuality. Coming to Jung as his analyst evokes the feeling of going to a lofty cathedral where mysterious transformations can take place. The deep dark well in the dream feels to the dreamer an unpleasant and frightening place, like the analysis and the descent into the unconscious upon which he feels he must embark.

At the archetypal level the dream conveys an understanding of the need to descend into the dark mysteries of the unconscious from which the dreamer could emerge reborn. At the more personal developmental level the dream may be conveying something about the dreamer's relationship to the mother's female body and the fear and dread that his relationship to her stimulates within him. The church can be viewed as a maternal symbol, as Jung has described so well. The deep, dark well could symbolize the maternal vagina as a dark and potentially dreadful place. Perhaps one component of this young man's homosexuality is his dread of the vagina and his primitive fear of the feminine. Neumann (1994) theorizes that fear of the female body emerges when the desire for bodily and sensuous contact is experienced as taboo, and when the female genitals are feared as the terrible, castrating "vagina dentata." According to Neumann, for a man the feminine as the "totally other" is something numinous; without the fateful confrontation with this numinosum, no life can attain to its potential for maturity and wholeness.

Jung's analysand needed to give shape to anxieties which he had been unable to integrate; he had given them symbolic form through the initial dream. Jung chose to focus on the archetypal, aesthetic and prospective components of the dream rather than on the bodily and infantile aspects; the aesthetic and spiritual components in the dream are given expression through the feeling tone of the transference. Jung describes the dreamer coming into analysis as though it were a sacred religious act to be performed in the mystical half-light of some awe-inspiring sanctuary. Like Bion (1962), I translate this desire as the analysand's developmentally appropriate need of having an intimate contained existence within Jung's mind where he can begin to help the analysand understand and transform what previously he has been unable to think about and experience.

The cause of the young man's homosexuality, according to Jung, was his overly close attachment to mother, which was secret and subterranean; the lack of separation between mother and son led to the deviation in sexual and identity development. Separation was critical for continued psychological growth. Jung (CW5) expanded on this theme: The male adolescent hero is involved in the task of separating from mother, represented symbolically as a devouring dragon. Through this confrontation with the devouring mother the adolescent self can become for the male a stronger centering force within the personality. From my perspective, the image of the devouring mother is also a projection by the adolescent of uninte-grated pre-oedipal fantasies of violent and destructive incorporation of the mother and her breast. These infantile fantasies are projected onto mother and then are experienced through projective identifica-tion as having an alive presence within her. When these pre-oedipal fantasies and impulses are integrated at both the personal and archetypal levels, the adolescent's experience of the Self as a center of initiative and meaningfulness can be consolidated. Successful psychological development in adolescence presupposes an emo-tional and affective revival of the infant's early relationship to the mother, especially her body and psyche. Adolescence, as a phase of the individuation process, offers a second chance to repair difficul-ties that have originated in the infantile period.

According to Jung, the adolescent's homosexuality was caused not only by a fear and dread of incest with mother, but also by an absence of male input and guidance. For Jung, the initiation into analytic treatment conveyed the meaning of an entry into the world of adult men. Through his understanding and his apprehension of the Self in the dreamer, Jung as analyst was able to provide a containing analytic space within his mind. There the analysand could feel securely held and healing and transformation could begin to take place. As analyst, Jung was able to respond to the analysand's need for maternal holding as he descended fearfully into the dark well; as analytical father Jung was able to provide containment by thinking about, digesting and interpreting his understanding of the uncon-scious aspects of the dreamer's psyche. A second dream reported by the young man:

> *I am in a great Gothic cathedral. At the altar stands a priest. I stand before him with my friend, holding in my hand a little Japanese ivory figure, with the feeling that it is going to be baptized. Suddenly an elderly woman appears, takes the fraternity ring from my friend's finger, and puts it on her own. My friend is afraid that this may bind him in some way. But at the same moment there is a sound of wonderful organ music.* (CW7, Par. 175)

According to Jung, the dreamer's presence in the church where a ceremony is taking place, officiated by a male priest, points to a ritual of initiation into manhood. The little Japanese mannequin can be seen as a phallic symbol which is essential in the ritual. The initiation ceremony into the realm of manhood involves the baptism of the mannequin/phallus. The friend standing with him before the altar was the dreamer's lover, who belonged to the same university fraternity. The fraternity ring symbolized their relationship. Jung believed that the dreamer was being led away from his homosexuality through the phallic baptism, which Jung related to a rite of circumcision. The elderly woman, who took possession of the fraternity ring, was leading the adolescent away from homosexuality and into a heterosexual relationship. This aspect of Jung's interpretation is difficult to accept fully; it appeared to negate the regressive, anxiety-evoking aspect of the maternal image. The woman may be, rather, the pre-oedipal mother from whom the dreamer needed to separate. She was viewed in the dream as possessive and domineering, perhaps wanting to take away the lover as well as the analysand's phallic sexuality. The older woman could represent the analysand's mother of infancy and early childhood with whom a psychologically incestuous relationship had existed, and from whom he needed to separate in order to affirm his sexual identity as disentangled from mother's unconscious desires.

The fear and dread of the powerful feminine/maternal figure aroused anxiety in the dreamer from which he had a strong need to escape. The beautiful organ music heard at the end of the dream may represent a manic flight from this deeper dread of the feminine. When there is an underlying incestuous element in the relationship between son and mother, the son experiences the mother as being in possession of his phallic sexuality and his penis which evokes severe castration anxieties. Much of the transient homosexuality of male adolescents can be viewed as an attempt to separate from the incestuous entanglement with mother and to forge closer links with masculine figures who can protect the young male from the dangerous and frightening allure of his incestuous desires.

Jung's views on adolescent male sexuality are dominated by the belief that the male adolescent needs to experience appropriate masculine identifications in order to develop a coherent identity. This process facilitates the separation from mother, who is viewed as potentially possessive. Our current understanding of adolescent sexuality points also to the need for the male adolescent to disentangle from the early pre-oedipal relationship with mother. The pre-oedipal mother is viewed as having both male and female characteristics; only later in the oedipal period is a clearer differentiation possible. From infant observation it is possible to view the mother's perception of the infant's sexuality as an important factor in the development of sexual identity. How mother relates to the masculine and feminine components of her own psyche and to her son's emerging masculinity are all factors that influence the son's later sexual development.

In my own work analyzing male adolescents with sexual identity conflicts I find that there are various sexualities that need to be acknowledged and respected. While for some male adolescents transient homosexuality represents an attempt at resolution of psychological conflicts originating in the pre-oedipal and oedipal periods, for others homosexuality is more of a true expression of the Self with a deeper ongoing meaning. The need to accept and acknowledge this path is of major importance for the analysis and for the adolescent's future psychological development. By focusing on the forms and transformations of erotic relationships rather than exclusively on the gender of the object of erotic desire, it is possible to help adolescents to a better understanding of their erotic and sexual life and the demands which their eroticism and sexuality make upon them. In addition, the qualitative aspects of their love relationships can become a focus of the analytic dialogue and help can be given to understand and heal difficulties in forming intimate and committed interpersonal relationships.

References

Bion, W. (1962). *Learning from Experience*. New York: Jason Aronson.
Fordham, M. (1995). *Freud, Jung, Klein: The Fenceless Field*. London: Routledge.
Gilligan, C. (1982). *In a Different Voice*. Cambridge, MA: Harvard University Press.
Neumann, E. (1994). *Fear of the Feminine*. Princeton, NJ: Princeton University Press.
Winnicott, D.W. (1960). *Maturational Processes and the Facilitating Environment*. New York: International Universities Press.

Gender Identity, Social Role and the Analytic Relationship

Anna Maria Panepucci

Genoa, Italy
Italian Association for the Study of Analytical Psychology

Depth psychology is often accused of having absolutized the intra- and inter-psychic dimension of the analytic relationship, and thus of paying scant attention to the real object. The setting is typified by self-referential attitude that leads to a confrontation of theoretical and technical models of analytic knowledge, rather than to a confrontation with external reality.

Despite this attitude, basic elements of a specific socio-cultural reality may assert themselves – in clinical practice, no less than in theorization – in subtle and insidious ways, instead of being recognized for what they are and turned into objects of investigation. Experiences that relate to social structure – formative experiences for the individual – persist even when, analysts interpret these experiences symbolically.

This premise grows clearer if we turn our attention to the analyst's identity in relation to the patient. The classical definition as a "mirror, neutral and bisexual" implicitly represses the analyst's sexual and gender identity, no loss than the limits imposed by gender. The most pernicious result of the repression of the analyst's identity lies in its allowing ideology, equally unobserved, to insinuate into interpretations; into the transference, countertransference and indeed into theory.

Philosophical thought has often called attention to the dangers of ideology. Bacon (1964) saw ideology as an *idola tribus* (tribal idol) and censured "false concepts that take possession of human understanding ... and dominate the spirit in ways that impede all access to truth" (p. 131). For Louis Althusser (cited by Ranciere, 1973), ideology "is a closed system, logical and rigorous, of representations (images, myths, ideas, concepts) and patterns of social behavior; and as such, it performs an historical function in a given and particular society" (p. 51). Ideology elaborates a system of ideas – political, juridical, philosophical, moral – which constitute a representation of the world and the human individual. But this representation is far from objective; it belongs to the sphere of imagination.

Some psychoanalysts (e.g., Grinberg, 1975; Maduro, 1983) see such representations as deriving from specific unconscious fantasies that originate in the history and nature of infantile object relationships and the identifications that accompany them. At this entirely psychic level, ideology establishes clear and certain models of identity by directing the individual toward specific courses of development.

Adorno (1966) stands at the crossroads of philosophy and psychology when he writes: "Identity is the original form of ideology; identity assumes the status of a norm of adaptation ... and specific vehicles, normative models and values. ... The love of abstract identity, and of naked self-preservation, constitutes a loss of identity." And again, "When rationality proves incapable of recognizing its own products, it ... turns into something specious, into mythology" (pp. 133-34). We must ask ourselves whether analyst and patient, as social subjects, can be immune to the coercions of ideology.

An historical look at the origins of psychoanalysis – born in the context of a patriarchal and therefore gender-based ideology – gives us reasons for doubt. In the name of a commonly-held truth the first analysts – both men and women – accepted the monadic theory of psychosexual development and applied it to clinical practice, despite its repression of the intellectual, spiritual and physical experiences of women analysts and patients. The women who studied with Freud appear to have been born like Athena from the mind of a single parent: Zeus, who swallowed the pregnant Metis and her wisdom.

Greek mythology too, with its own monadic theory, had images of Zeus, Dionysus and Hermes as boys, but not of Athena, Aphrodite, or Artemis as girls. Thus, the very roots of our culture appear to hold no representations of a process of female development. (The couple of Demeter/Kore does not suggest a line of development within the mother-daughter relationship, and its resolution required a violent, incestuous rape.)

Theory has given rigid definitions of what it means to be a woman or a man. A woman has been a non-man a "phallic" woman – who constituted an imperfect imitation of a man – or a "mother" and, – as a result of a split – a "sexual object." But, finally, she has remained an enigma.

The norm as simply a man, and no enigma at all. He was the model against which the other was defined. Everything at odds with his "nature" as a conscious, rational, active, potent, and moral being found ample vessel in the woman.

Such theoretical presuppositions, thanks precisely to their charge of ideology, found reification in social roles. In the words of Adorno (1966): "The squalor of the division of labor found its hypostasis in the concept of role, and was thus transformed into a virtue. The Ego ascribed to itself the very same functions to which society condemned it" (p. 249). Vertically – in terms of offspring – such rigid gender and role separations tended to turn identity into a question of imitation, rather than into any true process of the differentiation and integration of male and female qualities and functions. The norms promoted by ideology bonded nature and culture, sex and gender, gender and role, role and functions: obsessively dividing the features of the universe – both animate and inanimate – into "masculine and feminine," far outside the realm of sexuality.

Since the 1960s, we have witnessed a slow but constant disintegration of patriarchal society and ideology. We have learned to question its system of norms, its definitions of gender and role, its clear and certain models of identity, its emphatic insistence on the masculine as the model and fulcrum for the defining of differences at the socio-cultural level, as well as in individual psychic development. This process is a true and proper revolution that is taking place in each of us and all around us. We confront the difficult experience of a chaos in which social structures and the psychic life of the individual are thrown into disorganization, and we wonder where it is leading us.

In the reassuring language of metaphor, the old king lies ill, and the youngest of his sons – the least integrated – has to face a series of trials and enigmas in order to reach the waters of life and effect his regeneration. The old order no longer reflects the vital depths that give meaning to human existence, and the reality principle expressed by that order now appears to be faulty.

Psychoanalytic research – which "develops in terms of a natural process that reflects the emotional condition of the human beings it studies" (Winnicott, 1988, p. 49) – has likewise shifted. The studies of Stoller (1968) and of Money (1973) initiate a distinction between biological gender and psychic gender. They can correspond to one another, but do not have to do so. Gender identity seems to establish itself at about the age of 18 months and to develop slowly. It finds its basis, yes, in the child's biological gender, but it also depends on the conscious and unconscious expectations of the parents, on their introjection, and on the fantasies that the child develops about its parents and itself.

If gender identity can be disengaged from biological identity, it is not destiny. Here we discover the start of a road to still unknown processes of development, to strategies of evolution that differ from those implicit in a patriarchal society and, finally, to new definitions of masculine and feminine identity. Philosophy, here again, can be of some help to us: "Secretly the telos of identification is non-identity, which is something to be rescued from within it" (Adorno, 1966, p. 133).

When the true problem is seen to lie in an excess of identity – or in a mode of identity guaranteed by the persona – we can regard non-identity and the sphere of the unspoken no longer as shapeless, or as absence, or as a source of discomfort, but instead as a form of living that remains to be explored. Men and women who are free of coercive identities established by ideology no longer would be condemned to roles; the division of labor would no longer constitute the force that shapes the individual.

These premises lead us to make an assertion about analysis if it hopes to produce research that can deal with identity as a problem and challenge of the times in which we live, it must take account of the actual experience of analyst and patient as social subjects whose experience is marked profoundly by ideology, by the presence of male-centered criteria in a patriarchal ideology, and by the multiple registers – biological, social, and psychic – in which the analytic relationship articulates itself.

The concept of the countertransference has evolved from a symptom of the analyst's pathology into an instrument of analytic technique. Thinking back to this evolution, we may wonder whether ideology and its various derivatives – systems of representations, stereotyped patterns of social behavior, and deep psychic constellations – can be employed, once fully conscious, as tools of analytic practice and theoretical research.

Let us now take a look – in the greater light now being shed by the transformations that are underway – at the ways in which a number of specific socio-cultural assumptions on gender and role may continue to find expression in the man-woman analytic couple.

While asserting themselves in more veiled ways in the analytic couple of the male analyst and the woman patient – which reflects the model of the traditional man-woman relationship in the outside world – such assumptions may find more open manifestation in the woman-man couple, or in a comparison of the two. At times, the dynamics related to power are analyzed insufficiently, and the relationship runs the risk of mimicking a situation that the culture has produced.

The male patient with a woman analyst finds himself, in a position at odds with traditional social roles. Being observed, without being able to observe, lying rather than seated; can represent subjection to a power – even a sexual power – of which he has been deprived. He may then tend to deny the professional role – imbued with power – of the woman analyst, by reacting from the very start with an eroticized transference. Thus he attempts to re-establish a dominant position with respect to the woman as a sexual object, or he may attempt to place her in a subordinate professional role.

One patient – middle-aged and at the head of a flourishing commercial enterprise – gave play to both these responses. He proposed to me that our sessions be held on weekends, just as he worked on weekends with his secretary. Or a male patient can diminish the power of a woman analyst in the opposite way, denying her sexuality as a woman and recognizing nothing more than her professional capabilities.

A commonplace once shared by men and women alike – but with fear, by women – saw a woman's professional success to go hand in hand with a loss of femininity, as defined in terms of dependence and passivity. The desire to deprive women of power may also explain the belief, quite widespread at the start of the century, that women experience a far less conspicuous sexual drive. Desexualization is equivalent to dehumanization, or to an act of devaluation that can later, at times, be turned into "sanctification." Such a maneuver allows a male patient to enjoy the nutritive capacity of a woman analyst without its seeming to constitute a threat to his masculinity.

The woman patient with a male analyst experiences no transgression of social roles, and assuming a dependent position with respect to her analyst presents a lesser threat to her sense of identity. But the most profound differences between these two couples are witnessed at the level of the expression of erotic contents. Let us observe them from the point of view of the social stereotypes that appear in the countertransference.

Man Patient/Woman Analyst

The literature (e.g., Lester, 1985), informs us that the male patient tends to express sexual desire toward a woman analyst in a more veiled and indirect form. He experiences it rarely at the conscious level as a dominant theme, but more frequently in terms of projections outside the analysis and in acting-out. We see defense mechanisms against the sexual transference more than we see the transference itself.

The woman analyst's power seems to reawaken the male patient's fear of the phallic mother, inducing him to dwell at greater length on pre-oedipal struggles – played out primarily in terms of dominance and submission – and of sado-masochism. Thus the expression of strong erotic fantasies is inhibited. Then, when the pre-genital conflicts have been worked through, a strong erotic transference is rare.

The woman analyst may collaborate in setting up this typical configuration of the erotic transference. That is, she may be unwilling to recognize, accept and make use of her sexual fantasies about the patient, especially if he is younger than she. Thus, her defenses may reinforce the patient's.

The reason for this difficulty is that the man's relative subordination does not accord with typical feminine erotic fantasies, and that incest is socially less allowed to the mother than to the father. In addition, the woman analyst's facilitation of the expression of erotic contents might lead her to perceive herself – and to fear being perceived – as seductive. Nevertheless she may happen to dress with particular care on the day she sees that patient, thus acting out her erotic fantasies.

To dismantle the patient's defenses, inducing him to face an erotic transference, despite his insistent denial of it, could be experienced as a proposition, or as a way of carrying the embarrassing social role of the woman as an object – and not a subject – of desire. So, she may hide herself in a more reassuring, gratifying, and powerful maternal role, and thus create a resistance to the analysis. Analyses conducted by women tend to be longer than those conducted by their male colleagues, as a result of the different way in which the pre-oedipal relationship presents itself, but also because these analyses keep this relationship alive.

Chasseguet-Smirgel (1986) reports the recurrent dream of a woman analyst, in which her mother enters the studio, creates disorder and keeps her from doing her work. This dream perhaps gives warning against a facile and intrusive identification with the role of mother, as though there were no border between the maternal transference and the analyst's experience as a mother, or with her mother. The broken ear of corn (object of the cult of Eleusis) may be still working deep in the psyche: the representation of womanhood in a mother-daughter continuum, rather than the model of separation and differentiation between the two. Abstinence may be the woman analyst's specific risk, just as the risk for the male analyst is to pass from sexual fantasy to the sexual act.

As a man, Freud was both directly and indirectly aware of the male analyst's risks, and he prescribed unbending abstinence from sexual relations with the patient, but he did not insist that an analyst abstain from satisfying oral and anaclitic needs. He went so far as to serve breakfast to the "rat man." The woman analyst too like women in the outside world, may tend to oscillate between the roles of mother, sex object, and a-sexual professional before freeing herself from all of them and rediscovering her own identity.

Man Analyst/Woman Patient

With the male analyst and the woman patient, the erotic transference is experienced in more open, intense and persistent ways. This is the couple in which Freud observed and conceptualized the erotic transference and countertransference in Breuer/Anna O. and in Jung/Sabina Spielrein.

The woman, normally does not feel her dependence on a man to pose any threat to her femininity; she may even find reconfirmation as a woman in feeling and expressing admiration and desire toward the man. Greenson (1967) remarks: "Women feel more feminine in the company of the opposite sex, whereas men feel more masculine in the presence of men" (p. 400).

The male analyst, in turn, may contribute to the intensity of the erotic transference, sometimes encouraging the early expression of its sexual contents. He may anticipate these contents more than he analyzes them and he may be available to assume the role of a sexual partner. It is as though he assumes the roles of active man and the hunter, in allegiance to a widespread concept of virility.

An analyst in supervision reported that a young woman patient had dreamed of making love with Freud, whom this analyst clearly resembled. His response had been to ask, directly and almost as though with a personal interest, "Did you enjoy it?"

The anticipation and activation of erotic contents also may be a way in which the male analyst defends himself from a pre-oedipal maternal transference. Such a transference can threaten his sense of gender identity and provoke anxiety. He therefore deploys a phallic-narcissistic reaction, in repetition of his flight from maternal dependence. Such an acceleration of the sexual dynamics of the transference can represent a flight toward the oedipus complex, for the analyst no less than the patient, at a time in which the previous phase has not been worked through. Thus, integration of affectivity and sexuality may be hindered and sexual acting-out encouraged.

Sexual acting-out, in gratification of the patient's demands, permits him to reaffirm his identity as a man and to maintain an affective distance from her, by means of the activation of a split. The patient accepts gratification at this pseudo-genital level because it gives her the physical contact she desires, as an equivalent to maternal care and nourishment, without the risk of a state of fusion, or confusion, as might be the case with a woman analyst. (For much the same reason a male patient, too, experiences the maternal transference onto a male analyst to be less frightening than with a woman analyst.) In short, the male analyst shows a defensive tendency to read the request for maternal love as Oedipal; and erotic.

A price must be paid by the woman patient who does not work her way through separation and differentiation from the mother: Her sense of identity will remain uncertain and she will experience feelings of inadequacy. In addition, she will direct maternal requests and projections toward men and her relationships with women will be full of problems.

Society has taken a temporary form of libidinal organization – phallic narcissism – and used it to immobilize the libido into attitudes and personality structures that are marked by the repression of dependency and capable only of instrumental and temporary relationships. Thus, we have here a view of negative effects of the widespread use of a male-centered strategy: the offer of a hyper-invested penis, either real or fantasized, as the fulcrum of differentiation from the mother, for both males and females. But if this strategy loses efficacy – as a result of the weakening of patriarchal ideology – or simply fails to be deployed, the unresolved problem reappears. There is the risk – for men no less than women, both within and outside analysis – of the reappearance of anxieties of fusion and symbiotic undifferentiation, or of oral needs.

Prevalent pathologies, – such as alimentary disturbances, drug addictions, transvestism, and some forms of impotence force us to see the specific separation-individuation problems they share as signs explaining the dynamics underlying the current process of social transformation.

An indirect confirmation of the male analyst's role in activating or controlling the erotic transference may be found in the reports of numerous analysts. After difficult therapies that were marked by intense erotic transferences and countertransferences, these analysts have noted that their subsequent women patients showed a lesser tendency to develop erotic transferences.

The difficulties experienced by the male analyst in dealing with the maternal transference may lead to misinterpretations, such as, "You have to eat something before our session because you can't tolerate that a good father feeds you." A maternal function becomes paternal simply by virtue of being exercized by a man! Such a confusion in the definition of functions presupposes an unconscious connection between the old duo of function and biological sex; in the face of the possibility of "being" a woman, the male analyst takes flight from it. On seeing himself attributed with a feminine, maternal function, or on performing such a function, the analyst – like men in the outside world – seems to be afraid of losing his masculine characteristics. (A woman finds it easier to take on functions traditionally attributed to the opposite sex, partly because such functions are held in high regard, and partly because her sexual identity is more certain, as a result of the asymmetry of the processes of development).

The very fact of inquiring if a patient would prefer a man or a woman analyst may again presuppose the age-old confusion of sex and function. Or the male analyst's interpretation may suggest bisexuality when a woman patient brings in a dream of having been seduced by another woman in a climate of intense sexual excitation. Then the true problem, of the woman's drive relation with the° primitive undifferentiated mother – re-experienced with and by the male analyst – once again becomes unanalyzable, eluding all possibility that further development has been transformed into a question of "universal bisexual destiny." The problem lapses back into the unconscious, losing tension and robbing the relationship of tension.

We have examined a few gender differences in the countertransference. In particular, we have drawn attention to the way in which the woman analyst risks identifying with the role of the mother. We have observed also that the male analyst may respond to the maternal transference by narcissistic phallic reactions, by attributing bisexuality, by confusing biological sex and function. All these responses are defensive strategies and solutions that arise from a patriarchal society.

These examples seem to point – even within a particular setting – to an interpenetration of ideology, identity, theories of psychosexual development, and the course of masculine and feminine development in the real world. Ideology and theory are not neutral, just as the analyst is not neutral.

This prospect could encourage us to make ideology and its manifold derivatives a specific object of observation in the course of our constant efforts toward the transformation and reconstruction of modes of relationship and identity. It could also modify our collective and individual defensive strategies – different according to gender and source of specific afflictions and pathologies – and could eliminate the need for the sexualization of roles and could depolarize gender.

Translated from Italian by Henry Martin

References

Adorno, T.W. (1966/1982). *Dialettica Negativa* (Negative Dialectics). Torino: Giulio Enaudi Editore.

Chasseguet-Smirgel, J. (1986). *I Due Alberi del Giardino* (Sexuality and Mind). Milano: Feltrinelli.

Greenson, R. (1967). *The Technique and Practice of Psychoanalysis*. New York: International Universities Press.

Grinberg, L. (1975). *Identità e Cambiamento*. Roma: Armando Editore.

Lester, E. (1985). The female analyst and the eroticized transference. *International Journal of Psychoanalysis, 66*:283-293.

Maduro, R. (1983). I problemi dell'identità etnica in analisi. *La Pratica Analitica, 3*, 11-22

Money, J. (1973). *Man and Woman, Boy and Girl: The Differentiation and Dismorphism of Gender Identity from Conception to Maturity*. Baltimore: Johns Hopkins University Press.

Ranciere, J. (1974). *Ideologia e Politica in Althusser*. Milano: Feltrinelli.

Stoller, R. (1968). *Sex and Gender*. London: Karnac.

Winnicott, D.W. (1988). *Sulla Natura Umana* (Human Nature). Milano: Raffaello Cortina.

Visual Art, Sound and the Computer as Psychological Media

Art and Analytical Psychology

Picasso's Mirror

James Wyly
Chicago, Illinois
Chicago Society of Jungian Analysts

This is the third in our International Congress Workshops on Psychology and Art. My part continues a theme that I have been developing: transference and the transformative process in the making of art. Previously, I have explored Picasso's lifelong preoccupation with what happens when the artist makes a work of art, and I have suggested that his graphic meditations on this theme can teach us profoundly about transference and creativity in Jungian analysis. Now I am taking Picasso's ruminations on the creative process into three new dimensions: 1) carrying them into time, back into the seventeenth century and the culture that brought alchemy to its most profoundly psychological development; 2) carrying them into space, across the Atlantic Ocean to the high cultures of the Americas that the Europeans first encountered at the end of the fifteenth century; and 3) carrying them into mythology – American mythology – in search of an image that may help us to understand the archetypal nature of this transferential process and its essential relationship to artistic creation.

The image I am using to accomplish this journey is the mirror. All kinds of mirrors: the literal mirrors we find represented in the works we examine here; the works of art in which we see mirrored aspects of ourselves and our cultures; and the figurative mirrors we deal with in our consulting rooms, the mirror transference and the transference-as-mirror. These mirrors will take us on a journey back in time, across the Atlantic Ocean, down into the mythic level of the collective psyche, back to our time and our preoccupation with art and transference, and then back to Picasso again, with an answer to

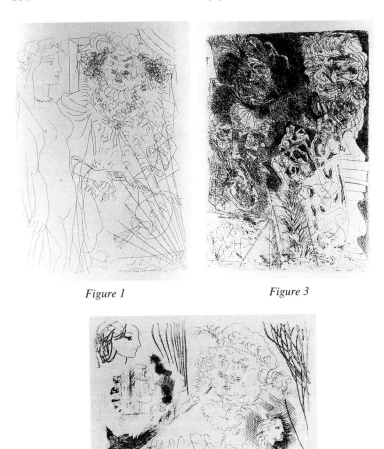

Figure 1   *Figure 3*

Figure 2

a seemingly rather banal but deeply provocative question that launches us on our journey: what is Rembrandt van Rijn doing in this picture (Fig. 1)?

Immediately we see that the work is the last of the four "Rembrandt" plates of the *Vollard Suite* – all made on two days in January of 1934 – and it is a takeoff on Rembrandt's late self-portraits. We are reminded of both Rembrandt's and Picasso's extensive productions of self-portraits, necessarily made with mirrors, as conscious acts of self-mirroring. But why is Rembrandt here? Why is he holding the hand of one of the Grecian or Cretan ladies who populate the rest of this series of 100 plates, almost all of which present a timeless, classical world far removed from Rembrandt's time-bound lace and curls?

If we examine all the hundred plates of the *Vollard Suite*, we cannot avoid perceiving Rembrandt as an intrusion, a kind of time-traveller who appears unexpectedly in the first of his four plates (Fig. 2). Bolliger (Ed. of Picasso, 1985) reports that Picasso told his dealer, Daniel Henry Kahnweiler, that the Rembrandt face emerged as he scrawled aimlessly on the plate, which he thought had been ruined by a defective varnish.

Figure 4

Rembrandt creates a disturbance (Fig. 3) when he gets into the classical world, for the classical bust – otherwise shown by Picasso with a serene countenance – appears upset here, as though it has become psychotic. Next he peers into the window at some half-dressed classical women (Fig. 4) who seem to disorient him. Then we find him in the plate we first saw (Fig. 1), hand in hand with one of the women, the sun behind him apparently reflected in a mirror that is just out of sight in the lower right corner of the work. Now he is serene. His disturbing voyeuristic adventure seems resolved and he is ready to paint; he has his palette and brushes in his hand. We recognize the subject matter to which Picasso returned in countless works throughout his life: the artist and his model.

But how did this transformation take place? And what effect does this apparition from the seventeenth century have on the *Vollard Suite* itself? One way of understanding this is to think about mirrors.

What happens when an artist such as Picasso's Rembrandt, brush or burin in hand, looks in a mirror and begins to respond to what it shows? To inform ourselves, we can consider some actual self-portraits by Picasso and Rembrandt (Figs. 5-12). Eight images. How many artists' faces have we seen? Two? Or eight? The mirror image, passed through the psyche of the artist, can be changed deliberately

Figure 5

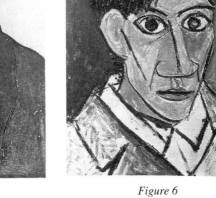

Figure 6

Figure 7

Figure 8

Figure 9

Figure 10

Figure 11

Figure 12

Figure 13

by the artist's will; but revelations are made which the artist did not control. I can hardly imagine that Picasso deliberately painted that horrifying image of his impending death into his 90-year-old face, for example. The mirror reveals unknown qualities when its image is fixed in ink or paint, and I think these are what Picasso and Rembrandt set out to discover in making these works. There seems to be an unconscious transformative process at work here, and we can verify its existence by examining a few more works of art. When Picasso shows an artist, the artist's model, and a work, the work almost never resembles the model (Fig. 13). Picasso knew that making art introduced a psychological factor which uncontrollably influences the result, and he cultivated it. These three works show us the level of awareness with which he approached this aspect of his art.

Since we have demonstrated that Picasso was fascinated by the transformative influence of the psyche in his own work, we can imagine with what kind of curiosity Picasso studied self-portraits – mirror images transformed by the psyche – made by other artists. He must have studied Rembrandt's many self-portraits profoundly, in search of the spontaneous effects of Rembrandt's psyche which Picasso's experience had taught him was visible there. We can understand, then, the level of astonishment with which he must have viewed Rembrandt's appearance in his own work. It is reflected in his comments to Kahnweiler on the day it happened. According to Kahnweiler, Picasso said, "Just imagine, I've done a portrait of Rembrandt. It's all on account of that varnish that cracks. It happened to one of my plates. I said to myself, 'It's spoiled, I'll just do any old thing on it.' I began to scrawl. What came out was Rembrandt. I began to like it, and I kept on. I even did another one (Fig. 3), with his turban, his furs, and his eye – his elephant's eye, you know. Now I'm going on with the plate to see if I can get blacks like his – you don't get them at the first try" (Picasso, 1985, p. xii). As Rembrandt gazed on the figures of Picasso's imagination "with his elephant's eye," Picasso could not have avoided wondering what transformations the earlier master's intrusion would bring to his world.

The transformative effect of the artist's eye. Picasso saw it when he looked in a mirror, and he assumed Rembrandt saw it also. But is this perception limited to the artist? Obviously not. If an artist portrays scenes involving mirrors he can lead us even farther into the realm of psychological transformation of images. Let us look, then, at another painting that clearly obsessed Picasso (Fig. 14). In the last five months of 1957, Picasso made no fewer

Figure 14

than 44 variations on this painting, the work of the Spanish painter, Diego Velázquez.

Velázquez' masterpiece involves the viewer in a very complicated set of mirrored relationships: doubtless one of its major fascinations for Picasso. Now we must review its construction, looking at it with Picasso's supposition about the transformative function of the artist's eye.

First we see Velázquez. He stands in the position familiar to us from so many artists' self-portraits, brush in one hand and palette in the other. He stands before a canvas and looks out at us. Was he painting us, or have we just interrupted him as he was working on something else? And what of Infanta Margarita María and her seven attendants – eight, counting the dog? They, too, appear to have been doing something else a moment before they became aware of our presence. Were they looking at Velázquez' work? Preparing the infanta for her inclusion in Velázquez' painting? Again, the canvas with its hidden surface keeps us from knowing anything except that our presence has made a difference. Everyone is reacting to us, even the man who was on the point of leaving the room, but who turns back to see what has happened.

And there is the mirror. It shows King Philip IV and Queen María Ana in such a way that we cannot avoid the fantasy that we are they. What do we see? That Velázquez' eye has turned us into the royal couple, that it has penetrated to the divine coniunctio at the foundation of our psyche? Or is it that our eye is shown to be at work here, and what we see is a reflection of Velázquez' possibly transformative painting? The deeper we go, the more mysterious it becomes. But one thing is clear: Like Rembrandt and Picasso, Velázquez was well aware of the transformative effect of the artist's eye, and he forces us into direct involvement with its mysteries. We cannot look at "Las Meninas" (The Attendants) without making contact, however furtively, with an imaginal king and queen.

So we are certain that Velázquez, like Picasso, was conscious of the transformative or psychologically revelatory function of the mirror. We could go further. Velázquez lived at the very height of alchemy's popularity, and he was a well-educated and worldly man. It is inconceivable that he would not have heard of the "royal couple" that was at the center of seventeenth-century alchemical thought. The fact that he has arranged the geometry of "Las Meninas" as he has demonstrates that he understood it in a truly "Jungian" way, as symbolic of inner, psychological phenomena.

And so did Picasso. Not only did he see what Velázquez saw; in typical fashion, he set out to go Velázquez one better – or 44 better, it turned out, for the creative impulse that set him on this course produced that many paintings on the alchemical theme.

Now let us look at the first painting of Picasso's series (Fig. 15). Here again we see Velázquez, towering before his easel, looking out at us. Again we find the courtiers and dog clustered around Infanta Margarita María, and again the chamberlain looks back from the stairs at the back of the room. But look in the mirror (Fig. 16). Picasso has made one crucial change. Where Velázquez painted the faces of the royal couple (Fig. 17), Picasso gives us a single face. And while its turned-up moustache resembles the one Philip IV wore in some famous Velázquez portraits, the face conspicuously lacks Philip's prognathous jaw and the moustache is identical to the one on Picasso's Velázquez. I believe the turned-up moustache reveals Picasso's entire game. The "king's face" in the mirror here is also Velázquez' own!

Figure 15

Figure 16

Figure 17

We can imagine that Picasso is in conversation with Velázquez, saying: "I see what you're doing. I stepped into your studio and you showed me the royal couple within me. But when you looked out at me, you were really seeing yourself. I know that couple is really you."

Velázquez has told us that the artist's eye sees into psychological depths when he looks at his model and Picasso has told us that those depths belong to the artist. Taken together, the two paintings would seem to say the last word on psychological projection. But Picasso has more to tell us, as the subsequent Meninas paintings show.

Figure 18

Figure 19

Picasso must have been entranced by Velázquez's audacious variation on the artist-and-model theme, in which the viewer steps into the role of model. As he continued to work with this conceit the question became, "If we continue to look at our subject – ourself – what happens? What further transformations do we perceive in this mirror?" Since I cannot show Picasso's entire series here, I shall describe it for you, using only a few examples. Fundamentally, three things happen: The colors become more important, the number of figures gradually diminishes to one, and the painter – whose enormous figure dominates the first work – fades away entirely. The image reflected in the mirror is the first to disappear, for in the first painting Picasso showed us the mirror's deepest secret; after that it lost interest for him. Now he is concerned with the mirror in its figurative sense, the mirror of the artist's eye. And as we look at the next illustrations let us give particular attention to the evolution of the figure of Doña Isabel del Velasco, the figure standing at the infanta's left (Figs. 18 & 19).

In addition to the group renderings, Picasso focused on individual figures from the original or on small groups of them (Fig. 20), such as Infanta Margarita María and her principal attendants. The series ends with Doña Isabel del Velasco, who stands at the infanta's left in the original. Two extracts from her final evolution are depicted (Figs. 21 & 22).

She began for Picasso as a stooping grotesque and evolved into this figure who bows to us, as though introducing her-

Figure 20

self. Do we not see here a transformation that occurred spontaneously as Picasso worked? And, given the assumptions we have had to make about projection, mirroring, and the artist's eye in these paintings, we must conclude that, in this last painting, we are contemplating something profound: an image of Picasso himself, which he shows to us as though it also belonged to Velázquez, and ultimately, to ourselves. The painter, the studio, the attendants all have faded and we – or Picasso – find ourselves face to face with a feminine image as full of delight as she is of mystery. Picasso has led us to an even deeper realization about projection: If we look long and deeply enough at what we project, we shall see aspects of ourselves that are unimaginably foreign to what we had believed we

Figure 21   *Figure 22*

Figure 23

were. Even a young lady from a Spanish court more than 300 years distant from us is a part of ourselves; her image is our creation. The mirror takes us to revelations that approach the divine.

For Picasso, to look at one's image, whether in a mirror or by way of the artist's transformative eye, led to the same place: a confrontation with the deepest levels of the psyche. It is interesting, then, to consider some of what we know about mirrors from cultures that appear to have valued them highly as instruments of revelation and transformation: the people who built the great pre-Columbian civilizations of the central part of the Americas.

Stone mirrors are relatively common finds in the oldest known mesoamerican burial sites, dating from at least 3500 years ago. Many of these mirrors, and the mirrors of the Olmecs who succeeded these almost unknown peoples, are deliberately made with concave surfaces. This gives them two suggestive characteristics: They invert the images they reflect, and they can be used to start fire by focusing the sun's rays. This implies that their makers were interested at least as much in the revelatory and transformative aspects of mirrors as they were in their reflective powers.

The warrior-god of the much later Nahua-speaking people whom the Spanish encountered was called Tezcatlipoca (Fig. 23). His name means "smoking mirror," and he is regarded as a personification of the polished obsidian mirrors used by these people; his characteristics must be those attributed to these black reflecting surfaces. He rules war and night, and is a patron of rulers, sorcerers, and warriors. He brings discord and conflict wherever he passes, and he is both a creator and a destroyer. He wears a smoking mirror on his head or on his back, so that contact with him is made by consulting the image it reflects. One source summarizes him as "the embodiment of change through conflict" (Miller and Taube, p. 164).

One is tempted to adopt Tezcatlipoca as the god of psychoanalysis. At the very least his attributes and the manner of consulting him – through meditating upon a reflected image – suggest the recognizing of unconscious projections and analysis of transference. With that we are back to Velázquez, Rembrandt, and Picasso; these processes are exactly what they, too, seem to have found when they consulted the mirrors of their art. It would be reasonable to suppose that, behind this place where art and psychoanalysis seem to meet, there lies an archetype; for lack of a better name I am calling it Tezcatlipoca, the archetype of self-reflection, the ability to contemplate something new and recognize it as one's own. Self-reflection with a capital "S."

Although we have some evidence that this archetype was understood fairly widely in the Americas from earliest times, such may not have been the case in Europe. There is something antithetical between religion based on self-reflection and religion based on faith. It is interesting to speculate that it is for this reason that Christianity kept Tezcatlipoca underground in Europe. His self-reflective process became the essence of the alchemical tradition, and there it was preserved for a select and often persecuted few. But the scientifically- and philosophically-investigative spirit of seventeenth-century Europe brought alchemical speculation unprecedented intellectual attention while the increasing diffusion of printed books gave it a far wider audience than it had enjoyed previously. Therefore, it does not seem too fantastic to suggest that the self-reflective quality we have seen in Rembrandt's and Velázquez' art represents a kind of artistic perception that seemed newly brought to light for their generation's European intellectuals. It could be that they were among the first Western painters to work with a real awareness that their superficially precise renderings of objective reality sprang from an unconscious source within them. At least Picasso seems to have seen this reality in their work, and it is the central mystery with which he worked throughout his life.

Our original question was, "what is Rembrandt van Rijn doing in this picture" (Fig. 1)? On the most concrete level, the answer is, "He is looking in a mirror." But now we know something more of what the act meant to Picasso, for clearly Rembrandt's mirror is something more than the one from his bathroom wall. We might go so far as to say that Rembrandt is consulting Tezcatlipoca; to Picasso he is engaged in a modern psychological act, for he is looking at something he knows is reflected to him from otherwise unknowable depths of his own psyche. For Picasso, this was the very essence of creativity, of making art, and I believe it is also the very essence of the analytic process.

We could say that Picasso identified for us the moment in European history when analysis became a possibility; he suggests to us that the artists and thinkers of the first half of the seventeenth century were among the first Europeans to begin to realize its possibilities. Velázquez was born in 1599, Rembrandt in 1606. Thus, we are speaking of a generation of artists who did their mature work between about 1620 and 1680. To broaden our perspective, let us remember that we are considering the years of the first mature flowering of opera, above all at the hands of Monteverdi; of the first generations of instrumental performers known as individual virtuosi, such as Sweelinck, Frescobaldi, Champion de Chambonnières, and Correa de Arauxo; and of the art of Milton, Corneille, the Le Brun brothers, Le Nain, and Bernini, among many others. We are speaking of the full flowering of the "high baroque"; now we may see it as a psychological phenomenon based upon a new ability to gain access to individual resources. Artists were known for their accomplishments executed in grand but completely personal, unique styles. It is no coincidence that this was also the time when a large number of important alchemical texts were published and diffused relatively widely.

Now we can see that Picasso identified a moment, already known as pivotal in the history of European culture, that was pivotal also in the development of human self-perception. As psychologists, we are only beginning to catch up with him. The implications of this development are tremendous, for it directs our attention to an enormous body of art that can inform us about psychological points of which we have only begun to be aware.

Igor Stravinsky also understood this point; he summarized it impeccably when he said, "One should worship god with a little art, if one has any; and if one hasn't, one can burn a little incense." At our best, we can follow Picasso in using our art to deepen our psychological understanding of who we are and what we are doing. If we cannot do that, at least Picasso has shown us a reflective attitude with which we can burn a little incense.

Whatever Happened to Paradise?

Christian Gaillard

Paris, France
French Society of Analytical Psychology

The painting we are about to explore hangs in the Städelsches Kunstinstitut (Städel Art Institute) in Frankfurt, Germany. It is by an unknown artist designated simply as "Oberrheinischer Meister" (Upper Rhinish Master) and was created in the southern part of Germany. It dates from around 1410 or 1420; that is, the period in the history of European art that is described as "international gothic." The painting (Fig. 1) is a small tempera on wood, only slightly larger than the area taken up by two open hands: 26.3 centimeters by 33.4 centimeters.

If you stroll from room to room in the Frankfurt Museum, and if you know how to allow yourself to be drawn in by a painting, your attention will be riveted by this one. The liveliness and richness of its colors, and the precise harmony of its composition, cause it to stand out from the masterpieces surrounding it.

The Scene: An Initial Approach

The scene appears to be happy, ideal, and soothing. To all appearances, its charm is complete, seeming to provide every promise of innocent pleasure. What gives the painting strength, however, and makes us pause before it is that, in spite of the foregoing, it is stubbornly enigmatic and, thus, proves to be strangely disturbing to anyone who lingers before it long enough to receive its impact.

A closed garden is inhabited by various figures, flowers, birds. The view looks down over a scene offered for contemplation. If one takes the time to wander through the scene at a leisurely pace, one gradually will make the round of the figures contained by the garden wall, one by one. Each figure is exactly where she or he belongs,

Figure 1. Paradiesgärtlein (Garden of Paradise)

absorbed in the appropriate pose and gesture, tangibly present and yet curiously absent as well.

A woman dressed in red is picking cherries, which she collects in a fold of her robe before transferring them to the wicker basket at her feet. A second woman, in blue, is drawing water from a fountain. Meanwhile, a third, seated on the grass and also wearing red, is with a baby and playing on a psaltery.

The viewer's eye returns to the central figure, draped in an ample blue robe and cape. Her crowned head is bent, absorbed in the reading of a book, in the heart of this garden. Would that be Mary?

Here is a "Garden of Paradise." Such is the title the painting is usually given. If this is indeed Mary, it is a representation of her in her eternal beatitude.

But why should she be holding a book? Is there a heavenly library available to the saintly following their tribulations down below? The garden is so inherently earthly that one begins to wonder if the female figure might not be Eve in Paradise before the Fall, instead of Mary in her eternal glory. But whoever heard of an Eve clothed in robe and crown, reading in the Garden of Eden? Unless it is the

Figure 2. La Madona del Rosetto

Virgin Mary, after all, at the moment she is awaiting the fate the angels are about to announce to her, a fate which is already written: Mary, just before she learns that she is going to be pregnant?

Eve, or Mary? But why choose one or the other? Instead, let us allow our gaze to float. Let us assume the enigma. In clinical practice, we learn to support the enigmatic pressure of a representation, to allow it to live, in order to get a more accurate idea of what is involved, and in order to search for the answer to what is being sought thereby.

One must also allow oneself to be guided by the surprise effect, by the astonishment provoked by the unexpected. Attention to the effect of surprise and the taste for the unexpected remain the best ways to confront the singular event presenting itself. This event is easier to grasp if we proceed by comparison, and make ourselves attentive to the relationships and differences this scene maintains with paintings we find to be similar to it.

The Closest Garden

What flowered, fenced-in garden most closely resembles our painting, by virtue of its structure and place in history? To my knowledge, it is "La Madona del Rosetto" (The Madonna of Rosetto, Fig. 2), a work found in the Castelvecchio of Verona, and attributed to Stefano di Verona. It is thought to have been painted in 1410; that is, either at the same time as or immediately before the painting in Frankfurt.

Here, too, as in the Frankfurt painting, the viewer looks down on a scene where a woman in a great blue cloak occupies a place of honor amid a profusion of flowers and birds. Again, as in Frankfurt, the eye travels around the center of the composition and then returns to it, contained by the fence of the garden, on which various species of birds are perched.

Also as in Frankfurt, the eye wonders about the contrast of blue and red in the clothing of the female figures: blue over red for the central figure; red over blue for the smaller female figure that mirrors her attitude from a lower part of the picture. Here, too, a fountain is an important element of the scenery.

The Differences

Yet the difference between the two paintings is striking. Both are painted according to the same structural organization, and obey, in appearance, the same representational pattern: a *hortus conclusus* (closed garden), in which the Virgin is the central figure. But their lives are quite different.

The move from Frankfurt to Verona implies a change of milieu and perhaps also a change of protagonist. In Verona, the woman ruling over the painting is undeniably the Virgin-Madonna of Christian myth, reigning over the golden trappings of eternity and surrounded by angels. In Frankfurt, this woman is a crowned noblewoman who, although still dressed in blue, may be simply strolling in the garden adjoining her castle, reading a book. As a result, her relationship with the flowers, fruits, and music, and especially with the women surrounding her in multiple mirror images of herself, is quite different: more immediately fleshly, and animated by another spirit.

A single detail conveys the degree of the change, as contained in the transformation of an important structural motif: the fountain. In Verona, the fountain is shown as a golden piece of liturgical jewelry, borne up by angels. In Frankfurt, the fountain is located quite concretely on the ground, within reach, with the ladle attached to it by a chain, making it possible to draw water.

The fountain, which appears in so much medieval art as a Fountain of Youth or a Fountain of Mercury, is depicted here as functional. It can be used. Even I, standing at the edge of the painting, might be able to see myself in its waters. Instead of transcendence supported by faith, and the uplift of religious transport, there is another type of communication: a woman beckoning, from the lower part of the painting, at my eye level; an invitation that might even be addressed to me.

From Farther Away

If we now place a little more distance between us and the two paintings, we note a distinctive change in the dominant hue, between one painting and the other, between Verona and Frankfurt. It goes from gold to green.

In Verona we are still quite close to the art of Ravenna and, therefore, to the icons and frescoes of Byzantine art, the icons and frescoes on a golden ground from early Christian times, which long gazed down on us from their position high on the altar and high in the dogmatic teachings of the Church. Much as we may be inclined to apply the modern psychological concept of "projection" to such phenomena, the pictorial evidence insists, rather, that the figures represented there held and maintained us beneath their gaze for centuries.

In the painting from Verona, and even more so in the one from Frankfurt, the viewpoints have been reversed. Now the scene is placed at eye level, even offering to our eyes a view from slightly above. And what do we discover? An open, animated scene, inhabited by multiple figures, which has become so human it almost seems that we could walk into it; a field which, in passing from gold to green transports us from a transcendent, eternal Beyond, existing outside time, to a garden space.

From the Sacred to the Profane

Already, in Verona, the Virgin Mary of Christian myth, wrapped in a great blue cloak covering her red robes, strangely pensive and sad – as a Piétà might be – has acquired a twin in the lower part of the painting, closer to us, a more human figure, garbed in red over blue, whom we recognize according to her traditional attributes, the wheel and the sword. She is Catherine of Alexandria, a virgin known to have been martyred in the fourth century of the Christian era who, later, was made patron saint of unmarried girls.

Both virgins are represented in all their glory and celebrated in accordance with tradition. But here they appear fated to meet with a Passion that is nearing, with pain which is, of course, still exemplary from afar, but which now better approximates human experience. What pain and what tragedy are thus inscribed in the scenery for the wonderment of our eyes?

In Frankfurt, the subject is even closer, visible in even greater detail. Certainly the noblewoman in blue is still in the center of the scene, but who can say with certainty whether this Eve-Mary is really Mary, or the Eve of Christian myth?

And who could the women surrounding her be? What is their purpose in this garden, which is no longer quite what it was in Verona, a mystical Rose Garden? I can recognize St. Dorothy, picking cherries, on Eve-Mary's right since I know that St. Dorothy is the patron saint of gardeners. The woman drawing water from the well would be Martha; I know the role she plays in the New Testament, in the life of another Mary. Meanwhile, St. Cecilia, the patron saint of musicians, would be presenting the psaltery to a babe who may be the infant Jesus.

Such a traditional reading of the painting would be intended to comfort. I do not doubt that most of the artists' contemporaries were content to see it in this way. But why should Catherine of Alexandria proliferate as a Dorothy, a Martha, and a Cecilia sometimes in red, sometimes in blue? Why incorporate such a marked alternation of red and blue?

I am aware that Martha, an ordinary girl, may be clothed in blue the way the Virgin Mary is traditionally shown. Dorothy, in red here, is a martyr. Cecilia, also in red, was decapitated, like Catherine of

Alexandria. The tragic history of these virgin martyrs, placed as they are as a counterpoint to the traditional celebration of Mary's virginity, tinges our sojourn in this supposedly paradisiacal garden with a note of sorrow.

The garden, in fact, deserves to be looked at more closely. As if in analogy to the now markedly halo-less heads of Dorothy, Martha, and Cecilia – a detail that brings them closer to the most familiar, most secular human universe – the garden is such a far cry from a mystical, allegorical rose garden that it could almost be taken for a botanical garden.

I have asked myself, of course, what flowers and what fruits are represented here. It is possible to make a scientifically accurate inventory of them, to identify each species. As might be expected, each of these species has its own function in the allegorical celebration of the virginity of Mary.

Amid this inventory, nevertheless, there is one rather singular plant on which we should focus our attention. If one peruses the circle of female figures that extends to the child playing the psaltery and begins again with the woman in blue, "Eve-Mary," we find, beside her at the foot of the table, a green plant with fuzzy leaves, presenting the following particularity: It is bearing fruit while still in blossom.

Incarnation as a Flower

Flower and fruit at the same time? Is that not an eloquent symbol for the concept of the promise and its fulfillment, a fulfillment which here seems to be offered for consumption? The prospect is an attractive one, a dream powerful enough to inspire faith in dreams. It is a wish that is as consummately ideal as that of an Immaculate Conception, or a Virgin Birth.

Moreover, the fulfillment of the dream is not located in some timeless and transcendent beyond, or reserved only for a select group of exceptional people. Here it is within hand's reach, in close proximity to the senses, arousing appetite and desire.

This paradise has become so earthly, the dream so arable, the flowers and fruits seemingly so ripe for nearly immediate enjoyment, that even though this strawberry plant may have served to celebrate the Virgin Mary, its presence here surpasses the role it might play as an allegorical symbol. Here it is a real living symbol offered up to the delectation and astonished questioning of a fifteenth century still in its early years.

The Taste for Symbol

As soon as we take note of the discreet, nearly hidden presence of the strawberry plant in the heart of the scene and have made ourselves attentive to this conjunction of flower and fruit – so seemingly innocent and botanical, yet so appetizing – our perception of the painting undergoes a transformation. We are induced to unfurl the fantasy-senses the painting has aroused in order to experience (rather than simply see) the sight of Dorothy reaching for the cherries, the taste of the water Martha is drawing from the fountain, the sound of the music from the psaltery Cecilia is holding, the fragrance of the flowers and the fruits in this garden – without any clear knowledge, of what we are experiencing.

Indeed, a symbol is alive inasmuch as it convinces the subject to live – in a tangible and real, albeit often enigmatic way – a hitherto unrecognized content. It is then up to the subject to acknowledge and explain what is going on with that symbol, a not always simple process.

The Newcomers

It is now time to wonder about the presence and purpose here of the group of male figures. Until now, I have left them on the edge of my commentary, as they are on the edge of the painting.

There is a group of three, apparently working toward a shared goal. Although one of them may be wearing a halo of flowers on his head – like Cecilia – and a pair of wings even more brilliant than those of the angels of Verona, it is difficult to see them as members of the chorus in some celestial Hosannah.

I can recognize the figure on the left as St. Michael, with St. George facing him, and St. Lawrence standing near the tree; the latter is recognizable because of the checkered pattern on his scarf. An archangel flanked by two holy martyrs should be enough to satisfy the audience for Christian iconography.

Here, however, they are dressed in the latest fashion of the day. This detail, coming as it does in 1410 or 1420, contributes to making the scene contemporary. This contemporary mood is so deliberately profane that the memory of their respective stories, their saintly histories, has faded into oblivion. As a result, St. George's terrifying dragon, reduced to a lizard basking belly up in the sun, would be soothing were not Satan present in the form of a dark monkey lurking under the flowers and fruits of the strawberry plant.

It is quite a novelty to see George, Michael, and Lawrence included, or at least waiting to be included, in this "Garden of Paradise." Never until now had men entered such a closed garden devoted to the celebration of Mary's virginity. What are they doing here? What sort of relationship, or non-relationship, links them to Dorothy, Martha, and Cecilia?

Composition and Structure

The answer lies in the composition of the scene. The two groups – the three women and the three men – are placed on either side of a table, another hitherto-unheard-of element in the usual closed-garden motif. The mystical Rose Garden of Verona certainly did not contain a table.

This table is an invitation to enjoy. Its vertical line leads the eye to the strawberry plant, with its flowers and fruits, as well as to Satan as a monkey. The table thus mediates a relationship between the group of women and the group of men, while keeping them apart. Moreover, the vertical line consisting of the table, strawberry plant, and Satan is reinforced by a second vertical line, the one formed by the woman in blue and the infant busy making music in the grass of the garden.

The two vertical lines separate the women and the men. The first, on the men's side, is about enjoyment, via the table and the strawberry plant; but it is also about sin, via the dark presence of the monkey Satan. The second line, which is central, represents the virgin birth of a child, without any apparent need for a man to participate in the conception. How will these men and women ever meet one another, in such an arrangement?

Suspense and Perplexity

The scene remains in suspense, heightened by the fact that nothing seems to trouble the serenity of the women; each is as perfectly whole and sufficient unto herself as the fruit tree, whose interlacing limbs seem to form a self-containing embrace. Could this be the key to the perplexity of the warrior George, the archangel

Michael, and Lawrence: the newcomers waiting on the edge of the painting? Michael, in particular, seems to be affected. Sitting with his head resting on his hand, his expression thoughtful, gazing out at us – almost as though he were thinking about the answers to our own questions – his pose is so striking, so expressive to us today, that one is tempted to describe it as melancholy.

We are definitely no longer in the happy time when Mary's virginity could be celebrated innocently. The mystical Rose Garden of Verona is far removed from the strange and troubling tension of this supposedly paradisiacal tableau. Michael, who for so long was an angel, and even an archangel, may have very good reasons to remain thoughtful, dreamy and melancholy, reflecting on the happy time of Christian myth, which is now part of the past.

What can be done? How do we go on from here? The question is rendered all the more insistent by the fact that the strongest line of tension in this scene consists of the gaze George the dragon-slayer is directing at Eve-Mary – still in blue – who, apparently, is impervious to this knowledge.

From One Story to Another

In the same way as we compared the Verona Rose Garden to the garden of Frankfurt, we shall now consider another painting (Fig. 3), dating from 1483, markedly later than the first two. It is a tempera on wood measuring 83 centimeters by 138, currently hanging in Madrid's El Prado museum. It is one of a series of four paintings that decorated a Florentine room from the time of the Medicis.

Why this work? It is yet another closed garden, as defined by the wall of green in the background of the scene, and the placement of the table, which itself forms an angle. But it is impossible to mistake this garden for the conventional, familiar Christian Paradise, or the Garden of Eden, even though the garden context may be appropriate. In this case, the garden is the setting that exposes to our view the most unexpected, violent, and rawest scene that can be imagined: a hunting scene, where the quarry is a woman. Let us now dare to formulate the question: Which of the three men – George, Michael or Lawrence – has risen, mounted a horse, and is now engaged in such a chase, sword held high and cape flying in the wind?

The quarry of the hunt is a woman, a nude woman, whose thighs are being bitten by two furious dogs, one black and one white, while the hateful horseman pursuing her is about to attack her and stab her

Figure 3. Storia di Nastagio degli Onesti

with his weapon. A notion that would leave the Upper Rhinish Master aghast, and worse yet for Stefano di Verona.

Yet the scene had been laid out for a genteel celebration, the women on one side and the men on the other, all dressed in their quattrocento party finery with a priest in the middle. The story represented here is a wedding party; the painting was commissioned as a wedding gift from Lorenzo de Medici to a Florentine noble-woman.

But, lo and behold, the musical harmony of the group has been broken abruptly. The men have been frightened out of their poise, and the women are rising hurriedly, jostling one another and upsetting the table in front of them, spilling the dishes and platters of food. The musicians have dropped their instruments – flute, lute, and tambourine – or flung them away with violence. The delightful music of the psaltery in the garden in Frankfurt is now gone irretrievably.

Assuming that the savage horseman is related in some way to the George, Michael, and Lawrence of Frankfurt, where does the naked woman come from, devoid as she is of any resemblance to a Virgin in blue? And, especially, what could possibly have led to such a revolution, to such a subversion of Paradise? This painting is the product of a tradition entirely distinct from the Christian one. Its author is one Sandro Botticelli. Although well acquainted with Christian virgin mothers, he is also an admirer of the Venus and Flora of Greek and Roman tradition.

Indeed, the bride-to-be rising behind the banquet table almost could be related to the Venus painted that same year, 1483, as she gazed so insistently at a sleeping Mars. As for the nude woman being pursued, she could be a cousin of the Flora who, the preceding year, was greeting the Venus known as Anadyomène or one who, already nearly nude, was being pursued by Zephyr in the famous painting "Spring" (which dates from five years earlier). Thus the Virgin Mary of Christian myth meets a setting in which Flora and Venus gambol, a setting that suggests other attitudes toward the male-female encounter.

The frame and the organizing motive of the three works we have seen up until now is still that of the closed garden built around a woman. What, then, is the source of the brutal and bestial lust seen here, which must certainly have been a surprise to the newlyweds who received the painting as a wedding gift, and which may have surprised Sandro Botticelli himself?

Similar Context; Altogether Different Story

To understand what is happening, it is important to know that the story illustrated here is very old; in 1483, it had been circulating for at least 130 years. It is an Italian story with nothing Christian about it, and it may even have reached the ears of the Eve-Mary of Frankfurt, since she was quite cosmopolitan.

The story was set down by Boccacio in his *Decameron*. A woman tells the story to a group of young women like her in the comfortable, worldly context of their exchanges – which must have been quite free – with the men accompanying them. In this story, a noble heiress is so proud of herself and her high birth that she wishes to have absolutely nothing to do with the men around her. Naturally, one of these men falls in love with her and tries to seduce her, but she remains impervious to his advances. So disturbed is he by the beauty's disdain that he soon loses himself in melancholy wandering, and eventually commits suicide. As punishment for this act of violence against himself, he is condemned to a Hell where he must perpetuate the hunt for the woman, an infernal hunt to which the beauty – who was too smug and sufficient unto herself – must also submit, with her own body, as punishment for her haughtiness.

Such is the terrible story that had been circulating for 70 years before the "Garden of Paradise" of Frankfurt was painted. The story had been told in Italy, seemingly playfully, to incite women to be looser and more open to men. Botticelli, at the request of Lorenzo de Medici, turned the story into a visionary painting presented as a gift to young Tuscan newlyweds to decorate their bedroom.

Are we not as far as possible – practically at its antipodes – from a Christian paradise? Are we not looking at the most violent compensation that can be imagined, at the most savage southern counterpart to the Christian celebration of the ideal, eternal virginity of Mary? Especially, is this not the revelation on the brink of erupting in the garden that Dorothy, Mary, and Cecilia were keeping to themselves as they sat at "Eve-Mary's" side? Is this not the same thing that was holding Michael, George, and Lawrence immobile in melancholy perplexity? Is this not what these women and these men, who have been saints for so long, wanted to keep in suspense to preserve their paradisiacal harmony?

[At the Congress this paper included an analysis of Dürer's black "Melencolia I" (1514) and Cranach's red "Melancolia" (1532), along with a reflection about incarnation. Space limitations preclude publishing these later developments.]

Translated from French by Anita Conrad

References

Miller, M. and Taube, K. (1993). *The Gods and Symbols of Ancient Mexico and the Maya*. London: Thames and Hudson.

Picasso, P. (1985). *The Vollard Suite*. (H. Bolliger, Ed.; N. Buterman, Trans.). New York: Thames and Hudson.

White, C. (1984). *Rembrandt*. New York: Thames and Hudson.

Picture sources:

Figure 1. Oberrheinischer Meister, 1410-1420.

Figure 2. Stefano die Verona, 1410, Museo Civico, Verona.

Figure 3. Sandro Botticelli, 1483, Prado, Madrid.

Frida Kahlo: Dynamic Transformations

Jacqueline J. West
Santa Fe, New Mexico, U.S.A.
New Mexico Society of Jungian Analysts

The tremendous popularity of Frida Kahlo's paintings suggests that her testimony speaks persuasively at this time. Her work is receiving so much attention, in fact, that people speak about Kahlo mania, or about Kahlo as an icon. A careful psychological analysis of the evolution of her work reveals the depths of the dynamics which render her paintings so compelling. Guided by the Aztec goddesses of dismemberment and death, Kahlo is relentless in her confrontations with agony, in her determination to portray psychic fragmentation and lifelessness. Her confrontation with the psychotic core and her steady development of psychic structures portray a healing for wounds abundant in our world – the abandonments, the incestuous attacks, the tragic accidents – which leave so many people broken in body and soul.

My object here is to weave psychological thoughts in and out of limited glimpses into Kahlo's life and her art. I have culled the biographical information from a number of different accounts, but depending primarily on Herrera (1983) and Zamora (1990). The paintings referred to in this text are among her better known works. Reproductions of them may be found in Zamora (1990), as well as in Herrera (1983) or in Herrera (1991).

Kahlo was born in Mexico City in 1907, the third of four girls. Her father was European Jewish. Her mother, Spanish and Indian, was a pious Catholic: stern, self-involved, and distracted. Overall, she was apparently quite painfully unattuned and unavailable to Frida, so that Frida's early development was affected adversely. Their relationship was highly ambivalent and strifeful. Without good-enough mediation, archetypal affects and images remain raw; they do not get transformed into manageable experiences. In their unmedicated form, they can overwhelm inadequately developed self-structures. In particular, they can damage the development of ego. Thus, early, inadequate mothering can lead to a personality ruthlessly dominated by the archetypes; this was the case for Frida.

The rancor that characterized Frida's relationship with her mother was in marked contrast to the closeness that characterized her relationship to her father. He was a quiet, intellectual and rather solitary man. Frida was unquestionably her father's favorite daughter and she totally adored him. He nursed her when she had polio at age six and he taught her about nature, scholarship, photography and art. Being a father's daughter, as Frida was, can be a very mixed blessing. The gain is often one of resilient ambition and proficient creativity. The cost is often one of alienation from the feminine source of Self and difficulties in relationships. In effect, such a girl must struggle with a demanding father complex. Instead of his firm and boundaried love and respect such a girl wins, or is handed, her father's heart. Emotional, if not physical, incest may result. Moreover, the girl is left with the feeling that she has defeated her mother. The hoped-for resolution of the oedipal situation, leaving the parents in union and the girl in anticipation of forming her own cohesive relationship, is not forged. Instead, seeds bearing the patterns of triangulation, betrayal and infidelity are planted. These issues pervade Kahlo's relationships. Meanwhile, the pre-oedipal issues that originated in the disturbed relationship with her mother and which became manifest in her vulnerability to assaults by raw archetypal reality, emerge in her painting.

As an adolescent, Frida led a rebellious and high-spirited life, strikingly defiant of conventional morality. When she was 18, tragedy struck. She was riding home from school on a bus when it was smashed and torn into pieces by a trolley car. She was thrown from the bus, terribly battered and skewered by a broken iron handrail from the train. No one, including the doctors, thought she would live. Her spinal column was broken in three places; her collarbone and two ribs were broken; her right leg had eleven fractures; her foot was dislocated and crushed; and her pelvis was broken in three places. In Frida's retrospective account, she reported that the handrail had entered her left hip and come out through her vagina. She added, with her typically challenging humor, that in this way she lost her virginity. Virginity was not the real question; whether the wound was literally as she so dramatically describes it is also not the question. What matters is the sense of brutal penetration, and the deep association of sex with horrific pain and tragedy. She wrote from the hospital that, by night "death dances around my bed." And death continued to dance around Frida for the remainder of her life. This was the first of some 35 operations she was to undergo, most of them on her spine or on her right leg and foot, many of them involving months of confinement to bed, often in restrictive body casts.

An initial recovery from the accident was followed a year later by a relapse that left her bedridden for months once again. Bored, Kahlo began to paint. At this point her sojourn through injury, suffering and transformation began to take form.

Shortly after she began to paint, Kahlo met Diego Rivera, whom she married the next summer, when she was 22. Rivera was already a successful artist, well known for his celebration of Mexican history and Communism – and for his philanderings, bravado, and violence. Frida certainly recognized that Diego's infidelities offered an arena within which the patterns of triangulation and betrayal that were planted in her early childhood could come to full fruition. She must have seen also, and explicitly appreciated, that Diego was violent. We talk clinically about trauma victims repeating their traumatizations; Frida had an uncanny sense of that when she wryly remarked sometime later that "I suffered two grave accidents in my life. One in which a street car knocked me down. ... The other is Diego."

In 1930, in the face of ruthless political oppression directed particularly toward the Communists, Kahlo and Rivera fled to the United States. Following difficult periods in San Francisco and New York, the celebrated couple went to Detroit, where Rivera was to paint murals for Henry Ford. It was in Detroit that Frida made her first truly creative breakthroughs. True to her story, these breakthroughs were ushered in by pain and trauma. Not only had Diego, by this time, had a number of acclaimed affairs, but also Frida had a tragic miscarriage. Shortly thereafter (1932), she painted *Henry Ford Hospital*. This painting is startling – and painful to view. Nothing is spared. Frida lies naked and weeping in the blood of the miscarried fetus. Her body is twisted as if in a grimace, though her eyes maintain their characteristically direct engagement with the viewer. She is small, helplessly stranded on the bed which, at a precarious angle, floats above an impenetrable ground. Blood red ribbons travel like umbilical cords from her hand, held against her still swollen stomach, to six objects floating strangely in the space around the bed. Their largeness relative to Frida gives the impression that they are in the foreground, closer to the viewer than to

Frida, almost as if she is holding them far out in front of her, pleading with us to see them and, through them, to see and understand her reality. When Frida spoke retrospectively about the six objects, she noted that the torso in the upper left is her way of "explaining the insides of a woman."

Indeed, this entire painting may be seen as an explanation of the insides of a woman, not only the insides of her body but also the insides of her experience. The literalness of this work is misleading. Most certainly it is a portrait of a physical event, the miscarriage. However, her physical suffering is inseparable from her psychic suffering. She is heartbreakingly alone. In this awesome confrontation with maternal failure, she lies like an abandoned child, not only unable to mother, but terrifyingly unmothered. Yet she asks to be seen. The ultimate desire of the child, to be seen, is a fundamental birthright. A mother's not seeing, not truly seeing, her child is maternal failure; it is miscarriage. Frida suffered dreadfully from having not been seen by her mother, from having been "miscarried"; in this painting she leads us through that suffering. There, in the midst of utter desolation, she bares her body – and her soul – so that she and the viewer can see her reality. This is a remarkable move. In this act of portraying her wound, she is making an effort to receive exactly that which she had been denied. This painting is indeed an explanation of the insides of a woman, an explanation with a plea to be seen, a plea to be seen – and loved – as she is.

The viewer in the case of this painting is not only Frida herself and whoever is her painting's audience; it is also clearly intended to be seen, and received, by God. This intention is conveyed through Kahlo's use of the style of *retablos*, which are small Mexican religious paintings. Noting the undeniable religious reference in this work, seeing that this painting is a plea to be seen also by God, we can sense that this work is an attempt by Frida to bring the divine into her healing. This is a prayer; it is work of and for spirit as well as of and for body and soul. However, in this prayer, this meditation on misfortune, she is not appealing to the Virgin, to a saint, or to Christ. She substitutes the various symbolic objects for the usual holy figure featured in a retablo. It seems that she knows that truth, the recognition of what is, through the portrayal of her "insides," is her way to healing, her way to salvation.

The painting of her miscarriage is startling and difficult, but one of Kahlo's next works, *My Birth* (1932), is almost unbearable to see. First of all, we witness this as if we are the midwife; there is no way to escape intimate involvement, even responsibility. What we are brought into involvement with, and feel responsible for, is death. The head which emerges from the womb is adult sized; the dark, joined eyebrows reveal that this is Frida. Her head hangs upon her long, thin neck, lifelessly delivered into a pool of blood. The mother's open legs are supported by hopelessly small feet; her belly is exposed. A sheet covers her chest and head, suggesting that she, too, is dead. On the wall, almost as a substitute for the mother's head, hangs an image of the Virgin of Sorrows pierced by swords, bleeding and weeping. This is a portrait of death, pervasive and relentless death. Recalling Frida's words, that this is "how I imagine I was born," we see that her image is that she was born into death.

It seems probable that this painting contains Kahlo's very recent experiences of the death of her own undeveloped child, as well as the recent death of her mother. Nevertheless, by portraying this as her own birth and death, she ushers us into symbolic and psychological reality. From this perspective, what are we to see? The most extreme image of an inadequate mother must be the mother who is unable to give life. This is Frida's declaration that her mother was in effect without life – and unable to give her life. This is the depiction of the ultimate betrayal, the ultimate failure, by the mother. There is no ambivalence here; Kahlo's image is ruthless and absolute. This is her expression of the raw and overwhelming archetypal experience that occurs when a child does not have a good-enough mother. This is her portrait of the decapitated Aztec goddess Coatlique with her dismembered daughter Coyolhaqui. In the Hindu pantheon, this is a portrait of Kali. This depiction of the destructive side of the great mother is Kahlo's way of showing us that she lives with this archetypal reality. Actually, her statement is not only that she lives with this reality but that, psychologically, it kills her.

Kahlo did other paintings during this period which portray similar confrontations with maternal failure, similar struggles with victimization and death, and a determination to describe the excruciating dismemberments that lie at the core of character disorders. These works powerfully portray the nature of reality with which borderline people in particular wrestle, whether they have a full character disorder or a more subtle underlying borderline pattern. Caught in archetypal fields of either-or reality, kill or be killed dynamics are pervasive. Developmentally, consciousness arrives with the differentiation of the ego. A child is led toward this differentiation through interactions with others who mediate the archetypal affects and images. The result is a differentiation, within the child, between Self and ego. For the borderline person, generally there is sufficient ego structure that a life pattern is maintained. Nevertheless, the inner struggles with elusive demons and death is relentless. Release from such a living hell comes as the person develops a capacity to make such struggles visible – conscious – to self and other.

This is the dynamic we see in Kahlo's early paintings. These insistent and ruthlessly honest descriptions of archetypal, core experience may be seen as her first attempts to provide herself with empathic mirroring. If these attempts are effective, we can expect her efforts to yield further development, rather than pathological repetition. Such development could be evident in the appearance of an observing ego in her next works.

Returning to Mexico, Kahlo and Rivera fought through a stormy divorce to a remarriage. Frida painted a number of remarkable testimonies to this period, many of which emphasize her feelings of abandonment and victimization. Ultimately, she worked her way into her famous series of self-portraits. These works, painted between 1940 and 1949, reveal an insistence on self-scrutiny. They reflect a wide range of feelings which Frida tracked religiously. She did not avoid suffering, she did not turn from pain, betrayal, and death. She carefully studied them and, as well, studied herself studying them. In these images, Frida is no longer lying down, overwhelmed; she sits erect. She is no longer completely submerged in the torture and devastation of her experience; she is now also carefully observing it. Thus, she loosens the grip of victimization. Her face and posture now express a self-willed determination, even defiance, a protective regality and arrogance. It does appear that by courageously and honestly depicting her torturous reality in her earlier paintings, she has gained ego development.

The almost mask-like quality of Kahlo's portraits, which people often see as defense, denial, or rage, may be seen alternatively as an accurate rendering of the nature of consciousness, which is required to look directly into those realms which some say lie well beyond description. She is looking at raw and chaotic archetypal reality: its brutality, ruthlessness, beauty and intensity. Its smoldering, potentially explosive power is contained by the steadiness of her gaze. She steadies herself in order to look – and she steadies herself by looking. Engaged in the mirroring she so badly missed, more from the perspective of the one who looks than the perspective of the one who suffers, she strengthens the observing ego and consequently supports the differentiation of and the relationship between the archetype and ego.

These portraits proclaim that Frida can now receive her own self-assertion, her own natural exhibitionism, without being persecuted by it. Just as the sensitive mother mirrors her child's grandiosity, Frida is now in a position to mirror her own strivings to announce her presence in the world. By mirroring her own grandiosity and exhibitionism, by supporting her own healthy narcissism, she is contributing to the development of her own more resilient structures. The risk, developmentally, is that the ego may become inflated. The ego can be dominated easily by the power of archaic grandiosity, losing its newly won differentiation. It then behaves as if it holds a conscious perspective but, in truth, it is merged with the Self. It becomes characterized by rigid and defensive versions of the various aspects of narcissism, such as unmitigated grandiosity, unleashed omnipotence, and relentless exhibitionism; the person becomes impenetrable, defensively self-sufficient, and arrogant. These qualities constitute what we recognize as a narcissistic disorder.

As one studies her portraits, it appears that Kahlo emerges with resilient and positive self assertion; she maintains the tension between ego and archetype without reverting to her early position of being overwhelmed and without falling into inflation. Frida's quite steady development of healthy narcissism evidently is what makes these works so irresistible and so remarkably popular. We sense in them the courage and fortitude of someone who is in the midst of transformation.

Kahlo's newly claimed development enables her to return, in a more evolved way, to the excruciating details of agony portrayed in her earlier works. In 1944, she painted *The Broken Column*. This is clearly a portrait of psychic as well as physical reality. The perspective and the stark style create a shocking and somewhat otherworldly impression. Frida dominates the foreground; she almost walks out of the canvas. She appears both two dimensional and split wide open. The ghastly opening in her flesh feels like a chasm. Nails are pounded into her naked body. An Ionic column, cracked and broken, stands in the place of her own cracked and broken spine and reminds us of her accident when she was penetrated by the rail iron. The column looks phallic, especially in conjunction with the bold femaleness of her torso and breasts. The cruelty of the steel corset, its starkness and rigidity, are unrelenting, even sadistic. There is an undeniably powerful erotic energy present. Here we see her struggling with – and examining – that combination of violence and sexuality which has its roots, at least in part, in her brutal accident. Kahlo once said, "I am not sick. I am broken." In her insightful way, this comment insists on a psychological and structural model in contrast to a disease model. Returning to the painting, we sense that the nails driven into her body allude to Christ and Saint Sebastian; they suggest spiritual triumph. Here, as well as in the portraits, Kahlo's martyristic transcendence of pain elevates her to the level of a religious figure, an icon. But she is not looking heavenward in prayer; she is looking, once again, directly outward – and inward. While anguished in both body and psyche, she remains present as the observer. Once again, she challenges us, and herself, to look – really look – at her reality. This is a reality of terrible torture, not only endured but also well examined. Here she stands, boldly maintaining the tremendous tension between herself as observer and herself as archetypal experience.

The relationship between ego and archetype is also studied in the unforgettable 1946 image *The Little Deer*. Kahlo painted this just before leaving for New York, where she was to undergo a massive operation, fusing vertebrae and implanting a metal rod along her spine. Another life-threatening, cruel operation and a predictably agonizing many months are ample explanation for this image of attack and suffering. Yet, in typical Kahlo style, this painting also clearly addresses powerful psychological dynamics. It portrays personal, observing and conscious reality in relationship to impersonal, instinctive and unconscious reality, once again. Frida's own head tops the body of a deer pierced by nine arrows. Magical beasts, part animal, part human are not unfamiliar images in Mexico – and in Europe; nor are saints pierced by arrows. But it is part of Frida's genius that she personally interprets mythology. Her gaze does not waver as she endures the suffering. There is a sense of inevitable death; the branch is broken and the opening in the dark and threatening woods is hopelessly far away.

The operation seemed to go well. Back at home, Kahlo painted *Tree of Hope Stand Firm*, also in 1946. This image is generally seen as representing Frida the tragic victim and Frida the heroic survivor. Psychologically, we could say that it also represents the torturous reality of borderline wounds caringly companioned by – that is, mirrored by – a watchful and hopeful, narcissistically-supported personality. The deep wound along her back reminds us that the borderline person endures torturous pressure from the ravishing power of uncontained archetypal reality. The upright figure who sits erect, instead of lying, resolutely holds a reflective and hopeful perspective, treasures gained through the painstaking cultivation of healthy grandiosity and exhibitionism and the consequent development of observing ego. This tension between ego and archetype – the tension of the opposites – which Jung saw as so critical to individuation, appears in multiple ways in this work. Night and day, sun and moon, mountain and crevice, black and white, red and gold all contribute to a tension that mounts toward a crescendo. This tension suggests a growing demand in the psyche for a synthesis, for the arrival of yet another phase of development.

A complicated attempt to step into this next phase appears in a remarkable painting from 1949, *Love Embrace of the Universe*. The tension between the ego and raw, threatening archetypal realities has led to a configuration wherein the ego is embraced by both poles of the archetypal realm. There is, however, a disquieting lack of resolution, which highlights the fact that Frida's paintings are portraits of a human psyche in process, not in completion. Incomplete, or unresolved as it is, the presence and power of love in this work are undeniable, as they are throughout her work, including the most ghastly and difficult pictures of torture, the complicated portraits, the observed agony, and now this.

Over the next years, Frida's health disintegrated steadily until her death in 1954. She lived out these last years as dramatically and remarkably as all the previous ones. She continued to suffer indescribable physical pain and she continued to love and fight with Diego. She clearly never reached the place from which she could extract herself from the power of the father complex and its associated dynamics of triangulation and betrayal. During these last years, she was more often than not on such massive amounts of drugs and alcohol that she painted very little and, when she did, her work did not have the quality of her previous paintings.

Overall, from one angle, it looks as if her self-destructive patterns won out, that she never made it "through" her process. She unquestionably did remain in the grips of some very destructive patterns. But, from another angle, it is abundantly clear that she bravely, creatively, and successfully wrestled with the phase of development that required attention. Confronted with chaotic borderline processes, she brought her torture into the light and developed a sufficiently strong observing ego to mirror her own healthy narcissism and to build more resilient self structures. She very successfully, even triumphantly, wrestled with chaos. Moreover, she gave us her testimony.

References

Herrera, H. (1983). *Frida: A Biography of Frida Kahlo.* New York: Harper & Row.

Herrera, H. (1991). *Frida Kahlo: the Paintings.* New York: Harper Collins.

Zamora, M. (1990). *The Brush of Anguish.* San Francisco: Chronicle Books.

Music and Analysis

Contrapuntal Reflections

Patricia Skar
Dublin, Ireland
Association of Graduate Analytical Psychologists
(Zurich Institute)

When I decided to apply to the Jung Institute in Zurich, many who knew me were surprised. "You're a musician," they said, "why do you want to become an analyst?" Some thought that I was giving up music to become an analyst. "On the contrary," I said. "I intend to do both." At first, this meant that I continued playing the piano and violin as I always had. But during my Zurich training, I started to see that my musician side could be brought into the analytic context as well.

I asked myself, "What do the processes of music and analysis have in common?" A primary task of analysis is to further a dialogue between consciousness and the unconscious, facilitating a new wholeness within the person. Music also bridges the two; it expresses in time the deep archetypal layers of the psyche. Music opens us to undiscovered aspects of ourselves, such as when we realize that a certain piece simply is as we are at a particular moment. T.S. Eliot (1969) speaks of "music heard so deeply that it is not heard at all, but you are the music while the music lasts" (p. 190).

Jung's concept of individuation can be seen as the process of making a coherent whole out of the disparate parts of our personalities. Music is similar, in making sound coherent, ordering it in time and creating a meaningful synthesis out of its contrasting elements. One reason that music affects us so deeply is that we identify with its sound-structuring process. This in turn promotes a re-ordering process within our minds. Jung said, "Individuation does not shut one out from the world, but gathers the world to oneself" (CW8, par. 432). Playing and listening to music brings us into emotional connection with one another. Music also unites us with our culture, whose development is reflected in its music.

The Piano, Performance, and Individuation

My own psychological development has been intimately connected with my musical development. I started playing the piano at the age of three and the violin at eight, and have continued to perform both instruments. When I entered my first Jungian analysis, in San Francisco, I was teaching piano. I noticed that my students' musical processes, as well as my relationships with them, were in many respects similar to what occurs in the analytic situation. As in analysis, I saw individuals confront the persona, shadow, animus and anima, in the context of what could be called an individuation process through music.

My experiences as a piano teacher seem, in retrospect, a natural prelude to becoming an analyst. I found that many people were coming to piano lessons for extra-musical reasons; learning the piano was often a disguised attempt at working on some other aspect of themselves.

"Lynn," who came to me in her late thirties, had studied piano throughout her childhood and adolescence and was quite an advanced pianist. I noticed immediately in her playing a lack of flow and a dryness and rigidity of sound; it was obvious that playing the piano was a rather limited, somewhat painful experience for her. I asked Lynn what she would really like to do at the piano. Without a moment's hesitation, she replied that she would love to be able to improvise on an idea of her own, or play popular or jazz music that appealed to her. Lynn had never ventured into this type of playing before, and was visibly excited at the prospect of being allowed to explore these clearly shadow areas of her musical development.

We decided together to approach playing the instrument as if she were a beginner, learning to let the energy for producing the sound come from the center of her body. Then we started working without a score, learning simple harmonic patterns over which she could create her own melodies. Within a few weeks she was coming to her lessons nearly ecstatic, saying that she had never dreamed this was possible: playing without being "bound to the notes" and actually creating music on her own. But Lynn soon realized that it would be a long process to build the repertoire of musical patterns she needed to give free reign to her ideas, and she became somewhat discouraged.

It was clear that she needed something more concrete to tackle in her practice. As a bridge between her former and new ways of playing, I suggested some transcribed jazz tunes. One that she particularly liked was Vince Guaraldi's "Cast Your Fate to the Wind." The title itself gives a good indication of the character of this piece, which was immensely freeing for Lynn. The expansive quality of the melody seemed to create "space" for her, and she began to move in a much rounder, more feminine way as she played. A syncopated, repetitive rhythmic pattern in the left hand had the effect of propelling her forward rather than keeping her "stuck" on the beat, a former tendency in her playing. This piece also gave Lynn the opportunity to confront a particularly difficult rhythmic problem for her, a triplet (three-note) figure in the right-hand melody against a four-beat division in the left-hand part.

This "three-against-four" rhythmic pattern is difficult for everyone to master technically at first. It somehow feels like the struggle between the masculine and the feminine. In this piece, the triplet figure has a round, lyrical feel which propels one forward, while the quadruple grouping has a more square solidarity. When the two rhythms are combined, three-against-four produces a tension of opposites that heightens the expression of the musical theme.

Since Lynn's dominant function was thinking, she diligently worked out mathematically where the notes should fall. She could play the measure slowly by itself, but could not fit it into the context of the surrounding music without the rhythm falling apart. Her intellectual approach, which had the effect of isolating this bar of music from its context, had to be sacrificed in order to bring the measure back into a feeling mode with the rest of the music around it. We did this by playing each hand separately, connecting the problem measure with the music around it, and feeling the flow of each part. Gradually she was able to put hands together and link up this problem section with the rest of the piece. It was a joy to see the abandon which Lynn developed as she "cast her fate to the wind" while playing this tune. She continued to learn other blues and jazz transcriptions, happily exploring sides of herself through the music that were quite remote from her conscious personality.

The psychological process she experienced through her piano lessons was in many ways similar to what occurs in analysis. First, there was an evaluation of her history at the piano, which had formed the "personality" of her playing. We could say that she had a faulty relationship with the instrument: it was necessary to go back to the beginning and "start over," finding a new way to approach the piano in relationship with another person. In analysis, the same process would involve forming a new, more positive relationship with the analyst than had been experienced with parental figures. With Lynn, the contrast of the freedom of the new way with the rigidity of the old patterns initially produced an inflation. This soon disappeared as Lynn realized the amount of hard work necessary to achieve her goals. Likewise in analysis, the analysand's positive or idealizing transference will often produce a "honeymoon" effect. But, as the analyst inevitably fails to fulfill all expectations, more realism begins to emerge in the analysand.

Through Lynn's struggle with the rhythmic problems in "Cast Your Fate to the Wind," we were able to see that her dominant thinking needed to make room for her inferior feeling, which in turn allowed the synthesis between three and four in the music to take place. Coming to terms with one's typology and how it affects the way life problems are approached is certainly an important aspect of analysis.

After establishing that her lessons with me were a safe container, Lynn worked through persona issues (performance fears), identified and integrated elements of her shadow (expressed through the jazz tunes), and confronted aspects of the negative animus. He appeared in the form of the critical inner judge, who always entered the scene when she was not making "good enough" progress. By facing these repressed aspects of herself, she became more "whole" musically and as a person. She was also able to free blocked areas of emotional expression in her body and gain access to new states of feeling that had previously existed only in the unconscious. And, as in analysis, a dialogue opened between the unconscious and conscious parts of her psyche, though here it occurred in the context of our musical relationship.

Jung and Music

As I began to think about how music creates a link between consciousness and the unconscious, I wondered what Jung had to say about music. I discovered, to my dismay, only a handful of references to music in the Collected Works. It was in his letters that I found Jung's clearest statement on music. He had received a request in 1950 from Serge Moreux, Director of *Polyphonie, Revue Musicale* (Paris) to write an article on "the role of music in the collective unconscious." He declined on the grounds of "age and health," but gave these few important words in reply:

Music certainly has to do with the collective unconscious – as the drama does, too. ... Music expresses ... the movement of the feelings (or emotional values) that cling to the unconscious processes. The nature of what happens in the collective unconscious is archetypal, and archetypes always have a numinous quality that expresses itself in emotional distress. Music expresses in sounds what fantasies and visions express in visual images. I am not a musician and would not be able to develop these ideas for you in detail. I can only draw your attention to the fact that music represents the movement, development, and transformation of the motifs of the collective unconscious. In Wagner this is very clear and also in Beethoven, but one finds it equally in Bach's "Kunst der Fuge" ["The Art of Fugue"]. The circular character of the unconscious processes is expressed in the musical form; as for example in the sonata's four movements, or the perfect circular arrangement of the "Kunst der Fuge." (Let-I, p. 542)

Jung had referred to "The Art of Fugue" before (CW14, par. 754) in connection with the importance of giving shape to the images that emerge from the unconscious. Jung suggested that a musical configuration of these images might also be possible, and offered Bach's "The Art of Fugue" as an example. I was reminded of my own impetus to learn this work, which came in the form of a dream where I saw myself playing it on the piano. At the time my energy was somewhat unfocused; I had several different part-time occupations. The day after the dream I bought the score to "The Art of Fugue" and was amazed at my strong attraction to the first of the 14 fugues; it became a sort of daily meditation for me. The piece seemed to have an amazing ability to organize my energies. I did not question this then, but simply accepted that the form of the music and my immersion in it were responsible. Jung must have sensed the special quality of this piece, to have named it twice in his reference to the archetypal quality of music. By giving me a dream where I was playing "The Art of Fugue," my unconscious was compensating for the lack of focus and order in my outer life. I was doubly lucky that I could buy the score and start learning the piece the next day!

When Jung mentioned the circular arrangement of "The Art of Fugue," he was undoubtedly referring to the process of inversion which characterizes the development of the fugue theme throughout the 14 fugues, which are all in the key of d minor. Strikingly, the theme itself, when paired with its inversion, produces visual circles if we line up, for example, the first five bars of Contrapunctus 1 and 4.

Contrapunctus 1 [BWV 1080,1]

Contrapunctus 4 [BWV 1080,4]

Repeated throughout "The Art of Fugue," this circular pattern is much like the process of individuation, which Jung described as the "circumambulation of the Self." He conceptualized the role of the unconscious as a counterpole to consciousness. Out of the collision of these two forces, the unconscious tends to create a third possibility. We could say that the entire 14 fugues of "The Art of Fugue" work on uniting the opposites inherent in the first fugal theme. This is a kind of musical analogue to the psychological process of individuation.

Individuation entails facing our typology and coming to terms with the inferior function, which often leads to the unconscious. The concert pianist and music therapist Margaret Tilly (1947) began analyzing music in terms of Jung's psychological types in the 1940s. She observed that people were more responsive to music that matches their particular masculine or feminine orientation and their typology. Tilly established rapport with her clients through improvising at the piano, intuitively grasping which type of music reflected the psychological make-up or psychic state of the person when therapy began. Once rapport was established, she then introduced music that would stimulate the inferior function, put moods in the context of a greater wholeness, or bring a new perspective on a situation by first experiencing it through music.

Tilly was an excellent pianist and could play the whole range of classical literature as well as folk music, popular music, and spontaneously improvised music. In 1956, prior to a trip to Switzerland, Tilly sent some of her case histories to Jung. He was so impressed with them that he invited her to his home to discuss her work. This may have been the first time Jung had encountered a performing musician who could relate music consciously to psychological processes. In fact, he told Tilly (1977) that music exhausted and irritated him since it "is dealing with such deep archetypal material and those who play don't realize this" (p. 274). Jung went on to say that he had always thought music therapy was sentimental and superficial, but that her papers were "entirely different." He asked Tilly to treat him as if he were one of her own patients and, as she alternately played and related case histories, Jung was more and more deeply moved. He finally said:

> *This opens up whole new avenues of research I'd never even dreamed of. Because of what you've shown me this afternoon – not just what you've said, but what I have actually felt and experienced – I feel that from now on music should be an essential part of every analysis. This reaches the deep archetypal material that we can only sometimes reach in our analytical work with patients. This is most remarkable.* (p. 275)

Music Therapy and Analysis

Nearly 40 years later, we have not come much closer to making music "an essential part of every analysis," as Jung suggested. Although one occasionally finds articles in analytic journals concerning music, these rarely contain any practical suggestions for using music in analysis. Why is this? With the importance of drawing, painting and sandplay in the mainstream of Jungian analysis, it seems odd that there is not an equal emphasis and ongoing research in the use of music.

One reason for this could be a lack of pioneers in the field – people who have had training both in music and analytical psychology – and who can envision, as Jung did when he met Margaret Tilly – the enormous potential for music in analysis. To explore this question further, I decided to look outside analytic circles and into the world of music therapy.

Music therapy as a profession is only a recent and specialized form of the continuing 30 000-year-old shamanic traditions of music and healing still being practiced throughout the world. Shamans use hypnotically repetitive rhythmic music to communicate with and dominate the spirit of the illness and also to enter an altered state of consciousness. The effect of this music is viewed today as a sedation of the left hemisphere of the brain (concerned mainly with language and sequential reasoning), activating the functions of the right hemisphere (spatial abilities, emotions, intuition and sense of rhythm). Brain scans have demonstrated that discordant sounds stimulate the left hemisphere, while concordant sounds activate the right hemisphere. Music with verbal content or which activates conceptual thinking creates a broader response across the two hemispheres. Since most tonal music would tend to activate the right hemisphere of the brain, we can easily see its potential for connecting us to emotion and balancing a state of consciousness dominated by left-brain, conceptual thinking (Robertson, 1993, pp. 23-25).

Researchers are also exploring a phenomenon called "sonic entrainment." Occurring throughout nature, entrainment is a locking in step of similar frequencies. Internally, we are constantly locking in rhythm with ourselves; our heart rate, respiration and brain waves all entrain to one other. Entrainment also happens when two people are having a good conversation; their brain waves oscillate synchronously. Frequencies and rhythms are now being used for relaxation, learning, stress reduction and treatment of disease. Most of this work is directed at entraining the heartbeat with an external rhythm, but there is also much research going on using specific frequencies to entrain the brain, mostly extremely low frequencies to induce the production of alpha and theta waves in the cerebral cortex. Alpha waves (from 7 to 13 hertz) are often associated with meditiational states, and theta waves (from 3 to 7 hertz) are found in states of high creativity and trance. Since the frequency of the electromagnetic field around the earth (7.83 cycles per second) is in the alpha wave spectrum of the human brain, some speculate that, when our brains vibrate at these frequencies, they lock in and entrain with the energies of the earth! (See Goldman, 1992).

The idea of resonating with the earth through sound is nothing new. According to tradition, the sixth century Greek mystic-mathematician-astronomer-musician Pythagoras discovered the "harmonic series," which is present behind every tone we hear and is the most important factor behind all musical practice and development. Pythagoras considered the whole-number ratios produced by the harmonic series to be archetypes of form, demonstrating harmony and balance that can be observed throughout the universe. He equated harmony of the universe with harmony of the soul or "inner universe" and saw music as a bridge between the two.

From the ancient Greeks to the twentieth century may seem like a huge leap in time, but the recently renewed interest in the science of music and healing is bringing us back to the concepts of Pythagoras. Although music has been used in healing since the earliest times, music therapy became a distinct modern profession in America only about 50 years ago. Since then there has been a remarkable development of the concepts and practice of music therapy, along with an increased interest in incorporating music in various forms of psychotherapy.

There are two obvious possibilities for using music in the psychotherapeutic context: listening to music or improvising music. A widely-used music therapy technique that employs music listening is known as "Guided Affective Imagery with Music" (GIM). This was developed by Helen Bonny who, in 1973, founded the Institute for Consciousness and Music in Baltimore, Maryland. In GIM, one listens to music in a relaxed state for the purpose of allowing imagery, symbols and feelings to arise and then be used for self-understanding. This is very close to Jung's idea of active imagination (see CW 8, par. 400), so a potential model for therapeutic music-listening in analysis could be called "active imagination through music." In both active imagination and GIM, the transcendent function is at work, bridging the gulf between consciousness and the unconscious. In active imagination through music, the music could be chosen by either the analyst or analysand to facilitate the investigation of a mood, picture, event, or dream. There might be a specific piece of music which has appeared in a dream or has particular associations for the client.

In analysis, sharing the experience of listening to music could be a catalyst toward deeper insight or aid in the release of repressed material. But another possibility may have a much greater potential for effectiveness within analysis: improvisational music therapy with instruments. In the course of researching different forms of music therapy, I discovered Mary Priestley's (1975) work. I immediately recognized that her method was highly relevant to Jungian analysis. "Analytical Music Therapy," conceived and developed by Priestley, Peter Wright and Marjorie Wardle in England in the early 1970s, employs words and symbolic music improvisations to explore the inner life of the client. It involves the use of simple tuned and untuned percussion instruments, such as drums, cymbals, xylophones, tambourines, and an unlimited variety of South American and African percussion instruments. Delicate instruments that have to be tuned, including most string instruments, are generally not suitable for analytical music therapy.

I trained with Priestley in individual music therapy sessions and gradually accumulated an array of simple percussion instruments, which I later brought into my consulting room. When clients asked about the instruments, I replied that they were there for us to use, like the drawing materials I always kept ready. Most clients seemed quite intimidated at first by the idea of playing any of the instruments, saying things like, "I was never any good at music," or "I wouldn't know how to play them correctly." Some (including a few who knew about my musical background) were afraid that I would be especially sensitive to their "mistakes." I explained that the nature of these instruments ruled out the possibility of "mistakes" and, as in spontaneous drawing, there was no critical standard by which their sounds could be judged.

Occasionally a spontaneous improvisation came out of the initial exploration of the instruments; other times a client would simply express an attraction for several specific instruments and perhaps have an interesting association to the sound. For example, one instrument, the "Caterpillar" (made of slats of hardwood attached to a flexible backing, and sounding like a falling set of dominoes when flicked), led a client to associate to tension in his spine. As another client played the small finger cymbals, she was reminded of a delicately embroidered pillowcase given to her by her grandmother.

When instruments are explored in the analytic space, the idea of play is introduced. Of course, it is just this thought of "playing" that may be intimidating to a client. In this context, a particular instrument or sound may lead back to an earlier developmental period. Priestley (1994) stresses that musical improvisation can reflect the developmental process. She even relates certain ways of playing music to Freud's psychosexual stages (pp. 157-61). In 1957 Heinz Kohut also compared the effects of music to the developmental stages. He postulated that music may offer a "subtle transition to preverbal modes of psychological functioning" (1978, p. 253). In addition, Kohut compared the concepts of primary and secondary process to the organizational features in music. For example, a simple rhythm (primary process) is often concealed under a sophisticated tune or variations of a theme (secondary process).

Apart from reflecting developmental stages and fixations, one of the most important things music improvisation can facilitate is the acting out of emotions. Music can release energy bound up in repressed memories, images, destructive patterns or physical symptoms. Some of Priestley's techniques, modeled on the work of

Melanie Klein, promote this expression of feelings. For example, in the "holding" technique, the client is allowed full self-expression through sound while being held symbolically by the musical matrix created by the therapist. Priestley normally plays the piano, an instrument ideally suited for "holding" because of its wide frequency and harmonic range. Also adapted from Klein, the "splitting" technique is used when a client has made a projection on another person and needs to reconnect to the emotion invested in that person. One may improvise as oneself first and then switch to becoming the other person, consciously owning the feelings that have been projected. Alternatively, the therapist can play the part of the other person, and a duet of the opposing forces takes place through the music.

I once worked with 60-year-old "Ann", who was carrying immense anger toward her ex-husband. She felt that he had never been able to see or hear her. When she tried to express feelings to him, he shut her out. I asked Ann if she could imagine what these interchanges would be like, expressed in sound. In this session, she had already been playing the deckadrum, a tongue/slit drum with 10 different pitches. Ann said, "My husband would be like this –" (playing very loud regular beats) – "completely rigid and unmoving!" I asked, "And how would you be?" She then played wildly, with varied rhythms and dynamics, all over the deckadrum. I suggested that I play the husband and she play herself. I chose a small but loud snare drum and beat regularly on it with wooden beaters. Ann's drumming alternated between a rather seductive soft insistence and frenetic pounding, as I continued my totally unresponsive, monotonous drumming. But as our eyes met, I felt that she knew I now understood what it had been like for her. Through the music, I was also connected to my own frustration in trying to penetrate this client's defenses. At the end of the session, Ann said, "It was like dancing – you followed me! I feel you really heard and understood me. Maybe something is moving now!"

In addition to improvisation, free or on personal themes, analytical music therapists use imagery techniques similar to Jung's active imagination. One can improvise on any theme that seems relevant to the feelings – physical or emotional – brought into the session. For example, in a training session with Priestley, my right shoulder and arm were hurting. She suggested an improvisation titled "Shoulder and Arm," which helped me to focus on the feelings inherent in that symptom.

What effects do the specific aspects of music have on us? Rhythm, the feeling of movement in time, is perhaps the most important element in music, since it is the driving and ordering factor behind the sounds. It has a stimulating or depressing effect on the rhythmic systems of the body (blood circulation, breathing, and heart rate). Rhythmic expression can reflect the dynamics of early and current relationships, and show the state of what Priestley calls "inner rhythm." For example, on her first day of trying my instruments, a client – who suffered from a lack of order and control in her life – played xylophones and drums without any discernible rhythm. At one point, I tried to play with her – a most frustrating experience because of the erratic nature of her sound patterns. This musical experience heightened my awareness of countertransference feelings, which had often made me want to impose rhythm and order onto her mostly disordered monologues.

The specific element most people associate with music is melody. It is probably first experienced as the rise and fall of the mother's voice. Tonal relationships in a melody provide possibilities for tension and relief: factors such as the frequency of and distance between consonant and dissonant intervals, the size and direction of the intervals, the fulfillment of expectations based on past associations, and manners of resolution; all appear to have an effect on the physical body of the performer or listener. But melody also appeals to the intellect; we must follow the notes of the melodic pattern if it is to make sense to us. This necessity is relevant for music therapy; if a client becomes overly emotional in a free improvisation, the therapist may be able to bring up the client's thinking function by playing something melodic.

Harmony provides the ground for melody; it is the underlying chord structure based on the key or scale of the music. Harmony can produce the physical sensations of tension and relief. To most people, consonant harmony feels agreeable and dissonant harmony disagreeable; tension is produced either by delaying the consonant or using the dissonant harmony. In music therapy, the skillful use of harmony can encourage the exploration of emotional areas. Using major chords tends to strengthen and soothe, while minor chords can mirror sorrow and yearning. An atonal tone cluster could act as a catalyst toward the expression of unconscious, disturbing feelings. (See Priestley, 1975, pp. 213-14.)

Another aspect of sound is timbre or tone quality. This results from a blend of the complex wave motion of the fundamental frequency plus its harmonics, and enables us to distinguish between different instruments that are sounding the same pitch. The timbre changes for each instrument as it moves from note to note, from low to high and from soft to loud; there is an infinite number of possible variations in timbre. The greater the number of harmonics and the stronger they are, the more rich, brilliant, cutting or strident the tone quality of a sound becomes. The timbre of an instrument often will provoke an association for the client. For example, as one of my clients played a range of tuned and untuned percussion instruments, she remarked that certain pitches or sounds were "dead sounds." This she correlated with "dead feelings inside," which she had had difficulty expressing.

All the elements of music can express and work successfully on aspects of the transference between analyst and client. Having improvised music most of my life, I initially found it difficult to unite my improviser-self with my analyst-self. Putting these two sides together meant holding two types of awareness: an inner, detached observer and an open receiver of the client's sound patterns. While improvising music, a pathway to the unconscious opens, making it more difficult to be protected and objective. Maintaining the analytic stance while improvising music means that one must be on the alert for such responses as a musical syntonic-countertransference reaction. But when the split-off parts of the client can be contained in the analyst's musical response, the door is open to reintegration and transformation.

Felix Mendelssohn wrote, "The word remains ambiguous; but in music we would understand one another rightly" (Jacob, 1963, p. 186). Sometimes one hears a thought or emotion that has never been accessible through words but is expressed in a client's music. One of my clients habitually raged at others' lack of caring and sensitivity to her needs. She seemed to have no access to sensitive mothering in herself, but as she played my delicate wind chimes, she immediately connected to a restful, quiet place, which in turn led her to a desire to paint and express her feelings. For a timid man, who constantly made excuses for a mother with whom he was actually furious, music became a vehicle for angry, strong feelings. When invited to express his feelings about his mother, he beat on the drum loudly for over 15 minutes. Afterward, he seemed visibly relieved and amazed at the strength of the emotion he had opened through his drumming. It then became easier for him to talk about his negative feelings toward his mother. The anonymity of the sound expression, which Priestley (1975) calls the "guilt-free medium of non-verbal sound" (p. 19), allowed those previously taboo angry feelings to emerge.

Concluding Remarks

Has music a place within analysis? We have seen how improvising music can activate the conscious and unconscious parts of the psyche, provide a guiltless vehicle for the expression of feelings and form a bridge of nonverbal understanding. For those who see the positive potential for music's use in analysis, the next question is: Would it be possible to include instruction in music therapy techniques within an analytic training program? Priestley recommended that analysts desiring training have individual training sessions twice weekly for six weeks, or three sessions a week for a month. A trained music therapist could also give analysts-in-training such a series of sessions, either individually or in a seminar. The reality of the music therapy encounter could then be experienced and evaluated by those interested in the possibility of using music in conjunction with their future analytic work.

Whether music is used actively in analysis or not, it remains an essential element in the consciousness and unconscious of us all. Music can lead us beyond the personal dimension into those deep archetypal structures which share a "common rhythm" with the order of the universe. Listening to and playing music help us rediscover an inner place of "unitary reality," where we are rooted in the cosmos and also in our individual selves. This is similar to Neumann's (1990) description of the awareness of the ego-Self axis: the "... experience of the harmony of the individual ego with the totality of its nature, with its constitutional make-up ..." (p. 43).

Analysis creates a facilitating environment for the process of individuation. I believe that music, with its powerful potential for connecting us to the deep layers of the psyche, could enhance this environment for the individuation process. Music is the only one of the arts that exists experientially in time. It can express directly the rhythmic and cyclic processes that make up our lives. I conclude with the words of pianist and conductor Daniel Barenboim (1991), who comes very close to my own feelings when he says: "... there is no better escape from life than through music, and yet there is no better way to understand life than through music" (p. 160).

References

Barenboim, D. (1991), *A Life in Music*. London: Weidenfeld & Nicolson.

Eliot, T. S. (1969). Four quartets. In *The Complete Poems and Plays of T. S. Eliot*. London: Faber & Faber.

Goldman, J. (1992). Sonic Entrainment. In R. Spintge and R. Droh (Eds.), *MusicMedicine*. St. Louis: MMB Music, 194-208.

Jacob, H. E. (1963). *Felix Mendelssohn and His Times* (Richard & Clara Winston, trans.). London: Barrie & Rockliff.

Kohut, H. (1978). Observations on the Psychological Functions of Music. In *The Search for the Self* (Vol. I). New York: International Universities Press, 233-53.

Neumann, E. (1973, 1990). *The Child* (R. Manheim, trans.) Boston: Shambhala.

Priestley, M. (1975). *Music Therapy in Action*. London: Constable.

Priestley, M. (1994). *Essays in Analytical Music Therapy*. Phoenixville, PA: Barcelona Publishers.

Robertson, P. (1993). The Great Divide. *BBC Music Magazine*, May, 23-25.

Tilly, M. (1947). The psychoanalytical approach to the masculine and feminine principles in music. *The American Journal of Psychiatry 103-4*, 477-483.

Tilly, M. (1977). The therapy of music. In W. McGuire & R. Hull (Eds.), *C.G. Jung Speaking*. Princeton, NJ: Princeton University Press, 273-75.

Auditory Imagery: The Acoustic Vessel*

Mary Lynn Kittelson
St. Paul, Minnesota, U.S.A.
Association of Graduate Analytical Psychologists
(Zurich Institute)

We seem to think that the ear is dispensable. We concentrate overwhelmingly on what is visual. Everything that we cultivate or build impresses through the eyes, by size and colour and shape. We ignore the miracle of the ear, which conveys images that are far deeper, more subtle and more penetrating than the eye. Light bounces off surfaces and conveys its message through a greater abstraction than sound. Sound goes directly into our bodies. What the aural can do to the inside of our brain, to the "within" of our lives, nothing else can do.

Yehudi Menuhin

The "eyes" have it! In doing dream and image work, we operate predominantly in the visual mode. Of all the senses, seeing is equated with understanding. "I see," we say. We image consciousness as light, not sound.

Yet analysis is a listening art. Sound, I believe, is the most important way that energy is exchanged in the analytic vessel. It is fitting, as well as fascinating, to be more ear-minded. We have a long way to go, in noticing that sound, resonance and silence are images.

Jung was apparently a highly visual person. But he did mention that images, the language of the psyche, are not only visual, but "feeling" and "acoustic," and that some people are "audio-verbal." He mentioned working with the hands, bodily movement and automatic writing as possibilities. He gave considerable weight to Klang (sound similarity) as a complex indicator; it accounts for "the

* Another version of this article appeared as "The Acoustic Vessel" in Murray Stein (Ed.), *The Interactive Field in Analysis* (Vol. 1). Wilmette, IL: Chiron, 1995.

largest number of indirect associations ... by far" (CW2, par. 22). As his ideas developed, Jung showed himself to be – centrally – a listener to the inner voice. He even advocated talking back, or active imagination. But attention to actual sounds, inside or out, is rare.

Really interesting are the dramatic auditory phenomena in Jung's autobiography: the knife handle, dining room table, and sideboard, all cracking dramatically at meaningful moments. Jung (MDR) relates that these auditory moments influenced him to study psychology, and that a later such moment emphasized his differences with Freud, especially about parapsychology. Auditory images, if anything, came to get Jung! They were fateful in his life, but their power remained unconscious.

Sound: Facts and Images

Sound is moving in every way. It occurs in a flow. And it moves what it contacts. Hearing literally makes us vibrate. It e-vokes – calls out – by its very essence.

"The world is more like music than like matter," says physicist Donald Hatch Andrews. Modern physics describes matter and energy as being in a state of constant, reciprocal vibration; they are inseparable. As Jung emphasized, objectivity (separation) is no longer scientifically accurate. Visual reality looks more distinct, sharp-lined, distanced. However, auditory reality is more vibratory, a flowing experience between inner and outer. The unconscious is associative, often diffuse, in reciprocal relationship with its surroundings. In the dark, in the dim or semi-conscious is exactly when we cannot see. Instead, it is where we hear well. Sound evokes a participatory style of consciousness.

Sadly, we have lost our healing connection with sound. Our auditory world is full of insensitivity and ugliness, chattering and noise pollution. Studies show that noise makes people miss more social cues and decreases the likelihood that they will help each other. It has been linked with poor school performance, ulcers, heart attacks, strokes, high blood pressure, psychoses and neuroses.

Nevertheless "sound" has a deep connection with healing. In English, the adjective "sound" means healthy, trustworthy. Sound is linked with both creation and redemption. In many mythologies – for example, Hindu and Judeo-Christian, as well as in Japan and Indonesia – sound is associated with creation and with the bridge between humans and the divine. (See Campbell, 1989.) Indeed, it is the religious realm that has maintained the ear center, with singing, chanting, playing instruments, gongs, muzzah cries, hymns, psalms, and the poetry of liturgies. God, we say, has a voice, and we listen for our own, still, small voices inside.

In the Judeo-Christian creation story, in the initial dark formlessness, a spirit, an energy moves. It becomes creative only when God speaks, when it is sounded vocally: "Let there be light" (Genesis 1:3). Indeed, sound brings light into being. This idea is echoed in the New Testament (John 1:1): "In the beginning was the Word." Oddly enough, science's theory of creation is similar. Here the sound is magnificent in its secular magnitude: the Big Bang. Indeed, physical evidence supports this idea. Jenny (1986) subjected liquids, powders and pastes, with little form, to different kinds of long tones. They took on the same exquisite patterns that are found in nature. His film looks like a miniature creation story. The longer the sound, the more differentiated these patterns became.

Shepard (1978) theorizes that the switch to the dominance of hearing may account for the development of imagination. At a certain time in evolution, mammals shifted from daytime functioning to nighttime. Dependence on vision shifted to dependence on hearing and smell. The nature of hearing is that stimuli are successive, needing pattern and ordering in time. Information became integrated cortically, not sensorially – the first step in human-like intelligence. By the time flora had spread, and thus the possibility of living in trees, in daylight, animals had developed deep-brain integrating and storing ability. "Holding of images would in time become the imagination" (pp. 16-17).

What happens when we hear? The human auditory process consists of two kinds of hearing. Conductive hearing is relatively simple. Sound energy bombards the whole of the body, skin, tissue, and especially the bones. With conductive hearing, you cannot stop sound; you can only increase or decrease it, holding the ears or closing the door. Selective or sensory-neural hearing is more complicated and more conscious, involving the outer, middle and inner ears. Sound waves travel to us, into the outer ears, which are cupped forward, and guide sound into the ear canal to the eardrum. Sound has entered flesh, incarnated, along the path of mattering. The eardrum further amplifies and channels the sound into the middle ear, where three tiny bones – the hammer, anvil and stirrup – further amplify it.

A membrane called the "oval window" provides the transition from the bone chain to the inner ear. The second transformation is from mechanical to hydraulic pressure waves, into a watery, inner world. In the inner ear, pressure waves press into the cochlea, also called the labyrinth. It is a closed, fluid-filled tube, curled up like a snail. Here, sounds are analyzed, including overtones. They create electro-chemical changes that send messages to the brain. This is the third transformation, from watery to electrical energy. (Also present in the inner ear are the semi-circular canals, the organ of balance and orientation in space.)

It is a lively, sparked path to the brain, where 1000 messages per second are interpreted. In electro-chemical energy, matter and energy most clearly – and mysteriously – meet. All this is happening, as we hear and listen within the analytic vessel.

The Acoustic Vessel

How does sound function in the acoustic analytic vessel? Auditory energy – sounds, resonance and silence – create both shape and revelation.

Sound as Shape

In its function of creating shape, sound usually begins the analytic process. The opening tones, the initial contact, usually occur by telephone, an unusually clear acoustic experience. Consciously honored or not, it is the first and freshest energy. It is a creative moment, from silence to mechanical "count-down" to electronic vocal connection. For the therapist, picking up the receiver, there is a sudden unknown voice sounding – sounding her* out – from the first moment onward. This "duet" is the real beginning of the work. Auditory perceptions and fantasies begin right here. Ear consciousness can catch these, note them. And what will follow? A few desultory phrases? A song in blues style? Jazz improvisation? An opera? Will it be solo, duet, quartet, or an entire symphony?

---

* For the sake of clarity, I use "she" to refer to the analyst and "he" to refer to the client.

During one such initial phone call, I was asking for an appointment with an analyst unknown to me. Amidst my anxious and hesitant tones and rhythms the analyst, to my ear, suddenly sang out: *"Lét's / Tăke ă chánce!"* This sentence rang out like the opening strains of a waltz. It sounded firm – engaging, and somehow old-fashioned. This proved to be an apt auditory image in retrospect, for the work that I did with this analyst did indeed begin in a whirl in which – to my amazement – he led with firmly structuring steps. My acoustic fantasy had been borne out.

A second way that sound creates shape is in the ritual shape of the hour, especially the entry and closure. This shaping might begin with "pre-sounds," such as a drawer opening, some pages shuffled, a buzz or bell at the door. Entry sounds move the partners into the work, footfalls (often distinctive) and verbal greetings, the "hellos" and name-sayings, with their distinctive melodies and rhythms. These ritual phrases shape the hour and carry it forward. In settling in, a coat hanger may rattle, a purse jingle; a zipper unzip, a Velcro strip loudly rip or, softer, a paper rustle (the first signal of a written dream offering?).

Often there are sounds of throat-clearing, breathing and blowing, a clearing of the spirit-pathways. The first stage in the hour is rather like musicians in their places before a concert, warming their instruments with their breath, re-trying their range, testing the vibration in the air, and the stretch between high and low. The partners are re-establishing a meaningful consonance and dissonance, so that they can be in concert once again. We remember. We re-create. We re-sound.

Toward the end, too, of any meaningful coming together, even in the briefest melody or social encounter, there is a striving for some resolution. A *decrescendo* – lessening of intensity, is called for, out of the space of heavy engagement. Like a musical coda, primary themes are briefly repeated at the end, in a faster, brighter style. This lighter coda can help bridge this deeper energy, to the pop-song energy of the sidewalk or roadway.

One analysand, in her first try at a women's "self-experience" group, showed me what she had not dared to do: an exercise, entailing jumping, fists clenched, shouting "ICH!" (I) at each landing. Now, in showing me, she jumped and gestured and shouted "ICH! ICH!" As the session progressed, we talked about other topics, circling this theme of self-affirmation. As she left, we suddenly found ourselves in unison, each making ich-like sounds, making a last round, a spontaneous final coda, on this theme. Only then did we say our usual good-byes. Such closings have the energy of an "amen," as a re-affirmation is re-sounded. Analyst and analysand are making a circle of knowing and safety around the awareness gained in that hour.

Only with the closing tones can the containing vessel be left. The ritual phrases of "Good-bye" and "See you next week" are sounded, as the session auditorily unwinds itself. The same footfalls, the same rustling of shoes and door and latches sound. Acoustically, the hour has made another full circle.

A third category involving acoustic shape is rhythmic patterning. Many clients have typical rhythms and climax points. The moment of highest intensity tends to occur at approximately the same moment, for example, ten minutes before the end of the session. Just as in an effective theatrical or musical piece, or in a good telling of a joke, a "sound structure" is laid to take the load of the "big moment." Only then can the top of the *crescendo*, the climax, be accomplished. Where this most vibrant moment is placed in the hour is important to the experience of its impact. When analysts describe their "sense" of the importance of something, they often are influenced by this sense of the analysand's rhythmic pattern.

Patterns, I suppose, are most necessary when orientation is difficult. In working with one analysand, I often became lost in a fog. Her communication seemed disconnected and convoluted – with long, vague silences. Eye contact was often minimal. Through the smoke-screen of her diffuseness, it provided a welcome orientation to focus on her rhythmic pattern. It was as rigid and fixed as the meter of a metronome. My immediate thought was how strongly it compensated her diffuseness.

As more intense contact ensued, I was clearly not to interrupt with any question or comment. Then, toward the end, this "main business" would come back with a shock, often after a pointed glance at the clock. This "climax point" in the hour was about three minutes from the end. BAM! She would strike and then retreat. She would drop an emotional "bomb," an extremely distressing moment or memory, and then get up to leave. Every hour, she initiated cutting off her session on the stroke, like an executioner, leaving herself – and often me as well – in an out-spilling turmoil. Her hours were a rigid, chronically sabotaged enactment.

Becoming conscious of this rhythm, this machinelike "un-success," brought more clarity to my often confused reactions. I felt, in working with her, that I was subjected to this pattern. Nothing I did, or did not do, could change it. Over the months, I realized that it was exactly this rigid pattern which was itself the defining experience. We – together – had to experience, again and again, this encasement in rigidity, this vague but heavy impossibility, which must have been her customary experience of human contact. As analyst, I had to try to "catch" and hold what she would drop. And I had to be made to fail, again and again. After about 20 months of struggle, the 57-minute climax all but disappeared. As her trust grew, her use of climax and rhythm not only allowed, but sometimes sought or even demanded, that she be heard and resonated to – within the hour. Being alive to the way that these patterns echoed, inside and outside the hour, offered image and helped me to trust, as the process unfolded.

Sound as Revelation

Of many possibilities of sound as revelation, I am mentioning three. One is sound synchronicity. It usually occurs in the form of unexpected sounds during the hour, such as happenings in the building, sounds of traffic, sirens, animals and insects, weather, things falling or breaking and some involuntary body sounds. It seems easy, and even "sensible," to ignore many such sounds, especially when they are repetitious or interruptive. However, Jung once wrote (in fact, to a fellow-sufferer of noises in the ear in old age): "You are quite right to remember the storm that interrupted our conversation. In a quite irrational way we must be able to listen also to the voice of nature, thunder for instance, even if this means breaking the continuity of consciousness" (Let-II, pp. 20-21).

During my work with one woman, a body therapy group that met upstairs would begin thumping, pounding, hee-hawing their way into our sessions. This occurrence was noteworthy, not only because this group was usually quiet, but also because their sounds followed us through three schedule changes. Since neither this analysand nor I ever tried to escape them, perhaps we were aware, on some level, that they were helpful in our difficult work. They would come when she had pulled back, withdrawing eye contact and falling silent. They seemed to shake her out of her stuckness, jarring her into response. She would jump and clutch at her heart area. We began calling them "devil-noises," connecting them with nasty and disruptive underground energies.

This woman's childhood had involved a basic disregard of, and scoffing at, her individual reality, especially her emotions. She had internalized these attitudes; this evil-sounding hee-hawing and thumping from the ceiling gave dramatic image to her discounting attitudes toward her own reality. They were synchronistic events, sounding forth, again and again, the energies that were trying to be felt and recognized, amidst great frustration. They stopped at about the time she began to risk more clarity about her hurt, aggressive and arrogant feelings. The work could move then to the human channel, to relational and transference energy, allowing gentler back-and-forth energies. This experience exemplifies fairly dramatic acoustic synchronicity; but there are many more, involving subtle and easily by-passed auditory events. (See Kittelson, 1996.)

A second category, simultaneity and flow, especially involves ideas of musical accompaniment and also poetic and symbolic listening. It describes listening to psychic energy and especially the analysand's voice, as it flows onward, in a many-layered way. This flow, these levels, are full of images. They are there for the hearing, if we can open our imaginations to them.

Perhaps my favorite topic is echo and return. The world is full of echo. It is everywhere, but not quite anywhere. Echo lives again when our ears are attuned to the way vibrations move back and forth with each other. It is important to clarify that "echoing" here refers to its acoustic sense; in our non-auditory way of talking, we say that we "echo" verbal content or emotions. In work attuned to audition, to change the sound of the communication is already a reworking of the image – the acoustic communication. It is not a faithful echo, for the original auditory image has been lost. In a genuine echoing process, the analyst keeps to the exact sounds, as originally expressed. She remains true to their melody, their timbre, meter, and rhythm, re-calling to the original moment in a resonant way.

In the myth of Narcissus and Echo, there are two cursed states, one of emptiness and insubstantiality, like Echo's, and the other, of longing self-enclosure, like Narcissus'. "Echo" is a wood nymph – charming, quicksilver, not quite fully formed, mingling, playing, mischief-making. Out in nature, echoes "ventriloquize" us back to ourselves. We discover ourselves at a startling angle of experience in relation to our own sounds. Receiving echo is not an easy matter. Echoes can be disturbing and tricky, and they carry a confusing mix of profundity and chatter. Things in Echo's realm are catchy, permeable, back-and-forth.

One familiar type is the echo of over-identification, where an analysand suddenly recognizes a word or sound or phrase as coming from someone or some place else: his mother, his brother, the locker room. He gets the chance to hear and react – in old and new ways – to these old, old strains. People also sound forth cultural, social and workplace sounds, and childish taunts that echo oddly from a past still encapsulated around the person. Songs are echoes too. Often dismissed, or reduced to their verbal content, such inner songs are like acoustic dreams or fantasies, and can be worked with as richly and fully.

Sometimes, during or after the analytic hour, it is the echo, the resonant repetition, that allows the meaning to "get through." One client dreamed, accompanied by warnings, that *she was supposed to rejoin her mother and her mother's invalid mother and bring them food*. As we worked, the word "invalid" began to take on a sense of echo, ringing oddly, persistently. At first, it meant crippled, unable, eliciting sympathy and care. But as it echoed on in the hour, it slipped into the arena of her college course on psychological testing, to scientific "validity." Now her mother-figures were not valid: unreliable and no longer useful to her life. In pulling her first into the familial, all-too-familiar position of binding sympathy, this echo tricked her into hearing, at least for a moment, the invalidity of these mother figures in her life.

Sometimes, a moment will have an echo, a resonance that is itself noticeable. An analysand's talk might sound as if she were muffled or alone. (See Berry, 1982.) And echo can even be a symptom. In her sixteenth month of analysis, one analysand reported that, especially under stress, her right ear would begin to echo what she was saying. The echo sounded in her ear as "not firm, weak." In the next hour, she reported that she had begun to talk to it: "I tell it that we know it is shaky now, and insecure, and that that is okay now," she said. It was a new, shy relationship. She and her echo had become reassuringly involved with each other.

This analysand was forced to hear her own insubstantiality, a focus of our work. The echo turned her into her own audience; she literally became her own auditory witness. Her own ears became filled with her sounding self. This echo suffered a blow when a medical doctor explained it somatically (a result of too little fluid in the ear), and it fled the analytic scene for several months. But then it returned. You can't keep a good symptom down! It stopped gradually over about two years. She had progressed considerably in depending on her own perceptions and values.

Echoing is actually a form of retro-hearing, which, like retrospection, is an essential part of the analytic process. A moment re-echoes, re-sounds in the ear. Imaginatively, it re-enters the very bones and cavities of one's being. Retro-hearing may simply be an experience of re-wonder, to deal with the impact of a moment. It may be a hearing anew, a shift in how something is heard. Retro-hearing not only clarifies the past; it fantasizes the analytic process onward.

Retro-hearing does not so much correct a situation, as add a layer to it. It is easy to find fault with certain moments in a session. But sometimes self-criticism is an abandonment of the resonance of the acoustic space. This resonance has its own necessity, and its own meaning. In "hindsight" it is easy to get pushy and, in a way, too clear, outside the resonance in which the partners were interacting. But in the work, it is not verbal articulation that matters most; sometimes, intellectual understanding is not even important. What matters is what is "telling": what it is that resounds in our souls.

Finally, an important part of the acoustic work occurs "around sound." In my work, I refer to: hearing something not there, hearing a field of sensed resistance, and hearing what is almost said. Lastly, there is silence, a particularly rich realm of auditory image. Wilmer (1994) and Federer (1989), among other Jungians, have been developing this area.

Clinical Indications

In all kinds of analytic vessels, acoustic work evokes a resonance, a deepening and containing atmosphere that encourages deeper listening. But acoustic work is especially important for some people and for some phases of work.

First, some people appear to be "auditory types" They are "ear-minded," that is, most responsive, to images in auditory form, perhaps to the sound of a person's voice or to a hum in the air. It is like speaking a foreign language to use visual (written) language or a picture. Process-oriented psychologists and neurolinguistic programmers have been exploring this area in terms of auditory and other sensory types; they offer useful skills.

Second, auditory processes call to early and basic levels of the psyche. Audition is one of the first systems to develop. At only four and one-half to five months fetuses jump, move their limbs and avert their heads in response to sounds. The womb is quite noisy, about 75 decibels, the volume level of a normal conversation. Auditorily, it is not so paradisiacal. A fetus probably hears mostly the digestive and muscular movements of the mother.

Fetuses and infants are highly responsive to voices, especially the mother's. One school, Audio-Psycho-Phonology, follows a process called "sonic birth." A mother's voice is recorded and then filtered to approximate how it might have sounded to the fetal ear, in water inside the womb. A typical reaction to such a tape, in the case of a 14-year-old autistic child, was to curl up in fetal position in his mother's lap and suck his thumb. The recording was then, step-by-step, reduced until the voice sounded like the mother's air-conducted sound, outside the womb. Then selective hearing could begin to function, and listening become differentiated (Joudry, 1984, pp. 50-51). This sonic birth process sounds like a literal enactment, in auditory terms, of D.W. Winnicott's idea: The task of the mother is to accustom her child slowly enough to the necessary loss of "paradise." It should occur in increments, a slow enough increase of frustration.

Acoustic emphasis is indicated, and perhaps necessary, in work which centers around infant and early childhood states. The sounds and resonances – and silences – that have surrounded infants and children are the primary way in which they have received meaning. This fact would seem to affect what we theorize as a child's reality, as well as the ways in which we, as adults doing analysis, fantasize about and remember our childhoods. Auditory work calls to the child: remembered, re-imagined, and recreated. For Jungians, this level of work is resoundingly in the "first half of life." It deals with the basic grounding of an individual psyche, the building of a stable enough ego.

Finally, and often linked with early wounding, some clients require acoustic work when they must deal with traumatic or formative acoustic experiences or images. For example, the analyst's vocal expression, the way she is talking or being silent, can activate a complex. Without a reactive and imaginative ear, the analysand's images and memories could be lost. Indeed, the vessel might never become established. When a voice – verbal meaning aside – is sounding like haranguing father or cold mother, like seductive or annihilating animus or anima, then that sound dominates its message. False questions about content will be futile, the vessel mired in impossibility. The analyst will feel useless and rejected, as all her accents, rhythms, and timbres are met with a dull thud. They must deal with that auditory cage, imprisoning the analysand.

Conclusion

The analytic process shares with music, poetry, theater and all of the arts that essential quality of reaching again to that original moment, that originality in life, which has so much to do with being vibrant, "young," creative – and just plain psychically sound. Auditory energy has a unique bond with the unconscious, one that makes acoustic work necessary and richly informative. Like a "royal road," it is a labyrinthine channel – to participatory consciousness.

So, what if we conceived of ourselves as auditory beings instead of visual ones? Our style would shift, and so would our availability to the world, inside and out. Centering in sound entails receptive interaction with the unconscious. Rather than "bringing light" to the unconscious, it means, first of all, being alive, resonant to it, such as it is. Here is a closing image: It is not only eyes that move during dreams, but also the tiny middle ear bones. REM can also mean "Rapid Ear Movement"!

References

Berry, P. (1982). Echo's passion. *Echo's Subtle Body: Contributions to an Archetypal Psychology.* Dallas, TX: Spring Publications.

Campbell, D. (1989). *The Roar of Silence: Healing Powers of Breath, Tone & Music.* Wheaton, IL: Theosophical Publishing House.

Federer, Y. (1989). *Silence: Non-verbal Aspects of Analytic Psychology.* Diploma thesis, C.G. Jung Institute, Zurich.

Jenny, H. (1986). *Cymatics: Bringing Matter to Life with Sound.* Videotape, Pt. III, Brookline MA: Macromedia.

Joudry, P. (1984). *Sound Therapy and the Walk Man.* St. Denis, Saskatchewan: Steele & Steele.

Kittelson, M.L. (1996). *Sounding the Soul: The Art of Listening.* Einsiedeln, Switzerland: Daimon Verlag.

Shepard, P. (1978). *Thinking Animals: Animals & the Development of Human Intelligence.* New York: Viking Press.

Wilmer, H. (1994). Unpublished lecture, C.G. Jung Institute, Zurich, Jan. 19.

Alchemy in the Computer?

The Interplay of Word and Image, Sound and Music

Manfred Krapp
Berlin, Germany
German Society for Analytical Psychology

Alchemy in the computer? In order to answer this question, we must examine the position of analytical psychology in the interplay of word and image, sound and music. Here the hypermedium computer has opened a creative arena in which all things can be represented by and transformed into one another. The computer simulates a modern *vas hermeticum*, which pays tribute to Mercury, the "tempter to expansion in the realm of the sensory world" (CW13, par. 299). He arouses veritable fireworks of sensual apprehensibility, warning: "If you don't know me exactly, you will destroy your five senses through my fire" (CW13, par. 267). Mercury has singed two of our senses already, sight and sound, and he is about to attack the tactile sense through cyberspace.

Analytical psychology cannot ignore the explosive liberation of psychic energy in the electronic vas hermeticum and its mercurial enactment of reality in word and image, sound and music. The bewitching and seductive sensuality of the communications media, their boundless malleability and the total availability of information have brought about a psychomental pollution that must be washed away. Jung wrote, "Whoever understands the images only partially, yet thinks that knowledge is complete, is susceptible to a dangerous error. For whoever does not regard his knowledge as an ethical duty is in bondage to the power principle" (MDR, p. 196, German ed.). The computer-generated images are subject to this ethical duty too. Let us continue with the alchemy of computer technology.

Representation of the world must not disintegrate into incommensurable pieces. ... The one world that exists is also the way it must be represented. With the advent of the computer there is one horizon not merely to the world but to our representation of the world. Because of the varied modalities through which it was acquired, the represen-

tation of the world has been fragmented. ... But now information is the way. ... The desired diversities become translatable into one another. ... In principle, a unification of the senses will be possible! The mind will be freed of its fragmentation. The plurality of the senses and of symbolic forms will be transcended. ... In the future, innovation will emerge from a creative transformation: an alchemy of representation. It was the dream of alchemy to transform any substance into any other; the new alchemy of the computer can transform any form into any other. (van den Boom, 1991, pp. 187f)

Alchemists imagined at length how matter could be given the desired form. According to Jung, this required ... "true and not fantastic imagination" (CW12, par. 218) as its "informing power" (CW12, par. 355). Alchemy sought a "parallel between alchemical production and human moral-intellectual change." Therefore, "form – which is human intellect – is the beginning, the middle and the end of the proceedings" (CW12, par. 366). This *"forma* works through *informatio* (also described as *fermentatio*). *Forma* is identical with *idea*. Gold, silver and so on are forms of matter, therefore one can make gold if one succeeds in impressing the form of gold (*impressio formae*) on the *informis massa* or the chaos, i.e., the *prima materia"* (CW12, par. 366, n47).

"Computers simulate brain processes. The images that form there are almost immediately ... transmitted from the brain to the outside." They are "dreams made exact" (Flusser, 1992, p. 29). Electronic simulations of psychomental activity make inner conceptualization transparent. The capacity of computers for representation and transformation is based on mathematics, on algorithms. Reality is scanned with precision, disassembled into its smallest components and reassembled. This is the dissolution and coagulation of alchemy. The superhuman calculating ability of computers can interconnect all things, so that impressive simulation models and graphic representations emerge. Complex structures of matter, including the brain, will be made comprehensible to the senses. Due to the self-similarity of so-called fractal patterns it will be possible, for example, to generate a mountain mathematically in a computer. (See Gleick, 1988.)

Computer graphics of chaotic non-linear processes can be quite similar to inner images. Thus, the pioneers of chaos theory – like the alchemists – anticipated their ideas, by imagination about nature. According to Flusser (1990), computation from data to calculated images has resulted in a new imaginative faculty. Thus, one can regard the computer as an auxiliary ego to the imagination. It elucidates the structure of nature ánd the correspondence of *imaginatio* and *informatio*.

In an alchemical laboratory, imagination has manifold expressiveness. Neumann (1992) sees alchemy as an expressive experiential process "that takes place with and in the world, in mankind and nature and its powers. ... The world as not-just-psychological is decisively involved" (p. 70). This statement also sheds new light on the "projection" of alchemy into matter. According to Jung, imagination is the medium between spirit and nature, "something incarnate, a subtle *'corpus'* of half-spiritual nature" (CW12, par. 394). It "is an active production of (inner) images, *'secundam naturam,'* a feat of genuine thought and conceptualization, not dreamed up out of the blue without plan or foundation – not making light of its objects – but seeking to grasp the inner condition of the idea that truly imitates nature" (CW12, par. 279). Here the ethical duty emphasized by Jung vis-a-vis the image includes the electronically-generated image. Imagination must relate to nature as to a higher principle. Therefore, the alchemical *opus* required, in addition to concentrated readings of alchemical writings, religious devotion and a meditative spiritual exercise. Only a spirit freed from the body can bring the adept into accord with the opus and with nature.

The soul is "identical with our empirical conscious existence only in part." It finds itself instead "in projected condition" and imagines the Greater. "This 'Greater' (*maiora*) corresponds with the 'Higher' (*altiora*) in the world-creating imagination of God which, however, because God imagines it, at once becomes substantial" (CW12, par. 399). With the help of the alchemical art and *Deo concedente,* this Greater can be realized. It corresponds to the idea of a *unus mundus* exactly as it corresponds to the modern holographic worldview. Human imagination implicitly contains information about a higher level, that is, the whole. The processes of consciousness in the brain are also holographically structured. Imagination and intuition then mediate among the various levels of consciousness. The unifying representational potential of computers opens a (holographic) view on the *unus mundus* by illustrating the correspondence of informatio and imaginatio.

The modern concept of information in physics is remarkably close to the alchemical informatio. "Today we are inclined to understand information as an extra dimension beside energy, as an ordering condition, structure or pattern" (Bischof, 1995, p. 211).

The capacity of complex organization in matter is defined as negentropy. This non-material principle of order, implicit in matter, finds explicit expression in the computer. Its potentialities for simultaneous information processing and mutual reinforcement, that is, structural linkage between interior and exterior, also transform the approach to the psychic. Could it also make insight into the Self "computable"? Then negentropy would become the paradigm of a depth psychology of consciousness.

From the entropy principle, Freudian psychoanalysis took as its point of departure a psychic apparatus directed purely toward the release of tension. But quantum physics has demonstrated that this mechanistic conception of an increasing shift from high-potential order to disorder has no validity at the subatomic level. Elementary particles are generated by negentropy, just as the organizational potential of the brain builds complex structures. Von Franz (1988) alludes to this when she speaks of the possibility that information, "through an ordering intervention, can allow the removal of an isolated system from a condition of entropy" (p. 88). For that, however, "the psyche must proceed from its passive-cognitive condition to an active-volitional one; in the first case information is an acquisition of knowledge, in the second a capacity for organization (= negentropy)" (p. 68).

The standardization of information through the digital code illustrates the correspondence of imaginatio and informatio. Before the computer era, the encoding of information was fragmented into different fields, at a cost in sensory perceptibility. Alphabetic writing and typographic printing have restricted sensuousness and physicality in the transmission of information, limiting it to the level of visual perception. Such an overcrowding of a single sensory level hinders the mutual coordination and reciprocal translation of the senses. This obstructs the faculty of imagination and the integrity of perception.

> *If Perceptive organs vary, Objects of perception seem to vary:*
> *If Perceptive organs close, their Objects seem to close also.*
> William Blake

Sense ratios change when any one sense or function – bodily or mental – is externalized in technological form. Imagination is that relationship among the perceptions and faculties that exists when they are not grown in material technologies. When so grown, each sense and faculty becomes a closed system.

The Reasoning Spectre
Stands between the Vegetative Man & his Immortal Imagination.
                                                                    William Blake

Referring to Blake's artistic perception, McLuhan (1968a) makes clear the effects of technology and the media on the capacity for imagination. (See also Krapp, 1995). Above all, alphabetical writing – which separates auditory from visual perception – shatters integrated perception as the basis of the imagination: "The phonetically written word sacrifices worlds of meaning and perception that were secured by forms like the hieroglyph and the Chinese ideogram" (McLuhan, 1968b, p. 93). The spoken word establishes a many-layered echo chamber between speaker and listener. Thus it produces a tactility that speaks to all the senses, received as integrated experience. In the non-alphabetical consciousness, a simultaneous auditory realm is realized, binding subject and object in a *participation mystique*. Writing "tears us away from the images that signify to our preliterate consciousness the world and ourselves in it ... so as to order the conceptions thus fragmented ('explicated') into intended lines, into countable, recountable, analyzable concepts" (Flusser, 1992, p. 17).

The ideogram offers more information than the linear alphabetic mode of writing, at one glance and in less space. The expressiveness of ideograms comes closer to nature and the Tao than our writing – even if, in the end, there is no word for Tao. "The beauty of Chinese writing is thus the same as that we recognize in flowing water, in spray and spume, in whirl and wave, just as in clouds, flames and mist in the sunlight. The Chinese call this kind of beauty 'following Li.' ... Li is the pattern of behavior that arises when one lives in harmony with Tao, the watercourse of nature" (Watts, 1983, p. 38). Chinese writing is closer to the true imagination of alchemy, than is alphabetical writing. Only with the help of the computerized images of chaos theory can Western science approach these flowing forms of nature.

With the diffusion of printing, the hitherto individual handwritten lettering went through homogenization and leveling. And in the daily life of print culture, ever more information is acquired through visually determined methods. The mechanistic worldview of Cartesian philosophy and science emerge, according to McLuhan, from the perceptual forms of linear perspective discourse. The separation of rational consciousness from the unconscious, of which Jung complained, must be considered also in this connection.

Analytical psychology is ... a reaction against an exaggerated rationalization of consciousness that, in striving to attain regular methods, isolates itself from nature and thus also tears people out of their natural history and transplants them into a rational present. ... Life becomes superficial, and no longer fully represents humanity. In this way much unlived life falls to the unconscious. One lives as one walks in shoes that are too narrow. ... We are isolated within our rational walls from the eternities of Nature. Analytical psychology seeks to break through the walls insofar as it excavates those visions of the unconscious which the rational intellect had formerly rejected. (CW8, par. 739)

The technology of the printing press perfected this production of regulated mental procedures and thus the separation of the images of the unconscious from consciousness. Here we see the necessity for an analysis of the media's changing the dynamic of consciousness and the unconscious.

Music becomes a remedy (Latin: re-medium) for these unidirectional conscious processes. Richard Wagner brilliantly grasped this connection: "One must remember the religious sects of the Reformation era, their disputes and treatises, to gain an insight into the raging madness which had seized letter-obsessed heads. One may assume that only Luther's masterful chorale rescued the healthy spirit of the Reformation, because it determined the feeling and thereby healed the letter-sickness of the brain" (cited in Bolz, 1990, p. 62). The music of Bach's chorales is a multi-media phenomenon in its joining of choral text, image and music. It has given back to humankind a complete sensory apprehension of a higher truth, which the iconoclastic stance of the Reformation sought to banish. Only the written Word of God, now accessible to all through the printing press, was legitimate. This furthered the ossification of religious symbols into dogma.

Schweitzer (1977) has described the integration of the different levels of expression in Bach's music, still unsurpassed especially in his chapters, "Poetic and Pictorial Music" and "Word and Sound in Bach." In the choral arrangement "Ach wie nichtig, ach wie flüchtig" ("O how empty, O how fleeting") from the Bach's Little Organ Book gives the choral text to the soprano. The two middle voices give an impression of fleetingness, and the octave interval of the pedal beneath them conveys the descent into emptiness.

Depth psychology presents the psyche almost exclusively through the spoken and written word. In training and control analysis the oral tradition lives, but theory has neglected the sound aspect of speech. Indeed Didier Anzieu "postulates a sound image of the self that precedes the body image developmentally. He ... criticizes the editor of Freud's Standard Edition for not having included in the index such key concepts as voice, sound and hearing" (Mahony, 1989, pp. 11-12). The researches of Tomatis (1987, 1994) show what fundamental truths were hidden in this sound image of the Self, about the influence on intrauterine development of the sound of the mother's voice and even of music such as Mozart's.

From about the fourth month of pregnancy, the embryo's hearing function is almost fully developed. A kind of communication develops between the maternal voice and the listening embryo, which answers playfully with reflexive bodily movements. The embryo is protected by the abdominal musculature from the outside acoustic world; it hears the voice of the mother through bone conduction via the spinal column and pelvic bones. The ringing musicality of the mother's voice, the sound that makes the music of life, thus exercises an immense influence on psychological maturation. If an adult hears the recorded voice of the mother suitably filtered to correspond to intrauterine conditions archetypal stages in the development of human consciousness become perceptible.

The initial matrix of communication is formed by the listening of the fetus to the mother's voice, its responsive movements and, from about the seventh month, its tactile exploration of its surroundings. This communicative stance determines the relationship of the ego to the unconscious. It is the basis of the anima function – equally so for both sexes. Analytic theory and methodology are based on the generative word of the father and thereby on the animus function. The musical-spatial "grasping" experience of the unconscious is the primary approach to the unconscious; out of it develop the iconic-imaginal and verbal-conceptual approach.

James Hillman made the pronouncement that: we therapists are too little conscious that we are singers. Yet Hillman offers no opportunity for singing, much less any musical accompaniment. The difficulty of modern humans in gaining entry to images of the soul is a result of the loss of an awareness of the auditory-musical dimension of language. If, like Hillman, we want to re-establish the original sense of images and to free the imaginal from the fragments of Reformation literalism, we cannot forget music and other sound. Print culture is the era of homogenized reverence for the image of the letter which, in an endless hypnotic monotony of typography, consists almost solely of straight lines, corners and (half) circles. One should not only replace the writing image with another image, but add a space in which the images order and move themselves. Reverence for the image and the musical ritual are bound to one another.

Singing (largely in contrast with speech and alphabetical writing) is represented in both halves of the brain. Music brings consciousness and the unconscious into an oscillating communication, on which its therapeutic efficacy is based. Abstract discourse screens psychic processes and straightens them out into a linear string. The simultaneity and many-layeredness of the psyche can be reconstructed only imaginatively and in retrospect.

> *Works of art have a strong effect on me, especially poems and sculpture, less often paintings. I was thus compelled ... to linger over them for a long time, and wanted to grasp them in my own way. ... Where I cannot do that, for example, in music, I am almost incapable of enjoyment. A rationalistic or perhaps analytic quality in me resists my being moved without at the same time knowing why I am moved or what moves me.* (SE10, p. 197)

Freud was able or willing to grasp art only in retrospect and with the help of analytic understanding. He could do little, therefore, with music. Jung, at least later in life, let himself be carried away by music. This is evidenced in the visit of a music therapist to Jung's house in 1950. After he had spent an afternoon in speaking with the therapist about music, he summed up as follows:

> *This opens an entirely new direction for research, of which I had never allowed myself to dream. What you showed me this afternoon – not only what you said, but above all what I concretely felt and experienced – leaves me feeling that music must from now on be an essential component of any analysis. It reaches deep archetypal material, which we only rarely attain in our analytical work with patients.* (Hinshaw & Fischli, 1986, p. 89)

Years earlier, in his correspondence with Sabina Spielrein, Jung had shown little understanding of her ambition to compose music. But perhaps for men like Freud and Jung, in love with their theories, there could be no proper place for a musical woman.

Today the inclusion of a musical entry to the psyche is becoming a necessity, because the electronic communications media present themselves imaginally-musically. According to McLuhan (1968b), an extension of the entire central nervous system (CNS) comes through the electronic media, and not just of a single sense, as with print. The connective potential of the electrical circuit can realize the parallelism and simultaneity of the neural network and thereby simulate the CNS in its interplay of the senses and even consciousness. Then humanity can experience itself as a totality, and not merely as fragments. "All humanity becomes our own skin" (p. 23). Although this must cause anxiety, "the age of anxiety and of electronic media [is] also the age of the unconscious and of apathy. But it is also significantly the age in which we get conscious of the unconscious" (p. 56).

The increasing communicative interconnection of people begins with the telephone. Already at the end of the nineteenth century, the telegraph combined simultaneously the most heterogeneous pieces of news and radically changed the journalistic scene. Radio allows expression to the human voice; original sound reproductions simulate direct auditory experience. Thus, the archaic emotional world of the oral tribal society comes back to life. Radio is the tribal drumbeat of the global village into which the world – and consciousness with it – is imploded by the simultaneous availability of information.

In the age of satellite and the information superhighway, the space – and time – relativizing communications net is nearly complete. Current events (e.g., the Gulf War) can be transmitted in real time. Audiovisual media produce a novel discourse of rapid moving images and simultaneous information. This discourse over-taxes the left-brained perceptual modes, which are organized by secondary processes. The discourse of the camera simulates the child's holistic tactile exploration of the world. Corresponding music makes the world even more appetizing. Television enforces "a form of interaction that once occurred exclusively through physical contact" (Meyrowitz, 1990, p. 232). This interaction necessarily leads to an inner and an interpersonal loss of boundaries similar to that in psychosis. Thus, a projective identification with reality is produced.

Now the pleasure principle is extended. To paraphrase Mann (1978, p. 191), perhaps this right-brained id no longer allows itself to be colonized by the ego. In the new mythical world of the media, logical-analytic discourse loses its dominating position. Modern humans are less at the mercy of the incalculable turbulence of nature, but more at that of the information flood.

In the sensory vividness of the new media, in their tactility, their human intimacy, and in their creation of bodily-instinctive needs, a long-repressed physicality breaks through. Its explosive release, moreover, opposes a counter-tendency toward disembodiment. If one can experience oneself floating in cyberspace, the boundaries of the body dissolve. In the novels of William Gibson, bodiless cybernauts roam unconfined in virtual spaces. Chips implanted in the brain make a direct brain-computer interface. The media-driven opening up of the individual and his or her exposed condition have produced a yearning for merging and rapturous dissolution of physicality. Psychoanalytically, we can speak here of a regression to the womb, to the re-establishment of an intrauterine state of suspension and of original communication. It appears, however, that the primal religio-mystical yearning toward overcoming physicality has manifested itself also in media technologies.

A music video of a concert by the pop group Pink Floyd illustrates the proximity of desire and numbness. The soaring sounds of the introduction to "Shine On, You Crazy Diamond" and the flowing, soaring movement of the camera direction produce a hypnotic trance and a yearning, melting condition. The camera forces its way into the brain through the eyes of the listeners. The ritual-performance of emotions by the electronic media is fascinating. In the radiant light of the laser, the solar hero appears, accompanied by his electric guitar, the modern lyre.

Wagner's "The Ring of the Nibelungen," is a parable of the danger of power over technology. The Tarnhelm (magic hood) is reminiscent of the cyberspace helmet. Hagen says:

> *I know the Tarnhelm,*
> *the finest Nibelung work of art:*
> *It suffices, when it covers your head,*
> *to change you into any form;*
> *if you long for the most distant place,*
> *it takes you away there at once.*

Space and time, like one's own identity, are dissolved.

How does depth psychology present itself in connection with media technology? The emergence of psychoanalysis at the end of the nineteenth century is unthinkable without the accelerated pace of life resulting from technology, including the telephone and the telegraph. Human perception as well was fundamentally changed. Freud used the telephone as a metaphor for the analytic process and for telepathy. Telepathy is perhaps the original, archaic mode of communication, which was later eclipsed by signals perceptible to the senses.

Freud's mediumistic view into possible extrasensory channels of communication from unconscious to unconscious is contrary to his logocentric stance, which would grasp the unconscious only by means of the conditions of linguistic abstraction. He hypostasizes the latent dream content, whose "multifarious logical relations" of dream thoughts to one another correspond to those of "sentence and speech." These dream thoughts underlie the "compression of dream-work ... whereby components are twisted, broken up and pushed together like drifting ice" (SE2, p. 310). Here Freud uses words to paint a beautiful image of the cubist organization of space, which Arnheim (1978) describes as "violent reciprocal interpenetration of independent unities" (p. 127). Dreamwork is thus, in a fashion unrecognized by psychoanalysis, a cubist artist!

"The work of Freud and Jung [thus] represents the arduous translation of a preliterate consciousness into literary conception" (McLuhan, 1968a, p. 102). Freud renders his understanding of the unconscious in a prosaic linguistic discourse. He tries to straighten out the distortion of psychic truth through regressive unconscious formations. In Jung's writings, the creative heterogeneity of the unconscious is revealed directly. The abundance of forms in the unconscious is the source of psychic energy and imaginal-mythic thinking that is a necessary complement to rational consciousness. From this point of view, in addition to its cultural anthropological significance, emerge Jung's therapeutic conceptions of amplification, transcendent function and active imagination.

Jung could not content himself with a logical-discursive rendering of the unconscious. His writings illustrating psyche by images point to the multi-media representation of psychic processes that is possible today. With their many-layered and interwoven structure and the various levels of text, footnote and image, Jung's works on alchemy anticipate the computer hypertext. Jung often allows the separate levels of image and text to collide sharply and to contradict one another. His rendering of the dynamic of the unconscious in word and image embodies an analogy to the cubist perception of space. Artists such as Georges Braque and Pablo Picasso have "consciously aimed for ... perceptual conflict. ... What mattered to

Figure 1

them was the irreconcilability inherent in absolute space itself."
Every element of a cubist picture "obeys its own spatial determinants." The spatial interrelation of these elements "is nevertheless
consciously irrational." Like cinematic fade-outs and fade-ins,
"opposing orders should be united into a whole" (Arnheim, 1978, p.
295). In its simultaneous multi-dimensional and non-perspectival
representation of space, cubism anticipates the perceptual mode of
the new media. Today the videoclip presents heterogeneous spatial
elements in a rapid rhythmic-musical succession of images.

Even if Jung (CW15) had little appreciation for Picasso, it is precisely the terse contrasts of Jung's representational style, for which he is often reproached, that place him on the side of the cubist. While Jung embraces a more honest, authentic view of the unconscious, Freud – with his uncomplicated self-contained literary prose – forces the unconscious into a polished formulation. Mahony (1989) compares Freud's style of writing with Cezanne: "Blocks of thought overlap, grouped around an aphoristic statement, mutually orienting and balancing one another" (p. 205). In his later work, Cezanne developed a technique of layering color surfaces, to reveal the deeper order of a representational space that lies beyond normal perception. The chromatic rhythm of the independent elements and their modulation made Cezanne a forerunner of cubism. Here one can see a certain analogy to Freud, when he arranges and coordinates the incongruities of the unconscious. But Freud relates to his functional-mechanistic conception of psychic apparatus, while Cezanne wants to free a higher spiritual order.

In Picasso's *The Veil-dance* (Fig. 1), inspired by African sculpture, the tension between individual picture elements draws attention, resolving itself when one sees the body rotating. "The rhythms of the body, the rhythm of space set against it, the search for balance in a composition which can capture the body in its movement and simultaneously allow it to be seen resting, although it has struggled against the picture's vertical form: The painter's hand controls these elements, which create volume through the play of hatched lines" (Daix, 1982, p. 32). It may be that Jung's cubist-like rendering of the psychic image can be exhibited optimally in the multi-mediality of computer hypertext.

At this interface of art, analytical psychology and the computer, media consciousness could emerge. Through its unifying sensory representational capabilities, the computer shows imagination in its correspondence with information. Like the alchemical laboratory, the computer gives substance to psycho-mental processes, makes nature's opus intelligible, and opens a (holographic) view of the unity of the world, unus mundus. Insofar as the computer compels ego-consciousness to relate to what Erich Neumann called the "creative void" – the non-ego – it sets the dynamic of the Self in motion. At the same time it establishes a relationship to the Thou. This communicative aspect is represented in alchemy by the *soror mystica*. Jung refers to the balance between ego and non-ego as *religio*, whose production by today's mass media consists in a regressive-pleasureful oral incorporation of the world and the Thou. As the opposite pole, the "true imagination" is needed. Only through its active and concentrated exertion can the computer be used as an auxiliary ego to the imagination in the sense of a negentropy of consciousness. Paradoxically, it seems that Western humans are equal to the challenge of technologies only with the help of a volitional ego, which has the mystical process as its substance and goal. According to Neumann (1953), "the mystic's interpretation of the elimination of ego [is] an error. ... Only with the help of the strongest concentration of the will and the sharpening of the personality toward this highest goal does the mystical inner way succeed. But this means, however paradoxical it sounds, that the ego evidently must attain first a heightened energy potential, in order to make its own suspension and transposition possible" (p. 182). True mysticism leads "to an intensified activity in the world" (p. 183), and a "clarification of the world" (p. 188).

References

Arnheim, R. (1978). *Kunst und Sehen*. Berlin: De Gruyter.

Bischof, M. (1995). *Biophotonen*. Frankfurt/M: Zweitausendeins.

Bolz, N. (1990). *Theorie der neuen Medien*. München: Raben

Daix, P. (1982). *Der Kubismus*. Stuttgart: Klett-Cotta.

Flusser, V. (1990). Eine neue Einbildungskraft. In V. Bohn (Hg), *Bildlichkeit*. Frankfurt/M: Suhrkamp.

Flusser, V. (1992). *Die Schrift*. Frankfurt/M: Fischer.

Gleick, J. (1988). *Chaos*. München: Knaur.

Hinshaw, R. & Fischli, L., Hg. (1986). *C.G. Jung im Gespräch*. Zurich: Daimon.

Krapp, M. (1995). Die neuen Medien und das Wahrnehmen der Imaginationsfähigkeit. In K-P. Dencker (Hg.), Interface II. *Bildwelten und Weltbilder*. Hamburg: Hans-Bredow-Institut.

Mahony, P. (1989). *Der Schriftsteller Sigmund Freud*. Frankfurt/M: Suhrkamp.

Mann, T. (1978). *Freud und die Zukunft*. Frankfurt/M: Fischer.

McLuhan, M. (1968a). *Die Gutenberg-Galaxis* (The Gutenberg Galaxy). Düsseldorf: Econ.

McLuhan, M. (1968b). *Die magischen Kanäle* (Understanding Media). Düsseldorf: Econ.

Meyrowitz, J. (1990). *Überall und Nirgends Dabei: Die Fernsehgesellschaft I* (No Sense of Place: The Impact of Electronic Media on Social Behaviour). Weinheim: Beltz.

Neumann, E. (1953). *Kulturentwicklung und Religion*. Zurich: Rascher.

Neumann, E. (1992). *Die Psyche als Ort der Gestaltung.* Frankfurt: Fischer.
Schweitzer, A. (1977). *Johann Sebastian Bach.* Leipzig: VEB Breitkopf & Härtel.
Tomatis, A. (1987). *Der Klang des Lebens.* Reinbek: Rowohlt.
Tomatis, A. (1994). *Klangwelt Mutterleib.* München, Kösel.
van den Boom, H. (1991). Digitaler Schein. In F. Rötzer, *Digitaler Schein.* Frankfurt/M: Suhrkamp.
von Franz, M.-L. (1988). *Psyche und Materie.* Einsiedeln: Daimon.
Watts, A. (1983). *Der Lauf des Wassers* (Tao, the Watercourse Way). Frankfurt/M: Suhrkamp.

*Analytical Psychology
and Religion*

The Altar in Human Groups

A Path to the Living God

Pilar Montero
San Francisco, California, U.S.A.
Society of Jungian Analysts of Northern California

Human altars play a role in awakening reflective collective consciousness. (An altar can be defined as an art form that functions as a threshold for communication with the immaterial spirit realm. The term "human altar" refers to the use of a human being to satisfy this purpose, whether it be as shaman, human sacrifice or other related role.) Also in groups there is the moment when their churning dynamic energy can be used to help them cross to a transpersonal perspective. For over 20 years I have studied the manifest unconscious patterns as they emerge in groups; I have glimpsed the new mythological forms that are not yet fully articulated in the broader collective but are hinted at in these reflective microcosms. My belief is that groups are units of life that can be awakened out of their regressive unconscious tendencies, to deliver more egalitarian, non-exclusive and sustainable decisions and products. I am using my experiences in consulting with groups to amplify the human altar as the medium that most descriptively portrays the transferential power of the consultant in fulfilling these aims.

Identifying the turning point in human consciousness is the critical issue here. My work with groups allows for a consideration of individuating groups, not unlike Jung's description of this phenomenon in the individual psyche. Addressing groups as units of life is an invitation to consider the emergence of a new archetypal form. My current interest builds on this possibility and takes it one more step: the awareness that groups of any kind can be moved to a level of functioning evolved enough to be considered as coming from a Self perspective, whether their life cycle is a few hours or hundreds of years.

The patterns of the new millennium seem more determined by the need for concerted action by a diversity of individual entities, rather than the behavior of homogeneous social structures more familiar to Europeans. For this reason, and because, as a Peruvian immigrant to the United States I am most attuned to these variations, I have explored the deceptively secular festive street parade as one reincarnation in the new world of the sacred human altar forms originating in ancestral Africa. In Peru, human sacrifices further elucidate the complexity of the human altar experience when its potential for regeneration is apparent, despite its shadow abode between colliding cultures. A current annual festival in the Andes dramatically brings to awareness the overriding power of the aboriginal home to honor Christianity's myth and message and yet absorb them into its local ancient form of worship and ritual.

Groups

I view groups as unified entities moving toward individuation, with individual members manifesting the conscious and unconscious energies of this quest. This view requires a group-as-a-whole perspective, with an individual playing each of the many roles the group uses to express the patterns ignited by its life force. Individuals in groups are faced with an onslaught of unconscious dynamics that threaten to obliterate them or inflate them beyond recognition. They must learn to identify and relate to these energies in a constructive manner; for service, commitment and responsibility are dependent on the fruitful interplay between individual and group life. This manner of studying groups is very much in line with our Jungian orientation that sees humanity as a function of the psyche and human events as translations of the elemental language of the psyche. We are embedded in the unconscious and not the unconscious in us. Inside or outside becomes a point of view rather than a location. Turning inward in groups and individuals means facing the deities and demons that drive us to our depths and heights. It does not mean looking inside oneself only, but inside the psychic apparition – whether it be an inner voice, image or thought, or the experiential environment in which we are lodged. This view is not dependent on typological preference, but rather affirms that both introverts and extraverts can get beyond the Cartesian split between psyche and world; the split is but the ego's perception of reality.

I find Jung's most creative formulation about the Self – the one most useful for our present purpose – is his definition of the Self as the central meaning, the highest value held by an individual entity.

The numinous then includes the secular, for we are dealing with values and not religious orthodoxies. The troublesome split between the sacred and profane is eliminated. Now we are free to ask how this divine spirit that can transform the fate of a group accomplishes its ends. We know the archetypal structures of the collective unconscious reach the psyche via images that can be visual, auditory, kinesthetic, and so on. We either make conceptual sense of images' meanings or we are transformed and healed through their raw beauty.

Jungian theory states that the *coniunctio* can occur directly but usually takes place in a medium. Borrowing from alchemy Jung calls this medium *Mercurius,* who is also the soul and the mediator between spirit and body. Thus, the Self cannot be known directly but via the *anima*: the image-forming mechanism that allows the archetypal forces to be transformed. As a function, the anima can be an altar: the symbol the psyche uses to bound the experience. This differs from the image of the anima per se, which is typically feminine. The meaning of the symbol is the purview of the *animus* logos function so that the *syzygy* – anima/animus – is the representation in relationship of how libidinal energy is dynamically altered.

In groups the anima, which functions for the purpose of transcendence, can be energized by a consultant, priest or shaman, either by formally offering him or herself as the central image carrying the transformative energy at the time, or by facilitating its appearance through the articulation of the image by some member of the group. The symbol then actively influencing the course of events will be translated into meaningful intellectual or behavioral work with the help of the consultant. Thus, when imaginal forms are illuminated in the service of energy that metamorphizes a person or group to the higher, more inclusive level of functioning which the view from the Self commands, an altar has been created. And, when this type of imaginal form is borne by a human being, the vessel can be called a human altar. I hope that my following lengthy amplifications of this symbolic form will elucidate how they overlap with the consultant role. First, let me explain how a group consultation is related to the human altar.

Group Consultation

My goal as a consultant has been to help a group become aware of the unconscious forces ruling it at any one time. Group members

react to having these images made conscious as individuals typically
do to any shadow material: They get upset and attempt to reject
them, or they accept the unknown and idealize the messenger/
consultant. The awareness of shadow is the golden means to individuation; the key is attaining a conscious attitude that invites the
unconscious to cooperate instead of driving it into opposition.

First, the language used by the consultant needs to correspond to
the characteristics and dynamics of the group at that moment. A help
is to voice the revealed in the original symbolic form and only later
to accompany the poetic word with intellectual elaborations – if the
group cannot digest its meaning. Second, timing is critical; the
purpose is to be in line with the growing edge of the group. The
consultant must keep a keen focus on the emerging Self of the group
in order to ride the wave that will lead it to its newly shaping
attitude.

Groups can be at any of the three stages of the coniunctio in their
development; an interpretation must take the stage into account. The
first stage which, in alchemy, corresponds to the separation of spirit
and soul from matter is about insight and the withdrawal of our
projections on the world. Colman (1995) has written brilliantly
about the scapegoat phenomenon. It occurs when a group, trying to
maintain its sense of wholeness and goodness, unconsciously loads
a group member with its shadow and – for all intents and purposes
– banishes that person from the group. My interest is the passage of
the group into the second stage of the *coniunctio* – when knowledge
is embodied consciously and the new attitude changes its behavior –
and into the third stage whence a vision of wholeness and the
interdependence of all life guides its mission. However, we need to
remember that all stages are active or potentially so at all times in a
group.

Let me describe one of these threshold crossings in a group. I
spent a weekend in a workshop of a very diversified and competent
group of women representing a group relations organization, which
was to be headed by a woman in the future. We had gathered, in part,
to plan a portion of an upcoming scientific meeting. The last few
hours of the workshop still had us playing and battling with issues
to do with gender, race, age and the like. Emotions ran high and no
viable structure for the scientific meeting was on the horizon. I was
a group member but, throughout the weekend, had felt free of the
group's entanglements because I desired little from it and, therefore,
could make some consultant-type statements. I decided to apply my

knowledge of groups to the current situation. I said the group was stuck because we had not consciously acknowledged that the future president of the organization was present and we needed to delineate a vision that represented the feminine in authority. This was an interpretation of a covert, competitive dynamic but stated as an intent that gave us a purpose. The group protested, saying that visions belong to the dimension of the sacred and we had practical assignments to identify. I insisted that we were failing exactly for that reason. That is, because the sacred depths were not being acknowledged we were caught in chaos and personal battles, we were defeating the group's highest value which was the seemingly impossible goal of integrating diversity – without obliterating differences – and still functioning in a united way. A silence followed. Suddenly a black woman said that she had had a dream the previous night; in it *she had seen a circular fire surrounded by snow. Wolves passed by it and smiled as they did so.* As if by magic, the group relaxed and proceeded to complete its planning work successfully and smoothly.

What had taken place? For a start, since the purpose is to transmute the group to a higher order of performance, the ego's grip has to be reduced. The ego and the Self, the individual and the collective, have to be brought together. This is not different from the generation of individual ecstatic states that can be produced in the various ways understood to "lower" ego consciousness. The better known ones are suffering; the seductions by the erotic or aesthetic; violent passions such as rage, fear, sex, exhaustion; huge surprise; steady and continuous drumming, chanting and dancing; and spontaneous numinous visitations. Many of these can be generated willfully in a group. However, groups are already in a state of lowered consciousness most of the time as they attempt to find a common denominator to control the disarray of human passions that govern them. Thus, the intent becomes to guide the energy present into a unifying channel so that the ecstatic openness that allows for the entrance of the desired divinity can happen. This is possible if, in a holding environment, the appropriate intent is induced in the group: one that is in line with the group's highest value, the Self, and in rhythm with the current emotional tone and dynamic language of the group. Now the vessel can come forth that allows the spirit to be embodied. The altar is being created.

In groups, the altar is normally an image which, no matter how humble, is wondrous in itself; the numinous is now visible. An altar is not just a means for the material to become rarified and for the spiritual to become dense enough to be humanly visible. It is also the face of the god for the people in its spell at that time. The consultant or group member in that role, in the shamanic or sacrificial function, on some occasions can carry the projected numen that makes of him or her the human altar. Here the image elicited becomes the garb for the changing effect. In the above example, however, the call for a vision alone would not have been enough to invoke the sacred attitude, for I was not carrying a human altar projection for group members. The power of the image was indispensable to allow for a perceptual shift into the transpersonal realm.

Action Altars

Moving altars that include the group as well as the shaman or priest have been described by Thompson (1993). This book and my own observations have inspired most of the material about African altars in this paper. The Pygmies and the San, a hunting and gathering civilization of Southern Africa, have simple but highly evocative rituals that seem to parallel the typical movement of energy in groups. They worship the forest and its spirits with yodel-inflected songs while they dance round and round. The spirits in turn receive this sacrifice of song and motion and grant game and honey. It is interesting that the forest also responds – when the dance and the yodeling attain the proper pitch – by the dramatic visitation of the Rafia leaf-covered maskers and the mystic hooting sounds of the pipe. Sometimes their aesthetic play is so powerful that they see forest spirits materialize. A bush may appear where there was none before or the ground is thumped rhythmically by a large leaf even though the air is still. It is worthy of note that the dress of these sylvan apparitions mirrors the natural altars the Pygmies use for sacrifice and the religious pipe hooting is similar to the yodeling used to invoke the apparitions. This is an example of groups crossing into the sacred and back. It suggests the divine need to reciprocate in a language comparable to that of the implorers, to allow for its comprehension and integration and use in everyday life.

The dynamic force that can transform or make things happen is symbolized by fire in all cultures. Fire was the central threshold dream image which shifted the group described above into a Self-directed state, and – among the Pygmies and the San – it is the energy source activating the conditions for crossing. Fire is the most precious gift of the forest; the rituals and natural altars created by the various Pygmy groups emphasize fire as the most blessed. Fires are used for divination, for clues to problems in blocking advanced well being, and for healing. The San also give primary importance to the ritual use of fire. They have, at the core of their culture, a circling dance of shamans moving around a central fire. These ecstatic healers – in trance – dance in concerted action, singing and clapping until they become like one organic being. The women also clap and yodel, heating up the mind as they do the ground. When in trance, the shamanic healers tramp on and pick up coals, for fire activates the medicine in them. Then they anoint patients with their sweat, for healing purposes. Blood may pour out of their nostrils when they are in an exalted state; this signals the passage from this world to the next. The blood – like the sweat and touch – are the strong medicine, good luck and blessings used to heal and strengthen their group.

Unity in Diversity

Unity in diversity is a topic close to my heart. It is both critical to post-millennial mythologies and personally relevant. It coincides with my experience migrating to North America, having grown up in Latin America, where my Caucasian roots were but one strand in the multiplicity of co-existing cultures and races. Also, all my ancestral power, riches and land were confiscated by a revolutionary government. I learned the hard way what the Peruvian Andeans, the Pygmies and the San knew from time immemorial: that the sacred pervades all of life and that nature is the face of God. A greater force is always there to be contended with, and is most noticeable when one is ill or in crisis. To put it crassly, private ownership is an illusion, for even our mortal lives belong to the state during a war. Yet I can only celebrate our capacity to meet life's tragedies with creations which allow us to soar beyond our limitations. The music and art history of virtually all humankind has been aesthetically blessed with the grandeur and beauty of structures consecrated to the meeting with the divine. The process whereby altars function to metamorphose energy in groups is not only mysterious but very difficult to comprehend. It deals with outcomes that need to remain embodied in other groups as tasks and decisions, even if the group entity that allowed for their origin no longer exists.

A dramatic manifestation of moving human altars are the costumed and masked protagonists of the mythological motifs enacted

in street parades in the Americas and the Caribbean. African ancestral patterns of worship reappear in miraculously modified forms in
these New World festivals. They are described eloquently in a book
(Nunley & Bettelheim, 1988) from which I borrow to illustrate the
reframing possible when altar forms are from one culture to another
and exhibited in a secular context.

Parades are a feast for the eyes and heat the body with a frenzy of
musical rhythms and songs. They are choreographed with mythological themes and magnificent costumes designed for this purpose,
meant not just to enhance audience involvement but to allow for
personal artistic and religious expression. They are reminiscent of
the old world shamanic aesthetics that significantly influence them.
These aesthetics assumed that all things had spirits and reorganized
the animistic world into new works of art, in order to control and
interpret it and thus to reorganize the human experience. Costume
designers aim for a similar ecstatic state, part and parcel of divine
possession. They emphasize scale, color and the richness of texture
for the heightening of affects. Masks and costumes which fully
cover the person are most informative about the interpenetration of
cultures and the ritual wearing for roles on the threshold of the
transpersonal realm. The viewer cannot see beyond the immediate
image to the person behind the mask; visual misinformation is
created that blocks the profane vision. At the same time, the visually
mysterious effect works on the person wearing the costume, who
flies mentally to other worlds. Indeed, the attitude required honors
the staying in sacred space, for death or illness may result if the inner
person stops flying. The fear of loss of soul, health or life powerfully
energizes the person and the sincere harmony with which faith and
action interweave takes us back to the transmission of African tribal
beliefs. These costumed characters – human altars in their own right
– can parade alone, but mostly they participate in choreographed
mythological enactments chosen from the locals' favorite liberation-
from-bondage motifs. As such these characters codify and enunciate
individuality while simultaneously declaring solidarity with people,
place or concept. At their best the characters mesmerize the collective with an aesthetically grand mirror of itself.

Altars of Sacrificial Death

Thus far we have dealt with the formation and function of human
altars in groups. However, the creation of altars – especially human

altars – has the implicit danger of real and symbolic sacrificial death. An example comes from my own work. Four of us consulted for a large group at the San Francisco Jung Institute for a public program weekend. By design, the four consultants embodied age, gender and ethnic diversity. The participants, however, turned out to be 98 percent Caucasian and homogeneous in most respects. In the last meeting of the large group, when typically the most poignant mythological themes of the conference achieve a fixed cohesion, members began to speak of us consultants as the gods. A sandtray-type play ensued where we were treated not just as representing the gods but as being the gods. When I became the focus, I found myself moving away from everyday reality into another very pleasurable consciousness permeated by air and light. I had become the threshold for the group's transcendence. I realized the danger to me only when I heard one of my consulting colleagues say he was worried about me because I looked drained of blood, that my face was deathly white. Most significantly, I was being rendered silent or stupefied and therefore unable to do any consulting. In such a way work groups unconsciously kill their members, consultants or leaders. When I heard the peril of my state in his words, I made a crash return into my flesh-and-blood self, released from the seductive other-worldly journey. This experience was energized by the unresolvable diversity issue that the consultant member engendered, given the values of this homogeneously Caucasian, sophisticated group. The experience was fueled also by the mystical projections the Jungian locale awakens in those who seek its shelter. It was but an exaggeration of what the consulting experience typically draws to itself. It illustrated also how readily the human altar can become the human sacrifice – a phenomenon all the more complex when the sacrificed one goes to death willingly. My discussion of the broadly complex topic of human sacrifice is limited to its occurrence in Peru where I recently witnessed a festival in which human lives were sacrificed voluntarily.

Blood sacrifice, the offering of humans and animals to the gods, is one of humanity's earliest forms of worship and was in the origins of most if not all religions. Human sacrifices are still being carried out in some places such as the Peruvian Andes; they are rare and legal only when voluntary and well integrated into rituals encompassing many communities. Clandestine, illegal occurrences do take place, however, and depend on the betrayal of poor people by seemingly unscrupulous shamans hired by a few well-to-do patrons who hope to ensure their wealth. Also, periodically a community may sacrifice a child to prevent or contain a natural disaster such as an earthquake or flood, or may even shed someone's blood to appease the spirit of a highway to prevent future accidental deaths in that area. Tierney (1989) most convincingly documents multiple human sacrifices with data gathered via his personal immersion in the cultures perpetuating these religious customs in the Andes.

I witnessed a variant of these ancient rituals in the annual Qoyllorit'y festival which takes place on a 17000-foot Andean mountain peak about 90 miles from Cusco, the classical Inca capital. The festival can draw as many as 70000 people from all over the land, particularly villagers who walk over rugged mountainous terrain to get there. It is most colorful because they are dressed in typical garb and because many villages send a group of musicians and costumed dancing troupes who choreograph a symbolic enactment meaningful to them and perform it repetitively. This organic weaving of vernacular music, dancing and drumming goes on incessantly for three days and nights.

The peak on which Qoyllorit'y happened was considered a tutelary deity in pre-Columbian times, drawing animal and agricultural offerings. During Inca rule, its cult was institutionalized and put in the service of a social cast that displayed its power and wealth with sumptuous festivities *in situ*. The Spanish conquest rooted Christianity in Andean society but was modified by the local practices and beliefs; a pantheon of Peruvian deities and saints emerged to take their place next to the European imports. The dark-skinned Christ of Qoyllorit'y is one of these hybrids. The story explaining his apparition and crucified imprint on a natural rock follows a typical Catholic form. Briefly, Jesus comes to a very poor, suffering but obedient boy. After many events, adults witness the final encounter; the apparition turns into the agonizing, bleeding Christ on the cross and the boy dies. A very large but simple sanctuary has been built on the mountain top encompassing the blazened rock. During the festival days, pilgrims crowd into it, holding lit candles dripping wax on their hands and requesting health, money or whatever wishes they hope to have granted.

At the heart of the worship are the *Ukukus*, the bear men. They are considered to be half divine, half human and are selected from the best of each village's crop of young men. They must excel in physical prowess as well as in goodness of character. They must also be very agile and capable of withstanding intense cold and exposure with little oxygen, for they are the ones who climb beyond the sanctuary to the highest glacier. There they spend the night challenging and surrendering to greater powers by doing the most daring of feats including handstands, jumping and running. Those who survive descend at dawn, carrying a block of ice on their backs on which reflects the light of the rising sun. They are in charge of bringing down the stars which as semi-gods they have grabbed out of the sky. The ice is delivered to the Christ in the sanctuary. The blending of ages and cultures is spectacular to behold.

We were shocked to hear of the one dead man the year I attended, the five the year before, and the equanimity with which the message was delivered to us by our erudite Mestizo guide and teacher of Andean mysticism. The eager, searching look in the clusters of villagers half way up the glacier that dawn belied the pose of acceptance communicated otherwise. Their eyes clearly mirrored fear and hope for the life of a son, relative or friend. Yet they offered their loved ones annually as transformative vessels in the hope of a better collective existence.

Almost as important was the order of the scene surrounding us those three days. Approximately 70 000 men, women and children somehow climbed this very high mountain, squatted at the foot of its glacier with no food, sanitary provisions or facilities of any kind and engaged in a multiplicity of religious and social exchanges in peace and harmony. This was a magnanimous intergroup event defying most of our social-psychological explanations. Obviously these pilgrims had the rhythm of centuries of custom and tradition to guide them. But it was grandly evident that their behavior flowed from the authenticity of belief in their spirits and in the vessels that could mediate their prayers. Each individual and his or her movements within their subgroups – and the subgroups themselves – seemed irrationally but intelligently linked by a web of invisible threads to the two interlocking spiritual centers. One was the god of the pre-Columbian moving altar embodied in the costumed Ukukus, dancing the slopes of the glacier to their possible death for the sake of one and all. The other was the familiar – to us – crucified Christ, at once an image for the ubiquitous scapegoat victim and an emblem for the conquest and subjugation of human life and soul.

During the arduous events of the festival I asked myself repeatedly: What is the victim's power? How does sacrifice accomplish its ends? I have gathered from my observations and readings that the essence of the sacrificial experience is the surrender: the moment when control is lost to the fear and excitement of the ultimate risk. Rational thought can explain the impact of the moment only clumsily and marginally, for the impact rests on the direct experience. Yet it is obvious that we are intoxicated by it and its capacity to discard the regularity and safety of daily existence. It seems to be accompanied by states of release, relief and guilt (he died instead of me), dramatic in the commingling of victim and participant killer. For here the latter also experiences immortality. If an event of this magnitude is to return a part of the human world to the gods, then our faith in the divine must be sparked and our current attitudinal disposition altered. In groups, parallels to these affects are noticeable when crossing happens and the means sacrificed for this purpose noted. When a group becomes aware that it has been captivated by a central projection and sees its pervasive and deceptive coloring of the reality it trusted, there is a massive release of affective energy. It unites the psyches present and propels them to a different standpoint – for good or evil, depending on the group's level of development and resources. This explosive state is pleasurable even if the data are painful and an ecstatic excitement is generated by the transforming libidinal energy which feels otherworldly or sacred.

References

Colman, A. (1995). *Mystery of the Group*. Evanston, IL: Chiron.
Nunley, J. & Bettelheim, J. (1988). *Caribbean Festival Arts*. Seattle, WA: University of Washington Press.
Thompson, R. (1993). *Faces of the Gods: Art and Altars of Africa and the African Americas*. New York/Prestel/Munich: The Museum for African Art.
Tierney, P. (1989). *The Highest Altar: The Story of Human Sacrifice*. New York: Viking.

Wana Jukurpa: The Medicine Snake Dreaming of Central Australia

Leon Petchkovsky
Wentworth Falls, New South Wales, Australia

Craig San Roque
Alice Springs, Northern Territory, Australia
Australian and New Zealand Society of Jungian Analysts

The authors traveled regularly to Central Australia during the 1980s, sometimes as clinicians, sometimes to lead Jungian study groups. We became involved with Healthy Aboriginal Life Team (HALT), an indigenous health education organization set up by Andrew Japaljari (AJ), a traditional *Walpiri/Pintubi* man, to meet and perhaps halt the ravages of alcohol and of gasoline-sniffing in the aboriginal communities in Central Australia. It was innovative at the time, because it used congruent cultural forms such as sand-painting iconography and an understanding of the mythological underpinnings of the kinship organization – the kinship/dreaming-totem systems – to get its message across. This kind of iconography and cultivation of kinship vectors is now normative for every health organization that aspires to address aboriginal people. It seems so obvious in retrospect. But back then, we just had an intuition that one reason that aboriginal people were having such a hard time was that, in their own words: "There is no dreaming for the grog, no dreaming for petrol." The mythic dimension that was missing was our starting point.

In March 1989, one of us (LP) shared a dream with AJ:

The dreamer is lying on the ground, on his back, quite ill. He has a heart condition [at the time, he in fact had a dysrrhythmia, which subsequently rectified]. *The locale is like the desert of Central Australia. He can see a wooden structure, a sort of scaffolding of ritual poles. There is a group of aboriginal persons approaching him, men and women. They are carrying a snake, which they apply to his chest and heart. Oil exudes from the snake. This is rubbed into his chest.*

AJ nodded non-committally and went about the day's business. The following day, he mentioned to LP that he had a dream, in which *he saw his father* [who was a *ngangkari* – native healer – and was still alive at the time]. *His father bade him approach, and sent a snake toward him for LP.* AJ took the dream as a positive sign for further discussions.

In May 1989 LP, by now back in New South Wales, received a phone call from AJ in Central Australia: "We have decided to call you Jungarrai, and to teach you about ngangkari business. When can you come?"

Central Australian society is exogamous, the two moieties each being divided into fours clans or sub-sections. Jungarrai/Japaljari form one father-son classificatory pair. Thus, a Japaljari's sons are always Jungarrais, and a Jungarrai's sons are always Japaljaris, which means that Jungarrais of different generations are in a grandfather-grandson relationship.

Earlier, CSR had given AJ a copy of Jung's *Memories. Dreams, Reflections* to read. AJ asked us, "What is your relationship to this fellow Jung? He seems to think *yapa* way" (indigenously). We pondered and one of us replied: "I suppose he's a sort of spiritual grandfather to us. After all, Leon analyzed with Irene Champernowne, who analyzed with Jung and then Toni Wolff; and Craig analyzed with Norah Moore, who analyzed with Michael Fordham." AJ said, "That's good. *Tjamu* [grandfathers] are the teachers; that's yapa way." We now had two sets of grandfather teachers. Jung and the Jungarrai grandfathers. A person who has not been given a sub-section name is in limbo in Central Australian aboriginal culture. The name establishes your relatives (*walytja*), dreamings (*tjukurpa*), songs (*inkanyi*), and sacred sites (*ngura*). And Jungarrai was one of the medicine (ngangkari) lineages. We had been put on the map.

Six years later, we are still students of ngangkari business, but there have been certain developments. In early 1990, CSR was invited by an aboriginal colleague to come up with a European story that would be the equivalent of tjukurpa: creation or dreaming stories which embody the law and back up customs, including methods of therapeutic practice sanctioned by tradition. Such a story would be useful in "holding the law for grog": helping traditional aboriginal people to handle the facts about alcohol. He resolved to research the stories, develop the most useful and prepare it so that, when he was asked, the story could be handed over at the right time in the right way to the right people. Dionysus had been invoked, and his name was *Sugar-man*. (The nearest equivalent to alcohol in the Western Deserts lexicon is *wama* or *pama* – sugar, honey, sweet sap – any highly concentrated source of energy).

CSR was offered work in the Alice Springs area as a psychologist/project officer for a local alcohol and drugs agency. Meanwhile, AJ and the grandfathers began to teach us medicine dreaming. They took us out to the beginning of the Snake Dreaming Track at Karrinyara (Central Mount Wedge). A year later, we were invited to the End, the sacred waterhole at Nyinmi in Western Australia, where the snake went into the earth to create a spirit site. We are currently being organized to fill in the stations between.

Our Western epistemological traditional is organized diachronically; Chronos rules. Aboriginal ontology is geosophic; time is measured as travel from one locus to another. *Ngura* (place), is all. As Swain (1988) points out, the ubiety and ahistoricity of the aboriginal world view struggles to accommodate a ubiquitous understanding of the religious universe predicated on Christian historic universalism: "Christ was born and died, in historic time, to save us all."

A new Hegelian synthesis is discernible however. The Walpiri now have "two laws" because they have taught *Wapirra* (God) to talk Walpiri. He is *kirdu* (owner) of the law, but they are *kundun-gurlu* (ritual custodians), who make sure the law is performed properly. Reciprocally, our own engagement with indigenous understanding, in particular the medicine dreaming, is in our view a proper Western task of reanimation. As Tacey (1995) put it:

Australia becomes an ideal place for the birth of a new dreaming, a dreaming which could be an important cultural experiment for the world at large. The thesis of white rationality is being eroded by the antithesis of black dreaming, but the synthesis will probably combine and transcend both.

A Jungarrai story points to some of the aspects and themes in the making of an indigenous healer.

Yarapalongu Wana Tjukurpa (the Medicine Snake Story)

There are two versions of the beginning. In the "male dispossession" version:

A black snake lived in a waterhole near Karrinyara. He was a Jungarrai. One day, a female snake, a Nungarrai (a sister) came to his waterhole from the East. He wanted to have intercourse with her (incest), but she fought him off. They had a huge fight, rearing up miles into the air, and she bit him on the head and won. He had to leave, and began traveling West.

In the other version, the male is a usurper who tries to appropriate the female's waterhole:

Two snakes were traveling from the East. They drove the Jungarrai snake from his waterhole in Karrinyara. He left, traveling West, and soon came to a Nungarrai snake's waterhole. She was a sister, but he wanted to have sex with her, and he wanted her waterhole. They had a huge fight, and she bit him on the head and won. He had to leave, and began traveling West.

The story of the medicine snake's journey to the west is told simply.

That Jungarrai was traveling West, traveling, traveling. And the Wakultjarra, like little wallabies they hit him with sticks, cutting him up real bad, cutting him to the bone, losing his flesh. They cut his balls, but he keep traveling right up to Lake Mackay [a waterless salt-lake] with the salt getting into his cuts, and hurting bad, but that Jungarrai he keep on going, until he got to Nyinmi, and the Kililpi [described as dog-like creatures, but also one of the Western Desert words for stars]. They cut his guts out, and his heart. Went three ways. His heart and blood went North to Balgo [an important medicine man site]. His guts and liver went South, and his skin, that eagle Walawurru lift him up, but skin was too heavy, and he drop him in the sea at White Point, near Port Lincoln. His spirit Kurunpa went into that waterhole at Nyinmi [another very important medicine man site], and ngangkari medicine men, they get their kurunpa, their mapanpa [healing energy] from that spirit. And his spirit was strong, and some kept going West, traveling to the sea at Newman.

Some of the themes we might discern are: the urge toward brother/sister incest, the struggle between male and female, and the ensuing usurpance/dispossession. These themes seem to us to be specific catalysts of the shamanic journey, rather than the broader individuation one of Everyman, which is more concerned with pulling away from incest with the parents, the *nostalgie de la boue* (nostalgia for the mud). Freud distinguished between *anaclitic* and *narcissistic* object cathexes, that is, attraction to the nurturing object versus the mirroring one. (See La Planche & Pontalis, 1973.) It took Heinz Kohut and D. W. Winnicott to affirm that mirroring was precisely psychic nurturing. Nevertheless, the shamanic neophyte's struggles orient more toward the contrasexual archetype (animus/anima) than the mother or father complex. The *berdache* (transsexual) phenomenon commonly described in Siberian and North American Indian shamanic cultures supports this view. So does the hermaphrodite of the alchemic adepts. We are forced to consider that the psychic healer may be an absolutely rotten analyst in that empathic nurturing Kohutian sense, but healing still occurs, out of a different principle: the urge of the autonomous psyche.

Consider the *Wana* story. Anima will not be integrated into ego. The female snake rejects her brother's hot advances, and he is thrown into the desert, to the cutting and mutilation, the castration, the death, and the spiritual renewal that is required. Only then will he have X-ray vision and the ability to extract the bad lumps of *mapanpa* that glow invasively in his patient.

There are solar hero elements evident in the travel from East to West, and the alchemical salt rubs many times into the wounds. But these elements are more general, and only to be expected in any difficult undertaking.

Post-script

There was some speculation about the effects of being placed in this story. Within a year, both authors' marriages of 25 years had failed, and they were on their personal journeys of exile and discovery: "salt getting into his cuts, and hurting bad." There is a traditional test that is put to the neophyte after he has completed his ngangkari training. He must demonstrate mastery of his powers by curing his first wife of an illness.

The *kumatjai* prohibition (one may not speak the name of the dead) virtually guarantees ahistoricity in the Western sense. There are no chronicles of the doings of great individuals. We believe, however, that there was a choice at the collective level, to go that particular way. "Walpiri do not passively drop things from cultural memory. Nor have they developed collective amnesia through an atrophy of their historical faculties ... significant events are not left to decay and be forgotten, but are rather stripped bare of their historic content as they are absorbed into places already saturated with mythical value" (Swain, 1988).

The reader is referred to CSR's (1986) detailed comparative discussion of indigenous aboriginal and Jungian analytic training programs.

References

LaPlanche, J. & Pontalis, J.-B. (1973). *The Language of Psychoanalysis.* London: Hogarth.

San Roque, C. (1986). Psychoanalysis, black and white: Towards floating a project on a cross-cultural psychotherapy training. In B. Wright, G. Fry, L. Petchkovsky (Eds.), *Contemporary Issues in Aborginal Studies.* Kingswood, NSW, Australia: Firebird Press.

Swain, T. (1988). The ghost of space. In: T. Swain & D. Rose (Eds.), *Aboriginal Australians and Christian Missions.* Australian Association for the Study of Religions at the South Australian College of Advanced Education.

Tacey, D. (1995). *Edge of the Sacred.* New York: HarperCollins.

Panel: Analytical Psychology and Religion

Introduction

Thayer A. Greene
Amherst, Massachusetts, U.S.A.
New York Association for Analytical Psychology

Jung's personal story and his intense explorations of religious questions provide the historical and psychological foundation for the open questions posed by the relationship between analytical psychology and religion. From his earliest dream of the ritual phallus to his boyhood image of God – destroying the Basel Cathedral with a mighty turd – Jung insisted on doing what his clergyman father had failed to do: approaching religion and, especially religious experience as an open question.

Like Jung, I am the son and grandson of Protestant ministers. Unlike Jung, I trained for the ministry and spent ten years as a University chaplain and parish minister before changing careers to become a Jungian analyst. I believe that the fate and future of our common life together on this planet will be determined by the nature of our individual and collective religious consciousness, as much as by any other factor.

What then are some of the most pressing religious questions of our time as they touch upon Jung's vision of the psyche and its religious function? First on my list is the rapid emergence of religious fundamentalism in a variety of countries and cultures and its frequently aligning itself with ultraconservative politics and nationalism. How do we explain this phenomenon from a psychological perspective? Why are an increasing number of educated and thoughtful people being drawn into the vortex of this collective vision? What is the fundamental psychic value that motivates them to adopt an adversarial relation to other viewpoints and other people?

Another development, in the United States at least, has been "New Age spirituality." In stark contrast to the collective quality of fundamentalism, this emerging phenomenon is highly diverse and diffuse in its orientation and focused primarily on individual experience, especially on intuitive and feeling values. Jung is often cited by New Age advocates as an authority for their viewpoint but, they tend to ignore or neglect his wisdom about the personal and archetypal shadow. What are we to make of the New Age phenomenon? Is it a sign of the emergence of the Aquarian Age or is it more an indication of religious confusion?

Finally, I must mention the re-emergence of the Goddess as an object of conscious religious value and worship. Repressed for centuries in the West, She is once again claiming her place in our individual and collective consciousness. Women and many men are responding deeply to her renewing presence. But how does an aging patriarchal culture become receptive to such a potentially transformative religious and psychological development?

Analytical Psychology and Religion for the Year 2000

J. Marvin Spiegelman
Studio City, California, U.S.A.
Society of Jungian Analysts of Southern California

My house shall be called a house of prayer for all nations.
(Isaiah 56:7)

Sir, to which sublime tradition do you belong?
   (Traditional greeting, in ancient times, for strangers coming
      upon each other on the border between Tibet and China).

The foregoing epigraphs express two ancient and differing longings in the human soul: that all humankind shall be as brothers and sisters, worshipping together in the one temple of the divine; and that each tribe, each nation, each religious tradition and finally all individuals shall acknowledge respectfully one another's differing faith. Reality, alas, shows a less favorable picture of this interplay of these opposites – the One and the Many – frequently one of suppression and domination of one side over the other. It is no longer customary for one religion to go to war against another, although "ethnic cleansing" in Bosnia and Muslim terrorism in the Middle East come close. And the world watches helplessly while that same border between Tibet and China is no longer one of peaceful greeting but witnesses the political religion of Communism crushing Buddhism in a conflagration among the many twentieth century political wars afflicting the end of our aeon.

It was one of Jung's major contributions to bring consciousness of such conflicting opposites back into the psyche and to show that the One of the individual soul is a reflection of the archetypal Many of the collective unconscious, residing in all humankind. The path of individuation, he showed, was the way that the multiplicity could be made conscious, lived and integrated into a unity that was both present in potential and needing to be achieved by hard psychological effort and experience. Such is the main work of classical Jungian analysis, constituting an important spiritual achievement in the century that is now ending.

The spiritual and political battles of our time have been accompanied by an ever-increasing world-wide contact among cultures and religions. Such encounters produce religious exchanges and syncretism that is now increasingly apparent, so that Buddhism, for example, dying in China and Japan, gets new life in America and Europe, and Christian priests from Africa renew faith among Caucasians.

This syncretism, and problem of the One and Many, reveals itself in dreams. In the second year of my first analysis, in 1951, I dreamed that a divine child was being born, attended by a Christian priest, a Jewish rabbi and a Buddhist priest. Part of my spiritual path, accordingly, has been ecumenical. The classic dream of this kind, however, was that of Zeller (1975) who told Jung this dream in 1949:

> *A temple of vast dimensions was in the process of being built. As far as I could see – ahead, behind, right and left – there were incredible numbers of people building on gigantic pillars. I, too, was building on a pillar. The whole building process was in its very first beginnings, but the foundation was already there, the rest of the building was starting to go up, and I and many others were working on it.*

Jung's response to Zeller's dream was that this temple truly was being built over all the world, as Jung too saw in dreams, and that it would take, he thought, about 600 years. This was also Jung's answer to Zeller's question as to what analysts were doing. A more recent and typical syncretic dream of a middle-aged Irish male is as follows:

> *I am at a Ferbrungen* [a Jewish religious celebration, with dancing and singing]. *I go into a levitation trance, spinning, eyes closed, balancing on one foot, arms extended but bent at the elbow in a 90-degree angle. I close my eyes, ask myself if God exists and answer, "I believe so." Opening my eyes, I've traveled a quarter length along the circumference of the circle we are dancing in. I bring my hands together in gassho* [prayer] *and bow to the circle of people, half of whom respond by bowing back; the other half are passive.*

The dreamer, raised as a Catholic and soon to become a Buddhist priest, while undergoing Jungian analysis, achieves ecstasy in a Jewish religious celebration, in a Muslim dervish dance. After acknowledging his belief in God, he comes to a Buddhist experience of enlightenment. That is surely syncretism!

At the same time that some individuals undergo religious development and achieve wholeness in Jungian analysis or along other spiritual paths that seek similar goals, the outer world is enduring increasing fragmentation, dissociation, even disintegration. Group life, including group religious life, often lacks the harmony, support, succor and meaning which all traditions have provided in the past. Meanwhile, the isolation of the individual, especially in cities all over the world, continues apace. Collective life within Jungian circles, as witnessed by battles, politics and intrigue, is no better – nor worse – than other groups and may be a fitting consequence of the Jungian emphasis on the individual along with a certain condescension toward outer "collectives." Not only is the traditional patriarchy being seriously undermined, but the emerging feminine aspect of the Self is far from being just the "good mother" and is filled with wrath.

Jung's great opus, *Answer to Job* (CW11), one of the chief contributions to the spirit in the twentieth century, gives us a picture of this historical development of the Self in the Western psyche. Jung's analysis makes apparent the necessity for contemporary individuals to be aware of our own darkness as a prelude to the further incarnation of the divine in the human soul. We lack, however, a vision of the global psyche – now in such turbulent transition – and need a new, global *Answer* to help us achieve some clarity and support in our lonely individual work.

In the meantime, our task as analysts continues to be that of consciousness-raising in our branch of the spiritual task of humankind at the end of the century, by remaining committed to our own religious attitude toward the psyche. In the face of the battles among and against fundamentalists, people allied with one or another orthodoxy of belief or behavior, it is of great importance that there are those, such as Jungian analysts, who are committed to the individual soul, its suffering and truths, while the collectives are mangling each other, yet also contributing to that same syncretic process affecting us all. We have no idea how long this collective *nigredo* must continue, but we can look for signs in the psyche itself to guide us on our path.

Love of Freedom

Arwind Vasavada
Chicago, Illinois, U.S.A.
Chicago Society of Jungian Analysts

Analytical psychology cannot be divorced from religion. The chief contribution of Jung is not so much in psychology as in the field of religion. He made us aware of the meaning of religion in life, and he made the terms "Self" and "religion" respectable in the field of psychology.

The West in the 1960s saw an influx of Indian gurus. People had visited them in India and brought them to Western countries. Young people used to flock by thousands to listen to them. Some devotees were in earnest and imbibed the flavor of Eastern wisdom. I wondered at this phenomenon. Some of the gurus did not know the language of the country. One who did not know English spoke in Hindi – which was not his mother tongue. The Hindi was translated into English by one disciple who did it well. Another disciple, however, did not know English very well but still she translated what he spoke. His words were secondary; his presence emanated depth of spirit, going straight to the heart of people. They were spellbound and came back again and again to listen to him and attend his intensive weekends. What was given and what was received by these people? Was it mere fascination? Was it eye-wash, a temporary involvement? It may have been for many but was not for all. Some of the gurus made homes in the countries to which they were called. The tradition they established continues. What does all this tell us?

It is clear that the Western world was awakened to a new dimension of knowledge, a knowledge that did not depend on books and techniques. People awoke to see that wisdom comes to one who is prepared to stake everything for it. It became clear, also, that wisdom cannot be codified or certified. Of course, there are institutions in the East where people go to learn wisdom and sacred texts are studied. But texts are secondary. Their study helps us to communicate in a certain language to certain kinds of people. It is, however, the life one lives that radiates wisdom and transforms one.

Is there nothing in the West similar to Eastern wisdom? Is there no such path traced out by anyone? It cannot be so. Human nature everywhere is the same. This call for total freedom, to discover one's foundation within is there. We have to look within to find it.

What shall we call the kind of life these persons live; is it based on a love of freedom? A scourge of smallpox blinded a boy of ten. All his hopes for studies and enjoyment of life were destroyed. He took a staff and roamed all over India. He went through all that life had to offer him, including scorn and pity, sometimes compassion. He went through all the deprivations life had to give him: hunger and thirst, heat and cold, disease and a near-death state. He often begged for food. When it was given, he ate too much and had stomach problems. He reached a stage where he could tolerate his dependence no longer. He sat under a tree and would not move from there until he felt free. If his life was worthwhile, he would survive; if not, he would die.

Hours went by and something happened. He felt a sense of strength within. He saw the world in a different manner. Everything felt different. There was a transformation. Needed help came and the perfume of wisdom attracted people and was valuable to all those who came for it. This person had nothing. He had nothing to lose. The world answered his needs and he felt fulfilled.

Another example. A professor of repute in a famous university, rich by education and means, but dependent on drugs for bliss. He quit his tenured job and traveled from the United States to India, by sea and land, going through many hazards to find a guru who would free him from his dependence on drugs. What was that quality and intensity of the pull that made him take this hazardous journey? He lost everything valuable in the eyes of the world. Why did he do that, and for what? And what did he get in return?

He found someone living in the foothills of the Himalayas, a person whose belongings were the clothes he wore and a blanket. People came to him for wisdom, remained with him as long as they wished and returned home. He had no degree or diploma; he did not study in any educational institution for gaining wisdom. He gave no diploma or degree to those who came to learn from him.

The professor also got nothing; rather, he lost his tenure and his worldly goods. In losing, he gained all. He felt he had found the answer to all his problems. He felt free from drugs and many other attachments. He returned home transformed. People flocked round him to listen to him. They felt a different kind of energy emanating from him.

These Indian gurus were not academically qualified. They did not go to universities or colleges, had no diplomas or degrees. Therefore, they gave none. Their basic needs were simple. They possessed nothing except what they had on their bodies. They asked nothing of those who came to learn from them. People stayed as long as they liked and went away when they chose. If there was any qualification required of them, it was their own intensity for gaining wisdom. They got what they put in. All kinds of people, from the highly educated to the uneducated, from rich to poor came to the gurus. They respected everyone and they were available whenever people called on them.

We find a similar story played out in the life of Jung. He learned what he had to learn from the university he attended and also from others such as Freud, Wilhelm and Zimmer. What was that inner call to Jung that he threw away the most coveted position in the International Psychoanalytic Association? Let us recall words of Jung:

> *Always the inner experience of individuation has been the most valuable and important thing in life. It is the only thing that brings any lasting satisfaction to a man. Power, glory, wealth mean nothing in comparison. ... The really important things are within. It is more important to me that I am happy than that I have the external reason for happiness. Rich people should be happy but often they are bored*

*to death; therefore, it is ever so much better for man to work to
produce an inner condition that gives him an inner happiness.
Experience shows that there are certain psychological conditions in
which man gets eternal results. [These conditions] have a divine
quality and yield all that satisfaction which man made things do not.*
(DS-I, p. 210)

In Jung's years of loneliness, when contact with Freud and his
image as an associate of the world-famous Freud died, Jung stayed
with death. This death was the starting point of his transformation,
the growth of his own wisdom and, consequently, his offering
wisdom to those who came to him.

All sorts of persons came to him, from all over the world, with all
sorts of expectations. Men and women with name and fame, high
degrees and diplomas came. Ordinary people came also. They got
from him according to their needs and according to the intensity of
their search. It did not matter to Jung who they were, so long as he
perceived a helpful contact between himself and them. Some
learned wisdom from him and went back and spread the word. An
important quality in the teaching of Jung, which is close to the way
of the guru, is that people from any religious background could
come and be helped. Why was it so? Jung had no preconceived
notion of the end of the journey, except that freedom from all kinds
of trappings is necessary. He saw that the cry for freedom, for
wholeness, is inborn in all human beings. The persons I mentioned
earlier were not formally educated. Although they possessed nothing but what they had on their bodies, the call for freedom – freedom
from all dependence – was of the utmost significance.

Like any genuine guru, Jung looked for the wholeness within and
was like a mirror to ever-present wholeness within others. For him,
belief was not important. Experiencing, seeing the divine, was all
important. For that reason Jung said to theologians, "It is high time
we realized that it is pointless to praise the light and preach it if
nobody sees it. It is much more needful to teach people the art of
seeing" (CW12, par. 14). This aspect of Jung's teaching, one that is
in total agreement with the way of the guru, attracted me the most
and brought me to Zurich to learn from Jung. I saw the guru in him.
Thus, my first question on my first meeting with him in Kusnacht
soon after arriving in Zurich was, "Dr. Jung, you are a guru. Why do
you deny that, as you do in your book *Psychology and Alchemy*?" It
was a shock later on when I saw that I had to study psychiatry in

order to get the diploma. I saw no connection between psychiatry and the way of Jung.

Jung did not start an institution for training. He taught all those who came to him, and not all of them had the qualifications we now require from a candidate for training. It is said that he did not even like the idea of starting the Jung Institute. He offered no diploma to his students, for example, C.A. Meier, Liliane Frey-Rohn or Barbara Hannah. In all respects, the way of Jung was like that of a guru.

What has gone wrong now? Is it because we have turned the paths of wisdom into a profession? Is it because we allow ourselves to be dominated by the requirements of the state? Do we see that requirements of states have divided us among ourselves? We sometimes do not admit a Jungian from one institution to another in a different state. Have we not lost a sense of community among ourselves? Let us ponder this question.

Archetype and Relation in Religious Experience

Eli B. Weisstub
Jerusalem, Israel
Israel Association of Analytical Psychology

There are two main trends in the modern psychological study of religious experience. The "archetypal" (Jungian) orientation describes an exclusively intrapsychic source of religious images and ideas; the "relational" emphasizes the relation to God as "wholly other" (Otto, 1923). I will reiterate briefly Jung's position, drawing from an article by Dourley (1995).

The unconscious is deity-creating. "The dynamic of the religion- and deity-creating function of the unconscious reflects a wholly intra-psychic dialectic." The psyche is strictly self-contained and "all extra-psychic agencies are excluded from the inner dialectic" between conscious and unconscious. "Such self-containment excludes in principle the possibility of a supernatural or transcendent world addressing the psyche from a position beyond the 'psyche'" (p. 177).

In analytical psychology the archetypes of the unconscious, especially the Self archetype, are imbued with numinosity and tend to be identified with the divine. The realization of a divine potential within led Jung to develop the thesis that there is a progressive incarnation of deity in humanity.

Does the incarnation of the divine in the human psyche exclude the possibility of a transcendent God existing beyond, as well as within the psyche? Jung considers the reality behind the phenomenon of psychic imagery. "It seems ... probable that the real nature of an archetype is not capable of being made conscious, that it is transcendent, on which account I call it psychoid" (CW8, par. 417). The archetype is "located beyond the psychic sphere. ... The ultimate nature of both (matter and spirit) is transcendental, that is irrepresentable" (CW8, par. 420).

Jung's need to be a scientific empiricist led him to a psychological reductionism of religious experience, akin to Freud's reduction of the psychological to the instinctual. Although Jung acknowledged a transcendental, irrepresentable realm beyond the psyche, his psychology of religion restricts itself to intrapsychic empiricism and thus does not easily allow for the existence of an extra-psychic God. Consequently, he downplayed the importance of faith.

Jung emphasized the importance of intra-psychic "knowing" as the significant religious experience. "It is only through the psyche that we can establish that God acts upon us: ... That which has no effect on me might as well not exist" (CW11, par. 757). To experience the profound depths of mystical and religious experience usually requires an openness and receptivity to the unknown. For it is here that one recognizes the limitations of the psyche. When faced with the unknown, we have no choice but to acknowledge all that is extra-psychic and beyond psychic comprehension. To call this realm the unconscious is insufficient. Because of this, Vasavada (1995) differentiates the unknown from the archetypal and collective unconscious. The unknown encompasses not only the unconscious, but all that we cannot know.

The Primacy of Feeling and Relation in Religious Experience

Otto (1923) was one of the first scholars to study the psychology of religious experience. The holy is, for Otto, not only an idea or an imagining but an experience of a primary feeling, which he refers to as the "mysterium tremendum. ... It is this feeling which, emerging in the mind of primeval man, forms the starting-point for the entire religious development in history. 'Daemons' and 'gods' alike spring from this root, and all the products of 'mythological apperception' or 'fantasy' are nothing but different modes in which it has been objectified" (pp. 14-15). The feeling, not the objectification in imagery, is primary.

The "mysterium tremendum" does not imply simply the inner experience of an archetype. Otto (1923) is referring to the relation to the divine as "wholly other." He calls the religious feeling, which is the experience of the numinous, "creature consciousness" or "creature feeling." It is the emotion of a creature who experiences its nothingness in the face of a much greater power, "The numinous is thus felt as objective and outside the self" (pp. 10-11). For Jung, even if the God-image is considered part of the psyche, the archetypal or "psychoid" aspects are beyond psychic perception. The divine refers to a reality that is experienced intrapsychically and yet is felt or intuited to be beyond the psyche. If the Self is experienced solely as boundaryless and infinite, there would not be an encounter with archetypal images or the Self; all would be one undifferentiated unity. The distinction between creature and creator and the relation to a creator are integral to Otto's understanding of numinosity. In the words of Kierkegaard (1849) the Self "reflects itself infinitely in relation to the Power which constituted it" (p. 147).

Apart from psychological explanations of the archetypal foundation of religion, Jung stated that the life of an individual is determined by a transcendent authority and that there is "the incontrovertible experience of an intensely personal, reciprocal relationship between man and an extramundane authority which acts as a counterpoise to the world and its reason" (CW10, par. 509).

The origin and goal of the religious quest is relational as well as archetypal. Analyzing Jung's emotional responses to the events in the Book of Job, Newton (1993) regards a combination of personal, interpersonal and archetypal factors as significant in the formation of Jung's religious ideation and feeling, and in his relation to God. The implication of Newton's work is that experience of the archetype of the Self, the God-image, is intimately connected to one's personal psychological development. The God-images we experience are usually not "pure" archetypal images. Religious "vision" is influenced by affect and by personal and cultural projections.

According to Buber (1952), religion is "only a matter of the human relation to God, not of God Himself" (p. 79). The I-Thou relationship is to other human beings, to nature and to God. All such encounters, experienced on the deepest level, form the basis of religious experience. Buber's and Jung's positions, seemingly at variance with each other, are complementary. Jung finds God within the psyche in relation to the archetypal God-image, whereas Buber's "I-Thou" experiences the Divine center in relationship to the Other, an extra-psychic orientation.

Throughout his life Jung continued to be open to new considerations. In a 1960 letter he wrote: "I quite agree with you: without relatedness individuation is hardly possible. ... I also agree with you that a religious experience depends upon human relatedness to a certain extent. I don't know to what extent." (Let-II, pp. 609-610)

The Divinization of Archetypal Images

In analytical psychology an aspect of the psyche, the Self-archetype, has been divinized and identified as the God-image. The divinization of Self archetypes (God-images) in empirical humans if taken concretely, results in the formation of a "God-man entity" (CW11, par. 758). The confusion between God and God-image in Jung's writings and the tendency to equate God-image with God may be due to a predominantly pagan (Aryan) influence. Noll (1994) contends that Jung's earliest ideas "are based primarily on the volkisch [national, racial] mysticism of sun worship. The most blatant survival is the central place of the concept of the Self in Jung's later psychology, which most commonly presents itself as an image of God or as an experience of the god within in the form of a circle or an Indian (Aryan) mandala." (p. 137)

Jung contributed to our understanding of religious development by making us aware that one can be guided by one's own God-image/s as they manifest in the process of individuation. The access to the spiritual source is within and need not be mediated by an externally represented God-image. The God-image may serve to guide us spiritually but it may lead also to a psychic inflation. Jung recognized that the indwelling of the divine spirit brings about the Christification of many that could lead to "insufferable collisions" (CW11, par. 758).

Acknowledging the shadow and our human limitations – including the limitations of our psyches – has a humbling effect that helps to diminish the tendency to psychic inflation. Recognizing and analyzing personal and interpersonal developmental influences on religious experience and respecting individual and cultural variability in God-images could help to prevent the spiritual inflation that leads inevitably to religious conflicts and war – all in the name of God.

Jung, especially in *Answer to Job* (CW11) turns to consciousness and the human factor to compensate for the lack in the archetypal God-image. Through becoming human, the archetypal divine aspect becomes morally responsible and compassionate. Only then do we arrive at a more integrated God-human entity, consciously incorporating opposites such as good and evil, male and female.

Eros and the Mystery of the Unknown

For the French philosopher Levinas (1989), being justifies itself by way of the ethical relationship with the Other. The individual becomes the site of transcendence. The realizable essence of God or the obligation inherent in the revelation is the unconditioned responsibility of being-for-the-other. Being-for-itself is conditional on being-for-the-other. A well developed relatedness function (Eros) reorients the psyche from an unconscious archetypal orientation to a conscious concern for the Other.

Without a deep sense of kinship and compassion for human beings, other creatures and the natural environment in which we live, humanity may not survive. A conscious religious attitude is necessary. We cannot rely simply on the archetypal psyche to show us the way. The archetypal psyche is grounded in dualism. It has the potential for destruction as well as creation. Faith in a positive God source is necessary to guide us in a life-affirming direction. The faith can be in a monotheistic God, in the Eastern way of self-knowledge or in Jung's conception of a positive, unifying Self. Faith is an inevitable factor in religious experience, even when the God-image becomes indistinguishable from God in a Self-God equation.

Jung (MDR) reflected on the importance of Eros, acknowledging it as "a kosmogonos, a creator and father-mother of all higher consciousness." In so doing he acknowledged the centrality of love, relation to others and to the Unknown. Religious meaning derives from the coming together of the relational and the archetypal.

In classical times, when such things were properly understood, Eros was considered a god whose divinity transcended our human limits, and who therefore could be neither comprehended nor represented in any way.

Man can try to name love, showering upon it all the names of their command, and still he will involve himself in numerous self-deceptions. If he possess a grain of wisdom, he will lay down his arms and name the unknown by the more unknown: ... that is, by the name of God. That is a confession of his subjection, his imperfection, and his dependence; but at the same time a testimony to his freedom to choose between truth and error. (MDR, pp. 353-354)

One arrives at a certain humility in the face of the unknown. We remain with a feeling of kinship with other humans and the rest of creation. As Jung wrote:

The more uncertain I have felt about myself, the more there has grown up in me a feeling of kinship with all things. That alienation which so long separated me from the world has become transferred into my own inner world, and has revealed to me an unexpected unfamiliarity with myself. (MDR, p. 359)

Jung and Eckhart: Their Conversation Today

John Dourley
Ottawa, Ontario, Canada
Association of Graduate Analytical Psychologists
(Zurich Institute)

Three places in the *Collected Works* Jung, using Meister Eckhart, illustrates his own understanding of the psyche and its religion-creating propensities. Jung's most significant appropriation of Eckhart is to be found in his elaboration of the relativity of the God concept (CW6, pars. 407-433). Jung here uses Eckhart to describe the dialectic at the core of the individuation process. Jung begins by affirming candidly that, within the containment of the total psyche, God and human consciousness are functions of each other; those who remain unaware of the unconscious origin of religion do not understand its nature.

Eckhart's description of his going forth from God into a creation that proclaimed the reality of God but in which no one was happy becomes for Jung a description of the movement of the ego out of the unconscious, with the realization that such birth alienates consciousness from its source. Jung describes the hazards of the ego's overcoming its alienation in reconnecting with its source, through Eckhart's somewhat obscure statement, "The soul is not blissful because she is in God, she is blissful because God is in her."

For Jung the soul is not blissful when she is in God. Bliss is forsaken when the soul's sense of God has been projected beyond the soul in the idolatrous identification of something or even someone as divine. The withdrawal of such projection restores divinity to its rightful place as a consciously recognized power within the unconscious. But this withdrawal presents the soul with a second danger to its bliss, namely, being swamped internally by the "flood and source" (CW6, pars. 426, 430) of an overwhelming unconscious.

But "the soul is blissful because God is in her." For Jung this state describes that of the unconscious coming to birth in the soul, mediating the energies of the divine to the ego. This makes both soul and God happy. This paradigm makes analytic work an always sacred work.

Such work is fraught with peril, as Jung admits in these passages. For the redemption of God involves the ingression of the soul and, by implication, the ego into the furthest reach of divinity which Eckhart terms the "Godhead." This ingression occurs in what Eckhart calls the "breakthrough," when he recovers his native eternity and divinity from which he is alienated but never wholly removed in time. Jung describes it as a process in which God disappears as an object and "dwindles into a subject no longer distinguishable from the ego" (CW6, par. 430). Jung's more than adequate psychological description of Eckhart's "breakthrough" thus becomes a description of the ego's furthest possible incursion into the unconscious.

Jung's major work on gnosticism (CW9-II) is the second significant locus of his use of Eckhart. In this work Jung equates Eckhart's experience and that of mysticism in general with gnostic and alchemical experience. Jung comments on an alchemical test in which the fire of the *deus absconditus* (concealed god) effectively is identified as the furthest reach of the psyche toward which all psychic life is directed and by which it ought to be governed as is a compass by the true north. The idea of attaining the deepest ingression into divinity, thus framed, can be also an immersion in Hell – perhaps implied in Jung's previous description of the dangers to the soul when in God or in the unconscious. Eckhart, Jung claims, went to this hell but, in the very passage Jung cites, Eckhart refers to a journey to a place "deeper than hell itself."

In these passages Jung again refers correctly to Eckhart's description of the "Godhead" as clearly distinct from God as trinitarian and as creator. Wholly divested of definition, the power of the Godhead is totally unconscious as would be a center of consciousness immersed in it. In a paradoxical statement worthy of Eckhart himself Jung writes, "As the Godhead is essentially unconscious so is the man who lives in God" (CW9-II, par. 301).

Yet for Eckhart it is only in this "living in God" that he fully recovers his natural divinity, from which he is alienated when relating to God as trinity or creator over against himself. Freedom from this relation to an alien God is what compels Eckhart's strange prayer, quoted twice: "This is why I pray to God to rid me of God" (Schurmann, 1978, pp. 216, 219).

Jung sees this moment of identity clearly but may be less comfortable with resting in or dwelling upon it than was Eckhart, due to its psychotic potential. Jung's reserve in this matter must be qualified by the tranquility, resignation and glowing memory of the state that informs Eckhart's remarks in that instant when he rested in unqualified unity with the divine, beyond the hell that may have been the price of gaining it.

Jung's third major appropriation of Eckhart is in his comparison of Eckhart to the Zen tradition. Here he uses Eckhart's term "breakthrough" to describe the ego's accessing the "non-ego-like self," in total release from the "'I-ness' of ... consciousness" (CW11, pars. 887, 890). In support of this position he cites the classic locus in Eckhart where Eckhart describes himself as "the unmoved mover," that is, as indistinguishable from God.

Jung deplores the ignorance of such experience in the West except in the mystical tradition, which flirts with heterodoxy or outright condemnation, as in the case of Eckhart. The Church is unaware of such experience and, when made aware, condemns it in the name of private revelation. In current Western culture only psychotherapy, by which Jung probably means his own, can foster the "disappearance of egohood" (CW11, par. 904) as a moment or stage in the emergence of the greater Self.

In an imaginary interchange Jung might well speak a word of gratitude for the personal spiritual help Eckhart provided him on occasion throughout his life. In the wider terms of cultural history,

Jung's appreciation of Eckhart would extend to the latter's early contribution to that stream of consciousness which culminated in such works as Jung's *Answer to Job* (CW11). In this work Jung makes psychologically explicit Eckhart's suggestion that God must create human consciousness to become conscious, in that process which Jung identifies as coincident with individuation.

Eckhart too might speak a word of gratitude to Jung inasmuch as Jung's hermeneutics would constitute so valuable a help in making conscious both to Eckhart and to modern people the meaning of his and our mystical experience. Yet Eckhart might ask if Jung had fully captured the furthest reaches of Eckhart's experience. Why is this important? Because Eckhart's experience might, in Jungian parlance, point to a dimension of the psyche that lies beyond the archetypes and is in some sense divested of the compelling need to seek their realization in human consciousness. Abiding in the moment of nothingness beyond archetypal urgency might well imbue subsequent consciousness with a more encompassing empathy, due to its immersion in the nothingness from which all form derives. Such empathy would become a significant resource for personal and collective survival and well being.

Nietzsche, Jung and the Death of God

Donald R. Ferrell
Montclair, New Jersey, U.S.A.
New York Association for Analytical Psychology

Friedrich Nietzsche's tragic life ended in 1900. Before descending into madness in 1889, he had given himself to the task of speaking about a crisis of the Western soul, the full expression of which, he believed, would begin fully to appear only in the twentieth century. He called this crisis the coming of the time of nihilism. He connected nihilism with a deep psycho-spiritual event he believed was taking place, largely unconsciously, within the Western psyche. One of Nietzsche's most dramatic metaphors for this complex event is "the death of God," when the time of nihilism will emerge fully.

To see that God is dead and remains dead, for Nietzsche, is to see
the end of life as we have known it for nearly 2000 years of Western
history. We have lost the eternal and transcendent ground for the
human venture in the cosmos and in history which the Western
cultural tradition has presupposed. Where God once was, there is
now only an unfathomable abyss. The death of God means "that
nothing is true and that everything is permitted." We get some sense
of Nietzsche's (1974) foreboding in this passage:

> *[The death of God] is already beginning to   ·*
> *cast its first shadows over Europe ...*
> *and how much must collapse now that this*
> *faith [in the Christian god] has been undermined ...*
> *for example the whole of European morality.* (p. 279)

Who of us today would want to see our spiritual situation or the
meaning of our culture this way? Can we not dismiss Nietzsche's
gloomy vision as an expression of his madness? Perhaps we are, as
Nietzsche's madman tells us, the "murderers of God." But has not
this murder of God been liberating for us as human beings? Does
Jung share this Nietzschean dread when he writes: "The destruction
of the God-image is followed by the annulment of the human
personality" (CW9-I, par. 170)?

For Nietzsche, the "monstrous logic of terror" that lies at the heart
of our cultural life after the death of God is what he means by
nihilism. To be godless citizens of the nihilistic culture Nietzsche
envisioned is to see how we create our own values and meanings.
Once we see this we discover that, just as we construct our symbolic
worlds of meaning and value by positing such structures, we can
also "unposit" – deconstruct – them by withdrawing our projections
of meaning and value. Nihilism – from Latin *nihil* (nothing) –
demands that we see how we create our own values and meanings.
This is the way that we have killed God, Nietzsche declares, and the
way that the human ego itself becomes something of a god. Thus,
nihilism arises out of the sense that nothing grounds or supports the
human world and the human venture in the cosmos beyond our own
symbol-generating/meaning-making capacities. In the nihilistic culture that is dawning, Nietzsche predicted, there will be a pervasive
experience of loss of meaning and direction. Increasingly, we will
be unable to feel grasped by a sense of transcendent purpose for our
lives.

Nietzsche saw that nihilism seeks to dismantle the cultural world based on the theocentric and logocentric moral and spiritual vision of the Western tradition and to unleash a monstrous logic of terror. While he was concerned about this destructive purpose in nihilism, Nietzsche also believed a constructive purpose would be served in clearing the way for the "transvaluation of all values," a process he saw as the overcoming of nihilism, at least in its self-negating form. This transvaluation Nietzsche thought of as a kind of "positive nihilism" in which the heroic – "Dionysian" – ego creates its own life-affirming values out of its encounter with the abyss of nothingness. The Superman of *Thus Spake Zarathustra* is Nietzsche's (1954) best known representation of this Dionysian ego, which he believed could overcome nihilism.

Jung was deeply fascinated and influenced by Nietzsche, because he embodied the radical experience of the loss of meaning that has been one of the hallmarks of life in modern Western culture. Nietzsche knew nihilism within his own soul.

Ultimately nihilism is, for Nietzsche, a code word that signifies, if Alice Miller (1990) is right, a profound wound to his sense of self that he was never able to mourn. This wound was delivered in Nietzsche's childhood by the significant others upon whom he was dependent. He defended against this wound, Miller argues, by attacking his introjected caregivers' symbolic equivalents, condensed in the symbol of the death of God. Moreover, if Jung is right, Nietzsche also defended against this wound by a split in his ego between himself as Nietzsche and himself as Zarathustra. This complex wound to Nietzsche's inner self had what Berger (1969) has called an "anomic" character; that is, it is meaning-destroying.

Jung (ZA), like Frey-Rohn (1988) after him, interpreted Nietzsche's psychology as driven by a dangerous inflation from the Self. In this state, Nietzsche's ego was progressively subsumed by the Self figure, Zarathustra. Inflation can be understood as the Self's incursion into the ego with "surplus" meaning in order to compensate the ego's vulnerability when it has experienced anomic events that it has not adequately mourned. Nihilism is both a radical and profound state of meaninglessness and, as in the life of Adolf Hitler of a demonically dark vision of meaning. It can be understood psychologically as the ego's becoming inflated by the abysmal, dark side of the Self. (See Ferrell, 1995.)

Jung, too, was aware of this abyss at the heart of life and of the profoundly destructive energies that could be unleashed in our encounter with the abyss. While he did not name it as nihilism, the descent of Nous (mind) into the dark embrace of Physis (nature) culminates, for Jung, in the death camps of Nazi Germany and the labor camps of the Stalinist Gulag. Of the creation of these massively dehumanizing structures and the nihilistic will to destroy that informed them, Jung says, "'The transvaluation of all values' is being enacted before our eyes" (CW9-II, par. 343). This is the monstrous logic of terror that Nietzsche feared.

It is not tragedy, however – as Nietzsche believed – but the religious symbol, that Jung asserts protects us from the destructive power of the abyss.

The religious myth is one of man's greatest and most significant achievements, giving him the security and inner strength not to be crushed by the monstrousness *of the universe ... [The religious symbol] is psychologically true, for it was and is the bridge to all that is best in humanity.* (CW5, par. 343)

Jung wrote these words at a time when he was about to enter one of the most profound crises in his life. If Kerr's (1993) reconstruction is correct, Jung was experiencing the beginning of the end of his relationships with Sabina Spielrein and with Freud. These profound losses seem to have destabilized his Self structure and opened him to the "confrontation with the unconscious."

The period from 1913 to 1918 that brought Jung, in Stevens' (1990) words, "to the edge of madness," was not only a time of extraordinary exploration; it was also a time of great loss. Central to Jung's experience of loss, following Homans' (1989) analysis, was the loss of his structure of meaning. Indeed, Jung (AP) tells us, that he became aware that he had no myth of his own. In the face of the anomic events of the loss of Spielrein and the rejection by Freud, Jung evidently experienced existentially what Nietzsche meant by the death of God. This experience was not merely the death of the God-images of traditional Judaism and Christianity, but the death of all external authority and the experience of nothingness that comes in the wake of the loss of such authority.

This time of his confrontation with the unconscious was a time of profound mourning in which Jung, with the help especially of Toni Wolff, surrendered to the task of letting go of the heroic attitude and the meaning structure built on it. Rather than dealing heroically with the pain of his loss of meaning, Jung patiently allowed the Self to manifest within him without completely identifying with it. He was prevented from this inflationary identification, I believe, precisely because he was able to mourn. To mourn is to acknowledge woundedness to the ego in the face of loss, and thereby to heal the wound of loss rather than to deny it by attempting to become omnipotent.

During his encounter with the unconscious, Jung's wounded ego was flooded with the surplus meaning that flows from the Self in its compensating function. His famous fantasy/dream of the appearance of Elijah and Salome, which Jung (AP) says took place in December 1913, seems to be structurally equivalent to Zarathustra's appearance to Nietzsche. In this fantasy/dream Salome tells Jung's dream ego that he is "the Christ," arousing profound anxiety in Jung, who responds to Salome, "This is madness" (p. 96). And yet, as Jung reports the fantasy/dream, he experienced a process that is analogous both to the myth of the crucifixion of Christ and the Mithraic myth of the lion-headed deity, Aion. Jung explicitly compares his fantasy/dream experience to the process of initiation of the ancient mystery religions, which held such fascination for him.

The images Jung reports from his fantasy/dream of Salome are reminiscent both of Jesus alone in the Garden of Gethsemane, surrounded by sleeping disciples, struggling to give himself over to the divine purpose; and of initiation into the cult of Mithra, the god who brings order out of chaos, the midpoint of the seven levels of initiation symbolized by the lion. Given Jung's struggle not only to find his own myth – his own ultimate purpose – but his sense of aloneness, abandonment and the cost of serving that purpose, as well as his own inner chaos, the Self spontaneously presenting him – in compensation – with the mythological equivalents of his own inner struggle.

It is a significant question, however, whether Jung remained permanently identified with these mythic images from the Self and, thus, remained in a state of inflation, as Noll (1995) has argued. Or was he able to experience the surplus meaning of the Self that flowed into his enfeebled ego in compensation, without becoming psychotically inflated as both Nietzsche and Hitler did? My argument, in contrast to Noll's, is that Jung did not become inflated, because he was able to mourn.

Thus, Jung was able to accept his deep vulnerability and loss and to experience the Self in a healing, rather than a destructive, way. Indeed, when Jung writes (CW9-II, par. 44n) about inflation, he refers to St. Paul's letter to the Church at Corinth. In this letter the

Corinthian Christians are told that they are in a state of arrogance because they have not mourned an episode of stepmother-stepson incest in their community, and thus are unable to act in a morally sensitive way.

Jung emerged from his confrontation with the unconscious, not in a dangerously inflated state, but in a more consolidated state in which his appreciation of the Self, the "god within," had deepened greatly in both its ordering and disordering functions. Out of this ordeal came his growing conviction that our vulnerability to loss of meaning, especially through the impact of anomic events, on the one hand, and our susceptibility to inflation in nihilistic states of unmourned meaninglessness on the other, remain among the most dangerous aspects of the human condition.

We may ask what the relevance of Jung's thought is to the problem of nihilism. In making the crucial distinction between the God-image and that to which it points, Jung keeps his own thought open to the "God beyond God" of Meister Eckhart and Paul Tillich, as Dourley (1981, 1992) has pointed out. Thus, Jung's thought is grounded in a sense of transcendence. However, in accepting that the God-images of Judaism and Christianity have lost their numinosity for growing numbers of people in Western culture, Jung implicitly acknowledges something like Nietzsche's pronouncement of the death of God – which might be better designated as the death of the dominant God-images of our culture.

In his deep concern to re-vision the God-image, Jung opened himself – whether he would have named it this way or not – to a confrontation with nihilism. Nihilism is the sense that our highest values, including truth, are nullified by the abyss of nothingness. Consequently, nothingness becomes the absolute in relationship to which the whole human enterprise is called into question as without ultimate validity, meaning or purpose. Gillespie (1995) argues that, behind this modern nihilistic sense of nothingness is the dark and terrible God of medieval nominalism who is a "terrifying, trans-rational, trans-natural God of will, an omnipotent God whose absolute power reduced nature to a chaos of radically individual and unconnected beings" (p. 255).

It is this God of medieval nominalism, in its Christian form, as well as the Yahweh of the Hebrew Bible, that Jung dares to confront in *Answer to Job* (CW11). By arguing that a more adequate God-image for our time would include this dark and destructive energy within a vision of God that includes both darkness and light, good and evil, order and chaos, consciousness and unconsciousness, Jung includes the nihilistic experience as one of the possible ways the Self is experienced by the human ego. By embracing the nothingness at the heart of nihilism as one aspect of the divine life, Jung honors the experience of nothingness without succumbing to it and allowing his thought to become nihilistic. Jung was not a nihilist; yet he knew the experience and had the courage to see that it, too, comes from God. Nihilism becomes a serious danger in its one-sided identification with the dark, irrational and destructive side of God. If nihilism is also the outcome of unmourned wounds to the ego, wounds related to the dark and destructive anomic forces in the Self, then it may be helpful for us to see how analytical psychology emerged from the experience of mourning.

In a post-Holocaust world that seems to be increasingly nihilistic, analytical psychology may play a significant role in helping us overcome nihilism. Frey-Rohn (1988) has argued that the overcoming of nihilism requires a new symbol to compensate the loss of the traditional God images around which human life has been organized in Western culture. From her perspective the overcoming of nihilism is ultimately a religious achievement: "a mystery within the soul" in which the meaning-seeking ego learns to relate to the Self as the transpersonal center within. Her suggestion presupposes that nihilism has not yet completely destroyed our sense of transcendence, that we can still experience that source and center within our own psyches from which meaning flows.

To honor Jung for helping to give expression to this new symbol after the death of God, is not to apotheosize him. It is to see, however, that to be grasped by the new symbol of the divine as the Self within, which Jung has helped to come to expression, is to be challenged to go beyond nihilism by going through it. It is to know the Self both as the source of meaning in its ontological fullness as well as the dark abyss that threatens us – and our precious structures of meaning – with annihilation.

In one of his last interviews before his death, Martin Heidegger looked out over the wrecked landscape of our culture and said, "Only a god can save us now" (Dreyfus, 1991). Jung's vision is more radical; God, too, needs to be saved. We may save ourselves by saving God. As heretical as that thought is in orthodox circles, and as infelicitous as it sounds to our secular ears after the death of God, it may be what is required of us. Even more paradoxical and in contrast to Nietzsche: perhaps we can save both God and ourselves by mourning what we have lost. If nihilism cannot be overcome by reason, perhaps it can be overcome by tears. "Blessed are they that mourn, for they shall be comforted" (Matthew: 5:4).

Wonhyo's Egoless Understanding and Jung's Symbolic Understanding

Zuk-Nae Lee
Taegu, Korea
Association of Graduate Analytical Psychologists
(Zurich Institute)

Wonhyo (a seventh century Korean religious leader who systematized Korean Buddhism) elucidates, in several works, an Eastern philosophical concept, *zi-kwan* – best translated as "egoless understanding." I find this concept to be basically similar to Jung's symbolic understanding. Both are concerned with the totality of the psyche.

Zi-Kwan implies seeing one's true self without ego. There are three important, closely interdependent aspects of this understanding: enlightenment, voidness, subject-object oneness. An examination of these three features will elucidate the whole.

First, enlightenment. Wonhyo distinguishes *tathāgata-garbha* – true self – from ego, false self. True self is characterized by illumination, or absolute understanding, while false self is marked by partial vision, or discrimination associated with ignorance. The illumination experienced in the state of egoless understanding is the awakening of a new consciousness. In this state, understanding brings non-discriminating differentiation, transcendent in nature.

To elaborate: This enlightened understanding is an intuitive, immediate awareness or discernment, whereas the understanding of conscious ego is a mediated, inferential or intellectual process. Through immediate awareness, the total reality is experienced; through mediated knowledge the particularity and partiality of reality are known. It is said that the enlightened understanding comprehends the changeless totality within ever-changing phenomena: non-discriminating differentiation. The totality itself is invisible, inexpressible and beyond the reach of all intellectual processes: transcendent. The enlightened understanding can be reached by a break-through of ego-consciousness to a true self.

Similarly, the symbol is understood as an expression of something unknown, and unknowable by intellectual processes. It points beyond itself to the archetype. Symbolic understanding occurs when there is a confrontation between the conscious ego and the archetypal level, the collective unconscious. That is, the ego experiences the transcendent in the archetype itself.

The archetype is the *lumen naturae* (light of nature), which brings light to consciousness. As lumen naturae the archetype is transcendent; to experience its effect develops ego-consciousness into Self-consciousness. That is, the Self is experienced and expressed as the true source of the ego. This transformation – the process of becoming egoless or experiencing the totality of one's psyche – is the aim of Jungian analysis.

The second aspect of egoless understanding – closely related to enlightened understanding – is that of the void. This understanding occurs through the illumination of true self, which makes void the ego. Making void the ego is achieved by the ego's dis-identification with mental contents, thus leaving no contents to understand. It is no longer preoccupied with the images of things, but merely reflects them. In this manner, the expansion of awareness takes place, in the same context as Laotze's "doing nothing" or "voidness," the pivot of Taoism. Laotze says, "Devote yourself to the utmost void."

In contrast, ego's making conscious the unconscious contents is equivalent to intellectual understanding only. Such identification makes the individual oblivious of the broader context of consciousness. This perspective limits reality. Such understanding through the conscious ego is of possessive and discriminative nature that results in subject-object dichotomy; egoless understanding is of void and transcendent nature leading to subject-object oneness.

In Buddhism the ego is a consuming affection; all Buddhistic teachings are related, implicitly or explicitly, to liberation from the ego. Wonhyo (1987) clarifies, above all, the meaning of voidness or nothingness in connection with the ego. The ego is characterized by clinging-to-itself, resulting in clinging-to-others. The clinging-to-ego is by nature exclusive not inclusive, rejecting not embracing, conflicting not harmonious, and diametrically opposed to the all-inclusive and all-embracing totality. Because of such characteristics of the ego, totality or total understanding is usually hidden from humans, who tend to see one thing from a particular frame of reference.

In contrast, with voidness of ego one is not bound by any particular realm or frame of reference, because voidness as a sphere of ultimate transcendence goes beyond all the polarizing dualities. A person's observation and understanding are beyond all frames of reference and positions. The frame of reference is set not on one specific stand or dimension, but on totality, in which diverse aspects will manifest themselves in harmony. Indeed, totality and harmony are inaccessible without a thorough eradication of the clinging or attachment to the ego. In such voidness or void-consciousness, the all-inclusive and all-embracing totality of true self discloses and renders things – living and non-living in the world – in the utmost fullness and vividness.

The void nature of Wonhyo's egoless understanding may be comprehended in analytical psychology as "letting things happen." Jung wrote:

> *We must be able to let things happen in the psyche. For us, this is an art of which most people know nothing. Conscious ego is never leaving the psychic processes to grow in peace. ... The conscious mind raises innumerable objections; in fact it often seems bent on blotting out the spontaneous fantasy activity. ... The exercises must be continued until one can let things happen. In this way a new attitude is created, an attitude that accepts the irrational and the incomprehensible, simply because it is happening.* (CW13, par. 20)

In such a process the transcendent function of the archetype is brought about, resulting in greater egolessness, the state in which the Self as psychic totality is experienced. For Jung the experience of the Self means the end of exclusive ego-consciousness.

The third feature, subject-object oneness, is called mystic, because there is no distinction between the knower and the known. This feature is closely interrelated with the first two features of egoless understanding, the enlightening and the void. This oneness, according to Wonhyo (1991), is an inner experience disclosed by the light of one's true self, making void the ego and thereby nullifying the distinction between subject and object. In the unity of all things, everything breaks through the shell of itself and interfuses and identifies with every other thing. One is all and all is one. All selves dissolve into one and exist only to the extent that they disappear into all other selves. The point here is the dissolution of the conscious ego, revealing the true self as illuminating light, which leads to subject-object oneness, a mystic experience.

Further, Wonhyo (1991) says that in the state of oneness there is no room for speech because, if we speak of a certain thing, it becomes the object, with ourselves as the subject and subject-object oneness exists no longer. Understanding in the state of oneness is a total union through ontological experience, non-differentiated and non-discriminated. In such a state, reality can be experienced immediately – with no medium of concepts and knowledge. Wonhyo (1986) refers to immediate intuition or immediate experience, entirely distinguished from intellectual understanding. Intellect is necessarily dualistic because it posits subject and object.

The mystic experience of subject-object oneness is identical with a numinous experience of the archetype, in the process of symbolic understanding. In this process, the experience of the archetype transcends the discriminative, dichotomizing nature of the conscious ego into the subject-object oneness of the Self. The healing power of the resulting numinosity is central to Jung's work: "The main interest of my work is not concerned with the treatment of neuroses but rather in the approach to the numinous ... The approach to the numinous is the real therapy and inasmuch as you attain to the numinous experiences you are released from the curse of pathology" (Let-I, p. 377).

Thus, the ego is transformed into the Self and all the contrary relations of the human being with the world manifest themselves harmoniously as an identity designated by Jung as *mysterium coniunctionis* can be regarded as analogous to subject-object oneness. (See Lee & Kim, 1995).

In summary, Wonhyo's egoless understanding is basically similar to Jung's symbolic understanding in that they are concerned with the realization of totality or oneness through the illuminating disclosure as true self, in which the ego has been transcended. In this context, I think that Jung understood Eastern thought as a whole to be a symbolic psychology and Eastern philosophers to be symbolic psychologists.

References

Berger, P. (1969). The Sacred Canopy: Elements of a Sociological Theory of Religion. New York: Doubleday/Anchor.
Buber, M. (1952/1957). *Eclipse of God*. New York: Harper Torchbooks.

Dourley, J. (1981). *The Psyche as Sacrament: A Comparative Study of C.G. Jung and Paul Tillich.* Toronto: Inner City Books.

Dourley, J. (1992). *A Strategy For a Loss of Faith: Jung's Proposal.* Toronto: Inner City Books.

Dourley, J. (1995). The religious implications of Jung's psychology. *Journal of Analytical Psychology, 40*-2, 177-203.

Dreyfus, H. (1993). Heidegger on the connection between nihilism, art, technology, and politics. In C. Guignon (Ed.), *The Cambridge Companion to Heidegger.* Cambridge, England: Cambridge University Press.

Ferrell, D. (1995). The unmourned wound: Reflections on the psychology of Adolf Hitler. *The Journal of Religion and Health, 34*-3, 175-197.

Frey-Rohn, L. (1988). *Friedrich Nietzsche: A Psychological Approach to His Life and Thought.* Einsiedeln, Switzerland: Daimon Verlag.

Gillespie, M. (1995). *Nihilism Before Nietzsche.* Chicago: University of Chicago Press.

Homans, P. (1989). *The Ability to Mourn: Disillusionment and the Social Origins of Psychoanalysis.* Chicago/London: University of Chicago Press.

Kerr, J. (1993). *A Most Dangerous Method: The Story of Jung, Freud, and Sabina Spielrein.* New York: Knopf.

Levinas, E. (1989). *The Levinas Reader.* Oxford: Blackwell.

Lee, Z.; Kim, H. (1995). Wonhyo's theory of mind in the perspective of analytical psychology. *Journal of the Korean Neuropsychiatric Association, 34*-2, 345-368.

Miller, A. (1990). *The Untouched Key: Tracing Childhood Trauma in Creativity and Destructiveness.* New York: Doubleday.

Newton, K. (1993). The weapon and the wound: The archetypal and personal dimensions in "Answer to Job." *Journal of Analytical Psychology, 38*-4, 375-396.

Noll, R. (1994). *The Jung Cult: Origins of a Charismatic Movement.* Princeton: Princeton University Press.

Otto, R. (1923/1979). *The Idea of the Holy: An Inquiry into the Non-rational Factor in the Idea of the Divine as its Relation to the Rational* (J.W. Harvey, trans.). London/Oxford/New York: Oxford University Press.

Stevens, A. (1990). *On Jung.* London/New York: Routledge.

Vasavada, A. (1995). *Complementarity between the Way of Jung and of the Guru.* Unpublished Manuscript. Presented to the Israel Association of Analytical Psychology, April 1995.

Wonhyo (1986). *Treatise on the Diamond Samādhi Sūtra* (D. J. Kim, trans.). Seoul: Yeolm-sa.

Wonhyo (1987). *Meaning of the Two Hindrances* (J.K. Kim, trans.). Seoul: Boyeungak.

Wonhyo (1991). *The Commentary and Expository Notes on the Treatise of Awakening Mahāyāna Faith* (J. H. Yeun, trans. & annot.). Seoul: Ilji-sa.

Zeller, M. (1975). *The Dream: The Vision of the Night.* Los Angeles: Analytical Psychology Club of Los Angeles.

Violence and Destruction

Violence in the Life of the Psyche

Rosmarie Daniel
Stuttgart, Germany
German Society for Analytical Psychology

A document of culture is always one of barbarism as well.
Walter Benjamin

The phenomenon of violence is extremely complex. My approach is one among numerous possible efforts to understand this phenomenon.

Though we as depth psychologists frequently meet with violence and destruction in psychic life, we have difficulties in naming it and allowing for its existence. Violence is a reality in life, and such realities are always psychically motivated. It would be nonsense to deny that we are "surrounded" by violence in outer life. In order to understand it and to do justice to it, we cannot merely fight it.

What is the contribution of depth psychology and of analytical psychology to the understanding of violence and destruction? Freud contrasts the unifying eros with the death instinct, which seeks violent separation and destruction. More in accordance with psyche, however, is Spielrein's (1986) view of destruction as the origin of everything that is in formation. According to this interpretation, sexuality – understood psychologically – consists of two contrary aspirations: to bring into formation and to destroy. Thus, she transcends the contrast of eros and thanatos later postulated by Freud. Both theses, however, are limited to the personal psyche, from which collective phenomena cannot be understood.

Jung's approach offers valid preconditions for approaching the phenomenon of violence without prejudice. Above all, the concept of archetypes is an excellent basis for understanding. Jung writes: "The world powers that rule over all mankind ... are unconscious psychic factors, and it is they that bring consciousness into being and hence create the *sine qua non* for the existence of any world at all. We are immersed in a world that was created by our own psyche" (CW8, par. 747). Thus, our ego is confronted with facts exceeding its possibilities for coping. In his essay "Wotan" (CW10), Jung speaks of the autonomous, objective, collective, psychic: the archetypal powers of the soul which, in former times, were personified as gods and characterized by myths. In my approach to the phenomenon of violence I stay with the picture in the myth, but also to the deed, and consider both an expression of the psyche.

In our work as depth psychologists we come into contact with violence and destructive energy every day in the transformation processes of our patients' psyches. Although Jung – in his concept of archetypes – has given us a good basis for understanding these phenomena, we do not take them sufficiently seriously. Have we, like Winnicott (1986), a sentimental relation to the human being and thus to his or her psyche? We as members of modern Western society are in danger of instinctively denying the "destructive factor on which the ability for the constructive is based" (p. 121).

The roots of this attitude are manifold and deep. The primary root is the postulate that the Christian God is only good. For this postulate the pre-Christian world of gods was sacrificed – an act of violence – and became the opposite of the completely good: evil as such. It was only in early Christianity that evil became significant as sin. With Plato there is the Kakon, the evil that is detrimental to virtue and is localized in the body. The immortal soul is the center of knowledge and self-knowledge; the mortal body is the sum total of the negative. Thus St. Paul can write of "the law of sin which dwells in my members" (Romans 7:23, Revised Standard Version).

As humans see themselves as the successors of God (the *imitatio dei* has always been important in religious life), human consciousness identifies with the completely good; other aspirations fall into repression. In this tradition, Jean-Jacques Rousseau defines human nature as basically only good and subject to change for the worse merely by external influences. In this view he approaches our modern attitude which alternately holds responsible culture, society, property, social inequality, influence by parents, and so on for all human behavior that diverges from the good. Rousseau fails to notice, however, that all these "exterior" factors are creations of the psyche.

In our society violence is associated with evil; hence we have a disordered relation to it. The German word "*Gewalt*" (violence, as well as power) is connected to "*walten*" (rule), with connections to land, possession, home. In modern meaning we can see a basic change; now "Gewalt" means force, arbitrariness. We encounter it relatively value-free only in its institutionalized form as *Staatsgewalt* (government authority), *Militärgewalt* (military force), *Waffengewalt* (force of arms), *Erziehungsgewalt* (parental power). Luther knew about the ruling aspect of Gewalt. In his translation of the Bible he spoke of the Gewalt of God, meaning God's power and glory. He took the view that all Gewalt originates from divine order: ecclesiastic Gewalt, which is effective through the word, as well as worldly Gewalt, which is effective through the sword. Existence as a human being – psyche, consciousness and culture – cannot be separated from Gewalt, indeed is based on it.

Violence in Myth and Rite

When we have eyes to see, we find violence at every turn, including in myths, fairy tales and dreams. Our biblical myth of human life after the expulsion from paradise starts with an act of bloody violence: Cain kills his brother Abel because God accepts Abel's sacrifice but rejects Cain's. In many myths of the creation, the formation of the world and thus of humankind and consciousness is synonymous with violence. In the Babylonian myth, Maruk creates the world out of the sea snake Tiamat which has been cut in two. In the Greek theogony Hesiod depicts Kronos cutting off his father Uranus' sexual organs as Uranus lies in perpetual embrace with Gaia, the earth. Kronos in turn is defeated by his son Zeus, who banishes him to the nether world together with the Titans. Here it becomes evident that one dominates who defeats the opponent by violence. That one causes change and thus a new formation – an episode of consciousness. The acts of the mythic heroes are almost always bloody and violent deeds. Heroes are described as fair, beautiful, strong – and violent.

Another mythological picture for the creation of the world is the cosmic sacrifice. In the Indian epic Rigveda the primeval creature Purusha is sacrificed and dismembered by the gods. The world order is made from parts of Purusha's body.

We can assume that the violence described in these stories is symbolic: about the deeds of gods, not of human beings. But then we have to disregard the existence of ritual deeds of humans and, furthermore, that mythologies depict ritual acts. The killing acts were perpetrated bloodily, not merely seen in a picture. Some scientists take the view that Palaeolithic hunters (ca. 70000 years B.C.) knew sacrifice of lives. For several millennia, bloody sacrifice of victims was a central part of religious activity. Moreover, we must not forget that there is also an act of killing – a crucifixion – in the center of the Christian religion. It is repeated ritually in the sacrificial meal of flesh and blood of Christ in the form of bread and wine. In the cultures of antiquity, sacrificial killing and eating of the victim were performed bloodily. There was the sacrificial altar off which "new blood has to ooze again and again" (Burkert, 1992).

According to Gronemeyer (1993), sacrifice is the beginning of culture and contains the most beautiful and religious emotions of humanity, as well as the most horrible. We can assume that being a human has been determined from the beginning by this close connection of religious shudder and violence to kill; this is even the seam that separates humans from animals. The early human seems to see the quarry not only as a piece of food but, in a kind of mystic solidarity, hits with axe or spear the self as a living being in the other living being. Simultaneously the human executes an act of differentiation between something alive – the self – and something dead which becomes visible in the victim. One can say that being a human is based in the encounter with the act of killing. According to Burkert (1992), the *homo religiosus* acts and becomes self-conscious as *homo necans*, as killing man (*operari* means to act and is connected to "opfern," to sacrifice). This act is psychic, spiritual. In the act of killing, life and death become one. The killed animal, which is like a sacrifice, serves as food and thus preserves life.

Phenomena of Violence Today

Civilized society lives off the cultural achievements of its past but maintains a great distance from that ancient world, in largely sterile surroundings. All imponderables, jolts, and the wildness of life in which the ancient humans had to find their foundation again and again are excluded or seem to be excluded. We are living in a complacent insurance society in which all possibilities seem to be cared for in advance, and in which we feel safe to a high degree. We are living in a positivized world with an explanation for everything. Negative phenomena which cannot be explained are disclaimed. The fears from which many people suffer are met with attempts at therapy. We try to keep out of our lives everything that might shake us.

In natural disasters, however, we still today encounter violence – if we really suffer from them and do not only participate as a television voyeur. We also encounter violence – the power of a ruler against whom we can do nothing – when death comes into our personal lives, be it through the confrontation with our own death, or through the deaths of relatives. Then from one moment to the next we are thrown into nothingness, into total negation, into the abyss; we have lost our safety and our knowledge that has an answer to everything. We must ask ourselves for the connection between this highly technical civilization and the violence escalating everywhere: violence among the young, in schools and in families and toward the civilian population in national and international trouble spots.

After the non-violent collapse of the communist system and the break-up of the iron-bound power positions of both world powers, we could enjoy for a short time the illusion that a non-violent time had dawned: a peaceful period. The violence that broke out all over the world has taught us to think again. It seems that the huge violence potential had been captivated within the rigidity of the two blocks of power, and now it breaks into open violence in a vast number of small trouble spots.

But what is the difference between this new violence and the earlier one? Violence in ancient times, and even as late as the Middle Ages, was ultimately creative; it had something to do with the founding of the world, with founding oneself in the world, with connecting oneself to God. Violence today seems to lack a recognizable context; it is irreligious and non-creative. It appears senseless, chaotic, and purposeless, even if it is aimed against something. It expresses something suggested in today's definition of violence: arbitrariness.

Our Western society is extremely violent, if mostly in disguise. You have only to stand by a highway as an unprotected pedestrian for the roaring, screaming, reckless driving to convince you of the violence of our society. Or think of the callous and brutal animal transports that roll over this very highway.

We are far from the attitude of ancient humans who continued to live via the killed animal. We recklessly exploit nature and environment; we encounter dead bodies without being touched in our being. Levi-Strauss said, "If we do not want to send any more people to concentration camps we have to start by not sending any more whales there" (1980, p. 262).

At all times humans have been subject to the *Herrschaft* (dominion) of the archetypal, of the power that exceeds human ego. This is not different today. But the rule was of divine origin, and this gave sense to human life. Today, the traditional religious contents do not prove binding for most people; the new gods are called science, technology and industry, money and market. Optimalization of profit is the aim and almost everything, including humans, is subjugated to it. Do people find sense in this?

Our civilization is in a deep crisis of values. Ethical, moral and religious agreements – which connected everything without question – have begun to falter. Our society is marked by deep untruthfulness; it disdains life and humanity, even if it speaks of "untouchable human dignity."

Everything visible in society – maltreatment of nature, of animals, of the weak – is within the individual psyche, too. Many of us are less and less able to accept these realities within ourselves. With many psychically sick patients this negative attitude toward being what they are is visible, especially in eating disorders and in grave narcissistic disorders. These patients identify with the collective trend.

Violence in Young People (especially those on the political right)

It is almost a cliché to say that a society has the youth it deserves. But it really is so; violence in the young reflects much of the terrifying reality of our civilization. The shadow of society becomes visible: the suppression or denial of death and violence, the increasing lack of relationships, the disregard for the weak. The apparent senselessness of today's violence reflects our society's crisis of value.

It would be naive to assume that the young in this society do not feel the crisis. It makes a deep impression on their psyches, all the more so if they are among the needy. We should not be deceived by their martial appearance; it is meant to disguise weakness. We must not be blind to its danger, but the political danger is less with the young people themselves than with the fascist tendencies that are widespread in the population.

To understand the phenomenon of violence among the right-wing young we must ask ourselves to what extent the adults in our society neglect their children. Parents are affected by our performance-oriented society. Its complex, hard-to-understand structures are too much for them; these structures leave almost no room for a human quality of life. In this unhealthy climate many parents exert pressure on their children to achieve and subject them to physical and psychical violence. In such a situation how can warmth, love and the I-thou relation be achieved? Where is the immediate, human reality, in this climate of media effectiveness and virtual reality? Isn't the violence in the family an expression of the desperate and senseless striving for a change, for getting out of this desert?

Violence is a part of the human psyche. It promotes consciousness and identity, and it is religious. It is connected with venture, courage and strength. But the violence experienced today, including right-wing youth violence, is cowardly; it is directed against the weak, the helpless, the different. But how and where do adults initiate their children to today's reality? Are children not left mostly on their own with no generally accepted rites that reliably introduce them to the adult world? Nothing in the prevailing culture promotes the finding of an identity for a young person.

In our civilization, all Gewalt (power but also violence) has been transferred to the institutions of the state, so that people are able to live peacefully and unendangered by open violence. As late as the Middle Ages this situation was completely different. Humans were much more prepared to exercise emotionally-based violence, and lived in comparative danger from sudden attacks such as by armed bands of robbers. No state power in the form of police came to help; individual self-defense was necessary. The image of the person with emotional and affective reactions and fitness to fight, was the knight. He roamed about in full armor, heavily armed. In the medieval knight novels, it becomes evident how easily the knight could be offended in his honor and how heated was his reaction to such an offense. The knights had a severe code of honor that canalized the individual's violence. The widespread knights' games (tournaments) featured violence in ritualized form. The opponent's death was not intended but it was accepted with approval. Fight and love defined the knight's life.

In today's world, which is externally pacified, there is no more opportunity for the young to prove their worth in a comparable way. And for those in some countries there are no more wars. (Please understand: I do not wish for war for our young people!) But we tend to put the spotlight only on the ugly, destructive side of war. Here we forget the psychic truth of the direct unity of destruction and life identified by Sabina Spielrein.

Almost all great epic poems are descriptions of seemingly never-ending battles. In the Bible, too, the language of war is used. Love and war belong together in the divine pair Aphrodite and Ares, as did love and fight for the knights. According to Hillman (1988), soldiers describe "in some cases increased vitality, a new sense for the beauty of earth and the nearness to the divine – the small history of their lives ... all of a sudden has got a transcendental glory" (p. 33). Is it not understandable that among the psychic desert of young people's lives, they are looking for an experience that is alive, that establishes them, that gives them identity and connects them to a superior power, that brings them to community, that helps them to survive in the difficult, extremely involved world in which they find themselves?

The repulsiveness of right-wing youths' violence should not keep us from trying to understand it. Hidden behind it are desperate, fragmentary and distorted attempts to find an identity, to feel oneself a person, to communicate, to be spiritually alive. These attempts are perverted and have criminal effects. By these attempts, moreover, young people push themselves even more into isolation and criminality, not least because the archaic form of these attempts does not fit into today's society.

The garments in which these adolescents dress up are dusted off from the National Socialist past. They are meant to shock the citizens with characteristics which, for the majority, should be left repressed and which, for a minority, are connected with horrible memories and associations. They also serve to differ, shockingly, from social common sense. The shock value increases the person's potency and contributes to finding an identity by erecting a counter-world to that of adults. Assembly in gangs strengthens the courage of the individual, and the law of the masses washes away limits of scruples which might still be present in some of the members.

Items from the Nazi past would not give rise to much worry, if it were all. But the National Socialists have revived the Germanic men's associations which terrorized their surroundings in the sign of death, such as the death-head under which the SS stood. (*Schutzstaffel* = Nazi "black-shirts.") In the attempt to revive the spiritual dynamics of the Germanic men's associations the god was revived, the archetypal reality that stands behind the men's associations: Odin, god of storm, of ecstasy, of the dead.

Incidents with the right-wing youths take place often. Usually they are under the influence of alcohol: in ecstasy. In their intoxication they hand over the last remnants of their own responsibility into the hands of the god of ecstasy.

We can discern fragments of the behavior of men's associations. The initiation to such an association demands of the initiate severe tests of courage and self-conquest. But the adolescents' violence shows cowardly behavior at first sight. Mowed down without distinction are the weakest of society: mentally ill, homeless and physically handicapped people. For one who wants to be accepted as a group member it is a test of courage to disregard the barriers of conscience and of the law and to attack a person bodily, contrary to the officially accepted ethics, even to kill.

A very significant element of the dynamics of right-wing youth violence seems to be the experience of crossing the border: the border of one's own conscience, exterior limits, and, as a group experience, crossing the borders of the ego – which are already uncertain. These young people act out of a feeling of being unable to rely on anything and anybody. They are young, but already disillusioned. They hate themselves as the weak and the outsiders in a hateful world that is too much for them. They project this hate on other weak people and try to destroy them. Some who cannot act out their hate on other people may commit suicide.

In the excesses of right-wing youths is a senseless circle of the barbarism of fragmentary archaic psychic conditions without a visible cultural result. Perhaps a warning signal for our society not to get stuck in barbarism? If the signal could be understood, it might produce a cultural result after all and re-unite the destructive aspect of violence with a constructive one.

Translated from German by Übersetzerteam, Stuttgart

References

Burkert W. (1972). *Homo necans*. Berlin, NY: de Gruyter.

Gronemeyer R. (1993). *Das Blut deines Bruders* (Your Brothers Blood). Wien: Econ.

Hillman, J. (1988). Die Welt des Mars. Gorgo. 15. Zurich: Spiegel.

Hillman, J. (1987). Wars, Arms, Rams, Mars: On the Love of War. Facing Apocalypse. Dallas: Spring Publications.

Levi-Strauss C. (1980). *Mythos und Bedeutung* (Myth and Meaning). Frankfurt: Suhrkamp.

Spielrein, S. (1986). *Die Destruktion als Ursache des Werdens* (Destruction as the Origin of Everything). Tübingen: Edition diskord.

Winnicott, D.W. (1984). *Deprivation and Delinquency*. London: Tavistock Publications.

Winnicott, D.W. (1988). *Aggression*. Stuttgart: Klett.

The Culture of Violence and Analytical Psychology

John R. van Eenwyk
Olympia, Washington, U.S.A.
Pacific Northwest Society of Jungian Analysts

By late 1994, according to the United Nations High Commission on Refugees, there were over 20 million refugees worldwide, with numbers increasing daily. The vast majority are trauma survivors who need psychological services. Ten years ago, for example, it was estimated that 20000 refugees who had been tortured were living in Chicago alone. Today that figure is generally believed to have doubled.

In 1984 the General Assembly of the United Nations defined torture as:

any act by which severe pain or suffering, whether physical or mental, is intentionally inflicted on a person for such purposes as obtaining from him or a third person information or a confession, punishing him for an act he or a third person has committed, or intimidating or coercing him or a third person, or for any reason based on discrimination of any kind, when such pain or suffering is inflicted by or at the instigation of or with the consent or acquiescence of a public official or other person acting in an official capacity. It does not include pain or suffering arising only from, inherent in or incidental to lawful sanctions.

"Lawful sanctions" refer to international law, which the United States and many other nations have not been willing to endorse. Indeed, the United States has never endorsed the Convention against Torture.

Today the term "torture" is subsumed under the larger heading of "organized violence": systematic efforts by governments or groups to demolish the capacity of other groups and individuals to resist their will. Organized violence is epidemic in the world. From Bosnia to Rwanda, Cambodia to the Philippines, El Salvador to Guatemala, South Africa to the Gaza Strip, organized violence is on the rise. As the study of analytical psychology spreads throughout the world, Jungian analysts gain the opportunity to provide invaluable services to this patient population. Jung's appreciation of symbols, respect for the patients' insights for deciphering their unconscious images, and esteem for diverse cultures create an excellent therapeutic atmosphere for working with traumatized refugees.

Many symptoms lend themselves to a Jungian treatment. For instance, the compulsion to have promiscuous sex may be an attempt to adapt to an uncertain future without one's mate. Similarly, a woman's belief that she has been kidnapped by aliens can symbolize what life is like under the strict, almost paranoid, domination of her father. Even denying the existence of God can be appropriate for one whose life has brought few of the satisfactions we all tend to expect.

The psyches of refugees who have been tortured display the characteristics of souls in crisis. Not surprisingly, the unconscious seeks to preserve its integrity during the ordeal of torture through processes remarkably similar to those outlined in Jung's research on alchemy. Understanding the psychological meaning and healing power of suffering, fragmentation, and the *nigredo* makes it possible to cooperate with the processes by which the unconscious attempts to restore the integrity of the psyche.

The Psychodynamics of Trauma

Trauma occurs when relationships become characterized by the misuse of power. Abusers are those who, when they cannot cope with the life tasks that confront them, abandon rationality (openness, dialogue, compromise, cooperation) in favor of violence. From their helplessness springs an unreflective – and, consequently, more regressed/less differentiated – use of power. Such regression inevitably leads to violence; physical, sexual, or psychological.

Archetypal Shadow

The misuse of power originates in the dynamics of psychological development. When consciousness becomes overly-invested in particular perspectives and behaviors, the unconscious proposes alternatives. This is rarely a smooth event. Jung called the psyche's ability to counterbalance consciousness through positing its opposite the "archetypal shadow." Although the archetypal shadow corrects the one-sidedness of the conscious attitude, it often leads to behavior that can be destructive. Thus, its activity is sometimes symbolized by such images as the devil incarnate, the snake in the Garden of Eden, the "fly in the ointment," the threat of chaos, or the Crucifixion. Anywhere that events seem to conspire against our control, we tend to see malevolent forces at work.

The archetypal shadow alternately destabilizes and balances consciousness in order for psychological growth to occur; without tensions of opposites, growth is not possible: "The shadow and the opposing will are the necessary conditions for all actualization," said Jung (CW1, par. 211). He cited the example of Lucifer (the "Light-Bringer") in relation to the will of God. Lucifer brings up possibilities other than God's, and by so doing preserves the Creation from being "just a piece of clockwork which the Creator has to wind up to make it function" (CW11, par. 290). However naive theologically, this statement is true to Jung's belief that creativity is a function of the chaos that ensues when opposites pull at one another, fragmenting whatever is caught in their conflict.

The figure of the trickster in folktale and myth is an important and ubiquitous personification of the archetypal shadow. This figure personifies the shadow side of ideals and beliefs about the nature of reality. The trickster takes on the "sacred cows" of a civilization, usually by portraying whatever a group cannot accept about its relationship to ultimate principles and idealized notions; then it is often perceived as primitive, immature, and worthy of little more than contempt.

Shadow Projections onto Groups

But "the so-called civilized man has forgotten the trickster," said Jung. "He remembers him only … metaphorically, when … he speaks of fate playing tricks on him or of things being bewitched. He never suspects that his own … apparently harmless shadow has qualities whose dangerousness exceeds his wildest dreams" (CW9-I, par. 478).

Rarely do humans recognize that the influence of the archetypal shadow comes from within. Rather, we project it onto individuals and groups. "As soon as people get together in masses and submerge the individual," Jung said, "the shadow is mobilized, and, as history shows, may even be personified and incarnated" (CW9-I, par. 478).

Nowhere is this more troublesome than in the violence of oppression. Arendt (1972) observed that "the chief obsession of the totalitarian mind lies in its need for the world to be clear-cut and orderly. Any subtlety, contradiction, or complexity upsets and confuses this nature and becomes intolerable" (p. 95). Alternate points of view, not to mention the attitudes of flexibility and openness that tolerate their expression, are intolerable to the totalitarian mentality. Possessed by their own fear of destabilization, oppressors seek to impose their will on others. Unfortunately, this activates others' resistance, which further exacerbates the oppressor's fear; a vicious circle.

Unable to tolerate the creative tension of differences of opinion, totalitarians side with one pole of the tension. Through slogans and intimidation they reinforce their chosen identity and suppress all others. Many of their subjects see this single-mindedness as a value. Jung understood the subtlety of their mistake: "A conscious capacity for one-sidedness," he said, "is a sign of the highest culture, but ... the inability to be anything but one-sided, is a sign of barbarism" (CW6, par. 346). Incapable of withstanding ambiguity, the totalitarian attitude becomes trapped in its one-sidedness. All other attitudes appear equally limited, and must be suppressed.

Involuntary one-sidedness makes the dominant individual or group too invested in its persona; the shadow appears and the conscious attitude collapses. "A collapse of the conscious attitude is no small matter," said Jung. "It always feels like the end of the world, as though everything had tumbled back into original chaos. One feels delivered up, disoriented, like a rudderless ship that is abandoned to the moods of the elements" (CW7, par. 254). Such disruptions become projected onto others, and the collapse of the conscious attitude truly "destroys life, for at such moments morbid ideas are also liable to take root, or ideals wither away, which is no less disastrous" (CW7, par. 254).

The only antidote to this chaos is to bring the fear and mistrust into consciousness. Unfortunately, by the time oppression reaches this level, matters are already out of control. Timmerman (1988), for instance, lived through the days of the Pinochet terror in Chile. He described trying to survive such mass hysteria: "The daily effort to overcome the tension caused by living constantly under threat, to avoid being arrested or kidnapped, to keep up with events is only part of the nightmare that opposition leaders must live with. They must also watch over their children, who are possible targets for reprisals. It is best to keep them out of politics and to keep them from being noticed as they go about their daily routine" (p. 89). To keep them from being noticed is a formidable task, for those in the dominant group become hypervigilant. They pursue fanatically the eradication of those upon whom their shadows become projected. When such collective shadow is let loose, catastrophic damage to the social fabric can occur rapidly, as individuals reinforce their shared paranoia with the power of the mob.

Deeply fearful of their own inclinations toward flexibility and adaptability, totalitarians suppress them, project them onto others and suppress those others. Any form of openness and acceptance, whether internal or external, must be eradicated.

> *It has often been noticed that the effectiveness of terror depends almost entirely on the degree of social atomization. Every kind of organized opposition must disappear before the full force of terror can be let loose. This atomization – an outrageously pale, academic word for the horror it implies – is maintained and intensified through the ubiquity of the informer, who can be literally omnipresent because he no longer is merely a professional agent in the pay of the police but potentially every person one comes into contact with.* (Arendt, 1972, p. 154)

As oppression spreads, fear of turns everyone into a potential agent of the state.

Symptoms of Trauma

Breakdowns in the social fabric destroy individual threads. Nevertheless, like the severe disruptions to individual functioning that are caused by eruptions of the unconscious, societal collapse can be as instructive as it is destructive. Here, too, archetypal forces are at work; imbalances are being addressed and new ways of functioning created. This is precisely what is happening in the Gaza Strip.

The Gaza Strip is the world's largest and longest-running refugee camp. At first thought to be a temporary situation, the displacement of tens of thousands of people by the creation of the state of Israel in 1948 seems now to be permanent. When Gaza fell to Israeli military control in 1967, travel was prohibited, an apartheid system of personal documentation was instituted, and manufacture, trade, and private enterprise were all but eliminated. Currently, 25 percent of the land and 60 percent of the water are controlled by Israeli settlers, who comprise of 0.5 percent of the 830 000 people in the Gaza Strip.

Under the occupation, Gazans have been subjected to random personal searches, home invasions and demolitions, arrests, and imprisonments without charges. While in prison more than 90 percent have experienced beatings and verbal humiliation; more than 80 percent prolonged periods of enforced standing, sudden and intense noises, and solitary confinement; more than 70 percent prolonged temperature extremes, starvation, the forced witnessing of others being tortured, sleep deprivation, deprivation of toilet facilities, and verbal humiliation inflicted on relatives; more than 60 percent periods of suffocation and genital abuse. Others have experienced the use of irritant gas, insertion of instruments into penis and/or rectum, rape, and electric shock.

Following release, almost 50 percent have had difficulty with social interactions, one-third have had difficulty adapting to family life, many experiencing marital problems. More than three-fourths continue to experience economic hardship directly attributable to the imprisonment experience. Families of those imprisoned were beaten, had household articles and personal belongings destroyed, and were threatened with rape.

Those who are subjected to organized violence tend to react in similar ways. Until recently, diagnosis has been limited to post-traumatic stress disorder, which lists among its symptoms anxiety, depression, grief, fear, suspicion, and paranoia. However, in a 1993 study, Ahmed Abu Tawahena, Ph.D., Mustafa El Maasry, M.D., and I assembled a list of symptoms and precipitating factors that seem to characterize survivors of organized violence. Among the more intriguing of our findings is that, because much of the trauma suffered under organized violence has yet to reach the "post" category, patients cannot escape the threat of violence. Such an implosion of the environment into the individual generates symptoms that resemble psychosis. Could this be evidence of the unconscious at work, attempting to restore balance to social chaos and to promote the healing of the psyche, both individual and collective?

The Gaza Syndrome

Patients at the Gaza Community Mental Health Programme have presented a peculiar syndrome characterized by delusions and/or intrusive/obsessional thoughts. Diagnoses of mood disorder with psychotic manifestations, delusional disorder, brief reactive psychosis, and schizotypal personality disorder do not describe these

Adaption Disorder: Aetiology							
		restraint	persecution	confinement	abuse	organized violence	torture
More Conscious		resistance anger		Healthy			
R S			fear	Pre-Morbid			
E Y			anxiety		Personality		
A M				isolation			
C P							
T T					withdrawal depression		
I O			Vulnerable				
O M			Pre-Morbid			loss of control helplessness	
N S			Personality				
S							
More Unconscious							intrusive thoughts delusions

REACTIONS / SYMPTOMS

symptoms accurately, for patients often realize how unusual and abnormal are their delusions and intrusive thoughts. Those affected rarely have any previous history of psychosis, manifest many decidedly non-psychotic behaviors, and do not fit the descriptions of brief reactive psychosis. We have found no organic factors that either initiate or maintain the disturbances. These symptoms seem to characterize anyone who must cope with ongoing violence. We have named this combination of symptoms "Adaptation Disorder" or "The Gaza Syndrome."

The symptoms of Adaptation Disorder correspond with six stages of increasing severity of organized violence (see Table). The six stages are restraint, persecution, confinement, abuse, torture, and organized violence. They are rarely as discrete as we have drawn them; each is mixed with the others to some degree. Nevertheless, each stage is a result of deliberate attempts to neutralize autonomy: physical, relational, or psychological.

During these stages, the specific symptoms depend on the strength of the pre-morbid personality and the severity of the trauma. For example, intrusive thoughts and delusions can occur earlier in the process if the pre-morbid personality is particularly vulnerable. When they appear early, illusions are rarely differentiated from reality and lead to delusional disorder. If the pre-morbid personality is healthy, they appear later. Then the illusions are generally recognized as such and experienced as intrusive thoughts.

Restraint refers to deliberately imposed restrictions on the free and autonomous exercise of human rights. These restraints can be economic, political, psychological, or spiritual. They include restrictions on travel, interruption of business activity, banning of political parties, censorship, and the closing of educational institutions and/ or houses of worship. Restraint is not solely a military or governmental activity. Families, spouses, and religious groups can all be agents of restraint.

Resistance and anger are normal responses to restraint. Depending on its severity and the vulnerability of the pre-morbid personality, however, the other symptoms I have listed may be present also.

To be restrained is to be limited. A more severe form of restraint is persecution, wherein one feels pursued or stalked. Healthy personalities will continue to display resistance and anger while also experiencing fear and anxiety. More vulnerable personalities will be less likely to demonstrate resistance and anger and more likely to display more severe symptoms, such as isolation, helplessness, and delusions. Nevertheless, unlike confinement and abuse, those who are persecuted often can band together for mutual support.

Confinement is the physical restriction of freedom of movement. While its primary form is imprisonment, whether in formal institutions or house arrest, it can also include kidnapping and the closing of borders. The goal of confinement is the eradication of free will, which often feels like an implosion of the environment onto the individual.

In addition to resistance, anger, fear, and anxiety, healthy personalities also experience isolation. Vulnerable pre-morbid personalities rarely feel anger and resistance but often experience more severe symptoms, those associated with increased violence. All confined persons, however, feel isolated, all routes of escape are closed off and there is no one to help.

Abuse is to confinement what persecution is to restraint when one is singled out for violence. Either physical violence or extreme intimidation are always present, as in shootings, police actions, war campaigns, terrorist activities. As the environment closes in on the individual, healthy personalities feel angry and resistant but also frightened, anxious, and isolated. Vulnerable personalities quickly withdraw and become depressed. As violations become increasingly uncontrollable, all abused persons feel increasingly impotent.

Abuse is the most variable of the six stages. The violence inflicted rarely remains sporadic, but expands rapidly into continuous, deliberate attempts to break one's spirit. As violence begins to characterize the confinement, even healthy personalities begin to break down, becoming withdrawn and depressed.

Organized violence and torture are profound escalations in violence, whether directed toward individuals or groups, that precipitate implosions of the personality. Ego boundaries collapse, will is broken, resistance becomes futile, isolation inevitable. An imploded personality is an impotent personality. Nothing works, possibilities disappear, isolation is complete. Simply carrying out the basic functions of daily life can be an impossible chore. Deprived of any healthy contact with the world, one withdraws into oneself.

Depending on the degree to which organized violence and torture become internalized, the symptoms are increasingly unconscious. Control is lost and cannot be recovered. Helplessness becomes a coping device. The healthy pre-morbid personality also experiences anxiety, isolation, withdrawal, and depression. The vulnerable premorbid personality probably will experience intrusive thoughts and delusions. As the violence continues, virtually all ego structures break down.

The sixth stage, torture, is characterized by perseveration. The torturer's goal is to permeate the victim's psyche. If survivors can be implanted with the personality (such as it is) of the torturer, control extends beyond the point at which the torture formally ends. Their personalities imploded and neutralized, survivors belong to their oppressors. Everything they do repeats the torture experience. They become the walking wounded who remind their communities of the consequences to be faced for any resistance to the oppressor.

Once the stages of organized violence are complete, the internalized oppressor is a factor in virtually all aspects of survivors' lives, for their egos have been destroyed. The only mitigating factor is the survivor's unconscious, but it often expresses itself in ways that feel foreign. Intrusive thoughts and impulses, for instance, feel to survivors as if something or someone is speaking to them from inside their heads. Such intrusions create tension and conflict which may lead to compulsive behaviors employed to counteract negative consequences.

Delusions, on the other hand, consist either of the belief that something is occurring that cannot be substantiated by consensus, or the compulsion to engage in behavior contrary to one's best interests. In the delusional stage, survivors have little or no insight into the self-generation of their beliefs or compulsions.

The Analytic Response

The psyche's attempt to heal itself, whether through integrating the internalized dynamics of the abuser or through "ventilating" the experience of abuse, often looks like disorder to our colleagues in other disciplines. However, none of these symptoms is unfamiliar to the analytical psychologist, and to consider such symptoms to be hostile to the healing process is to create a therapeutic environment in which trauma survivors can be subjected to further abuse.

Consequently, understanding symptoms in the light of the psyche's attempts to heal itself is essential for utilizing them for the survivor's benefit. For example, a survivor who was imprisoned in Gaza for seven months without being charged felt isolated, believed that he was living in his own world, and began to feel that people were watching him. Soon a Ginneiya (Arabic for fairy) began to tell him that he was the awaited prophet, God's successor on earth. He also felt that the Ginneiya was sexually involved with him; he could feel her hand fondling his sexual parts, and his penis inserted into her. He often had an erection. He also had other visual experiences of mice and snakes in the dark, as well as profound feelings of guilt.

This man's delusions and intrusive thoughts compensate for the humiliation and social isolation he has experienced. In his delusions he is a special person, highly exalted above others. But the images also take him into the darker regions of his soul, where the horrors he has experienced take the form of mice, snakes, and darkness. When we explained how his symptoms reflected his psyche's attempts to heal itself, the images were able to activate his perceptual and interpretive functions, thereby reinforcing his ego.

Jung noted how the psyche's attempt to balance itself is reflected in the imagery employed by the alchemists. Torture, fragmentation, and dismemberment are archetypal themes, as are *coniunctio* and *hieros gamos*. Rejoining that which has been split apart creates new, more complex and highly organized unions. This process is the essence of individuation, but it is not the essence of torture.

When one is either tortured or forced to endure other forms of organized violence, the usual alchemical processes are interrupted. No longer are the elements allowed to seek their own destiny with the assistance of the inner alchemist. Rather, any potential for transformation is systematically frustrated by the manipulations of the torturer. Consequently, the personality of the survivor becomes locked in the enduring grip of the internalized influence of the torturer. At this point, the psyche's efforts to shake itself free from the torturer – nightmares, sleep disorders, delusions, intrusive thoughts – actually perpetuate the suffering of the survivor, who becomes trapped in the past.

To amplify the psyche's efforts to heal itself we must employ a number of techniques. First, we must establish a temenos wherein the survivor can be safely contained during the perseverations of the torture experience. Second, the survivor must be empowered. Fortunately, we are usually sufficiently ignorant of the survivor's background. Thus, they become the experts who teach us. Finally, we must interpret the chaos of the psyche as attempting to liberate the survivor. Nightmares, delusions, and intrusive thoughts, which feel so out of control to the survivor, reflect the psyche's ultimate resistance to being controlled. So far all this differs little from classical analysis.

Matters get sticky when we embody the rubedo – the blood – of the alchemical process. Survivors have been emptied of their ability to resist the torturer. Their psyches are locked into cycles of unending chaos. If they are to be rescued from drowning in the unconscious, we must jump into support them. In so doing, we encounter the internalized torturer. Once the remnants of the torturer's influence are identified in the symptoms of the survivor, we can engage the internalized torturer.

Especially in the case of delusions and intrusive thoughts, this can be a formidable task indeed. Essentially, we must be able to stand toe-to-toe with the torturer and battle for the soul of the survivor. To do so requires that we become familiar with our own potential to be torturers. In treating torture survivors, "it takes one to know one." We must acknowledge and integrate our power, our violence, our sadism.

Only then can we understand what torturers do. What needs are met by violating others? What kind of genius leads to the refinement of technique? Who is lurking inside the unconscious of the survivor? Most importantly, how did the torturer gain access to – take up residence in – the psyche of the survivor? Fortunately, we are assisted in this battle by two powerful allies.

The first ally is the survivor's unconscious psyche, which seeks its own healing and responds to the analyst's efforts. Explaining, for example, that nightmares reflect the psyche's independence from external control, whether that of the torturer or the survivor, is a first step toward restoring survivors' faith in their own autonomy. Once they can accept their nightmares and begin to complete them by "dreaming them onward" in waking life, the nightmares usually abate and are replaced by more moderate images.

Further, the psyche presents to the survivor's ego essential information about the healing process. Here we are on familiar ground. What other branches of psychology often view as chaotic distortions of normal psychic functioning we see as a language to be understood. Delusions and intrusive thoughts have meaning.

The second ally is the survivor's ego. The analyst who engages the internalized torturer provides a model for the survivor to do the same. Torturers who once dominated survivors are confined to the consulting room and called to account. Engaging, listening to, and working with the survivor's symptoms challenges the influence of the internalized torturer. With each symptom that is successfully integrated, the survivor is empowered.

Summary

Organized violence generates a unique set of symptoms. To the trained analytic mind, these symptoms are adaptive. Often they allow survivors to remove themselves from pain. Sometimes they mobilize resources. At other times, they attempt to balance psychological damage of catastrophic proportions. The severe symptoms that resemble psychosis seem to be an inevitable part of any landscape characterized by unrelenting violence from which there is no escape. The symptoms often contain an element of truth that is expressible in no other way. They are a testimony to the strength and health of survivors. We should work with them, not oppose them.

It is not sufficient, however, to confine ourselves to working with the psyches of survivors. Practices of organized violence are not simply psychic residues; they are deadly viruses that infect countless people every day. From a public health perspective, we must work to eradicate the virus. We must enter the public arena to expose and to defeat organized violence wherever it exists. We must work to create in the world around us a temenos that reflects that of our consulting rooms. We must bring analysis into the world.

References

Arendt, H. (1972). *Crises of the Republic.* New York: Harcourt, Brace, Janovich.

Timmerman, J. (1988). *Chile: Death in the South.* New York: Vantage Books.

One Lone Springbok

Analytic Work and Destruction of the Natural World

Patrick J. Tummon

Cape Town, South Africa
Association of Graduate Analytical Psychologists
(Zurich Institute)

In August 1993 I was driving with my family on a dirt road through a vast semi-desert landscape in Namibia, when I spotted a lone springbok several hundred meters into the veld – an unusual sight, as they are very much herd animals. I pointed it out to the others and slowed down to give them a good chance to see it. Both six-year-old Oisin and I were moved almost to tears by its aloneness, while his nine-year-old sister was more pragmatic, saying that at least it was alive. I quickly added that it surely had companions hiding in the mountains to our left, an idea which my wife Brigitta supported. For the moment Oisin's tears were held at bay, as were my own.

I am not sure if Oisin remembered just then, but I certainly did, that we had read just a few weeks earlier, how in the last century, one might have seen herds of over ten million springbok on their migrations through southern Africa. This knowledge made it more difficult for me to hold back my tears and helps explain why the image of that lone springbok in the vast landscape – empty of any other large mammals – has become a very moving image. It was a symbol for me of our damaged relationship to the natural world, locally and globally. (To get some idea of how beautiful the springbok are, see the de Kock [1995] video.)

Some Natural History

Springbok (gazelles) were just one of the many kinds of antelope that filled the plains of southern Africa before these lands were taken over by agriculturists. Because of their short reproduction cycle, however, their populations would explode, given a few years of reasonable rains, so that they far outnumbered other antelope species. Herds of many millions frequently were seen, by early European settlers, migrating across southern Africa in search of fresh pastures. (See, Skinner, 1993.) Not unexpectedly, the Bushpeople – the indigenous hunter/gatherers of southern Africa – ate a great deal of springbok and referred to it in their stories with deep affection (van der Post, 1961). The last big migration to be reported was in Kareekloof 700 kilometers northeast of Cape Town in 1896; the herd was estimated to be 24 kilometers wide and 160 kilometers long. According to McFarlan (1992), these vast herds of springbok are the largest known herds of mammals ever recorded in human history. Today one has to drive over a thousand kilometers northeast from Cape Town to the Kalahari Gemsbok National Park to see, if one is lucky, a herd of a thousand or more, and then only after patchy rains. The decimation of the springbok population of southern Africa is a microcosm of what has happened to large mammal populations the world over. This destruction, which inevitably involved the annihilation of whole ecosystems, is tied closely to the human population explosion that has been underway ever since the development of pastoralism and agriculture.

The Human Population Explosion

The hunter/gatherer adaption had been the environmentally-stable strategy of hominids for well over two million years. Then about 40000 years ago the rate of technological change began to increase, leading to a slow growth in the human population. (See Ponting, 1992.) This combination of technological change and human population growth eventually led to food shortage, which in turn brought about the domestication of sheep in the middle east 11000 years ago. The global human population at that time is estimated at four million people. The growth in population (outlined below) since then speaks for itself.

Given that there are over 1400 of us today for each single hunter/gatherer 12000 years ago, it is surprising that there are significant populations of non-domesticated mammals left on earth at all. Moreover, the spiraling destruction of natural ecosystems means that the earth future generations inherit will be much poorer in terms of species diversity. This destruction is not the first massive trauma inflicted on the biosphere, but it is by far the worst for which humans

Human Population	Time	Adaptations (in ascending order of numbers involved)
4 million	10000 BC	hunter/gatherer = H/G
5 million	5000 BC	H/G, pastoralism = P, agriculture = A
50 million	1000 BC	A, P, H/G, urbanites = U
100 million	500 BC	H/G, P, A, U
200 million	200 AD	H/G, P, A, U
1000 million	1825 AD	H/G, P, A, U
2000 million	1925 AD	H/G, P, A, U
3000 million	1960 AD	H/G, P, A, U
4000 million	1975 AD	H/G, P, A, U
5000 million	1987 AD	H/G, P, A, U
5750 million	1995 AD	H/G, P, A, U
7000 million	2010 AD	P, A, U, ?

are responsible. We live in a time of ongoing genocide, with between 20 and 100 species of flora or fauna being annihilated daily.

Why is homo sapiens (sometimes referred to as homo sapiens sapiens = the double wise human; what self-conceit and self-deception!) in danger of diminishing greatly the capacity of the biosphere to support human life? Such a question forces us to ask how a relatively insignificant species of ape, which we were five million years ago, evolved into the awesomely destructive predators we are today? While this may seem an impossible question to tackle, evolutionary psychology/anthropology is beginning to offer some convincing insights into the origins and complexities of the human psyche (e.g., Barkow et. al., 1992; Maryanski & Turner, 1992; Pfeiffer, 1985; Ridley, 1994; Wright 1994).

Human Evolution

In brief, this evolutionary process involved intense selection pressures for strong social cohesion on apes, who moved from a tree-dwelling habitat with weak social ties (except between mothers and dependent young) to ground-dwelling. Predation pressures also selected for a more upright posture, which led to bipedalism. Bipedalism had the effect of selection for the larynx further down the throat, which facilitated a wider repertoire of vocal sounds. This repertoire led eventually to human speech as we know it today.

Competition for resources and predation pressures also maintained strong selection pressure for increasingly complex cognitive capacities, which were specifically designed to extract food and shelter from the natural environment, in competition not only with different groups of the same hominid species, but also with other mammal species. These pressures also favored cognitive capabilities that facilitated living in a social group. The hunter/gatherer way of life emerged in response to these conflicting pressures. (See Maryanski & Turner, 1992.)

The Evolution of the Brain

Modern individuals (anyone born during the last 50000 years), are born with exquisitely complex information-processing capacities operating largely unconsciously and at amazing speed, which develop to varying degrees and at different times during the life of an individual. The central function of these capacities is to enable individuals to negotiate their journey through life from birth to death within a social group and, until recently, with in a complex and sometimes very dangerous natural environment. Evolutionary theory goes further, stating that all these capacities were selected because they promoted the reproductive success of the sets of genes that carried the information programs for these capabilities.

Significant from a Jungian perspective is the growing consensus among researchers that humans are "hard-wired" from birth to interact with life in particular ways and are not born with a large general learning mechanism, as many suppose (e.g., Tooby & Cosmides, 1992). Jung said the same thing when he wrote "archetypes force [humans'] ways of perception and apprehension into specifically human patterns" (CW8, par. 270). His idea of deep-structured organizing principles in the human psyche that have resulted from our evolutionary history is being substantiated by evolutionary psychologists/anthropologists.

I find it heartening to read for instance, that "evolutionary psychologists argue that the human psyche has a number of specialised and domain specific Darwinian algorithms," that Darwinian algorithms are "specialised learning mechanisms that organise experience into adaptively meaningful schemes or frames" and that they "are assumed to focus attention, organise perception and memory, and organise procedural knowledge that will serve to guide decision making behaviour" (Walters, 1994, p. 289). Here one sees Jung's archetypal hypothesis taking on a contemporary Darwinian form.

The Shadow of Evolution: Deception and Self-deception

Crucial to our understanding of the destruction of the natural environment is the role that the capacity for deception and self-deception has played in our history. Our capacity to deceive others – and our conscious selves – as to our real intention is not unique. Indeed, deception – and detection of deception – is an intrinsic part of the competition for resources in life: from the molecular level, to plants, insects, fish, birds, reptiles, mammals and humans. (See Rue, 1994; Wright, 1994.) Our emerging complex capacities to relate to our social and natural environments have included a propensity to cheat others to our own advantage and an unconscious monitoring of others' attempts at cheating. This propensity to cheat, to detect cheating, and to counteract it, is as old as life itself and cannot be eliminated. It can only be curtailed among humans by appropriate social sanctions. It is a genetically-encoded propensity that can affect every domain of psychic life and hence it is an intrinsic part of what Jung called the Self. We all need a certain level of deception and self-deception in our lives for healthy psychic functioning. But when deception leads to serious disadvantages to ourselves or others, serious problems may arise.

Shadow Play: Deception and its Curtailment

The mythology of the Bushpeople demonstrates this tension between deception and its curtailment in quite a humorous fashion. One of the central figures in their mythology is the Mantis who frequently tries to trick others in his group. His deception is invariably uncovered by Ichneumon, a dwarf mongoose, a vigilant little animal. A central story (Bleek, 1923) describes how in a time of drought, and hence little meat, Mantis miraculously grows a magnificent eland from a piece of old shoe. He hides this eland from the others but eventually Ichneumon discovers his secret and reveals it to the others. They proceed to kill the eland when Mantis is away. He returns to find them dismembering the eland and is greatly upset. They ignore his protestations and refuse to believe him when he claims that he would have shared the eland with them, if they had given him the chance. This story not only demonstrates that deception does not pay, but also that the urge to accumulate valuable assets for oneself alone leads to the loss of everything.

Thus, the relatively egalitarian structure of hunter/gatherer societies was achieved only by keeping the tendency to selfish behavior and all the associated acts of deception in check from childhood to old age, by mythology and social sanctions. These societies lived in a constant tension between reciprocity and cheating, a tension that maintained relatively equal access to resources for everyone.

Shadow Looms Large

When climatic changes and wasteful hunting techniques reduced available antelopes in the Middle East, hunter/gatherer groups were forced to domesticate animals and to develop more intensive food-gathering techniques. These in turn led to the construction of a social cage, which inhibited the freedom of individuals and caused the breakdown of the egalitarian structure of the hunter/gatherer complex. When this move was followed by the domestication of plants – agriculture – the concentration of power became even greater, simply because there were more resources available in a given area. A priestly caste, followed by kings, quickly emerged. These castes took control of food distribution and so gained access to maximum resources for themselves, to the detriment of the majority of society. (See Ponting, 1992.) Deception played a central role in this development.

Mythologies were developed which legitimized this position, particularly of those highest in the hierarchy. While the distribution of resources remained grossly uneven, there was little the majority of people could do. Most were too busy working in order to survive, on relatively poor diets compared to that which existed in hunter/gatherer societies. Here one sees the human capacity for deception and self-deception writ large, taking on highly codified forms supported by military power, for the first time in human history.

The mythologies of hunter/gatherer societies seek to ensure a relatively egalitarian social structure with strong curbs both on deception and on any individual accumulating more resources than another. Urban societies, through complex deceptions, have mythologies and rituals that reinforce massive discrepancies in access to resources.

The Shadow and Nature

Our evolutionary history, in relation to the natural environment, was one of increasing capacity to understand natural ecosystems, all that implies in terms of brain functioning, and an increasing capacity to use this knowledge to extract – with relative ease – sufficient food and resources for survival. This capacity evolved in such a way that it left the natural environment capable of supporting future generations in the same way.

This reciprocity with nature – neither taking too much, nor too little – broke down with the advent of agriculture and urbanization. Their impacts on ecosystems were radical, killing all the larger undomesticated mammals and replacing indigenous vegetation with a few domesticated plant species. But the urge to a more balanced relationship with natural ecosystems is inherent in human nature, creating a tension in individuals of societies where this balance seems not to be achieved. (The heartbreak that the Bushpeople felt when dispossessed of their land is beautifully captured in Watson's poem "The Broken String," reprinted below).

Since the vast majority of humans have lived on the edge of poverty during the urbanization process, the individual's personal survival was the overriding concern, rather than what was happening to the natural ecosystem. Even when there were misgivings about destruction of natural ecosystems, most individuals were powerless to effect any change in the patterns of expanding urban settlements that spread around the world.

The Epic of Gilgamesh

If the majority of individuals had no choice, what of those who had some choice? What went through their hearts and minds? Did they feel that something was amiss, that the urge to take more and more from nature and from other humans was going too far? Was there not something within the psyche that tried to pull them back into a more balanced relationship with nature? The answer I suggest is "yes"; the epic of Gilgamesh from ancient Sumer illustrates this struggle beautifully.

The Sumerian epics were composed around 2100 BC while Gilgamesh, the historical being of Uruk, is thought to have lived around 2700 BC. Copies of the epic were circulating in the Middle

East for about 2000 years – a testimony to how deeply it resonated with issues of central importance to those in power.

The epic begins singing the praises of Gilgamesh: "He who has seen everything, I will make known to the lands I will teach about him who experienced all things … alike. Anu granted him the totality of knowledge of all" (Kovacs, 1989, p. 3). It goes on to sing his praises as the builder of the great wall of Uruk. He is two-thirds divine, one-third human. What a marvel of creation! Here you find none of the vulnerabilities of Mantis, the trickster god of the Bush people. Gone is the focus on vulnerability to selfishness and deceit, to be replaced by assertions of massive power and total knowledge. In the classic despotic tradition, Gilgamesh terrorizes his subjects, both men and women, who plead with the chief god of Uruk to save them from his tyranny. Anu calls on Aruru the mother goddess to create a rival, Enkidu, equal in strength to Gilgamesh – which she does. Enkidu is completely at one with nature, runs and lives with wild animals and sets free those caught in traps.

Here we have polar opposites in the male psyche: the massively inflated dominating one versus the idealized innocent "natural" male. Enkidu is brought out of his oneness with nature by a beautiful temple harlot, who seduces him beside a waterhole in the wilderness. Afterward the animals flee from Enkidu, much to his distress. Subsequently, the harlot dresses him and brings him to Uruk, where Enkidu engages Gilgamesh in a fierce wrestling match. Gilgamesh eventually wins. Enkidu submits to Gilgamesh and they are friends for life, perhaps even lovers.

The main body of the epic deals with Gilgamesh's and Enkidu's pillaging of the cedar forest of Lebanon, followed by their killing the bull of heaven. Enkidu continually attempts to dissuade Gilgamesh from this rape of nature, but Gilgamesh refuses to heed Enkidu's misgivings. Gilgamesh also ignores his own persistent nightmares that warn him of the folly of his intentions. Eventually "the gods" decree that Enkidu must die. After one more adventure alone, in search of immortality, Gilgamesh returns empty-handed to Uruk, a lonely and disillusioned man. The epic attempts to hide the destructiveness of his life by ending with praises for the king who built such magnificent city walls.

In this summary of the epic I have left out many fascinating details, whose meaning is certainly worth exploring, but space limitation necessitates focusing on the central theme of the relationship between Enkidu and Gilgamesh. Enkidu represents, I suggest, a deep complex set of interrelated cognitive capacities – the result of our evolutionary history, which facilitates a deep connection to natural ecosystems.

This profound knowledge and empathy helped restrain any exploitation of the ecosystem beyond what was necessary for survival. Gilgamesh, on the other hand, represents the power drive running amok, no longer restrained by the culture of the hunter/ gatherer society, abusing all under its power, including the natural ecosystem. The epic, rather than being a healing reconciliation between these two opposing potentials, is the grim story of how the power drive assimilates all the other potentials in the psyche to its own ends, the only limitation is that of existing technology and the number of people involved. Human history over the past 10000 years can be viewed as the gradual globalization of the Gilgamesh epic.

The current alarming rate of destruction of natural ecosystems is unprecedented in evolutionary terms. It is in some sense unnatural, and hence should be easy to reverse. Unfortunately, evolutionary theory cannot support such optimism. Given that most current ecological destruction is carried out mainly by a combination of impoverished slash-and-burn farmers and multinational business corporations, it will take enormous social pressures to counteract the vested interests involved. Fortunately, however, social pressures for change are increasing as more and more individuals begin to realize the potential disastrous results of current trends on the capacity of the earth to provide a habitable home for all of us. Let us hope that a new resolution of the Gilgamesh epic will emerge before it is too late for us and our children.

The Therapeutic Frame

What are those of us, who spend most of our working hours within the confines of the therapeutic space, yet who care for our home – the planet earth – to do? I will share some of my own troubled musings on this issue.

It came as a painful shock to me as I walked in mountains not far from Zurich over a decade ago, with my two-month-old daughter on my back, how few birds, trees or plants I could identify. It brought tears to my eyes as I realized what a gaping hole there was in my life. The feelings that arose were similar to those one encounters in one's journey in therapy when one meets again consciously, for the first time perhaps, the unmet childhood longings in relation to one's parents.

It was as though the unmet potential for the growth of a complex and differentiated relationship to the natural world imploded in on me and left me grieving. An important strand in my life since then has been my effort to recover from this loss. I have been fortunate to spend time in the bush of South Africa with people who care deeply for their environment, who know it well, and who are generous in their sharing of their love and knowledge of that ecosystem. I regard myself as an enthusiastic learner, with much to learn.

As a therapist, my explorations have led me to conclude that:

(a) The individual's relationship to the natural environment is an important one, with an archetypal core that can be addressed meaningful within the therapeutic frame.

(b) In the same way that my relationship to my intrapsychic and interpsychic needs mediate my effectiveness in journeying with clients in their explorations of such issues, so too does my inner and outer relationship to the natural environment determine my effectiveness in mediating this issue for my clients.

(c) My clients also can mediate this issue for me.

(d) This mediation operates as an intrinsic part of the overall therapeutic process; sometimes in the background or not present at all, other times at center stage.

(e) Psychic wholeness or harmony is not possible without a positive engagement with the natural world.

(f) The resuscitation of a sense of gratitude to the natural world for what we take from it is an important factor that can be mediated in the therapeutic setting.

In my relationships with colleagues I long to see the emergence of this issue as one that engages our hearts and minds. An engagement, I hope, that will lead to this topic's becoming a significant issue, both in the training of future analysts and in our own ongoing education. Also, I would like to see the constitution of the IAAP revised to incorporate some form of environmental ethics as guiding principles.

I conclude with Watson's poem, mentioned earlier. Watson (1994) has rendered in poetic form stories collected from Bushpeople in Cape Town in the 1870s. These Bushmen were imprisoned in Cape Town for stealing sheep from farmers who had stolen their lands. The poem describes the heartache of a hunter who is stripped of his land.

Song of The Broken String

Because of a people,
because of other,
other people who came breaking the string for me,
the earth is not earth, this place is a place now changed for me.
Because the string is that which has broken for me,
this earth is no longer the earth to me,
this place seems no longer a place to me.
Because the string is broken,
the country feels as if it lay empty before me,
our country seems as if it lay both empty before me,
and dead before me.
Because of this string,
because of a people breaking the string,
this earth,
my place is the place of something –
a thing broken –
that does not stop sounding,
breaking within me.

References

Barkow, J.H.; Cosmides, L.; Tooby, J. (1992). *The Adapted Mind: Evolutionary Psychology and the Generation of Culture.* New York: Oxford University Press.

Bleek, D. (1923). *The Mantis and his Friends.* Cape Town: Maskew Miller.

de Kock, T. (1995). *Springbok of the Kalahari.* Johannesburg G.T.V.

Kovacs, M. (1989). *The Epic of Gilgamesh.* New York: CBS College Publishers.

Maryanski, A. & Turner, J.H. (1992). *The Social Cage: Human Nature and the Evolution of Society.* Palo Alto, CA: Stanford University Press.

Mc Farlan, D. (1992). *Guinness Book of Records.* Enfield: Guinness.

Pfeiffer, J. (1985). *The Emergence of Human Kind.* New York: Harper & Row.

Ponting, C. (1992). *A Green History of the World.* London: Penguin.

Ridley, M. (1994). "The Red Queen: Sex of the Evolution of Human Nature." London: Penguin.

Rue, L. (1994). *By the Grace of Guile:* The role of Deception in Natural History and Human Affairs. New York Oxford University Press.

Skinner, J.D. (1993). Springbok Treks. *Transactions of Royal Society of S.A.* (Vol. 4B), 291-305.

Tooby, J. & Cosmides, L.M. (1992). The psychological foundations of culture. In J.H. Barkow et al., 1992.

Van der Post, L. (1961). *The Heart of the Hunter*. London: Hogarth.

Walters, S. (1994). Algorithms and archetypes: Evolutionary psychology and Carl Jung's theory of the collective unconscious. *Journal of Social and Evolutionary Systems, 17* -3, 287-306.

Watson, S. (1994). *Return of the Moon*. New York: Sheep Meadow Press.

Wright, R. (1994). *The Moral Animal*. New York: Patheon Books.

After Such Violence

A Reconceptualization of Jung's Incest Theory[*]

Claire Douglas
Malibu, California, U.S.A.
Society of Jungian Analysts of Southern California

Something deep in the collective insists that incest is secret and not to be discussed. A feeling of profound sadness accompanies the subject. In part this is because many of our patients have experienced early childhood abuse, most often at the hands of a close male relative, an abuse not infrequently compounded by being repeated by their former therapists. Working with these patients in the aftermath of such violence and mirroring the reality of their pain is sorrowful, harrowing, and sometimes treacherous work. The sadness comes also because we as Jungians often misunderstand the phenomenon of incest and fail to keep up to date with research inside and outside our field, nor do we read Jung thoroughly or realize the full scope of his ideas on incest. Instead, we tend to remember one or another partial concept and use it as if that were its totality. This dishonors the complexity and profundity of Jung's thought. It also does a disservice to our patients. How we theorize about our patients and their process powerfully affects their treatment.

The prevalence of sexual abuse is well known. Studies in the United States (e.g., The Harvard Mental Health Letter, 1990) made during the 1990s put the figure of adults who recall childhood sexual abuse at from 10 percent to 50 percent Most often the child is female and the perpetrator a male relative. There is an ever increasing sexualization of young girls in music, advertising, entertainment, and the culture's female objects of desire seem to be getting younger and younger. A contemporary backlash against recovered memories and its corrective – but too large a swerve – away from certitude also complicates the issue.

---

[*] An abridged version of the paper presented at the Congress.

For our patients, who bear the physical and emotional scars of incest, basic trust has been shattered and the sense of self violated and replaced by the introjection of the abuse. A helpless, fragile, yet persecutory self-concept often takes its place, one full of loneliness, shame, and self-disgust. This broken self has difficulty in basic relationships, in negotiating with others, and in playing. Its sense of community with fellow humans has been ruptured and, in its place, the damaged child and adult tend to hover around abusive people and situations as moths repetitively approach the all too familiar and destructive flame. Many researchers now find a high correlation between childhood sexual abuse and not only psychosis but post-traumatic stress syndrome, borderline personality disorders, multiple personality disorder, anxiety neuroses, depression, lack of biological regulation (especially in the immune system) and neurological dysfunction.

We reap the harvest of centuries of violence toward the feminine, within both men and women. An abused boy's inner feminine tends to be doubly victimized by the boy's – later the man's – over-identification with this wounded feminine aspect and/or a compulsive quest for virility and heroic accomplishment. Not only is an abused girl's outer feminine dishonored and injured and her connection to her body warped but her inner masculine tend to split into a male abuser and its rigid and merciless judge.

The three masters of depth psychology – Pierre Janet, Sigmund Freud, and Carl Jung – all agreed on the actual damage done by early childhood sexual abuse, including incest. Janet (1898) found that memory traces of the event, though unconscious, act as *idées fixes*, that are often unerasable. The patient's life becomes hostage to these ideas and a full life may be prevented by the fixation. Janet (1929) found also that incest trauma often causes the personality to stop its development, leaving the patient frozen in fear – incapable of learning from experience or of future growth.

Freud's discovery of childhood sexuality and his conception of the Oedipus complex – the development of the child through a stage of incestuous longing for the parent – form the background of his theory. Originally, however, Freud thought that his theories depended on his discovery that hysterical patients had been sexually abused. He believed that he had discovered the root cause of hysteria: the child's sexual trauma following parental breaking of the incest taboo. This theory was first published in 1895, after appearing in letters as early as 1893. He concluded, "I find it's the closest relatives, fathers or brothers, who are the guilty men" (Freud, 1954, p. 195).

Two years later, however, in a letter to his friend and confidante Wilhelm Fliess, Freud wrote that he had abandoned his seduction theory. Westerlund (1986) notes that Freud's change in theory came about at the time of his self-analysis and his recall of the memory of his own possible sexual trauma. According to Jones (1953), as early as February 1897 Freud was writing to Fliess that he might not be capable of sustaining his theory because to do so would be to implicate his own father. Freud was realizing not only that parents could have sexual feelings for their children but that his father may have acted on such feelings. This caused Freud a period of profound turmoil. A dream he related at about that time may show the way he resolved this crisis. *He saw a sign in front of him which stated "You are requested to close the eyes"* (Freud, 1954, p. 171). Freud did so. From thenceforth it was the child in himself and in others who became responsible for the incestuous thoughts and desires. It was they who desired their parents, not the other way around.

Westerlund and other, mostly female, neo-Freudians believe that Freud's lack of belief in his patients had far-reaching consequences for all women. Many also note the inadequacy of Freud's theory of development and the problems this has caused, particularly for women.

Jung's ideas about incest are strikingly multi-faceted and complex. In the general index to his *Collected Works*, there are two full columns of references under "Incest." In his letters (Let-I & Let. II), there are more personal exchanges that elucidate, elaborate, and sometimes contradict Jung's more theoretical writing. The seminar on Dream Analysis (DS) contains an extensive analysis of a patient's incestuous dream. The subject is mentioned only twice, however, in the *Visions Seminars* (VS) and there is no listing in the index for the 1925 *Seminar on Analytical Psychology* (AP) or the Zarathustra (ZA) seminar. The *Freud/Jung Letters* (FJ) incorporate a highly personal discussion, over many letters, of the two men's theoretical agreements and disagreements on this subject. They also contain Jung's confession to Freud, as Freud had once confessed to Fleiss, that Jung had experienced sexual abuse as a youth. Later exchanges on their respective theories of incest keep to the theoretical plane. These letters came at a crucial juncture in Freud's and Jung's relationship. A good case could be made, as, Kerr (1993) does, that the break between Jung and Freud came to a head and final rupture over their discussion of incest – their differences here crystallizing the incompatibility of their views.

Jung's references to incest can be organized under the following headings: the child, Jung's criticism of Freud's seduction theory, archetypal symbol versus reality, its extension in his alchemical studies and, finally, the incest archetype in the transference-counter-transference. Organized this way, Jung's thoughts on incest form a totality out of which something new can grow. Jung's ideas on incest are different aspects – polarities even – of one whole. Keep in mind that Jung's mandala of ideas, as well as our own, are representative of a "given moment [and have] inevitably the quality peculiar to that moment" (CW11, par. 970). The essence of Jung's views concerning whether children are the initiators of incestuous feelings comes in a 1926 lecture:

The Oedipus complex is a symptom. Just as any strong attachment to a person or thing may be described as a "marriage," and just as the primitive mind can express almost anything by using a sexual metaphor; thus the regressive tendency of a child may be described in sexual terms as an "incestuous longing for the mother." But it is no more than a figurative way of speaking. The word "incest" has a definite meaning ... and as a general rule can only be applied to an adult who is psychologically incapable of linking his sexuality to the proper object. To apply the same term to the difficulties in the development of a child's consciousness is highly misleading. (CW17, par. 144)

Jung stays remarkably consistent on this subject. He recognizes children's normal sexuality and grants the possibility of incestuous wishes but lays their cause, if present, at the parent's door. He often repeats that incestuous longings occur in adults, not children. If they are present in a child, then the psyche of the parent needs to be explored and treated. One of the more comprehensive and concise statements of this position is in an article where Jung writes of a child's night terrors:

Freud ... explains this fear as due to the collision of the child's incestuous tendency with the incest prohibition. ... I have no doubt that children can have "incestuous" tendencies in the extended sense used by Freud, but I doubt very much whether these tendencies can be attributed ... to the child's psychology *sui generis*. ... The child psyche is still under the spell of the parents' psyche, especially the mother's, and to such a degree that the psyche of the child must be regarded as a functional appendage of that of the parents. (CW10, par. 61)

Thus, Jung is in tune with cross-cultural studies today which find that the Oedipus complex – rather than being biologically deter- mined – is a product of our specific Western culture and pattern of family relationships. For Jung, a child's and infant's sexuality is a biological reality; the pattern in which the sexuality is molded depends on the child's culture and parents.

Jung's view of children's incestuous wishes as indicative of their parents' psychology is a major disagreement with Freud's seduction theory. Jung often acknowledged Freud's work but even in 1912 was dissenting publicly:

I am unable to vindicate any particular strength to incestuous desires in childhood. ... I even do not seek the reason for regression in primary incestuous desires or any other sexual desires. ... A purely sexual etiology of neurosis seems to me much too narrow. I base this criticism not upon any prejudice against sexuality, but upon intimate acquaintance with the whole problem. ... I found [that Freud's hypothesis] works to a certain extent, but not always and not everywhere. (Quoted by Kerr, 1993, p. 419, from an unpublished typescript of Jung's talk.)

Jung objected to Freud's seduction theory on other grounds as well: he found it reductive, concretist, and soulless. Jung's researches showed him that the incest taboo was only one of many taboos and he knew, from his clinical work, that neurosis can derive from many more complexes than the sexual ones. Jung also criti- cized Freud's thought process as typical of the unconscious thinking of an extravert (probably of the feeling type) in that Freud held to a single idea and ruthlessly exaggerated it.

In his letters to Freud during 1912, Jung raised most of these points but also argued for a symbolic rather than concrete interpre- tation of the incest taboo. As he pressed his case, his enthusiasm led him temporarily to lose sight of the reality of incest:

Just as *cum grano salis* it doesn't matter whether a sexual trauma really occurred or not ... it is psychologically quite immaterial whether an incest barrier really existed or not, since it is essentially a question of later development whether or not the so-called problem of incest will become of apparent importance. (FJ, p. 506)

Jung's introverted intuitive thinking made inner reality and the- ory as important, if not more important, than what happens in outer reality.

Yet for Jung as analyst, the reality of his patients' suffering kept him connected to their experience. Throughout his work, when he discussed the treatment of neurosis, Jung insisted on taking outward events seriously. For instance, in a series of one patient's dreams (DS), Dreams 16 and 24 held incestuous contents which Jung took as objective threats to the patient's children. Jung insisted that the patient understand the incestuous element in the dream in order to prevent it. Elsewhere, Jung is even more objective:

A genuine realistic value must be attached to the abnormal sexual fantasies of a neurotic in so far as he allows his actions to be influenced by them. The fantasies not only hinder him in adapting better to his situation, they also lead him into all manner of real sexual acts, and occasionally even to incest. ... It would be of little use to consider the symbolic content only; the concrete aspect must first be dealt with. (CW4, par. 551)

Jung's ideas on the objective treatment of incest show that Jung would not have used our Jungian method of archetypal interpretation as the method of choice with specific patients and their objective situations. Jung held, and through his writing, asks us to hold, both poles – the subjective and the objective – and see which, or which mixture, best suits a specific circumstance and case. Jung, the psychiatrist, analyst, and healer, is often lost sight of as we immerse ourselves in his theory. In 1948 Jung advised a colleague who had consulted him about a patient: not a neurotic with incestuous fantasies, but a woman suffering from the consequences of incest.

I have never come across a case where a woman actually had a child by her father, but I've seen a number of cases where [incest with father and mother] might easily have happened. ... The actual event of incest means nearly always a terrific blow to the psychic structure, except in cases of very primitive minds. ... Its effect is a fixation to the time and circumstances of the incest as well as to the person of the perpetrator. ... The main point is that incest arouses an archaic level of the mind ... in which one finds a highly archaic meaning of paternal incest.

When one has to treat such a condition, one ought to get the patient to reproduce the (unconscious) fantasies around the incest, applying the method of active imagination if the dreams don't produce the necessary stuff. (Let-I, pp. 499-500)

Jung's comments agree with recent findings in neurological and biological research about the long term sequella of trauma.

Jung's concern with the reality of incest and treating those suffering from its consequences and, at the same time, his creation of a symbolic view was, as he wrote, "a pretty complicated business" (Let-I, p. 500). Unable to accept Freud's myth of a father-enforced incest taboo, Jung studied worldwide myths of an ancient mother world. Jung replaced Freud's limited and paternalistic incest myth with a far more profound one that includes the maternal, the unconscious, a reconnection to the earth and the feminine, all seen through masculine eyes: the perspective of the hero. Jung found the hero myth to contain the central archetypal motif of son-mother incest. The hero returns to The Mother in all her protean forms, to be transformed and reborn. Jung elaborated the many forms of this myth in *Psychology of the Unconscious* (CW-B). This book can be read as Jung's coming of age; it was a work that not only signaled Jung's irreconcilable differences with Freud but also his own discovery of the symbolic meaning of incest – a taboo that only a hero can break.

For Jung, the hero myth represents "our own suffering unconscious, which has an unquenchable longing for the deepest sources of our own being; for the body of the mother, and through it for communion with infinite life in the countless forms of existence" (CW-B, par. 317).

The incest prohibition causes the longing – both holy and romantic – which in turn gives rise to the religious impulse, perhaps "too narrowly understood as incestuous" (CW5, par. 342) in that it included not only the myth but other human longings, such as for beauty, spaciousness, and a sense of the good. Thus transmuted, Jung found that the effect of the incest prohibition was to spiritualize the libido. In more mundane terms: The libido longs for a return to the mother; this is prohibited, and so the libido is freed to be creative in its search for another object and to develop through – and past – regression.

Jung's story of the hero could be read as his own story. Jung was a hero who broke the incest taboo by voluntarily descending into the unconscious; he fought with the dragon in the underworld, and returned with her treasures of individuation – a state of consciousness that could transcend the opposites. There are shadow elements in this story that Jung told and lived and that we, his students, inherit. Jung identified himself with the hero who can and did break taboos in his subjective descent to the mother. This identification with the taboo-breaking hero discovering new worlds may have allowed him also to break the incest taboo, objectively, with various *sorors* who accompanied him in the work (Carotenuto, 1983; Kerr, 1993; Douglas, 1993). Here Jung's symbolic interpretation of incest, and his idea of the taboo-breaking hero as a paradigm for individuation, puts Jung and his followers in a realm between two worlds: the archetypal and the concrete. Jung knew that this boundary area – where personal psychology, objective reality, and the archetypal intersect – is an area full of perils.

The questions of the opposites, of symbolical son-mother and brother-sister incest and the hero myth are developed further in Jung's alchemical studies. The archetype of incest, rather than its objective reality, now has captured Jung's interest and concern:

The archetype of incest is also at the back of the primitive notion that the father is reborn in the son, and of the hierosgamos of mother and son in its pagan and Christian form; it signifies the highest and lowest, the brightest and darkest, the best and most detestable. It represents the pattern of renewal and rebirth, the endless creation and disappearance of symbolic figures. (CW14, par. 178)

In alchemy, Jung found incest to be a symbol not only of the union of opposites but union with oneself as well. Jung also described it as a form, often a sinister form of the *coniunctio*. Whether son-mother or brother-sister union, "Both forms are familiar to alchemy and constitute the prototype of the royal marriage. This endogamous mating is a variant of the Uroborus, which, because it is by nature hermaphroditic, completes the circle in itself" (CW12, par. 496). Jung also felt that the incest motif had profound spiritual implications. He demonstrated that the alchemical process was similar to the analytic one in that both work with projections but also bring about radical change and that in both there is some inevitable confusion of actuality and symbol.

The main forms of the incest archetype that Jung found in alchemy continue the hero motif involving: a) the hero's – and now the *prima materia*'s – descent; b) the hero's "incest" through absorption – burial or being swallowed up – by the mother, earth, ocean, or matter; c) the hero's punishment for breaking the taboo – by his decay, burning, drowning, bursting, or death; d) his transformation, renewal, and rebirth into a new form.

The other great myth in alchemy, and in Jung's discussion, is the incestuous marriage of the brother-sister pair. It is an alternative Grail myth, for there is a wounded and sterile king whose land has become a wasteland. Jung interpreted the king's condition, psychologically, as a state of spiritual sterility. The king is advised to marry his son and daughter together in order to make his land fruitful.

Jung saw in these archaic alchemical myths proof of the age-old human urge for healing and higher consciousness, for renewal and individuation. He found that the brother-sister pair, the pair he spent most time studying and describing, was analogous to the *artifex-soror* pair in alchemy and the analyst-analysand pair in analytical psychology. Jung felt that both pairs were working toward similar goals and suffered similar perils.

Jung linked the alchemists' work and early depth psychology, stating: "The natural archetypes that underlie the mythologem of incest, the hierosgamos, the divine child etc., blossomed forth – in the age of science – into the theory of infantile sexuality, perversion, and incest, while the *coniunctio* was rediscovered in the transference neurosis" (CW16, par. 533).

As the alchemist was drawn into the matter he or she was seeking to refine, so too does the analyst get drawn into the field of the analysand. Jung wrote of the transference/countertransference problems this created as the analyst was absorbed into "the peculiar atmosphere of family incest" through projection, a sense of unreal intimacy, fascination, resistance, and doubt. Jung asserted the reality of these incestuous feelings in any thorough-going analysis but questioned, rather than answered, their cause:

Is it a genuine incestuous instinct or a pathological variation? Or is incest one of the 'arrangements' (Adler) of the will to power? Or is it a regression of the normal libido to the infantile level, from fear of an impossible task in life? Or is all incest-fantasy purely symbolical, and thus a reactivation of the incest archetype, which plays such an important part in the history of the human mind? (CW16, par. 368)

Jung concluded that the incestuous longing that can occur between analyst and analysand in the consulting room is highly problematic yet potentially as healing as any other descent and rebirth:

The existence of the incest element involves not only an intellectual difficulty but, worst of all, an emotional complication of the therapeutic situation. It is the hiding place for all the most secret, painful, intense, delicate, shamefaced, timorous, grotesque, unmoral, and at the same time most sacred feelings which go to make up the indescribable and inexplicable wealth of human relationships and give them their compelling power. (CW16, par. 371)

Jung described the phenomenon of this fascinating and repellent attraction in a most feeling way. He charted the stages of transference-countertransference, however, through an enigmatic series of alchemical pictures: the *Rosarium* illustrations (CW16), that provide an almost dreamlike screen for active imagination. They appeared so ambiguously because transference-countertransference was still too young a topic to appear more clearly in clinical consciousness. What we have learned since then rests on Jung's and the other early depth psychologists' work and personal experience.

Conclusion

First, Freud's and Jung's changes in their theories of incest, seduction, and sexual trauma over time, away from the actual and toward the symbolic, may have discouraged us from investigating and observing the traumatic consequences of actual incest. Yet those who adhere to a purely objective treatment of incest lose much of what Jung has to offer. Those who interpret solely on an archetypal and symbolic level alienate victims of actual incest from their own reality: the ability to face the often denied, rejected and repressed sense of what happened to them. The subject of incest is too often a blind spot for Jungian analysts, though Neie (1985), Kugler (1987), Roy (1988), Kane (1989), and Douglas (1990, 1992) have written on it, most often emphasizing the need for analysts to pay more attention to the actual events in their patients' lives as well as considering the archetypal realm. Jung could hold both the subjective and the objective meaning of incest; the archetypal and the factual. We need to do this tactfully and delicately, sometimes holding the symbolic in silence until the patient finds a way to it or when a dream, perhaps, indicates that the patient is ready. This delicacy in timing and sensitivity of when and how to interpret is the art of our science.

Second, Jungian analysts bear an extra burden (and temptation) because of Jung's romantic relationships with patients and former patients. His interpretation of the hero myth as a myth of one who breaks the incest taboo for the purpose of his own healing, renewal, and transformation along with identification with the hero contains potent shadow elements that also enter his discussions of brother-sister incest, alchemy, and transference/countertransference attraction. Since our psychology is, as Jung said, a personal confession, I believe that much of Jung's best writing occurs when he is working out this personal problem. His "personal confession" enlightens but also shadows his work on incest and especially on what he calls the incest archetype in analysis.

Taylor (1982), Zabriskie (1982), Pederson (1988), Matthews (1988) and Rutter (1989) are among the Jungians who have best examined this heritage and how it is played out unconsciously by analysts who break the incest taboo through therapist-patient sex. Patients with histories of prior sexual abuse are especially vulnerable, for this is the very field they need to bring into analysis with them. The result of the patient/therapist incest destroys the analysis and impedes the possibility of future therapy. The analyst's abandonment of abstinence abandons the patient and has destructive consequences. The shattering of the analytic container is a narcissistic abuse of power on the part of the therapist (see Springer, 1992, for a cogent study of the psychology of such an analyst). An analyst who gratifies his or her own needs this way manifests serious pathology in using a patient in order to have the analyst's own Grail wound healed. He is, "an adult who is psychologically incapable of linking his sexuality to the proper object" (CW17, par. 144). A heated transference/countertransference is not to be rejected or cooled down, for it is just here that healing can and does occur, and where love and hate and the other opposites can intermingle. But the container must be held in order for its contents to burn symbolically and efficaciously. An analyst who concretizes the symbolic, through sexual acting-out, breaks the container, and violates a sacred trust.

Many non-Jungian clinical findings cite the double wounding this concretizing inflicts on patients who must deal with their original abuse, the profound damage analyst-patient sex causes, along with the great difficulty their future therapists face. It is a lengthy process to help these doubly-abused patients to rebuild their trust and sense of appropriate boundaries.

A disconcerting amount of incest-taboo breaking has occurred in the Jungian community in the supposed sanctuary of analysis. The many causes include our reluctance to broach this subject directly in training, our faulty theorizing that tends to focus us solely on archetype and symbol; and the ease with which narcissistic acting-out can be disguised in archetypal or alchemical vocabulary.

There is an ethical double bind that can present itself in treatment. On one side: Incest cannot be judged as wrong because love is healing and is so much better than indifference. On the other: You can't imply, feel, or even think that any incestuous experience could be good. Some people suffer from "frank" incest, a familial and/or analyst-inflicted abuse of sexuality. Other people suffer from "missed" incest: parental withholding and/or the analyst's coldness, distancing, and indifference so that the child or patient never feels desirable. Maybe "incest" isn't the appropriate word for all we are talking about. The word, as Jung once suggested (CW-B, par. 342) may be too narrow for his meaning.

My next to last conclusion starts with a question. Is incest the proper word to use now for union with oneself, for the hero's descent, for the archetype of union, for the heat and desire in the transference-countertransference, and for each of the various other meanings Jung loads on the term? Words have lives of their own, and their usage changes as the culture does. After such violence toward children, documented in the years since Jung's death, can we still use the word incest and mean by it what Jung meant? The word has grown too weighted with too many children's pain.

In many cases where Jung once used the word "incest," Edinger's (1988) "lesser coniunctio" is a more apt term. He writes that the lesser coniunctio occurs "in the familiar territory of the Oedipus complex" (1988, p. 212). He goes on to describe the lesser coniunctio as a product of lust and primitive instinct. It is dangerous, contaminated; subject to further procedures; producing a killed, maimed, dismembered or fragmented product. The lesser coniunctio appears, subjectively, when the ego identifies with primitive forces rising from the unconscious and, objectively, when object union is contaminated with power and unmodulated "unregenerate desire" (p. 215). This formulation fits many of the places where Jung's use of the term incest no longer carries an appropriate feeling tone. And maybe "kinship libido" is a more appropriate term for endogamous love and relationship – that which contains eros in order for it to develop and do its healing work.

Finally, and this is the subject of a new discourse, the hero's quest – its search for transformation through an anima figure, and the incest archetype this quest depicts – is seen through the eyes of the hero. This quest seems unreflective of women's, or the feminine's, experience of the archetype; it fails to communicate what goes on within a woman in reference to her perception either of integration or of incest. Our culture, in its new recognitions of the feminine, seems to have entered into a new stage of consciousness that needs new words and new myths. I hope that many of us, both men and women, are in the process of creating that myth.

References

Carotenuto, A. (1983). A Secret Symmetry: Sabina Spielrein between Jung and Freud. New York: Pantheon.

Douglas, C. (1990). *The Woman in the Mirror: Analytical Psychology and the Feminine*. Boston: Sigo.

Douglas, C. (1992). Oisin's mother: Because I would not give my love to the druid named Dark. A study of incest. In M. Stein & L. Corbett (Eds.), *Psyche's Stories* (Vol. 2). Wilmette, IL: Chiron.

Douglas, C. (1993). *Translate this Darkness: The Life of Christiana Morgan*. New York: Simon and Schuster.

Edinger (1988). *Anatomy of the Psyche: Alchemical Symbolism in Psychotherapy*. LaSalle, IL: Open Court.

Freud, S. (1954). *The Origins of Psychoanalysis: Letters to Wilhelm Fliess*. New York: Basic Books.

Janet, P. (1898). *Nevroses et Idees Fixes*. Paris: Alcan.

Janet, P. (1929). *L'Evolution Psychologique de la Personnalité*. Paris: Chehgine.

Jones, E. (1953). *The Life and Work of Sigmund Freud* (Vol. 1). New York: Basic Books.

Kane, E. (1989). *Recovering from Incest: Imagination and the Healing Process*. Boston: Sigo.

Kerr, J. (1993). *A Most Dangerous Method: The Story of Jung, Freud, and Sabina Spielrein*. New York: Knopf.

Kugler, P. (1987). Childhood seduction: Physical and emotional. *Spring*, 40-80.

Matthews, J. (1988). Response to "Sexual abuse of children: Incest archetype in theory and practice." In *The Family: Personal, Cultural and Archetypal Dimensions*. National Conference of Jungian Analysts, San Francisco, CA.

Neie, W. (1985). *The Princess and the Sorcerer: Consequences of Sexual Abuse in Childhood and Considerations for Therapy*. Unpublished typescript diploma thesis. Zurich: C.G. Jung Institute.

Pederson, L. (1988). The dysfunctional coniunctio. Paper presented at the North-South Conference of California Jungian Analysts. Carmel, CA.

Roy, M. (1988). Sexual abuse of children: Incest archetype in theory and practice. In *The Family: Personal, cultural and archetypal dimensions*. National Conference of Jungian Analysts, San Francisco, CA.

Rutter, P. (1989). *Sex in the Forbidden Zone: When Men in Power – Therapists, Doctors, Clergy, Teachers and Others – Betray Women's Trust*. Los Angeles: Tarcher.

Springer, A. (1992). Paying homage to the power of love: Exceeding the bounds of professional relationship. Deutsche Gesellschaft für Analytische Psychologie, Conference, Berlin.

Taylor, C. (1982). Sexual intimacy between patient and analyst. *Quadrant, 15-1*, 47-54.

Westerlund, E. (1986). Freud on sexual trauma: An historical review of seduction and betrayal. *Psychology of Women Quarterly, 10*, 297-310.

Zabriskie, B. (1982). Incest and myrrh: Father-daughter sex in therapy. *Quadrant, 15-2*, 5-24.

Clinical Issues

Mutual Influence in the Analytic Relationship

Jungian and Psychoanalytic Views

Claire Allphin
Oakland, California, U.S.A.
Society of Jungian Analysts of Northern California

That transference and countertransference are inseparable is now a widely held view. Jung wrote about this in 1929, in different words. In more recent years analysts have been writing about how to think about and use these inner responses to clinical material. I am seeking to integrate Jung's work on the psychology of the transference, in particular his use of the *Rosarium Philosophorum* (CW16), pictures from an alchemical text to illustrate the process with some of the more current views of the mutuality of the analytic process.

Jung described these pictures as steps in the process. He wrote, "The patient, by bringing an activated unconscious content to bear upon the doctor, constellates the corresponding unconscious material in him, owing to the inductive effect which always emanates from projections in greater or lesser degree. Doctor and patient thus find themselves in a relationship founded on mutual unconsciousness" (CW16, par. 364). Jung did not write, however, about the necessity of the analyst's examining his or her inner experiences to determine the meaning before speaking about, or acting on, them. The result of this omission has been that analysts, and therapists of many persuasions sometimes act precipitously on their inner experiences without thinking enough about the effect on the analysand. My central point is that analysts need to attend to their inner experiences and use them to understand the analytic situation. This understanding can then be used to avoid acting on these experiences in ways that are traumatic for the patient.

The main theme in the picture series is a symbolic fusion of bodies resulting in the emergence of the soul. Thus is explicated the core of the analytic process. The analyst's fusing with the analysand creates a wholeness that results in a connection to the soul in each of them. This connection, in turn, permits a birth of new realization of the psyche in the analysand and a change in the analyst as well. Because each person is unique, each analytic process will be unique.

The social constructivists postulate that the analytic dyad creates its own history. Hoffman (1992), a psychoanalyst, writes, "Even if, for all practical purposes, the long-range goals of the analysis are fairly well established (and, of course, even those are subject to revision), the immediate means and ends are not fully knowable in the constructivist context, and both may be regarded, at least partially, as in the process of being created by the participants" (p. 294).

Another psychoanalyst, Burke (1992), considers the personal reactions of the analyst as a potential source of invaluable information. He defines repression and projective identification as understandable only in relation to the subjectivity of the analyst. Burke writes that the strategy of asymmetry and mutuality is to discover the relationship through the experience of both patient and analyst. When mutuality includes analysts' disclosure of their inner experience, it is important to examine the meaning for the patient either before or after such disclosures. The asymmetrical aspect of the relationship has to do with the power imbalance: charging fees, taking vacations, keeping the time boundary and – of major significance – the analyst's obligation to consider the meaning for the patient of all that occurs in the relationship, and to consider the patient's needs as primary.

What patients tell us about their past and current lives is colored by who they are, and how we hear what is being told to us is colored by who we are. Most important are the unconscious processes that are going on in each of the partners in the analytic relationship, and the vulnerability of each to the other because of the intensity of the involvement. Jung maintained that the pictures in the *Rosarium Philosophorum* could be seen as illustrative of these unconscious processes and vulnerabilities occurring in the analytic relationship. Hoffman, Burke, and other contemporaries of ours have written about how to think about and use these occurrences.

I think of the fountain, depicted first in the series, as the analytic container. Jung says it contains the divine water and is also called the uterus. Thus, we have an image of the analytic container as a place where the fetus can grow and from which a birth can take place. The fountain is symbolic of the structure that contains both participants, and of the processes that will produce psychic development in the patient and changes in the analyst as well. Realization of the potential for this development will depend upon the two participants, who will be influencing each other throughout the process. The match will be a good one for some and not for others.

In Figure 2 (see illustrations p. 539ff), the king and queen are clothed and their left hands are joined. Jung writes, "The left-hand (sinister) side is the dark, the unconscious side. ... The left is inauspicious and awkward; also it is the side of the heart, from which comes not only love but all the evil thoughts connected with it, the moral contradictions in human nature that are expressed most clearly in our affective life" (CW16, par. 410). The contact of left hands may be indicative of the affective nature of the relationship. This is of dubious character, a mixture of heavenly and earthly love complicated by an implication of incest.

I experienced this complication when, in the first hour, I fell in love with a male patient who was the opposite of me in many ways. In the first hour there is a great deal that is unconscious between analyst and analysand. It is awkward because we do not know each other, and the relationship has the potential of being wonderful and terrible at different times. But at this time much is unknown, hidden under the clothes, as it were. The feelings I had for my patient lasted for an evening and did not return until much later in our work together.

In order to make conscious use of their experience within the analytic relationship, analysts must take responsibility for what they know about themselves. Rather than thinking primarily about what they need to do to "help" patients, analysts need to experience how what they do or say affects patients, and how what patients do and say affects their analysts. Analysts' realization and understanding of their own experience provide the key to resonating to the experience of patients. Patients' responses to our resonance tells us what aspects of our experience are useful to patients. In this process we find out about ourselves. Ultimately, we must differentiate ourselves from the other in order to know the other.

This mutuality of influence is understood most easily when the analyst has had a life experience similar to the patient's. I once sat silently for a whole session as the patient cried about the loss of her mother. I had tears in my eyes as well and felt very close to my patient as I thought about the losses in my life, resonating with what it meant to my patient to have lost a mother toward whom she felt love and respect and very little, if any, negative feeling at the time. In this hour the patient and I were, as in Figure 3, naked together, experiencing a union informed by the spirit. The spirit, descending from above in the picture, is the mediator, that which keeps the experience symbolic, not to be acted upon. This experience was a stark encounter with reality: no false veils or adornments and the shadow not hidden. This patient was usually talkative and intellectual, not often showing emotion. Thus, she had an encounter with her shadow; she was revealing vulnerability to me. I believe that she was influenced by my openness to my own feelings of loss. I was influenced to open myself in her presence because of her need to be more herself and to have me experience her in a more authentic way. In this experience of fusion when the feelings are positive, the analyst is vulnerable to taking action. The analyst's awareness of both the symbolic nature of the relationship and the power imbalance is protection at such times.

In Figure 4, the king and queen are immersed in the bath, symbolizing a descent into the unconscious – the equivalent of a "night sea journey." At such times the analyst may need to be more available for phone contact or extra sessions, enlarging the holding environment because of the fragmentation the patient is feeling. One of my patients called me several times a day during a period when she experienced a fragmentation precipitated by her husband's leaving her for another woman. She was suicidal, felt there was nothing to live for, and threatened to kill herself and her child. This is a precarious time and one in which the analyst needs to hold her own experience of this kind of fragmentation while holding the patient's. At such times, the analyst may experience these feelings as well. Healing occurs when the analyst stays connected with the patient by knowing inwardly the patient's experience.

The analyst who experiences the depth of the fragmentation and despair may become frightened for the patient. This may lead the analyst to take or suggest action in order to stop the patient's feelings. Such a concretization of the analyst's experience can produce a break in the connection, an emotional abandonment of the patient. Instead, the analyst's fear can be a key to the patient's experience. By finding inner courage and maintaining the connection, the analyst enables the patient to find the courage to suffer this tumultuous time. This is not to say that people who are suicidal never need interventions to keep them from acting on suicidal feelings, especially when there is not sufficient connection with the analyst, or when the patient is taken over by impulsivity, or is in a psychotic depression.

In Figure 5, "Nigredo," coitus takes place in the water, the unconscious. The two are united as in the analytic relationship. That it takes place in the unconscious indicates the union is symbolic. Jung says, "Absence of symbolism ... overloads the sphere of instinct" (CW16, par. 460). That is, acting out the union in a physical way overloads the experience so that it loses its symbolic meaning. The picture symbolizes each taking in parts of the other that are in fact unknown parts of themselves. The opportunity to learn about these parts as belonging to the Self is lost and the patient's soul has been violated. Because of the power imbalance in the analytic relationship, what the analyst says and does always has a powerful impact, usually more powerful than the impact of the patient's words and actions upon the analyst. In this relationship, mutual influence is not the same as equal influence.

A variant of "Nigredo" is "Fermentation" (Fig. 5a). Here the figures in the water are winged, representing the spirit.

Death is the theme of Figure 6. From the vantage point of the ego, the descent that began in the marriage bath has hit bottom insofar as there is now a realization of new potentialities of the self.

In Figures 4 through 6, beginning with immersion and ending in death, the analyst needs to know the experience and not be unduly afraid, in order to stay connected with the patient's feeling. When my patient was threatening to kill herself and her child, even though I was physically present, responding to phone calls, and meeting for extra sessions, evidently I could not be fully present emotionally because of the fear I had that my patient would act on her threats. As a consequence, my patient turned her rage on me and left therapy because, I believe, she felt abandoned by me. This was mutual influence; my patient experienced my fear which kept her from feeling held as she experienced this fragmentation.

In Figure 7, "The Ascent of the Soul," the soul leaves the body after the death and decay. Jung says this is a time in the work when the patient is aware of the collective unconscious. It is a tenuous time, something like a schizophrenic state, a time when latent psychoses may become acute, a time when an awareness of the non-ego can occur. There may be a feeling of disorientation, of alienation and disconnection from people. A male patient sobbed in terror as he experienced himself as though in outer space, floating, without any human connection. Since such experiences occur when analyst and analysand are joined as one body, the analyst is likely to be affected profoundly by this archetypal experience and must allow the fear of it to inform the process. The analyst needs to tolerate "not knowing" at this time: not knowing where this experience will lead. As I sat with my patient, I felt afraid. As I imagined the state my patient described with terror in his voice, I could feel the disorientation and terror of the aloneness. I said, "I'm here"; "It's okay"; "I'm with you." In that hour he experienced a profound change: He was no longer so afraid of the darkness in life. He and I mutually influenced one another. He was influenced by my openness to this kind of experience, my knowing the experience of alienation. I was influenced by his experience. The asymmetrical aspect is that I was familiar with these states and could feel with him, not stopping his process out of my own anxiety.

Jung says of Figure 8, "Purification," that the falling dew indicates the divine birth is at hand. This means that more than intellect is necessary in the transformation process. The dew shows the return of the soul. In the analytic relationship more is required than intellectual understanding; there needs to be a feeling connection to the unconscious material and between analyst and analysand. Jung says the falling dew is the opposite of the black state that results from the union of analyst and analysand. From death comes life; there is light from above. When the patient who experienced himself in outer space returned, he felt a new awareness of what was important to him. He began to question the type of work he was doing and then to make some changes that were more in line with his needs and desires. I felt his excitement in wanting to do more for himself. I also felt that I would miss him as he began to talk about setting an ending date for our work together.

In Figure 9, "The Return of the Soul," the two birds at the bottom left of the picture are symbolic of a divided pair of opposites, meaning that, although the hermaphrodite seems to be united, there is still unconscious conflict. There is always doubt and when one side comes up, the opposite is not far behind. When my patient was feeling ready to set an ending date, conflict arose between us because I thought there were other areas to work on and did not wholeheartedly agree that he was ready to stop. He felt I was trying to hold onto him for my sake. Then I would swing to the opposite and feel it was time to stop; this led him to talk about not feeling ready to stop. This back-and-forth went on throughout the termination process. The conflicting opposites are ever present in such situations.

The last picture, "The New Birth" (Fig. 10), shows the union of opposites, a wholeness. Jung says that images from the unconscious are only anticipations of wholeness, which is always beyond our reach. When my patient left, he felt the same expansiveness as the figure in the picture. I experienced the other aspects in the picture that represent the confusion and the disorientation. I vacillated between thinking he was ready to leave and feeling he could do more work with me. I was aware of not wanting him to leave because I felt abandoned by his leaving. We were close, and I would miss him. Though he was leaving on a positive note, I wondered whether I had helped him enough. Was he unable to go further because of my limitations? I was left with these dark thoughts and feelings as he experienced the light and excitement of going out on his own. It is possible I had these feelings because I did not stay with his experience for a long enough time. When I spoke, saying, "I'm here," he may have felt abandoned because I became too afraid to stay in the frightening, alienated place. In this mutual process he may have been influenced, by my fear, to truncate his experience.

Several situations illustrate the integration of Jung's ideas about this process with current psychoanalytic views. These situations manifest, also, a major characteristic of mine as a clinician. I feel strongly about beginning and ending sessions on time.

Early in the work with one patient she wrote the check to me at the end of the hour. I became increasingly uncomfortable about not being able to end the hour on time, and for several weeks, it felt to me as if the check writing took longer and longer. I wondered whether or not to say anything. I thought about how my style is to begin on time and end on time and wondered, as I have in the past, if I am too rigid about this. I wondered how to bring it up with the patient. Finally, early on in an hour, I said something like, "I wonder if it is hard to leave the hour because there is not enough time to get what you need from me?" This question brought up feelings in the patient that she expected me to criticize her for what she was doing, but instead, she was moved by my concern for her. She referred to this interchange over the several years we worked together as an important indication of my difference from her critical and demanding parents. This seems to be an illustration of Figure 2. My patient and I were still clothed, we were just getting to know each other. Unconscious processes were occurring which brought up expectations about me that related to her life history. There was mutuality in that, even though I feel strongly about ending hours on time, there are patients who write checks at the end of hours with whom I do not feel as agitated as I did with this patient. I think, therefore, that I was being influenced by this patient to react, which I had a propensity to do anyway, so that she could have a different experience with me than she had with her critical and demanding parents.

I was uncomfortable also with a patient who took off her shoes at the beginning of the hour and then spent several minutes at the end of the hour putting them back on (they had laces) before writing the check. In this situation, I had less time than usual between sessions. Consequently, it felt even more imperative that my patient leave on time. I hesitated to question her because I knew my feelings had to do with the way I had arranged my schedule, and I did not say anything for a year or more. Finally, because of more intense than usual discomfort at the end of an hour I somewhat teasingly said to the patient, "I wonder if you don't like leaving me and extend the time by putting on your shoes and writing the check after the hour is up?" She laughed and said she didn't think so. The behavior continued in subsequent hours. I finally changed my schedule to have the usual ten minutes between hours and was somewhat more comfortable.

Eventually, this patient began to talk about her feeling that I was not interested in her, just as her mother had not seemed to be interested in her. I believe I did not deal with her about the ending of the hour because I wanted to avoid conflict, just as her mother had done. My patient had been a child with much vitality and feistiness; she may have made her mother feel helpless as I was feeling about ending the hour on time. I believe her experience with her mother was influencing me to relate to her in this way, and my fear of confronting a feisty child was influencing her so that she could not speak about her feelings to me. I was not aware of the mutuality of influence that was occurring when I spoke about the ending of the hour and made the decision to change my schedule. This experience illustrates the asymmetrical aspect of the relationship instead of the mutuality: I changed my schedule instead of thinking about the meaning of the interchange, which might have led me to think of mutuality and the transference, thereby understanding what the patient needed from me that was different from what had happened with her mother.

These situations illustrate my central point about the effects on each other of the two people in the analytic relationship. I know I am unusually uncomfortable when I cannot end hours right on time. I have told myself and patients, at times, that an important way the container is established is by the time boundary, and I do indeed become anxious when the hour is extended beyond fifty minutes. I also know that I am uncomfortable when I cannot do things such as returning phone calls immediately, so that the ten minutes in between hours are important to me. Is keeping the time boundary really only for my sake, or mainly to help the patient feel contained? I am talking about only a very few minutes, not about extending the hour for eight or ten minutes. How am I affecting my patients with this issue that is my own?

Each of us brings our past and current experience to the hour and injects it into the other, consciously sometimes, but more often unconsciously. Many of my patients pay me monthly, or hand me a check at the beginning of the hour. Thus, I suspect that the patients I have mentioned were writing checks at the end of the hours because something in them knew this was a problem for me and that each one was trying to change me and be changed by me in a process that disturbed my equilibrium and put pressure on me to interact in some way that disturbed the patient's equilibrium. Discomfort with the old way needs to be created so that a new way can be entertained.

This brings me to the most important aspect of the power imbalance and inequality between analyst and analysand: sexual desire. Because the two influence and are influenced by each other, feelings of desire are not unusual in the relationship. The analytic relationship can have an intensity and intimacy that in other circumstances would include a sexual relationship. Returning to the example of the patient with whom I fell in love in the first hour, I was overtaken by feelings for him, thought of him all evening, and then the feelings left. He was very different from me in many ways. At our first meeting I did not know, consciously, how different. As I came to know him more, and we became more intimate, he began to have sexual feelings and fantasies about me. When this first occurred, I did not feel the same toward him. It was only after several years that I again felt a sexual attraction toward him. My speculation about this relationship is that, at the beginning, I was unconsciously influenced by his need to have me value him as a man as he went through primitive, early feelings and reactions about being infantilized by his mother and father. I think he needed me to hold the memory of my sexual attraction for him so that he would not lose himself entirely in the early experience with his mother, who wanted him to continue needing her.

I believe the patient was influencing me with an unconscious, non-overt seductiveness that affected me because of my propensity to be attracted to a man who was so different from me. This presented the potential for me to develop some aspects of myself that I projected onto him, just as he saw in me, consciously or unconsciously, undeveloped aspects of himself. During the period when he was feeling sexually attracted to me and I did not have reciprocal feelings I believe I was again being influenced by him unconsciously to be more nurturing than seductive with him. His sexual feelings were more about needing mothering at that time than a sexual relationship. Since his mother had been seductive with him early in his life, he would naturally seek to be related through his sexuality. Later, when at times there was a more mutual and adult intimacy between us, I could feel a sexual attraction to him.

The major complication of mutuality in the analytic relationship is that the analyst holds the power and has to take responsibility to be aware of and responsive to the patient's needs rather than the analyst's own. Thus, when I raise a question with my patient about writing a check at the end of the hour, some patients will comply by writing the check some other time. It might be easy to detect such intimidation but my own desire to end the hour on time may keep me from noticing it, or I may minimize the importance of the patient's reaction because of my need to end the hour on time.

Mutuality of influence is ever present but it behooves the analyst to be conscious of the fact that the power difference is also ever-present.

References

Burke, W. (1992). Countertransference disclosure and the asymmetry/mutuality dilemma. *Psychoanalytic Dialogues*, 2-2, 241-271.

Hoffman, I. (1992). Some practical implications of a social-constructivist view of the psychoanalytic situation. *Psychoanalytic Dialogues*, 2-3, 287-304.

ROSARIVM

Wyr findt der metall anfang vnd erste natur /
Die kunst macht durch vns die höchste tinctur.
Keyn brunn noch wasser ist meyn gleych/
Jch mach gesund arm vnd reych·
Vnd bin doch jtzund gyfftig vnd dötlich·

Succus

Figure 1

PHILOSOPHORVM.

Nota bene: In arte nostri magisterij nihil est Secretum
celatū à Philosophis excepto secreto artis, quod artis
non licet cuiquam reuelare, quod si fieret ille ma
lediceretur , & indignationem domini incur‑
reret, & apoplexia moreretur.   Quare om‑
nis error in arte existit , ex eo, quod debitam

Figure 2

PHILOSOPHORVM.

seipsis secundum equalitatē inspissentur. Solus
enim calor tēperatus est humiditatis inspissatiuus
et mixtionis perfectiuus, et non super excedens.
Nã generatiões et procreationes rerū naturaliū
habent solū fieri per tēperatissimū calorē et equa
lē, vti est solus simus equinus humidus et calidus.

Figure 3

ROSARIVM

corrūpitur, necp ex imperfecto penitus secundū
artem aliquid fieri potest. Ratio est quia ars pri
mas dispositiones inducere non potest, sed lapis
noster est res media inter perfecta & imperfecta
corpora, & quod natura ipsa incepit hoc per ar
tem ad perfectionē deducitur. Si in ipso Mercu
rio operari inceperis vbi natura reliquit imper‑
fectum, inuenies in eo perfectionē et gaudebis.
    Perfectum non alteratur, sed corrumpitur.
Sed imperfectum bene alteratur, ergo corrup‑
tio vnius est generatio alterius.

Speculum

Figure 4

CONIVNCTIO SIVE
Coitus.

O Luna durch meyn vmbgeben/vnd susse mynne/
Wirstu schon/starck/vnd gewaltig als ich byn·
O Sol/du bist vber alle liecht zu erkennen/
So bedarsstu doch mein als der han der hennen.

ARISLEVS IN VISIONE.

Coniunge ergo filium tuum Gabricum dile-
ctiorem tibi in omnibus filijs tuis cum sua sorore
Beya

Figure 5

FERMENTATIO.

Hye wird Sol aber verschlossen
Vnd mit Mercurio philosophorum vbergossen·

Figure 5a

PHILOSOPHORVM.
CONCEPTIO SEV PVTRE
factio

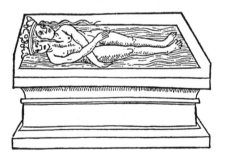

Hye ligen konig vnd koningin dot/
Die sele scheydt sich mit grosser not.

ARISTOTELES REX ET
Philosophus.

Nunquam vidi aliquod animatum crescere
sine putrefactione, nisi autem fiat putri-
dum inuanum erit opus alchimicum.

Figure 6

ROSARIVM
ANIMÆ EXTRACTIO VEL
impregnatio.

Hye teylen sich die vier element/
Aus dem leyb scheydt sich die sele behendt.

Figure 7

PHILOSOPHORVM

ABLVTIO VEL
Mundificatio

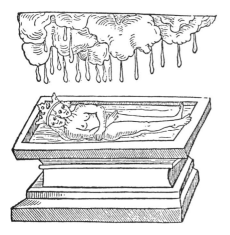

Sie felt der Tauw von Himmel herab/
Vnnd wascht den schwartzen leyb im grab ab.

Figure 8

PHILOSOPHORVM

ANIMÆ IVBILATIO SEV
Ortus seu Sublimatio.

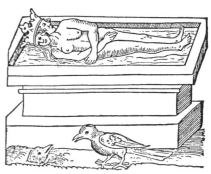

Sie schwingt sich die sele hernidder/
Vnd erquickt den gereinigten leychnam wider.

Figure 9

PHILOSOPHORVM.

Sie ist geboren die eddele Keyserin reich/
Die meister nennen sie ihrer dochter gleich.
Die vermeret sich/gebiert kinder ohn zal/
Sein vndötlich rein/vnnd ohn alles mahl.

Figure 10

Fermentation in Jung's Alchemy

Beverley D. Zabriskie
New York, New York, U.S.A
New York Association for Analytical Psychology

True Fermentation few workers do understand,
That secret therefore I will expound to thee
George Ripley

Among depth psychologists, Jungian analysts share a distinctive appreciation of psyche as a dynamic between conscious and unconscious. Yet we are also distinctly disparate in our clinical use and understanding of transference and countertransference. Jung's emphasis on individuation beyond adaptation and his reluctance to found a school, insist on a system, or model a technique are often cited for our lack of consensus. Indeed, Jung offered few narrations of specific cases. However, he did present a model of depth analysis through the phenomenology of alchemical experiment and theory. In this model, our theory, knowledge – and confusion – are embedded.

In the Western alchemical conceit, the original oneness of reality might be achieved again by a reintegration of the elements of the outer world that mirror the individual's inner state. The elements and their derivatives – the mercurial inspirations of air, the sulphuric inflammations of fire, the salty incarnations of earth and influences of water – must be rebalanced for the sake of reunion. In the extension of this imagery to psyche and our practice of psychology, these elements are seen in various degrees of balance and imbalance, while their language may be used to describe a range of therapeutic stances.

Some Jungians stay earthed in the personal and historical, following a developmental path; others go with the flow of whatever is raised by dream or ego or analyst, while others are inspired by an "aerial" overview of meaning. One group projects onto the other a literal, non-symbolic approach; shamanic inflation is projected in return. Some seek to add warmth and melt resistance with a mix of personal sharing and archetypal anecdote; others maintain analytic abstinence to tend the fire and hold the heat in a well-closed vessel. What one offers as incarnating human bonding – from helpful advice to extra-analytic connections – to another's eye is binding obstruction of individual embodiment. While poetic, these expressions suggest differences that go far beyond language, image, type, ethic, or temperament to fundamental questions about Jungian analysis and the quintessence of working as a Jungian analyst.

The Alchemical Context

Jung unpacked alchemy's mating metaphors in a two-part explication: an essay "The Psychology of the Transference" (CW16) and a later volume, *Mysterium Coniunctionis* (CW14). In Jung's alchemical psychology, three central tenets converge: his formulation of psychic energy, his concept of "psychization" (assimilation of a stimulus to a pre-existent psychic pattern), and his view of the unconscious as process. The first evolved from a Freudian drive theory to a psychic physics. The second was informed by the kinship libido and instinct sacrifice of tribal initiations and the voluntary sacrifice of the Mystery rites. The third emerged from the insights of modern science, the intuitions of alchemy and William James' psychological vision and pragmatic philosophy.

Psychic energy, psychization, process. These are the mercury, sulphur and salt; the spirit, soul, and body at play in Jung's retort for the meeting of conscious and unconscious. They are also at work in the psychotherapeutic effort to transcend the distance between them.

Jung had followed the Freudian Herbert Silberer in comparing the changing intensities of transference and countertransference with alchemical transmutations. This led to "The Psychology of the Transference," Jung's most explicit treatment of transference-countertransference. It consists of allusions to an illustrated sixteenth century alchemical text, the *Rosarium Philosophorum*, (Rosary of the Philosophers). Here, in the alchemists' musings on "feminine" matter reminiscent of the Roman Catholic rosary's meditations on Mary as mediatrix, Jung perceived the same non-dogmatic and empirical engagement with the realities of psyche and matter which he demanded of himself.

The outer operations on the substances, the inner movements of soul between body and spirit were the concern of the 20 *Rosarium* engravings. In them, the original oneness of the world fountain flowed into the two – male and female, King and Queen, Sun and

Moon – who were also the four insofar as they contained all the
elements, and could become one, in bifurcated and fused hermaph-
rodites and ultimately in the accomplished synthesis of the integrated androgyne.

Jung studied the *Rosarium* as a pre-psychological, empirical
account of the phenomena of individuation. He reproduced the first
half of the *Rosarium* scenes in his commentary on transference and
countertransference dynamics in an analysis. (By implication, the
second set of images address individual and collective psychic
experience beyond psychotherapy.) He continued his work on the
royal pair imagery in *Rosarium* and other adepts' writings in
Mysterium.

For Jung, the first ten images depict the initial fluid condition
experienced in psychotherapy. As psychic energy is brought to bear,
there is movement out from original unconsidered states of fusion.
Through increasing exposure and revelation, the king and queen –
the separate perspectives of conscious and unconscious – lose their
ground in the mutual disorientation of the fifth image, Death, a
submersion of soul in the dark waters of the *nigredo*. Soul then
departs from the incarnation in which it has been held, and ascends
to join the spirit hidden in the clouds (Fig. 8). The dynamic soul-
spirit returns to revivify the blackened body (Fig. 9), and so releases
the reflective feminine, lunar consciousness of the swan-winged
creature balanced on the moon. The hermaphroditism in this *albedo*
(white) suggests the strangeness of the newly accomplished stance.

Once the albedo is achieved – following the alchemical dictum
that return to chaos is essential to the work – another phase of the
opus begins; the new reflective capacity must be tested in the
suffered experience of the *rubedo*. As in any course of change, there
is fermenting throughout, but there is also a specific operation of
fermentation, the winged lovers consorting in the clouds (Fig. 11).
Their wings have been won, first seen in the pecking birds (Fig. 9),
borrowed from the swan (Fig. 10).

In the original *Rosarium* sequence, which Jung evoked in his
study of the transference, fermentation begins the "reddening." Yet
Jung takes fermentation out of order. His doing so is the concern of
this paper.

In Jung's scheme, the winged pair is an abrupt airy intrusion
between the submersion of the unwinged couple in the nigredo (Fig.
5) and their putrefaction (Fig. 6). The redness is off color between
the depressive black and the musing white to come. It is as if the

fermentation (Fig. 11) is brought into the psychotherapeutic process which Jung sees suggested in the first ten tableaux. Indeed, ten years later, in *Mysterium*, Jung declares that the modern human cannot bring about even the soul/spirit union alone, but needs the analyst's guidance with dreams. Then, when it comes to "the reuniting of the spiritual position with the body" (Fig. 9), which "means that the insights gained should be made real" (CW14, par. 679) – "when it comes to the question of real experience the analyst can no longer help" (CW14, par. 752).

Perhaps Jung's change is inconsequential; each adept had the license and mandate to experiment with the operations, test and change the recipes. Indeed, Jung was excited that "the alchemical opus was not a collective activity rigorously defined as to its form and content, but ... an individual undertaking on which the adept staked his whole soul for the transcendental purpose of producing a *unity*" (CW14, par. 790). As a cyclic or timeless process,

> *the time-sequence of phases in the opus is very uncertain. We see the same uncertainty in the individuation process, so that a typical sequence of stages can only be constructed in very general terms. The deeper reason for this "disorder" is probably the "timeless" quality of the unconscious, where conscious succession becomes simultaneity ... "synchronicity." ... We would be justified in speaking of the "elasticity of unconscious time" on the analogy of the equally real "elasticity of space."* (CW16, par. 468, n8)

In alchemy, however, "each of the vessels in a laboratory was supposed to exercise a mystical influence upon its contents and was chosen at the appropriate juncture with this in mind" (Raphael, 1965, p. 98).

As we know from Jung's association experiments, anomalies signify complex, disturbance, ferment. And so we attend to the unusual, the out of order, the mistaken. Through the crack of the unexpected, the hole in memory, the slip of tongue, the unconscious emerges. Thus, questions about Jung's disordering the images are worth pursuing, especially as we turn to the Transference essay as a clinical handbook and his most "technical" text.

The lovers of the later scene are unquestionably different from those of the earlier. But the *Rosarium* itself calls the image (Fig. 6) "conception" as well as "putrefaction," and alludes to a fermentation image: the sower burying seed in the ground so that it may explode its skin for the next vegetation. Jung's transposition may be read also as insight into latent psychological initiation, or shamanic transfiguration.

As our theory is embedded here, so too will be our disagreements. In the talk of the *Rosarium* – as the gold of consciousness, the ferment of our work – infuses and ripens and brings our efforts to completion, "it is as the ferment of the paste, or the coagulation of the milk in the cheese, or the musk in a good smell" (Fabricius, 1989, p. 140). It is through Jung's involvement with Fermentation that we look at our legacy.

Transference and the Psychization of Libido

In his Transference study, through the alchemical concept of the *coniunctio*. Jung moved from the merely reductive view:

> *The transference phenomenon is ... one of the most important syndromes in the process of individuation. ... By virtue of its collective contents and symbols it transcends the individual personality and extends into the social sphere ... back ... to the original and primitive order of human society and forward ... to an inner order of the psyche.* (CW16, par. 539)

Jung's placement of transference between instinct and a psychic inner order is to be understood within the view of the unconscious as a dynamic process and of psychic energy as "a psychic analogue of physical energy ... a more or less quantitative concept" (MDR, p. 208). This notion of differing intensities of psychic energy opened Jung to the alchemical sensibility of conversion through mutation and to the extension of instinctive libido into psychic energy. Instinct is neither to be suppressed nor repressed, but both integrated as pure instinct and also tapped for psychic activity since, as a psychic phenomenon, instinct would be "psychized" (CW8, par. 234). Through psychization "the reflex which carries the stimulus over into its instinctive discharge is interfered with. ... Before having discharged itself into the external world, the impulse is deflected into an endopsychic activity" (CW8, par. 241).

In the *Rosarium*, psychization is shown in the nigredo (Fig. 5). In Jung's terms, psychization is a meeting between conscious and unconscious in "the ego-personality's coming to terms with its own background, the shadow," (CW14, par. 707). Here a natural process becomes an opus wherein "instinctive energy is transformed, at least in part, into symbolical activity. The creation of such analogies frees instinct and the biological sphere as a whole from the pressure of unconscious contents" (CW16, par. 460). This freeing is achieved through *reflexio*.

> Reflexio *is a turning inwards.* ... *Instead of an instinctive action, there ensues a succession of derivative contents or states which may be termed reflection or deliberation. Thus in place of the compulsive act there appears a certain degree of freedom, and in place of predictability a relative unpredictability as to the effect of the impulse.* (CW8, par. 241)

Thus, "the stimulus is ... transformed into a psychic content, it becomes an experience; a natural process is transformed into a conscious content" (CW8, par. 243). In alchemy, this occurs in the dissolving of the existing matter. In psychotherapy, the transformation is the dissolution of the overvalued drives, desires, attitudes through the felt experience of the analytic transference and depth understanding of its frustration and meaning. In Jung's schema, it is also the relativizing of the ego personality through contact with the archetypes of the objective psyche.

The move from instinct to symbol first brings a dimming of the ego's orientation in the dawning awareness of illusion, projection, and limitation. In the momentum of individuation, the lights by which we have waked are extinguished, and in our dreams' diffuse light, first appears the nearby shadow, then the more distant anima or animus, and ultimately the Self. Through the darkest ordeal of initiation, we move toward the most sacred moment in the mystery.

Instinct, including the sexual, is not dissociated nor disclaimed, but is retained and symbolized: "*Sexuality*, like hunger, undergoes a radical psychization which makes it possible for the originally purely instinctive energy to be diverted from its biological application and turned into other channels" (CW8, par. 239).

A stunning alchemical insight sees the body seeking release from the demands of soul as much as soul requires liberation from body; for in soul's need for expression and yearning for union, it can enslave the body just as it might be enslaved. While "absence of symbolism, overloads the sphere of instinct," instinct and body also need to be freed from symbolic demands they cannot carry. As it follows the stimulus toward a realization in imagery, coitus is still coitus, but also becomes *coniunctio*. Then, a potential new perspective is born of "a union of two figures ... the daytime principle of

lucid consciousness, the other a nocturnal light, the unconscious"
(CW16, par. 469).

The Beads of the Alchemists' Rosary

Jung saw the regressions and progressions of fixed and released
libido in the collapses and revivals of the alchemical corpus. The
first passage in the *Rosarium* moves through black to white, from the
oneness of the fountain to the cosmological couple or royal pair
through whom earth and water re-meet fire and air, while their salt
and sulfur interplay with mercury. Both are mortified and fixed in
deadly fusion as two become one, their differences melting in their
immersion in each other. This occurs first in the more feminine
water, more congenial to queen, more hostile to king as the steady
solar day-time conscious is encompassed by the lunar night-time
unconscious.

For mutual liberation, soul in masculine form (Fig. 7) extracts
itself from the fused male-female, leaving the abandoned body
apparently morbid and lifeless. After the first sacrifice – the soul's
separation from the body – the union of spirit and soul, is achieved
– out of sight. Conceptions continue in hidden gestation, both below
in the dormant bodies and above in the clouds where the restless soul
joins spirit in impregnating coniunctio. Jung translates this as "the
attainment of full knowledge of the heights and depths of one's own
character" (CW14, par. 674). The rain of birth waters (Fig. 8) refresh
the dead pair below, pouring forth the homunculus (Fig. 9), the non-
biological child of the soul-spirit mating.

Moistened by the fluidity both of the shadowy nigredo and of
spirit's dynamism, there is an awakening into a consciousness
whose potential vitality is suggested by the pecking birds (Fig. 9).
Via the soul, spirit contacts and enters body. After the second
conjoining of spirit-soul with the embodied reality of the person's
being and life, there is rebirth as a lunar personality. Now the
psychized body is moon-struck, infused with spirit-soul and arises
into the albedo, appearing in the second or white conjunction as the
stunning lunar hermaphrodite (Fig. 10). Through the psychization of
libido, imaginal energy is now released, allowing the formation of
the white stone, the transmuting power that transcends the psychic
divide. Its firm hold on the reptilian and balance on a moon sliver
suggest its equilibrium between instinct and illumination. The fruits
of the moon tree, grown in "the white foliated earth," the residue of

a harrowing experience, and the white or silver ferment of the swan wings are the harvest after the dissolution and descent. As the goal and fruit of analytic work, reality is now both symbolic and concrete. With the capacity both to be and also "not be" – to transcend the ego – one may muse, meditate, reflect. In mystery terms, the old light has been extinguished through the voluntary sacrifice of the nigredo; the new light is moonlight.

This is the accomplishment of the second thing, the *rebis*. It is called an everlasting food, a white tincture that replenishes itself, a white foliated earth. The woodcut of ten, the denarius, is "the culminating point of the work beyond which it is impossible to go except by means of the *multiplicatio*" (Fabricius, 1989, p. 140). The alchemical ten symbolizes the return to unity on a higher plane. Beyond this there is no counting and no knowledge. Unity occurs through the seminal capacities of the white stone or silver ferment, the reflective approach that gives essence to the multiplicities of earthly existence.

And then comes a new aim: the yellowing of the white foliated earth, the ability to engage with reality through the transition from the private, introspective naked lunar silver state to the ready garb of the hermaphrodite (Fig. 17). The movement toward the more complete personality is initiated by the Fermentation.

Fermentation

> *But Here King Sol Is Tight Shut In*
> *And Mercurius Philosophorum Pours Over Him* (CW12, plate 268)

Fermentation is a key to the opus. Sol's fire and air have mingled with Luna's water and earth; solar light has met dark Moon. But in the volatile, mercurial nature of things the king loses his tight closure on queen. What has joined together comes asunder. The winged pair personify fermentation.

> *The wings denote its incipient volatility due to the engaging of its solar, centripetal and its lunar centrifugal energies (the king and queen) which spiral into the process of fermentation. ... The interpenetrating solar and lunar principles upon the cross made by the elements together make up the sign of Mercurius, with the wings of volatility jutting upwards.* (Zolla, 1981, p. 65)

Fermentation marks an ending and a beginning, for it is the conversion of organic substances into new compounds in the presence of a ferment. As a noun, ferment is blend, brew, combination, composite, compound, concoction, mixture, leaven, yeast. As a verb, it is akin to agitate, bake, boil, bubble, burn, churn, foam, fume, roast, seethe, simmer, smolder, bloom, blossom, bud, develop, flourish, flower, germinate, grow, sprout. The *Rosarium* instructs the alchemist:

> *Sow your gold into white foliated earth, which by calcination is made fiery, subtle and airy. Gold is the ferment of the work without which nothing is done, because it is the leaven of dough, the curd of milk in cheese, and as musk in good sweet things, and with it the composition of the greater Elixir is made, for it lightens up and preserves from the scorching, which is the sign of perfection.* (Fabricius, 1989, p. 140)

As the seeds (semina) of metals, Sol and Luna are ferments which help prepare the elixir or medicine of metals, which then tinctures or colors them.

In the undoing of what was done, solar seed has been left in lunar body. Sol and Luna are as corn, sown by king and queen in white foliated earth. In the swelling golden ferment, the seed sprouts from the shell of the husk from within. It breaks out, breaks through, ruptures old skin – suggesting the violence and pain felt when the protected temenos must be left for the sake of embodiment and realization. It is now separation that allows the seeds sown in psyche to ferment and distill.

The Philosopher's Stone was a ferment which could insinuate itself between the particles of imperfect metals, thereby attracting to itself the particles of its own nature: the white stone, or silver ferment, would yield silver; the red stone, or golden ferment, would yield gold. In our language, the ability for imaginal consciousness and passionate synthesis gathers energy to itself and affects all it touches.

In alchemy, "ferment whitens confection, forbids combustion and holds tincture that it flies not away, it softens bodies and makes them enter by course and conjoins them." In the *Rosarium*, Hermes warns: "This does not take place at once since it is not the intention of nature to do so; but it takes place by means of the copulation, that is, little by little (Fabricius, 1989, p. 140). A verse ascribed to Goethe states:

> *Long Is the Quiet Spirit Active in Creation*
> *Time Alone Strengthens Subtle Fermentation*

"A winged dissolution, a fermenting copulation, a putrefying glorification carries the process from *albedo* to the *citrinitas*" (Fabricius, 1989, p. 143). The final androgyne, in order to quicken and grow, to receive the invisible rays from the sun and the moon, and to develop into a mineral seed, needs the fire of fermentation. As the two opposite substances of the joined bodies are mixed with juices, they are ground to a fine black powder, place in a sealed retort and grilled at the special low heat of fermentation necessary for the transformation.

To effect this, the alchemist must keep up a moderate temperature, and a yellow color will tinge the substance with orange hue as the "voluntary sacrifice in the citrinitas of the riches gained in albedo reflects the inexorable process ... of new adjustments" (Zolla, 1981, p. 143). This sacrifice is sometimes shown as the lunar egg or rebis fermenting, cleaving and dying while winding its way toward the splendor of the sun. As the growing light of solar illumination helps the adept to discern the limitations of the lunar, the sower alchemist is under a power requiring the death and fermentation of the white gold gained in conjunction. It must again putrefy so that the opus will be more completely fulfilled as the adept gets beyond the Self.

As one comes to know that one cannot live by reflection alone, one is drawn to risk the integrity of the discovery and fantasy outside the laboratory, and to move into life. This often occurs by following the projections of anima and animus toward those who, as Jung once said, represent the likeness to the difference in ourselves.

Then, when the projections must be withdrawn, from "the decomposed substances of the metals, the so-called seed of gold supposedly germinated, and subsequently the soul of matter was restored to its body, the revived element" (Raphael, 1965, p. 97). After incubating in the intensities of the therapeutic retort, analyst and analysand sense the limitations of the transference which must be frustrated and contained, and of continuing only to reflect on the understood. The soul returns to the matter of how one lives one's life. The protected circle wherein trust, stability, and focused attention have allowed a birthing of a truer reflective self becomes a place of departure toward the space beyond the temenos.

Fabricius (1989) sees the lovers in clouds, trysting no longer in feminine waters but in masculine air. Their wingedness is not sudden, but rather an evolution from the two birds (Fig. 9): the single bird and the winged white reborn rebis (Fig. 10). The copulation complete, Luna forces Sol to withdraw. Then the winged sun of solar perspective descends into the Mercurius-filled basin.

In the tales of the separated lovers – of Isis and Osiris, Eros and Psyche, Rapunzel and her blinded lover, Romeo and Juliet – their blending is preceded by the torments of fermentation, a "harrowing of hell." These stories "correspond in alchemy to the fermentation of the androgynous primal matter" (Raphael, 1965, p. 45).

The fermentation also represents "the particular experience of spiritual elation that flares up between mystics of the opposite sexes ... in which mystical transcendence is intensified by the peculiar vortex of spiritual energies that leads to the formation of an androgyne subtle psychic being" (Zolla, 1981, p. 25). According to one observer, in the Christian tradition "the alchemical process of fusion through fermentation shares the aim of early Christian ascetic couples: to liberate the animating principles through fermentation and fusion of the subtle bodies" (Raphael, 1965, p. 25).

Jung sees fermentation as a "variant," Sol and Luna locked in a "steaming" embrace in the hot water of a "boiling solution" (Fig. 5) – still in the midst of the psychotherapeutic affair. Its winged and airy look seems flighty when placed between death and putrefaction, and it does not capture the sense of loss in separation that begins the reddening phase of the opus. While it is indeed again a conception born in death, it is not the loss of self felt in fusion but in separation.

Following the adepts' recipes, the analyst fostering fermentation must maintain the moderate fire of attuned attention to the seeding within the analysand's psyche, holding steady as parts are internalized so that the other may take leave and separate. After the initiatory sowing, at the end of the transferential coupling through fermentation – the gain through loss, the "voluntary sacrifice ... of the riches gained in albedo ... an inexorable process of new adjustments" (Zolla, 1981, p. 143) – the new conceptions and germinations may be birthed as the new center of the personality.

Jung (CW16, par. 459) stressed the air aspect of the winged Sol and Luna in water as spirits, creatures of thought, a combination of air and water, spirit and body in fermentation. To his eyes, they become two vapors which gradually develop as fire increases in heat and which rise as on wings. As they themselves become spirit, he says "the real meaning therefore is Goethe's 'higher copulation' ":

> *No more shall you stay a prisoner*
> *Wrapped in darkest obfuscation;*
> *New desires call you upwards*

To the higher copulation. (CW16, par. 462, n11)

This "higher copulation" seems to move away from the earthed process of seed dissolving in the ground.

There are many ways for this conjunction to fail, sometimes through an analyst's involvement in coagulating concretizations which kill the symbolic, or a withdrawal into those sublimating spiritualizations which disembody. When Josef Breuer fled from Anna O.'s fantasy that with his seed she was having his child, that their termination date would be a birth day of the fruits of their labors, the first fermentation in psychoanalysis fizzled. In an unfortunate repetition, Jung wrote that his analysand Sabina "kicked up a vile scandal solely because I denied myself the pleasure of giving her a child" (FJ, p. 207). Jung's later regret was expressed with fermentation's imagery: "I ... deplore the sins I have committed, for I am largely to blame for the high-flying hopes of my former patient" (FJ, p. 236).

Fermentation seems to reveal a "hot spot" in Jung's psyche and thus in our therapeutic tradition. Not only did he change its place, but in his commentary in the Transference essay, Jung spins into an odd digression. He asks whether the analyst can "give good advice under all circumstances," and whether it is "not essential to the true art of living, sometimes, in defiance of all reason and fitness to include the unreasonable and the unfitting within the ambiance of the possible" (CW16, par. 462). He then goes on to reflect on an intrapsychic and transferential danger for the fermenting pair: "Although the two figures are always tempting the ego to identify itself with them, a real understanding even on the personal level is possible only if the identification is refused. Non-identification demands considerable moral effort" (CW16, par. 469).

Jung acknowledges that in both psychotherapy and life, "the maintenance of a moderate fire" which "does not scorch the King and Queen" (CW16, 448), as recommended by the alchemists, is in the highest degree difficult. For it means keeping to a middle way between the physical and spiritual components. In his forays into the dark waters and sublime heights of psychotherapy and psyche, Jung had his own "hot spots" that created detours from the middle way. Jung came to feel that

> *without the conscious acknowledgement and acceptance of our fellowship with those around us there can be no synthesis of personality. ... The inner consolidation of the individual is not just*

the hardness of collective man on a higher plane, in the form of spiritual aloofness and inaccessibility; it emphatically includes our fellow man (CW16, par. 444)

At times this feeling led him to blend the contents of the retort with the stuff of outer life. According to von Franz (1975): "This explains why Jung, in contrast to therapists of many other schools, cultivated private personal contact with many of his patients; many of them later became his students" (p. 226).

Today we would not extravert or concretize kinship libido in this way. Jung gives a clue as to why his patients became such figures of his personal life when, at the end of his memoirs, he reflected: "I had no patience with people – aside from my patients. ... I had to learn painfully that people continued to exist even when they had nothing more to say to me. ... when the spotlight cast its beam elsewhere, there was nothing to be seen" (MDR, p. 357).

Conclusion

Alchemical fermentation involves sowing the substance with a metal, a psychological force, to increase its capacity for transmutation – adding the symbolic to the actual – and so increase the stone, the capacity to make meaning conscious, in quantity. Through fermenting experience, there is a transformative process from the unconscious to the conscious, to the reflected and the realized Self. Experienced as intrapsychic process, of the unconscious and the conscious in mutual contact, and as interpersonal interaction as one psyche affects the other, ferment germinates. If identified with, inter-personally; if concretized or acted out transferentially, it spoils and rots. The husks of the primitive are not removed from the kernel of emerging individuality, instinct does not cross the threshold of psychization, the capacity for reflexio is not realized.

Why did Jung include fermentation within the nigredo of shadow integration of psychotherapy? Within his brilliant understanding of depth analysis as alchemical process, is there temptation for a premature fermentation after mortification? Are we prone to illicit elations or quick sublimations? Are we prone to false ecstasy of archetypal identification or to overpersonalizations of the transference which may tear the neck of the vessel, thereby both overheating the retort and cooling the heat needed for the lives of analysand and analyst alike? Do we fly too soon from leaden depression into flights of fantasy about magical meanings? Do we lure our clients to fly with us, thus aborting our own and our clients' individuation, that value which we consciously hold so dear?

In the therapist, we may see the impulse to shamanize, take wing, rather than analyze – take apart; in the transferential field, it may impel the analyst to confuse personal and interpersonal with the "trans-subjective" and transpersonal: to soak in a hot emotional bath, or soar in the exaltation of a special "oneness." The danger is that the imaginal and symbolic take on a "ruddiness" that offers substitute gratification, replacing the experiential satisfaction which is the domain not of the *opus* but of life.

Seen reductively, misplaced fermentation can over-leaven, curdle, intoxicate, rot the stuff of the psychotherapy, and simultaneously leave the draught of life thinned and watered down. Conversely, following Jung's notion of symptom as vector, we must look also at his mutation as far-seeing intuition – of the instinct-archetype, matter-mind, body-spirit linkage that returns the fertility of the mystery religions which, if not concretized, is transformative. The attitude, the means, the analogy through which Jung pursued his investigation did not loop him back into psychoanalysis. Rather, he took both sexuality and the transference beyond the biological and adaptive, beyond the personal.

While our mishandling of fermentation may threaten our clinical tradition and current context, the winged fermentation also gives image to Jung's gift of a sensibility that includes the archetype-psyche-instinct reach regarding spirit-soul-body in the winged couple: as ancient as the mating of Isis and Osiris, as contemporary as last night's dream and today's meeting. In bringing this alchemical process to our attention, Jung re-presented the possibility of integration between body and spirit, between one's given reality and dynamic potential linked in and through the soul of engaged human experience.

References

Fabricius, J. (1989). *Alchemy*. Wellingborough: Aquarian Press.

Raphael, A. (1965). *Goethe and the Philosophers Stone*. New York: Garrett Publications.

von Franz, M.-L. (1975). *C.G. Jung: His Myth in Our Time*. New York: Putnam's, for the C.G. Jung Foundation of New York.

Zolla, E. (1981). *The Androgyne*. New York: Crossroad.

The Many Ways of Working In Psychotherapy with Children and Adolescents

Jung's Ideas as a Basis for Different Kinds of Therapeutic Work

Alice Merz
Zurich, Switzerland
Swiss Society for Analytical Psychology

Analysts who specialize in therapies for children and adolescents focus on the special qualities of a child and the symbolic expression of the child-soul in the reality situation of everyday life. Since 1980, at the Zurich Institute a student can choose to study and train in one of three programs: work with 1) adults; 2) children and adolescents; 3) children, adolescents and adults. In April 1995, of 375 registered students, there were 28 were in the children's program and 24 in the combined program. To date there are 40 diplomates from the children's program and 10 from the combined program. Interest in these programs grows yearly.

Five papers were intended in this panel. However, Gisela Broche had to withdraw as a presenter due to health problems. Christina Kuster and Anna Kohler chose to have their papers included in summary form only.

The fact that the Zurich Institute offers professional training of analysts for children and adolescents owes much to Gisela Broche. With great energy, courage and conviction she persuaded the Curatorium to expand the training options. In the winter term 1979-80, for the first time in the official program of the Institute, special lectures and seminars were offered for students who wanted to become analysts for children and adolescents. Gisela Broche became the first director of the children's program.

The following four lectures are presented by analysts for children and adolescents trained here in Zurich. They would like to give you an idea of the variety of approaches we put into practice. Also, analysts of adults may find certain of our approaches worthy of consideration.

Mourning: Work with Maternally Bereaved Children and Adolescents

Annika Bugge

Vienna, Austria
Austrian Society for Analytical Psychology

In recent years I have worked with maternally bereaved children and adolescents who, prior to entering therapy, had not mourned the loss of their mothers: young clients from families whose members showed a pattern of repressing their feelings, especially grief. My object here is to describe what may happen to children who were not allowed to mourn and how therapy can help them to reconnect with the buried emotions of grief.

None of these reasons for these clients' coming for help was the mother's death. The widowed father generally saw no connection between the child's problems and the early bereavement. These young clients were referred to therapy two to ten years after their loss, for a variety of other symptoms. Most of them struggled with a fragile self-esteem which they covered with a cheerful, brave persona. They impressed me as having been forced into a false maturity at the expense of their emotional nature. Separation anxiety, little trust in the reliability of relationships, psychosomatic ailments, sleep and eating disturbances and suicidal fantasies were some of the most apparent symptoms. What concerned me was not just their presenting symptoms, but the maladaptive patterns they had developed, to protect themselves against the pain of mourning, feelings of rejection and fear of being abandoned further. I got a sense of these young clients' unconscious bond with the destructive and death-dealing aspect of the negative mother archetype, a bond that sabotaged their need and drive for individuation and the development of ego-identity and autonomy.

What happens to the child who never could work through dependency on the mother because the bond was prematurely and violently broken through bereavement? How does this child fill in the personality's "holes" without the continuing experience and memories of a safe place that such dependency allowed? The danger is especially apparent if this child is affected with what John Bowlby has termed "pathological mourning." In my experience, the bereaved child who is not allowed to grieve is likely to carry deeply within the psyche through later years an insufferable burden of which distress and rage are a part and which may become the potential seeds of self-destruction and depression.

An example of pathological mourning is provided by Bowlby (1990) in his biography on Charles Darwin, who lost his mother when he was eight years old. Bowlby gives impressive examples from Darwin's life that show how he remained cut off from his feelings and memories about his mother. One of these episodes occurred when Darwin's cousin, who was also a close friend, lost his wife. In Darwin's sympathy letter we find the striking sentence: "Your affectionate account of the loss of your poor wife was forwarded to me ... I truly sympathise with you though never in my life having lost one near relation, I daresay I cannot imagine how severe grief such as yours must be" (p. 78). There is no indication in Darwin's autobiographical material that he later went through a mourning process. Furthermore, Darwin evidently could not see a connection between his health problems, his depression and anxiety and the early loss of his mother.

The characteristics of a mourning process as described by Bowlby are helpful in understanding how a child may work through a loss. Bowlby describes the child's emotional reaction to the loss of the mother in three main phases: protest, despair and detachment. Those of us who work with children know how painful and difficult it can be to establish contact with a deeply distrustful child who, out of emotional or concrete abandonment, has moved into a psychological defense of detachment, denying the wish for relationships. Often I have been deeply concerned about the abandoned child's fight against bonding with the therapist. The need for love often seems so loaded with vulnerability that the only defense the child has – as a means of warding off painful feelings of dependency or loss – may be a wall of ice or breaking off the therapy. By rejecting a gentle and caring approach, these children seem to have no inner container for love. Yet we know how desperately they long for warmth and togetherness. We need to be aware that abandoned children may have had no one onto whom it seemed safe to place their love. If this is the case, they are likely to fear being subjected to rejections and hurts from us, similar to those they experienced in the past. Perhaps one of the most difficult tasks is helping these children to restore their trust in a world that can bring them safe and reliable relationships through which they can explore and find their inner helping images.

The family dynamics of these bereaved children are important. My young clients have taken over patterns of pathological mourning belonging to the family. Consequently, it is important to include the family in our analytic work. In these families I observe two distinct patterns for dealing with the loss. First is the family that reacts to the death with distance and withdrawal from one another. They do not share their suffering and grief. The clients coming from families with this pattern generally fight against positive bonding to me as a mother figure. The other pattern I observe is the family that reacts to the loss with intense feelings of closeness; yet they fail to support each other in their grief. The children from these families often show a strong propensity to dependency on me.

Further, I have become aware of a negative power energy in the home environment which leaves little room for feelings and genuine relatedness. As the child's mourning process is evoked through the mother-child relationship constellated within the transference, I witness how the expression of grief at home has met with rationalizations and educational measures. Seen from the view of analytical psychology, this deficiency in the child's emotional environment seems to result in constellation of the negative animus as described by Asper (1992). That is, the beginning of an animus structure in the psyche of the abandoned child constellates a negative animus response in the surrounding adults, whose own mourning may be split off.

An example from my practice shows what may happen to a young client who was not allowed to mourn the loss of her mother. Anna, who had just turned five when her mother died of cancer, came into therapy at 16 because of her failure to keep up with schoolwork. She suffered general anxiety and had symptoms of an agitated depression. Her identity crisis was deep. Drugs and alcohol had become a habit, and I was concerned that she would fall into total chaos. The adolescent "being in charge" part of Anna struggled during the first months of her therapy against a positive bonding with me. She wanted to reduce her sessions from once a week to fortnightly. The message that it was not safe to trust a woman was noticeable in such remarks as, "I don't need any woman friends. I have always got on better with men."

In her initial sandplay picture, Anna drew with her hand a huge spider. She made no comments to this picture. I saw the symbol of the spider, at this stage in our work, from its negative aspect: Anna was caught in the web of the Terrible Mother. Fear, ambivalence, mistrust, aggression and a negative transference marked the beginning of our work. Much later, the positive aspect of this archetypal symbol – a potential for centering – became noticeable as Anna became more conscious of her psychic conflicts and her mourning process. In the Bible the spider is associated with death. (See Isaiah 59:5.) Could it be that Anna symbolically communicated to me an important theme of her therapy: her mother's death and Anna's dark fate? Her picture also provided me with insight into the family complex, where the mother's death had become a taboo subject. In addition to allowing memories of the deceased it is important to explain the reality of death to the child. This explanation is an important base for healthy mourning to proceed.

At home, the mother's memory was repressed to the extent that photos and objects belonging to her were removed from the premises. Anna did not refer to her mother on her own accord. When I asked, Anna told me in an indifferent manner what she could remember. My attempt to convey my empathy for her early loss was brushed off in a harsh tone of voice. She warded off any reference to feelings of sadness or anger that I sensed in the hour. I equated this type of response with her negative animus. In the countertransference she made me know within myself what it felt like to be brushed off and not taken seriously and understood.

After a year of therapy, she began to occupy herself with having a child. A medical examination revealed a phantom pregnancy. It seemed that Anna, who was not grounded in her feeling life, tried to work through her mother's death on an archetypal level by somatizing her pathological mourning. After a long period of working on her child fantasies Anna told me that she felt her preoccupation with having a child had to do with her mother who, as a result of her premature death, had not been allowed to carry out the function of mothering. Symbolically, Anna expressed here her need to be emotionally connected to her mother, to keep her mother alive within her. This insight seemed to mark the beginning of her conscious mourning process. Her preoccupation with literally having a child diminished.

I had now become a positive mother figure. Anna began to open up and could show her shame in place of finding her tears silly and childish. She told me of how she had felt guilty and ashamed for not having had any feelings for her dead mother. I have found these feelings to be deep in these young clients who have developed a strong persona that served as an adaptation mechanism in a home environment that failed to meet their emotional needs.

When Anna had been in therapy for three years, she had gradually developed trust in my ability to receive and understand her sad, desperate feelings. It was now possible to link these emotions that welled up in her, when she was separated from people she cared for, to her feelings as a little child when she was separated from her mother, first by her illness and then by her death.

Being more in touch with her feelings also meant connecting to the pain of longing for the mother and of mourning a childhood she had never had. It is this deep longing for the ideal good mother, which is also felt in the transference, that these young clients need to become conscious of, in order to separate their excessive expectations from the more realistically fulfillable ones.

The example of Anna's therapy shows how the abandoned child, through bonding in the transference and the process of mourning in the analysis, may find helpful symbols that can be internalized and thus help to sustain the child on the path to self-discovery and future psychic development. However, we can well imagine that the path of the maternally bereaved child will not be easy; the early abandonment trauma conspires to keep this child vulnerable in self-esteem and basic trust.

These clients' bereavement trauma and their incomplete mourning process hamper their natural impulse to individuation. In my experience, these individuation impulses are freed after the child reconnects with the split-off emotions of the trauma, emotions that were re-experienced in the mother-child relationship, as constellated within the transference or through symbolic play. It has been an important experience for me to observe, once our trusting relationship had developed, how the impulse to mourn is released in these young clients. I have been touched and impressed by the relief brought to my young clients as they are helped to express, to understand and to articulate the intense emotions of their abandonment complex. Thus, they are linked to their early loss and, eventually, to a more hopeful way of dealing with it.

When the adult can stand the child's despair of loss, we can learn a great deal from the child and thus help her or him to accept and carry the burden of a dark and painful fate. Those who work with these children need to be empathic, but also able to maintain their emotional strength by being connected to their own "bereaved child."

Just Being There

Rutger Schoeller
Tägerwilen, Switzerland
Swiss Society for Analytical Psychology

With pacifier in mouth, sword in hand, pistols in holster and paint on shoe soles

Pacifier, paints, sword and pistol are all linked to key experiences of just being there in my child psychotherapy practice. With "a pacifier in my mouth" I followed Niki's path through the deficiencies of early childhood and experienced leaving my ego standpoint behind. With "paints on Sahra's sleeves" I came to realize that having to relinquish the principles of one's upbringing can reactivate ego development. Ken's "pistol in the holster and sword in hand" illustrates an almost unbearable paradox with which I am confronted repeatedly as an analyst: concentrating on the "problem side" of the child and forcing me as analyst to redefine my own ego-boundaries.

Pacifier: Niki

Sixteen years ago, with my new degree in psychology, I was working for the Department of Psychology at a university. Niki, a ten-year-old boy from a children's home, came to me for treatment. Unfortunately, two walls of the therapy room had one-way mirrors which could not be camouflaged. This might be useful for a student eager to observe, but was macabre for both child and therapist.

The reasons for Niki's tantrums and the extent of his destructive potential were obvious to me as soon as I set eyes on his file: desolate family background; a mentally retarded alcoholic mother divorced from an equally addicted husband, incapable of even a minimum of attention to her children; thus, a case of total neglect as found so often in the records of the juvenile authorities.

First session. Niki was investigating the various articles in the room: a pacifier, a baby's bottle, some diapers and a child's pot. I am beside him, watching him stare at the pacifier. Spontaneously, I leaned forward and stuck the pacifier in my mouth. Niki looked at me seriously but with a smile on his face. I offered him the pacifier and he put it in his mouth. Shortly afterward he took it out and murmured to himself, "So he uses one!"

I feel myself wavering: "Did I influence the procedure; was I too hasty?" I had put the pacifier into my mouth without thinking, perhaps out my own experiences as a boarder at school and as counselor in a children's home. The oral needs of children in such a home are great. I felt my own longings, accepted them and granted them the right to exist. Is that personal weakness or professional strength? Had I introduced my personal aspects too hastily, thus anticipating Niki's development?

During the course of therapy it became clear that my instinct had been correct: Niki needed regression. More important than what we do is what we are. The child's Self in conjunction with the analyst's Self determine the therapy framework. As a result of my own analytic self-encounter and supervision, and in the Balint-style group supervision with colleagues after completion of training, my unconscious mind had been stimulated. I had learned to trust my Self. Is it not precisely this Self-confidence that makes correct therapeutic action at the right moment possible?

In the following sessions there was regressive play. Niki lowered the window blinds, darkening the therapy room. He placed blankets on the floor and asked me to lie down, put the pacifier in my mouth and yell like a baby. He was to be the mother and brought me the bottle with milk or lemonade. I was to have a midday nap; he was the mother working in an office. Then I had to assume the role of a two-year-old child and throw wooden blocks around; he was scared that I'd hurt myself.

Suddenly the uncomfortable thought occurred to me: What if someone is looking through the one-way mirror and can see me, an established university lecturer, lying on the floor screaming like a baby? I could endure it because of my conviction that this role-play was an absolute necessity for the psyche. I let myself fall back, acutely aware that the therapeutic vessel must have no leaks: no one-way mirrors, no intruders or spectators – not only for the protection of the child's psyche but also for protecting the analyst from prying eyes. The protection of closed doors, a darkened room and privacy are most conducive for psyche development, even if the danger of emotional or even sexual exploitation cannot be discounted completely.

Niki reversed the roles; he was now the baby and I was to be "Mapa" (Mama + Papa). Thus, he was able to regress to early childhood and to experience whatever had been lacking in his life. In the following sessions he experienced again and again the transition from the passive, screaming, orally pacified baby to the aggressive, disappointed infant who must learn to step out of the uroboric relationship and see himself as a separate being. Niki liked me to cuddle him a great deal and to show great pleasure when he had finished his bottle. Thus he could experience early childhood. At every session he took a further step in his development until I no longer had to be the infant; I was now only Mapa.

My instinctive, spontaneous action of putting the pacifier in my mouth first, served a transitional function: leading the way into a childlike, primitive, archaic world and helping Niki back into this original state where he was able to experience all the motherly love and attention that was missing in his own life. I had to be before he could become. This was not make-believe. The hungry baby inside me really existed and I let it cry. When I let it happen, Niki was able to let it happen, too.

My experience with Niki illustrates the importance of role reversal: the analyst temporarily becoming a living transitional object by relinquishing for a time the usual role of adult specialist and assuming an identity of the small child. Niki really felt, "I can do it if it's all right for a grown-up to do it, too!" Like a shaman I climbed down into Niki's primeval world: not only in sympathetic thought but literally, in flesh and blood. Hence Niki was able to follow – with a pacifier in his mouth.

What effect did Niki's story have on me? Where was my personal gain? Perhaps in the first-ever and consequently lasting experience that I was of value as a "Mapa." (At that time my two sons had not been born.)

Paints: Sahra

Six-year-old Sahra had been sent to me suffering from enuresis resulting from a severe urinary tract infection – unnoticed by her parents – and from parental neglect and cruelty. Her frequent urinary infections had become a desperate – and vain – attempt to awaken parental instincts in her mother and father.

Session 28 (of 89). Sahra wanted to paint a picture, chose a large sheet of paper and large pots of liquid colors. Wanting me to paint, she sat in front of her blank sheet, observing what I did. I was sitting in front of a large blank sheet, wondering what I should do. If I went ahead she might be tempted to copy me. If I did nothing, I wouldn't be complying with her wishes. She also did not want us to paint a picture together.

Before long she asked me impatiently when I was going to start painting. I replied that I hadn't the slightest idea what to paint. She answered "Paint just anything!" staring me in the face. "Don't you really want to paint?" she asked me. "Oh yes, I'd like to paint but I'm waiting until you start," I replied. She said, "But I don't want to start, I want to see what you are going to do."

I see that I must take the first step toward the unconscious. I start by choosing yellow paint and make a yellow spot on the upper part of the sheet: the sun. The symbol of spiritual enlightenment? She immediately paints a yellow spot at the top of her sheet.

I pleaded with her to tell me what I should paint. She wanted me to paint the sea, a ship and the sun. I painted them, slowly, observing what she was doing. She was painting a green meadow with flowers and butterflies. As she worked, Sahra applied paint more and more thickly. The paint was covering her sleeves and dripping onto the floor. (She had refused to put on a coverall.) I thought of how her mother would scold her about the paint on her sleeves. I thought of my beechwood parquet flooring, relieved that it had a protective surface; I could wipe it clean after the session. Sahra suddenly exclaimed, "Your picture is much nicer than mine," and painted over her picture with brown. I reflected that I ought to have used my better judgment not to paint a picture. Her lack of self confidence was evident. I encouraged her, "But Sahra, your meadow and flowers turned out very well." Too late; they had been painted over, and I was in the role of the adult art critic.

While she was painting she wet herself and the urine ran from the chair onto the floor. I tried to remove the paint from her pullover and wipe up the urine. I comforted her – "That doesn't matter – I'll mop up after – it's perfectly all right to do it here." Thus, a mother-child relationship had formed with me in the role of a protective, caring mother. The creative aspect in painting was less important than regression to the anal phase of development when she was able to splash around with paints and urinate at the same time.

An early-childhood experience was made possible for Sahra when I withdrew from the normal values of upbringing. The important factor was not cleanliness or even artistic creativity, but being in harmony with Self, coming to terms with reality: a feeling for what was needed now, receiving the libido that was directed at her by my allowing the paints and urine to splash down. I withheld any desire for order and discipline. The authoritarian environment had to take a back seat, leaving a healing, caring, protective attitude of just being there to ensure development of the psyche.

In the following sessions Sahra frequently painted pictures dripping with color and even managed to flood the sandbox with water. I managed to keep calm, holding back until Sahra found her Self and began a new phase of ego-development in which she identified with her mother and played with dolls, bossing them around and swearing at them.

In a further session it was my turn for role-play again. I had to be the servant bringing her – the queen – fried eggs while she sat enthroned on a chair balanced on a table. Once again my ego was stretched to its limits.

As in the case of Niki, I felt needed. The lack of parental love and attention prompted Sahra to exploit me as a servile object. I, too, was a victim of a lack of parental responsibility, when Sahra's parents neglected to keep our appointments or to pay my fees. I often considered terminating therapy, but the thought of her desolate situation made me continue. I knew that I could help her and I wanted to do so. It feels good to be needed but if I had too many patients with parents like Sahra's, I would take less pleasure in my job.

Pistols and Sword: Ken

Phallic aggressive instruments illustrate an analytic attitude of persona which Paul Brutsche once described as an attitude of "ego-parenthesis": professionally-induced weakening of the analyst's ego-standpoint.

For just over a year I have been treating Ken, aged 10, for neurotic reactions and a hyperkinetic syndrome. For the past few sessions it has been "Mr. Schoeller, can we play at cowboys again today?" I sigh to myself, "Not again!" However I reply "Yes, of course" – pause – "If you want to!" I notice again how boys, in particular, prepare themselves for role-play by arming themselves to the teeth.

Several sessions ago, Ken had armed himself with all four pistols – sticking two in his belt – as well as all the swords and a machine gun. He also had a pistol in each hand and wore a knight's helmet. He let himself be photographed in a proud, macho pose: omnipotent phallic ostentation which I was supposed to admire. "Hey – Mr. Schoeller, don't I look just great?"

Now Ken distributes the weapons: swords, pistols, machine-gun, bow and arrows. I get the damaged pistol and a shotgun without the firing pin. He builds himself a cover with chairs and boards. I try to do likewise but, with little material left, I find it difficult to hide myself behind a single wooden plank. I think, "Just my luck!" Ken places a piece of rock crystal on the table which I am to steal. I think, "So that he can shoot me dead!" To my surprise this does not happen immediately. I can return to my cover unharmed. But then he appears and shoots the door open. "Hands up! Hand over the stone! [I hand it over.] Surrender your weapons!" They may have been lousy weapons but now I have nothing to defend myself with. Ken fires three shots at me.

Again the decision: what to do next. Should I fall down wounded or even dead? Should I give myself up, which could arouse feelings of guilt in him, or follow the dictates of my own ego: remain seated and unimpressed? I decide to ask him what I should do. As usual the answer is: "Fall down dead. Count to ten and then get up!" And then what? I have to go toward him and take back the stone. I get a pistol back. I fall to the ground with a crash – a trick learned, fortunately, in judo: Count out loud to ten, creep from under cover and go to him. More shots. Again I fall. Again I count to ten. And so it continues.

I get tired of this procedure. Indeed I am aware of diminishing professional empathy and increasing vital ego-interests in fantasy form. Any minute now I'm going to start shooting! Who am I? Must Ken's omnipotent self-experience progress at the expense of my ego boundaries and tolerance limits? I think: "Blasted, subjective, archetypal Hell! I don't think I can take much more of this!"

I retreat under cover again and gain some breathing space. Ken, who is obviously aware of my diminishing patience, wants to reassure himself, "But Mr. Schoeller, you would never have shot!" Almost at the end of my tether I reply, "I haven't a chance!" Now he proposes, "You are the policeman now and have to come and arrest me!" I don't get very far – more shots and again I am on the floor. He tells me that he is now "going crazy" and is shooting around like a madman.

These role-plays usually end with Ken's wanting to play in the sand and have his photograph taken, to take home. Sometimes I say that I would like to have my turn of shooting because I am always the one to be shot. Then I pretend to shoot around as if berserk, but always aiming at a target; otherwise I might just shoot him by mistake!

While the next ailing-ego drama is being set up in the sand-box, the "overkill" continues. Tanks and soldiers, of course: Switzerland against Germany. The Swiss with bullet-proof vests and much better-equipped; the Germans – such idiots. He takes out the pistols and shoots at the Germans. I am glad that I am not sitting in the sandbox but my nationality (German) begins to prickle! At the end of the session Ken takes his leave, a photo of the sand-box battle in his hand. He helps my bruised ego. "You are great at playing cowboys!"

The role of pistols and swords as images of phallic spiritual libido in the process of breaking away from, and coming to terms with, the grip of the matriarchal sphere is clear as a transference and counter-transference phenomenon.

These scenes illustrate the professional drama in an analyst's conflict between professional image and ego requirements. As analysts of both adults and children, we suspend our own ego requirements in order to empathize with the needs of others. The knowledge and experience of our professional persona protects us from emotional contagion, and yet permits a certain degree of infection. We achieve this protection in child therapy by means of the analyst persona and by sacrificing the demands of our own egos. We become involved in something that is not normally compatible with us, such as lying on the floor and bawling like a baby or, as in my case – a pacifist – having to shoot with a pistol or to fight with sword in hand.

This sacrifice means being willing to reach a stage where I no longer know what the terms "healthy" or "abnormal" imply, or indeed who, beyond the ego I am: baby, vengeful policeman, wicked robber, Mapa, teacher, doctor or whatever. I am a void, just being there: waiting to be used; damming up my ego aims, needs and desires.

Within the confines of the therapy room, we embark on a night-sea journey, without knowing either the journey's end or the route to be taken. I am led by the images, hints and clues that arise in the child's spontaneous play toward the possibilities for development. In the process of regression to its own original, primitive or archaic being, the childlike soul recovers from the harmful effects of social demands and restrictions. At one time the reflex cried out and resisted in vain within the child, but it can be re-activated.

Recovery through this state of just being there has its price: fees – usually the concern of the parents – and sacrifice of the analyst in ego-limitation and its accompanying stress. The longer therapy concentrates on the problem side of the child, the greater the ego-stress to the analyst: aversion, reluctance, irritation, one's desire to be on the winning side for once. I must awaken in my patients those aspects that I have to silence within myself.

It is possible to resolve the paradox of ego-awakening in the child and ego-silencing in the analysts. First we bring about a direct experience of coming together, a meeting of equals. A situation of equals can exist only when I don't know, when I am just being there and when I can make no sense of a situation. Then, suddenly, intuitive knowledge starts to form, independent of any acquired, adult knowledge. The healing moment comes when the child can find and give way to self-expression, feeling respected and approved. Then I realize why I, the analyst, had to lie on the ground with sword, pistol or pacifier: because parental, analytic knowledge also tumbled to the ground.

What happens if I am professionally unqualified, not a good father, not a first-rate specialist, can't be bothered to play? Suddenly I start to influence pedagogically: wipe the floor when the paint drips down, clean the hot-plate on the cooker when the milk boils over. The child thinks, "Aha, he really would prefer to keep things neat and tidy: no mess after all!" In so doing, I demonstrate my limitations to the child and to myself; I do not make a coming-together possible.

Nevertheless, I have never come across a child who has been unable to cope with this "sobering experience," nor have the thera-peutic processes been affected adversely by it. From conversations with older, more experienced colleagues I realize that the older they get, the less they are prepared to become involved in situations like these. They drop games which they used to play in younger years and are no longer prepared to crawl under the table – and not only for physical reasons. They were more willing to indulge childlike needs early in their careers because they themselves still had childhood needs to be satisfied or lived out in play.

When I play with a child, I am also my own playmate. In the same way that a child matures, the analyst's inner child, too, recovers from tormenting deficiencies. I believe that as our work progresses, the potholes in our own childhood development begin to fill up. Inasmuch as we differ as personalities, our methods of treatment are dissimilar. It must be possible to experience these situations on a symbolic, imaginary level. However, at the moment, I work in the manner I have described.

It is important that we say "yes" wholeheartedly to what we do and participate in, so as to be able to say "no" freely at another time.

Translated from German by Catriona O. Aichinger-Brown

Parallel Development of Mother and Child (summary)

Anna Kohler
Geroldswil, Switzerland
Swiss Society for Analytical Psychology

In my therapeutic work, I attempt to establish a fruitful connection between fairy tales and painting. In my experiment with five children and their mothers, on the parallel development of mother and child shown by means of drawings, I selected Grimm's "The Nixie of the Mill-Pond" as the basis for my experiment. The interesting point of this tale is that, in the course of the story, the role of the hero is transferred to the woman. She becomes the person who carries the action.

It was my intention to involve the mothers of the children in therapy more actively into the developmental process by sending each of them forth on her individual path as a fairy tale heroine. The tale provided these women with support and structure in the unconscious realm which directly confronted them in this painting experiment.

I chose women who had participated for at least one year in my regular talks with parents. The mothers painted once a month in a group for 90 minutes, while the children painted during the same week in their individual therapy hours. At the beginning of these hours I read consecutive chapters of the fairy tale. The first picture they painted was meant to get them into the right frame of mind. In the second picture they were urged to portray what moved or touched them most in the fairy tale. We agreed that nothing was to be said at home about the drawings or the experience but that I would look at and discuss the pictures with each mother and her child separately at the end of the experiment. My objectives were as follows: 1) a clearer demarcation between the personalities of mother and child; 2) relatedness rather than unconscious, interfering symbiotic entanglements.

One set of pictures was painted by a 42-year-old working mother bringing up her child alone, and her 10-year-old son. If we look at the parallel development of this mother and her child, we can observe certain common features at first: their resistance at the first painting session, replaced at the second by a burst of energy from both of them. From the third painting session onward, the developmental path of the mother clearly leads inward. Her archetypal pictures point to a time marked by the ability to wait, a time of patience; she must collect herself at first and digest her newly gained impressions. This corresponds to her nature and the phase in life through which she is passing. Her son incorporates movement and activity into his pictures. He wants to know, to experiment, to apply. This tendency is compatible with his nature and his age. In both mother and son, painting triggers an increase in energy, which leads to more open conflicts and tensions between them. They must find a new form of relationship, so as to be able to support in a positive manner the separation tendencies of them both.

It was interesting and gratifying for me to learn that, at a subsequent meeting my colleague at the Psychiatric Service for Children barely recognized the mother whose entire appearance had changed in a positive sense. In contrast to an earlier time, her participation in the talk had become confident and spontaneous.

The son has become a Boy Scout. He likes camp life and now wets his bed only rarely; bed-wetting is not a major problem in his activities. The development processes experienced by the five mothers and their children during the experiment differed widely depending on age, sex and existing personal problems. The women found painting together in a group both supportive and stimulating. They felt a common bond by the knowledge that each of them had a child in therapy with me. The agreement not to talk during the painting sessions, and the fact that their personal situations were not known, gave them a feeling of protection and security. The women found this experiment to be an opportunity to get in touch with themselves.

For me, the crucial point in the experiment was the decision of each child to engage in this process together with his or her mother.

The children were proud and at the same time curious to discover how their mothers could express themselves in painting. The work the mothers did on themselves furnished the children with more psychic space to develop their own personalities.

Psychotherapy with Severely Mentally Retarded Children and Adolescents *(summary)*

Christiane Kuster-Neumüller
Zurich, Switzerland
Swiss Society for Analytical Psychology

My presentation at the Congress had two parts. In the first part, I discussed the subject theoretically; in the second I gave practical examples, using relevant slides. This paper is a summary of the first part.

Interest in psychotherapy with severely mentally retarded (developmentally disabled) children and adolescents has increased only slowly, during the last 10 to 15 years. There had been a belief that a more-or-less normal intelligence is necessary for this treatment.

Jung's pioneer work, in noticing and explaining seemingly incoherent remarks of schizophrenic patients, was fundamental to his lifelong research. But basic questions regarding mentally handicapped persons remain neglected by Jungian psychology regarding, for example: the stability of the boundaries between consciousness and the collective unconscious how archetypal images appear and the efficacy of psychotherapy with these individuals.

Quite often, children who have sustained early emotional injuries have not been fully able to develop or use their intelligence. Behavioral symptoms of these children are well known. But if mentally handicapped children show the same symptoms, often they are interpreted as belonging to the retardation rather than to the early emotional injury.

Mentally handicapped children often have brain damage from various causes, which influences not only their intellectual capacities, but others as well, such as mobility or perception. Moreover, the family of such a child has experienced a terrible shock after a traumatic birth and discouraging diagnostic information.

After birth the child, which we see as a symbol of the Self, may have lain crippled before the exhausted mother. These traumatic experiences can influence most particularly the mother-child relationship through unconscious rejection by the mother or compensating overprotection. Grimm's fairy tales "The Little Donkey" and "Hans my Hedgehog" tell what reactions occur when a child is born who does not fit the wishes and images of the parents. These fairy tales also show that such a child may go through an individuation process, after long suffering.

Currently, such children receive a great deal of intensive medical care, therapy and parental interest because they are handicapped. This attention also has a dark aspect: The child may develop the identity "I am handicapped" instead of "I am." While these children slowly become more independent, they may fear not being loved and losing identity. These problems may become a neurosis.

The aim of psychotherapy is not so much to increase such clients' intellectual capacities as to help them to find a way out of suffering and to develop their potential. Mentally handicapped children in psychotherapy sometimes cannot speak or make themselves understood. Others cannot draw or make a sandpicture and often do not know what dreams are. Consequently, these children are not able to give into therapy the kind of unconscious material that we believe is necessary for understanding. But it is expected that we as therapists can have an empathic knowing of what is going on in these therapies and also have trust in the self-healing capacities of the client.

In my experience, severely mentally retarded children and adolescents are able to express their inner conflicts and be active in psychotherapy. In the therapeutic process it becomes clear that the archetype of the Great Mother contributes to emotional healing. These children stay mentally retarded at the end of therapy. But they have developed a strengthened self-esteem for tackling everyday life.

Translated from German by Hazel Friedli-Long

References

Asper, K. (1992). *Schritte im Labyrinth*. Tagebuch einer Psychotherapeutin. Olten: Walter Verlag.

Bowlby, J. (1981). *Charles Darwin*. London: Hutchinson Ltd.

Prenatal and Perinatal Influences in Contemporary Jungian Analysis

JoAnn Culbert-Koehn
Santa Monica, California, U.S.A.
Society of Jungian Analysts of Southern California

Therapy must support the regression and continue to do so until the prenatal stage is reached. ... The so-called Oedipus Complex with its famous incest tendency changes at this [prenatal] level into a Jonah-and-the-Whale Complex, which has a number of variants.

C.G. Jung

Speaking of birth trauma at the 1989 IAAP Congress in Paris, I felt shy in presenting my hypothesis that what had caused me deep emotional pain in my certification interview was memory of my own traumatic birth. From my infant-psyche point of view, leaving the container of the training program stirred feelings about leaving the womb.

Drawing on the writing of D.W. Winnicott, I emphasized the physical and psychological experience of the birth process, and the period immediately after birth. Since 1989 I have begun also to look at the impact of prenatal experiences which, like the birth experience, can be observed in transference/countertransference phenomena. The works of W.R. Bion, Yvonne Hansen, Neil Maizels, Erna Osterweil, Michael Paul, Alessandra Piontelli, Otto Rank, Lynda Share and Frances Tustin have helped me to explore this area.

Although Jung made some disparaging remarks about the literal aspects of birth trauma – for example, calling it "a famous obvious truism" (CW2, par. 842) – he strongly emphasized pre-birth influences, most notably in relation to his concept of the collective unconscious. References in his works to destiny, fate and vocation also emphasize prenatal influence. One of the most interesting such references occurs in the 1935 Tavistock lectures (CW18, par. 205), mentioned in Bair's (1978) biography of Samuel Beckett.

Beckett's analysis with Bion had reached an impasse. As a farewell to the analysis, Bion is said to have taken Beckett out to dinner and to hear Jung at Tavistock. Beckett was taken with Jung's view of complexes, since his experience of creativity was about being seized by an autonomous force that demanded expiation. A casual comment by Jung affected Beckett deeply:

> *In response to a question about the dreams of children, Jung mentioned a ten-year-old girl who had been brought to him with what he called amazing mythological dreams. Jung could not tell the father what the dreams signified because he sensed they contained an uncanny premonition of her early death. Indeed, she did die a year later. Jung said, "She had never been born entirely."* (Bair, 1978, p. 209)

It was the words, "She had never been born entirely" which, according to Bair, profoundly affected Beckett, who

> *seized upon this remark as the keystone of his entire analysis. ... He was able to furnish detailed examples of his own "womb fixation," arguing forcefully that all his behavior, from the simple inclination to stay in bed to his deep-seated need to pay frequent visits to his mother, were all aspects of an improper birth.* (Bair, 1978, p. 209)

No one's personality is so uncomplicated that any single trauma or memory explains everything. But the events around one's birth, or the days immediately following birth, leave a profound imprint and tend to be re-experienced at times of separation and transition. When they are not experienced consciously, they have a dark, pessimistic, agitating, stifling, debilitating, sometimes terrifying impact. These earliest memories often have both physical and psychological correlates and frequently carry a seeming life-and-death urgency which Bion has described as "catastrophic anxiety." Patients experience intense pain – but a more intense sense of gratitude and relief – when these pre-verbal birth memories are made conscious in the analytic process. I feel that, as Jungians, we have a responsibility to learn more in this area and to build on Jung's early intuitions.

Prenatal Life

Freud noted in 1926 that there was more continuity between prenatal and postnatal life than the dramatic caesura of birth would lead us to believe. In recent years we have impressive new data that confirm Freud's idea. Piontelli (1992) observed infants in utero and afterward. She found that temperamental differences can be observed in utero and continue to manifest in the life of the developing child. One dramatic example was an infant, Julia, who actively mouthed and licked the umbilical cord. As a young child she was sensuous and self-absorbed. Brought to treatment at age three, Julia always had pockets filled with food, once as many as eight pockets.

Paul (1988) has observed the prenatal experience, indirectly, in his Los Angeles consulting room. A woman patient dreamed *she was in an autopsy room watching the end of a postmortem, which then transformed into an embalming scene.* "She saw the circulatory hook-up clearly and, as the process was begun, she awakened screaming from her dream and could not shake off the hideous sensation of being flooded and engorged with fluid" (p. 555). At the time of this dream her choking phobia returned. She questioned her mother, who reported having toxemia which was exacerbated during her pregnancy prior to the patient's birth.

In my own practice I have observed dramatic examples of prenatal trauma. "Beth" has been in analysis for many years. When she began treatment, she was suffering from anxiety and psychosomatic problems. She felt overwhelmed with responsibilities that left little time for herself. Her mother had cancer while pregnant with Beth and underwent radiation treatment during that time. Beth often felt that things were "coming at her," that the world was not safe. She had never had a safe place to be a baby or little girl. These themes dominated the treatment.

Recently Beth and her husband moved into a new home. The previous home was smaller, cozier, near the ocean, womb-like. The new home felt larger, lighter, more out in the world, part of a more established neighborhood. The session after the move, Beth lay on the couch sobbing, holding her head, contracted in pain. She said, "I hate the new house and the new bedroom; there are no curtains and too many windows. The light is streaming in, and I feel bombarded and exposed. My husband likes the new windows with no curtains and the bright carpet. I'll never feel comfortable. I can't get comfortable." As she talked I felt her fear that I would not hear her or comprehend her terror. The verbal crescendo and despair were building, and I said quietly, "Do you think this might have to do with your experience in the womb with your mother's cancer and radiation treatment?" Her hands came down from her head as the agony began to subside. She cried then very quietly and we could begin to talk about the pain.

Sarah, another patient with prenatal trauma, comes four times a week. During the first years of treatment I had, two days a week, an office without windows. Although I preferred the office with windows, Sarah preferred the womb-like "dark one." As the analysis proceeded, it became clear that Sarah's depression intensified before her younger sister's birthday each year and before her own birthday. In the weeks before her birthday, she would feel as though her body were filling up with dark fluid. She felt such pressure in her head that it seemed as though her whole body might explode. She would say that she couldn't get comfortable and was afraid of dying when away from me. She would also feel pain in her teeth. She might visit a chiropractor or an ENT doctor during this time, also without relief. In the somatic countertransference, I experienced her extreme feelings of lethargy and fatigue.

Sarah's mother suffered from high blood pressure and smoked excessively during her pregnancy with Sarah. When I offered the interpretation that the womb might have been toxic and that maybe she had indeed been in a life-or-death situation, Sarah's fear of dying began to diminish. She also felt that as a baby in utero and after birth she had gone "mindless" to blot out the pain. Although she felt grateful and relieved when an interpretation was made, it has taken several years for the physical symptoms to become identified cognitively. In the periods before her birthday, what seemed important for me was to stay alert and active, to ask her to report on what was happening in her body and mind. I experienced a strong countertransference pull toward fogginess, sleep and mindlessness. Over time I learned not to identify with her despair or her terror but to stay respectful of her feelings and help her verbalize her intense pain.

A third example is my patient "Robert," who knows from his mother's medical history that she suffered from hypertension during her pregnancy with him. This was a high-risk pregnancy, and Robert was delivered by caesarian section. In the period before his birthday he is always more depressed, lethargic, and tense, as if awaiting a catastrophe. After the birth date passes, the depression and anxiety lessen. During this time he often draws pictures that look like in-utero creatures that are developing but may be aborted. A recent dream was of *two very sad-looking in-utero babies, with Robert looking into their eyes and seeing sadness.*

All the patients just described are extremely sensitive to stimuli from the environment and to receiving projections. All are hypersensitive to others' needs but resentful of being in this role. It is hard for these patients to focus on their own desires, for they feel guilty and fear punishment when something good is happening to them. They long for a secure, protected womb in which to develop.

Rosenfeld (1987) discusses Felton's (1985) work on fetal osmotic pressure and quotes from her work with autistic children and their mothers. Felton hypothesized that dissociated contents in the mother's mind which she found disturbing were activated during pregnancy and seeped into the child's unconscious. Felton called the process "osmotic pressure." The fetus seems to be helpless to ward off such pressure. Children from such a prenatal environment may be phobic toward their mothers. "They are terrified that they may ... have to guard against something very frightening which is being forced into them" (Rosenfeld, 1987, p. 277). They may feel also they have too little skin or boundary. The patients I have described in this section reflect many of these characteristics.

The Birth Process

Paul (1988) discusses the feeling of pressure as being central to the birth process. He notes that the word *pressure* derives both from Middle English and Old French, *pressen, presser*.

> *Literal and directly connected senses of pressure include: to exert a steady force; to press to death; to execute; to compress; squeeze; extract. Figurative senses of pressure include: to bear heavily on; to reduce to straits; to beset or harass; to oppress; to crush; to distress or afflict; to weigh down; to burden (mind, feelings, spirit); to produce a strong mental or moral impression; to urge on, compel, force.* (p. 564)

These images and feelings can help us understand the infant's experience of birth.

Movement from inside the mother's body to outside it may result in sudden overstimulation and painful feelings of being raw or cold. This movement is a dramatic moment often replayed in child play and possibly re-enacted in analysis. Leaving the consulting room may evoke such painful birth feelings. Several patients have told me how "out in the cold" they felt when my consulting room door closed. One of Paul's patients dreamed of feeling very small and unprotected after birth, like a shrimp without a shell. The patient had had a difficult birth, and Paul's countertransference experience was of this patient verbally beating against him. I have noted patients doing this before vacation breaks – asking repetitive questions in an extremely aggressive and invasive way – beating against me as if trying to get inside my body to avoid the pain of separation.

With Paul's patient it was possible to reconstruct that her mother had developed uterine inertia that resulted in caesarian section. During each of her menstrual periods this patient would beat verbally at Paul and call him at home. He surmised and interpreted that her menstrual periods were experienced as if she were giving birth to a damaged baby, which had been pounding against the uterine wall again and again, attempting to emerge. Paul points out that each birth is nothing less than a major stage in evolution which required millennia in the history of phylogeny to occur. In a human birth, this transition from inside a watery environment to an outside gaseous one occurs in a matter of seconds.

From my own practice comes an example of how the image of birth comes up at the time of a potential life transition. "Judy's" birth was induced. She comes from a family in which there is a generational difficulty with separation. Judy's birth was difficult and her mother suffered from depression from the loss of a parent shortly after the birth. Judy is in a new relationship with the most suitable man since I have known her. This man is bright, in her profession, and available. He also likes her! In the past she has picked rather unavailable men. Several months prior to the session here described, a fourth session had been added with the idea that if she could experience more contact in the analysis, perhaps she could tolerate more intimacy outside the analysis.

Judy is partly excited by the new relationship but also terrified of the feeling which she states is the horror of being more separate from me and from her parents. She tells me she is thinking of *Alice in Wonderland:* "This new relationship feels like falling into a rabbit hole." There is terror in her voice when she asks how could Alice tolerate her adventure? Things going from big to small, changing sizes, growing, shrinking, unfamiliar. She seems to intuit the feeling of havoc that will be unleashed in her by this new relationship to me as well as the boyfriend if she can let the adventure continue. She says Alice has to meet all these strange people (parts of herself, her feelings). "It doesn't feel safe to me. I'm not Alice. I'd want to be home with Mom."

Near the end of the hour Judy told me a recurring dream from her childhood. *She was going down into the ground by wooden stairs. Maybe it's the underworld; there's no going back, and it's scary going forward as in the rabbit hole. There is scary stuff in the passage. You have to go through to get out.*

In a subsequent session she begins by saying she noticed she was angry driving over to the session. She said that I had pushed her out at the end of the last session, after I had said it was time to stop. She kept talking, and I had said, "We really need to stop." This upset her, as she thought it was an especially good session and wanted to savor it. My comment made her feel that I just tolerated her and that my office was a factory. Near the end of the session, having talked about her ambivalence and resistance to her new boyfriend, she said, "I just want to be a cute kid, forgiven for everything and allowed to act young. Not a stiff, married, traditional adult." After a pause, she added, "I'm over 40, and I still want a perfect childhood."

I said she seemed to be longing for paradise, that maybe she was longing for the womb. Offered the new relationship and the feelings and anxieties it stirred up, parts of her wanted to go forward while a lot of her wanted to go back. Paradise. As a countertransference reaction I now had images of her grandmother's home on an East Coast beach where Judy remembered the happiest times of her life. The atmosphere in my consulting room seemed very fluid.

Judy then said in an uncharacteristically soft way (unlike her frequent changes of subject after an interpretation), "I wonder what my experience in the womb was like, and what my life would have been like if I hadn't been induced." She now began to speak of her grandmother's summer house. "The summers in that home were the best part of my life. The grass was soft, and it was a big place with a lot of land and huge trees where I could climb. I was more on my own there than at home. My imagination felt free. I could be on my own and not be discovered. The house was like a castle with secret places. I felt really safe there."

For patients with premature, induced or caesarian births, the movement from inside the mother's body to outside can be viewed as a traumatic loss. Paul (1988) suggests that the patient may feel robbed or ripped off. Osterweil (1990) suggests that the patient can feel expelled. Certainly Judy felt mechanically pushed out at the end of the previous session. Such patients may attach in tenacious ways that may be difficult for the analyst to understand and endure. Breaks in analysis, as well as life transitions requiring separation and loss, will bring up the desire to remain in the womb along with the hatred and terror of being born.

After Birth

Winnicott (1975) emphasizes the period immediately following birth: In order for satisfactory development to occur, the baby needs a mother who can welcome the newborn and actively adapt to its needs. The baby needs a sense of continuity, to be in a state of being. Winnicott postulates that if this does not take place, if the baby's mother is not available due to excessive narcissism, depression, or ill health, the baby will adapt by splitting off its own needs. A premature defensive and precocious use of mind occurs, causing rupture in the mind-body connection, often resulting in psychosomatic illness.

A young woman who came into treatment with me two years ago provides a dramatic example of this pattern. Among the reasons Linda sought treatment was a conflict about whether to get pregnant or to continue her studies. Some of her apprehension about pregnancy related to fear of being left by her husband if she was not advancing in her career. It became clear that her father's divorcing her mother had upset what she believed was an "ideal" family. Seeing her mother as quite helpless to function independently after the divorce made her fear pregnancy, even though she felt she would enjoy mothering and was reasonably secure with her husband. When she began to see that she could indeed function differently from her mother, she became pregnant within four or five months.

No sooner was Linda pregnant than she became very ill: vomiting profusely all day and unable to take in nourishment. She was exhausted and bedridden. She seemed to need to be a baby herself and to be completely taken care of and fed special amounts of baby food. In preparing to become a mother, she needed first to be a baby again. She had been the baby of the family, although the quality of mothering seemed geared to her mother's needs, not her own. At the time of the pregnancy, the poor quality of her own early mothering was still unconscious and thus somatized.

Nevertheless, she was more stable during the last months of her pregnancy and had a natural delivery. She described this as a powerful spiritual experience. The birth was a time of deep connection to her husband and a reclaiming of her body. Linda had been a dancer in her early twenties and was able, during the pain of labor, to dance to music to facilitate the birth. It is my guess that she had an easy birth herself and that both her own prenatal and postnatal periods were tougher.

Linda gave birth to Greta and took her home from the hospital the next day. Her husband took time off from work. The nursing went smoothly, and the three of them settled in. I did not know until she told me several months later, but Linda kept the house quite dark and allowed no visitors for at least three days (the period after birth that Winnicott sees as critical). Linda wanted the transition out of the womb to be gradual for her baby. I wondered what her own experience after birth had been. When visitors did start coming to the house to see Greta, Linda experienced it almost as a violent intrusion. Since Linda's mother was very socially oriented, I wondered if Linda, as a new born, had felt impinged on by her mother's narcissistic need for many visitors. Perhaps Linda was protecting her baby the way she wished she had been protected.

The Birthday Anniversary Phenomenon

Another source of evidence that birth can be stored as traumatic memory is manifested in the range of affects that come around a birthday. I began noting this phenomenon with several female patients who described their husbands as emotionally distant around their own birthdays each year. The women all reported that in the weeks before their husbands' birthdays, the men were depressed, provoked fights, and resisted making plans to celebrate. Each wife would insist on a celebration, only to have it spoiled; the husband would either be ill or provoke violent conflict on the evening of the planned celebration. These men had no conscious memories of or curiosity about their births, although they described poor relations with their mothers.

After observing this birthday celebration phenomenon, the wives began to accept their husbands' discomfort at such times, to lower their expectations, and to avoid making special plans. This seemed to reduce the tension in the marriages at birthday times.

How is prenatal and birth memory stored? What kind of memory is it? Share (1994) has reviewed the literature on infant memory. She states:

Recent and very significant research data ... lend support to the possibility that the earliest affective and perceptual experiences/ traumas can be stored in the unconscious, the conscious, or both, and are capable of retrieval in infancy, early childhood, and even adulthood. Additionally, researchers have tentatively located a place (the thalamoamygdala circuits) where such memories of affective experience may be stored and processed. (p. 142)

Linking Freud's ideas about types of memory with Terr's (1988) work on trauma, Share states that there are two types of memories getting clinical attention. "Burned-in" behavioral memory is one type of memory, which is comparable to Freud's perceptual memory; Terr's verbal memory is a second type, similar to Freud's memory image.

Share points out that authors such as Donald Spence, Ernst Kris and Scott Dowling – who insist on the impossibility of reconstructing specific infant memories – are referring to "verbal memory." This kind of memory comes from a verbal child, age three or older. Verbal memory becomes modified, distorted, and overlaid with current experience and does not lend itself to veridical reconstruction.

Behavioral memory is traumatic, pre-verbal, intense and often re-enacted. The McGough Group of Irvine, California reported in the *New York Times* that this type of memory imprints on the amygdala. Large amounts of epinephrine and norepinephrine are released and may affect the indelible way this type of memory consolidates and imprints.

Share (1994) suggests that both types of memory are important in analytic work. "Using reconstructive *and* narrative approaches in working with these two types of respective memories, we could reach the human experience of our patients at the beginning while at the same time understanding the variations and developments that change such experience over time" (p. 143). Reconstruction is more possible from behavioral memory, which will be re-enacted and felt in the somatic countertransference. Behavioral memories will be present also in dreams. The narrative approach is more applicable to our work with verbal memory.

Birth Trauma and Classical Jungian Analysis

The dynamics of personal birth trauma may need special attention in the context of Jungian analysis. Patients with birth trauma have special problems navigating a transformational process. For example, while many patients in the *mortificatio* (psychological death) phase of an alchemical transformation process may feel a fear of death, birth-traumatized patients need special help to separate their feelings and fantasies about death from the literal danger of death because of the traumatic birth imprint. Birth-traumatized patients often have somatic symptoms during the mortificatio stage and seek medical attention. Often there are feelings of impending catastrophe or doom that can be felt by the analyst in the counter-transference. If the patient's terror can be understood and related to the birth or prenatal trauma, the depression and grieving related to the psychological death necessary in the mortificatio stage can be faced, and the patient eventually can move forward.

During the *separatio* stage of an alchemical process, patients with birth-related anxieties may feel persecuted by overpowering affects of being mutilated, cut up or forced out; separation is not seen as part of growth and individuation but as catastrophe. Separation anxiety may be acute before times of actual separation, bringing up the threat of death. Feelings of being raw, skinless and overly exposed may be acute following separation. If the analyst does not help the patient face these painful feelings, forward movement will be evaded and an impasse in treatment may occur.

Birth and/or prenatal trauma may even erupt in a *coniunctio* stage of an alchemical process. Bion (1966) has said that prenatal trauma can be split off successfully, only to manifest at any time in adult life. It does not manifest, necessarily, during infancy or early childhood.

Ruth, a patient of mine in her forties, dreamed that *she and her boyfriend were getting married and were at the hospital to adopt twins. At the hospital she found out she was one of the babies. The baby in the dream was like an egg out of a shell – an embryo, the dreamer wondered? It needed to hold her hand. It had a tiny arm that reached out and touched her finger.* Ruth awakened from the dream shaken. It reminded her of how terrible her prenatal embryonic state must have been. Her mother told her that the night after Ruth was conceived, she realized how bad her marriage was – that it was doomed. The mother stripped naked, started drinking, and got hysterical. Her sister came to the apartment to calm her down.

The dream comes up at a time of making a new relationship. This patient has had a difficult time coupling with a man. Do this memory and her associations surface as she tries to couple and create a new relationship, reminding her of the rupture in the parental couple and in the mother-child bond? This dream may bring knowledge of the original trauma which, when integrated, will no longer need to be reenacted. In the dream, Ruth makes contact with the embryo, perhaps leading to a new life.

Maizels (1985) suggests that there is an ongoing conflict throughout life between those parts of the personality working to stay in the darkness of the womb and those parts wanting to change, to move forward into the light. His work on birth anxiety and the pull toward the womb may also help us take another look at the conflict between Fordham's and Neumann's description of the first year of life. According to Samuels (1985), Fordham describes an infant as being sufficiently developed to be capable of some separation from the mother after birth. Neumann postulates an extra-uterine year in which mother and baby are one psychologically. Perhaps both views are true. Parts of the personality a la Neumann remain merged with the mother in an in-utero or womb-like state of mind still unborn while other parts of the mind are born, go forward, and are separate from the mother. What if both states of mind continue to coexist and conflict throughout life?

Concluding Remarks

Tustin (1988) warns us to be gentle in our dealing with mismanaged physical and psychological birth because we are dealing with elemental states that normally remain deeply buried and not investigated. There is an enormous sense of rawness and extreme vulnerability related to birth trauma. Trying to analyze such early states seems rather like trying to put a nightmare under a microscope; to write about such early states often seems awkward and clumsy but not to do so seems a professional dereliction.

When we talk about birth, we are talking about an experience that is both universal and deeply personal. It is both known and mysterious, physical and psychological, individual and archetypal. The physical process of birth affects the psychological birth process. The psychological process of either mother or fetus may affect physical birth.

When exploring this area of psyche, both analyst and patient may encounter intense pain and chaos in the transference/countertransference. Of necessity there will be periods of terror and waiting in the dark. These difficult analytic junctures are compensated by the patient's relief that the analyst attempts to understand where the patient is stuck and is willing to traverse this difficult territory. There can also be moments of awe for both patient and analyst that the body and psyche hold these memories until we are ready to make the descent.

References

Bair, D. (1978). *Samuel Beckett: A Biography*. New York/London: Harcourt Brace Jovanovich.
Bion, W. (1966). Catastrophic change. *Bulletin of the British Psychoanalytic Society*, 5, 18-27.
Felton, J. (1985). Personal communication quoted in Rosenfeld (1987).
Maizels, N. (1985). Self-envy, the womb, and the nature of goodness. *International Journal of Psychoanalysis*, 66, 185-192.
Osterweil, E. (1990). Notes on the vicissitudes of intra-uterine experience. Oral presentation, Los Angeles, CA.
Paul, M. (1988). A mental atlas of the process of psychological birth. In J. Grotstein (Ed.), *Do We Dare Disturb the Universe?* London: Karnac.
Piontelli, A. (1992). *From Fetus to Child*. London/New York: Tavistock/ Routledge.
Rosenfeld, H. (1987). *Impasse and Interpretation*. London: Tavistock.
Samuels, A. (1985). *Jung and the Post-Jungians*. London: Routledge & Kegan Paul.
Share, L. (1994). *If Someone Speaks, It Gets Lighter: Dreams and the Reconstruction of Infant Trauma*. Hillsdale, NJ: Analytic Press.
Terr, L. (1988). What happens to early memories of trauma? *Journal of American Child and Adolescent Psychology*, 27, 96-104.
Tustin, F. (1988). Psychological birth and psychological catastrophe. In J. Grotstein (Ed.), *Do We Dare Disturb the Universe?* London: Karnac.
Winnicott, D.W. (1975). *Through Pediatrics to Psychoanalysis*. New York: Basic Books.

Rage and Psychic Transformation

Takao Oda

Tokyo, Japan
Association of Graduate Analytical Psychologists
(Zurich Institute)

A sufferer can transmit his disease to a healthy person whose powers then subdue the demon, but not without impairing the well-being of the subduer.

C.G. Jung

In his study of the archetypal wounded healer, Meier (1949), further developed Jung's idea. When analysts realize the wounds of their patients and receive them into their own psyches, an archetype is constellated. The archetypal healer is vulnerable to woundedness, often in place of the patient. The capacity to accept is one of the fundamental prerequisites of being an analyst. Such a kind and warmhearted attitude comes from the analytic culture.

In the analytic relationship with borderline persons, however, it is often impossible for analysts to maintain kind and warm feelings toward their patients. This is especially true when those patients are strongly influenced by *participation mystique* (mystical participation). A patient's demanding, manipulative and aggressive attitude toward an analyst sometimes makes the analyst angry. An analyst who is under the influence of mystical participation with a patient may harbor anger or even rage toward that patient. The therapist's anger and rage come partially from the "talion law of revenge" (the principle of "an eye for an eye"). Lambert (1972) discussed the talion law and gratitude from the viewpoint of transference/countertransference, and as an unsolved problem. Although I agree with him, there are other kinds of anger that can be analytically important.

Quoting from Racker (1968), Lambert (1972) distinguishes between neurotic countertransference and countertransference proper. It is impossible for us to differentiate completely between those two types of countertransference. When we have analytic relationships with borderline patients, mystical participation or projective identification and projective counteridentification develops. Consequently, analysts are strongly influenced by their own developmental problems. Resolving the unconscious fusion with our own inner parents is one of our major tasks as analysts.

Archetypal Basis of Anger and Rage

Experiencing affirmative rather than aggressive feelings is important for the construction of the analytic container. However, when we treat severely wounded patients, we often face our own anger and rage toward them in our effort to help them find healing. Anger works, sometimes destructively but often constructively; it facilitates psychic differentiation and transformation, for analysts as well as patients. This kind of aggression, which functions differently from the talion law of revenge, has an archetypal base and is activated in the close, mutual relationship between the analyst and patient. A Japanese fairy tale (Seki, 1978) illustrates transformative anger and rage.

The Serpent Bridegroom

Once upon a time, a wealthy man had three daughters. A long spell of dry weather dried up his rice field. The wealthy man told himself that he would marry one of his daughters to the man who could fill the rice field with water.

The next morning when the man went to the rice field, he saw that it was filled with water and a big serpent, the spirit of the pond, was slowly moving there. The wealthy man was at a loss as to what to do and he took to his sickbed.

First the man asked the eldest daughter to marry the serpent. The eldest daughter refused. Then the father asked the second daughter the same thing, and she did not accept. Lastly, the youngest daughter was asked by her father to marry the serpent. She accepted her father's request and told him that she would do anything he asked of her.

The youngest daughter asked her father to make a device for slaying the serpent; a gourd stuffed with cotton containing thousands of needles. The youngest daughter went to the pond where the serpent dwelt, and announced to the serpent that she was going to marry a lord who would be able to sink the gourd into the pond. The serpent ran the needles into his body as he moved to sink the gourd. The serpent shed blood and died.

*After the daughter slew the serpent, she went on a journey, leaving
her father and two elder sisters. On her way, the daughter met an old
frog woman. Because the daughter had slain the serpent who was the
natural enemy of frogs, and so saved the lives of many frogs, the old
woman gave her a magic skin. When the daughter wore the old
woman's skin she took on the appearance of a genuine old woman.
People did not know that the daughter was a young woman and thus
she was safe and protected.*

*The daughter continued on her journey, wearing the skin of the old
woman. On the way, she took on work as a live-in maid for a wealthy
man. The eldest son of the wealthy family chanced to see the
daughter as she was reading one evening. She was not wearing the
old woman's skin. He fell in love with the daughter. The wealthy man
found that his son's lovesickness came from his desire for the
daughter. The son and the daughter were united in marriage and
lived happily ever after.*

The daughter's rage is not described directly. In fairy tales, only
the skeleton of a story is told, and characters' feelings are not usually
mentioned. We readers therefore have to supplement the tales by
using our imagination to amplify the skeleton of the tales, and
adding our own feelings. Those feelings consist of omitted ones and
ones of which the heroes and heroines are unconscious. I believe that
the youngest daughter slayed the serpent because she was in a rage
against him. The daughter would not have slain the serpent if she
had not experienced rage.

Why was the daughter so enraged against the serpent? In "Beauty
and the Beast" type tales, the father rules his daughter. The father
asks his daughter to marry an animal and she agrees to do so. The
daughter in "Beauty and the Beast" is passive. She does not get
angry at either her father or the beast.

The youngest daughter in the Japanese tale told her father that she
would do anything he asked of her. In this she resembles the
daughter in "Beauty and the Beast." The rest of the tale, however, is
completely different. The daughter seems to accede to her father's
request but all along she is planning to slay the serpent. The daughter
has been ruled by her father; the bridegroom is weird and has power
over the daughter. She is in an unreasonable situation, in that she
must pay the penalty for the promise her weak father carelessly
made to find a way out of his difficulties. The daughter saves her
father by agreeing to his request. However, she is in a rage and
prepares to attack the threatening serpent. Both the father and the
serpent totally disregard the daughter's individual nature.

Projection and Compelling Power

In "Beauty and the Beast," the daughter accepted her father's request to marry the beast, and she actually married him. This passive woman's love for the beast broke the spell over the prince who had been transformed into a beast by a witch. From the outset the daughter in the Japanese tale had no intention of marrying the serpent. Thus, we find a woman of action. This type of woman also appears in Grimm's "The Frog King," but there the princess is immature and in a more or less fused relationship with the frog.

My concern is with anger and rage in the analytic relationship. The talion law of revenge is one of the problems; aggression that comes from this law hurts the patient's psyche and will always function destructively.

Aggression, however, comes not only from the talion law of revenge. Analysts may use their patients' and their own feelings of aggression for analytic purposes. Furthermore, if analysts can experience patients' aggression and contain their counter-aggression psychically in the inner vessel, the analysts will be able to keep themselves stable, not influenced by the talion law. Aggression that is experienced psychically is different from that which comes from the talion law. This kind of aggression helps the object to transform. A patient's aggression toward an analyst may facilitate the analyst's transformation. An analyst's aggression toward a patient may facilitate the patient's transformation. This transformative anger or rage, unlike that of the talion law, is beneficial to analysis and healing.

In our role as analysts, we receive many sorts of projections from our patients. Projection in general, to say nothing of projective identification, is always more or less demanding and manipulating. I associate the analytic relationship with "Beauty and the Beast." A beast image may be projected onto the analyst from the patient, and onto the patient from the analyst. If the analyst can endure receiving the projection of the beast image, and the patient can endure similar projections from the analyst, the dynamism of healing will occur through the archetypal "coniunctio": marriage between Beauty and the Beast.

In the Japanese tale, the daughter's attitude toward the non-human being is completely different from that of the daughter in "Beauty and the Beast." The youngest daughter projects her archaic parents and primitive male image onto the serpent, but she does not marry him. The daughter faces and slays the non-human being, and she overcomes the fusion with the inner parents and the primitive male figure. Whereas up to the present she was forced to live as a daughter undifferentiated from her parents and as a primitive female, she now rejects the serpent's projection and the mystical participation with him. Psychoanalysts call such mystical participation, with splitting, projective identification.

We may think of the daughter in the serpent bridegroom tale as a patient. Simultaneously, we can view the daughter as a therapist figure. In the latter case, the primitive serpent becomes the patient. We associate borderline patients' demanding and manipulative attitude with that of the serpent who does not consider the daughter's free will. The serpent's or borderline patient's mystical participation has compelling power.

Borderline patients suffer from fusion with others, especially with their parents. Furthermore, their psyches easily split into opposites, for self-protection from these destructive inner parents. When patients project a good mother image on the analyst, they expect the analyst to give them anything they want. If these patients' wishes are not fulfilled, the projected good mother is immediately transformed into a bad, destructive stepmother. Borderline patients demand to be special. The analyst may be influenced by such an attitude; patients unconsciously rule the analyst.

The analyst can be wounded by these patients' aggression. The more patients are unconscious of their own demanding attitude, the more the analyst gets angry. Superficially, the anger or rage seems to be influenced by the talion law of revenge. The analyst's aggression, however, comes mainly from the analytic situation in which the analyst is not allowed to behave freely, as an ordinary human being.

Transformative Aggression

In the serpent bridegroom tale, the serpent is slain by the youngest daughter. I imagine that the slain serpent is transformed into a human being: the eldest son of a wealthy family. The fact that the youngest daughter has faced her own rage has facilitated both her own and the serpent's transformation processes.

In discussing the tale in my book (Oda, 1993), I associated a female borderline patient with the daughter and the analyst with the serpent bridegroom. The daughter, having slain the serpent, has achieved her independence. When a borderline patient expresses abandonment rage against us, we may feel counter-anger, arising partly from the talion law of revenge. At the same time, however, we get wounded and feel depressed and sometimes symbolically slain.

In the female borderline patient's dream, the analyst image was slain by her inner aggressive male figure, and her symptoms began to improve. The patient projected primitive, weird and demanding parents and the primitive male figure onto the analyst and, in rage, slew this image of the analyst. Similarly, the daughter slew the serpent and transformed him as well as herself. The patient became more separated from the analyst and somewhat conquered her mystical participation by slaying him.

The youngest daughter in the serpent bridegroom tale had to overcome the fusion with her father. She told her father that she would do anything that he wished because she was his child. The daughter did not have a personal mother, but she had to be differentiated from the collective, archaic and destructive mother. She did this by slaying the serpent. This demanding serpent, who attempts to force the daughter to marry him, represents the father who rules his daughter and the destructive collective mother as well.

Archetypal aggression can facilitate differentiation of the subject from the object. This kind of aggression is crucially important in the analysis of severe cases such as borderline personality disorder and schizophrenia.

Earlier I associated the analyst figure with the serpent bridegroom, slain by the daughter. Alternatively, we may associate the patient with the serpent bridegroom who intends to rule the daughter. Borderline patients try to dominate the analyst by involving him or her in mystical participation.

Directing anger at the other, and receiving anger from another are archetypal opposites. If we cannot accept both aspects – experiencing anger or rage and being wounded by it – we are unable to handle aggression psychotherapeutically. We can realize and use our patients' and our own aggression as a tool only when we are highly conscious of our own anger or rage and able to live through it.

Meier (1949) studied the archetypal wounded healer and the archetypal opposites of wounding and being wounded. He quotes the oracle of Apollo: "He who wounds also heals" (p. 5). While Meier made a large contribution to analytical psychology, he did not discuss the analyst's experiences concerning aggression, here and now. My concern is with the transformative function of aggression:

not only the patient's aggression but also the analyst's anger and rage.

Clinical Example

A 38-year-old female borderline patient was suffering from depression with bulimia and suicidal ideas. Three and a half years after beginning analysis with her, I asked her to pay for a telephone conversation with me. She verbally expressed her aggression toward me, telling me that she would not be able to rely on me for help because I could not understand her depressed and wounded psychic condition. She also told me that I was not kind enough to her when she was suffering from this condition, and that she would never come to see me again. Borderline patients easily feel abandonment rage and demand that the analyst be superhuman.

Before this incident I had always felt wounded and depressed because of a fused relationship with this patient, when I was the object of her anger and rage. This time, however, I felt anger and rage, and saw an image in which I was cutting down a serpent with a knife in the intermediate realm between me and the patient when she told me that she would not come any more. The patient's sympathetic therapist figure had changed abruptly into a destructive one. She blamed me for not understanding her feeling of misery. She could not see the real analyst but projected her idealized and destructive analyst images onto me alternately, and she did not allow me to be myself. I associated the youngest daughter's slaying the serpent with thousands of needles with my own image of cutting down a serpent with a knife.

Different mechanisms are simultaneously at work in the inner realm at such a time. As analyst, I was the object of the patient's anger and felt wounded and depressed. As the serpent bridegroom being slain, I may have helped the patient to transform into a more differentiated person, separated from her archetypal parents. Simultaneously, however, I experienced anger and rage against the patient. I may even have slain her in my imagination. And thus I may have facilitated the patient's transformation, just as the daughter changed the serpent bridegroom into a human being by slaying him.

I felt angry with the patient. On a deeper level, I felt rage against the archaic parents and the primitive man who ruled her life, as in the fairy tale the daughter slew the serpent who represented these figures. I may have felt also a sort of abandonment: counter-anger as a talion law of revenge when the patient said that she would never come back to analysis.

It is necessary for us to face our own complexes and to be differentiated enough from our archaic parents to use archetypal transformative aggression as a tool of analysis. When we are able to do so, the influence of the talion law of revenge in an analytic relationship will be reduced considerably. On the other hand, we must maintain neutral and composed feelings separate from our wounded and aggressive feelings. This separation is indispensable in preventing the acting out of our own feelings.

Constellation of Anger

Two weeks after the patient quit analysis, she asked to resume. During these two weeks, I realized that I had directed my anger and rage not only against the patient but also against her demanding parents and the primitive male figure who ruled her. The frog prince of "The Frog King" is considered to be both the primitive male and the witch who rules him.

After having lived through rage against the patient in my psyche, I am now able to maintain a relatively stable relationship with her, not only when she projects a warm and sympathetic therapist image but also when she projects a destructive therapist image. It is necessary for us as analysts to experience our own aggression, in order to help our analysands to become considerably differentiated and independent from their inner parents. We must work actively toward overcoming our fusion with the personal and the archetypal parents. If we can live through our own aggression in relationship with patients, it is possible to offer a place where anger can be constellated and so facilitate both the patient's and the analyst's transformation.

Two weeks after the patient resumed analysis, her suicidal ideas and bulimia had improved considerably. She brought the following dream:

> *I am living in an apartment with my mother and my son, who is in elementary school. We three go to a department store to shop for a set of eight wooden sewing boxes which contain sewing needles and thread.*
>
> *My son interrupts a saleswoman with some questions while she is explaining the boxes to us. The saleswoman orders my son to be silent and to hear her out. I protest against the saleswoman's*

conduct. I tell her that she should not interfere in my son's talking, and that my son is allowed to say anything. It is not her job to teach my son how to behave. Her job is to explain the boxes to us.

At that moment my mother, who is behind us, begins to say something. It seems to me that my mother does not stand up for my son but for the saleswoman. I get angry with my mother who interferes in my son's and my affair. I slap my mother on the mouth. Astonished at being slapped, my mother soon goes home alone. She is lying in bed wrapped in a futon mat.

The scene has changed. Perhaps I have already moved to a new house without my mother. Or perhaps I am going to move from the apartment to a new place. There are lots of things to be moved, or goods already moved, lying around.

The patient told me that, after the dream, she actually got angry with her interfering mother. This dream shows the patient at first in fusion with the inner mother. Then, however, the patient is enraged by the saleswoman's and mother's interfering attitude. In the dream the patient slaps her mother on the mouth. In the second half of the dream the patient's rage against the archetypal mother facilitates her differentiation from the mother. The patient is overcoming her relationship of fusion with the archetypal mother. The therapist's transformative aggression may have facilitated the constellation of archetypal anger against the demanding inner mother.

Fusion and Differentiation

As in the fairy tale "The Girl without Hands," borderline patients symbolically cut off their hands continuously, due to their own aggression. Indeed, this patient was suffering from a wrist-cutting syndrome in her college days. These patients' self-injury comes from their inability to experience anger and rage psychically, and also from their being in a relationship of fusion with their parents. If we try to work analytically with borderline patients, we must help them to become more differentiated by experiencing anger and rage against their inner parents and the primitive opposite sex. We also must resolve the fusion between those patients and ourselves.

As a child, the patient I have been describing felt abandoned and misunderstood by her mother. The patient married a man who was a mother's boy. Although they lived far from her parents' house, she was still not separated from them. The patient's personal relationships were not going well, especially with women. Though the patient disliked her mother, she had not been able to express her anger against her in everyday reality or in her dreams. When the patient saw unknown women in the city, she felt physically invaded by them.

In the dream, the patient experienced psychic rage against her mother for the first time. Borderline patients cannot express their aggression toward their parents because they are afraid of being unable to live independently of them. These patients must experience anger and rage in order to become psychically differentiated. When we try to cooperate with borderline patients analytically it is necessary for us to accept their aggression and to become wounded, and sometimes even to be "slain." At the same time we must experience our own anger and rage toward such weird and threatening patients who embody both their archetypal parents and the primitive figure.

One may say that the anger and rage discussed above, facilitating psychic transformation in patients, is the archetype of transformation that Jung discussed. The concept of this archetype is useful in analysis.

I emphasize the following idea: When we psychically experience anger and rage against our demanding, manipulative inner and outer patients, the aggression for facilitating transformation is constellated. Then the analyst and patient are more differentiated than when a state of fusion existed. When the aggression for facilitating transformation is constellated, both the patient and the analyst will fight against their demanding inner parents and the threatening, primitive inner figure.

Rage as a facilitator of transformation is a common motif in "The Serpent Bridegroom" and in "The Frog King." If we compare the youngest daughter and the youngest princess, the former is much more conscious of her own conduct in that she slays the serpent by using her own wisdom. In the serpent bridegroom tale, the serpent may have directed his rage against his inner parents and the female figure. Only when the daughter slays the serpent who represents the demanding and manipulative inner parents and the invading male figure does the serpent become separated from his inner parents. Transformed into the eldest son of wealthy family, he marries the transformed daughter.

A similar transformation process occurs in "The Frog King." The frog was able to direct rage against the witch, who had changed him from a human being into a frog, only when rage was directed against him by the youngest princess. At that moment, the frog succeeded in overcoming his fusion with a demanding, destructive, archetypal mother and was transformed into a human being. There is another difference however between the youngest daughter and the youngest princess. The princess is primitive and is in a more or less fused relationship with the frog. She promises the frog all that he wishes if he will bring her golden ball back again, whereas the youngest daughter can maintain a proper distance from the serpent.

Summary

The analyst must experience his or her own rage and anger toward manipulative patients who are fused with primitive inner figures and archaic parents. Within the alchemical vessel, the analyst imagines a pair of persons; the therapist who experiences rage and the patient who receives it. If the analyst can consciously live this aggression against the patient within a vessel in the intermediate realm, an archetype of transformation will constellate. At that moment, the patient will confront his or her own archaic parents and primitive figure and differentiation will be facilitated. Fairy tales illustrate the archetype of transformative aggression. The case of a female borderline patient exemplifies the dynamics of anger and rage within a clinical context.

References

Lambert, K. (1972). Transference/counter-transference: Talion law and gratitude. In M. Fordham, R. Gordon, J. Hubback & K. Lambert (Eds.), *Technique in Jungian Analysis* (Vol. 2). London: William Heinemann.

Meier, C.A. (1949/1967). *Ancient Incubation and Modern Psychotherapy* (M. Curtis, trans.). Evanston, IL: Northwestern University Press; new revised edition 1989: *Healing Dream and Ritual*, Einsiedeln: Daimon.

Oda, T. (1993). *Mukashibanashi to Yumebunseki: Jibunoikiru Joseitachi* (Fairy Tales and Dream Interpretation: Women Who are Living through Themselves). Osaka: Sogensha.

Racker, H. (1968). *Transference and Countertransference*. Madison, CT: International Universities Press.

Seki, K. (1978) *Nihon Mukashibanashi Taisei* (Vol. 2, Collection of Japanese Fairy Tales). Tokyo: Kadokawa.

Manic-Depressive Psychoses and Analytic Concepts

Wolfgang Kleespies
Berlin Germany
German Society for Analytical Psychology

Manic-depressive psychosis has been the subject of much less psychoanalytic literature than have the schizophrenic psychoses, for various reasons. One is the widespread assumption that affective psychosis – another name for manic-depressive psychosis – is a rigid illness that can be treated by analysis only to a limited degree. Also, this illness often disappears spontaneously without a single thera-peutic word exchanged with the patient. And this psychosis may have an abrupt and spontaneous onset for no recognizable psycho-logical reason. Where should one begin the discussion?

To begin with, the biological factor is so obvious that we have abdicated our psychotherapy centered on verbal exchange. Also, this illness belongs to the most severe psychological disturbances; under such circumstances it seems pointless to start an analysis. The analyst's sense of being at a loss would be conveyed in the counter-transference.

Most striking about manic diseases is the intense inner excite-ment, coupled with a flood of associations, leading to psychotic acts that may make compulsory hospitalization necessary. A comparable problem pertains in psychotic depressions. The depressed person often shows no affective modulation, but sits opposite one with a fixed mimic expression or is filled with self-condemnatory or guilty feelings. Frequently such patients no longer can carry out simple daily tasks and are barely able to follow complicated trains of thought. Often they have the deluded conviction that they are hopelessly ill or inferior, and they are not open to any suggestions to the contrary.

A manic-depressive illness consists of a unipolar state – mania or depression alone – or bipolar, in which manic and depressive phases alternate cyclically. In the manic phases the patients often have no awareness of their illness, hence lack motivation for therapy. In depressive phases there is inflexibility and a lack of tolerance for stress. Moreover, due to their extreme narcissistic needs, severely depressed persons cannot endure the reserved behavior of the analyst and suffer from unbearable emotional tension. If one can reclaim a pre-established deeper transference, it is easier to get access to the patients during a time of acute illness. Generally, however, one is limited to the symptom-free interval for clarifying questions of indication of therapy, the goals of treatment and the prognosis.

The Etiology of Manic-Depressive Psychosis

Biological factors, especially genetic, probably play a role in the development of affective illnesses. This statement is supported by studies on families, twins and adoptions. It is not known definitely, however, whether this illness is transmitted genetically or by family environment. Within a specific family, particular forms of reaction and problem-solving can be passed on. Stierlin and others (1986) have established, for instance, that a characteristic of manic-depressive families is judging their surroundings by mutually exclusive categories. "Somebody is either good or bad, honest or dishonest, controlled or uncontrolled, responsible or irresponsible, etc." (p. 278).

These judgments make it difficult for those concerned to find a middle way. Consequently, the illness has extreme manifestations. The patient's self-image is one of being damned and totally bad, or completely good, blessed or great. These extremes in the psyche concur, especially in depression, with the psychoanalytic theory that an archaic, sadistic super-ego imposes obsessions, punishments and unfulfillable expectations. This super-ego structure is found in all forms of depression: of psychic, hereditary or somatic origin. In analytical psychology also, a great deal of attention has been paid to the formation of opposites. Jung mentioned manic-depressive illnesses rarely, but he made interesting observations. In his preface to the autobiography of Custance (1954), who described his maniacal experience in detail, Jung pointed to the visibly developing structure of opposites in the author's manic psychosis: "The mania lifts the inhibitions placed by the consciousness on the unconscious: the result is crude opposites shimmering in all colors and forms which nothing can alter." And: "As a result values become apparent in an undifferentiated black and white system" (CW18. par. 830).

Jung found further that in mania no individuation is possible, since all ability to have relationships and to be self-critical is lacking. This striking tendency toward extremes is revealed in the judgments and opinions of the patients, the mood swings in depression and mania, but also in behavior.

A patient of mine, acting at the height of her psychotic depression, had her furniture picked up by a moving firm and took her other possessions – including her certificates and diplomas – to the rubbish dump. She possessed nothing except the clothes she was wearing. When she came to me later after having been released from the clinic she appeared strangely quiet and content. I discovered subsequently that, in order to save her very existence, she had made a sacrifice to the cruelly demanding demons of her depressions; otherwise she probably would have committed suicide.

The Problems of Diagnoses: Psychogenetic and Psychodynamic Factors

With manic-depressive patients, I have often discovered triggering moments which were psychodynamically relevant. They must be sought carefully for they may be well hidden. Each trigger leads on to a biologically predetermined conclusion, which develops according to its own law.

The psychotherapist need not draw a clear boundary between an illness that is psychogenic and one that is caused by somatic (biological) factors. In both we are dealing, from the psychotherapeutic point of view, with the person's inner life; that is, with a suffering human being. The notion of a biological basis taken by itself says nothing either for or against the feasibility of psychotherapy. We all have neurophysiological bases for our thoughts and feelings. Archetypes originate, as Jung has pointed out, in our inherited brain structure. Everything depends largely on room for maneuver in the development of the psyche.

Although manic disease is easy to recognize, it is not possible to make an accurate diagnosis of a depressive illness by psychological means alone. All depressive conditions have a similar psychological configuration, independent of how strong the constitutional contribution is. In diagnosing a manic-depressive illness, phenomenological as well as psychological facts must be taken into consideration.

These facts include the typical course of the illness with its phaselike character, then the monotone form with agitation or dynamic evacuation and low spirits in the morning, as well as the possible appearance of typically depressive delusions with ideas of guilt, sin, insignificance or hypochondria. Combinations of all these can occur.

As early as 1917, Freud (SE10) concluded that the melancholic suffers from reduced self-esteem. The bereaved normal person behaves completely differently. Although an important part of his or her life is lost, the person retains self-esteem and integrity. The bereaved depressive, on the other hand, behaves as if a part of his or her self-esteem has been lost. The lost person is important, even indispensable, for self-esteem. At this point we can raise some psychodynamic considerations.

As Neumann (1980) has described, developmentally the relationship to oneself and thus to an emerging self-confidence depends on the relationship to the primary objects. In effect, these are archetypal experiences which the child has. They can be extremely negative or they can develop in a positive way, making one able to withstand stress. "Self-confidence depends almost entirely on the original relationship with the mother" (p. 47). Thus, the relationship of the ego to the Self, or as Neumann calls it, the ego-Self axis, is shaped decisively by the mother. On this axis between ego and Self runs a complicated reciprocal cooperation which is all-important in psychological development.

According to Jacoby (1985), a great difference in the basic feeling about life depends on whether the individual feels like one of those loved and favored by the gods or like one rejected and cast out by the gods, male or female. I think that the father as well as the mother can have a decisive formative influence on a child's self-esteem.

Manic-depressives have always been cast out by the gods. Most analytic authors today agree that, in addition to the tendency toward symbiotic fixation and dependency in the regulation of self-esteem, narcissistic disturbances play a decisive role.

Analytical Psychologists seem to agree that manic and depressive illnesses are based on a disturbance of the ego-Self axis. McCurdy (1987) comes to that conclusion by examining the connection of the Dionysus myth with affective illnesses.

When dealing therapeutically with these illnesses it is important to recognize archetypal themes. These themes of worth and worthlessness, of greatness and littleness, are encountered in mythology, too. I am thinking, in particular, of Hephaistos, the son of Zeus and Hera, who was born with multiple disabilities; most striking was a limp. Not wanting to accept him, his mother threw him out of Olympus. In analytic language this experience corresponds to an object loss and is a severe narcissistic injury. According to the myth, Hephaistos later lived in a volcano. Seen psychologically, he embodies an affective condition of narcissistic fury caused by rejection. This fury can express itself in aggression against oneself or others, but it can create a flow of energy and submerge the ego, as in mania. It is emotional energy that overflows all barriers like a volcano: formless and uncontrolled.

In mania there is characteristically an inflation of the ego with archetypal grandiosity that sweeps away constricting self-images. Hephaistos, however, also developed and changed. He became a master at forging and, thereby, of the volcanic energies – an apt image for psychological energies. His ego directed and guided them, whereas the manic person sinks into the whirlpool and is carried away. A therapeutic goal can be deduced from this: ability to control one's impulses.

Actually, the manically ill have very little control over themselves. They exaggerate and are finally overwhelmed with ideas, usually grandiose ones. Such patients are able to work themselves into a manic-euphoric condition which can become addictive. Consequently, they are not prepared to take medication or they stop taking it shortly; they are not prepared to relinquish euphoria.

In a depressive psychosis ideas of guilt, insignificance and sin prevail. They may have their source in the early stages of development; the child can obtain the impression that it is asking too much of life and that it has no right to do so.

These notions develop into a complex, perhaps a deeply rooted inferiority complex. It may be rooted in archetypal experiences of personal unworthiness and activated later by such triggers as object loss, narcissistic injury, even by professional success. (Since success is a contradiction to the conviction of inferiority, it can cause a depression.) An older patient became hypochondriacally depressive after having a professional promotion late in life. Psychotherapeutic consultations proved to be fruitless. It was only after his eventual retirement that he felt healthy again.

In narcissistic conflicts two different forms of reaction are possible. A depressive decompensation can develop or, in compensation, a latent superiority complex blooms. The complex then develops into a manic flood of grandiose ideas or, as Freud expressed it, the negative archaic super-ego is thrown overboard.

Early in life the child forms ideas of its own insignificance, as well as fantasies of superiority or delusions of grandeur. The latter are more pronounced, the more the inferiority complex burdens the ego. The groups of fantasies lie close together; each group forms one complex. Presumably the way is paved for a reaction in one or the other direction early in life and later, activated by a given trigger. In the event of illness, either mania or depression may emerge: an inflation with positive or negative grandiose ideas. Thus, the archetype of the Self deluges the ego and occupies it. Since inflation means the collapse of ego-Self axis, the intensity of this inflation makes the difference between neurotic and psychotic illness. Psychoanalytic authors such as Rado (1956) and Fenichel (1945) point out that the too-great intensity of the negative self-image leads to psychotic depression.

Clearly it is not always possible to escape the sense of helplessness and inferiority by means of grandiose ideas. Apart from a biological predisposition to manic energies, psychodynamic factors play a role. Perhaps they could explain why in one case a depression occurs and, in another, a mania. A thought of Mentzos' (1991) is of considerable interest. He suggests that two different pathogenic parts of the super-ego could exist.

A part of the super-ego that comes from the father may be warded off more easily in a manic manner than a super-ego coming from the mother, because a super-ego from the mother is more archaic and thus more dangerous. The consequence is then depression. I find the parts that are threatening in varying ways are represented in a single parent and not necessarily distributed between two parents. From the point of view of Analytical Psychology we should seek relevant archetypal configurations that were predominant at onset of the illness. In most cases I have been able to see significant archetypal configurations that existed at the outbreak of a mania or a depression. It is not possible, however, to make conclusive statements regarding this hypothesis.

Therapeutic Concepts and Case Material

In therapy one procedure in particular has proved to be worthwhile. If a patient comes to me for treatment initially during a pronounced phase of illness, my top priority is supportive therapy relating to the here and now. The patient must have the feeling of being accepted. The severity of the illness generally determines whether in-patient treatment would be more effective – as in the event of suicide attempts or danger to others. Usually I also prescribe medication, which can become problematic, of course, if one is asked to conduct an analysis later on. Each case must be considered individually. To proceed therapeutically it makes me feel more secure to form a psychodynamic hypothesis about the causation of the illness. The patient must be ready to probe inward and to look for deeper connections. Often one finds also – apart from the phaseal disturbances – obvious neuroses, and can approach a therapy by dealing with these first.

I also believe that positive countertransference is very important; one must be able to imagine tolerating a longer depressive or manic phase with the patient. In manic phases the therapist must be able to tolerate frustration so as to bear the patient's possible rude remarks and attacks.

Some authors (e.g., Kohut, 1974) consider mania as untreatable in principle. My experience has not confirmed this. However, most authors today agree that one should not begin treatment during a mania in full force, because of the lack of relationship. Then, in the symptom-free interval one can work on the manic or depressive material and on the patient's self-control.

In my experience various settings have proved effective. First, the standard analytic procedure with modifications. I never treat these patients lying down. Because of the intense bond they have to other people, there must be a reliable, clearly defined person sitting opposite. Otherwise, intense anxieties or inhibitions can occur. Two to three sessions a week are usual, but the analyst's emotional attention is more important than the frequency of sessions. Too reserved an attitude is obstructive. At the same time, one must not be too oral-giving, but avoid catering further to the patient's desires.

In mania there are no elements of an individuation process – for example, the ability to form relationships – as has been pointed out by Jung (CW18, par. 830). There is only an enormous self-obsession. The attractiveness of the euphoric condition must be lessened in favor of arduous development, a process that can last many years.

The goal is to repair the ego-Self relationship: a large and difficult aim. Everything depends on surviving the meeting with the shadow in a productive manner. Here we are confronting the parental images and the early archetypal images of grandiosity and inferiority. Especially with mania, success depends on the patient's finding a way out of grandiose self-centeredness toward development of relationships.

A further treatment is an analytically-oriented procedure aiming to stabilize the ego-Self relationship in a particular way, for instance through achieving more psycho-social competence. Here one session a week is usually enough.

Finally, we have the "dynamically oriented consultation." The therapist supports, accompanies and helps the patient to recognize and discuss emerging conflicts. Examples of these different methods of procedure follow.

Example 1: Frequent analytic therapy. The patient is 36 years old, has had several manic phases and works for a church. He began with individual sessions in order to establish the therapeutic relationship firmly, and then participated in group therapy. This combination proved helpful. His egocentricity and problems with closeness and distance could be treated better in the group situation, as could his lack of control over emotions and impulses, which caused him considerable difficulty at work.

He was born out of wedlock and never knew his father. His mother had ambivalent feelings toward him and appeared to be ashamed of his illegitimate birth. She feared what other people said. Collective norms appeared to be more important to her than her son's feelings. He said of his mother: "I could never confide in her. She was terribly afraid and uncertain regarding other people and let it out on me in an hysterical way." His mother tended to have rigid, crass opinions. There was only black and white and she often rejected her son when he did not come up to her expectations. On such occasions she would say something like, "You are the absolute end; I don't want to even know you anymore."

He received more affection from his grandmother who lived in the same town. When the patient was four years old his mother married. He did not feel accepted by his stepfather, but saw him as a competitor who was taking the mother away.

In our first sessions the patient demonstrated that he was very crude in his judgment of other people. He also saw things in extremes. He could express himself in a critical way about someone one day and be great friends with that person the next. This tendency corresponds to the behavior patterns that Stierlin and others (1986) describe as typical for families of manic-depressives; they judge and act according to black and white categories.

The patient first suffered a manic phase when his girlfriend left him with their child, because she felt neglected by him. Actually, he was afraid of being close to anybody and felt completely out of his depth in the role of father. After the separation it looked as though he were going to have a crisis. He was able to overcome it, however, by developing a compulsive work mania.

In a short time he passed his exams. In this way he proved his superiority and his independence. He didn't care that his girlfriend had left him; he didn't need women. Finally he became so arrogant that he left the church. Now his mania broke out completely. Leaving the church was supposed to be an additional proof of his independence. Instead, he was forsaking his religious basis which had supported him up to then.

Seen from a psychodynamic point of view he suffered a double loss; the experience of losing his mother repeated itself. When she did not like something about him, "she didn't know him anymore." The rejection by his girlfriend corresponded on an archetypal level to the rejection of the negative all-powerful mother. Unfortunately, in his grandiosity, he also cut himself off from his last remaining positive basis. It was the support of a giving, transpersonal, positive mother – mother church – whom he left. He had nothing left to live for and nothing from which to derive comfort. Consequently, he developed an excited mania, driven by unconscious fears.

Regarded mythologically, the patient had been driven from Olympus by Hera and had even helped her to drive him out. Old archetypal conceptions about his inferiority, his own lack of substance were reactivated and threatened to inundate him. In this situation "the volcano was boiling"; his ego was inflated with compensatory grandiose ideas.

Once again we find a structure based on opposites: inferior self and superior self. For instance, he was convinced that he could get and marry any woman in the world. This manic fantasy obliterated the separation situation; it was as though it had never happened. Finally he made himself conspicuous in public by behavior that was too familiar and excited; he had to be committed to a clinic by the police. After his discharge he came to me for treatment.

The first night in the clinic in the half-dark of the emergency ward he had a hallucination:

He was among freemasons, in a holy, secret place. People were working everywhere. Men in white overalls were walking around. He was sitting before a large block of stone and, with sweat on his brow, he was carving the following words in the stone, "Become a man."

He found the words strange and he kept thinking about them. Only later on in his therapy did he realize what they meant. It occurred to him that the freemasons regarded the human soul as a stone that had to be hewn. It signified the effort and strain required for the development of our souls; you didn't get anything for nothing. Eventually it became clear to him that he would have to abandon his pride and ideas of grandiosity. "Become a man" meant for him to "Become more modest, to develop more relationships to others, get more involved with other people." The prerequisite of course, was to have more of an identity. He was lacking in masculine identity and had to obtain it.

A dream in which, once again, a stone played a role was helpful. He dreamed that

I as his therapist was highly praised by his girlfriend. We were in my office. Instead of responding to the praise, I retreated into a red, phallus-like stone, which reminded him of the Celtic megalith stones. I closed the door and started to do other things.

Our analysis of the dream revealed that he saw me as demonstrating an independent, masculine identity. I was able to fence myself off and not to be tempted by words of praise – for which the patient was very susceptible – but could turn away from women, autonomously.

These dreams marked his unconscious tendencies to achieve what he needed: an idealized father figure. The reappearing motif of the stone is interesting. He associated it with the great steadiness and permanence that he needed so desperately. Here he met the stable, unchanging qualities of the Self – for which the stone is frequently a symbol – which compensated for his manifold disquiet. Here we met once again the structure of opposites between the contents of the conscious and the unconscious.

The entire analysis was filled with tensions between opposites, which tortured the patient. During the day he fought disparate tensions and moods, such as feelings of being lost, alone and depressive; manically exalted moods. He had had them as long as he could remember. The red stone symbolized on an archetypal level the achieving of the "lapis," the alchemical image for the goal of the individuation process. In the lapis opposites are united.

In the following years of treatment it was possible for him to learn gradually to restrain himself and actually notice what concerned other human beings, such as the other members of the group. He proved to have an amazing sense of empathy but had never shown it out of fear of losing himself. Only slowly did he grasp the fact that he could find himself only if he forgot himself.

Here another dream was helpful; it underlined the problem once again and proved to be a turning point in his self-centeredness. He dreamed that

> *he was going to communion. Members of the group were also there. He said in the dream, "I also belong here," entered the circle, took the communion cup, drank it up greedily in one gulp and to the very last drop.*

Something was wrong. One can view the communion circle and the relationship of the patient to it as a representation of the ego-Self axis. This axis was still disturbed. The patient could not learn about himself through greedy selfishness and the exclusion of others. One is secure and part of the group only when one accepts others.

The patient gradually transferred this awareness not only to the group but also to his personal life. He had been married and had a small daughter. On his own initiative he has remained at home for a year to look after his child and the home. In this way he is learning to take other people – above all those close to him – into consideration.

Example 2: Analytically-oriented therapy, one session a week A 34-year-old student was suffering from manic and depressive phases. It was fairly easy to establish two conflict areas which lay at the root of the illness: the relationship complex and the achievement complex.

The achievement complex was manifested in the patient's inability to complete three courses of study; he had broken off each of them. Since he had no hold on the outside world, the therapeutic goal was to support him in his search for a profession. He suffered from great fears of failure and had hardly any self-confidence. Thus, it was impossible to start another course. His father had discouraged the patient consistently, in whatever he had undertaken. When he showed his father anything he had made by hand the father always said, "What's that supposed to be?"

An oedipal conflict with his father had never taken place, since his mother greatly disliked any kind of aggression. She was reserved in regard to men, hated sex, and seemed to be very inhibited. She tended toward depressions. The patient developed clear passive-feminine characteristics and, in order to please her, was never aggressive.

Preceding each of the manic phases there had been an experience of failure. The problem, therefore, had to be with the achievement complex. He failed because of his own perfectionism. An old negative image of the powerful, archetypal father was activated every time achievement was asked of him. This image blocked him and cut him down to size the moment he wanted to feel on a par with his father.

In the myth of Bellerophon, he became too daring and wanted to fly to heaven with his horse, Pegasus. An angry Zeus made a fly sting the horse and throw Bellerophon, who from then on wandered the world, lame. At least my patient was able after his failures to rebel manically against the father figure and momentarily at least to shake off his negative power. However, he was not able to transform his mania into productive forms. In his manic phases he appeared outgoing and flashy, wore sunglasses, traveled around a great deal and was arrogant and demanding toward his parents.

The factors that triggered the depressions were much more severe. Each time, disappointments in love hurt him narcissistically. He was unable to develop ideas of grandiosity to counteract his childhood experiences. The depressions were characterized by self-denigration and self-accusation, which could not be mitigated. Such patients seem to maintain a negative grandiosity and isolation while they are ill. They do not let anyone near them and outdo any conceivable critic in their self-accusations.

In the interval between mania and depression, it was important to pursue a clear aim: a job and thus an anchor in the outside world. He decided to train to become a financial expert.

I could not support or praise him unequivocally. He was afraid that he would become dependent and feel under pressure to do well. His main achievement in therapy was to control the demands he put upon himself; he projected on me an alternative and mild father figure who did not oppress and discourage him. He has finished his training: the first exam he has passed since his Abitur (university entrance exam). Nevertheless, the relationship problem still remains in the therapy.

Treatment in Private Practice

In private practice, once-a-week treatment is usual, not due to lack of time but because it is often enough. The important consideration is that the therapeutic relationship remains constant over a long period of time. A deeper treatment is either not indicated by the degree of chronicity or is not desired by the patient. Many patients expect support and are happy when, by means of a Lithium therapy, for instance, the illness phases stop. They do not want to or cannot come to grips with deeper therapy. If you take into account the structure of their personalities, sometimes they can be prevented from getting into dangerous or conflict-laden situations, or they can be helped out of them. I have several patients who have learned to come to me in time when a manic phase is beginning. Between such times, these patients have developed enough self-perception and ability to control themselves that frequently, through intensive discussion, large blunders can be avoided. Acquiring increasing control represents one of the fundamental therapeutic improvements.

Conclusions

It is possible to use analytic therapy profitably in manic-depressive illnesses, with a few modifications. Very often a specific psychodynamic can be found with which one can work. There is not much choice of means, however, because of the peculiarities of character: being quick to take offense, propensity for symbiotic behavior, intolerance of frustration and, above all, deep-seated grandiose ideas and inferiority complex. Modifications take into account the identified intrapsychic conflict.

Translated from German by Maureen Metzger

References

Custance, J. (1954). *Weisheit und Wahn* (Wisdom, Madness and Folly). Zurich: Rascher.

Fenichel, O. (1945). *The Psychoanalytic Theory of Neurosis*. New York: Norton.

Jacoby, M. (1985). *Individuation und Narzissmus* (Individuation and Narcissism). Munchen: Pfeiffer.

Kohut, H. (1974). *Narzissmus* (The Analysis of the Self). Frankfurt: Suhrkamp.

McCurdy, C.D. (1987) Manic-depressive psychosis: A perspective. *Journal of Analytical Psychology, 32*, 309-324.

Mentzos, S. (1991). Psychodynamische Modelle in der Psychiatrie. Göttingen: Vandenhoeck & Ruprecht.

Neumann, E. (1980). *Das Kind* (The Child). Fellbach: Bonz.

Rado, S. (1956). The Problem of Melancholia. In *Collected Papers* (Vol. I). New York: Grune & Stratton.

Stierlin, H.; Weber, G.; Schmidt, G.; Simon, F. (1986). Zur Familiendynamik bei manisch-depressiven und schizoaffektiven Psychosen. *Familiendynamik, 11*, 267-282.

Depression and Suicide

David Rosen
College Station, Texas, U.S.A.
Inter-Regional Society of Jungian Analysts

The subject of depression has been relatively unexplored in analytical psychology, as compared with Freudian psychoanalysis. This discrepancy is especially striking when dealing with the topic of suicide. Indeed, Jung – unlike Freud – never wrote a separate essay or book on either depression or suicide. My hope is to contribute to more effective Jungian-oriented treatment of depression and enhanced suicide prevention.

Depression

Freud's classic work, *Mourning and Melancholia* (SE14), contrasts normal bereavement with pathological depression. Unlike in mourning where there is actual loss through death of a loved one, in melancholia the loved one lives but is lost as an object of love or gratification. The despondent individual feels anger toward the lost love object but, because the anger cannot be vented on the loved one, it is turned against the self by way of the person's own ego. This depressive backlash can be made much worse by guilt feelings (from a harsh superego) for harboring such anger in the first place. Abraham (1917), a follower of Freud, attributed depression to a blockage of libido. He claimed that, when people gave up their sexual desires without gratifying them, they felt unwanted and unloved with resultant self-reproach and self-degradation.

When Jung was still a Freudian he, too, viewed depression as blocked libido or an "I am stuck" condition. However, when Jung broke from Freud he experienced his own severe depression and the loss of his false (Freudian) self, which was tied to the completion of "The Sacrifice," the last chapter in *Symbols of Transformation* (CW5). Jung's break from Freud also yielded a breakthrough when he experienced melancholia as regression into a symbolic womb (the *prima materia* or collective unconscious), a regression that resulted in "loss of soul," followed by psychic death and rebirth. Jung discovered that the sacrifice of his hero identity – loss of ego – created an emptiness that allowed the spirit to enter and repossess his lost soul.

Post-Jungians express different views about depression and its value. For example, Odajnyk (1983) claims that depressions are useful and healing only if the ego stays intact and defends against the pressing drives and fulfills needs of the unconscious. This sounds more like a Freudian or neo-Freudian view. In contrast, my position is that the ego must die symbolically for meaningful change and healing to occur. Steinberg's (1984) thinking is similar to mine. Using a redemption model, he sees successful analysis of depressed individuals as involving a death of the negative parental introjects (which the depressed person tends to project onto others) and the rebirth of a newly constituted ego that is linked to the Self. Later, Steinberg (1990) outlines Jung's view of depression as purposive, creative, and potentially transforming through a death-rebirth experience.

Depression also operates as a normal biological conservation-withdrawal mechanism which protects the individual and allows for periods of rest or incubation, such as sleep or renewing retreats. When a person's psychological conservation-withdrawal mechanism is operating, the individual is in a state of adaptive depression. This is not an abnormal reaction, but a natural, perhaps essential process, much like Storr's (1989) concept of solitude as a necessary state for active imagination, creativity and the reviving of mental health. Depression becomes abnormal or pathological only when the individual remains locked in a state of darkness and inactivity, instead of progressing beyond it and ideally transforming it.

Oscar Wilde said, "Where there is sorrow, there is holy ground." Similarly, my view of depression is archetypally and spiritually based. Like Jung, but unlike Freudians and present-day biologically based psychiatrists, I see depression as a potentially favorable affect which is linked to the quest for meaning. My approach to understanding depression is a holistic one and involves a systems model. As illustrated in the diagram, it is necessary to view depression as having four factors: biological, psychological, sociological, and existential/spiritual. Like Jung, I consider soul (as reflective of the fourth factor) the central element in the healing process.

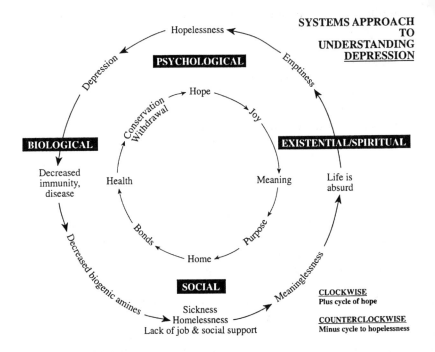

Suicide

When depression becomes abnormal and the person remains in darkness and despair, suicide becomes a reality. Menninger (1938) maintained that we (analysts, therapists, and healers) bear a responsibility to avert suicide.

Freud postulated two fundamental drives in the human psyche: sexual (libido or life instinct) and aggressive (*destrudo* or death instinct). In suicide the aggressive or death drive is turned against the self. Often suicide is an act of disguised murder.

Menninger refined Freud's concepts and posited three necessary components in order for suicide to take place: the wish to kill; the wish to be killed; the wish to die. The ego becomes the murderer and the victim becomes the self. Menninger also emphasized that the suicidal person has a wish to be rescued; this wish forms the basis for suicide prevention and all therapy with depressed and suicidal patients.

The French writer Albert Camus challenges us to deal with the only real philosophical issue, which is suicide. He resolves the issue by rejecting suicide and focusing on hope and the future. Shakespeare, through his character Hamlet, presents us with the same essential dilemma: to be or not to be. It seems that Shakespeare was using his writing and active imagination to transform his suicidal "false self" into his inspiring and creative "true self." Winnicott (1986) claims that if the true self is unable to emerge, the result will be suicide or self-murder by the false self, that is, the dominant negative ego identity.

The Jungian view regarding the prevention of suicide was addressed by Klopfer (1961). He inferred, based on Jung's essay "The Soul and Death" (before Jung's letters concerning suicide were published), that Jung would be opposed to suicide. Klopfer felt that suicide represented a longing for spiritual rebirth, but he characterized the essential issue as involving a symbolic death of the ego that has lost its connection to the Self and hence to the purpose and meaning of life. The ego has to return to the collective unconscious and the womb of the great mother to reestablish this contact and to be reborn with a new meaning for life. Jane Wheelwright (1987) has a similar perspective and phrased it this way: "Our periods of depression, which are like small deaths, can be used in a sense, as practice for our exit ... It is a misinterpretation of this process which, more often than not, leads people into suicide. The downward pull and immobilization that accompany deep depression are mistaken for sensations of physical death rather than of the psychic death which, as a matter of course, precedes psychic rebirth" (p. 407). Now it is indeed clear from Jung's letters that he was against suicide unequivocally as a crime against the Self. (Let-I, p. 434; Let-II, pp. 25, 278-79).

Hillman's (1964) work is provocative philosophically, but dangerous and of little use clinically; he is critical of psychiatric treatment, suicide prevention, and – amazingly – hope. Nevertheless, to Hillman's credit, he discusses the inherent transformative drive in suicide. However, he regards suicide as a rational deed to be understood and accepted and he recommends that analysts maintain "dispassionate scientific objectivity" toward the act. Since depressed and suicidal patients are hypersensitive and vulnerable, they could perceive such a cold, detached neutrality as "countertransference hate" and such perceived rejection and abandonment could precipitate an actual suicide. Kirsch (1969) also criticizes Hillman's approach because he downplays and even ignores valuable medical assessment and treatment as well as suicide prevention.

In my view, preventing suicide – which is often related to depression and nearly always associated with hopelessness – involves killing the suicidal part of the ego (which I term "egocide") and undergoing transformation. This is accomplished by analyzing to death the negative and self-destructive part of the ego (often represented by the shadow), which leads to symbolic death and new life. By confronting the vibrant and varied symbols at the core of depression, it can be turned into a fountain of creative energy. Through active imagination and work in the creative arts, suicidally depressed patients can transform their self-destructive false selves into meaningful true selves. (See Rosen, 1996.)

Egocide and Transformation: The Case of Jung

After the break from Freud, Jung plunged into a dark abyss of severe depression and the depths of the collective unconscious. He went through a suicidal crisis in December of 1913 and underwent egocide (killing the negative ego) prior to contacting his inner Elijah. In a dream Jung (MDR) *teamed up with a dark-skinned savage and they shot and killed Siegfried*. When he awoke a voice within Jung said, "You *must* understand the dream ... at once! If you do not understand (it), you must shoot yourself!" Jung tells us that he was frightened because in the drawer of his night table lay a loaded revolver. Fortunately for him, and for us, the moment of egocide came and Jung realized, "The dream showed that the attitude embodied by Siegfried, the [German] hero, no longer suited me. Therefore, it had to be killed" (p. 180). Thus, Jung and a representative of his "primitive shadow" psychically murdered this negative aspect of his dominant Freudian ego-image and identity. Jung then fell deeper into the depths of the archetypal world, where he met Elijah.

Soul Attack, Disability and the Healing Process

There is an ancient history of associating depression with injury to the soul or its loss. By the soul, I mean the enlightening spirit or life-giving force that gives rise to those stabilizing, integrating powers that make a being whole and a person fully human. Such a person can find meaning in life and experience optimism, sensitivity, receptivity, empathy, and creativity. When the soul is attacked or a person feels disconnected from its life-sustaining force, the individual feels dead and is often so depressed that he or she wants to commit suicide. The "soul attack" victim becomes disabled or "not able" to function.

The etymological root of healing is *haelen*, which means to make or become whole. Hence, healing involves a process toward wholeness that culminates in integrity and having meaning and purpose in life. Shamans, based on healing their own severe depressions associated with loss of soul, were able to help similarly troubled individuals to heal themselves. In fact, the forerunners of modern mental health professionals were shamans or "doctors of the soul." The archetype of the "wounded healer" is near and dear to the hearts of many Jungians. Hence, it is critically important to have a clear, life-oriented philosophy that includes finding meaning for ourselves and helping others to do the same.

Plato described one of the seats of the soul as the heart, and therefore made a direct connection between the heart and soul. Thus, there is an archetypal basis to the popular song "Heart and Soul." The heart and soul represent the vital essence of the body and the psyche, which have been artificially separated for too long. Damage to the heart and soul often is self-inflicted, activated by negative mother and father complexes and the subsequent taking in of harmful poisons such as nicotine and alcohol. Heart and soul attacks are therefore associated with the possibility of the loss of heart and soul – death.

We need the term "soul attack" in our everyday discourse, just as we now have the term "heart attack." Why? Primarily because it would help in overcoming the stigma associated with depression and suicide. Thus, treatment and prevention programs would become more accepted. The American populace seems to be receptive to the word "soul" as indicated by Thomas Moore's (1992, 1994) best-selling books. It seems that people easily could grasp the meaning and importance of dealing with "soul attacks."

Paralleling our treatment approach to heart attack victims and Coronary Care Units, there ought to be Psychical Care Units providing acute intensive treatment for patients with soul attacks, specifically for the care of their souls. Acceptance of the term "soul attack" might direct more resources to effective treatment, rehabilitation, and prevention of severe depressive and suicidal states. Persons with soul attacks are just as disabled as those with heart attacks. In both cases there has been a death and loss. With heart attack victims there is a death of cardiac tissue and time is needed for healing and regeneration. Following the acute phase, a slow and caring process is required with follow-up outpatient treatment to prevent future heart attacks. With persons suffering from soul attacks there is psychic damage and symbolic death – egocide. Egocide (in contrast to suicide) allows for the false self to be shed (symbolic death) and new life to begin, based on one's true self. Just as a heart attack can be precipitated by a stressful event (e.g., loss of job), a soul attack can also be precipitated by a loss, such as divorce. Egocide allows for the needed death of a part of the person's identity, but the whole person lives. As in any crisis, there is danger – in this case of suicide – but the opportunity also exists for self-actualization.

How can the subacute and chronic treatment phase be financed? In addition to health insurance, disability insurance is often available to assist persons in their regenerative and long-term healing processes. The treatment process involves four factors: biological, psychological, social, and existential/spiritual. We must always address each of these factors. For soul attack victims, the healing process may involve anti-depressant medication, psychotherapy, new job training or group therapy, as well as assistance in becoming reconnected to the soul and thereby re-establishing meaning and purpose in life. We must advocate more than the bare minimum – more than just a "cure" and "survival." While a cure and survival are critical, a premium should be placed on caring for the soul and an on-going healing process.

Healing, if attained, would ensure rebirth and life without self-inflicted harm to the heart or soul. The experience of a life-threatening soul attack allows for the transformation of depression, an end to the preoccupation with acts to end one's life, and for the spirit to enter the previous void of suicidal melancholia. A key aspect of this healing is to transform destructive energy into creative products and constructive actions. Art therapy and what Jung termed "active imagination" are essential medicine for the soul.

References

Abraham, K. (1927). *Selected Papers on Psycho-Analysis*. London: Hogarth.

Hillman, J. (1964). *Suicide and the Soul*. New York: Harper & Row.

Kirsch, T. (1969). Comments on "Suicide and the Soul." *Existential Psychiatry*, Spring, 102-108.

Klopfer, B. (1961). "Suicide: The Jungian Point of View." In N. Farberow & E. Shneidman (Eds.), *The Cry for Help*. New York: McGraw-Hill.

Menninger, K. (1938). *Man Against Himself*. New York: Harcourt, Brace, & World (A Harvest Book).

Moore, T. (1992). *Care of the Soul*. New York: HarperCollins.

Moore, T. (1994). *Soul Mates*. New York: HarperCollins.

Odajnyk, V.W. (1983). Jung's contribution to the understanding of the meaning of depression. *Quadrant, 16*; 45-61.

Rosen, D. (1996). *Transforming Depression: Healing the Soul Through Creativity*. New York: Arkana/Penguin.

Steinberg, W. (1984). Depression: Some clinical and theoretical observations. *Quadrant, 17*, 7-22.

Steinberg, W. (1990). *Circle of Care: Clinical Issues in Jungian Therapy*. Toronto: Inner City Books, pp. 119-144.

Storr, A. (1989). *Solitude: A Return to Self*. New York: Ballantine Books.

Winnicott, D.W. (1986). Fear of breakdown. In G. Kohon (Ed.), *The British School of Psycho-Analysis: The Independent Tradition*. New Haven: Yale University Press.

Wheelwright, Jane (1987). Old age and death. In L. Mahdi, S. Forter, M.L. Little (Eds.), *Betwixt and Between: Patterns of Masculine and Feminine Initiation*. La Salle, Il.: Open Court.

The Animating Body

Psychoid Experience In Analysis

Giles A. Clark

Sydney, Australia

Australian and New Zealand Society of Jungian Analysts

In 1946, Jung put forth a hypothesis of a "psychoid" level or quality of the unconscious psyche: "Since psyche and matter are contained in one and the same world, and moreover are in continuous contact with one another and ultimately rest on irrepresentable, transcendental factors, it is not only possible but fairly probable even that psyche and matter are two different aspects of one and the same thing." (CW8, par. 418).

The psychoid may be understood best as a dynamic idea that describes all real physical and psychic experience at depth: psychic reality in its most fundamental sense, where experientially (in perception and apperception) psyche and soma are indistinguishable. Psychic energy and body matters are two aspects of the same phenomenon: a unit of meaning. Furthermore, this psycho-physical experience is of a process that is energetic, relational and purposive.

The psychoid has to do not only with an individual, intrapsychic level of life, but also with an area of experience where bodily sensations are symbolic. They occur through primitive sensations, proto-symbols and psychosomatic metacommunications, which are felt both inside us and in relationships. These experiences painfully unite us in something we unconsciously make together, arising out of an as yet unmet need to share in something undeveloped and uncoordinated.

In work with regressed patients, symbols and sensations are transferred by projective identification into the analyst. The analyst, infected at the level of the autonomic nervous system senses the symbols vitally through animal imagery and somatic symptoms (in dreams and illness). This is an embodied countertransference in which we find what I call an "animating body" which is "consubstantiated."

That is, our two psyches – in certain emotionally-loaded, regressed situations in analysis – discover or create a common mixed, affective sense of body – an embodiment of unconscious emotions in which we both share. This "body" can be either a sensed or – if more symbolically developed – an imaged body, or both. At the psychic pole, unconscious physical communications and subliminal body language produce associative imagery from memory of intra-psychic and internalized interpersonal relations, perhaps also from internalized fetal relations. Psychically, early relations often seem to be imaged or symbolized by an animal body or by interacting bits of non-human bodies. Consequently, I use the expression "animating body." These animal-like symbols and sensations have to do with very early part-object, pre-verbal stages of development, an infant's part-object relations among zones of his/her own body and their instincts and impulses, and relations with bits of mother, fantasies or mother's body and her insides.

Insofar as there is imagery – not just psychosomatic sensations and symptoms – these not-wholly-human animating images seem to derive from a later (over the age of one-year) psychic imagery, but they are symbols of pre-image experience, even of intrauterine relations. Jung speaks of the "bond" of the transference neurosis in which

Spirit and matter together. ... form an impenetrable mass, a veritable magma sprung from the depths of primeval chaos. ... They emit a fascination which not only grips ... the patient, but can also have an inductive effect on the conscious of the impartial spectator, in this case the doctor. ... He too becomes affected, and has as much difficulty in distinguishing between the patient and what has taken possession of him as has the patient himself. (CW16, par. 363)

Indeed, Humbert (1986) says that regression

puts the analysand back into that initial experience in which the object takes shape through a dual relationship where bodies impose their own reality. It is here in the body, where the early traumatic incidents were imprinted, that their re-activation takes place. ... In these archaic zones the patient's illness has a certain power and it "makes" the analyst in the same way that the child "makes" his mother. The analyst can then be present without quite understanding what is going on. (p. 11)

A case exemplifies not understanding what was going on as a slow and painful but necessary way to create a deep understanding in a consubstantiating or psychoid sense. "Pat" described herself as half Parsee and half Anglo-Indian; her father a Parsee, her mother an Anglo-Indian. A brother two years older than she had been killed in a car crash when he was in his early twenties; Pat had a sister about two years younger than herself. Pat was 32 when she first came to see me. Her presenting problem was a frighteningly murderous impulse at her job – in intensive care with babies. But she said also that the real reason for seeking therapy was the "terrible issue of the murder of my father by my mother." She felt mother had killed him by "nagging and bullying him relentlessly." Nags and bulls were to become significant symbolic metaphors.

It emerged that she and her sister had been sexually assaulted by the father when Pat was six or seven. She used the expression "he was so vigorous," an idiosyncratic expression that I did not forget. Yet she still regarded father as good and mother (who collusively blamed her for the sexual activity) as all bad and witchy. This was a defensive splitting, but also the first sign of a tangled internal knot.

After a certain amount of time she had a powerful dream full of Mithraic (and perhaps Zoroastrian) bull imagery.

A doctor (analyst) jumps onto the bumper or chest of a car-bison and wraps his legs around its bumper or neck "like a woman's position in a sexual act." The doctor's erect penis is jabbing into the neck or throat of the car-bison. The doctor holds onto the mud-guards or horns and pulls off the head of this creature, climbs into the headless torso and disappears. The head, now definitely a bison's, is still alive and dangerous and attacks the dreamer, who awakes in fear.

This initial dream vividly describes the subsequent analytic relationship: a life and death struggle in which the phallic analyst is sacrificed by being absorbed into a (dead?) body. Then Pat's savage nature becomes split off further and turns on herself. However, insofar as it seemed that I was soon to disappear – like the doctor in the dream into the "bestial body" it was vital (to me and to Pat) that I undergo this process and come out the other side, alive. Similarly, it was vital for Pat eventually to re-unite the severed head and the sundered body – which represented so many terrifying splits. But this dream of attack, castration and potency anxiety also contains a memory, as we shall see.

She also told me of a recurrent dream/nightmare of riding on a gray hunting horse. Her view in the dream is always from the rider's position – of the horse's neck and head seen from behind – but the horse always jumps to its death, over a cliff or into a fire. She loved her dream-horse and felt it was her "body power." It is certainly about a powerful, even phallic sense of body, but incorporating – for Pat – violence and destruction as well as sexual and gender confusion. After these dreams, Pat became increasingly angry and murderous in her feelings toward me. I began to feel ill, initially just during the sessions, but later after them also.

After about 15 months, there was a summer break of three weeks. When she reappeared I was surprised to see that she had cut off her long hair and was wearing extraordinarily masculine clothes. She presented me with a copy of a letter which she said she had written to her doctor, requesting to arrange for a sex change. It turned out that this letter was a fake, but its meaning – her symbolic needs and communication to me through it – were real: an expression of her confusion over uniting her internal parents, her need to identify with me and her feeling of failure to achieve these aims. In the confusion of trying to sort out the implications of the letter and her change of appearance, she said, "I have told you many lies over the year."

Thus, the historical and therefore identity chaos increased. She wanted me to know what had actually happened to her in the family, and why. She needed me to be her idea of a parental mind: digesting, sorting out and thinking for the physically and mentally pained baby. But the analyst/parent cannot know the baby's mental or physical pain from the inside or experience the baby's identity. Nevertheless, the more I could be made to suffer her turmoil, the closer she felt I would identify with her.

She agreed that she needed to come four times a week. With this intensification, Pat became even more restless or, if physically still, so tense that it was painful to sit with her. Sometimes she lay on the couch, sometimes she huddled on the floor, and sometimes she sat up. When sitting in the chair she would stare pointedly at me. Any actual or perceived flicker in my face, particularly a diversion of my eyes, was reacted to as if it were my frightened, guilty and treacherous flight from her. I linked this to her father, and later to her own sense of guilt. But increasingly my interpretations were met either with a disdainful silence or by her screaming at me, "You are bloody mad!" Both maneuvers succeeded in making it very difficult to think and to find words. Indeed, as always with a regression into a psychotic transference, verbal interpretations became inappropriate and not taken in. For Pat they felt like further phallic incestuous intrusions, narcissistic and selfish, stemming from my clumsy needs.

Her recurrent shouts of "You are bloody mad!" were, for a few weeks, her only words. She shouted them not only when I said something, but also when I was silent, which increasingly I was. Eventually she stopped the shouting, stopped all words – and we sat in silence for several weeks. This protracted silent phase was physically uncomfortable; I ached and felt sick. Moreover, occasionally she induced a sexual sensation and, in one session, she broke the silence by whispering, "I've got you." Her immediate curling up and hiding of her face after this remark seemed distinctly more erotic than angry; at that moment I saw her spider-like weaving a web around me and venomously sucking me out.

After this she returned again to the wordless physical tension and the environment of silent projective identifications. I felt as though my body were being made to do all the work, and that survival was my main concern.

Bollas (1987), in what he calls an "informative regression," distinguishes four stages of regression and recovery within the countertransference. He describes the second stage as one

> *of terror over survival, as the analyst is overcome by a dreadful silence that immobilises his psyche-soma. This is understood as the patient's presentation of maternal hate, of death wishes against the aliveness of the child. The fear, however, is due to the child's responsive destruction, expressed by the analyst's countertransference. The analyst, having split his personality, has projected his (mother's) hate into the environment, leaving him only a part analyst.* (pp. 350-351)

This stage changes when events occur that mobilize the analyst's fury into speech; aggression becomes a means of survival.

It was my analytic role to embody for Pat someone who she could feel was a sensitive, suffering but also strong and eventually clarifying embodied mind. She brought a dream in which *I was probing the anus of her gray horse.* She shouted, "I hate you, you are attacking my horse." Then she leaped up from the couch and attacked me, biting and kicking. I thought that I ought to be interpreting this event in an analytically correct way, trying to understand for myself and her what she was trying to do, and to whom. Actually, I physically defended myself. My physical self-defense made her yell, "You are attacking me," to which I rather cowardly replied, "No, I am defending myself." She said, "No, men don't defend themselves; they only attack, you bugger."

I was able to take up "men only attack [and] bugger" and it turned out that her brother had tried to sodomize her when she was about 12. Then she said that in fact he made her masturbate him onto her chest and neck and that he "would come so vigorously." The expression "he came so vigorously" sounded loud bells; the dream image of the doctor with his penis/knife in the bull's throat took on a new significance. This brother was both an aspect of her father and a split-off, needy part of herself. His later fatal car crash was experienced by Pat as a terrible punishment for her guilt. A few sessions later she brought the following dream:

> *I am staying at a farm, and I wake up. It is a cloudy, drizzling morning, about 4:00 AM. The cockerel is about to crow and I want to watch the cock crowing. So I go outside and wait and listen for him. Then I hear the first crow so I know where to go to see him. He is standing on a heap of rotting compost. At each crow he creates an image of sunrise. When the cock is not actually crowing the weather is still cloudy. Then I notice that the cockerel has been plucked. His plucked body is bleeding from where the feathers have been torn out of him. His naked body is plump. His naked neck is thin and scraggy except when he crows, when it becomes strong and muscular. I know that in some way he is the ugly crucified Christ.*

This dream of a plucked cockerel who was also Christ, and obviously a wounded phallic symbol too, even an image of an erect penis (father's and brother's), suggests many questions about the analytic relationship. In particular because my own initial pre-analytic dream (from 15 years before this) was of a crucified Christ as an ugly plucked chicken covered with green mold. Through my personal associations and interpretations of my dream and my understanding of Pat's dream, I saw the cockerel/plucked chicken image as symbolic of our similar psychic experience, of our attacked, abused and/or denied bodies. The difficulty was that Pat's dream of a cock felt to me as though a seminal part of me had got into her. I was her brother, her father and her phallic mother. Here, in our transference/countertransference *unus mundus*, I felt that I had been unconsciously seduced into an invasive assault. Or had I unconsciously assaulted her with my own projective identifications? Or had she made me feel intrusive? And, the other way around: I felt raped by my dream. Was it that she had got into me too much and/or got too much out of me? Whose dream was it? Whose cock? Whose Christ? Whose body? I now think that the cock-Christ was a shared symbol, somatic and psychic, our animating body which incorporated us both. Her dream and our two bodies were attributes or aspects of a single shared psychosomatic dynamic substance: our psychoid developmental-relational energy. As Jung wrote in 1934, "In the deepest sense we all dream not out of ourselves but out of what lies between us and the other" (Let-I, p. 172).

To link the first and last of Pat's dreams that I have recounted: a) the sacrificial bull = the potent animal body through which revitalizing change may eventually happen = the analytic body; and b) the sacrificial weapon = the analyst's (father's/brother's) desired and feared phallic potency. These two elements (bull and man) come together as one in: the sacrificial body, Christ-as-cock = the embodiment of the ugliness of abuse = the (counter)-tranferentially wounded analyst-as-savior.

Our struggles to make sense of the cockerel dream and to understand its place in our history eventually enabled Pat to begin to accept the limits of her power to possess and control her world. She became a more peaceable person, her constipation ceased and, as we disentangled ourselves, my countertransference pains ceased too.

A regression such as I have described is a relationship wherein the psychotic part of the analysand's personality forcibly projects its mad and bad fragments into the analyst. The analyst frustrates the patient in not obeying the desires of the patient. The patient seeks to make both the ideal of oneness and the lethal hate more effective, using means more affective than symbolic. Toxic, somatic projections are used in a process of psychotic, psychosomatic fusion: a sick and sickening union that is functionally necessary, in order to communicate affectively and thus effectively.

Wiener (1994) has put forward the hypothesis that "many psychosomatic patients may be suffering from particular disturbances in vitality affects [unnamable feelings] emanating from the time when sensuous communications between mother and baby can critically affect emotional development" (p. 345).

Wiener is then able to make her valuable distinction between body-talk and body-language. She hypothesizes that

> body talk *is a consequence of the kind of preverbal communication between mother and baby where there may have been a bad fit in terms of vitality affects. In later life, this can manifest itself in the form of "body" or psychosomatic problems which cannot be put into words but are often recognisable through the quality of the interpersonal transference dynamics.* (p. 348)

She uses the words "discomfort" or "dissonance" as being evident in the "doings" of early body talk. Pat is operating very much in the discomforting "body talk" mode – where the analyst has to let him/herself be "done to" for a protracted period.

The consubstantiating experience of a shared world of psychic and psychosomatic animation – a body of mutual experience – is actually an environment formed unconsciously out of the patient's chaotic internal relations and made interpersonal by the unconscious projective identification of these messy relations into the analyst or, perhaps, into which the analyst is sucked. Because this environment is created unconsciously, we sense it as if it were a psyche-soma experience into which we unwittingly (passively) fall and in which we find ourselves together, sharing in it animatedly. The analyst's task is to "think like bloody mad" and to find a way out of this sometimes sickening confusion into our separateness and differentness. The analyst needs to think through his or her affected and infected autonomic nervous system, its sensations and primitive symbols, and thus help the patient – (and the analyst) – to a new psyche-soma coordination.

> *Countertransference is the fundamentally useful tool that it is, only to the extent that the analyst's conscious personality is open to his own serpent mind: the more he can let in, contain, and know what is going on in his own autonomic nervous system, the more he will know his sympathetic and parasympathetic responses to his patients, and be able to help his patient to his (the patient's) serpent mind.*
> (Peters, 1987, pp. 374-376)

We can understand psychoid substance as a vitalistic force or urge which energetically permeates the psyche-soma and reaches out to mate with the human environment – with other embodied vitalistic persons. Initially this is the mother's body, or experienced aspects of it, including the insides of the mother and her mind. The infant then introjects these experiences. But the fundamental core of this vital energy is the pre-objective, pre-image, urgent process of energetic relating. It seems that this core is like a primal vital spark that instinctively lives itself out between me and the world. If – at the beginning of life – this urgent primal force is thwarted, its vitalism is damaged and a pathological, often psychotic struggle for survival develops.

The order of damaged developmental events in the transference seems to go something like this:

1) Initially, as felt from the inside, we find that we are both in one shared active environment. We have created our shared natural psychic universe around us. The fantasy is: "I love you absolutely and shall for ever because you love me absolutely and shall forever. You are mine and we are therefore one."

2) Then, disillusioning experience changes or develops the fantasy: "I simultaneously find that you are not one with me but are separate, different; you have a separate body and a separate mind and live in a different world. This is terrible and intolerable. I hate and envy you your separateness; I cannot have you because you do not love me absolutely and eternally."

3) "Therefore I must force us into a shared environment. I must force you to be one with me, and me to be one with you – force us into love."

4) "Simultaneously, I hate and envy you so much that I must kill you. So I shall wound you, hurt you, make you ill and sick unto death." Thus, this commonly sensed environmental field which the analysand has created is now simultaneously: a) a place full of inactive oceanic reverie and bliss; and b) an active battlefield of bullet-like projections and psychic germ warfare. It is both good and bad, pleasure and pain, loving and hating, sex and sickness, a life and death-struggle.

5) But first the analyst and then the analysand discover a paradox: that the apparently loving side, the blissful inactive oneness, is deadly; and that the murderous hate, pain and sickness are energizing, vitalizing, animating.

6) Even more paradoxically: this terrible animating body – which is so fierce, disharmonious, sickening and disassociated – brings life and unites us.

The animating body is consubstantial between us and inside each of us, healing internalized inter-personal wounds and psycho-soma rupture. This forceful psychoid level of experience is affective in the metacommunications between the autonomic nervous sensations and symbols experienced between two persons, as discussed in the example of Pat.

In regressed analytic relations this process can be sickening and near-deadly, as well as erotic, healing and enlivening. Symbols and sensations are often experienced similarly: The analyst's dreams, fantasies and sensations belong equally to the patient and to the relationship; these contents feel simultaneously confusing, invasive and mutual but demanding differentiation, interpretation and the making of a sense of autonomy. However, this mutative process can be realized only when the consubstantial "animating body" has been lived out, thought through and eventually translated into a limiting, separating but commonly understood language.

References

Bollas, C. (1987). Regression in the counter-transference. In L.B. Boyer & P. Giovacchini (Eds.). *Master Clinicians on Treating the Regressed Patient.* New York: Aronson.

Humbert, E. (1986). Wellsprings of memory. *Journal of Analytical Psychology, 33*-1, 3-20.

Peters, R. (1987). The eagle and the serpent. *Journal of Analytical Psychology, 32*-4, 359-381.

Wiener, J. (1994). Looking out and looking in. *Journal of Analytical Psychology, 39*-3, 345-349.

Analytical Psychology and Psychopharmacology

Concetto Gullotta, Grazia Cerbo, Liberiana Pavone,
Adriano Pignatelli, Daniela Palliccia,
Fabrizio Alfani, Vincenzo Caretti
Rome, Italy
Italian Association for the Study of Analytical Psychology

Bellica Pax, Vulnus Dulce, Suave Malum
(A warring peace, a sweet wound, an agreeable evil)
John Gower

Many of us deal with patients who take psychotropic drugs, either regularly or occasionally, while undergoing psychotherapy. This double approach is necessary for more serious cases. However, it is applied not only to treat clear psychotic symptoms or serious depressive manifestations, but is much more widespread than we are inclined to acknowledge. There is, in fact, embarrassment among many of our colleagues regarding this problem, an embarrassment that sometimes verges on hypocrisy and a consequent refusal to acknowledge the extent of this phenomenon and its importance for the future of our science.

We (the authors of this paper) decided to deal with this issue by means of a study group made up of analytical psychologists, some of them with a medical-psychiatric background, others with a philosophical background. In addition to the general interest that this issue arouses, we have been urged to investigate by the extensive publicity which, in recent years, has been given to the pharmacological treatment of psychic disorders – particularly in relation to depression – accompanied by a barely disguised critical attitude toward the schools of depth psychology. A far greater trust in the curative properties of drugs, together with a skeptical attitude toward psychoanalytic treatment, are expressions of deep anthropological and cultural changes. The full extent, characteristics and future implications of these changes are beyond our grasp.

During an interview (Evans, 1964) in 1957 Jung expressed his position against drugs, stating that they alter the deepest moral structures of a person, thus paving the way for suggestion. It must be noted, however, that Jung's observation dates from the outset of modern psychopharmacology. Over the last 40 years an improved knowledge of the drugs' acting mechanisms and of neurophysiology has made possible selective use of psychotropic drugs. It is legitimate, therefore, to ask ourselves what view is valid today: Do we share Jung's negative opinion? If we do, how do we justify resorting to combined therapies for some of our patients?

These questions, deliberately provocative, appeal to the experience of each of us. They imply a critical attitude toward our clinical practice and our degree of consistency with psychological theories of reference. We are asking: Does Jungian theory allow for biological intervention, or is the recourse to drugs excluded *a priori* from the theoretical foundations of analytical psychology?

If asked in terms of extremes the question can produce an ideological confrontation and lead to disputes that are harsh and pointless. From an epistemological and methodological point of view, perhaps ideological confrontation is not the most suitable attitude with which to tackle the question of the use of drugs during analytic treatment. While respecting individual differences, the confrontation should allow for an appropriate detachment. There is danger, as witnessed by many authors from different analytic schools, of arousing bitter disputes.

Even within our study group we had to acknowledge the emergence of emotions and aggression which each of us initially interpreted as a manifestation of not sufficiently analyzed personal dynamics. Subsequently, we were able to recognize the partiality of such an interpretation; we did not deny it entirely, but we relegated it to the background, as part of the inevitable network of human relationships. It seemed to us more productive to observe how the issue of the use of drugs during analytic therapy – a subject which may appear neutral and academic – had affected us deeply. Perhaps it is connected to the unfathomable and individual choice by each of us to embrace the profession of analyst. The intimate and final decision that tipped the balance in favor of this work reflects an inexpressible aspect of our personality, an aspect touched upon by the analytic theories which describe it while its essence remains confined within the subjective dialogic experience. Although inexpressible, this deep nucleus represents the foundation of confidence in our personal foundations and in our identity as analysts. It seemed that the opposite polarities of such deep nuclei were studded with our reflections, evoking in each of us shadow aspects of our professional choice.

It is understandable, therefore, that the activation of these emotional elements brought about a temporary paralysis of both the theoretical elaboration and the psychological reflection, during which our group experienced an extreme difficulty in communication. Each of us tried to describe and explain to the others his or her point of view, at the same time acknowledging one's limited comprehension of the other person. We found ourselves in a situation that, similarly to the images of the *Rosarium Philosophorum*, we could define as *nigredo*, in which the clashing of the opposites brings about chaos and paralysis.

It is important to us that we experienced all this within a group. Indeed, each of us, as if an autonomous complex had been provided with consciousness, was able to observe the other person, express convictions and recount one's own experience, not disengaged from a deep affective drive that characterized individual autonomy. The presence of a variety of individuals obliged us to face the irreducible aspects of the problem. Therefore, in the conclusions drawn from our work, we do not propose a univocal solution regarding the clinical use of drugs. We describe how the psychological experience and the theoretical reflection of our group showed us that the very nature of the problem mirrors the polarity through which the knowledge and its underlying archetypal structure are established.

Theoretical Aspects

Drugs and psychotherapy constitute the elements of a conflict that is underway between biological psychiatry and dynamic psychiatry and even, in a more radical manner, among medical science, clinical psychology and psychoanalysis. This conflict finds no immediate solution and, indeed, prompts further questions. For example, must drugs be rejected because they pollute the analysis a priori? Or should their presence be tolerated, since they help the patient to keep the illness under control, thus promoting the analytic work and the therapeutic relationship? Further, is it possible to adjust the interpretations, the strategies and all the consequences of the medical model to those of the analytic model? Finally, what place does the confrontation between the body and the mind have in the patient's life, in the analytic relationship and in the therapist's orientation?

Our reflections pivot around these questions and demonstrate – with the help of the psychological model – that the dispute between drugs and psychotherapy takes on a prominent role in the process of individuation of both patient and therapist. In the model of analytical psychology, our reflections also demonstrate how the terms of this conflict may find an interpretive hypothesis both on an epistemological level and on that of clinical practice. From an epistemological point of view, the theory can be understood as an archetypal category. The psychopharmacology-psychotherapy dilemma would not express a contraposition inherent in the nature of things, but rather the psyche's tendency to represent a certain element of experience in the form of a pair of opposites. On the clinical level, the problem is that of assessing whether it is appropriate to prescribe drugs in some particular clinical circumstances and interpreting the symbolic meaning taken on by the drug within the therapeutic relationship.

The reciprocal inference of these two levels constitutes one of the main reasons why this subject arouses affect. Often, while discussing clinical experience, one is unaware of being overwhelmed by the ethical and psychological aspects. At the same time, one is influenced by personal clinical experiences when the problem is dealt with theoretically.

In the scientific literature on the subject the discussion always moves into psyche-matter dualism: the symbolic meaning of the drug in a transference relationship versus its chemical and biological effect. This dualism is the focus of our attention.

Jung was long involved with the relationship between psyche and matter. Drawing from his personal and clinical experience, he tried to supply the theoretical tools to overcome, from an epistemological viewpoint, such a contraposition. As we know, he believed that there is a continuity between the physical and the psychical.

In biological evolution, the purely physiological processes predominate. As life evolves, vital functions appear, capable of developing their own autonomy and thus progressively disposing of automatisms contingent on the biological processes. At this stage the psyche begins to reveal itself. Jung expressed this concept in detail (CW8, pars. 376-377), holding that the psychic appears where it is possible for the vital phenomena to evolve greater autonomy, no longer constrained by the causative determinism of physical laws. Therefore, the psyche is not governed by physical laws, with their cause-effect relationship, but belongs to a different order of phenomena whose behavior is analogous with the processes that take place in the subatomic world.

The findings of quantum physics on the nature of phenomena at the subatomic level offered Jung further support for the validity of his concept of the relationship between psyche and matter. His theorical formulations are found in his work on synchronicity. Although fascinating and exciting on an intellectual level, they appear far from the common clinical experience. Just as the theories of modern physics seem to clash with the convictions suggested by common sense, at first glance these theoretical reflections seem unable to contribute to our therapeutic practice.

In order to reduce the gap between theory and clinical practice it is appropriate to refer to the therapeutic process as described by Jung and as it emerges from our own experience. Here, however, a new difficulty arises: A single phenomenology of psychological development during an analytic treatment does not exist. Jung himself recognized that the phenomena he described (CW16) take place only in a limited percentage of cases. We refer, thus, to the process of individuation as a metaphor of all the possible ways in which the transformation of conflicts in creative polarities can reveal itself. The reference to the process of individuation thus forms the link necessary to connect the events of the daily clinical practice with theoretical reflections on the relationship between psyche and matter.

Clinical Considerations and Conclusions

In Jungian theory the process of individuation refers as much to psychological development outside psychotherapy as within the relationship of analyst and patient. In the process of individuation, via the vicissitudes of the libido and conflictive experiences, the transcendent function emerges. As concentric rippling follows the dropping of a stone in a pond, so the transcendent function gives access to the symbolic dimension, promotes awareness of unconscious contents, mediates between the opposites and allows for the compensation of the unilateral attitude that consciousness may assume in conflicted states.

How can pharmacological intervention alter the psychic processes we have described? To answer, the therapist must assess whether in an individual patient, at a particular time, within a specific therapeutic relationship, the use of medication is likely to hinder or promote the process of individuation.

We believe that medication – a molecule endowed with a specific chemical-biological activity – is not capable of promoting or of hindering the psychological development of an individual. "Psychic," for Jung, refers to an autonomy from the deterministic laws that govern biological phenomena. If we share this opinion, we cannot believe that the medication significantly alters the psychic sphere of existence.

At the same time, deciding whether to use drugs may have significant consequences for the subsequent psychological development of the patient. The main consequence of the use of medication is not the biochemical effect of the elements but rather the symbolic meaning that the drug takes on within the therapeutic relationship. Thus, it is not possible to express a final opinion on the appropriateness of the use of drugs in the course of analytic treatment. Such a decision can be reached only within the individual therapeutic and existential experience.

This experience can be influenced by several factors in the psychic world of the patient and that of the analyst. An element common to all cases in which a medication is being used is the potentiality to activate the conflict between psyche and matter. Indeed, even if one member of the analytic couple fantasizes a pharmacological treatment, such a conflictual polarity may arise within the relationship. The contraposition of psyche and matter is characteristic of our culture; scientific and technological development makes this conflict ever more intense. Hence, psychopharmacological progress and advancement of a new organicist vision of psychic disorders may bring about a further radicalization of such contraposition. The possible risk is that a unilateral attitude favors only one pole of the problem, confining the other to the shadow.

The possibility of combining the poles of the question resides, above all, in the analyst's ability to confront this dilemma. Without such confrontation there is no possible access to that symbolic dimension which, alone, can offer a genuine integration. The individuation process evolves within a historical frame, through the confrontation with present-day issues that do not find an immediate explanation in the analyst's psychological concepts. When these issues involve fundamental aspects of our way of conceiving the psychic life (as is the case in the conflict between psyche and matter), it is inevitable that they activate responses linked to our sense of professional identity. This development of the analyst's sense of identity can be difficult; it can be likened, rightfully, to the alchemical *opus*.

Such development is necessary. If we are skeptical about the progressive recognition of an organicist attitude toward psychic disorders – which tends to support and intensify the split between psyche and matter – we must recognize that denying the existence of the problem can lead depth psychology to a progressive alienation from the most crucial issues of the contemporary world, with the subsequent loss of its transformative and dynamic potential.

Theoretical reflection on these issues shows us the relativism inherent in our therapeutic activity; it helps us to acknowledge the emotional echo that our psychological theories can evoke. Jung phrased this idea in this way: "He who cannot understand the art of 'theorizing' cannot be a doctor. ... The doctor should encourage not only in himself, but also in the patient a way of conceiving and understanding the illness which enables him to treat, and the ill person to recover his health or at least to cope with his condition" (CW16, par. 218). How can we deny that today our "way of conceiving and understanding the illness" cannot ignore the developments of the neurosciences and of psychopharmacology? We are not advising our colleagues passively to accept theoretical methods and models of organicist psychiatry, but we emphasize the necessity of a theoretical effort by which the drugs-psychotherapy problem (which evokes the body-mind conflict which, in turn, refers to that of psyche-matter) may be overcome creatively.

This theoretical effort should never be considered exhausted. Jung said that every patient needs a new theory, and it is the analyst's task to create, accordingly, a way suitable to that single patient of understanding the particular illness. Therefore the conflict between drugs and psychotherapy may be resolved only by capturing the symbolic meaning within the specific therapeutic context. Such a resolution, being an integral part of the individuation process of both the therapist and the patient, should not be determined a priori, but sought each time in the relationship between them, according to the particularities of the single case.

Translated from Italian by Grazia Cerbo and Rolando De Angelis

Reference

Evans, R. (1964). *Conversations with Carl Jung and Reactions from Ernest Jones*. New York: Van Nostrand.

Research and Jungian Psychotherapy

Outcome Studies

Part I

Georgia Lepper
London, England
Society of Analytical Psychology

A handbook edited by Bergin and Garfield (1994) deals in a reasonably even-handed way with all the major psychotherapies: cognitive, behavioral, humanistic and psychodynamic. One of its important findings, a conclusion that has been building over the years, is that outcomes do not vary much among different modes of psychotherapy. It seems to be less the theoretical base of our practice than some other factors that account for the growing evidence that psychotherapy is a successful treatment. This conclusion has been demonstrated in part by "meta-analysis," a method of aggregating studies so that a larger statistical base is formed than individual studies can support in themselves. According to Kazdin (1994), some of these aggregated studies have shown that, on average, a client who is treated by psychotherapy is better off at the end of therapy than 76 percent of the members of a control group who have received no treatment.

While such a finding may be good news for the future of psychotherapy in the mainstream of health care, it leaves open some important questions: 1) What are the factors that account for psychotherapeutic change? 2) How do we relate process factors to outcomes? 3) Even if psychotherapy is effective, is it cost-effective? How does the provider or funder of health care define cost-effectiveness, and what part do researchers play in defining it?

These findings suggest some lines of inquiry that might support a Jungian approach. One significant conclusion is that the "therapeutic alliance" is one of the important common factors in positive therapeutic outcome (Kazdin, 1994; Lambert & Bergin, 1994). It was Jung who first suggested that it is the "'rapport,' or relationship of mutual confidence, on which the therapeutic success depends" (CW16, par. 239) and that "the personalities of doctor and patient are more important for the outcome of the treatment than what the doctor says or thinks" (CW16, par. 163). Contemporary research confirms these intuitions. The problem for researchers now is to understand of what significant elements the therapeutic alliance might consist, and how to evaluate it in terms of outcome.

At present, outcome research is dominated by research methodologies current in academic psychology. These have remained primarily within the traditional scientific paradigm, characterized by quantitative methods. Important among these are various forms of factor analysis. Factor analysis seeks to identify key variables, and to establish correlations between them. The effect is a research strategy that follows a kind of input-output logic: the investigator identifying and assessing key factors initially and, after an intervening process such as therapy, assessing those factors for any changes. Important methodological problems include the means by which variables are identified and contrasted. My colleagues' and my presentations of research studies will demonstrate these methods.

These methods have been highly effective at mapping the field and isolating those factors that appear to be correlated with positive effects. They have also generated the question: If the therapeutic relationship is a key factor in positive outcome, how can we identify the factors operant in such a process? It is here that the "qualitative" methods – now enjoying wide currency in social science, and beginning to be incorporated into psychology – could come into their own. This trend in thinking has led to an alternative understanding of social inquiry and to the systematic study of meaning based on the experience of subjects, "phenomenology." It is to this trend of twentieth century thought that Jung properly belongs; the contemporary research methods that have evolved within this strand of thinking include a specifically Jungian contribution to psychotherapy research.

I do not see "quantitative" and "qualitative" as opposing "truths." I see them as complementary, open-ended, and equally governed by a proper respect for empirical analysis. Thus, they follow directly in the rigorously empirical spirit of Jung's original research.

What kind of perspective can we as Jungians bring to the problems of research in psychotherapy? I have already indicated one potential area: the empirical study of the "therapeutic alliance." Researchers (Henry et al., 1994) in the field of psychodynamic therapy have suggested that the psychodynamic process is not readily amenable to quantitative methodology. However, important questions about the function of the alliance in the psychodynamic process can be studied qualitatively, through the increasingly sophisticated techniques for studying human interaction that are current within the phenomenological tradition. It is perhaps through these methods that the important elements in psychotherapeutic change can best be identified and subsequently evaluated as factors.

There is a second possible line of inquiry that may be of particular relevance in the context of different cultures and systems of health care. In the United States, a largely free-market system prevails, with private insurance schemes acting as funders to individuals. In continental Europe, typically, a statutory insurance system provides universal coverage, under strict guidelines from government. In the United Kingdom, health care is delivered primarily through the National Health Service, funded by taxation, and (mainly) free at the point of delivery. Social science research demonstrates that treatment decisions are not based on a simple input-output model. They are part of a complex social process, which includes individual and collective values and attitudes, as well as costs and funding constraints. "Qualitative" methodology can look at the effect of context on the characterization of the problem, the rationality of decision-making, and the process of making choices about treatment.

To give some flesh and bones to this way of thinking, here is an example from a study of physical medicine, where the "objective" facts of the diagnosis were quite clear. The context is the British National Health Service. The condition in question was a congenital heart defect in children, requiring major surgical intervention, with considerable risk and pain. In a study (Silverman, 1981) of the interaction between pediatric consultants and parents, it was demonstrated that the process of diagnosis and the discussion of treatment were very different depending upon whether the children were "normal" children, or Downs syndrome children – in whom heart defects are common. In the case of Downs syndrome children, pediatricians and parents cooperated in arriving at a diagnosis which indicated "no treatment" in view of the risk and pain involved. "Quality of life" for the child was seen by both doctor and parent as the main criterion of outcome.

In contrast, in the case of normal children, the interview was managed by the pediatrician in quite a different way. In this case, the doctor first had to tell parents who had not already come to terms with a damaged child that their child was seriously ill. Subsequently, the study shows that the interview was managed to support the choice of surgery, with all the risk and pain that would involve. Indeed, it is media practice in the United Kingdom to report the case of a child with a life-threatening condition, for whom it has been said that there is no treatment. The media follow the enormous lengths to which parents, friends and community have gone to raise money to send the child to the United States, where a possible life-saving – but highly risky and painful – treatment (usually surgery) is available.

These are social decisions, characterized by qualitative judgments as well as by "facts." Even in the case of an apparently "objective" diagnosis, the interpretation of symptoms is a complex act. It is not context-free. It involves anticipating a variety of possible, and only partly predictable, outcomes. The choice of treatment is heavily dependent on that context.

Relating this model of outcome to the question of the cost-effectiveness of psychotherapy – whether psychotherapy is being provided privately, within a managed insurance scheme, or in the context of an integrated health care system – will make substantial differences in identifying and evaluating outcomes. Are diagnostic decisions measured, as they are in traditional outcome studies, in terms of symptoms? How are they are interpreted in terms of available resources? And what kinds of values do they express, in terms of perceived human need?

Psychotherapy, like any form of treatment, plays its part in a culture of care. It might be well to investigate how therapist and patient arrive at an understanding of the nature of the problem, what might be done to make it better, and what might be agreed by them in the end as evidence of a successful outcome. A study of this "collective" process might lead to a reliable measure of what effectiveness means to both therapists and patients, and what they consider to be worth the price.

Part II

Wolfram Keller

Berlin, Germany
German Society of Analytical Psychology
In association with R. Dilg, G. Westhoff, R. Rohner, H-H. Studt
and the Psychotherapy Research Group in Analytical Psychology, Berlin
(D. Baldus, R. Väth-Szusdziara, C. Weitze, R. Huntzinger, G. Betzner, H.
Krause, P. Affeld-Niemeyer, A. Göttke, S. Loesche)

Jungians are not part of the tradition of empirical psychotherapy research. They consider themselves obligated to the individuality of their patients. Thus, they are skeptical about the results of such research with its claims of generalization. Jungians are, however, not the only ones with this skeptical outlook. Other psychoanalytic schools are hesitantly – and only under increasing pressure from health-care administrations – ready to make an empirical analysis of the quality of their treatment.

Despite a large number of empirical studies on the effectiveness of psychotherapy, there is a lack of studies on the efficacy of long-term analyses with a naturalistic (non-laboratory) design that include analysts in private practice. This is particularly important because the effectiveness of shorter and less expensive psychotherapeutic procedures may result in no insurance coverage for long-term analysis.

Against the background of an increasingly critical professional situation, the C.G. Jung Institute in Berlin initiated in 1991 a study on the efficacy of Jungian long-term analyses in the Department for Psychosomatic Medicine and Psychotherapy at University Medical Center Benjamin Franklin, which was financed by outside research funds. In order to carry out this study in an acceptable time and financial framework, my co-workers and I decided on a retrospective naturalistic multi-level design. A publication of the main results is in preparation. An outline of our plan follows.

Objectives

1. Proving the effectiveness of long-term analyses (more than 100 sessions) and examining the stability of treatment results by a follow-up study six years after treatment.
2. Evaluating cost-benefit data.

3. Justifying Jungian psychotherapy and analysis to the cost carrier and the health-care administration.
4. Implementing research strategies in the area of outpatient care as a measure for quality assurance.

Methods

The members of the German Society (all working with adult clients) were asked to participate. Seventy-eight percent responded to our inquiry; 24 percent participated in the study.

The central component of our study was the follow-up examination of our former patients via a questionnaire six years after termination of psychotherapy or analysis, and the recording of treatment-seeking data from health insurance companies five years before and after treatment.

The participating analysts documented, on the basis of their notes, all cases of outpatient Jungian analysis, psychotherapy, short-term psychotherapy and group therapy, including dropouts, that were completed in 1987 and 1988. This documentation was done by means of a basic questionnaire on clinical and demographic data along with characteristics of the therapy setting, all from the start of therapy, plus overall assessment of the patient's state at the end of therapy. Thus, the selection of a sample of 111 cases via a follow-up questionnaire could be checked in its essential variables against the total of 353 documented therapies completed in 1987 and 1988. The selection of the participating therapists was checked via a survey of all Society members with respect to central characteristics of therapist and setting. An ICD-10 (International Classification of Diseases, version 10) classification concerning the time before treatment was established by independent raters, based on the request for coverage of the cost of therapy. On this basis the severity of disease was assessed according to the method by Schepank (1987).

Results

The results of this retrospective study show the effectiveness of Jungian analysis and psychotherapy for most of the study participants from several assessment levels of observation on the basis of different success criteria. Treatment proved effective from five different perspectives:

1. In the sustained improvement from the patient's point of view, comparing health status before treatment to the subsequent health status. Using self-assessment, 70 to 90 percent (depending on the success criterion of the study participants reported good to very good improvements in physical, psychic and socially relevant areas – including subjective experience of disease.

2. In the therapist's overall assessment of the patient's state at the end of therapy and the relatively high agreement with the patient's follow-up assessment six years after the end of treatment.

3. In the psychometric test studies of the actual state of health in terms of symptoms, personality and changes in experience and behavior, compared to a random sample of healthy subjects and other clinical groups.

4. In the expert rating through clinical interviews of a subsample (in the Berlin region) of 33 patients, at the follow-up examination by independent examiners and by the significant decrease of the severity of disease compared to the pre-treatment status. (Severity of impairment was measured according to the Schepank method.)

5. In the reduction of the time on disability leave and in hospital five years before and after treatment and, additionally, in comparison to the average such days for all patients, from a large health insurance company for the study-relevant years one year before and after termination of treatment.

More than three-fourths of the patients examined here underwent analysis (rather than psychotherapy); thus there was empirical proof of effectivity for long-term analyses which is still demonstrable after a mean of six years. Improvement of the patients' physical state and social functioning five years after therapy also results in a marked reduction of health insurance claims – disability days, hospital days, number of visits to a doctor and drug intake – of a large number of the treated patients and, thus, in a reduction of costs.

Work Disability and Hospital Days Recorded by the Insurer

Using health insurance data, the number of days on work disability and in hospital were recorded for each patient five years before and five years after therapy. Conclusions were drawn from these changes on the effectiveness of therapy and the incurred costs. Thus, a reduction of work disability and hospital days after treatment can be regarded as a global measure of therapeutic success.

This elegant and increasingly important procedure for recording administrative health insurance data presents difficulties, however, in research practice and methodology. Obtaining data from health insurance companies is cumbersome and time-consuming. In addition, in order to calculate the number of days on work disability, the patients must have been continuously employed. Hence, many patients were excluded. Our sample was reduced to 47 patients for the work disability days and 58 patients for hospital days. The size of our sample is at the lower limit for a statistical statement.

Comparing the number of sick days per patient the year before and the year after therapy, there was a reduction in the mean number of days on sick leave from 24 to 8. The reduction had a statistical tendency with p=.054, just missing the 5 percent significance level.

Similar results were obtained regarding the number of days in hospital: The average number of such days in the year before therapy was eight per patient, compared to only one day in the year after therapy. This reduction is statistically significant with p=.037. Similar results were obtained within the five-year observing period.

To illustrate effectiveness in comparison to average patients, we have added the preliminary results of the pre- and post-therapeutic comparison between the health insurance coverage data of this study and the statistical characteristic data of all those with compulsory insurance in one of the major health insurance companies (Barmer Ersatzkasse, BEK). Comparing the administrative data of the cost carrier of our sample with the statistical mean of all members of BEK one year before and after therapy, figures were determined for the study-relevant years. For a comparison, our data have been calculated for 100 policy holders.

Before beginning therapy, our sample had 1456 sick days per 100 cases. This figure was clearly higher than the mean value of all BEK policy holders for 1985: 1083 sick days per 100 cases. Thus, our study population was clearly "sicker" than the average BEK policy holder. In the year after therapy, however, the number of sick days of our population was clearly below the 1989 average of the health insurance company: 820 versus 1229 days. The one year pre/post-reduction of sick days in our population was 47.3 percent.

A similar effect could be demonstrated in comparison of the hospital with the BEK: Our population had a sum of 912 hospital days per 100 cases one year prior to treatment. The corresponding mean value of the BEK in 1985 was 164 days per 100 cases. In the year after therapy (1989) our sample had 116 days in hospital per 100 cases and the corresponding mean value of the BEK in 1989 was 167 days per 100 cases. Thus, the one year pre/post-reduction of hospital days in our study sample was 87.3 percent.

Discussion

Cost-benefit considerations as success criteria play an increasingly important role for health-care administrations. As we have shown in this study, psychotherapy apparently has a long-lasting effect on patients' seeking medical treatment. Though complete recording of these data requires great care and a methodologically reliable procedure for interpreting the data (Richter et al., 1994) once these prerequisites have been fulfilled, together with the clinical results and the longitudinal change in health care utilization data, we have the convincing arguments for the effectiveness of Jungian psychotherapy.

Part III

Seth Isaiah Rubin
Sausalito, CA
Society of Jungian Analysts of Northern California

Four considerations motivated the development of this paper. The first, a true open question in analytical psychology is: What role, if any, will psychotherapy outcome research play in our field? Psychotherapy outcome research is conspicuous by its absence. What does this absence mean? Is it merely an expression of a correctable one-sidedness that grew out of the significant spiritual orientation of analytical psychology, or is it an indication of a fundamental opposition to scientific empiricism as it is understood currently in the health sciences?

Let us turn our attention to a report of the American Psychological Association (1993). This important, controversial report sets out the rationale for and the definition of empirically-validated treatment. The criteria for such validated treatments are displayed in two tables, one of which (p. 10) is:

Table 1
Criteria for Empirically Validated Treatments: Well-Established Treatments
1. At least two good group design studies, conducted by different investigators, demonstrating efficacy in one or more of the following ways:
a. Superior to pill or psychological placebo or to another treatment.
b. Equivalent to an already established treatment in studies with adequate statistical power (about 30 per group; cf. Kazdin & Bass, 1989).
2. Many single case design studies demonstrating efficacy. These studies must have:
a. Used good experimental designs and
b. Compared the intervention to another treatment as in 1a.
Further criteria for both 1 and 2:
3. Studies must be conducted with treatment manuals.
4. Characteristics of the client samples must be clearly specified.

The second consideration is that follow-up is a hidden link between therapy and research, integral to both and often found missing in each. Follow-up serves two purposes for analysis, one for the analyst and the other for the analysand: 1) Follow-up enables the analyst to learn about outcomes over time, and 2) The contact between the analyst and analysand during follow-up serves as a "booster," consolidating and strengthening the analytic gains for the analysand. Follow-up for properly designed research provides the basis for determining whether and how the analytic interventions work in the long run. Are the gains maintained? Is there a "sleeper" effect; that is, do the true gains emerge only after analysis is completed?

Third, follow-up implies measurement but does not restrict the research to measured variables only. Qualitative research methods have a definite place in open-minded and critical-thinking psychotherapy process and outcome research. In the best of all research, the qualitative and quantitative methods complement each other, much like the conscious and unconscious positions of the psyche.

Fourth, Table 1 represents the "Gold Standard" not only because of the high value of this sort of research but because of the tremendous expense it entails. These studies are much more expensive in terms of money, time, and effort than are retrospective studies. Their expense is one of the major reasons for conducting retrospective research: It is more practical.

What about criterion 3 in Table 1? A paragraph from the report addresses this issue:

> *It should also be noted that there are many other studies of dynamic therapy that do not qualify as providing efficacy evidence based on the criteria that we have applied. These studies were mostly conducted before the advent of treatment manuals. With dynamic therapy in particular, the use of treatment manuals is crucial to accomplish some degree of treatment specification. This is because the dynamic rubric encompasses a wide range of treatments and because therapists of various styles and levels of training characterize themselves as dynamically oriented. Thus, for studies of dynamic therapy in which no treatment manual was used there is a real question about what therapy was actually delivered by each of the participating therapists. In light of the large number of APA members who practice psychodynamic psychotherapy, in the interest of the profession and the public, we conclude that it is critical that more efficacy evidence on the outcome of psychodynamic therapies for specific disorders be obtained if this clinically verified treatment is to survive in today's market.* (APA, 1993, p. 2)

My response is that the use of a training manual seems antithetical to the practice of Jungian analysis. As Jung himself was so fond of pointing out, it is the personality of the analyst rather than the technique he or she employs that makes the crucial contribution for success in analysis. What the treatment manual does is attempt to eliminate or at least reduce the personality of the analyst through "standardization and precise definition of treatment."

In 1992 I initiated a new research effort at the San Francisco Jung Institute with the help of Wayne Detloff, Hal Batt, Cathy Skarica and the Institute clinic's six psychology interns. All new patients in the clinic are invited to participate in the research project and fill out the current, widely-used Symptom Check List-90 (SCL-90) and the Inventory of Interpersonal Problems (IIP) at intake, after every six-months interval of therapy, at termination, and during follow-up (six months, one year, two years, and five years after termination). A specially designed intake form is administered during intake only. So far, we have collected intake data on 13 patients and six-month therapy data on three patients. Now that the procedures have been tested and refined, we anticipate adding at least 20 new patients to the research project during the next year.

In the future, the project will be extended in three directions: 1) Seasoned Jungian analysts will be recruited to participate; 2) True randomized clinical trials or quasi-experiments will be designed by adding control and comparison groups aimed at establishing the empirical validity of Jungian analysis; and 3) Instruments pertaining to Jungian analysis will be designed and tested. We are developing an instrument to measure Capacity for Symbolization and one to measure Individuation. We intend to include the perspective of the analyst as well as the perspective of a qualified third-party (perhaps another analyst), thereby approaching the ideal of the multitrait-multimethod matrix approach set forth by Campbell and Fiske (1957). The creation of a treatment manual for Jungian analysis is a true open question, one that I hope we can examine more substantially in the future.

References

American Psychological Association (1993). Report of the Task Force on Promotion and Dissemination of Psychological Procedures, adopted by the Divison 12 Board.

Bergin, A. & Garfield, S., Eds. (1994). *Handbook of Psychotherapy and Behavior Change* (4th ed.). New York: John Wiley & Sons.

Campbell, D.T. & Fiske, D.W. (1959). Convergent and discriminant validation by the multitrait-multimethod matrix. *Psychological Bulletin, 56,* 81-105.

Henry, W.; Strupp, H.; Schacht, T.; Gaston, L. (1994). Psychodynamic approaches. In Bergin & Garfield (1994).

Kazdin, A. (1994). Methodology, evaluation and design in psychotherapy research. In Bergin & Garfield (1994).

Kazdin, A.& Bass, D. (1989). Power to detect differences between alternative treatments in comparative psychotherapy research. *Journal of Consulting and Clinical Psychology, 57,* 729-758.

Lambert, M. & Bergin, A. (1994). The effectiveness of psychotherapy. In Bergin & Garfield (1994).

Richter, R; Hartman, A; Meyer, A.; Rüger, U. (1994). Die Kränkesten gehen in eine psychoanalytische Behandlung? Kritische Anmerkung zu einem Artikel in Report Psychologie. Zeitschrift. für psychosomatische Medizin, *40,* 41-51.

Schepank, H. (1987). *Psychogene Erkrankungen der Stadtbevölkerung: Eine Epidemiologische Feldstudie in Mannheim.* Heidelberg/New York: Springer.

Silverman, D. (1981). The child as social object: Downs syndrome children in a paediatric cardiology clinic. *Sociology of Health and Illness, 3-3,* 254-274.

Couples, Families and Groups

Systems Theory and Jungian Psychotherapy

Paula Pantoja Boechat
Rio de Janeiro, Brazil
Jungian Association of Brazil

Family therapy began in the 1950s – in Palo Alto, California, USA. A group of researchers from the Mental Research Institute (MRI), were seeking to understand the etiology of schizophrenia. They thought of initiating a study of family interactions and found that Bertalanffy (1933) had formulated some principles that seemed to be universal and applicable to several different systems, whether biological, physico-chemical or of a diverse nature.

The Palo Alto group – composed at first mainly by Bateson, Jackson, Haley and Weakland and later including Watzlavik and Beavin – developed Family Systems Theory. This theory uses for understanding the human system the same principles described as responsible for the regulation of every other system, including the cybernetic one.

But what is this we are now calling a system? The simplest definition of a system is an ordained composition of elements in a unified body separated from the rest of the world by recognizable boundaries. Systems theory as applied to the family holds, for example, that the family as a whole behaves differently from the sum of its individual members. The theory also describes some laws that govern the processing and storing of information: the adaptability, the capability for self-organization and the development of strategies for the behavior of the system. If there is any change in one element of a system, the whole system will be changed. The behavior of one person within a family is therefore dependent upon the behavior of the other members.

Thus, whatever causes a modification in one member will modify the family as a whole. Similar to any other system, the family is the origin of its own modifications. In this respect, systems theory holds that it would be too simple to say that one anorexic episode, for example, could be explained only in terms of past experiences of one person. It is necessary to understand the system where this symptom arose. It belongs to the whole system and not only to one of its "elements," the "identified patient."

This element is expressing a symptom that has connections with the past; it has a psychodynamic explanation. But in systems theory it is a matter of concern to find out what function this specific symptom has in the homeostasis of the whole family. The family tends to stability, through processes of feedback that can be activated when there is an intent of change.

Behavior is a reaction to rules imposed by an individual's family group, usually unconscious rules. Through communication the members of a family transmit and receive information and behaviors. It is impossible not to communicate. Even when you do not answer a question that was posed to you, you are communicating. The equilibrium of the system is established, not always in ideal terms of healthier relationships, but in terms of adaptability to the environment.

Systemic Homeostasis and Jungian Homeostasis

When Jung says that the Self promotes a compensation in the psyche, he makes a systemic statement. The Self can be seen as an inner spirit that has the function of organizing the individual in a self-regulating and relatively closed system of psychic energy. Jung understood the neurotic or psychotic symptom as having a teleological intention in the individuation process and a homeostatic effect on the person's psychic energy. Thus the Self, the archetype of the supraordinate personality within us, is always sending messages (communicating) in the direction of our individuation process, of our psychic health.

In systems theory there is not such a guiding structure; in the search for homeostasis all elements of the system participate equally. In the individuation process, Jung sees a hierarchy between Self and ego, with the Self leading the ego to a healthier homeostasis. In systems theory, in which all the elements search for homeostasis, sometimes the illness of a family is the attained homeostasis.

Systems theory maintains that the illness of a person intends to bring homeostasis to the whole family system, but also assert that such an identified patient incarnates the possibility of redemption for the whole group. Therefore, both the neurotic or psychotic symptom in an individual, and the identified patient in a family carry the same teleological meaning. According to systems theory, groups of people – couples, families and even psychotherapeutic relationships – can be viewed as feedback circuits. The behavior of each person affects and is affected by the behavior of every other; anything someone tells someone else about him or herself is connected to the relationship existing between them. Whenever we cannot answer why there was a behavior, the question should be changed to what for; a clearer answer is likely to emerge. This is true for system theory and also for analytical psychology.

Jung tells us that the psychotherapeutic relationship, too – viewed from the standpoint of the therapist – is not neutral. The therapist perceives, understands and is affected by the world through the psyche and its subjectivity. The alchemical retort, where two substances react to each other to promote a final transformation, is a metaphor of the therapeutic relationship.

Thus, countertransference plays a very important role in the therapeutic system, and is one of the most important sources of knowledge. When people are involved in an intimate relationship, they share characteristics. This can occur knowingly in the projective identification or in an unconscious communication. There exists no clear way to know where I end and you begin. In the language of quantum physics: "The macroscopic systems are always related in their microscopic states" (Zohar, 1990, p. 169). Similarly, we can understand the contagious aspects of the unconscious within families, when the speech of one member reveals non-expressed thoughts of the whole group.

Also, we can understand how Jung describes a dream he had which showed him his countertransference and revealed to him much about his patient. When Jung dreamed of this patient, she represented an aspect of himself, which also belongs to the patient. Jung writes: "The patient, by bringing an activated unconscious content to bear upon the doctor, constellates the corresponding unconscious material in him. ... Contents are often activated in the doctor which might normally remain latent" (CW16, par. 364). This statement has many connections with the new idea of constructivism in systems theory, which I shall discuss later.

According to systems theory, the input in a given system can be amplified and bring about change or can be neutralized to maintain an old stability. In the former case, the feedback mechanisms are positive; in the latter they are negative. From this hypothesis derives the strategic therapy.

Strategic therapy is directive, consistent with the principles of cybernetics; it is – like systemic therapy – a derivation of communication theory and a clear plan of action. This plan is goal-oriented, directed toward the particular behavior game the family is playing. By employing directive intervention methods, the therapist tries to clarify the problematic aspects of the family's interactional rules. Reinforcing the symptom – amplifying the problem – the strategic therapist is convinced that he or she feeds the system back in a positive fashion, thus forcing it to change. This strategy brings good results but also the idea that the therapist can predict the results and provoke the change.

In my experience, pursuant to constructivist therapy, the strategics went back, thus, to linearity or causality. The therapist who does something specific will provoke the patient (or the system) to react by making a specific change. (There is always a direct or indirect suggestion.) The illusion of power – that knowledge of the function of the communication promotes the change – brings some therapists to a sense of "omnipotence." This theory is called "first order cybernetics."

The Concept of Double Bind

Studies of families with a schizophrenic element have allowed for the conclusion that the emergence and maintenance of such an ill element is essential for the stability of the system. Further, researchers came to the conclusion that the system will react quickly and efficiently to any internal or external attempt to change the organization. Thus is maintained a negative but stable homeostasis. Where we try to understand a certain family's dynamics, we must pay attention to its communications.

Psychosis can be seen as an incurable and progressive disease of an individual's mind, or as the only possible reaction within a context of communication: a reaction that obeys and perpetuates the rules of that communication. According to systems theory, if there is a schizophrenic element in a family, it has a very typical way of communication: "double bind" communication. Bateson and others (1956) describe it as follows: 1) At least two people are necessary with one of them as victim; 2) The experience occurs many times in a long-term relationship with that person; 3) One negative primary communication is given; 4) A secondary communication that contradicts the previous one is given also; 5) A third communication which forbids the victim to escape the field occurs. Eventually it becomes no longer necessary to have the victim exposed to those five steps. This person has now learned to perceive his or her universe in double bind patterns.

Later, this double bind description was changed in terms of people caught up in a communication or "in an ongoing system which produces conflicting definitions of the relationship and subsequent subject distress" (Bateson et al., 1962). The terms now are not victim and victimizer, and the phenomenon of double bind is seen as more systemic. There is not a schizophrenogenic pole against the schizophrenic one. More clearly defined, the communication is schizophrenic and the most fragile link of the chain shows the illness of the group.

The way to escape a double bind situation is to comment on the discrepancy of the binding messages; that is, to metacommunicate. Metacommunication occurs when we communicate about communication, to define the relational sense of the message. The metacommunication is the shadow of the communication; if there is no place for shadow, there is double bind and there is illness.

Students of systems theory found eventually that double bind situations are found not only in schizophrenia, but also in humorous or paradoxical situations. Double bind can be source of creativity as well as pathology. Bateson (1972) and Wynne (1976) clarify the creative aspect of the double bind. Individuals whose lives are enriched by double bind and those who are confused by it have something in common: They adopt a double perspective.

In psychotherapy, if we can only perceive and clarify the hidden aspect of what is told or felt, we are not accepting transcontextuality. Yet Jung was always able to understand and clarify to the patient not only what was told and felt but also the multiplicity of transcontextual truth hidden in a symbol. In symbols we can see many faces, polarities, shadow and light, positive and negative perspectives.

As the double bind was first described, it conveyed the impression that it was synchronous. But not to be forgotten is the repetition of the experience through time: double bind bringing, for example, disease or creativity, as well as therapeutic use of double bind. But the therapist must be conscious of the transference-countertransference double bind, to avoid being confused and paralyzed in the work. Thus, once more, it is important for us to understand and recognize the shadow aspects of transference and countertransference.

If we were not so concerned to have a single truth for the family's or the patient's situation, we would not need to interpret everything as resistance. If we so interpret, we give the patient the message that we want to help but we also want him or her to remain ill. That is a paralyzing double bind message.

"Reciprocal double bind" was described by Jay Haley in the schizophrenic family. Elkaim (1990) brings this concept to the understanding of couples' relationships. These double bind situations correspond to an internal coherence of the system; it is a choice the couple makes, to maintain the homeostasis of their marriage.

Elkaim uses the term "official program" (OP) to describe what each member of the couple wants to receive from or to be changed in the other member, and "map of the world" (MW) to describe the marks that each member of the couple has earned in the past. This map is present in the member's psyche, influencing his or her attitudes.

An example is found in the marriage relationship of some Olympic gods. Zeus and Hera, as we know, had a very difficult marriage relationship. Hera was faithful to Zeus; this faithfulness was expressed clearly in the fact that she found fulfillment only in her relationship with him. In the Greek myth she is called Teleia, "perfect one." She attained her perfection in marriage. Zeus, on the other hand, was called Teleios, "the bringer to perfection" (Kerényi, 1975, pp. 96-98). Zeus was never faithful to his wife, a fact that provoked her revengeful attitudes against his lovers and their off-spring.

Their ancestral family began with Cronus – the father of Zeus and Hera – who used to devour the children from his marriage with Rhea, as soon as they were born. Rhea decided to ally herself with their younger son, Zeus. She gave Cronus a stone to eat in lieu of Zeus, saving him and thus destroying her marriage with Cronus.

Hera was doomed to be faithful because she was afraid to repeat her mother's behavior and, by so doing, destroy her own marriage. Zeus was unfaithful, to avoid the destiny of his father Chronus, who was faithful but was betrayed by his wife. Also, when Zeus was unfaithful, he was obedient to the role his mother gave him to play.

Also important for us to know is the way Zeus and Hera fell in love. Slater (1971) tells us that when Zeus perceives himself "unable to win [Hera] directly, he resorts to a stratagem. ... He decides to take advantage of her maternal instincts ... by assuming the disguise of a cuckoo suffering from the winter winds, which Hera warms at her bosom. He then resumes his true shape and ravishes her. Thus it is not through any masculine aggressiveness or sexual irresistibleness that Zeus becomes Lord of Hera, but through a childlike appeal" (p. 131).

Zeus was the great "Don Juan" of Olympus. Yet he only showed how frightened he was of women and of being betrayed. The relationship that threatened him least is the one with Hera. He knew she was unable to be unfaithful to him. But even then, he avoided getting too near her and kept running away. Zeus was afraid to envision his mother in the faces of the women he related to, but still he kept looking for her. Thus, in Zeus' OP he wanted to be loved as a husband, but in his MW he had the blueprint that women could love only their children.

Hera, in her OP wanted the guarantee that Zeus was always going to be her husband, but at the same time she knew, through her MW, that the relationship which brings safety is the one between mother and son.

What makes the reciprocal double bind so frequent in marriage relationships is the "matching" of the members' OPs and MWs. I observe this matching very often in my psychotherapeutic practice.

Pseudomutuality

Another interesting concept in systems theory is pseudomutuality, described by Wynne and others (1958). Pseudomutuality is a miscarried solution for the people who are striving for relatedness and for identity. These authors point out three kinds of relationship: mutuality, non-mutuality and pseudo-mutuality.

Mutuality corresponds to the relationship between people when there is a recognition and acceptance of changing role assignments; individual differences are welcomed to enrich the relationship. This is a rare condition.

Pseudomutuality is found mainly in psychotic families. In these families, there is a major necessity of adaptation to the group, in contrast to the differentiation of each person. Here, any movement of independence or any open assertion of a feeling of personal identity provokes anxiety at unmanageable closeness or distance. Even when there is no psychotic element, these families generally lack spontaneity, creativity and humor, and have rigid boundaries with regard to the external world.

Nonmutuality is a relationship wherein there is no emotional involvement, such as is typical between a seller and a buyer in a shop. If the encounter comes to take more time and personal involvement, it becomes mutual or pseudomutual.

For Wynne and his co-workers, schizophrenia is the result of a failure to develop an individual ego, clear and stable; this failure is related to a deficiency in the family relationship. The role assignments or the expectations that elements in a family have toward one another are not, in themselves, schizophrenogenic. The expectations are healthy when there is flexibility in their being projected, integrated, reprojected, worked through and modified according to the needs of the family members and not only the needs of the family as a whole.

It is the denial of individual differences that makes a family pathological, or one of its members ill. In Jungian terms, each individual's persona (or role assignment) and each individual shadow must constantly be made conscious and worked through in the family relationship, if one wants to relate mutually and develop in the individuation process. If loss of individuality occurs, either through fusion with or absorption by stronger organisms, the family and the individuals are sick.

Each step toward individuation demands communication and negotiation. It is necessary to have individuality, but at the same time solidarity and mutuality.

Mutuality, Individuation Process and Related Individuation

In the Heidelberg Family Therapy Institute (Simon, 1984), the concept of "related individuation" was developed. The concept refers to the ability to differentiate each person's internal world into clear communications about needs, expectations, feelings and perceptions. The internal world of each element must exist in a highly differentiated way, but must also be marked off from the ideas, expectations and demands of the others. The degree of related individuation shows the degree of mutuality or pseudomutuality existing in a relationship.

For Jung, individuation means becoming a single, homogeneous and unique human being. As he put it: "Only what we really are has the power to cure us" (CW7, par. 281). I believe that there is no such thing as individuation of the family as a group, but only individuation of its members. The relationship of the Self and each individual ego is something that happens intrapsychically and expresses itself extrapsychically. Nevertheless, the influence of the environment, mainly of the family, is important because it can ease or confuse the search for individuation. There may be a conflict, more or less acute, between the roles lived by each member of the family and the appeals of the process of individuation, the appeals of the Self. In the pseudomutual family there is an effort to adapt to the script determined by the relations within the family, instead of an effort for individual differentiation.

For me it is important to understand the individual and the system. I believe parts of the individual belong to the family system, and parts of the system belong to the individual. Once I have a systemic perception of the individual, I understand more clearly when a transformation in the patient has a good or bad homeostatic response from the family.

Constructivism

In individual therapy, the therapist must be conscious of the therapist-patient system; the therapist is not a mere observer but a co-participant in building the reality. The observer becomes part of the observed.

Constructivism is a new school of systems theory that places itself against traditional epistemologies which say that cognition is the expression of a reality that exists independently of the observer. Constructivism says that any observation about reality is primarily a statement about the observer. The subject-object split is no longer important. Rather, constructivism views cognition as an aspect of interaction. This new theory is now called "second order cybernetics."

Life develops through processes of learning. Systems are organized in ways that clarify an interactional domain in which the quest for survival can be pursued. In this way, we can see living systems as cognizing systems and life as a process of cognition. (See Maturana, 1978).

The first wave – or first order – cybernetics has been focused on systems' maintaining their organization. It is based on the assumption that the observed can be considered as separate from the observer.

The second wave – second order cybernetics or constructivism – is focused on systems' changing their organization. It includes the observer's role in constructing the reality that is being observed. Maturana (1978) brought to us some important elements to explain the constructivist theory:

1. The concept of structural coupling says that what comes to be does so in the intersection of a specific system and an environment. Thus, it is impossible to describe any therapeutic situation without knowing that we are included in it.

2. That which really matters in psychotherapy, touching the therapist and constellating change, is the intersection of the world maps of the therapist and the patient.

3. In psychotherapy it is not truth or reality that matters, but the mutual construction of reality. Different couplings bring about different but compatible worlds. Thus, there is not only one possible solution, but multiple solutions connected to the relationship between the members of the therapeutic system (therapist and family, or therapist and individual).

Resonance

With these explanations in mind, we come to the concept of resonance. (See Elkaim, 1990.) Resonance manifests itself in a situation where the same rule is applicable to the patient's family, to the therapist's family of origin, to the institution where the patient is received, to the supervision group, and so on. Thus, resonance is made of similar elements that are common to different systems that inter-relate.

We can see that Elkaim must be talking about something that Jung described as synchronicity. When I reminded you of Jung's dream with his patient, I was talking about synchronicity. There we could see an aspect of the patient that was part of Jung's psyche. Synchronicity, as we know, cannot be understood in terms of classical physics, but only in terms of quantum physics. Here the elementary particle can be wave and particle simultaneously, depending on the observer's position.

As Zohar (1990) writes, "Like the elementary particle's system, we too (our characters, our beings) are quantum systems. ... The quantum self in its particle aspect reveals a very significant individual integrity and nevertheless, through its wave aspect, reveals itself simultaneously in relationship with culture as a whole. This gives us a structure for personal identity and personal responsibility, but at the same time for the intimacy and group identity" (p. 169).

References

Bateson, G. (1972). *Steps to an Ecology of the Mind*. New York: Ballantine Books.

Bateson, G.; Jackson, D.; Haley, J.; and Weakland, J. (1956). Towards a theory of schizophrenia. *Behavioral Science, 1*, 251-264.

Bateson, G.; Jackson, D.; Haley, J.; and Weakland, J. (1962). A note on the double bind. *Family Process 2*, 157- 161.

Bertalanffy, L. von (1933). *Modern Theories of Development*. London: Oxford University Press.

Elkaim, M. (1990). *Se Voce Me Ama, Nao Me Ame: Abordagem Sistêmica em Psicoterapia Familiar e Conjugal*. Campinas/São Paulo: Editora Papirus.

Kerényi, C. (1975). *Zeus and Hera: Archetypal Image of Father, Husband and Wife*. Bollingen Series, *LXV*- 5. Princeton, NJ: Princeton University Press.

Maturana, H. (1978). Biology of language: The epistemology of reality. In G. Miller and E. Lennenberg (Eds.), *Psychology and Biology of Language and Thought*. New York: Academic Press.

Simon, F. (1984). *Der Prozess der Individuation: Über den Zusammenhang von Vernunft und Gefühlen*. Gottingen: Vanderhock & Ruprecht.

Slater, P. (1971). *The Glory of Hera: Greek Mythology and the Greek Family*. Boston: Beacon Press.

Wynne, L. (1976). On the anguish and creative passions of not escaping double-binds: A reformulation. In C.E. Sluzki & D.C. Ransom (Eds.), *Double-bind: The Foundations of the Communicational Approach to the Family*. New York: Grune & Stratton.

Wynne, L.; Ryckoff, J.; Day, J.; Hirsch, S. (1958). Pseudomutuality in the family relations of Schizophrenies. *Psychiatry, 21*, 205-220.

Zohar, D. (1990). *O Ser Quântico*. São Paulo, Editora Best Seller.

I Love You, Let's Separate

Michel Cautaerts
Brussels, Belgium
Belgium Society of Analytical Psychology

Why talk about the couple? Because some people do not want, or do not need, individual help. Because analysis affects the couple. Because there is sometimes synergism between marital therapy and individual therapy. And finally, because in order to be able to enter a commitment with a partner we must stop projecting the peculiarities of the unconscious onto his or her unfamiliarity. To stop such projecting we must go to the origin of our fears and recognize – if we can, without being petrified or paralyzed – the figures of the gods, of the primordial forces, the archetypes constellated by the relationship.

If a man is fleeing a woman, and if the woman is hesitant when faced with the man, it is Nyx – black night – and her daughter Thanatos that they are both more afraid of than each other. These strange figures are projected onto the unfamiliar, the other sex. Is it because Nyx is the mother of a lineage that seems to have refused to develop toward greater awareness? Who does not feel perturbed before the most terrible of couples, Life and Death?

From the view of the unconscious, the couple is an archetype, a matrix that preforms meaning. One of these ancient figurations is syzygy, the conjunction-opposition of the sun and moon. Somewhere between pathological dissociation and creative dissociation the couple is connected with the pressure of the unconscious on the conscious and the compensation of that pressure by cohesive forces.

We are concerned with four couples: the parental couple, the "life couple," the internal couple – which becomes conscious only gradually – and the transferential couple. In research on the couple there are inevitably areas where these four merge or overlap, similarly to marital life. The transferential couple and the internal couple are the main themes of Jung's work. I shall discuss the life couple but not the parental couple.

The Life Couple

Conscious Development and the Personal Unconscious

Partly conscious, partly unconscious, the couple holds the life of the mind and the life of the body together. The future partners recognize each other by reading each other's conscious and unconscious. The relationship will endure only if their unconscious is animated and if the archetypes interact.

In order to enter a relationship the partners practice courtship; they orient themselves in relation to each other, eliminating what does not please or what they think cannot appeal. These exclusions constitute the courtship shadow. Initially, the couple's complementarity is based on the structures of consciousness: gender identity, psychological types. These structures, in effect, create the typological shadow.

The couple builds a conscious contract that defines the couple's territory and modes of operation, and is connected with psychological types and defenses against the unconscious. Conscious contracts are an amalgam of the personal and family ideas and habits of each of the partners and of gender stereotypes. When a couple seeks counseling, this contract is called into question.

It is in the couple that our "soul incarnate" is put to the test. Each partner creates meaning on the basis of the emotions and sensations he or she experiences daily. The incarnation of the one comes up against the different incarnation of the other: a different way of qualifying perceptions and using them to form a world view. The meaning the individual sees will be colored by the trials of previous relational experiences and, ultimately, by the relationship with the mother.

One aspect of incarnation is bodily: sensations that are accepted or desired, bodily pleasures and habits. The other aspect of incarnation is the way in which certain archetypes – puer-senex, for instance – influence us more than others.

After a while the repressed contents in each partner begin to exert pressure. Repressed material is usually not far removed from consciousness; the couple can talk about it. It is the genealogical shadow that intervenes here, made up of all the instances where families of origin have interfered.

We work on this shadow with recollections of the parents. One good technique is to use the classical genogram (genealogical diagram) or, better, the "landscape genogram." In the latter (Pluymaekers & Neve-Hanquet, 1992), the clients draw up a creative picture of their families: highlighting the myths, false secrets, habits and influences. This method also reveals defects in symbolization dating from previous generations and occurring as archetypal imagoes or instances of acting-out in the following generation. The "projective shadow of the couple" is akin to the mechanism of projective identification; it is composed of the elements that the partners have split and deposited in the couple and that have been "petrified" and immobilized by archaic defense mechanisms.

As a containing partner develops, he or she manifests the content which the other partner has projected onto him or her. The archaic defenses of the projecting partner play a role. If that partner has dissociated, he or she has done so for the sake of survival and forming an ego. The projecting partner does not know how to reintegrate what has been projected. The containing partner is faced with the choice of continuing to serve as container or destabilizing the projecting partner.

The Vicissitudes of the Normal Developmental Process of the Couple

One partner may want the other to continue to carry the projection of being only a parent. Sometimes the mother of renewal (mixture of mother and anima) is projected with the wish that the spouse contain the dissociated state. For example, a man who could not understand what was disturbing him told his wife that her womb was "a cemetery." He was expressing an inverted, blunt wish for rebirth.

The problem of guilt and shame is the inability to come to terms with one's shadow. The shadow can be projected onto the partner: The projecting partner takes command in order to control the other and avoid the confrontation. If the dangerous parts of the Self are projected into the other and cannot be reintegrated without dissociation, the other becomes the scapegoat. Sometimes the animus or anima takes possession of the ego of one of the partners. And finally, the partners may cling to the couple in order to avoid loneliness. Tisseron (1992) says that it is impossible to confront this situation if there has been no mother to whom the child could cling.

The partners make decisions which, at best, lead to sacrifices – relinquishing certain values for higher values – and, at worst, will lead to mutilations. When they sacrifice part of themselves on the altar of the couple, the underlying motive is often to allow the neurosis or the splits to persist.

A new and more rigid "conscious contract" is established. Any changes one might wish to make will come up against archaic defenses. There are several possible solutions: 1) The couple live on common ground; 2) They become fixated in collusions (Willi, 1982), obeying an established system so that each partner can avoid being confronted with what has been split. (One of the two, or indeed both, may live outside the couple, a situation that is unbearable for the other partner.); 3) The relationship breaks down because the containing partner ceases to contain.

Jean Van Eyck's work, *Arnolfini Wedding* (Fig. 1) depicts, at first sight, an ordinary couple. But it conceals and – in the mirror – reveals a different problem: the reflection of another, unconscious couple in the mirror of the relationship. Jung quotes *Cantilena Riplae*:

> The Mother's bed which erstwhile was a Square
> Is shortly after made Orbicular
> And everywhere the Cover, likewise Round
> With Luna's Lustre brightly did abound. (CW14, par.438)

Life Couple and/or Internal Couple?

A further stage can occur in the couple's relationship, giving rise to an inversion of forces and problems. As Humbert (1983) says: "It can happen that the action of the anima and animus becomes unbearable and re-triggers the questioning, which then relates to the nature of the forces with which the ego is identifying; the result is the recognition that those forces are collective in nature" (p. 128). Movements suddenly occur that complicate the relationship. The partners do not understand and are disoriented. Their points of reference concerning their identities – one of which is the couple – disappear for a while. Archetypes have been constellated, and it becomes necessary for the partners to detach themselves from the roles they induce.

The atmosphere changes. The shadow was relatively precise, but here matters are blurred: the territory of mood and affect in the case of the anima and of rigid opinions in the case of the animus. The relationship seems to have lost its meaning. The partners may get caught up in endless quarreling, but they are unable either to separate or to stay together. The ego must detach itself from its

Figure 1

identification with the archetypes in order to acquire more flexibility and freedom. The psychoid is animated. The interplay of the interaction, overlap of the individual shadows and the animus/anima figures is what we call the psychoid shadow of the couple or the archetypal shadow.

Working Hypothesis

The shadows of the couple, especially the projective shadow and the psychoid shadow, are inaccessible or accessible only with difficulty in individual therapy. To become apparent, they require the physical presence of both partners at the session. The psychoid shadow of the couple is particularly dense and often can be perceived by the partners only with the help of an experienced third person.

If the partners identify with the archetypes, the life couple becomes an archetypal couple, in which the roles take over the partners, so to speak. They suffer in their incarnation since the "body of the gods" is different from our own bodies. Further, one cannot talk to someone who is identified with the archetype.

How can one bring about differentiation? By identifying what is redundant; a certain interaction's inducing – without the intervention of consciousness – a certain role such as the warrior, the witch, the princess, the king. Young-Eisendrath (1993) has developed this approach.

Once triggered, the role exhausts the energy. It is not possible to talk about it; the body is implicated in the partner's reaction. Narcissistic equilibrium is affected each time, and the subject feels tricked, no longer allowed to speak, going through a nightmare, or playing an absurd role.

If the partners can differentiate these dictated roles, they can distinguish among an archetypal dramatization – connected with an unconscious identification and flaws in the incarnations of the previous generation – an effort to seek meaning, and a defense against the frightening archetype.

If the partners detach themselves from their identifications, what was experienced as biological fertility becomes an effort on the part of both partners to renew both themselves and their relationship. The creative process is resumed through the work on projections. The couple will continue to exist only if this work promotes renewal. The progressive integration of the internal couple and the life couple is necessary, prompting the partners to travel the road of development many, many times.

In the first part of life the body is an object of pleasure or a tool for living. In the second part of life it is a source of information.

Marital Therapy Practice

> *People want to be loved? Not so. They want to be preferred. ... It is terrible, because you are asking a companion to be at the service of your wounded narcissism, and that really is not what he, or she, is there for.* (Humbert, 1994, p. 25)

The Session Procedure and the Couples' Questions

I see couples for about ten sessions of one hour each. My purpose is to identify the shadows and enable the partners to perceive them. Each partner seems to want to be preferred by the therapist, to form a couple with him or her. To acquiesce would be to create perverted triangles, as described by Hochmann (1971). To refuse is inappropriate. The therapist can refer this behavior to the following three questions, which couples ask.

1. The partners want to be helped to understand: communicating, clarifying confusions of attitudes – extraverted or introverted – and of functions.

2. They want to know what is at issue between them: who or what takes over the relational sphere of the couple. Family imagoes? Intrusions in the name of the law of blood ties? The question is on the borderline between this complex of problems and another: What are the couple's implicit contracts?

3. The couple want to know what is dictating their roles. The answer is the archetypes. Every therapist has a frame of reference for obtaining a clear picture of the principles involved: invariable protocol (Caillé, 1991); collusions (Willi, 1982); Greek mythology as the figurative, internal representation of the archetypes, my preferred framework.

This internal frame of reference enables the therapist to identify the specificities of the discrepancies between the real couple and the archetypal couple. The symbolic language of the partners is respected in the therapist's formulations. A clinical example is the case of two young people who have been living together for two years and are separating. They are unable to commit themselves. Their relationship has been one of two children who shared the same fear of being deserted or trapped. Through analysis the woman discovers incest in her childhood. She has known about it, but has been unable to face it. Eventually she dreams that *she vomits black matter*. She is thus vomiting the shame of what happened to her, which left images of men colored by a Chronus who was arresting her life and her development.

The Themes

Two of the themes that couples bring are the child and the parents. The *child* is an overdetermined symbol. 1) The partners feel like children in the presence of the therapist. 2) The partners are children of the previous generation. 3) Their actual children put pressure on the couple to live without pretence, or are "parentified" and sometimes even determine the couple's sexual behavior. 4) The split of the original child, promulgated by the parents in the past and maintained by the unconscious couple, must be remedied. 5) The puer aeternus manifests in both its aspects: refusal to develop – to make the sacrifice required when one reaches adulthood and sexual initiation – and the evolution of new forces mobilized by the individuation drive. A clinical example:

Anne is separated from her husband. The man she met at happy gatherings has become cold and distant since they married. He reasons with her but shares none of her emotions. When he says that he adores his daughter, there is no discernible feeling in his words; this is a maneuver aimed at making Anne – who has left him – feel guilty. He wants power and nothing else. He talks about seeing her again only because she is the stake in the contest with the new man in her life. As long as he could regard his wife as empty-headed, he felt secure. She was entertaining, "like a puppy." But now that she has acquired a sense of freedom, he cannot stand it. In response to her vivaciousness and freshness, her husband – who has aged before his time – never misses an opportunity to lecture her or to keep reproachfully silent.

The theme of the *parents* is governed by a different law from the couple. The family falls within the province of kinship bonds, the couple only within that of commitment. To what extent can a man and a woman sever the bonds of kinship, fusion and identification that have united them with their parents? What vengeance will they bring upon themselves? Where are they to place themselves between the law of kinship and the law of commitment? Since mythological times humans have recalled the struggle between solemn oaths and the evaluation of circumstances. In the couple, solemn assertions mask unquestioned family beliefs.

A genealogical shadow is connected with the families from which the partners have come. For example, Romeo seems dominated by sensations, which he demands in grandiloquent discourse. Juliet, a feeling type, gives precedence to the relationship, especially since this is her second marriage. Unconsciously, Romeo is still tied to his mother. Juliet has a cold mother and an infantile father. Romeo's archaic intuitions make him suspicious of his wife to the point of accusing her of lesbianism if she has a woman friend. Juliet does not dare to use her objective reasoning to put an end to these accusations. The father's absence – an accustomed state for Juliet – and possession by the mother for Romeo are understood by neither partner. When Juliet is reprimanded, she thinks she is facing a father; actually she is facing a demanding son-lover, who wants to impose a model of femininity on her. In Anne's case, there is no parental couple in the partners' original families. Both partners went through analysis, but were unable to break the vicious circles in their relationship.

In *Hommage à Appollinaire* (Fig. 2), Chagall shows us a modern illustration of a timeless and androgynous couple. Their bodies are joined and form wings. The world is represented by the figures and letters on the clockface. The nocturnal opens at the bottom of the painting. The colors and the inscription are reminiscent of those of Van Eyck. Has development prompted what was in the center of the mirror in Van Eyck to emerge in Chagall?

Archetypal Points of Reference

The first archetypal point of reference consists of primordial forces: Chaos, Gaea, Chthon, Nyx, Eros. These forces underlie the psychoid and accompany its emergence. Chaos: chasm, opening, cleft; the fear of heights. Earth (Gaea) and her three layers: the upper layer, which bears crops; the middle layer (chthon), which holds the dead; the deepest layer, night (Nyx). Eros or, rather, the two Eroses: 1) the original Eros, which prompts the primordial forces to produce what they contain within themselves; 2) the rational Eros, who accompanies Aphrodite after the castration of Uranus.

Figure 2

Ramnoux (1959) writes that there are three forms of dread that correspond to Gaea's layers: 1) the dread of being let go, without support; 2) the dread of density, of the tenacity of the rock that holds roots and of the clay that holds the dead, the obsessive fear of being buried alive or clutched by jaws; 3) the dread of insubstantiality and of smoke, the dread of falling into a bottomless pit or of being buffeted by the winds. (Psychologically, the terrors and fascination of confusion, the dread of being unable to grasp a firm hold which Tisseron, 1992, has named as the source of shame.)

The second archetypal point of reference is the generation of the gods. Theogonies such as Hesiod's (1953) are full of images of evolution representing the archetypal roots of the genealogical shadow. Gaea – Earth – produces a companion of like stature:

Uranus, the starry Sky. He does nothing but beget children who never leave Gaea's womb. Hesiod (1953) says:

> *After these came cunning Chronus, the youngest and boldest of her children; and he grew to hate the father who had begotten him. ... Sky took pleasure in doing this evil thing. In spite of her enormous size, Earth felt the strain within her and groaned. Finally she thought of an evil and cunning stratagem. She instantly produced a new metal, gray steel, and made a huge sickle. ...* [Chronus seizes the sickle and castrates his father. Aphrodite is born of Uranus: sperm and blood, mixed with the foam of the barren sea, Pontos.] *"Aphrodite ... a goddess tender and beautiful, and round her slender feet the green grass shot up. ... Eros [Desire] and beautiful Passion were her attendants."* (Lines 137-201)

Chronus, in turn, swallows the children he begets with his sister Rhea. Rhea hides their last-born, Zeus, who enters into conflict with Chronus and finally defeats him. In order to ensure his power, Zeus then swallows Metis, a woman who uses ruse and cunning.

The series of fantasies that haunt families and groups, as Bejarano (1974) has described, is endless: devouring, dismemberment, joined parents, oral and anal primal scene alongside incest, murder, theft and struggles for power. We find exclusion and inclusion, from the mother's womb to the father's belly, from the mantle of the family to that of society.

These archetypal figures correspond to the energies that possess men and women. They also illustrate the non-integrated masculine, the archaic animus, the unconscious feminine, the narcissistic anima.

The third archetypal point of reference is The Zeus (Metis)-Hera-Ares-Aphrodite quaternion. Ares is the only son of Hera and Zeus, who hate him; he springs from the shadow of the Olympians. There is no cold distance or ruse plotted in secret. Nor is there any territory; that is reserved for Poseidon, Hades and Zeus. A dancer and warrior, Ares is energy, fire, enterprise, ardor, immediate and impetuous presence. A rebel, he is the only one to denounce iniquity in order to defend his children. Devoid of cunning, he sometimes falls prey to the hubris of the poltroon who defeats him, "not in combat but through devious promises and perjuries" (Vernant, 1985, p. 40). His conquests are achieved on the bonds of the night, Nyx, the dread of falling through space and being buffeted in all directions, or of Styx, the guarantor of Horkos (the oaths). He was imprisoned in a jar by trickery and deprived of the divine power of instantaneous travel.

Ares is a god of proximity, who belongs to no one and is certainly not the favorite of those who claim to lay down the law in the name of fate or principle. The Greek endeavor to attain measure and distance through the word was perforce distrustful of this figure of emotion. Ares intervenes whenever life is arrested because the distance between two clans, two opinions, two ways of doing things becomes too great. He does not belong to either camp. Ares takes on a positive aspect of our civilization of control and distant reserve; he brings back warmth of contact where distance and rigid or perverse controls have sterilized life. His energy emerges in the couple whenever it becomes necessary to accept change and to confront opposites. The therapist enables the partners to invest the energy of conflict in building up a new couple system which is open to achieving identity and then individuation.

Aphrodite is the goddess of emergence. From the birth of Aphrodite onward, Eros is presented in a favorable light in the Theogony. As Rudhardt (1986) puts it, "In the dialectic between desire and courtship, the two partners who are in love each have their share of initiative" (p. 17). Vernant's (1989) addition is: "The birth of Aphrodite, who unites and brings together persons who are separated by their individuality and are opposites by virtue of their sex" (p. 156).

Golden light, bond of love, awakening of the senses and of the emotions, the mirror of Aphrodite offers those who stop to look at the beauty of emergence, the lightness of moire silk, the depth of a love devoid of self-interest. Aphrodite is the joy of the right movement, the sparkle of an eye, a breeze that caresses the skin, the calm after the storm, the water lily on the dull blue-green of the depths, the smile of a child, and tender desire. For lovers, she represents the pleasure of discovering each other and, above all, the vision of God in each other's eyes.

The person in whom this archetype is constellated enters the relationship without focusing on the obstacles. As my little son put it: "He doesn't think of his life at all any more; he only thinks of his joy." The original child awakens in the souls of the lovers: puer aeternus, no doubt, but with a strength that will make it possible to foil the snares of confinement by the father or the mother. Born of asymmetry and severance, Aphrodite makes them forget the family and kinship rights. Her power of enchantment deploys a force that obliterates all vows and leads to decisions that later seem incomprehensible even to the person who has made them. Aphrodite is the marvelous superfluity of flowers – but not fruit (Demeter's work); she is the "vision carrier" (Bolen, 1984). Under her eye, the male feels ready to undertake anything, recognized by her for his specific characteristics and exalted for his personal qualities.

Here is a clinical example: A young woman has been ill-treated by a cold mother and an inattentive father, she has a sadistically jealous brother. The brother represents the mother's intuitive jealousy of the qualities she senses in the child. An Aphrodite woman has numerous relationships with men. With some men, it is their attentiveness that appeals to her; with others, their taste of beauty and their creativity. Throughout the first part of her life, she meets with repeated misunderstandings; she is such a good listener that they confuse this exclusive attentiveness of the moment with love or desire. But when she refuses to marry them they are frustrated and jealous and accuse her, quite wrongly, of being a vamp. She thinks she is unintelligent; in her family only cold, rationalizing intelligence is valued, whereas in her the intelligence of the heart prevails. An encounter with an Ares-type man, who is emotionally close, a man who has a fighting spirit but is not hurtful, eventually awakens in this woman the possibility of love.

Among the shadows of Aphrodite are the Erinyes, who were born of the blood of Uranus. Horkos was the appanage of the Erinyes. In the ancient concept of justice, the Erinyes personified vengeance, which is sometimes passed on from one generation to the next. It is they who pursued Orestes after his crime.

Hera yielded to Zeus only on condition that he promised to marry her. Jealous of his privilege, she watched over him; she was more a spouse than a mother.

The fourth archetypal point of reference is the Oresteia. With Aeschylus' *Oresteia* (1974) the Greeks illustrated the transition from the law of kinship, which dominated families and small communities, to the law of commitment – the basis of the couple. They also tried to establish a form of justice which, rather than being based on oaths and solemn declarations, was founded on common law – the examination of circumstances – and sentiment.

Couple partners will need the courage of Ares as well as Aphrodite's trust in life, if they are to survive certain crises. It is difficult to separate from one's family, from the group to which one belongs or from one's theories which, as Humbert (1983) puts it, serve as surrogate mothers.

We are used to Oedipus, but less accustomed to Orestes. The Oresteia followed a curious course of development – a phenomenon, perhaps, of the collective unconscious. Authors are attaching more and more importance to Electra. Yourcenar (1954) makes her myth the story of a family secret, in which Orestes is the son of Clytemnestra's love-making with Aegisthus in the absence of Agamemnon. Orestes learns who his father was just as he is confronted with the death of Aegisthus.

Cycle Of Transformation: The Ares-Aphrodite Couple

The partners in a couple know the roles they are playing and the roles they have seen around them either in real life or in fiction. Identifying those roles can serve as a basis for marital therapy. I propose the following. Ares and Aphrodite are figures of transformation from the predominance of the ego to that of the Self. In equilibrium, these opposites generate harmony. In opposition, they produce discord, unhappiness. In regression, they retrace the cycle of transformation. Ares may revert to Chronus, the intemperate. Ares was imprisoned in a vase; Chronus imprisons a couple in a closed definition of the relationship. Aphrodite may become Rhea, who inspires severance and hatred and promotes dissonance so as to make the relationship dynamic again.

If the opposites become even more regressive, Ares becomes Uranus – the starry sky, the creative mind. And Aphrodite becomes Gaea, who is unceasing fertility but also pure instinct and thus produces both monsters and progress. Regression is followed by a clinging to a figure of stability: Chthon, the unchanging earth. Fascination with this archetype, or the wish to end the unbearable in the face of despair, can plunge a person into death or can plunge the couple into the will to paralyze all movement.

The scene of perpetual, aimless, undirected agitation, empty talk for the sake of relieving anxiety, uncoordinated movements, tics or starts: Nyx is terrifying, like a manic crisis or a non-ritualized trance. Chaos, the abyss, the chasm, is the opening – black and white – of the nightmare that shakes and informs at the same time. That opening can be the suicidal lure of the abyss.

In progression, Ares and Aphrodite develop toward other deities. The Zeus-Hera couple is the will to establishment and to democracy, but it can soon develop into tyranny unless it is shaken by crises.

Zeus is a factor of order but, if accentuated and rigidified, it is a sterile order. For Hera, the couple comes before the family, whereas for Demeter the relationship with the children overrides the couple's relationship. Athena and Artemis, virgins and warriors, give precedence to the masculine and are thus the opposite of Hera and Demeter. With Poseidon it is the emotional that predominates; with Hades it is the esoteric, paranormal processes and all the beliefs they involve, as well as material wealth.

As to Artemis and Apollo, the rival brother-sister couple, Apollo is the cold defender of objectivity; he keeps his distance and sees himself only as the image of his father. Artemis makes the passage between savage nature and the laws of the city. The industrious Hephaestus tends to lapse into fascination with objects. The figures of Ares and Aphrodite take on the appearance of Orestes and Electra. This is the stage in the differentiation process where parental ties are severed. The more differentiated the figures become, the more they multiply. Art presents them to us in roles with which we are more familiar.

Why This Schema?

Couples create if they are capable of renewal, of integrating the products of the psychoid into their daily lives. I propose that the therapist use a mythological frame of reference because the polysemy of the archetypes allows greater flexibility of adaptation to the particularities of the couples who seek therapy. In addition, the presence of a figure in the conscious mind evokes that of its opposite in the unconscious: that of the partner or that of the couple. The therapist's attention is thus drawn to what is emerging. Further, given the diversity of couples, it is important that the therapist have a point of reference. Some will find it in theories. I prefer to enshrine it in the creative symbolic, since it is in this sphere that the soul feels more respected, more alive, more present.

Translated from French by Carolyn Loane

References

Aeschylus (1974). *The Oresteia* (D. Young, trans.). Norman, OK: University of Oklahoma Press.

Bejarano A. (1974). Essai d'étude d'un groupe large (Study of a large group). *Bulletin de Psychologie de l'Université de Paris*. Numero special, 98-122.

Bolen, J.S. (1984). *Goddesses in Every Woman*. New York: Harper Colophon.

Caillé, P. (1991). *Un et un Font Trois. Le Couple Révélé a Lui-même* (One and One Made Three. The Couple Revealed to Itself). Paris: E.S.F.

Hesiod (1953). *Theogony* (N. O. Brown, trans.). Indianapolis/New York: Bobbs-Merrill.

Hochmann, J. (1971). *Pour une psychiatrie communautaire* (Toward a Community Psychiatry). Paris: Seuil.

Humbert, E. (1983). *Jung*. Paris: Editions Universitaires.

Humbert, E. (1994). *La dimension d'ainer*. Paris: Ed. des cahiers jungiens de psychanalyse.

Pluymaekers, J. & Neve-Hanquet, C. (1992). Travail sur les familles d'origine et genogramme paysager (Work on family of origin and landscape genogram). In *L'histoire de vie au risque de la recherche, de la formation et de la therapie* (sous la direction de Ch. Leomant). *Etudes et seminaries, 8*. Paris: Centre de Recherche Interdisciplinaire de Vaucresson.

Ramnoux, C. (1959). *La nuit et les enfants de la nuit dans la tradition grecque*. Paris: Flammarion.

Riplaeus, G. (1649). *Omnia Opera Chemica*. Cassel.

Rudhardt, J. (1986). *Le role d'Eros et d'Aphrodite dans les cosmogonies grecques* (The role of Eros and Aphrodite in Greek cosmogony). Paris: Presses Universitaires de France.

Tisseron, S. (1992). *La honte: Psychanalyse d'un lien social* (Shame: Psychoanalysis of a Social Link). Paris: Dunod.

Vernant, J-P. (1985). *Mythe et Pensée chez les Grecs* (Myth and Thinking among the Greeks). Paris: Éditions La Découverte.

Vernant, J-P. (1989). *L'individu, la mort, l'amour. Soi-même et l'autre en Grèce antique* (Individual, Death, Love: Self and Other in Ancient Greece). Paris: Gallimard.

Willi, J. (1982). *La relation de couple. Le concept de collusion* (The Relation of the Couple. The Concept of Collusion). Paris: Delachau et Niestlé.

Young-Eisendrath, P. (1993). *You're Not What I Expected*. New York: William Morrow.

Yourcenar, M. (1954/1971). *Electre ou la chute des masques* (Electra or the Fall of the Mask). Paris: Gallimard.

The Social Dreaming Matrix[*]

Peter Tatham
Totnes, Devon, England
Independent Group of Analytical Psychologists

Helen Morgan
London, England
British Association of Psychotherapists – Jungian Section

"The Social Dreaming Matrix" has been developed since 1982 by Gordon Lawrence and his colleagues at the Tavistock Institute and elsewhere. Beginning with a social dreaming workshop in 1993 we have been excited by the potential of this new form of exploration of social issues through dreams. The link between this work and Jungian concepts is reflected in Lawrence's (1991) essay, headed by a quote from Jung, "The dream is a little hidden door in the innermost and most secret recesses of the soul" (CW10, par. 304).

The application of social dreaming to Jungian thought has opened exciting possibilities. Jung saw the dream as a spontaneous, creative expression of the unconscious psyche that arose to comment upon, and compensate for, deficiencies in any conscious situation. Since archetypal theory implies that dreams can be seen also from a collective angle, dreaming might be "intending" to inform and transform the social and political context of the dreamer as well as the personal situation. As individuals of the late twentieth century, we dream within a context that is in a state of flux. Increased communications mean that the conscious mind is bombarded with images reflecting the divisions, conflicts and uncertainties of our world. In our daily work as analysts we are involved in exploration of the dream as it relates to the personal unconscious of the individual as well as the connection to an archetypal, collective aspect. The Social Dreaming Matrix provides a possible arena within which that collective angle might have expression.

[*] This paper was written following the Congress.

We saw the Congress as an arena for analysts familiar with the concept of the collective to attend to the unconscious processes that might occur within those present. People came to Zurich, in middle Europe, from all corners of the globe, at a time approaching the end of the millennium. For five days we would listen, speak, think and discuss. We also dreamed. We wondered what dreams we would experience there and what might those dreams tell us about the nature of the collective context in which we found ourselves? Might those dreams, if explored from the perspective of the social rather than the personal, shed light on the open questions with which we are faced and which were to be the theme of the conference? The Social Dreaming Matrix was a means of investigating these questions.

In the Social Dreaming Matrix participants met to share their dreams. The primary task of the event was to associate to one's own and others' dreams that were made available to the Matrix, so as to make links and find connections. It was not necessary to bring a dream to take part; neither was it necessary to participate every day. There were at least 80 participants every morning.

The term "Matrix" means "womb" or "a place out of which something grows." The chairs are set out in the form of a spiral or a snow flake. It is not a circle and the concerns are not those of group work. The door was left open and people could enter at any time during the hour. Thus, while the time and space for the event were established, the individual relationship to boundaries was not the focus. Nor were the usual transference issues. As convenors, our roles were to hold time and task boundaries, to record the dreams presented and to comment on themes where it seemed helpful. We gave attention to the dream and to thinking about the images presented.

While it is not possible in a short paper to explore the content of the dreams presented, certain themes emerged that related to the task and context of the Congress itself. Ancestors and parents appeared in the dream images and associations to our struggles to find an appropriate relationship to our theory parents were made.

The death of Jung was a recurring theme. On the first morning there was a dream of *a body buried in cement which the dreamer was trying to get rid of but the body kept re-emerging. Everyone was upset and tried to hide it*. Associations centered round the image of the body of Jung which seems to refuse to die. Do we have to find a way of finally burying this body? Does not the dream also pose the question of how we can set Jung free?

There were also dreams of siblings, cousins and second cousins. If we look at analytical psychology on a generational basis, these dream images could be thought of as posing the question of how we talk to each other when we are even more distantly related than second cousins. How do we retain a sense of family across the continents, both geographic and philosophical?

The Tower of Babel appeared as a theme in a Congress paper by Kaj Noschis. Prior to this paper a dream was presented in the Matrix of *a mountain with four rocky pinnacles on the top. Within it was a beautiful place, like a Chinese landscape with waterfalls and willow trees. At the bottom of the mountain was a rainforest full of animals and shanty towns.* As these images permeated the Matrix, a paradox arose. It is our nature to keep our eye on the top of the mountain, to aspire to the city of God; yet do we not need to attend also to life in the shanty towns at the base if we are to live in the world of humans?

There is the wish to unite to build the City of Humans that is like the City of God, and to speak with one tongue. Yet the reality is that we speak in many tongues. Throughout the Congress we were listening to papers in four languages; without interpretation we could not have understood each other. How are we to manage the variety of tongues spoken by the different schools within Jungian thought? In the Tower of Babel story it is God who demolishes the tower and forces diversity of language. While we must work to manage the diversity within our profession, perhaps it is inevitable that we never achieve unity, for this would mean stagnation and hubris – characteristics the psyche seems to abhor.

Perhaps the power of the Matrix is that within it many tongues may be spoken without one having to have authority or power over others. A "multi-verse" rather than a "uni-verse" develops within which a plethora of meanings can co-exist. There is no answer, no "right" interpretation or response. Instead, the Matrix offers a container with elastic boundaries that can stretch to take in and hold each new meaning. Again, the dreams conveyed the notion that the direct approach, although appealing, often fails. There were many images of attempts to "get over the top" of hills, slopes and mountains. Vehicles were unevenly weighted and veered off to one side as they slid back down hill. Banks could be negotiated if the angle of assault was altered. Thus, instead of aspiring to the beauties of the mountain top, we cannot neglect the places we inhabit down below. While respecting the sacred, its glorification may lead to an inversion into its negative opposite, and the mundane – even the profane – needs attention.

It was not just the plethora of meanings and associations to a particular dream that could be held within the Matrix, but the dreams themselves – when seen in relation to each other – asserted plurality. When a dream image arose that looked as if it were leading us in a particular direction, another would come up that implied the opposite. One participant told of a dream in which *a large white bird had to be shot, a necessary act*. In the same session another image was offered where *the dreamer was leaving Zurich and a large white swan came to see her off at the station*. Within two dreams we had the malign and the benign white bird. In the context of a conference entitled "Open Questions," it seemed that the images from the unconscious were determined to keep to this task and not allow us to close down with answers.

Perhaps surprisingly, this was not a frustrating or unrewarding experience. People spoke of a sense of wholeness, of the Matrix as a healing experience in contrast to some of the more conflictual, "political" aspects of the Congress. While in many arenas we have to close options by making choices, electing representatives and deciding policy, perhaps there is also a need for arenas in which we can collaborate in exploring uncertainty and paradox. Because issues of power, authority and responsibility were not the matter of the Matrix, because the role of the dreamer and of the person associating to it is a truly democratic one, the individual is free to engage with others in exploration and a sense of "communitas" develops. It is not that the Matrix avoids the difficulties of human connectedness – the dreams themselves raised some painful themes of shame concerning racism, gender, splits and divisions, political in-fighting within the Congress, shadow and evil – but people were able to engage with each other to explore such matters around the image of the dream.

The currency of the Matrix seems to be paradox. Despite large numbers, participants said that they felt this to be a place where each could be heard. It was a collective experience where not everyone spoke and where often you did not know who was reporting a dream. And yet the individual was not lost. The Matrix offered a container which gave a space for the difference of individuality to be "held" by the collective. The "problems" were provided not by the conscious ego but by the images of the dream. The focus was not the individual but the collective. Hence the tensions and clashes between individual egos could be put aside and something more unconscious, more collective had voice. The assumption was that people could manage their experience for themselves and, indeed, within this large collection of people there were no indications of regressive behavior – of fight/flight or dependency – that one might expect within such a large group. Rather than feeling denied, individuals felt, on the whole, attended to.

Keats' concept of "negative capability" where questions can be kept open "without any irritable reaching after fact and reason" comes to mind. The Matrix does not offer a place where difficult questions can be answered, but it does allow them to be asked. The lesson it may offer at a time when tensions are high is that, instead of directing our energies at finding answers, it may be more helpful to ask within what sort of container we need to work, that can contain open questions.

Reference

Lawrence, G. (1991). Won from the void and formless infinite: Experience of social dreaming. *Free Associations*, 2-2, 259-293.

Analyst-Training

Who Is Apt And Worthy To Be An Analyst? (summary)

Urs H. Mehlin

Gockhausen, Switzerland
Association of Graduate Analytical Psychologists
(Zurich Institute)

My concern is with the following issues:

1. Are there objective criteria to determine the qualifications for the analytical profession?

2. If yes, is it possible to evaluate such criteria during training?

3. How valid are exams and other means of testing?

4. How do examiners and training analysts deal with their own shadows? (E.g., power, weakness, prejudice.)

Since we apply selective means during training at different stages (selection committees, examinations, supervision), it is only fair to use some criteria, well knowing that these are too general to apply to every individual case. Without such reflection, however, decisions tend to become too subjective and casual. In the selection committee for the child analyst program at the Jung Institute in Zurich, we have formulated criteria under the following categories:

1) Ability to make contact and to communicate with children and adults.

2) Capacity for introspection and integration.

3) Imagination and creativity.

As general criteria I propose:

Open-Mindedness	*versus*	Rigidity
Ability to reflect		Tendency to (co-) acting-out
Reliability		Incalculability
Carefulness/attention		Carelessness
Relatedness		Ego-centeredness

Exams in "postdoctoral" training present a specific problem, since they stimulate by definition some regression on the side of the

examinee. The "initiates" meet, so to speak, the "initiands." Considering that situation, exams should fulfill at least two conditions:
1. Relation to the practical requirements of the analytical profession.
2. Consideration of the specific interests and talents, that is, the "individuality" of the candidate.

These conditions presuppose, in the examiners, some awareness and tolerance concerning one's own complexes. Such complexes detract from validity of judgment, as does a positive or negative countertransference in selection interviews or examinations. A helpful underlying question is: "Would I trust the candidate enough to send clients?"

Even with all attempts to formalize and to define criteria, the determination of professional aptitude in the analytical field remains – and must remain for each individual case – an "open question."

Panel: Power and Eros in Training

Introduction

Eli Weisstub
Jerusalem, Israel
Israel Association of Analytical Psychology

The interplay of power and eros is central to the success or failure of analytic training programs. The dominance of power over eros is at the core of many problems arising in the training process.

In a training institute, power struggles between training analysts may be based on political and theoretical differences, as well as interpersonal conflicts and disagreements about what constitutes a "Jungian" analyst. A dominant analyst or group of analysts may have the power to determine the selection of applicants, the course of training, the theoretical orientation in training and who will finally be accepted to qualify as an analyst. Candidates may suffer because of unresolved power issues in individual training analysts or within training committees.

At the same time, power may have constructive function in training, especially in establishing professional and ethical standards. The balance, often delicate, between the power of authority and the eros necessary for a positive training process can be disturbed easily. When eros is not consciously and responsibly dealt with, it can create severe problems. Training analysts may not be sufficiently aware of the importance of their supervisory role and may become involved in an overly personal relationship with trainees, consequently blurring boundaries required for optimal training. The necessity for maintaining objectivity and ethical responsibility is as significant in training as it is in personal analysis.

In other instances training analysts, appreciating the positive significance of eros and relatedness in the training process, tend to be overly strict, rigid, authoritarian and unsupportive to candidates.

When guidelines for training and supervision are not clear, the authority manifested by training analysts/committees may be misused. Mystification of training and the initiation process in becoming an analyst may lead to confusion and excessive anxiety and fear. Serious consideration of power and eros issues could contribute to fairer and more constructive analytic training.

Awareness of the need to discuss these subjects openly led to the formation of a panel of analysts experienced in directing training programs, as well as analysts who have completed their training only recently. The panel participants represent various cultural and training orientations.

One Analyst's Experience

Elisabeth Adametz
Berlin, Germany
German Society for Analytical Psychology

A very dear man brought me to read Jung's *Memories, Dreams, Reflections* (MDR) when I was 19. About 17 years later, I began my analytic training. In the meantime, I studied medicine in Vienna – my father's home city – and in Hamburg, where my mother lives and where I was born. I worked for several years as a physician. In January 1993 I finished my analytic training and since then I have been working as an analyst in Berlin-Kreuzberg.

In May 1986, led by eros, I moved from Hamburg to Berlin and picked up the application forms from the Institute for Psychotherapy. I found the secretaries so unwelcoming that I had to recover in the park across the street. The standards seemed unreasonably high and unfulfillable. My situation was desperate. So far I had developed myself as much as I could on my own, but now I needed help to go on, including connecting my work and psychoanalysis. Eight months later, shortly before the application deadline, I mustered the courage and applied. In the interviews I was as present and empathetic as possible: friendly, very open, but discrete about my secrets. We were able to establish a rapport and I received inspiring ideas to think about.

I was accepted – fortunately – since I had already started to be skeptical toward Freud and his disciples and had begun to idealize Jung and his disciples. At the Berlin Institute both schools are taught, along with child and adolescent analytic therapy. Lectures and seminars are partly interdisciplinary and are always open to all students. There is a good exchange between the students of a particular year.

When I started training, we were initially admitted only for one year. Admission to continuing training was decided on the basis of a group examination. There was also a limited "reporting system": The training analysts declared their consent for each step of the training with a signature, with or without objection. The contents of the training analysis were not to be disclosed. Now however, both the probation year and the "reporting system" have been abolished. Interested students and some training analysts debated this proposal for years. Decisions about progress – now in the hands of supervisors and the training committee – are supposed to be completely independent of the training analysis. Training analysts confirm only the number of sessions to date and whether the analysis has ended. In considering power and eros in training situations, my focus is on the training analysis which is generally considered the most important learning experience of the training.

The problem of countertransference was first mentioned explicitly in a letter from Freud to Jung in June 1909, in answer to Jung's intimation of his muddled relationship with Sabina Spielrein, in which there was much eros and much misused power. Freud said in his opening address to the Second International Psychoanalytic Congress in Nuremberg in 1910, "We have become aware of Countertransference ... and therefore demand that [the analyst] begin his work with a self-analysis" (SE11, p. 144). In 1912 Freud wrote "I would count to the many merits of the Zurich Analytical School that it ... has established the rule that anyone who would analyse others must first himself undergo an analysis with an expert" (SE12, p. 117).

As I knew no analysts, I chose from the institute's list the training analyst whose name had the most vowels. His call time was before 8 a.m. and I imagined him to be in the bathroom when I called him. I was speaking from an open public telephone in front of a construction site, on my way to work. The dialectical process began immediately. I asked him about a time: he replied "You mean, if I have space." I was brave enough to ask him to speak louder. He explained the way to his house too exactly; I had a city map and was not a little child. And meeting on Friday at 8 p.m. made me suspicious. Didn't he have anything better to do?

I didn't know this part of Berlin. It was idyllic countryside. The house was not very big, the garden not very orderly. A girl with a bicycle also wanted into the house; she confirmed that I was in the right place. There he stood on the staircase, smiling at me in a friendly way, as if he had been expecting none other than me.

Now I could be really open – which meant that I didn't have to tell him anything – at least not before we had agreed about working together. When I left, after an hour, we had made a second appointment. I felt rather disenchanted. Whom had I expected? Would this young, friendly family man be able to understand me at all? I had watched his face, listened to his voice, perceived his empathy, and noticed a mental agility that I liked.

He seemed to me to be handsome enough, friendly enough, bright enough – but not much more. I decided nevertheless to try it. I learned only later, from Winnicott, that there is nothing better than good enough.

At the Berlin Institute the progressive Freudians let their patients sit in a chair and they treat them less frequently; the progressive Jungians make their patients lie on a couch and treat them three or four hours per week. I realized that I had fallen into the hands of a progressive Jungian only at the end of the second meeting. Until then I had taken the couch to be obsolete, at least in its tangible form. We decided to start the analysis.

That night I awoke with the feeling of a terrible explosion, and I had to scribble it on a piece of paper to get it out of my system. I was not unconscious of my anxiety, but it was so strong that I had to split off part of it. In a subsequent dream, a rather moderate anxiety revealed itself. *A young wild pig raced through all the rooms of my apartment with such a speed that I could only stand there astonished.* This was the starting point of the analysis. (After a few weeks he moved to an office downtown, according to his plan that I had known all along.)

We spent the first two years mainly trying to develop mutual understanding. We struggled over words, trying to reach a common language. To me it was a matter of life and death to be understood exactly – to the point of splitting hairs – not too fast and not too slow, not too soon and not too late. I was unremitting and merciless. He often defended himself, but was ready anew to try to understand me at each session. A turning point for me was a dream in which *my analyst promised to guide me to the point of no return.*

By this time I had come far enough in my training that I could begin analyzing under supervision. In the interviews with my first patients, I sensed their unspoken massive anxieties about beginning treatment. Their anxieties recalled my previous split-off anxiety about beginning my analysis and about having to lie on the couch. I was enraged and blamed my analyst, and was nearly overwhelmed by the brunt of this feeling, but this time it was possible to integrate it. I felt less rigid in the sessions and dared to look at him. By now, we had come to know each other so well that I could begin slowly to dive into dependence and very early experiences of my life. I trusted him to sustain me, to protect me and not to misuse his power. I knew he would be there with absolute reliability and sufficient frequency, which at that time meant four times a week. Without his help I wouldn't have dared to enter my deeper self. At this time mistakes or impatience on his part triggered inner catastrophes. To recover I was completely dependent on his help. This time of complete dependence, in which I worked simultaneously as a doctor in psychiatry and analyzed my own patients, lasted about nine months and ended with a dream about *the birth of a healthy baby.*

Around this time I cut off my long pigtail, which I had had for 20 years, because I didn't need its magic power any more. Three years later, after finishing my exams, I ended my analysis. I had planned to go happily and gratefully, but I woke up that morning full of hate and carried it into the last session. It was a great comfort for me to feel that he did not return my hate. I could tell him about my dream of *blind parents, who were expecting their third seeing child.* It was a dream which I forgot and which he recalled to me six months later, when I returned, worried but not knowing exactly why. It proved to be necessary for us to repeat our parting.

Were there any influences due to the training situation in my analysis that differ from other analyses? It troubled me that we had the same profession; I would have liked to have been able to tell him something entirely new. Also, doubts about him and our analysis sometimes led to doubts about the method and about myself as an analyst-to-be. Nevertheless, I found it fruitful to analyze and to be analyzed at the same time.

We training candidates have to pay for the analysis ourselves, because we are supposed to be healthier than the health insurance stipulates. Ferenczi's standpoint of 1923, that training analyses should go even deeper than others, has been realized. It seems ironic that we must have a minimum of 300 sessions, which is also the maximum granted by the health insurance in well-founded special cases. In 1985, the average duration of a training analysis at the Berlin Institute was 458 sessions, with a tendency to increase.

After some time in the Institute I came to rely on the discretion of my analyst and knew that he left meetings during times when I was discussed. Not all analysts are willing to do this. For me, it was extremely important that he learned first hand from me what I had experienced in the Institute, what was said or written to me, what I planned and what I wanted to say or to write myself.

Another difference, also very important to me, were the occasions in the Institute or at conferences, where we met incidentally. We are both in favor of the "non-reporting" system. In preparing this text, however, I often found myself calling it the non-responding system; I experienced it that way as well. Thus, in public I often felt ignored by him, which hurt me deeply. There were many visible reasons to feel envious and jealous. At the same time there was a certain nearness, an undisturbed, anonymous observing or listening. I felt horror and joy. There was always a confusion about the nature of our relationship. All structures of the analytic frame were missing. We needed about 20 percent of our sessions to try to work through these incidents, and we didn't always succeed. I regret that there was little power and eros left over for other things during my training.

Now I consider myself as relatively independent; I have a profession I am suited for, and with which I am mostly pleased. I am now in a position to learn from my daily experiences with an emotional attachment.

Translated from German by Elizabeth Adametz and Timothy Cox

The Role of the Training Analyst

Paul Brutsche
Zurich, Switzerland
Swiss Society for Analytical Psychology

I begin with two simple hypotheses. The first is that power in training is based psychologically on an unconscious misconception of the role of the training analyst (TA). The second is that the negative effect of power consists mainly in the training candidate's becoming too much attached to the training analyst and the analyst's views and values, thus losing the inner connection to the candidate's psychological creativity.

A TA may become identified with one or more of several problematic roles:

1. *Teacher-persona:* looking perfectly competent. The assumption is that the candidate needs a professional authority in order to be guided safely. It is not only personal vanity that leads the TA into this. The candidate needs to perceive the TA as someone superior and competent, in order to trust that, with time, the candidate will develop the necessary self-assurance. The TA's persona results from the interaction of the role and the candidate's expectations, plus all the imaginary demands generated by the training institution.

The TA becomes dedicated to an unconscious program of power over a candidate, who must be guided correctly toward professional competence. But then the candidate's psyche and the psyche in general are not valued as powerful realities in themselves.

2) *Therapeutic cynic:* assuming that candidates are naive believers in therapy, lacking grounding in reality, overestimating their capacities and fascinated by the sublime concept of individuation. Instead of being encouraged to pursue a religious search for meaning, they must be brought down to earth to acquire real analytic skills. Such candidates exist, but only a cynical TA would take for granted that candidates in general can be described so cynically.

Such a cynical TA would then act as a mediator of a shadow point of view, a sober enlightener and a pragmatic disillusioner. The shadow's business here would consist in forcing candidates to adopt a more realistic understanding of themselves and of reality in general.

This role is justified by a candidate's exaggerated self-estimation. But I have seen examples where this enlightened pathos of sobriety has resulted in a profound wounding of the soul. Some candidates have looked for a religious dimension in their training analysis. Not only did they not find it but they found themselves programmed toward mere professional training.

Power is present insofar as the TA becomes identified with the task of self-criticism which the candidate is assumed to avoid. But this presumption is wrong and so is the strategy that is used to fight it. This disrespectful shadow strategy produces in the candidate feelings of uncertainty, insufficiency and diffuse injury.

3) *Soul guide*: mediating the wisdom of the soul, knowing exactly how much analysis the candidate still needs, and the candidate's hidden talents.

The TA actively supports the candidate throughout the training program, with valid recommendations for preparation for exams, choice of supervisors, ideas for papers the candidate must write, and helpful bibliographical hints. If conflicts with the Institute arise, the TA is on the candidate's side and hints that institutions and regulations are always a little bit suspicious.

Also for matters of private life the TA is able to provide some practical hints. The unmarried male candidate could match quite well with a particular female candidate. The candidate feels emotionally dependent, owing feelings of everlasting respect and thankfulness to the TA. All this renders a healthy and objective distance quite difficult.

4) *Mediator of higher values*: referring to the archetype of the Self and functioning as a priest. Hence the TA must teach about Jung the "right" way, distinguishing between the orthodox and the dissident followers, between those who still take the objective psyche and the language of dreams seriously and those who follow the wind and run after the idols of developmental psychology and vocational politics. When the TA is functioning in this manner, according to this view, direct contact with persons who themselves had direct contact with Jung is the only guarantee for legitimate understanding. Whoever lacks this immediacy of succession – whether the first, the second or third generation – and the charisma that accompanies it, is considered to be "liberal."

This priestly role produces adepts and disciples, an ideological annexation that brings power into the picture. Power is involved even when one renounces it in opposition to the big institution that is said to be governed by it, and when dreams are awarded the only legitimate authority. In this pretention to possess the truth, and to convey it to the elect few, lies the blind presumption of power. The TA turns into an inflated preacher about the right way to live and to work as a Jungian. At the same time the boundary separating the TA from the candidate is crossed. The candidate is forced to become a follower and eventual steps toward autonomy are marked by a lifelong bad conscience.

5) *Identification with the archetype of the* mana *personality:* carrying the guru function, becoming the ideal person – as a therapist and as a human being.

Under the influence of this archetype the TA tries hard to personify individuation, using self-quotes in claiming to be an original: "as I often say." Standard expressions belong necessarily to the TA's repertoire, along with some extraordinary interests that increase the aura of being someone special. Some carefully culti-vated oppositions are needed: a little bit of natural science, some mystical experience and knowledge in nonanalytic areas, with preference for those which show an intimate bond to nature.

Such narcissistic self-portrayal does no serious harm, as long as it is done in an obvious and rather silly way. But this behavior, accompanied by the inner conviction that one is special as a person and a TA, becomes dangerous. For then a narcissistic attraction takes place toward the TA as the center, making it difficult for the candidate to develop autonomy. Only people around the candidate will notice how often he or she mentions the master's name. Standing practically for the voice of the Self, all the master says seems to come from the candidate's innermost center. Nonetheless, a powerful annexation has taken place, including the candidate's adoption of the TA's personal traits: gestures, language, even lifestyle.

I have put in parallel the singular aspects of the individuation process: persona, shadow, anima/animus, Self, mana personality. Why? I don't mean it as an amusing game. Nor do I do it because of referring every type of classification back to the concepts of analyt-ical psychology. In training the archetypes of the individuation process enter the scene but, when the corresponding role identifica-tion with its binding effect occurs, the TA's basic attitude is wrong. What is wrong with this attitude?

It is wrong because of the wrong assumptions: that the TA must represent something greater, mediate something higher, play an active role and transmit personal experience. Almost necessarily, the TA falls under the spell of the individuation archetype in transgressing boundaries: personal boundaries and those set by the training function – responsibility for the personal growth of the candidate.

What could be done to avoid these assumptions? Four points come to mind.

1) *A more modest image of one's role.* It is not greatness that makes a trainer. Not human or professional greatness. Not even moral greatness. I heard once about a colleague who, at being appointed to an important function at the Institute, decided for himself that, from now on, he would try to become serious and exemplary. This was the most disastrous thing he could do to himself and to his candidates.

2) *Return to one's own person*: to one's own dreams, fantasies and questions. Resist the temptation to pass on and market one's own personal insights. The French philosopher Blaise Pascal once said that the reason wars happen is that people can't stand to stay at home alone. The trainer who is too much involved in the candidate's business succumbs to this expansive tendency of power in general.

3) *Less active doing.* The German word for "power" is "Macht," which has the same root as "machen" (to make). Power almost always has something to do with excessive activity. If the TA would withdraw a bit and trust a little more the process and experience of the candidate, less doer energy would enter the field.

4) Give up the idea that, with words, one can pass on one's experience to the candidate. St. Ignatius of Loyola, in his spiritual exercises says, "It is not by hearing and knowing many things that one nourishes the soul, but by tasting them personally from inside." The dangerous aspect of power is to consider one's own truth as the only one.

What, all in all, is demanded of the TA, is to become a good-enough trainer.

The Flame and the Tree

Margaret Jones
London, England
Society of Analytical Psychology

A passage from Jung's *Seven Sermons to the Dead* has provided both a focus and a container for my reflections on our subject. In the fourth of the sermons, Jung – as Basilides – speaks of the two "God-devils," the growing one and the burning one:

> *The burning one is EROS in his form as flame. It shines and it devours. The growing one is the TREE OF LIFE; it grows green, and it accumulates living matter while it grows. Eros flames up and then dies away; the tree of life, however, grows slowly and reaches stately stature throughout countless ages.*
> *Good and evil are united in the flame.*
> *Good and evil are united in the growth of the tree.* (Hoeller, 1982, p. 53)

The flame, eros, burns and consumes matter and the tree grows powerful because it accumulates, conserves and consolidates matter. Two elemental facts and faces of nature: complementary, not opposed. As with any institution the tree, the growing one, functions to serve itself and, by growing in strength and stature, it provides shelter and nourishment for those who are drawn to seek its shade or enjoy its fruits. A powerful organism and a potent symbol for those conservative forces that dwell in us and our institutions as in nature. Its complement is the burning one, the flame, which ignites and transforms, through its intense heat releasing the seed to germinate, regenerating through destruction, ensuring new growth and renewed vigor.

Which is more powerful, the flame or the tree? The answer of course, is that they are mutually dependent. Without flammable material, there would be no fire; without the fire that germinates the seed, there would be no new life. Thus it is in society and in our profession: the growing one, that which consolidates and represents power – the organization – needs the burning individual vision and courage to risk all, no less than the individual needs the organization or group to realize or validate that vision and to provide fellowship. Zinkin (1989) wrote movingly of the paradoxical relationship of individual and group:

> *The Grail stories present ... the opposition between individual and*
> *group, in that it is the heroic individual who is destined to reach [the*
> *Grail], but for the benefit of the group. Both the transformation of*
> *the group and the transformation of the individual is brought about*
> *in the course of the story. ... The group has no function, no meaning,*
> *no existence without the individual who will complete it. This*
> *individual, like Perceval, has a moral duty towards [the group] but*
> *also, as Jung says, it would be suicidal of him not to join [the group].*
> (pp. 378-385)

A threat to individual vision is inherent in the current training and working "climate." (By "individual" I mean the individual candidate within a training program, the individual training institute within the body of training institutes and the individual analyst within society.) There are pressures for standardization of training programs and competition within the therapeutic world. There is the public focus which has recently been turned so uncompromisingly on the business of therapy and the abuse of trust and power which is revealed almost daily. There are the ever-increasing demands for proof of results and the ever-increasing requirements – personal, academic and professional – which candidates must fulfill.

Now I pose a question and attempt a response: If the continuing transformation of the group is indeed dependent on the continuing transformation of the individual, is there anything we can do in the arena of training to validate and safeguard the space within which candidates undertake the arduous journey of training? If there is, then not only the individual but also the group stands to benefit. The training experience can offer the individual the opportunity not only to learn, but also to grow, and real growth is always painful as it requires the dismantling of existing structures – a trial by fire. There is one thing we can do, practically. The peer training group can be – paradoxically – of great value in protecting the space an individual trainee requires in order to gain maximum benefit from the process of training. Let me share some personal observations from the past ten years.

Individuals applying for training seem to begin to bond with each other even during the process of selection which, at the Society of Analytical Psychology (SAP) in London, requires them to participate in a half-day of unstructured group discussion and small group interaction. Years later, they often refer back to the events of that day, clearly having experienced it as a significant shared ordeal. When a new group meets they reconnect over the remembering of the "selection day." A sense of group identity begins to form; the group is felt to have a particular personality. They may not comment on it themselves – they are in the process of being it – but those who come into contact with them comment on it. A "bright group," a "caring group," a "competitive group," a "troubled group." Very similar to the experiences connected with the birth of a child: the bonding and the projecting of hopes and fears onto the infant, in this case, the infant group.

I have noticed the solidarity of a group's identity reinforced by the trials of each member of the group. Consequently, while they may experience and address their personal intra-group conflicts when they feel safely by themselves – perhaps within the meetings which are scheduled twice a term with their group tutor – they will close ranks immediately if they feel criticized or undermined from outside. In the face of the shared experience of collective pressures – from training organization, family, friends, society, as well as personal stress and strain – the group can act, paradoxically, as a protector and preserver of individuality. The members share information about particular troubles they may be experiencing and allow and even create spaces for each other while these individual "dark nights" are being negotiated. In this willingness to accommodate, support and nurture each other, the group members demonstrate their unconscious sense of being alone with only each other in a harsh and uncaring world. It is the "night sea journey," which they have embarked on individually and as a group, that unifies them. Edinger (1992) wrote:

> *It sometimes seems that the goal of the individual's psychic develop-*
> *ment is to come ever closer to the realization that his own personal,*
> *unique individuality is identical with the eternal archetypal individ-*
> *ual. Uniqueness and universality merge as one takes upon himself*
> *the fate of being an individual.* (p. 57)

The essence of what the group can carry seems to be the containment of this working out of individual uniqueness within the context of the small universe of the training group.

In summary, whatever emphasizes collective norms and requirements, whatever measures and standardizes, whatever aims for acceptance, validation and approval may also devalue individual difference and creativity, discouraging challenge and deviation. This seems to me to present a profound challenge to those who value the work of Jung and wish to help others to learn about and train in the practice of analytical psychology.

Agents of Transformation

Jean Kirsch

Palo Alto, California, U.S.A.
Society of Jungian Analysts of Northern California

Analytic training requires an attitudinal shift of such magnitude that one might call it a spiritual transformation. The ability to enter into an intimate and durable analytic relationship requires a special kind of attunement and self-possession; the practicing analyst must be conscious enough to carry both the regressive transference and the weighty Self projections of the prospective transference. Furthermore, the attitude necessary to conduct an analysis is often resisted by candidates. They may evade learning its art and science, despite their conscious desire and intent to be thus transformed. This resistance must be met by the intelligent and compassionate use of power and eros by the teaching analyst: power – the authority to exert influence – and eros, careful and related engagement with the other. Power and eros are essential agents for the transformative process of analytic training. (For this discussion, "teaching analyst" refers to any analyst – except the personal analyst – who assumes any of the educative and evaluative roles instrumental in the process of training. The analyst who supervises the candidate's therapeutic work is the "control" or supervising analyst.)

Training is a dialectic in which a gradient exists between the authority to influence and expectations of the process. We usually we think of authority as flowing from the teacher toward the student and expectations as flowing from the student to teacher. Yet the gradient oscillates; influence and expectations issue from both sides of the dialectic in a productive give and take. Although it would be misleading to ignore the hierarchy of training and the power differential that exists between teaching analyst and candidate, it is incorrect to assume that the candidate is powerless to have significant impact on the quality and the outcome of training.

Power and eros are active agents in the dynamics of the training dialectic; they are also the principles that govern it. To explore the dimensions of these opposites, I draw upon Jung's definition of eros as the principle of relatedness, a daimon in and of itself encompassing the opposites of love and hate. Power I define as the principle of creativity, another daimon, which embraces the opposites of construction and destruction. Either eros as relatedness or power as creativity can be corrupted and perverted to become what Jung called, after Nietzsche, will-to-power. Will-to-power can build magnificent structures and inspire passionate erotic attachments and it can motivate sublime achievements, but it is an unwieldy force in training, for will-to-power oppresses and hinders growth of candidates' knowledge and skills. In training we are better served if we strive for balance and moderation, relying on conscious effort to sustain the tension between opposites that comprise the dialectic, and to create a "training space." Ideally, this is a free and protected space in which candidate and teaching analyst explore archetypal themes through play with the images and affects that arise in the teaching situation, whether that be a seminar, control sessions, or an evaluative meeting with the training committee. This space will collapse if either excess of authority or unrealistic expectation and projection overwhelm the psychological state of either teaching analyst or candidate, leading to a perversion of power or eros. Will-to-power then takes the place of the creative and related play with image and affect that prevails in the ideal "training space."

If the dialectic collapses in the direction of authority, training will become indoctrination through the analyst's abuse of power. Conversely, it will collapse into triviality if the analyst relinquishes authority to the candidate.

If the dialectic collapses in the direction of an inflated or deflated expectation of analytic training (e.g., if either teaching analyst or candidate is caught in a paranoid or idealizing projection), the authority to influence and the capacity to be influenced is perverted. Training then promotes imitation and identification with the admired or devalued teaching analyst; the particular myth of analysis dominating the local training body becomes the central dogma of the ritual of training, with Jung's *Collected Works* as its sacred text.

A situation dominated by either extreme squeezes the spirit out of training, strangles transformation. Whether training in its perverted form exemplifies indoctrination or imitation, power and eros are used for personal or institutional advantage, and do not act as creative agents for growth and learning in an atmosphere in relatedness. Training loses its principles and is neither creative nor caring. Thus, when either power or eros is unprincipled, training is dominated by will-to-power. Values are perverted. Eros becomes self-serving. Power reverts to authoritarianism.

Nobody undergoes the transformation from non-analyst to analyst without intense affect. Just as a personal analyst must be able to receive and withstand powerful affective transferences, so must the teaching analyst be able to tolerate whatever is generated by the candidate's decision to undergo the transformative process of analytic training. An incoming candidate is an established adult person, with strongly developed notions of role and identity, who agrees to assume yet again the student position, which requires a potentially humiliating deintegration/integration process. Most candidates protest against this process and its state of not-knowing. Not-knowing can be a frightening experience, especially when initiatory veils shroud the training process, which expects personal development and demands an intuitive grasp of psychological meanings, in contrast to a process that emphasizes didactic presentations and states objective criteria by which progress is measured.

Additionally, the projection of Self is not carried readily by the larger training body, though most candidates make this kind of projection. I believe that the defensiveness one often observes in a candidate during training is largely a mixture of anxiety about not-knowing and disappointment that the organization and its members do not embody the idealized Self. Anxiety mounts. Candidates challenge, either overtly or covertly, the evaluating committees, seminar leaders, authors, analysts, supervisors and all institutional processes with an array of actions and arguments that exceed the critical questioning that is integral to learning. At a deep unconscious level defenses of the Self are activated. Teaching analysts, singly or in groups organized to oversee training, are likely to respond defensively and demandingly to this phenomenon. Then the perversion of power and eros becomes a real possibility, sometimes even under the rubric of "initiation." When this perversion occurs, the teaching analyst must sustain authority and stay empathically related to the individual candidate and to the candidates as a group, who often will band together for mutual protection. Teaching analysts walk a tightrope. Called upon to treat candidates as "junior colleagues," they may verge on denial of the candidates' psychological vulnerability. In their attempts to address the candidates' manifold anxieties, they may cross the bounds of training and invade the personal analysis, or, alternatively, patronize and infantilize the candidate.

One of the most vital relationships in training is that between control analyst and the supervised candidate. It is transformative when there are definite elements of power and eros constellated, when the "divine spark" is struck between them. In personal analysis such a strong affinity can mislead analyst and analysand to believe that a personal love relationship is meant. This can occur also in control analysis; then, of course, training goes awry. In control analysis, there is yet another possibility for going astray from the task of training. The transformative potential in the supervisory relationship may be so great that the two can be led to believe that a personal analysis is meant. Also, when the power of transference has a special appeal for the control analyst, it may not be easy to sustain a focus on the teaching aim. The aim of control analysis – the formation of an analytic attitude – differs greatly from that of personal analysis, which aims to explore the essential being and potential wholeness of the candidate. The control analyst, to be effective, must be able to assert authority and maintain relatedness in the service of the transformation required to develop the analytic attitude.

What about unresolved personal transference issues toward senior members of the analytic community? Feelings of envy, jealousy, impotence and resentment or their opposite – inflated feelings of omnipotence, triumph, and disdain – may inhibit the teaching analyst's effectiveness or be projected onto the candidate. The teaching analyst may seek resolution of these feelings vicariously through the candidate's development. Many unresolved transferences lie at the root of corrupted power and eros in training.

Sometimes, the teaching analyst's internal doubts and conflicts stem from objective situations. The institute may have been established in an atmosphere of cultish devotion to Jung that is difficult to outgrow. Thus, the power and eros inherent in the training relationship may have been misused, historically, to promote identification with and imitation of its senior analysts who enjoyed standing in for Jung. If there is institutional sanction for this kind of influence, the training body will operate along dysfunctional lines. In this situation the analysts as a group have relinquished all claims to the creative deployment of authority and influence, relying instead on indoctrination, identification and imitation and, when that fails, pedantic authoritarianism. Relatedness disappears and training occurs in an atmosphere of stale niceness, or worse, petty vindictiveness.

Sometimes there are institutional rivalries along theoretical lines, such as one between the "developmental" and "classical" Jungian groups. Should a teaching analyst who feels strongly about one side of this argument disqualify him/herself from participating in training a candidate whose personal analyst declares emphatically for the other side? Or should such pairings be encouraged, on the ground that a difference in emphasis will vitalize the teaching relationship to the professional benefit of both candidate and analyst?

Power and eros, in their principled form as creativity and relatedness, when held in balance with the give and take between the authority to influence and the expectations of the training situation, will constitute a "training space." In this space the dialectical relationship fosters formation of an analytic attitude in the candidate; it is the responsibility of the teaching analyst to sustain the tension between these opposites through knowledge and compassionate use of insight.

Crossing Cultural Boundaries

Rodney Galan Taboada
São Paulo, Brazil
Brazilian Society of Analytical Psychology

If there is a "modern man," he is so as long as he refuses to identify himself with Christian anthropology. The originality of "modern man," his novelty in relation to traditional society is exactly the desire to consider himself as a historic being and to live in a radically unsacred cosmos.

Mircea Eliade

The professional preparation of an analyst is a complex system of intentions and procedures which from candidate selection to the maturation phase is much more similar to the religious education model than to the training of a technician. The activity of a Jungian analyst is situated on the border between modern and classical thinking. It is from this epistemologically ambiguous position that this activity's virtues and problems derive.

Brazil has an emerging economy based on immense natural resources, with an enormous effort in technological modernization and consolidation of democratic political practices. This modernization process, however, is far from established. In Brazil, feudal practices and sophisticated technology centers are found side by side.

Brazilian society is multiracial and made up of three major cultural influences: Aboriginal, European and African. These ethnic groups are well blended, forming an embryonic culture that is differentiated even from other South American countries.

The migratory currents from the end of the last century and the beginning of this one brought Portuguese, Italians, Spaniards, Germans, Arabs and Jews to Brazil. These, in addition to the Japanese, make Brazil an outstanding example of tolerance and pacific multiracial coexistence. Differing from other American countries, where the various ethnic groups were kept isolated, in Brazil these populations continue to blend. Thus, the average Brazilian descends from several nationalities.

In Brazilian culture, the archaic and the modern exist together, creating an ambiguous character, or else a multifaceted character that at times reminds us of a primordial chaotic condition. This characteristic has often been pointed out as our great fault, but it holds our best quality, tolerance.

If modern humans rely on the denial of the mystic to privilege the rational, Jung has shown how this dissociated modernization process is the cause for humanity's suffering. Jung said: "The man who has attained consciousness of the present is solitary. The 'modern' man has at all times been so, for every step towards fuller consciousness removes him further from his original ... *participation mystique* with the herd" (CW 10, par. 150).

The modernization of humanity is an irreversible process; it is based on a desire for consciousness and liberation from the unconscious. Therefore, the major task of the analyst is to recognize the legitimacy of the desire for modernization and to avoid the dissociation from consciousness of the archaic values that aim at the search for wholeness. When Jung pointed out the irreconcilable distance between consciousness and the unconscious in modern people as a the cause of their suffering, he also pointed out the role and purpose of the analytic process; that is, to help modern people to understand the nature of their suffering and to correct the deviations resulting from this dissociation.

For a "Third World" analyst who works in a society where the modernizing impulse to fight anachronistic and archaic structures is intense, the task is even more complicated. If the modernization is seen as urgent economically and politically, the dissociation from traditional values and the progressive substitution of values foreign to our culture are dangers that must be considered.

In the "Third World" we are great consumers of technology produced in the "developed" world. This consumption is dangerous; together with goods that make up indispensable modern-life equipment, we have imported a series of behavior patterns, foreign to our cultural background, that have set us apart from our search for a true cultural identity.

The benefits of personal analysis in Brazil are currently accessible only to a small portion of the population which for economic and cultural reasons have been in touch with this process. Analysts also stem from a restricted cultural elite that has had access to formal higher education. Because the professional preparation of an analyst is long and expensive, it is a privilege of a social class that is deeply engaged in modernizing values. In deciding to invest a few years in preparation as an analyst, a psychiatrist or psychologist is searching for differentiation and elitism and thus is inevitably receding from the popular roots of his or her culture. This contradiction is the great challenge for an analyst in the developing countries. How can highly differentiated and expensive knowledge be applied without dissociating from the more profound roots that make up the national culture?

Perhaps the worst inheritance of colonialism is the pattern left in our minds that despises our own traditional values and substitutes for them imported values, uncritically. According to this pattern, anything foreign is better than whatever is national. This is rooted so profoundly in our way of being and thinking that it refers not only to material goods, but – even more regrettable – to intellectual production. We are taken by a terrible cultural inferiority feeling. This feeling has stopped us from thinking for ourselves and appreciating our own ideas. Thus intellectual production in the Third World is a difficult process, which requires a tremendous effort in the fight against the dragon of internalized prejudice.

In the preparation of a Jungian analyst in Brazil, the dialectical relationship between modern and archaic has been converted into a heroic effort to maintain a conscious unity, of modern elements with the root values of our culture. These values characterize our soul as a nation and culture.

The "developed world" offers deplorable examples of intolerance and insensitivity, while the pacific coexistence of races, beliefs and cultures is an undeniable value of the Brazilian soul. The duty of Brazilian analysts, therefore, is to understand how these multiple influences have coexisted without major conflicts and to contribute to the modernization process of Brazilian society in decreasing social injustices. We must do this without losing track of the more profound layers of our unconscious sources related to the Aboriginal world, to the African world and to the different European and Asian cultures that now make up our background.

Over the last two decades the interest in analytical psychology in Brazil has increased greatly. This is due, in great part, to the systematic work of the Brazilian Society of Analytical Psychology. Since its foundation and affiliation with IAAP, it has established qualitative standards for the preparation of Jungian analysts in two units: São Paulo and Rio de Janeiro.

The institutionalization of analysts' preparation assumes the exercise of power. This power is exercised from the moment the institution gives itself the right to select and evaluate candidates up to the moment the Society chooses an ethics board. The power exercised by Jungian societies throughout the world consists of issuing the title, "Jungian analyst." Its value is proportional to the possibility and ability of these analysts to remain faithful to the essence of the work and at the same time to make it available to more people. Without this collective vision of the purpose of our practice, we risk this universal value's becoming an exclusive benefit for a few privileged people.

Jungian analysis is more than a simple psychotherapeutic method. It is the duty of local societies, and the IAAP, to prepare the Jungian analyst not only for private practice but above all to seek the common welfare. The concept of individuation is at times confused with a theoretical defense of individualism. It is important that this theoretical mistake, made only by those who have not truly understood the depth of Jung's work, be counteracted not only by our words but mainly by our actions.

Thus, the challenge to Jungian societies worldwide is to work hard in the task of crossing the boundaries that separate people and races. This is the only way we will be acting truly according to the theory of the collective unconscious, which makes us alike in our differences. Concerning this conflict, Jung said:

> *Our psychic process are made up to a large extent of reflections, doubts and experiments, all of which are almost completely foreign to the unconscious instinctive mind of primitive man. It is the growth*

of consciousness which we must thank for the existence of problems; they are the dubious gift of civilization. (CW8, par. 750)

References

Edinger, E. (1992). *Ego and Archetype.* Boston/London: Shambhala.
Hoeller, S. (1982). *The Gnostic Jung and the Seven Sermons to the Dead.* Wheaton, IL: Theosophical Publishing House.
Zinkin, L. (1989). The Grail and the group. *Journal of Analytical Psychology,* *34*-4, 371-386.

Supervision In Training (summary)

Sherry Salman
New York, New York, U.S.A.
New York Association for Analytical Psychology

Barry Proner
London, England
British Association of Psychotherapists-Jungian Section

This workshop, following on the successful workshop held at the 1992 Congress in Chicago and organized by Marga Speicher, was well attended by participants from Brazil, Denmark, Germany, Great Britain, Israel, Italy, the United States, and elsewhere. The intention for this program was to provide a container for support and discussion of issues regarding the supervision of candidates in our analytic training programs. We provide such containers for candidates, but often do not offer the same to ourselves. Supervisors also need supportive and confrontational containment, so that the power dynamics inherent in the supervisory situation can function creatively, not destructively. Participants shared their experiences as both supervisors and supervisees.

The specific questions, anxieties, issues, and concerns that emerged from the discussion are summarized here:

1. There is a creative tension between two kinds of needs: that for didactic learning and that for facilitating a candidate's natural development and style. It is important for the supervisory process to encompass and hold this tension of needs, which we often experience as opposites in the supervisory process. What are the various ways in which supervisors frame and struggle with these opposites for themselves, and for the candidates? In what ways do we work to encompass and contain both these needs? What seems to work and what doesn't?

2. Each generation feels that it knows more than the one before. From our modern standpoint we criticize – probably rightfully so – the more laissez-faire supervisory attitudes of our predecessors. The

development of an analyst was considered by many of them to spring almost entirely from the personal analysis, the soul journey, typological considerations and the unique expression of the Self in the role of analyst. This development was grounded in the subjective experience of an encounter with the objective psyche and subsequent sanctification by a tribal elder. There were very few "rules of the road"; the entire ritual of analysis was in relative infancy. This situation was rocky and dangerous, but flexible and potentially very creative.

Now we find that there are objective considerations to working analytically that can be taught and there are guidelines to which we expect analysts to adhere. In short, we posit certain fundamentals that supervisors are responsible for imparting via the supervisory process. But how do we remain conscious of the tendency for fundamentals to turn into fundamentalism or – conversely – for the candidate's freedom of discovery and movement to become chaos and countertransferential acting-out?

A related question is: How should we respond to the great differences in supervisory styles? These include the more permissive – mainly giving support and encouragement – versus the rigorous, even dogmatic in the conception of analysis, demanding certain capacities and activities from candidates. The problem of combining rigor with support and encouragement surfaced many times, together with mention of the vulnerability and anxiety felt by candidates during their first analytic work. A dominant theme was whether supervisors should expect candidates to work in a particular way, or should they listen to the candidate and adapt themselves to the work the candidate wishes to do when it is not what the supervisor had in mind? This question raised strong feelings.

3. There was a great deal of concern for the difficulties a supervisor faces in trying to hold these issues in awareness, and also an acknowledgment that we do not know whether there is consensus regarding the fundamentals among, or even within, the various training institutes. (This was suggested as a topic for future discussion.) In addition, questions arose as to the differences in the form of supervision and in its requirements: How many supervisors? For how long?

4. Participants discussed problems they encounter in the supervisory process. For example, what to do when supervisor and candidate do not respect each other or personalities clash? Further, considerable anxiety was expressed regarding the problem of evalu-

ations during the supervisory process: the difficulties this process poses for both supervisor and candidate. Questions were raised as to how we as supervisors make judgments and evaluations in a related way. There was a suggestion that a supervisor write self-evaluations about the work with a particular candidate, before evaluating the candidate. There was some concern about supervisors' having difficulty maintaining conscious relationships with each other when they are critical of each other, and what effect this has on the supervision of candidates.

There was a suggestion that supervisors write evaluations only in terms of "impediments to learning" rather than in clinical terms regarding complexes. Others felt this would be impossible. Some participants felt that the personal supervisor, like the personal analyst, should be exempt from the evaluation process altogether. Issues were raised of persecution, judgment, nepotism and identification. It was suggested that evaluation of the supervision be done at regular intervals by a panel of three other analysts. It was clear that evaluation within supervision deserves a forum of its own, and that it is important to maintain continuing dialogue among supervisors and between supervision and the training process.

5. These issues led to a discussion of the interface between analysis and supervision. There are analysts who engage in discussions of an analysand's cases in analytic sessions. Such discussions can gratify the wish of candidates (and analysts) for the analyst to be also their teacher who will impart knowledge of the analytic process including, by implication, impressions of the candidate's own analysis. It was thought that most analysts avoid this minefield. The obverse appeared to be more troubling for participants: When, if ever, is it necessary for the supervisor to comment on the psychology of the candidate, or even to make an analytic intervention? Are there occasions when such comments become necessary in order to deal with a difficult transference problem, whether positive or negative? There was a move to discriminate with increasing clarity between the suffering experienced, by both candidates and analysts, during analysis versus during supervision.

6. Many issues arose about the training and educating of supervisors. Can supervisory skills be taught? Should they be taught? What should the prospective supervisor learn, and what are the qualities we expect to promote? It was suggested that all analysts, particularly supervisors, avail themselves of at least one hour of supervision a month all their working lives.

This workshop generated feelings, anxieties, and questions. The co-chairs and participants felt the discussion was worth pursuing as an on-going event, and that, in the interests of depth of exploration, future such sessions might profit by focusing on only a few of the specific issues that arose at this Congress.

Past and Future

Report from the Psychological Club of Zurich

At the Congress delegates' meeting, John Beebe reminded the delegates of his request, made at the Workshop on Jung and Anti-Semitism during the Paris Congress of 1989 and forwarded to the Psychological Club of Zurich. The Workshop's Chairman, Jerome Bernstein, asked for a clarification and, insofar as possible, an atonement for the existence of a Jewish quota in the Club, earlier in the century. The President of the IAAP received from the Club a letter dated July 12, 1993. The letter included the report of a study group of the Club which had been presented to the Club's Executive Committee. Both Beebe and Bernstein have expressed satisfaction with the tone of the letter and thanked the Club for its responsiveness to the 1989 request. A translation of the Club's letter and the study group's report follows:

To: Thomas B. Kirsch, M.D. (President)
International Association for Analytical Psychology

Honored Ladies and Gentlemen:
At the annual membership meeting of the Psychological Club of Zurich on May 28, 1993 the members were informed of activities in the Club during the 1930s and 1940s with regard to limitations in the admittance of foreign and Jewish applicants. A member of the Executive Committee reviewed the minutes of Members' Meetings and Executive Committee Meetings during those years, and gave a report. The report was supplemented with verbal testimonies by members who had witnessed the events first-hand. This discussion had become necessary because of inquiries and questions from several Jungian Societies.

The membership meeting entrusted a study group with the task of preparing a summary and opinion to be presented to the Executive Committee see below. We are grateful that Dr. Siegmund Hurwitz, who was one of the individuals affected by those events, made himself available to be part of the study group.

There is no question that today we regret the events of that time. In other respects we sincerely hope – and unfortunately it is only a hope – that all discrimination against anybody, especially against Jews, is a matter of the past.

With friendly greetings,

Study Group (signed):
M. Hofer, J.C. Reid, Ch. Altmann, S. Hurwitz, A. Schuh, R. Schweizer
Executive Committee (signed):
A. Ribi, J.C. Reid, Ch. Altmann, W. Niederer, H. Sulser

Report re: Question of restrictive conditions concerning admission for membership in the Psychological Club of Zurich.

In the mid-1930s hesitation became apparent with regard to the acceptance of foreigners of Jewish and non-Jewish origin. Partly it became difficult to receive membership fees from foreign countries, and partly there was resistance against what was perceived as *"Überfremdung"* (too many foreigners). The problem was discussed at the annual membership meeting in May 1936; from that time on, a posture of resistance against a disproportionate increase in Jewish membership manifested itself. According to a note in the minutes of this meeting, Jung expressed the following view: "Professor Jung refers to remarks about the Jewish question in other places. He stressed that Jews are an important cultural factor in Europe, even though their racial difference cannot be denied. If they produce a bad effect, then the person who is being affected must seek for reasons within himself or herself. The Club should expose itself to such effects and consciously deal with them, instead of holding others responsible for an unpleasant influence."

It was said also, however, that admission to the Club was as a rule very restrictive at that time. Restrictions were based, however, on individual suitability and not on "a question of race." No resolutions were made at that meeting.

From that time on it was left to the Executive Committee to decide on the admission of foreign and Jewish applicants. The question was discussed in the Executive Committee meeting of April 1940, and reference was made to the customary tradition of cautious admission policies.

In 1944 the Statutes of the Psychological Club of 1916 were revised; the 1944 version remained in force until 1991 with only minimal changes. Neither the Statutes of 1944 nor those of 1916 included any mention of restricting the number of Jewish members or guests.

Nevertheless, in the Fall of 1944, the then Executive Committee wrote an internal eight-page commentary on the new Statutes, in which the Committee stipulated the practical implementation of many different regulations. This commentary was distributed among the members of the Executive Committee and was regarded as secret. This document, dated 7. December 1944, contains the following sentence: "The number of Jewish members may under no circumstances exceed 10 percent of total membership, and the number of Jewish statutory guests should not exceed 25 percent." About three weeks later, in the Executive Committee meeting of 29. December, this "Jewish clause" was modified. The expression "under no circumstances" (*keinesfalls*) was replaced by "if possible" (*womöglich*) and it was agreed that it would be possible to exceed these percentages if the Executive Committee voted unanimously for acceptance of a Jewish applicant.

Soon afterward, in the meeting of 25. January 1945, the Executive Committee again discussed the *numerus clausus* (closed number) for Jewish applicants and reached the conclusion that it was in accordance with the need to preserve the social structure and the character of the Club. It was stated further that the Executive Committee consequently "perforce" would have to "assume the responsibilities accruing from the enforcement of these regulations."

The last time the question of admission of Jews in the Club came up for discussion was during the membership meeting of April 1950. According to a statement by an individual who, at that time, was affected by the regulation in question, C.G. Jung gave his support for the Executive Committee to abolish any special regulations regarding Jewish applicants. After the official part of the membership meeting a discussion was held and it was concluded that there was general agreement that the regulations contained in the Commentary by the Executive Committee "at that time were due to extraordinary circumstances and should be canceled."

Sources

Minutes of the Members' and Executive Committee Meetings from 1936 to 1950. Commentary regarding the Statutes distributed to the Members of the Executive Committee, dated 7. December 1944.

English translation compiled by John Beebe in consultation with Jane C. Reid, Peer Hultberg and Samuel van den Bergh on the basis of English and German language documents received from the Analytical Psychology Club Zurich.

Reflections from the Presidency

Thomas B. Kirsch
Palo Alto, California
Society of Jungian Analysts of Northern California

As this is my *Schwanengesang* (swan song) as president of the IAAP, I take this opportunity to give you some personal reflections on the experience. First, it has been a great honor and privilege to serve all of you in this capacity; it certainly has been the high point of my professional life. The single most meaningful part of the job has been meeting colleagues and the friendships that have developed from these encounters. I look forward to the continuance of these friendships, albeit under different circumstances. Second, the presidency has allowed me to return frequently to Zurich, which has always been a second home. I feel that I have come to know the Swiss, and that experience has been a most meaningful one.

Let me backtrack a bit and tell you how I first came to know the IAAP. As many of you know, my parents were first-generation Jungian analysts who worked closely with Jung and for whom Jung was the central figure in their lives. Growing up under these circumstances produced a host of complicated reactions. One of those reactions was to get me into Jungian analysis in Zurich in 1958, so that I was there at the time of the first IAAP Congress. Already then I began to hear about the shadow problems between individual analysts and between groups of analysts. My analyst, one of the founders of the IAAP, made a strong analytic suggestion (or is that an oxymoron?). He said, "You should get out of here during the Congress; this is no place for you now." I went to London and returned to Zurich as the Congress was ending. The atmosphere was still electric, and analysts were gossiping about this and that. Only analysts had been allowed inside the hall: no visitors, no spouses. Both my parents had presented papers there.

That was my first glimpse of the IAAP, and one that faded into the background during the ensuing years, when I returned to the United States and finished my medical, psychiatric, and Jungian studies. Facing military service, I was assigned – by a stroke of good fortune – to work for the National Institute of Mental Health, administering projects in community mental health and research. I never dreamed that this experience in administration would be useful, but it has been invaluable during my IAAP presidency. In the 1960s, though, I saw it only as a necessary evil.

My first IAAP Congress was 1971 in London. It was very exciting for me to be with the "grown ups." Unbeknownst to me I was nominated for second vice-president, but I lost the election. By the 1977 Congress, I presented my first paper to this body and Jo Wheelwright, my mentor, nominated and promoted me for the position of second vice-president. This time I won, and the merry-go-round began! Adolf Guggenbühl was the president, Jim Hillman his honorary secretary, and to them I was still "kid Kirsch." It is hard to describe what those first six years were like. I was rather dazed, learning the ropes. It takes a long time to learn the ropes of the organization, and I am grateful for the six-year period as second vice-president. There is a move today toward limiting the length of time in each position to one three-year term, but I think that should be on an individual basis. Perhaps it was due to my youth, but those two terms were advantageous to me. Also, I feel I have been more effective the past three years than the first three years as President. I entered the IAAP with the notion that I would take it one term at a time. I told myself I could always leave, if it was not right for me, and could return to a quieter, more introverted life.

In 1983 Hannes Dieckmann became president. The 1986 Congress was in a divided Berlin, and the German Society did a wonderful job organizing the Congress. Hannes and I worked very well together. We were shadow figures for each other, the German and the dispossessed Jew, but that was part of the challenge. Berlin was a difficult place to be for many Jewish people, including me. After all, my family had been from Berlin, and my father a founder of the Jung group there before World War II.

By then I was first vice-president and well on my way toward understanding the different aspects of the job. I always believed Hannes was spending too much time on the job and thought, "If and when I become president, I won't give so much of myself. I will just cut through the paperwork and make the necessary decisions; it does not have to be so time-consuming." I suspect that Verena Kast now thinks the same thing about me; that I should delegate more, have less discussions, reach decisions more quickly, have the meetings go faster, and so on. Well, somehow that is not the way things go. The time and energy requirement for the job is just what it is – enormous! Those of you who attended the delegates' meeting on Wednesday will understand what I mean.

When I assumed the presidency at the Paris congress in 1989, the pattern of a president serving two three-year terms had been firmly established. The organization had grown from slightly under 1000 members in 1977 to about 1800 in 1989. The various tasks had been well defined, but nothing prepared me for what was going to happen in the last four months of 1989, and the repercussions of those world events upon analytical psychology. As the Congress in Paris adjourned, Hungary was opening its borders to East Germany. This was the first crack in the Eastern European-Soviet Bloc, which spread so quickly to all the former Soviet satellite states. Within a few months after the collapse of Communism in Eastern Europe, we were receiving letters from all the former satellite countries, asking how they could study Jung and analytical psychology. Could we supply books, lecturers, analysis, and so on? There had been sporadic contacts prior to 1989, but the dramatic political changes accelerated the process greatly.

With enthusiasm for the rapidly changing political situation, the Executive Committee of the IAAP sent me as a representative to Russia to see what was possible for analytical psychology. Thus, in May 1991, my wife Jean and I went to Moscow and Leningrad; our mission was to explore the possibilities of publishing Jung in Russian and to investigate the state of psychotherapy and analysis there. We found a small group of young, psychodynamically-oriented psychologists who were hungry for whatever we could bring them. Then, through Renos Papadopoulos, a series of seminars on basic Jungian psychology was initiated.

With the help of the Van Waveren Foundation of New York City, we brought them the *Collected Works* in English and began discussions on translating the series into Russian. Finding an appropriate publisher in the former Communist state was not easy. We signed one contract, but only one book was translated and published. Four others were translated, but they have been pirated away by the translators because our publisher lost interest and went into other business ventures. Incidentally, IAAP wasted no money on that venture since we paid the publishers only upon publication, not upon translation. We are now in the process of negotiating with a new publisher. Russians are avid readers, and these editions are printed at a minimum of 25 000 copies. The one that was published sold out quickly.

Having grown up during the Cold War, I was quite intoxicated to be there in Moscow, a stone's throw from Red Square and the Kremlin, paving the way for the introduction of analytical psychology to the eager Russians. The negotiations for the translations were not easy, as the infrastructure of the country – telephone, post, and so on – were at a 1930s level. Initially, it was necessary to be there to get things done. There were very few telephone lines into Russia, and a letter could take as long as six months to be delivered. Once it took 300 times dialing to get through from California, and then the connection was bad. An extremely frustrating business! An inordinate amount of time, money, and energy were being spent on this.

About this time (October 1991) I had the following dream: *I was commuting from London to Moscow. I was running to get on a commuter plane, but I could not catch up with it. I awakened running helplessly on the tarmac.* This dream helped me to see that I was commuting, psychologically, between Europe and Russia. Not possible! It was like an intoxication. I withdrew some of my energy from Eastern Europe, realizing that there were many other responsibilities closer to the basic needs of the IAAP that required attention.

In spite of the difficulties, we have been able to have a significant influence on the development of psychotherapy in post-Soviet Russia. Jungian psychology is on the map there, and we have achieved a great deal under difficult circumstances. As evidence, note how many guests from Eastern Europe are attending this Congress.

What has happened in Russia has occurred less dramatically in other parts of the world such as Mexico, Korea, Australia, New Zealand, South Africa, with a beginning in China. It gives me a great deal of pleasure to have participated in this organic expansion of analytical psychology.

Let me outline briefly some of the basic responsibilities of the president's job. David Richman of San Francisco, when introducing me there at a meeting, described my duties:

(1) Running the Executive Committee meetings, a challenging task with our individuated colleagues; (2) overseeing Congress plans; (3) hammering out professional standards and guidelines that can fit diverse Jungian groups; (4) mediating intramural and inter-personal group problems; (5) admitting individual members as Jungian analysts in countries where groups do not exist; (6) presenting the

Jungian point of view at eclectic professional conferences; (7) tracking and mounting a response to those who misrepresent themselves as Jungian analysts; (8) negotiating publishing issues concerning Jung's works.

Underlying all this has been my strong feeling that it is vitally important to keep all the different parts of the Jungian world under one roof, the IAAP. This continues to be a daunting task, as the impulse to split is ever present.

I appreciate Don Sandner's paper here; its generosity represents the best from the San Francisco point of view. However, I wonder and many others wonder why splitting up to now has not happened in San Francisco, as we have the same ideological struggles as in other groups? In my opinion it has to do with the fact that Jo Wheelwright and Joe Henderson, with their interest in psychological types, genuinely valued a psychology of differences from the very beginning. More importantly, they had a mutual respect even when they strongly disagreed with one another – which they often did. They did not try to change each other, and so far this tradition has held. During my term on the Executive Committee of the IAAP, many splits in societies have occurred. Why? Behind the theoretical differences lie narcissistic wounds and power issues, in which ideologies play their part. There has been a breakdown of mutual respect and a divorce takes place. Wheelwright and Henderson have had a "marriage" which at times was rocky, but it has held, God willing.

Fortunately, I have had wonderful support from a number of people who have been essential in making the whole organization function. For the past six years Ursula Egli has worked tirelessly on tasks large and small; in a quiet, efficient, and gracious manner, so that I look well organized when I am not. Without her ever present skills, carrying on any other professional activities, such as a private practice of analysis, would have been most difficult. The vice-presidents, Verena Kast, Luigi Zoja, and Eli Weisstub all have risen to the occasion whenever called upon. My honorary secretary, Murray Stein, has been a tremendous support with his marvelous organizational skills, intelligence, and vision of analytical psychology. Executive Committee members Gustav Bovensiepen, Lorie Paulson, Joanne Wieland-Burston, Christian Gaillard, and Luigia Poli have done fine jobs when called upon and have helped the IAAP run smoothly. I need to single out Andrew Samuels who, both on and off the executive committee, has been a sympathetic soul with his global knowledge of people and analytical psychology, and has been helpful in some very delicate situations. Bob Hinshaw has been a roving ambassador mediating between the Zurich Institute and the IAAP, overseeing the translations of Jung into Russian, and generally turning up at just the right time.

I have had friends and mentors, *des éminences grises*, Adolf Guggenbühl and Joe Henderson, who have lent their support with the most delicate and confidential situations. In San Francisco John Beebe, Tom Singer, and David Tresan have been my most long-standing local friends to whom I could turn. Finally, my wife, Jean, who has borne the daily intrusions of the telephone and fax into our lives and has entertained gladly numerous out-of-town visitors. I cannot thank her enough for just being there and listening to me go on and on about one thing and another.

The IAAP as an organization needs many changes. The Constitution which was written in the 1950s needs a major overhaul. It seems to the regular member that there is a small power elite and little possibility of communication between a member and the executive committee. It takes too long to work one's way up the ladder to become president. How does one get new people on the executive committee? How do we get smaller societies onto the executive committee? These are all issues for the new committee to work on.

What about the future of analytical psychology? There are many pressures impinging on our field both from the outside and the inside. First of all, let us look at the outer situation. After a period of rapid growth in analytical psychology and depth psychology in general, there are intense economic and social pressures against analytic psychotherapy all over the world. Various insurances, both governmental and private, no longer are willing to support payments for analysis in the same fashion. Many people are looking for the quick fix, looking to Prozac and its progenitors, and to short-term psychotherapies, and are less willing to undergo the long, expensive road of analysis. In the United States the number of people wishing for Jungian analysis has not kept pace with the increase in the number of analysts. There may be too many of us! We may need to lower our fees so that more people can afford us, and more of us can stay in practice. I hear about many young analysts who are not able to make it financially. Young analysts, except graduates of the Zurich Institute, tend to remain where they were trained. Some analysts probably will need to move to cities where there is a need for analysts.

On the inner level, we continue to be creative, incorporating new ideas into our work, and develop in new directions. Thus, the topic of this Congress, "Open Questions." However, many of us are concerned: Where will this multiplicity lead us? What is central to being a Jungian? My understanding of what it means to be a Jungian has been my foundation for the decisions that have come before me. I have reacted intuitively; most of the time it has turned out all right. However, whatever it means to be Jungian in today's world remains elusive. Is it working with dreams in a particular way? Is it working with the Self? Acknowledging that the psyche has a basic spiritual aspect? Is it the belief in archetypal theory? Having a symbolic attitude? The dialectical nature of the analytic process? Dialectical relationship between the ego and the unconscious? We have many different clinical variations in our practices. How do we evaluate them as Jungian? How do we know whether someone is Jungian, and what does that mean?

Jung referred to his psychology as analytical psychology. Most of us do not go around calling ourselves "analytical psychologists." The term has never caught on in a collective sense. In the United States we often refer to ourselves as "Jungian analysts." I do not like the label "Jungian analyst," as if our theory and practice followed one person only. "Jungian" is a term for each of us which seems to symbolize our own unique relationship to the unconscious and to Jung. We have discussed the fact that we are mourning Jung at this Congress. I wonder when we will be able to call ourselves analytical psychologists or an equivalent term and have it mean something?

There are at least two opposing forces that I see from the point of view of the president of the IAAP. On the one hand we have those practitioners who gravitate toward psychoanalysis, Kohut, Klein and object relations. The individual Jungian analyst incorporates more or less of these other theories and methods into his or her practice. Some Jungians feel that, with the psychoanalytic addition, they have truly found the right way to do analysis. I sense among this group a tendency of some analysts to value the other theories above their Jungian orientation. Freudian psychoanalysis and its off-shoots have the real answers.

At the other end of the spectrum are those who feel that Jung's work has become so diluted that it is time to return to Jung: only his work and very few others. These people have been referred to – erroneously, I believe – as "classical" analysts. I see them falling into a kind of fundamentalism. In view of the trend toward fundamentalism in other sectors of our contemporary world society, I fear that this Jungian purity is another form of fundamentalism. It is essential that we reflect on this movement and try to understand its meaning. Richard Noll is speaking to this shadow phenomenon in Jungian circles.

On the other hand, I see myself most influenced by Jung's way, but open to many other approaches to the psyche, depending upon the circumstances. Thus, I see myself as Jungian, probably even a classical Jungian, but completely convinced that other analysts and theorists have much to teach us about the psyche. I certainly agree that transference/countertransference is central to doing analysis. As imperfect as analysis is, it is a way of life for me. I am enormously grateful to my own analyst in San Francisco and generally feel good about the work I do with my patients. As I talk with other colleagues who have done the work for many years, I realize the limits of any analysis. It is an imperfect work done by ordinary human beings.

The tension between these two extremes in analytical psychology is great. One wonders if the center can hold against these opposites. The value of these international Congresses is in bringing many of us together and giving us a chance to dialogue with those with whom we are in strong disagreement. It is through this dialogue that the *tertium non datur* (third not given) has a chance to emerge.

With some writing and lecturing projects ahead I plan to remain active professionally and to keep in touch. I would like to reiterate what a valuable experience these 18 years have been for me and to thank you all again for your support. I wish Verena Kast and the new executive committee all the best for the next years.

Author Index

Subject Index

RECENT TITLES FROM DAIMON:

Heinrich Karl Fierz
JUNGIAN PSYCHIATRY
Foreword by C.T. Frey-Wehrlin
Preface by Joseph Wheelwright
illustrations and index
430 pages; paper
ISBN 3-85630-521-1

This newly translated book is the life work of the well-known psychiatrist and co-founder of the renowned Jungian "Klinik am Zürichberg" in Switzerland. From the contents: Meaning in Madness / The Attitude of the Doctor in Psychotherapy / Psychological-Psychiatric Diagnosis and Therapy / Psychotherapy in the Treatment of Depression.

C.A. Meier
Personality
The Individuation Process
in the Light of C.G. Jung's Typology
Carl Gustav Jung never produced a systematic treatment of his own work – he was always moving forward. His assistant-of-many-decades, Carl Alfred Meier, made it his life-task to gather and present in detail the various aspects of Jung's far-reaching discoveries. This final volume of Meier's work addresses the human personality in its encounters between consciousness and the unconscious,

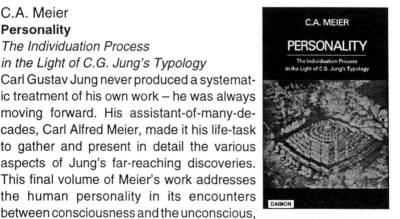

a process referred to as *individuation*. In describing such encounters, the author extensively explains the notion of Jung's *psychological types*. (192 pages)

Verena Kast
SISYPHUS
The old Stone, a new Way
A Jungian Approach to Midlife Crisis
ca. 130 pages, paper,
ISBN 3-85630-527-0

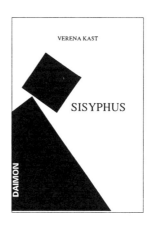

Verena Kast refers to Sisyphus as the "myth of the forty-year-olds," who often experience their lot in life to be a Sisyphus task. Are our human efforts all in vain, or is there some meaning to be found? In the end it is a struggle with death itself.

Verena Kast deals with a problem that also fascinated Nietzsche and Freud. ... This book is packed with down-to-earth experience, clinical anecdotes, wit and insight.

Murray Stein

Alan McGlashan
Gravity and Levity
The Philosophy of Paradox
162 pages

This book heralds a breakthrough in human imagination, not a breakthrough that may take place in the future, far or near, but one that has already occurred – only we may not have noticed it. Life, as the author shows, is open-ended and full of paradoxes. Its principles cannot be understood by logic and causal reasoning. We can only come to terms with life if we accept that there is no final answer to it and that adjusting to life's natural rhythm is the key to finding release from the horrors and problems around us.

SUSAN BACH

LIFE PAINTS ITS OWN SPAN

ON THE SIGNIFICANCE
OF SPONTANEOUS PICTURES
BY SEVERELY ILL CHILDREN

DAIMON

Susan Bach
LIFE PAINTS ITS OWN SPAN
On the Significance of Spontaneous
Paintings by Severely Ill Children
with over 200 color illustrations
Part I (Text): 208 pp., part II (Pictures): 56 pp.
Life Paints its own Span with over 200 color
reproductions is a comprehensive exposi-
tion of Susan Bach's original approach to
the physical and psychospiritual evaluation
of spontaneous paintings and drawings by
severely ill patients. At the same time, this
work is a moving record of Susan Bach's
own journey of discovery.

Mary Lynn Kittelson
Sounding the Soul: The Art of Listening
"In this delightful, phenomenological account, Kittelson writes in lively pursuit
of the language of hearing, an ode to the persistent primacy of the ear. ...
It's right here, she says, just around the corner from our noses.
Kittelson's ear awareness finds side-doors into the topic. She lets us in on a
secret as intriguing as Freud's footnote about the gradually diminishing sense
of smell in human beings: we have a lapsed instinct for interiority. For turning
inward, for spiraling deep into the dark, for following evocative reverberations
to their source." — from the Foreword by Nor Hall, Ph.D. (300 pages)

Forthcoming: A Festschrift for Laurens van der Post
The Rock Rabbit and the Rainbow
edited by Robert Hinshaw
Authors from around the world have combined
their talents in a tribute honoring this one-of-a-
kind writer, soldier and statesman, a man of his
time. Contributions include: Joseph Henderson: "The Splendor of the Sun"; Alan McGlashan: "How to be Haveable"; Ian Player: "My
Friend Nkunzimlanga"; Jean-Marc Pottiez:
"Rainbow Rhapsody"; T.C. Robertson: "A Triad
of Landscapes – a Day in the Veld with Laurens"; and numerous other essays and works
by Aniela Jaffé, Jonathan Stedall, Harry Wilmer, Jo Wheelright, C.A. Meier and many others.
(ca. 240 pages, illustrated)

The Rock Rabbit
and the Rainbow
A Tribute to
Laurens van der Post

ENGLISH PUBLICATIONS BY DAIMON

Susan Bach – *Life Paints its Own Span*
E.A. Bennet – *Meetings with Jung*
George Czuczka – *Imprints of the Future*
Heinrich Karl Fierz – *Jungian Psychiatry*
von Franz / Frey-Rohn / Jaffé – *What is Death?*
Liliane Frey-Rohn – *Friedrich Nietzsche*
Yael Haft – *Hands: Archetypal Chirology*
Siegmund Hurwitz – *Lilith, the first Eve*
Aniela Jaffé   – *The Myth of Meaning*
               – *Was C.G. Jung a Mystic?*
               – *From the Life und Work of C.G. Jung*
               – *Death Dreams and Ghosts*
Verena Kast   – *A Time to Mourn*
               – *Sisyphus*
Hayao Kawai – *Dreams, Myths and Fairy Tales in Japan*
James Kirsch – *The Reluctant Prophet*
Mary Lynn Kittelson – *Sounding the Soul*
Rivkah Schärf Kluger – *The Gilgamesh Epic*
Paul Kugler   – *Jungian Perspectives on Clinical Supervision*
Rafael López-Pedraza   – *Hermes and his Children*
                         – *Cultural Anxiety*
Alan McGlashan – *The Savage and Beautiful Country*
               – *Gravity and Levity*
Gitta Mallasz (Transcription) – *Talking with Angels*
C.A. Meier   – *Healing Dream and Ritual*
               – *A Testament to the Wilderness*
Laurens van der Post – *A «Festschrift»*
R.M. Rilke – *Duino Elegies*
Susan Tiberghien – *Looking for Gold*
Ann Ulanov – *The Wizards' Gate*

Jungian Congress Papers:
Jerusalem 1983 – *Symbolic and Clinical Approaches*
Berlin 1986 – *Archetype of Shadow in a Split World*
Paris 1989 – *Dynamics in Relationship*
Chicago 1992 – *The Transcendent Function*

Available from your bookstore or from our distributors:

In the United States:

Continuum   *In Great Britain:*
c/o Publisher Resources   Chiron Publications   Airlift Book Company
P.O. Box 7017   400 Linden Avenue   26-28 Eden Grove
La Vergne, TN 37086   Wilmette, IL 60091   London N7 8EF, England
Phone: 800-937 5557   Phone: 847-256 7551   Phone: (607) 5792 and 5798
Fax: 615-793 3915   Fax: 847-256 2202   Fax: (607) 6714

Worldwide: Daimon Verlag   Hauptstrasse 85   CH-8840 Einsiedeln Switzerland
               Tel. (41)(55) 412 2266   Fax (41)(55) 412 2231
               e-mail: 106020.3115@compuserve.com

Write for our complete catalog!